THE LONGEST MINUTE

ALSO BY MATTHEW J. DAVENPORT

*First Over There: The Attack on Cantigny,
America's First Battle of World War I*

THE LONGEST MINUTE

THE GREAT SAN FRANCISCO EARTHQUAKE AND FIRE OF 1906

MATTHEW J. DAVENPORT

ST. MARTIN'S PRESS ≋ NEW YORK

Published in the United States by St. Martin's Press,
an imprint of St. Martin's Publishing Group

THE LONGEST MINUTE. Copyright © 2023 by Matthew J. Davenport. All rights reserved.
Printed in the United States of America. For information, address St. Martin's Publishing
Group, 120 Broadway, New York, NY 10271.

www.stmartins.com

Designed by Jonathan Bennett

Library of Congress Cataloging-in-Publication Data

Names: Davenport, Matthew J., author.
Title: The longest minute : the Great San Francisco Earthquake
and Fire of 1906 / Matthew J. Davenport.
Other titles: Great San Francisco Earthquake and Fire of 1906
Description: First edition. | New York, NY : St. Martin's Press, 2023. |
Includes bibliographical references and index.
Identifiers: LCCN 2023025153 | ISBN 9781250279279 (hardcover) |
ISBN 9781250279286 (ebook)
Subjects: LCSH: San Francisco Earthquake and Fire, Calif., 1906. |
Earthquakes—California—San Francisco—History—20th century. |
Fires—California—San Francisco—History—20th century. |
San Francisco (Calif.)—History—20th century.
Classification: LCC F869.S357 D384 2023 | DDC 979.4/
61051—dc23/eng/20230524
LC record available at https://lccn.loc.gov/2023025153

Our books may be purchased in bulk for promotional, educational, or business use. Please
contact your local bookseller or the Macmillan Corporate and Premium Sales Department at
1-800-221-7945, extension 5442, or by email at MacmillanSpecialMarkets@macmillan.com.

First Edition: 2023

10 9 8 7 6 5 4 3 2 1

To every San Francisco firefighter,
past, present, and future

Contents

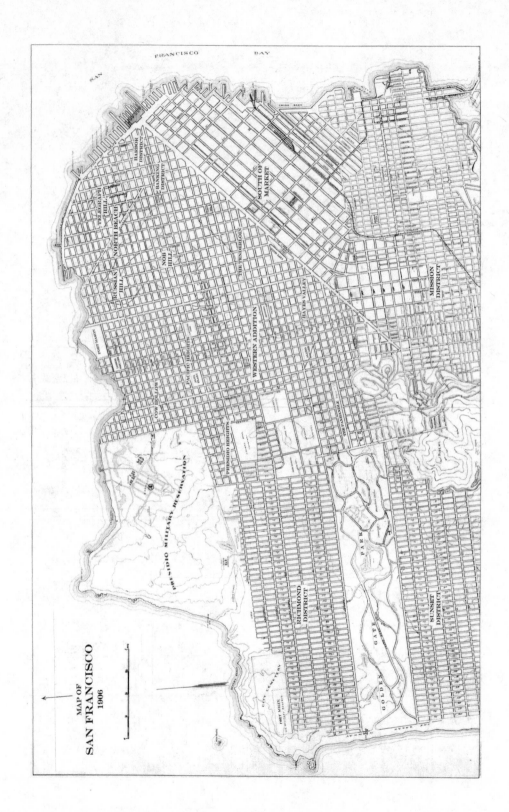

MAP OF
SAN FRANCISCO
1906

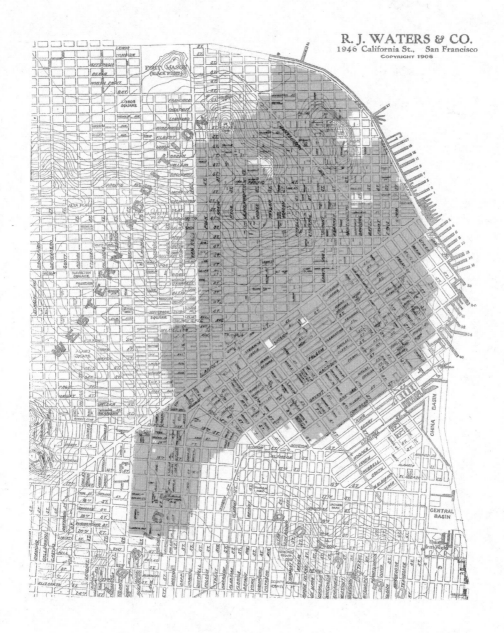

FACING PAGE: Map of San Francisco, 1906.

THIS PAGE: Map of San Francisco with darkened portions
showing the area destroyed by fire April 18–21, 1906.
(Courtesy of the Bancroft Library)

There is a crime here that goes beyond denunciation.
There is a sorrow here that weeping cannot symbolize.
There is a failure here that topples all our success.

—John Steinbeck, *The Grapes of Wrath*

THE LONGEST MINUTE

Prologue

A PRIL WAS MORE than half gone, and spring in the city was cool and dry. Temperatures had reached seventy degrees just once all year and no rain had fallen since the first of the month. The sun rose earlier each morning to fight persistent fog as days grew longer and nights shorter, and onshore breezes carried squawks of seagulls and the churn of side-wheel steam ferries into downtown streets where noise was constant.

Iron-wheeled wagons rattled behind hooves clip-clopping on paving stones. Tall buildings echoed coughs of automobile engines and whistles of wheelmen and the jolts and lurches of passing cable cars. Bells played each hour from parish churches, synagogues, cathedrals, and a century-old mission. Newsboys in flat caps yelled "One nickel!" hawking dailies of the *Examiner, Chronicle,* or *Call.* Sidewalk merchants called out offers of fresh fruit, or fish, or knife sharpening, or shoe shining. And unhoused people sought "enough money to get a bed," which could be found in many of the city's thirteen hundred lodging houses for as little as two bits (25 cents) per night—more for a room with electric lights, and more still for one with a telephone.

Wind from the northeast brought sea air's scent of salt and brine and the smell of the waterfront fish market. An acrid taste of sulfur floated from foundry smokestacks, and an earthy scent of coal or wood fires carried in smoke coiling from nearly every city chimney. Bakers on Polk Street propped doors open to lure in customers with aromas of baking bread or layer cakes or pies, a pleasant escape from the street smells of urine or horse manure or the foul stench of

Clay Street's wholesale butchers or trash burning at the Sanitary Reduction Works down South of Market Street. And in a time before antiperspirant and deodorant were widely sold, body odor carried in the drafts of passing crowds, disguised here and there by a whiff of cologne water or perfume.

San Francisco in 1906 was America's largest city west of St. Louis. It was home to more than 400,000 souls, and rarely was a bare head seen. Men in bowlers and fedoras walked downtown streets where clothiers pushed the "snappiest hat of the season," the Broadway high telescope, still on sale the week following Easter. Women topped with feathered three-story flower-pot hats beneath white linen parasols shopped Kearny Street's storefronts of milliners selling velvet (not velveteen, underlined) toques trimmed with or-naments, plumes, or roses. Fishermen and longshoremen hauled and carried under tweed fiddlers and wool sailor caps. House cooks and maids hurried to butchers' and grocers' shops in bucket hats and scarves. Policemen patrolled in custodian helmets. Bellboys served in pillboxes.

Conversations were frequently colored with accents—Irish, German, Italian—and often in another tongue. More than three-fourths of San Francis-co's residents were immigrants or children of immigrants, and most others were from midwestern or eastern states. Messages to family and friends back east or overseas could be dispatched at any of four dozen offices for Postal Telegraph or Western Union throughout the city. And tastes of home could be found among the city's hundreds of restaurants offering international fares—Japanese, Turk-ish, French, Chinese, Mexican—a choice of cuisines as reflective of the diverse populace as the city's fifty banks, which included the French American Bank, Russo-Chinese Bank, German Savings and Loan, and Bank of Italy.

For "amusements," sophisticates preferred musicals at the Tivoli or operas at the Grand Opera House. Tickets were cheaper for comedies at the Alcazar, burlesque at the California Theatre, or vaudeville at the Orpheum, and cheaper still for families to roller-skate afternoons and evenings at "The Big Place," Mechanics' Pavilion. Adults could watch newfangled motion pictures in the Lyceum Theatre for a dime, and children for a nickel. Coppersmiths and iron-workers finished shifts at any of the city's sixty-six foundries and bet their day's wages on weeknight boxing bouts at the athletic club in the Mission District or plunked down two bits for bleacher seats to watch baseball South of Market at Recreation Park, where the San Francisco Seals played home games three or four afternoons each week.

This "Queen City of the Pacific" was home to the West Coast's busiest port and roughly twice the size of California's second-largest city, Los Angeles. San Francisco's tallest skyscraper, the Call Building, and the dome of City Hall both soared higher than any other building west of Chicago, and the "[f]ire and earthquake proof" Palace was still one of the largest hotels in the country. But just beneath the modern, cosmopolitan veneer was the unmistakable character of a frontier town still outgrowing dirt streets, and six years after stepping into the twentieth century, the city kept a foot firmly planted in the nineteenth. Storefronts for phonograph dealers and electricians flanked coal merchants and mining companies. Blacksmiths and horseshoers worked beside photographers and auto mechanics. Coal scuttles were sold on the same shelves as Pocket Kodak cameras in department stores where customers could also pay to see 3-D images on a stereoscopic viewer or moving pictures through a handheld animatoscope. Dray horses pulled horsecars along rails crossing those of electric streetcars while the city's eighty-six carriage and wagon sellers faced fresh competition from twenty-six dealers of the new motor car. And every afternoon at dusk, the San Francisco Gas and Electric Company's electric streetlights illuminated sidewalks paced nightly by lamplighters venturing to neighborhoods where they hoisted wick-tipped poles to ignite gas streetlamps.

As nighttime came, the waning crescent moon of mid-April cast a faint silvery light on concrete curbs and brick sidewalks of dark alleys where saloons, billiard taverns, and gambling houses filled with the smoke of 5-cent cigars and penny cigarettes. The clamor of vice spilled out the swinging doors of grog shops and singsong houses lining the waterfront's Barbary Coast, where beer-moistened air carried tawdry tunes from steam pianos, gramophones, and banjo players. Oil lamps cast an orange glow over greasy tables where sailors and deckhands paid two dimes, one for the beer and one for the girl—before staggering behind darkened doorways of brothel parlors and "cribs." And in the waning hours each evening, policemen walked the night's unluckiest in handcuffs to the Hall of Justice's city prison, where a booking desk register listed drunks, vagrants, and pickpockets.

And thus the day that would bring catastrophe before dawn began like any other. While most of the city slept in the small hours of Wednesday, April 18, 1906, even before ice wagons and milk trucks began their routes, the busiest waterfront on the Pacific Coast teemed with life. Patrons staying past the last calls of dance halls and gambling saloons stumbled home as first light brought the whistles of steam tugs and the rattle of coal carts, and dray horses clopped across wharves hauling wagons filled with the morning catch to the fish market.

The pearly light of a warm, clear morning shimmered on the waves of the bay and washed the gray Colusa sandstone of the Ferry Building, and a steady easterly breeze sent waves slapping against the wood pilings of its seven ferry slips while periodic gusts lifted the flag into snaps atop its 245-foot tower.

In a time before bridges spanned the bay and many railroad lines terminated in Oakland, the Ferry Building was the nerve center for up to fifty thousand daily commuters and visitors to San Francisco. Double-decker steam ferries arrived and departed its slips on average every fifteen minutes between 7:00 a.m. and 8:00 p.m. connecting with piers in Oakland, Sausalito, Tiburon, San Rafael, and Alameda. Its tower, modeled after the twelfth-century Giralda bell tower of Seville, Spain, heralded the time of day with twenty-two-foot-wide clockfaces on each of its four sides—then the largest in the United States and readable from a considerable distance up Market Street or out on the bay. Inside, a nine-hundred-pound swinging weight kept time for the pendulum clock, built by E. Howard & Company in Boston, which was installed with a double three-legged gravity escapement to avoid being thrown off excessively by the steady pushes and tugs of strong winds on its eleven-foot-long minute hands and seven-and-a-half-foot-long hour hands. Each week, a worker climbed ten flights of stairs and a series of steep ladders to wind the mechanism and correct the time, which as regulated ran fast—on average two and a half minutes fast each day. That Wednesday morning, its hands struck five o'clock roughly three minutes early.

On a street corner three blocks from the waterfront, police sergeant Jesse Cook walked patrol, on duty in the downtown's harbor district since midnight. As church bells through the city chimed the five o'clock hour—on time and a half hour from sunrise—Cook unlocked a blue police box, phoned the central switchboard for his hourly check-in, and continued patrol. He walked a sidewalk with well-worn curbs along a brick-paved street lined with wood-frame and brick storefronts. In the predawn light, fruit vendors and produce merchants raised canvas awnings and walked horses from alley stables to hitch to delivery wagons loaded with the daily stock.

Jesse Cook was forty-six and a California native. Married with two daughters, sixteen and nine, he was slim and of above-average height, with a thin face of light wrinkles and a full mustache salted gray from seventeen years patrolling San Francisco's streets. Most recently he'd served as sergeant of the Chinatown squad, and in the months since his reassignment to the Harbor District Police Station, Sergeant Cook worked to know his beat completely.

He learned which Barbary Coast saloons closed last and which commission produce houses opened first. He stayed current on which businesses did not employ night watchmen so his officers could safeguard their buildings during off-hours. And he aimed to personally know every sailor and teamster and dock worker and warehouseman.

Seasoned locals remembered a time just a generation earlier when the city's shoreline was six blocks further inland and most of what became these streets sat beneath the shallow waters of Yerba Buena Cove, backfilled during the manic growth of the gold rush. Prospectors and new residents had extended the city's crowded shores by heaping sand and dirt and garbage in with the wooden remains of grounded ships and abandoned transport boats. This "fill-land" was then leveled, and roads and buildings were stacked on top.

Just as Sergeant Cook knew the world above, he also knew what lay beneath. He understood the concrete sidewalks and brick buildings and alleys of tightly wedged basalt paving stones that he patrolled—and on which one-sixth of the city's more than 400,000 residents lived—formed a brittle shell above soft sand and mud encasing trash and rotten boat carcasses atop a sedimentary layer of old bay clay. In his words, this part of the city "was all filled in land, filled in on mud."

Sergeant Cook carried a cigar to share with his friend, fruit merchant Tom Burns, for a pre-workday smoke, something of a morning custom. As Cook walked the sidewalk looking for Tom, he paused in front of the wholesale produce store Levy & Levy, where he saw the owner's twenty-two-year-old son, Sidney Levy, trying to calm a delivery horse.

"What's the matter with your horse?" Cook asked.

Sidney answered, "I never saw him act like that before."

The horse was "pawing at the street," neighing loudly and acting "very nervous."

Cook heard a noise that did not belong. Then a steady rumble. Then the ground moved. He knew it was an earthquake.

The ground started shaking and the sounds swelled to a roar and Cook knew worse was coming. He looked back to the west up the Washington Street incline and saw a shockwave speeding toward him through the ground "like the waves of an ocean coming down the hill and the buildings seemed to be rocking in and out."

Mindful he was standing beside a two-story-tall brick building, Sergeant Cook jumped from the sidewalk into the open street just as the waves hit.

Adrenaline carried his legs out further from the buildings. "The whole street was undulating," and convulsions ripped through the ground, popping the paving stones up in swells faster than he could run. His feet landed everywhere but where he aimed, and he struggled to stay upright. A steady, earsplitting roar filled the air and drowned out all other sound except church bells clanging off-key with each jolt. The ground jumped up and dipped down, then pulled sideways, jarring him further off-balance with every step.

As he neared the street's center, it "split right open" in front of him in a burst of sand and brick. The ground liquefied, and an eight-inch iron water main shattered and water gushed up onto the street.

Cook's momentum carried him toward the "gaping trench." He long-jumped across it, landed on a sidewalk, then halted and backstepped as the building before him leaned in and collapsed. Keeping his feet under him, Cook scrambled to the refuge of a large doorway as the shocks grew "fiercer and sharper." In the distorted space around him were others huddled shoulder to shoulder in the same shelter. And above and beneath the deafening rumble were screams and crashes and horse whinnies and church bells clanging. And there was trembling and dust and gushing water.

Through a shaking blur Cook saw the brick front of the building across the street begin to peel away and collapse. On the sidewalk below it he saw Tom Burns, the friend he'd been looking for. And he saw a fruit seller and a clerk run out the front of the store and reach the sidewalk just as two floors of bricks slammed the scene flat in an explosion of dust.

Cook turned his face away and pressed his eyes shut as the debris cloud enveloped him. He clung white-knuckled to the frame of the doorway, holding himself upright. The ground twisted under him "like a top, while it jerked this way and that and up and down and every way" and the sidewalk "felt like it was slipping into the Bay."

Breeze blew the debris cloud clear to expose a six-foot-tall pile of bricks and chunks of masonry on the street. Buried beneath were the fruit seller and the clerk and, for all Cook knew, his friend Tom Burns.

It was a few seconds past 5:12 a.m. on Wednesday, April 18, 1906. Jesse Cook, the veteran police sergeant who prided himself on knowing how things on his beat and in his city were going, found himself huddled in a doorway with strangers wondering when the shaking would finally end. Cook knew only that in the slow passing of those few crowded seconds, he had seen the ground open, buildings fall, and men die. Unable to see beyond the street corner or the moment, he had no grasp on the scope of disaster then unfolding.

By the time the shaking stopped, hundreds across the city were already dead, most killed while sleeping in their beds. Flimsy lodging houses of three, four, and five stories collapsed and sank into landfills. Beneath broken streets, iron water mains—like the one Sergeant Cook had hurdled—had cracked and shattered. Power and telephone lines were twisted and torn, cutting off communications and disabling alarms. It was the strongest earthquake even the oldest residents of the city had ever endured—still today one of the strongest in the recorded history of California—and for those who survived its long moments of violent jolting, the worst was yet to come.

Flames ignited in dozens of businesses and dwellings and spread like a brushfire through city block after city block of clustered, dry wooden structures. Survivors in the path of the spreading blazes fled their homes with what could fit into wagons or trunks or be carried to the open ground of parks or onto ferries to evacuate as individual fires grew into a firestorm. People pinned in ruins and rubble were doomed to asphyxiate from toxic smoke or incinerate in the flames. Firefighters responded everywhere they could, fighting against time as much as fire, digging to rescue at least a few trapped souls before flames overtook them. But in most places, with little to no pressure at hydrants, firemen could only pull last reserves of water from emergency cisterns or precious trickles from hydrants. With little water to stop it, and fed in places by onshore winds or by new blazes started with black powder or dynamite in the hands of amateur demolition crews, the firestorm devoured the city—block by block, business by business, home by home—without pause for three days and three nights.

News of the earthquake and fire traveled faster than news had ever traveled before—over telephone lines and telegraph wires and even through wireless signals. The nation and world read details of the earthquake within hours of it striking, and over the coming days, AP wires carried the latest on the slow destruction of San Francisco by fire. Newspapers in towns and cities nationwide issued "Extra!" editions and evening issues with news of the spreading inferno, all bought by readers eager for updates. It was the first such event to be followed nationally in almost real time, giving it unprecedented attention and immediacy. And having struck in a city filled with professional photographers and in a time when cameras were cheaper and more widely available than ever before, it became the most-photographed disaster of its time. Vivid images of skyscrapers engulfed in flames and an entire city leveled to an apocalyptic ash heap of ruins—even motion pictures of the aftermath captured on hand-cranked cameras—were seen far and wide, adding life to sterile newsprint and closeness to a distant tragedy, capturing the attention and imagination of people coast-to-coast and making it America's first truly national disaster.

When the last fire was extinguished, the smoke cleared to reveal a dystopian wasteland and laid bare the breadth of destruction and depth of loss. In many of San Francisco's largest districts and neighborhoods, nearly every resident had lost their home, church, library, theater, grocery store, butcher shop, bakery, dry goods store, drugstore, and favorite restaurant and coffee shop. Most downtown employees lost their workplaces, and every South of Market child lost their school. Every inhabitant of Chinatown lost their home, and every merchant, their store. The city's downtown banking and harbor districts (the current-day Financial District) were reduced to stripped skeletons and rubble, including all fifty of its banks. City Hall was shaken to a crumbled shell and had many of its vital records incinerated by the firestorm that had destroyed the city's landmarks and largest homes and gutted its tallest buildings and grandest hotels. Seventy-five church sanctuaries were destroyed, including all three cathedrals and five of the seven synagogues. On one end of a city block, four lodging houses packed with tenants occupying more than one hundred rooms had collapsed and burned so quickly that only a handful of people escaped, and the ash of incinerated residents mixed with the ash of their flattened rooms, along with the dust of other wooden flats jammed into the same block—just one of more than five hundred blocks stripped, leveled, or vaporized.

Never had a major American city been so totally destroyed. But within days, newspaper coverage of the disaster shifted to optimistic stories of rebirth and rebuilding, part of a concerted effort by city leaders and business owners to persuade displaced residents to return and reassure potential developers that San Francisco was a safe bet for investment and growth. "GREAT BUILDINGS ARE TO RISE FROM ASHES" ran the headline of the *Chronicle* one week after the earthquake. Front-page stories highlighted "a spirit of unity" that had "arisen out of the fire" and would lead to "the making of a grander city." Reporters insisted "the calamity should be spoken of as 'the great fire' and not 'the great earthquake,'" and they began to refer to the disaster as "the great fire" to avoid a perception of San Francisco as earthquake-prone. And the Board of Supervisors fixed the total dead at the misleadingly low number of 478, while thousands were still unaccounted for and remains were still being found.

Rubble was cleared and homes were rebuilt and businesses reopened, and in the first few years that followed, the anniversary of the disaster served mostly as a benchmark for the progress of the city's rebirth. "SAN FRANCISCO WILL CELEBRATE TODAY THE ACHIEVEMENTS OF ONE YEAR OF RECONSTRUCTION" read the April 18, 1907, headline of the *Chronicle*. "SAN FRANCISCO'S REBUILDING IS WONDER OF WORLD" declared the *Examiner* on April 18, 1908, and on the 1909 anniversary, the *Call* headlined "HOME AGAIN AFTER THREE YEARS." In 1915, the city hosted the Panama–Pacific International Exposition, a world's fair to acclaim the completion of the Panama Canal and showcase San Francisco's nine-year recovery and celebrate "the rebuilding which has obliterated almost all traces of the disaster."

In the decades that followed, the city's skyline grew to surpass its former heights, and "1906" became a universal touchstone for all parts of the disaster—the earthquake, the fire, the injury and death, the loss of one's home and pets and all material possessions. "1906" was a common answer by survivors to questions of what happened to their childhood home, their first job, their father's store, the school they once attended, or how a loved one died. It became shorthand for the fate of a church's first sanctuary or the elegant interior of a hotel, and the reason why, on many city streets, not a single house or restaurant or store or apartment building predates that year. "1906" came to be invoked by residents of all ages and races and classes as a unifying reminder of shared suffering and collective fortitude. "1906 Survivor" was employed as an honorific title for aging survivors who would appear at annual commemorations and share their memories, an exclusive club that dwindled each year until its last known member passed in 2016. And now in a time with the last survivor gone and no living connection to the city that was, "1906" has endured as San Francisco's historical demarcation line between its current life and its former.

Today, as with the label itself, 1906 is reduced mostly to numbers, recited as quantifiable benchmarks to wedge the catastrophe into its assigned slot on the list of historical disasters ranked by scale. Research seismologists and geophysicists and geologists have studied the data for more than a century to tell us the science: the seismic event that struck the morning of April 18, 1906, was a tectonic earthquake that ruptured 296 miles of the San Andreas Fault with an estimated moment magnitude of 7.9. And thanks to archivists and librarians and genealogists and historians, many of whom painstakingly worked to correct a distorted historical record, the quantifiable loss suffered in San Francisco during the Great Earthquake and Fire is now also widely known: every home and business in more than twenty-eight thousand structures covering more than five hundred city blocks—nearly five square miles—was destroyed. Approximately a quarter million residents or more were made homeless, and it has been estimated that more than three thousand people were killed.

From a distance of 117 years, it is difficult to reach the city as it once was, its sights and sounds and smells and grandeur and grit. And even more difficult to topple tall tales that have ascended to new heights over the past century, many defended with rigor worthy of a better cause. To tell this true story as it happened, to strip away legend from fact and attempt to comprehend what people underwent in those days and hours and seconds, I have worked to sift back through the historical ash and rubble. Letters and diaries and telegrams and unpublished memoirs of eyewitnesses—residents, visitors, firefighters, police officers, soldiers, sailors, guardsmen, city officials—written privately for family histories or published for a wide audience still survive, as do official and unofficial reports and transcripts or recordings of interviews given through the rest of the century and into the current. I have found many of these dutifully preserved in the files of city and university libraries, museums, historical societies, and archives. Others I have obtained directly from ancestors of survivors—letters and photographs they found tucked away in closets or basements of family homes, unseen for decades, a few shared publicly here for the first time. Collectively they add color to monochromatic images and sound to silent-film reels. They give us a better understanding of San Francisco's first life and the disaster that ended it. And most importantly, they add testimonial corroboration to physical and documentary evidence to reveal how a natural disaster led to such unnatural devastation.

Municipal ordinances and contracts predating 1906 reveal a city and county with public works of water, electricity, gas, and mass transit all in the grip of a few private hands. I have combed through these records and decades of building ordinances and insurance maps and reports of the private water company together with documented recommendations of city engineers and a fire chief's annual requests and repeated warnings—now ringing almost cinematic in their foresight—that highlight extremes of overconfidence in the face of fire hazards and seismic danger and defiance to almost every safety measure. These chronicle a history of city officials approving cheap construction on unstable fill land and nonenforcement of already inadequate building and fire codes, leaving the city's poorest neighborhoods a flammable tinderbox of collapsible death traps. And they document decades of reliance on a water company more intent on preserving its monopoly through bribery of city officials than updating or strengthening its water system in neighborhoods where population growth had far outpaced its dated capacity for even basic needs.

In the National Archives at San Francisco, located in San Bruno, I combed through transcripts of insurance trials conducted in the months following the disaster. Many of these have not been previously consulted and are most revelatory, containing sworn testimony from hundreds of eyewitnesses—business owners, night watchmen, barbers, cooks, bartenders, firefighters, soldiers, police officers, water company engineers, even the city's fire chief and mayor—answering probing questions about what they saw and heard and felt and what actions they and others around them took. These verbatim accounts reveal how and where many of the fires started and how quickly they spread. They expose the near-total failure of an outdated and insufficient water system entirely vulnerable to ground movement. Together with contemporaneous reports of first responders, they highlight the impossible circumstances thrust upon firefighters who worked to the end of their physical and mental tethers and managed, often with improvisational cleverness, to save lives and battle a citywide firestorm. And when read in conjunction with records from the coroner and the Department of Public Health and funeral homes as well as letters from relatives of people missing since the earthquake, all collected over several decades by a city archivist determined to finally build a more complete list of the disaster's dead, they have enabled me to reconstruct how and where many residents and visitors to the city were injured or killed.

But even when the fatalities are mapped and the origins and paths of fires followed and the actions of firefighters understood, there are questions historical records can never answer. Was thirty-six-year-old Sarah Corbus asleep or awake when the chimney crashed through the roof and crushed her to death in bed? When the Kingsbury Hotel collapsed around forty-year-old Margaret Fundenberg and her fifteen-year-old son, Edwin, visiting the city from Pennsylvania, did they both die instantly? Or did one or the other or both survive, trapped in the wreckage, doomed to asphyxiate from lethal smoke, or burn alive and conscious in the flames that followed? And when a rescuer chopped against time through one of the floors of the same collapsed hotel before being forced out by the fire, who was the man yelling from below that "three persons" were pinned in the wreckage on the other side? Who were the other two? What were their final conscious thoughts?

For all the questions the voices of San Francisco's past prompt, they tell us there was no universal experience during those three April days in 1906. How the earthquake impacted each person depended on the strength of the buildings around them and the firmness of the ground beneath them. Whether someone was afforded hours or days or only minutes or seconds to evacuate their home before fire reached them was determined by the closeness and flammability of structures on their alley or street and their proximity to businesses filled with combustible materials. The speed or ability of firefighters to stop a small fire from growing into a blaze or a blaze into a firestorm depended on the water pressure in a district's hydrants and the water level in its cisterns. Thus, someone's odds of losing their home and all their possessions as well as their ease of escape or chance of injury or death was determined by their location in the moment of impact—not their proximity to the epicenter or fault but their position on an urban minefield of hidden quicksand and ramshackle firetraps.

The earthquake itself did not destroy San Francisco or even cause most of the damage or deaths. It was one minute—roughly, give or take—of shaking sparked the three-day disaster that left the city as it was before 5:12 a.m., April 18, 1906, a place and time unrecapturable forever. Nothing beyond the earthquake was inevitable, not the extent of structural damage or the fires that resulted or the reach of the inferno or the numbers made homeless, injured, or killed. Thousands of lives had been placed at the short end of fortune's stroke, their fate sealed before the ground moved. The roots of the disaster set in violent motion that Wednesday morning reached back more than half a century to days of bonanza, when man's hunt for gold grew a waterfront village into the largest city in the American West. It is there where the first seeds of devastation were sowed and our story begins.

1. Seeds of Disaster

A T ITS END, as in its beginning, the face of San Francisco's first life was shaped by the defiant hand of man fighting stubborn forces of nature. Sixty years before its busy streets splintered and crowded buildings fell, the peninsula on which it stood was a stark landscape of sand dunes, marshland, and mudflats punctuated by shallow streams and steep hills. The city then was barely a town, no more than a shoreline dotted with a few dozen wooden buildings. Its streets, unshaded and unpaved, could be stirred into dust storms by the strong bay winds and melted into quagmires by occasional winter rains.

For thousands of years, the land was home to the Yelamu, a community of Ramaytush Ohlone peoples who adapted to the habitability challenges of a dry, sandy peninsula and lived near the few freshwater streams and on the waterfront where they found sustenance in the shellfish and traded with inhabitants further inland. The Yelamu numbered approximately two hundred or more when their land was settled by Spain in 1776 with the construction of a presidio on the bay entrance and the establishment of Mission San Francisco de Asís, later commonly known as Mission Dolores due to the nearby fertile creek, which settlers named Arroyo de los Dolores. Rather than learning the local language or cultural practices, the Spanish sought to "proselytize" and "civilize" the Yelamu and other local Ramaytush Ohlone peoples, while forcing many into indentured servitude. The Spanish also brought in large numbers of livestock, and the ecological transformation and introduction of diseases such as smallpox, measles, typhus, scarlet fever, and influenza led to the collapse of the Yelamu community and eventual disappearance of its people.

Surrounded as it was by one of the greatest natural sheltered harbors in the world and with a climate mostly free of summer heat and winter snow, the shallow cove on the peninsula's eastern waterfront established itself as an important provisioning port for ships traversing the North Pacific. After falling under the rule of Mexico in 1821, the mission was secularized, and the emerging waterfront settlement grew into a year-round trading market and was named Yerba Buena for the fragrant herbs that grew wild on local sandhills. In the summer of 1846, the town consisting of a couple of stores and hotels, a mill, a warehouse, a school, and barely two hundred residents was claimed by the United States without a shot fired when the captain of the USS *Portsmouth* marched with seventy of his men ashore to the town's adobe Custom House and raised an American flag on the plaza later named Portsmouth Square.

The next year, Yerba Buena was renamed San Francisco to match the bay, and in January 1848, gold was found more than a hundred miles away in the sand of the American River in the western slopes of the Sierra Nevada mountains. News of the discovery spread by spring, with a prospect of riches trumpeted in San Francisco by local store owners and the town's two newspapers—the only ones then published in the territory. With a population lured out to the Sierra Nevada foothills by the hope of instant wealth, the town nearly emptied of its people. And as word spread over the coming weeks and months, gold hunters arrived, and the city became their port and supply center. Over land came Mexicans from the south and Oregon settlers from the north, then voyagers sailed into the harbor from Alaska, the South Sandwich Islands, Canada, Chile, Peru, and Hawaii. Malaysians and Chinese and Australians crossed the Pacific, and after President Polk announced in his December 1848 message to Congress that California had an "abundance of gold in that territory . . . as would scarcely command belief," Americans traveled from the East Coast, as did many Europeans, braving months-long journeys that included arduous treks across the Isthmus of Panama or perilous voyages around Cape Horn, all converging to flood the town in one of the greatest peacetime migrations in modern history.

San Francisco began the year 1849 as a trading village of fewer than two thousand residents, and by year's end it was a city of more than twenty thousand. Construction soared—quick, makeshift, and cheap—of shops and warehouses and gambling saloons and boardinghouses. And wood-planked shanties. And tents, everywhere tents, of blankets or canvas, covering earthen floors packed tight with all of their worldly possessions, living spaces doubling as small shopfronts peddling bagged spices or barreled flour or stacked lumber or used mining supplies. The emerging urban center was built primarily by and for single men, who composed most of the ballooning, transient population, resulting in very few residential structures planned or suitable for permanent residency. As the city grew from the waterfront, wooden and canvas edifices spread along the ungraded dirt streets of the area's first survey—aligned roughly on a north/south axis on a grid expanding from the central plaza (later Portsmouth Square) with no regard to intervening hills, creeks, marshes, or gullies—and grew rapidly to fill the newly surveyed blocks to the south of (and parallel with) Market Street, mapped on a diagonal from the port southwestward toward the heights of Twin Peaks, the two prominent hills crowning the center of the peninsula.

Billowed sails of barks and clippers propelled tens of thousands of gold hunters through the Golden Gate—the strait so fortuitously named before the gold rush—and into San Francisco's provisioning waypoint, and as crews dropped anchor and headed for "the diggings," most of the vessels were abandoned, transforming the eastern waterfront into a crowded thicket of tall masts. Shallow Yerba Buena Cove was jammed with deserted transport boats and even a few larger ships pulled in at high tide and grounded for use as lodgings or storeships on newly mapped water lots for purchase. Martin Roberts, a lumber importer who arrived from New York in 1849, purchased two abandoned vessels on a water lot and fitted one for his wife and baby daughter, then on their way to join him. He also purchased a land lot in the city to build a home, but it would be crowded among the unsightly shanties and lean-tos that already filled the cramped dirt streets lined with canvas houses. The population of a city was wedging into the infrastructure of a village, and still the rush continued. As a visiting reporter noted, "San Francisco seemed to have accomplished in a day the growth of half a century."

City planning was hurried by the tsunami of new residents, and from the start it was shaped by fire. On Christmas Eve 1849, a large blaze began in a gambling saloon and, fueled by winds, it devoured downtown's tinderbox of wooden shanties and painted canvas tents. It burned through the night and into Christmas Day before its progress was finally halted when a makeshift bucket brigade abandoned trying to extinguish the fire and instead covered unburned structures with mud and formed a firebreak by demolishing buildings with black powder. The blaze destroyed most of the business district and caused more than $1 million in damages (equivalent to more than $38 million in 2023). City leaders called a special meeting of citizens to take the first steps toward organizing a volunteer fire department to protect against the next inevitable blaze. Three fire companies were formed around three hand-pump fire engines, led by men with previous experience as firefighters in eastern cities. And residents rebuilt quickly but cheaply. "Scarcely were the ashes cold when preparations were made to erect new buildings on the old sites," a local journalist observed. "These, like those that had just been destroyed, and like nearly all around, were chiefly composed of wood and canvas, and presented fresh fuel to the great coming conflagrations."

Five months later, a larger blaze burned through three hundred buildings—many of which had been rebuilt after the first fire—and was still spreading when volunteer firefighters formed another firebreak by pulling down wood-frame structures, halting its advance. Damages exceeded $4 million. The fire chief protested the lack of water available for his firefighters, so city council approved funding for an emergency water cistern and passed an ordinance requiring all homeowners to keep six buckets filled with water. Again, wooden and canvas structures were rebuilt quickly, and again, just five weeks later, a larger fire followed. This time it was caused by a clogged chimney in a home bakery, and stiff summer winds spread flames clear to the waterfront, growing into a firestorm that melted iron and glass and caused more than $5 million in damages, the most devastating yet.

In response, the city expanded and reorganized the fire department and budgeted for more firefighting equipment. And more businesses rebuilt with sturdier, noncombustible masonry and added iron shutters, improvements proven wise by another fire that fall that incinerated a sea of older wooden buildings covering four city blocks between Washington and Pacific Streets near the waterfront, stopped again by the intrepid efforts of volunteer firefighters.

The following spring, a three-day fire, fueled in part by newly installed elevated wood-plank roads and sidewalks, reduced 1,500 buildings across eighteen blocks—three-fourths of the city, including the entire business section—to ashes, causing more than $12 million in damages. One volunteer who worked a water pump for more than six hours fighting the flames wrote to his wife of "over one thousand homes enveloped in flames at once, a perfect sea of fire." Martin Roberts "worked all night" saving the lumber inventory on his lot and returned to his family's moored houseboat exhausted. Just six weeks later, during yet another round of rebuilding, another blaze consumed ten city blocks of structures, including the hospital, Custom House, and City Hall.

After six major fires in eighteen months, most downtown structures were rebuilt with brick and stone, such as the four-story Montgomery Block, the city's first "fireproof" building (and for a brief time after its 1853 completion, the tallest building west of St. Louis). A new city building code established a downtown fire district where no canvas or wood-frame structures could be built and where open fires and candles were banned. Iron shutters and metal roofs were also added to buildings to increase fire resistance. The paving of streets and sidewalks began, replacing wood planking. Reserve water cisterns were finally constructed. And as the city approved more funding for firefighting equipment, a growing number of residents volunteered for duty as firefighters. Companies were formed by groups of friends and neighbors, often of the same national heritage: the Lafayette Hook & Ladder Company was formed by French immigrants, and the Hibernia Engine Company by Irish. The city paid for engines and wagons, but much of the equipment and protective gear was purchased with donations from wealthy citizens or the firemen themselves. Martin Roberts, busy working on the expansion of wharves and building his own home, organized a fire company and served as captain, and he stored his company's pump engine on his front yard until a firehouse was built a block away. Eventually, more than twenty volunteer fire companies were available to respond to fires, all in healthy competition for the best response time.

California was admitted to the Union as the thirty-first state in 1850, and San Francisco's hotels and stores and gambling saloons were brimming with the currency of gold. Miners on their way to or from the diggings paid for liquor and women and lodgings and gambled with gold lumps or dust poured from leather pokes onto scales that topped every bar and card table and store counter. "A copper coin was a strange sight," a journalist observed. That same year, the federal government established an Assay Office in the city to not only test the purity of miners' gold but establish a uniform standard for fineness, weight, and value. Private smelting companies were authorized to issue coins meeting these standards until Congress officially established the San Francisco Mint downtown on Commercial Street, the first in the West. Completed in 1854, the three-story "thoroughly fireproof" cement-covered brick structure housing vaults and a foundry converted $4 million (equivalent to more than $142 million in 2023) in mined gold into coins in just the first year.

San Francisco's population topped fifty thousand by 1853, and city planning lagged behind city expansion as developers flattened nonconforming dunes and hills with steam shovels to grade for streets and hauled the sand and mud to fill ravines and creek beds south of Market Street—to depths in some places of forty feet or more. And most was hauled to the waterfront, where it was dumped into Yerba Buena Cove and down in the coastal marsh of Mission Bay along with trash and the wooden remains of abandoned boats, adding hundreds of acres of landfill real estate to the city's shoreline for even more new construction. Within the decade, many of the city's boardinghouses, hotels, and businesses sat on dozens of unstable city blocks atop "fill" or "made" land.

And blocks beyond downtown filled with wood-frame apartment buildings and houses as more tenants stayed and resident families grew. Martin Roberts finished building a house at the corner of Stockton and Washington Streets for his family to move from their water lot just as his wife gave birth to their second daughter, Grace, in 1852. One of a soaring number of native-born San Franciscans in the nation's newest state, Grace traveled with her parents to Washington, DC, at the age of eight and met President Buchanan at a reception, where he took her hand and remarked, "You are the oldest native Californian I have ever seen."

By the time the rush for gold waned in the mid-1850s, the city had matured from a mud-lined town of tents and shanties into a wood-frame and brick-walled mercantile center where new fortunes were made in maritime trade, agriculture, and manufacturing. Banks had emerged to offer more opportunities for commercial ventures, institutions which with the mint coaxed order from the chaos of messy dealings among merchants from mismatched world markets. Enterprise flourished in the densely concentrated heart of the city, beating to the rapid pace of a waterfront teeming with Pacific commerce, and the legacies of many of the era's entrepreneurs would prove immortal. Among them was Italian immigrant Domenico "Domingo" Ghirardelli who decided, after his general store burned in one of the 1851 fires, to open a confectionery shop downtown selling chocolate, candy, liquors, and spices, and later became world-famous for his delicious, sweetened chocolate. And James Folger, who traveled from Nantucket to the Golden Gate in 1850 and made enough money to buy a controlling share in the spice and coffee mill where he worked, from which he shipped roasted ground coffee to towns and mining camps throughout the Pacific Northwest. And Levi Strauss, a Bavarian immigrant who started a dry goods store near the waterfront in 1854 and eventually partnered with a customer who was a tailor to patent a new idea of riveting denim pants, giving birth to blue jeans.

In 1865, when news of the start of the Civil War four years before took a dozen days to reach San Francisco on horseback, word of Union victory arrived within hours via telegraph. And with the city topping 100,000 residents during the war and nearly 150,000 just five years later, the greatest challenge for city planners through the urban hyper-expansion and frenzy of construction was supplying fresh water to a growing population on a hilly peninsula with inadequate springs, only a few small lakes, and no large reservoirs in a climate of limited rain. Early on, fresh water from the springs of Sausalito was ferried across the bay in barrels and sold by street vendors by the bucket. Soon, private companies formed to send water into the city, one through wooden pipes across the peninsula from Mountain Lake, and another through flumes and tunnels from a reservoir formed by damming Lobos Creek, but both sources proved insufficient.

Seizing the chance to profit from the mounting demand, a resident financier acquired from the state legislature an exclusive contract to build a water supply system for the city and county of San Francisco, and together with other investors formed Spring Valley Water Works. After absorbing its only competitor, Spring Valley's control of the city's water supply was complete, a monopoly preserved for many decades through political favors and outright bribery of city and county officials. Armed with eminent domain rights, the enterprise—renamed the Spring Valley Water Company—grabbed land around the Pilarcitos Creek down in San Mateo County and redirected its water up the peninsula through redwood flumes and wrought-iron pipes more than ten miles to San Francisco, crossing mudflats and marshland on the way. City leaders commissioned the company to build reservoirs and pumping stations and a pipe distribution system throughout the city, projects overseen by Hermann Schussler, who was splitting his time as the company's chief engineer and a consultant to hydraulic mining companies.

Having forfeited the public issue of water to private interests, San Francisco's governing body, the Board of Supervisors, did no better with setting safety standards for new construction. After the fires of 1849–51, many downtown buildings had been rebuilt with "fireproof" materials, but as the city grew over "made" fill land, no laws forced developers to test bearing capacities of soil or drive foundations to safe depths based on a new building's height or weight. As residential streets expanded westward across the peninsula, most new homes had wood frames, and South of Market, businesses and tall boardinghouses were constructed as cheaply and as close together as possible. When the city finally did update building codes to mandate fireproofing of wooden beams and trusses, spacing between structures, and setting thickness and brick/mortar-quality minimums on load-bearing walls and chimneys and flues, the tardy rules did not apply to existing structures, and favored developers were granted exceptions.

In 1866, after the state legislature approved a paid fire department for the city and county of San Francisco to be managed by a board of fire commissioners, volunteer fire companies were disbanded, and a paid-call fire department was placed into service. The company structure of the volunteer department remained, their company names changed to numbers and organized around six newly purchased horse-drawn, steam-pump fire engines with large boilers that built pressure to pump water from hydrants or reserve cisterns and apply to a fire. As these were far more powerful and efficient than the old manual hand-pump engines, the city allocated funds for more new steam engines and horses to pull them. And while many veterans of the volunteer force stayed on, new firemen were recruited and trained for paid positions, though the new department would still rely on a large force of "on-call" firemen paid per call.

San Francisco's population grew even more with the completion of the transcontinental railroad in 1869, finally linking the commercial center of the West Coast with the East. And within San Francisco, the local invention in 1873 of what newspapers then called an "endless-chain, stationary-engine, up-hill railroad"—soon known as the cable car—connected the city's landscape, pushing more development up to the top of its steep hills and into the western sandhills. David Colton, who had made his millions in gold and real estate, had built a neoclassical villa not far from Grace Church at the top of the California Street hill, and after the Clay Street cable car began running, the "Big Four" founders of the Central Pacific Railroad—Mark Hopkins, Leland Stanford, Collis Huntington, and Charles Crocker—staked their claim on the hilltop with baroque, Victorian, and Italianate mansions, followed by silver baron James Flood, whose Classical Revival home was built with Connecticut brownstone shipped around Cape Horn. Newspapers spilled sufficient ink about California Street's "aristocratic thoroughfare" of gaudy palaces built by the "nabobs of Nob Hill" to give the hill its name.

The cable car transformed transportation across San Francisco as many horse-cars and steam-powered streetcars of other passenger railways were converted to a cable system. New cable car companies were formed and new tracks carried passenger-filled cars into the newly graded streets of the Western Addition, extending residential growth out to the Presidio and newly developed Golden Gate Park, keeping middle-class and upper-middle-class residents of newer, more distant neighborhoods connected with downtown. And new cable car lines followed, rolling through North Beach and over Russian Hill—named for the hilltop cemetery of Russian seamen discovered by early settlers—and Nob Hill and down through the banking and harbor districts. Cars of a funicular cable railway even climbed Telegraph Hill, named for the first telegraph office built on the peak (replacing earlier wooden pole-top semaphores) to signal the arrival of ships through the Golden Gate. New lines of rail slots also cut the length of Market Street, and within a few years, electric overhead lines were installed South of Market for trolleys rolling from the waterfront to the Mission District and beyond.

Public and private development soared, raising the countenance of the city to its new station as the "metropolis of California." At noon on February 22, 1872—the 140th anniversary of George Washington's birth—the cornerstone was laid for a massive new City Hall, planned as a "municipal palace" occupying an entire city block. In 1874, a new US Mint was completed on Mission Street after four years of construction, an imposing granite and sandstone structure of Greek Revival style housing vaults that would eventually store one-third of the nation's gold reserve and a foundry that within three years would be minting nearly 60 percent of the nation's annual output of gold and silver coins. And the seven-story Palace Hotel was built on Market Street, which at its opening in 1875 was not only the city's tallest building but its most elegant, and with 755 guest rooms, it was the largest hotel in the United States.

The 1880 census counted 233,959 residents in San Francisco, and as ever, most were immigrants. The population explosion of the gold rush had turned the city's northeastern piers into a business gateway for fishermen from Italy, Spain, Mexico, and South America. In the years that followed, the area between Russian Hill and Telegraph Hill became known as the "Latin Quarter" for its concentration of Spanish and Italian speakers, and the North Beach district, with its growing population of Italian Americans, would become the city's "Little Italy." In the 1880 census, the population of North Beach and the Latin Quarter was included in the broad "white" demographic, which accounted for 90 percent of the city's official population and included native-born Americans and Californians and those of other non-Asian ancestry, such as Germans, Australians, Russians, Mexicans, French, and Irish.

The city's Black residents were classified then as "Colored" and composed less than 1 percent of the total population. Some of the earliest pioneers of Yerba Buena had included people of African descent, like William Leidesdorff, a West

Indian of Danish African ancestry who arrived in town as a merchant captain and operated the first steamboat in San Francisco Bay as well as the town's first hotel and commercial shipping warehouse. As a successful businessman—and with his biracial identity mostly unknown at the time—he was appointed the port's American vice-consul by President Polk, and after the territory fell under US control, he was elected to the town council and served as town treasurer. When he died of typhoid fever in 1848, flags on ships filling the harbor were flown at half-mast and the *California Star* declared "the town has lost its most valuable resident."

When gold fever spread through the abolitionist press and free Black communities, many African Americans joined parties taking overland routes to the gold fields. So too did many from the South, brought by white owners as slaves, some of whom gained or purchased freedom for themselves and their families after arriving. Quite a few found success starting and operating businesses, like Mifflin Gibbs and Peter Lester from Philadelphia, who ran the Pioneer Boot and Shoe Emporium; Henry Cornish, who ran a furniture and clothing business on Battery Street; and George Washington Dennis, an ex-slave who ran a livery stable. More than 450 Black residents were counted in San Francisco in 1850 when California was admitted to the US as a "free" state, but they were denied the right to vote as well as equal testimony rights in court, and slavery was effectively practiced before and after statehood, especially after the passage of the California Fugitive Slave Law.

Forced outside the white power structure, San Franciscans of African descent built and maintained their own society. Frustrated by worshipping from the segregated pews of First Baptist Church, a few Black parishioners established the First Colored Baptist Church—later renamed the Third Baptist Church—of San Francisco in 1852, the first African American Baptist church west of the Rockies. That same year, the first African Methodist Episcopal Church of San Francisco—the First A.M.E. Zion Church—was organized. A former slave from West Virginia established the city's first Black periodical, the *Lunar Visitor*, and the city's first Black newspaper, *Mirror of the Times*, followed. With African American children excluded from early city-run schools, a "Negro Children's School" was established in the basement of an A.M.E. church. Black ideological leaders set up the Athenaeum and Literary Association, a center for intellectual life and one of the city's first circulating libraries, predating the public library by more than two decades. And after the Civil War, freed people journeyed west and steadily added to the city's African

American community, which grew from 1,176 in 1860 to 1,330 in 1870 and 1,628 by 1880.

In that same 1880 census, 21,790 of San Francisco's residents were singled out as "Chinese," the only demographic segregated by national heritage, comprising more than 9 percent of the population. Gold hunters from China had been among the first to enter the Golden Gate in 1848 and join the diverse populace filling the city's streets. Even then, the Chinese—derogatorily called "Celestials" and "Coolies" by many of the city's English-speaking immigrants—were singled out for racial ridicule and stereotype. "There were hordes of long pig-tailed, blear-eyed, rank-smelling Chinese, with their yellow faces and blue garbs," declared a book of the city's early history published in 1855, reflecting a prevailing xenophobia that would translate into social, political, and legal exclusion.

By the end of the gold rush, Chinese laborers composed as much as one-fourth of mine workers, and they filled an estimated 85 percent of the jobs on the California Pacific Railroad, where they played an instrumental role in construction of the transcontinental railroad. They worked long days through the unshaded heat of summer and cold Sierra winters, leveling ground and laying track and building bridges and blasting through mountains with gunpowder and dynamite. They slept in unheated tents or caves and survived the perils of boring through rock walls and loading dynamite while working in wicker baskets slung from ropes or balancing on timber frames of bridges high above gorges and canyons. When the railroad work ended, most laborers returned to San Francisco to find jobs, and in the economic depression of the 1870s, Chinese residents became the scapegoat for every ill from crime to unemployment. Editorials on "the Chinese problem" filled local newspapers. "The Chinese Must Go!" became a rallying cry for politicians, especially leaders of the newly formed Workingmen's Party, which united its white, working-class members with racial grievances aimed at Chinese laborers and elected sufficient members to the state legislature in 1878 to pass a ban on voting by anyone of Chinese ancestry.

In 1879, a new state constitution chiseled anti-Chinese prejudice into the bedrock of the state charter. When admitted to the Union as a "free" state in 1850, California's first constitution—like most states at the time—restricted voting to white male citizens. During Reconstruction following the Civil War, the 1870 ratification of the Fifteenth Amendment extended voting rights to Black male residents, and while the federal Naturalization Act of the same year also extended naturalization to residents of African nativity or descent, it specifically excluded Chinese residents. And both changes were reflected in California's 1879 constitution, which vested the right to vote in every male citizen "*provided,* no native of China . . . shall ever exercise the privileges of an elector in this State." A new section titled "Chinese" was also added to the constitution, forbidding corporations or state, county, or municipal governments from employing "any Chinese or Mongolian," and requiring the legislature to regulate, restrict, and remove Chinese residents by all legal means and "discourage their immigration by all the means within its power."

By 1880 in San Francisco, the Workingmen's Party held the offices of mayor, sheriff, auditor, and district attorney. Anti-Chinese ordinances were swiftly passed, and existing zoning and public health laws were enforced selectively to purge neighborhoods and lodging houses of Chinese tenants and the city of Chinese-owned businesses everywhere except the twelve-square-block community many Chinese residents knew then as *Tong Yun Fow*, Cantonese for "Town of the Tang People." San Francisco's Chinatown would expand in size and become the largest concentration of Chinese Americans—and the most densely populated neighborhood—in the United States.

Nationally, the Chinese Exclusion Act was enacted in 1882, banning further immigration of workers from China to the United States and barring reentry to previous residents—including those born in the United States—resulting in the detention of Chinese residents returning to the city from trips abroad to visit family. One was twenty-one-year-old Wong Kim Ark, who was born in San Francisco to Chinese immigrant parents in 1873. When his parents returned to China in 1890, Wong stayed to live and work in the city he knew as home. But when he returned by steamship from visiting them in 1895—even though he was prepared with an identification document signed by three white residents who knew him to be a born-and-raised San Franciscan—the officer in the Custom House refused him permission to land and ordered him held by the ship's captain. Wong applied for habeas corpus, and after five months in floating detention, his petition was heard and the federal district judge ordered him released. The US Attorney's office appealed to the US Supreme Court, and in 1898 the court ruled that the citizenship clause of the Fourteenth Amendment—itself barely older than Wong—"includes the children born, within the territory of the United States, of all other persons, of whatever race or color, domiciled within the United States." Thus, the landmark case of *United States v. Wong Kim Ark* secured birthright citizenship for all children born of immigrants in the United States, a durable precedent that still stands today. But in its day, San Francisco's leaders remained undeterred, and strict enforcement of exclusion laws tailored narrowly around the ruling forced American-born Chinese residents to carry their birth certificates or identity cards anytime they left the confines of Chinatown.

Cultural differences—Eastern religious practices of Taoism and Buddhism, the Cantonese and Mandarin languages, the "bound feet" of Chinese women, the long braids (called "queues") worn by many Chinese men—were often singled out by white residents for mockery, and many of them passed on the most dreadful lies to their children, instilling not just resentment but fear. Etta Siegel, brought to America from Romania by her parents when she was not yet three years old, was from a young age "scared to death of them" because she was warned by her parents to "stay away, be careful or they would kidnap you." It was not until her later years that Etta understood the racist fables she was taught were fiction: "They were just as 'fraid of us, I'm sure, as we were of them."

But the fear felt by San Francisco's residents with Chinese ancestry was real and based on a shared experience of ridicule, legal exclusion, imprisonment, and even violence. Residents of Chinatown were surrounded by a city largely hostile to their neighborhood's presence, a city led by men who had tried to expel them before and would seize on any reason to try again.

San Francisco's population approached 300,000 by 1890, eighth by size in the United States and the largest west of St. Louis. The city's first skyscraper, the ten-story, steel-frame, red sandstone de Young Chronicle Building, was completed that year with a clock tower climbing 218 feet above Market Street. Not to be outdone, the Spreckels Call Building across the street followed and soared 315 feet to the top of its baroque dome. West of Van Ness Avenue, fresh rows of Stick-style, Eastlake, and Queen Anne Victorian houses popped up in the Western Addition neighborhoods of Cow Hollow and Pacific Heights, and empty lots were bought up for more construction in the new Richmond District and Presidio Heights neighborhoods along newly graded streets through the leveled sand dunes between Golden Gate Park and the Presidio, and in the Sunset District south of the park.

To meet an ever-increasing need for water in the city, the Spring Valley Water Company claimed more land in San Mateo County, built a dam to divert more creeks and runoff into additional reservoirs, and ran more flumes and pipes up the peninsula. The company even pushed into the valleys and creek system of Alameda County, prompting Oakland merchants and officials to protest the company's encroachment into their local water sources. And until stopped by a series of court rulings, San Francisco received water for all "municipal purposes" free of charge, allowing Spring Valley to compensate by driving rates up on its individual customers, prices considered "extortionate." But beyond complaints by residents of Spring Valley's high rates and poor service or talk on the street and in newspapers of the company's corruption and undue political influence, it was the city's fire chief, Dennis Sullivan, who reported to the Board of Supervisors that his firemen were "handicapped by the lack of water, the want of pressure, and the dearth of hydrants." And his was a voice difficult to ignore.

If institutions are "the lengthened shadow of one man," as Ralph Waldo Emerson once declared, then the man casting the shadow of the San Francisco Fire Department by the mid-1890s was Dennis Sullivan. Clean-shaven with a cleft chin, discerning eyes, and closely trimmed reddish-brown hair, Sullivan was a man of "wonderful physique" and "perfect health" who carried his shorter stature with a squared, upright posture. Sullivan originally joined an engine company of the fire department at the age of twenty-five as a blacksmith, a skill he had refined since his early teenage years in New York. His work ethic and attention to detail earned him a higher-paid position as a stoker, then promotion to hydrant inspector, then district engineer, then assistant chief. After the 1893 death of long-time chief David Scannell, Sullivan's "extraordinary adaptability to the work" won him the respect of his peers and appointment as chief of the department at the age of forty-one.

The new chief arranged for a drill tower to be built for training his firefighters, conducted inspections of all reserve water cisterns throughout the city, ordered that all officers maintain in their homes a bell connected with the central fire alarm office, and required all battalion chiefs to live within one block of their firehouse. For his part, he made his home[1] with his wife, Margaret, on the third floor of the Bush Street firehouse for Chemical Engine 3 downtown. Sullivan earned a reputation for personally responding to most fires, no matter how far removed from his quarters, sometimes even beating the first engines to the scene. "Chief Sullivan arrived in less than five minutes" of the alarm and ahead of his engines, a newspaper reported of a February 1894 fire, where he called in a second alarm and was disturbed by the "scarcity of hydrants" available for his responding engines and low water pressure in the few nearby.

---

1 The Sullivans also owned a house on 49th Avenue (present-day La Playa St.) out in the Richmond District.

He had already witnessed the deadly effects of the lack of water the previous summer when a blaze in the Western Addition burned a block of homes to the ground and took the lives of three firemen because "hydrants were too far away and too few." And he noted it again at another three-alarm fire a few months later when a grocery store and the San Francisco Press Club were gutted by a blaze that his firemen again fought with "weak streams" of water.

Chief Sullivan wasted no time in making a strong case to the Board of Supervisors for drastic changes. Pointing to the "alarming increase in the number of fires each year" and the steep jump in average monthly fire alarms from fifteen to forty-one over the previous five years, he lobbied for building codes stronger than the existing "faulty and contradictory" ordinances that had fostered a landscape of structures "built almost entirely of wood." Reminding city leaders that his firemen were charged with the protection of residents crowded on a peninsula "far removed" from any neighboring city's ability to render aid in the event of a major fire, he requested funding for more engines, hoses, and firehouses, and he urged the board to make the department full-paid, eliminating reliance on part-time "on-call" firemen.

And in what was reported as a "scathing report on the city's lack of water," Chief Sullivan took direct aim at the Spring Valley Water Company, calling the feeble water pressure and lack of hydrants "wholly inadequate" in the event of large fires. Sufficient water was delivered into the city from reservoirs through transmission mains, but it was conveyed to most streets through four-inch and six-inch distribution mains with capacities outpaced by new construction that had doubled and tripled the water needs for each block. Larger mains could deliver sufficient water to meet the needs of added residents through additional service pipes, unlike the existing, smaller mains, which resulted in low pressure, especially when more than one or two hydrants on the same block were used, forcing fire engines on a second or third alarm to relay water from hydrants three and four blocks distant. This was especially true South of Market where, along some blocks, a 250-foot stretch of street lined with apartment buildings housing hundreds of residents was fed water through multiple service pipes from a smaller distribution main—four-inch diameter—as compared to a six-inch-diameter main on Nob Hill that along the same length of street supplied one or two houses. This led to water pressure challenges in crowded, poorer sections of the city even in the absence of a fire emergency. Chief Sullivan identified more than fifty streets—most of them South of Market—where larger eight-inch to twelve-inch mains were needed, lobbied for 320 new hydrants, and after his men found most of the city's reserve cisterns unfilled, unusable, and all in a neglected state, he urged the Board of Public Works to fix, fill, and better maintain them.

In 1896, San Francisco elected a new mayor, thirty-five-year-old James Phelan, an Irish Catholic millionaire son of a forty-niner. A lifelong bachelor of medium height with a closely trimmed beard gone prematurely gray, Phelan was far more interested in public service and his own ideas of urban improvement than the commercialism that had made his father's fortune. He was anti-Asian, supported racist Chinese exclusion and zoning laws, and eventually would run a statewide campaign to "Keep California White." His municipal focus in his 1896 campaign was eradication of the bribery and political favors that had plagued City Hall for decades, and along those ethical lines, as historian Walton Bean noted, "He was immune to the temptations that afflicted politicians of lesser character and inferior financial independence."

Phelan was elected and reelected on a platform opposing civic corruption and served with an eye toward reform, specifically aiming to gain public control of the city's water supply. During his tenure, he managed to enact a new city charter, a portion of which restored accountability by providing for rotating membership of municipal boards, appointed annually by the mayor in staggered terms. And after Chief Sullivan's repeated urgings, the Board of Supervisors approved a "full paid" professional fire department, paying all firemen to be "continuously on duty" rather than "on call." And new firefighting equipment was added, including more steam-pump engines and more of the new chemical engines, which carried tanks of water and smaller containers of soda powder and acid that, when mixed and added to the water tank, caused a chemical reaction that pressurized the contents, forcing a stream through the hose and acting as large extinguishers.

In 1899, the new City Hall opened after twenty-seven years of construction (the cornerstone had been laid when Mayor Phelan was ten) to little fanfare. It was the largest municipal building in the west and boasted a dome taller than the capitol and third tallest in the world. But beneath its brilliant, original design and imposing façade ran deep scars of graft, and a quarter century of different architects and conflicting designs applied in eight separate construction phases with a laundry list of contractors cutting corners to fund kickbacks fostered doubts in the quality of materials and workmanship. Grand juries heard testimony about "large sums collected for work that was never done" on the massive dome, use of substandard materials such as unreinforced masonry, and "slipshod work" covered with plaster and paint. Before it could be occupied, more money was necessary for repairs to rusting ironwork and falling plaster ceilings. Once opened, it was already dated, "a dark and dismal pile of masonry," lacking ventilation or heat, and "architecturally a horrible nightmare." In the end, it cost the city more than $5.7 million (more than $200 million in 2023). As San Francisco entered a new century, City Hall presented a conspicuous monument to civic corruption and a broader, cautionary metaphor of dangerous instability in a city where a seismic menace lurked just beneath a grand but brittle exterior.

The threat of earthquakes hung constantly over San Francisco, as it does today, even if it was not as widely discussed then, or its science developed or causes understood. The city sits on the junction of the earth's two largest tectonic plates, the Pacific and the North American, two of more than a dozen gigantic plates forming our planet's surface kept in slow but constant motion by thermal energy in the mantle miles below. Rock masses along plate junctions are strained and stretched and crushed by the forces of these sections of land mass and oceanic crust colliding or slipping or pulling apart. Where they meet along the North Coast of California, the Pacific and the North American Plates are both gradually moving to the northwest, but the relatively faster movement of the Pacific Plate causes the slower North American to appear as if it is creeping to the southeast. This constant oppositional ground movement has turned the Bay Area into a giant shear system marked with displaced crust and crossed with faults where the ground has fractured in the past, not only scarring the land but shaping its unique beauty into a scenic embodiment of the mobile and active surface of the earth. The Santa Cruz Mountains and Marin Headlands were thrust up along the San Andreas Fault, and the Oakland and Berkeley Hills along the Hayward Fault. Movement of rocks along faults formed Napa Valley, Portola Valley, Monterey Bay, Tomales Bay, and the sand-covered plain we know today as Silicon Valley. Even the deep-water-protected port of San Francisco Bay itself—the trait that made the city the wellspring for the gold rush—was formed by movement along faults.

Periodically, the forces of energy constantly loaded into the region by the applied dynamic stress of rock masses between the creeping motion of the two colossal plates overcome the forces of friction holding them together, causing a sudden and violent break along a fault, resulting in an earthquake. Parked as it is midway between the San Andreas Fault and the Hayward Fault, the peninsula on which San Francisco sits has been shaken at irregular intervals by earthquakes. The original adobe chapel at the Presidio was toppled by a severe shock in 1812, and another in 1838 cracked the brittle adobe walls on other Presidio structures and in Mission Dolores. After 1849 (when records were regularly kept), earthquakes were recorded each year, ranging from "slight" to "violent," some causing swells in the bay or even tidal waves, a few causing structural damage, injury, and death. In 1865, author Mark Twain was present to experience "the heaviest earthquake shock" and witnessed falling buildings and the panicked rush of frightened residents into the streets: "Never was a solemn solitude turned into teeming life quicker."

In October 1868, the entire Bay Area was shaken by a rupture along the Hayward Fault, causing what would be known—at least until 1906—as the "big" one, "the great earthquake." Streets split apart and walls of brick buildings cracked or collapsed. Structures on "made" land—which lost its solidity and liquefied in the shaking—were "totally demolished" by catastrophic settlement, and both the original City Hall and Custom House were "badly damaged." Throughout the Bay Area, more than one hundred people were injured and thirty killed—six in the city, some from falling walls, chimneys, and cornices. The Chamber of Commerce formed an earthquake committee for the purpose of "providing against the effects of earthquakes by improvements in building," to which were appointed scientists and engineers and architects to make recommendations for upgrades in building materials and structural design. It was another full year before the report was submitted to the chamber, which "was accepted without reading and placed on file." And for unknown reasons it was never published.

Even without a public report, the committee's conclusions were no secret to builders, and architects and engineers did study the structural damage caused by the earthquakes of 1865 and 1868, and some changes did follow. Most of the city's buildings had wood frames, which offered flexibility in response to ground movement but were prone to collapse without diagonal bracing. And most buildings concentrated in the city's downtown area—particularly within the designated fire limits—were timber-joisted masonry, where outer walls of brick and mortar bore the loads of the inner structure—wooden floors and columns and ceilings and roof supported by timber trusses and joists anchored into the masonry. The thick, heavy, rigid outer brick walls with low tensile strength—little resistance to snapping or cracking—were largely inflexible to ground movement, and lateral shearing motions of earthquakes caused them to crack or collapse, dropping the roof and inside floors. And if joists and trusses supporting the inner floors and roof were insufficiently anchored, even just a few inches of lateral movement of the outer walls could cause a pancaking of the interior living space within a standing outer shell.

Architects and engineers recommended lowering chimneys and using better masonry mixtures and thoroughly cured bricks less prone to cracking. To reinforce brick masonry walls, iron rods could be inserted through the mortar and anchors used to secure wooden joists and girders to outer walls, recommendations for new construction and for retrofitting existing structures. Builders responded and by the 1870s, some new structures employed sufficient strengthening methods to be heralded as "earthquake proof," such as the Palace Hotel with cross walls tied to strong exterior walls reinforced within iron banding, and the new mint built with iron reinforcing rods within the masonry behind its sandstone exterior atop a floating foundation of deep concrete and granite basement walls. New building codes codified a few of these recommendations, requiring that walls be anchored with iron to wooden beams and foundations laid of stone or brick to resist settlement. But the new code did not apply to existing structures, and with its new requirements inadequately enforced by overworked inspectors, most safety upgrades would be left entirely to market forces. And while pricier hotels such as the Palace and Grand and later the St. Francis and Fairmont spent more on added structural safety, there was little incentive for tenement landlords or owners of lodging houses in working-class districts to assume the cost of structural retrofitting for the safety of tenants, and no building codes required it. Through the minds of civic leaders and developers ran a hope that earthquakes—especially 1868's "big" one—would simply be forgotten.

But unavoidable reminders visited the city a few times each year, usually in the form of "long rolling" tremors or a "sharp, undulating shock," a few severe enough to make tall buildings shake "like the snapping of a whip." These shudders and minor earthquakes rippled through the ground beneath the city when the bedrock holding together the two shifting plates fractured along one of the region's smaller faults, or along a distant section of a larger fault. But the long portion of the San Andreas running through northern California—and directly alongside San Francisco—was locked together as it had been for many decades even as the rocks beneath the ground on each side continued moving, constantly contorting the crust and loading the fault with massive amounts of elastic strain. The small, periodic breaks along other faults could not accommodate the two plates' continuous creeping movement, and eventually the overwhelming, opposing forces of strain and friction would reach a violent breaking point. It was inevitable: another "big" one would strike the Bay Area, sooner or later.

As year after year passed, the additions of gas lines and electric wiring and more densely jammed, wood-frame structures in the crowded city compounded the hazards to follow the next great earthquake with the additional risk of widespread fire. And every year with increasing urgency, Chief Dennis Sullivan urged the Board of Supervisors for changes. He listed locations where more hydrants were needed, a list that grew longer after the repeated reply from the Spring Valley Water Company's engineer Hermann Schussler: "the company declines." Sullivan stressed the need for an auxiliary saltwater system for the downtown banking and harbor districts patterned after that of the city of Boston. And he recommended that a large seawater reservoir be built on the high elevation of Twin Peaks connected with hydrants "to ensure a sufficient supply of water in case of a large conflagration." And a "light-draught, high-power" fireboat "of good speed and large pumping capacity" for protection of the waterfront to ensure an open lifeline for water traffic. And larger water mains to replace "the small and inadequate" mains of many streets. With frustration firmly rooted in the immovable Spring Valley Water Company's increasingly inadequate water delivery system and refusal to spend on improvements, Sullivan finally wrote the board that "as the carrying out of these recommendations depends upon the will of a private corporation, very little has as yet been accomplished."

In 1901, after intervening in a labor fight and siding with employers by using the police force against striking workers—a move that drastically eroded his popularity in a city where more than one-third of the population paid union dues—Mayor Phelan declined to run for another term, unable during his tenure to accomplish either of his grander goals of eliminating Spring Valley Water Company's private monopoly or removing the supervisors who enabled it. Into the political vacuum stepped millionaire lawyer, real estate investor, and political boss Abe Ruef. A native San Franciscan who stood five feet, eight inches tall with a receding black hairline and a full dark mustache beneath a prominent nose, Ruef was a studied master of patronage and political favor. Recently frustrated by his inability to overcome the Southern Pacific Railroad's continued control within even the local Republican Party, Ruef spied an alternate path to municipal power in a new political party then forming out of the city's recent labor disputes, the Union Labor Party. And after packing the convention with his chosen delegates, the man known to locals as "the power behind the throne" found his perfect candidate for mayor in his friend and client Eugene Schmitz.

Also a native San Franciscan and the same age as Ruef (they both turned thirty-seven by the 1901 election), Eugene Schmitz was "a commanding figure of a man." He stood six feet tall, had a head full of curly black hair, sported a thick mustache and goatee, and dressed impeccably. A concert violinist, former conductor of the Columbia Theatre orchestra, and president of the musicians' union, Schmitz was both cultured and amiable. And married with two children, he was also a practicing Catholic of German Irish descent, helpful with three of the city's largest, overlapping voting blocs. After giving speeches written by Ruef in a campaign financed by Ruef, Schmitz won the election and was sworn in the following January. Abe Ruef acted officially as unpaid "legal advisor" to the new mayor, meeting regularly with seekers of favors or jobs, followed by payments of political contributions or "attorney's fees" to his law firm "for advice in matters of municipal law," after which Ruef would "share his fees" with the supervisors and the mayor. Schmitz's administration—soon referred to as the "Ruef-Schmitz" government—would halt the momentum of even modest reform, undermine the new charter's civil service organization by appointing paid loyalists to important public boards, and erode what little accountability had been previously forced on Spring Valley's monopoly.

By 1902, with a population nearing 400,000, more of San Francisco was made of wood than any other major American city (93 percent of its structures, compared with 70 percent in Boston, 20 percent in St. Louis, and only 6 percent in Philadelphia). In New York City's Manhattan borough, the National Board of Fire Underwriters found "very little frame construction." And Chicago, with stronger building codes thirty years past its own citywide conflagration, had rebuilt responsibly and was only 44 percent wooden. The San Francisco Board of Supervisors passed an updated building ordinance in 1903 mandating fireproof roofing and incombustible materials in future construction, prohibiting additions or expansions to existing wooden structures, and mandating fire escapes on all buildings. But the new code did little to reduce the risk of fire or improve durability against seismic threats in the city as it currently stood. And enforcement of the new standards was in the hands of Mayor Schmitz's appointees on the board of the Department of Public Works—led by his own brother—who granted permits for the most favored developers regardless of noncompliance.

National recommendations for use of steel or reinforced concrete in construction of taller structures were ignored by officials indebted to the bricklayers' union, resulting in more use of brick masonry, which lacked elasticity and was more likely to crack or crumble under the stress of an earthquake. Because the new code yet again did not apply to existing structures, within the "fire limits"—expanded to include more of downtown, the banking and harbor districts, and a portion South of Market where supposedly only "fire-proof" structures would be allowed—a third of the buildings were wood-frame and nearly two-thirds were timber-joisted masonry (with outer load-bearing brick-and-mortar walls but floors and roofs and columns of timber, boards, and planks, most without fireproofing), proportions that would not improve before 1906. And while the city also approved initial funding in 1905 for the auxiliary seawater reservoir on Twin Peaks for fire suppression, construction fatefully would not begin until after 1906.

In the middle of this tinderbox, Dennis Sullivan had during his decade as chief managed to upgrade the fire department itself into one of the most modern and efficient in the world. 584 full-time firefighters practiced multiple times daily with their equipment, building instinct and muscle memory that was triggered into quick action when the alarm sounded. They worked out of forty-five firehouses with thirty-eight steam engines and seven chemical engines. There were also a dozen ladder companies, ten truck companies, and enough dray and trotter horses stabled in every company house to hitch three to each steam engine and two to each chemical engine and hose wagon for more power and speed up the city's steep hills. It was a state-of-the-art fire department tasked with the impossible: protecting a city of wood with insufficient water.

A cautionary omen reverberated across the nation in early 1904 when a major fire destroyed more than 1,500 buildings in downtown Baltimore. The following year, the National Board of Fire Underwriters formed a committee to rate the fire risk in major cities. In New York City, the committee found the probability of fire devastation "light" and concluded "a general conflagration over a major portion of the city is practically impossible." But in San Francisco, the risk of fire was "alarmingly severe," due to highly combustible, poorly built, wood-frame buildings, a general absence of firebreaks, congested occupancy of tall structures, and "almost total lack of sprinklers." The board found only 2.2 percent of buildings within the city's designated fire limits to be "fireproof," and down in the poorly zoned mix of residential and commercial streets South of Market, the few "fireproof" buildings were surrounded by flammable wood-frame or timber-joisted masonry. Any large blaze, the board declared, would be "unmanageable from a fire-fighting standpoint."

This "alarmingly severe" rating assumed the water system would work and predicted that even with sufficient pressure in hydrants, any localized fire was likely to spread into an "unmanageable" disaster. One wonders what language of alarm the board would have added had it accounted for the fault line that ran alongside or crossed many of the water system's supply pipes and tunnels from reservoirs in San Mateo and passed within one hundred yards of the Crystal Springs dam itself. Or what cautionary words the board might have used had it factored in seismic risks where the city's entire water supply flowed through wooden flumes over creeks and soft marshland and was delivered to neighborhoods through water mains which were—as Chief Sullivan had warned time and again—too small to provide sufficient pressure for even a two-alarm fire in most places, reaching homes and businesses and hydrants through an intricate web of cast-iron pipes that sprawled through the sand and mud of unstable "fill" and "made" land. And with most of the city's sixty-three re-serve water cisterns—the backup system in case of water shortage—only half filled, a few entirely empty or filled with trash, and all in a poor state of repair, the risk of a widespread inferno was higher than even hyperbole could reach. "San Francisco has violated all underwriting traditions and precedents by not burning up," the board concluded. "[T]hat it has not done so is largely due to the vigilance of the fire department, which cannot be relied upon indefinitely to stave off the inevitable."

2. The Day Before

EIGHT-YEAR-OLD WILLIAM DUNNE was enjoying a two-week Easter vacation from school in mid-April 1906. His father, an Irish immigrant, worked as a liquor merchant, and his mother, a California native, worked as a midwife. William loved baseball, playing cards or checkers, and listening to the phonograph in the parlor of his parents' flat. His folks did not own an automobile—and would not buy one for many years—so to get around they hired horse-drawn buggies or paid a nickel each for cable car rides. On Sundays, they would often venture out to Golden Gate Park with other neighbors, picnic for an early dinner to beat the fog, or ride the ferry across the bay to Marin County, where they would take an electric train up to picnic in Muir Woods.

As with so many San Franciscans of his generation, William felt "pride and identity" in his neighborhood, which for him was the Mission District. Built between Potrero Hill and Twin Peaks and centered around the eighteenth-century Mission Dolores, its streets were home to working class and wealthy alike, and its residents were mostly Irish and nearly all Catholic. Corner grocery and sundry stores capped long blocks of narrow, wood-framed, flat-front, and slanted-bay-windowed Italianate homes and apartment houses mixed with occasional fenced yards surrounding a few palatial estates, some dating a half century back to the expansive years following the gold rush. Young William delivered newspapers through these streets for extra money and played tennis at the park where people left community rackets and balls on the court

("I never had to buy a racket and I very seldom ever had to buy tennis balls"). San Francisco, as William knew it, "was a big city with country manners."

"In my generation," he later said, "you measure everything before and after the fire and earthquake." People like William who knew San Francisco as it was before the tragedy would often refer to the time before the earthquake as not just another time, but another place. It was as if the city they knew died and what was later reborn was a "new city."

Tuesday, April 17, 1906, was the last full day of life for the city young William and so many others knew, and it dawned gorgeous and pleasant. Up in the Italian American community of North Beach, the sun shined through the gray clouds puffing from smokestacks over the sea of wood-frame dwellings that were home to fishermen, produce sellers, brickmasons, and shopkeepers. Merchants and patrons in Broadway Street's tailor shops, drugstores, and ristorantes scoured the morning issue of *L'Italia*—"The First and Largest Italian Daily in the United States"—for updates on known deaths from the April 5 eruption of Mount Vesuvius near Naples, and dozens answered the newspaper's call to contribute at its Montgomery (present-day Columbus) Avenue office or the nearby Italian Consulate to a fund set up for the victims. $650 had already been raised and $80 more would come that day from local wage earners in amounts of 25 cents, 50 cents, or $1, for some a full day's pay. As the day's temperatures rose into the mid-60s, the residential slopes of Telegraph Hill saw children on their Easter break from school playing hopscotch on sidewalks so steep they were "cleated like the gangplanks of a river steamer," as a local reporter observed, and where impromptu games of baseball ended with "the lucky batsman knocking the ball on the tops of the houses half a block below."

Down at the Ferry Building, forty-three-year-old Melissa Carnahan and her husband, William, in town from Pennsylvania to visit her family, had ventured from the St. Francis Hotel to join the crowd stepping onto the morning ferry to Sausalito. After crossing, they rode the train up the zigzag tracks ascending Mount Tamalpais, the highest peak in the Marin Hills, where the clear day afforded them a beautiful panorama of the Golden Gate and the San Francisco skyline. After lunch, they took the train down and ferried back, enjoying the view on the fogless day. As they returned in the early afternoon, on a waterfront pier beside the ferry slips, chains clanked and pulleys shrieked and trucks rattled beneath a puffing steam crane emptying the holds of the tall-sailed Italian merchant bark *Elisa* after it made fast to the pier more than a month overdue. The crew disembarked, reportedly "tired, but well" after 210 days at sea. Their journey had brought them from Hamburg to Staten Island, then south around Cape Horn where they hit rough weather, spotted three icebergs, and sailed against northwesterly gales in dense fog and lost a sail. Their cargo was more than six tons of concrete, which builders in the city with delayed construction projects had been awaiting.

As on any other weekday afternoon, commuters and visitors stepping from the Ferry Building into the city were "confronted by a confusion of tracks" of rail lines crisscrossing the brick paving stones of East Street (present-day Embarcadero), jumbled with wagons and pedestrians amid the steady parade of cable cars, a congestion problem Sunday's papers reported would soon be remedied by a planned pedestrian footbridge. A crowd stood in a bunched line at the double turntable where United Railroads' Market Street cars painted by line—red, blue, green, yellow, white—rolled on and were swung around and aimed back up Market. Conductors exchanged transfer tickets for a nickel from each rider as they boarded, most opting for open-air bench seats to enjoy the day's warm weather. With a clang of the roof gong, gripmen pulled grip handles back with a squeeze of their ratchet lever, and as iron jaws tightened on the whirring cable below, cars pulled as many as 130 passengers at a time forward for an eight-and-a-half-miles-per-hour ride up Market Street's wide thoroughfare past the city's tallest buildings, largest banks, and grandest hotels. Newspapers in recent days had reported on United Railroads' plan to convert its cable car lines in the city to faster, larger electric streetcars, something most business owners and merchants opposed because of "unsightly" overhead wires that city leaders pledged would never clutter the open vista of Market Street.

Inside Market Street's forty-year-old Grand Hotel, an eclectic, four-story homage to Second Empire and Italianate styles, Terry Owens, the chief of the Denver Fire Department, was staying with his wife and baby, vacationing from Colorado seeking to cure his monthlong cold. He was surprised by the "many wooden blocks" of the city—not just the high number of wooden structures, but especially their concentration downtown. "Bad place for fires," he told a local reporter that day in an interview to be printed in tomorrow's paper. In the afternoon, Chief Dennis Sullivan stopped by the Grand Hotel and gave the visiting fire chief a ride in his buggy to a blaze down in the Mission District. Impressed with the prompt response and efficient work of the fire crews, Chief Owens judged them "the best of a class that I have ever seen and I have visited every big department in the United States." And he effusively concluded, "I see now why San Francisco has been free from disastrous fires; her men are too prompt and too intelligent. It does my heart good to watch them work."

Cable cars continued up and down Market Street in the early evening, and the Market/Hayes green line rolled out through the newer neighborhoods of the Western Addition within one block of the Fell Street flat where twelve-year-old Marion Baldwin looked from her second-floor window facing the grass Panhandle of Golden Gate Park. Her parents were dressed up to attend a banquet at the Palace Hotel. Her father was in a tuxedo, and her mom in a satin dress "looked just like a queen." With their permission to visit her friend Bertha who lived on the corner, Marion walked downstairs and out to the street where she saw the "hack-man"—the hired driver—on the carriage waiting for her parents. She walked on to her friend Bertha's, and they worked on drawings until after dark.

Electric lights brightened downtown streets and buildings against the night's falling darkness. In Chinatown, where red-and-gold-lacquered lanterns lit brightly painted green-and-yellow wooden balconies projecting from brick Italianate buildings along Dupont Street (present-day Grant Avenue), wide-eyed tourists slowly walked past the glowing windows of bazaars and curio shops filled with jades and porcelain. Barbershops along Waverly were closing and toy peddlers had mostly retired for the night, but fortune-tellers still sat at their folding tables hoping for a few evening customers. A few herbalists in closely spaced storefronts kept their doors open past dusk, advertising their pulse diagnosis to sell more cures of bark, roots, nuts, and flowers from their drawers, and dried meat dealers still stood at their sidewalk racks, hoping to unload their last bits of dried duck, oysters, and frogs. Workers climbed the steps of Waverly Place's pastel-painted brick Tin How Temple for evening prayer ceremonies, and just beginning their night's work were madams in the doorways of brothels and "singsong houses" lining Sullivan and Bartlett Alleys. Narrow sidewalks lined with closed display stands concealed a subterranean maze of cellars and basements packed with card games of *dou dizhu* or tables crammed with tired workers reading one of several neighborhood newspapers: *Mong Hing Yat Bo* (Chinese Daily World), *Tai Tung Yat Bo* (Chinese Free Press), or *Chung Sai Yat Po* (Chinese-Western Daily). And above the streets, through thickets of laundry lines and balconies lined with potted plants, conversations in Cantonese and Mandarin carried through open windows.

Two blocks from the edge of Chinatown's confines, beyond where its residents dared not roam for fear of harassment, arrest, or worse, Dupont Street opened into Union Square, a grassy city block crossed by walkways lined with hedges and trees. The square was dominated by the Dewey Monument, an eighty-five-foot-tall column topped by the *Goddess of Victory* statue, dedicated three years before by President Theodore Roosevelt as a tribute to naval victory in the recent Spanish-American War. Buildings surrounding the square were dwarfed by the twelve-story St. Francis, the newest and tallest of the city's grand hotels, where Melissa and William Carnahan had dressed in formal wear for dinner after returning from their Mount Tamalpais trip. They took the elevator down from their sixth-floor room to the hotel's impressive gold-and-white dining room. There they dined with Melissa's three cousins, then walked out to Union Square and mingled with the night crowds.

Much of the talk on the streets was of the opening of opera season, specifically the premiere of *Carmen* that night at the Grand Opera House on Mission Street. The world-famous Italian tenor Enrico Caruso was in town headlining in the part of Don José, and famous soprano Olive Fremstad was playing the lead role of Carmen. In this golden age of opera, Fremstad and especially Caruso had generated much print in San Francisco newspapers since their arrival with the rest of the touring Metropolitan Opera company on Easter Sunday.

The opera company had premiered the night before with a performance of *The Queen of Sheba*, which was well attended and well received. The *Call*'s headline read "BRILLIANT ASSEMBLAGE CROWDS GRAND OPERA HOUSE," and reported of "grandeur never equaled here before." But Monday night's premiere was widely considered a warm-up for the real thing, or as described in the *Examiner*, "the predecessor of the storm that awaits Caruso and Fremstad tonight." Tickets for balcony seats started at $7 (more than $232 in 2023), and box seats cost $65 each (more than $2,160 in 2023).

The night was still warm, and downtown was windless. At the opera house, the air itself was charged with anticipation. Open carriages and automobiles clogged Mission Street, delivering the city's wealthiest to the main entrance. A steady stream of tuxedos and dresses and tiaras flowed up the steps, through the main corridor, and around the elaborate crystal fountain in the grand vestibule beneath a moonlit skylight. Reporters who had covered many previous opera premieres would effuse that "the dresses seemed more beautiful, the jewels more brilliant and the people more interested and interesting."

The theater was a grand space trimmed in shades of pale blue. Tiers of elegant luxury boxes rose high above either side of the stage, which was boasted to be the largest in the country. And behind the floor seats, three tiers of balcony seats receded at angles affording every attendee a splendid view. Famous society photographer Arnold Genthe was among the crowd taking their seats for the show. Maybella Tevis and her husband, William, the millionaire banker, sat up in a box. Also in a box was twenty-four-year-old actor John Barrymore, spending his final night in town after completing his run of performances in *The Dictator*. He was to sail for Australia the next day with the rest of his touring company, and of that night's audience he observed, "[A]ll of San Francisco and his wife was there."

At 8:00 p.m. the curtain lifted. Every seat was filled. Caruso's "ringing tenor woke up the house on his first phrase," wrote a reporter. "Caruso has the kind of tenor that rings in the ears long after it is heard and seems to echo in the memory at call." Former mayor James Phelan thought the singers "a brilliant company." And twenty-two-year-old Stanford sophomore Laurence Klauber, sitting up high in the gallery with a friend, thought the Italian tenor was simply "the goods."

The audience gave a standing ovation that reportedly included at least two curtain calls and lasted ten minutes. Twenty-nine-year-old James Hopper, a former college football star, coach, and lawyer who was now living his passion for writing as a reporter, was so moved by the performance that he walked the city block slowly back to his paper, the *Call*, saying to himself, "Surely, what I have felt tonight is the summit of human emotion."

Laurence Klauber and his friend walked out of the theater and into a post-show traffic jam—a "string of carriages" clogging the streets and blocking in the electric trolleys—so they had to run six blocks down to catch a car. Others avoided the traffic by walking up one block for a late dinner at Zinkand's, a German restaurant popular with theater patrons. Photographer Arnold Genthe walked eight blocks from the opera house to his home on Sutter Street. He fell asleep, as he would later recall, "with the music of *Carmen* still singing in my ears."

Back across town on Fell Street, time had gotten away from Marion Baldwin, still drawing with her friend Bertha, whose mom called up the stairs to tell Marion the street lamplighter had already been by. Startled by the late hour, Marion dropped her pencil, then ran downstairs and out the front door and into the dark night air feeling "ashamed and guilty." Her parents were still at their dinner at the Palace Hotel, and the street was quiet and empty, "no wagons or horses." She reached home, used the hidden key under the mat to unlock the door, went inside, changed, rushed upstairs to her bed, put her head down, and "went right to sleep."

In Chinatown, above the family liquor store on Washington Street that he had operated since his father's death the year before, fifteen-year-old Hugh

Kwong Liang went to sleep on a narrow bunk in a cramped, second-floor flat he shared with his cousins. The room was lit by the glow of the Chinese Grand Theatre across the street. Two blocks away, Lily Soo-Hoo, who had turned seven two days before, shared a bed with one of her older sisters in their parents' third-floor apartment. Kept awake by the family's cats, which were restless and "making lots of noise," she stared at the blue eyes and gold hair of her prized "beautiful French doll" as she tried to get to sleep.

Down in the Mission, eight-year-old Gregory Lighthouse had enjoyed the "delightful" evening playing outside in Garfield Park one block from his parents' 24th Street home. But he had stayed out past his curfew, and now in his bed he felt guilty and found it tough to get to sleep. And a few blocks away, another "Mission boy," eight-year-old William Dunne, fell asleep on his small bed in his parents' room, ready to wake up to another day of his Easter vacation.

At midnight, switchboard operator James Kelly and relay operator Charles Daley began their shift in the central fire alarm office, a large third-floor space with windows overlooking Portsmouth Square. The night had turned cool, and they kept a fire burning in a brick fireplace. The central switchboard was connected by an electric line to each of the more than three hundred fire alarm boxes on street corners throughout the city, so thickly located in the downtown area that, as Charles explained, "a man could stand on one corner and by looking four ways he would be apt to see one box if not two or four boxes." Painted red, the boxes stood out prominently, with "FIRE ALARM STATION" in white lettering on each, followed by the words "FOR FIRE BREAK GLASS PULL HOOK DOWN ONCE AND LET GO." Inside large buildings, private lines from wall alarms also connected with street boxes.

When the handle of any street box or building alarm was pulled, a signal traveled to the fire alarm office's central switchboard, where a ticker-tape machine punched out a four-digit number denoting the alarm's location. At the switchboard, James was connected by telegraph with every firehouse, battalion chiefs' homes, and restaurants frequented by firefighters of certain companies. Three or four fire companies local to the alarm box location would be sent, and their battalion chief would ride in his buggy with his telegraph operator, who would unlock the alarm box and, on the telegraph key inside, tap out messages to the switchboard. If the fire needed more engine companies (ten firefighters each), the chief's operator would tap out a second alarm ("10–2") for six more companies, or a third alarm ("10–3") for another six, and he would signal once the fire was contained.

By the time James and Charles came on duty that night, an alarm had been pulled on the box at the corner of Bay and Mason Streets. The fire was burning at the Central California Canneries warehouse, a substantial two-story brick building that occupied the block on Mason Street between Bay and North Point Streets up in North Beach. The company's night watchman and his wife and brother, who all lived inside, had been saved an hour earlier by a neighbor who saw smoke coming from the second-floor windows, pulled the fire alarm, broke into the warehouse, woke them up, and got them out.

When the bell rang on the alarm panel in the three-story O'Farrell Street firehouse of Engine 2, the night watchman checked the box number, saw his company was to respond, sounded the house gong to wake the rest of the company, and pressed the button to turn up the firehouse lights. The button also released the horses from the stable in the back of the street-level apparatus floor, and they lined up beneath their hanging harnesses. The captain, his lieutenant, and the seven other firefighters of the company rushed down the spiral stairs from their second- and third-floor quarters, pulling up suspenders and rubbing sleep from their eyes. Men lowered and secured collars and harnesses onto three engine horses (set up to take no more than "12 seconds," a procedure rehearsed daily). Two horses were hitched to the hose wagon, which carried lengths of folded cotton hose and helmets and protective turnout coats. A fireman swung open the tall, wide firehouse double doors to the street, and the captain confirmed the location of the alarm by matching the box number with the one at Bay and Mason Streets.

Two firemen ensured the horses were hitched securely to the front of the engine, while at the rear, after checking that the boiler was full on the water gauge, the engineer kicked the valve connecting with the wall heater pipe shut and used a match or kerosene torch to ignite the wood-shaving kindling inside the firebox beneath the boiler. Up on the seat in the front of the engine, the driver slapped the reins, and as the horses yanked the engine from the house, the engineer stepped onto a narrow foothold behind the back coal tray for the one-and-a-half-mile ride up to the North Beach fire, holding on to a side rail and using his free hand to shovel coal through the boiler door to stoke the growing fire, a bumpy trip over brick and cobbled streets affording enough time for the fire to heat the boiler to sufficient pressure for pumping. Behind the engine followed two horses pulling the hose cart, with a driver up top and the rest of the firefighters hanging on to the sides.

When their company arrived at the fire, the driver pulled the engine near a hydrant, jumped down, unharnessed the horses, walked them a safe distance away, and covered them with blankets. As the hose wagon rolled to a stop, firemen jumped off and donned coats and helmets. One carried a spanner wrench to the hydrant and spun the outlet cap off with a kick followed by quick hand turns; another connected a stiff suction hose from the engine to the hydrant; and others connected a cotton hose to the engine and ran its unfolding length up toward the flames. At the hydrant, a fireman wrenched the rear stem nut to open the stream, filling the suction hose to the engine where the engineer shoveled coal into the firebox and watched the needle on the brass pressure gauge. When it reached 40 PSI, he opened the release valve, the hose stiffened along its length, and at its end two hosemen aimed the brass nozzle and threw water on the flames. The remaining firefighters pulled another hose from the wagon and connected it to the engine, ready for the engineer to signal pressure had reached at least 80 PSI, when they could open a second line on the flames.

The night air was dry, and onshore winds fed the fire. Glass in the windows on all sides of both floors shattered in the intense heat. By 1:00 a.m., flames shot from window openings as the blaze sucked oxygen from the air venting through the warehouse. Sweat ran down the blackened faces of firefighters who endured oven-like temperatures and choking smoke, attacking the yellow and orange flames through every opening in the cracking masonry.

Hearing the initial alarms in his Bush Street quarters, Chief Dennis Sullivan made the twenty-block trip to the blaze in his two-seat buggy with his driver behind his trusted horse, Brownie, to personally supervise. On arrival he directed his operator to send a second alarm from the alarm box. The ticker-tape machine at the fire alarm office punched out a "10–2"—ten dots, then two dots—and James Kelly tapped out the second alarm to six more engine companies in the surrounding area. Gongs sounded in firehouse after firehouse, and, as with Engine 2, watchmen and officers and drivers and engineers and hosemen of company after company carried out their jobs with muscle-memory precision and arrived at the cannery to join the battle.

By 1:30 a.m., more than one hundred firefighters were playing powerful hose streams into the warehouse blaze and soaking the walls of neighboring buildings on surrounding streets with hoses running from ten fire engines pumping from street hydrants a block and two blocks away. And with flames still intensifying and threatening to spread, Chief Sullivan directed his operator to send a third alarm, calling in six more engine companies.

In the small hours of the morning, after a post-opera dinner with fellow company members and gracious greetings of late-night fans lingering in the Palace

Hotel lobby, Enrico Caruso finally retired to his fifth-floor suite. His valet slept in the adjoining room along with three dozen traveling trunks. Each of the Palace Hotel's large guest rooms boasted its own fireplace, bathroom, and telephone. When completed in 1875 at a mammoth cost of $3 million (more than $80 million in 2023), the Palace could boast not only its size but especially its opulence. Its landmark was the "big and bulging" central Grand Court of marble floors surrounded by the ornate balconies of seven floors climbing to the massive domed skylight above. Five safety-catch hydraulic elevators (known then as "rising rooms") carried guests to lavish bedrooms finished with oak floors and thick redwood paneling in Louis XIV style.

And it was safe. Constructed with cement-covered brick walls wrapped in interlocked iron rods, the "basket-work of iron enclosed in brick" with its own water supply and emergency hoses on every floor boasted to be earthquake-proof and fireproof. Fading somewhat in the shadows of the St. Francis and the Fairmont, the Palace was no longer San Francisco's tallest or newest but was still the grandest. Most of the Metropolitan Opera company members, including the manager and director, were staying at the Palace. And the most famous among them, Caruso, had chosen his suite, in which President Grant had once stayed, for its elegance. French chandeliers lit satin-covered walls, an English marble fireplace, and Turkish carpets, and a Persian bedspread covered the bed. He dressed down in a nightshirt for sleep, "happy" with his performance and with the audience's effusive reception, and he "went to bed feeling very contented."

One block away stood the sixteen-story Call Building, the city's tallest and part of Market Street's "newspaper row." Inside, reporter James Hopper finished writing his article about the opera around 2:00 a.m. He left, crossed Market, and began walking the sidewalk up the Post Street incline for six blocks to his room at the Neptune. The night struck him "as particularly peaceful," but when he passed a boardinghouse's livery stable, he heard horses inside screaming "with a sudden, shrill cry" and "the thunder of a score of hooves crashing" against the stalls. A stableman in the doorway remarked of the horses, "Restless tonight; don't know why."

By the time Hopper reached his six-story corner hotel, he had climbed Post Street to a point affording him a view "of the big buildings below, the Bay beyond with the red and green lights and the long silhouettes of ships at anchor, and still farther, the familiar hearth-like glow of the mainland towns." But the heights of Nob Hill and Russian Hill blocked from his view the harsh glow of a fierce battle still being waged twenty blocks away in North Beach by more than 160 firefighters against the flames of the cannery fire.

Hopper passed through the quiet lobby of his hotel and entered the elevator.

"Fine night," the operator remarked.

"Beautiful," Hopper responded.

He reached his third-floor room and was in bed by 3:00 a.m. Still stirred by the opera, his sleep was restless and his dreams were filled with the voice of Caruso and the cries of the horses.

At the cannery, the firefighters won the battle, finally extinguishing the blaze around 3:00 a.m., but not before it destroyed 20,000 cans of food and caused more than $50,000 in damages. While his firefighters watered down the hissing, smoking embers, Chief Dennis Sullivan rode his buggy back to his Bush Street quarters, a three-bedroom flat on the third floor of Chemical Engine 3's firehouse. As was his custom on returns from late-night calls, he retired to the guest bedroom so as not to wake his wife, Margaret, who was asleep in their bed.

In the fire alarm office, Charles Daley tapped out a signal at 3:05 a.m. to all companies and chiefs that the fire was out. For the next two hours, firefighters and inspectors roamed the warehouse's charred, water-soaked ruins. Horses pulled the last engine from the scene just as daylight began breaking through the morning mist. It was 5:00 a.m.

Bells atop old St. Mary's Church in Chinatown and Nob Hill's Grace Church sounded the hour in unison. Predawn light spilled down the wide expanse of Market Street, and electric streetlights clicked off, block by block. But the lights of "newspaper row" shined as they had through the night, through the windows of the Examiner Building and the towering Call Building next door and the Chronicle Building across Market. Through front lobby doors shuffled employees in suits wrinkled from a long night of writing and editing and formatting the morning issues. *Examiner* news editor Jack Barrett stood on the corner with two coworkers waiting for his ride. Looking up Market, he noticed the sunlight "spread its brightness on the roofs of the skyscrapers, on the domes and spires of churches and blazed along up the wide street with its countless banks and stores, its restaurants and cafes." At that hour on that corner, "the city was almost noiseless."

Chronicle newspaperman Frank Ames stood on the same sidewalk at the far end of the block, looking through the large windows of the Palace Hotel. He stared at the "bright and inviting" lights of the Grand Court, where servers readied tables for awakening guests.

Examiner reporter Fred Hewitt and two coworkers crossed Market's empty pavement and strolled together along a sidewalk and stopped as they met two police officers on a walking patrol. After a brief conversation, the policemen headed toward their station, and the newspapermen walked on to "within a stone's throw" of City Hall and its ornate, imposing dome.

Three blocks away, police officer Harry Schmidt spoke briefly with his shift sergeant, Jesse Cook, then walked patrol past storefronts of fruit and produce merchants just opening. He stepped up onto the sidewalk in front of C.W. Gould & Co., a frequent stop on his beat. He entered and made his way between stacked orange crates to the back of the store for a drink of water.

In that moment, on a street corner one block away, Sergeant Jesse Cook spoke with young Sidney Levy about what could be making his delivery horse act so excited. It was 5:12 a.m.

3. It Seemed Eternity

THOMAS CHASE'S MORNING walk was hurried. Already a few minutes late for his early shift as a ticket clerk at the Ferry Building, he fast-walked down a sidewalk three blocks South of Market. Also called "South of the Slot" for being south of Market Street's cable car slot, the district Thomas walked was a working-class neighborhood of factories and clustered, cheaply built lodging houses painted with ads and overcrowded with transient laborers and immigrant workers. "North of the Slot were the theaters, hotels, and shopping district, the banks and the staid, respectable business houses," author Jack London wrote of Market Street's class demarcation line. "South of the Slot were the factories, slums, laundries, machine-shops, boiler works, and the abodes of the working class." Smoke from fifty of the city's sixty-six foundries wafted through its narrow alleys and well-worn streets where congested tenements shared party walls with blacksmith shops and taverns, wedged in among railroad yards and warehouses. Its sidewalks at the five o'clock hour were almost empty, and the air was warm and dry, what many locals called—with pardonable erroneousness—"earthquake weather." Thomas noticed the pleasant "clear and bright" conditions, and he particularly noticed the stillness: "not a breath of air was stirring."

This part of the South of Market district east to the waterfront was built above what was once the shallow waters of Mission Bay. As with the streets near the waterfront a few blocks north, this "fill land" was an unstable layer of mud and trash and rotted wood leveled off atop the thick sedimentary layer of old bay clay and topped with brick streets, concrete sidewalks, and heavy buildings. Its hidden threat snaked south and west in fingers of soft "fill" stretching deep into the city, and the crowded urban landscape above was little more than a brittle veneer masking deep voids where marshy lake beds and creeks once ran.

One of these underground spurs of soft soil reached west beneath the city more than two miles through South of Market and into the Mission. There it crossed Valencia Street directly beneath the Valencia Hotel, fixed on a stone foundation but perched on ground that was soft, sandy fill to a depth of more than forty feet. When it was constructed in 1888, the four-story building (then the Hillenbrand Hotel) was the tallest in the district, and in 1906, updated only in name, it still dominated the street, with bold five-foot-tall letters reading "VALENCIA ST. HOTEL" painted across the top of its wood siding visible for blocks.

At 5:12 a.m., predawn light began to shine through the Valencia Hotel's front windows and glass-paned double front doors into its lobby, where the night clerk was making his morning wake-up calls to roomers—weekly and monthly boarders—for work shifts or early trains. Off the back of the lobby in the all-night cafe, two groups of men played cards, drank coffee, and a few, having worked night shifts, sipped beer. Henry Powell, a police lieutenant on his morning patrol, checked in with the clerk, then walked through the cafe where "[e]verything was peaceful and orderly."

At that moment, seven miles from the peaceful lobby of the Valencia, the force of decades of accumulated strain and shear stress from the creeping of the Pacific Plate against the North American Plate overcame the strength of the rock crust and erupted in a break along the San Andreas Fault. The focus—the point of the break's initiation—was at least five miles beneath the seabed where the fault runs beneath the forty-foot-deep Pacific waters of the Gulf of the Farallones, and the epicenter—the point on the water's surface directly above the focus—was only two miles west of San Francisco's western shore. The break was horizontal, a strike-slip fracture where the crust on each side moved horizontally past the other. And the movement was right lateral, so for a person standing on either side of the fault line, the ground on the far side of the fault ripped loose in a rightward direction. The moment magnitude was an estimated 7.9 with a release of accumulated energy in the elastic rebound of the crust—the springing of bedrock back into its original shape after snapping loose from years of strain—roughly equivalent to detonating more than eleven million tons of TNT (greater than seven hundred times the force of the atomic detonation over Hiroshima).

Seismic shockwaves shot out in all directions. Initial primary waves pulsated through the ground and seawater at the estimated velocity of nearly three miles per second, compressing and dilating—pushing and pulling and pushing and pulling—the water and rock and soil as they traveled. Stronger secondary waves followed through the ground at slightly slower velocities of roughly two miles per second with the resulting shearing forces violently shaking the ground from side to side. Primary and secondary shockwaves reached the ground's surface quickly and at full strength because the rupture was relatively shallow, and the surface waves combined side-to-side jerking with up-and-down motions and crossed the ground like swells of water crossing a still pond.

Clarence Judson, a thirty-six-year-old railroad mechanic, was wading into the surf of Ocean Beach on the western shore of San Francisco. He had left his home three blocks away—where his wife, Nellie, their two-year-old son, Robert, and their newborn twin girls, Anita and Florence, were still asleep—and walked the road through the sand dunes to the beach for his customary early morning swim. Clarence left his shoes, robe, and hat on the sand, walked into the water, and was chest-deep when "a breaker larger than usual came in and shot away up the beach." It almost took him off his feet, and before he could get out, "instantly there came such a shock" that it threw him to his knees. He tried to get up but was thrown down again. Clarence, "dazed and stunned," was "tossed about" by larger and larger waves, his "ears full of salt water and about a gallon" in his stomach. Three times he was "thrown down" and "only by desperate fighting" did he escape the crashing tides of water and reach the sand.

"The motion of the quake was like the waves of the ocean—about twenty feet between crests—but they came swift and choppy, with a kind of grinding noise." Clarence tried to run through the sand to grab his shoes, robe, and hat, but he felt "paralyzed." Each successive shockwave shook the ground so violently, he could not get his feet to land where he aimed: "I reached for my shoes and landed with both feet onto my hat, twice." He managed to get into his shoes and robe "after being thrown to the ground a few more times." Worrying for his sleeping wife and babies, he ran staggering "like a drunken man" through the sand dunes onto the road, already "badly cracked," toward his house "at top speed."

Leading tremors whipped through the Richmond District, and less than a half second after smashing ashore, they reached Ernest and Louise Adams, asleep on the second floor of their wood-frame house on the north end of 24th Avenue. Their bedroom window afforded them a view over Lobos Creek and the sand dunes of China Beach, and on a clear day they could see across the waters of South Bay and the Golden Gate to the heights of Mount Tamalpais above Point Bonita Lighthouse and the Marin Headlands. The violent shock threw Ernest out of bed, and his first waking impression was feeling the morning air fill the bedroom and seeing the side wall "dashed to the ground." The floor was moving beneath him, creaking and jerking as the shaking grew stronger, and with his wife he "crawled down the stairs amid flying glass and timber and plaster" and made a dash for the street.

To the south, the shock rippled through Golden Gate Park, almost empty at that hour. The force toppled pillars of the park's stone gates, snapped large sections of trees down onto cracking walkways, damaged the Temple of Music, collapsed the roof of the Sharon Building covering the indoor children's playground, and turned the "earthquake-proof" Sweeny Observatory atop Strawberry Hill into ruins.

To the north, the vibrations swept east through the hills of the Presidio military post, opening cracks through the grass of the parade grounds and throwing chimneys from the Army General Hospital. Soldiers sprinted from the two-story enlisted quarters, expecting the structure to topple and trap them inside. The earthquake jolted the two-and-a-half-story wood-frame quarters of Major William Stephenson, who awoke to his "bed sliding about on its castors" and the house "jerking, swaying and groaning like a ship in a heavy sea." He lay in bed hearing plaster crumbling onto floors and picture frames crashing and glass shattering and expected "any jerk to be the last."

But the jerking continued as the wall of devastation barreled east from the open Presidio grounds into the residential streets of Cow Hollow and Pacific Heights, where seventy-eight-year-old Eugenia Poston likened the leading wave of tremors to an "unwonted stir" of a "hollow rumble, creaking, crashing." The retired schoolteacher "sprang up, or was thrown out" of bed by the stronger secondary waves that followed: "the convulsive upheaval of Mother Earth, rocking, twisting, wrenching, as if torn from her moorings." She grabbed her robe, ran to the door as tables and chairs danced out of her way, and reached her hallway where "the side wall seemed to have sprung from the roof—light poured in from above—and plaster, lathes, brick—was falling through the opening."

One mile south, surface waves shot east from Golden Gate Park and beneath the narrow, two-story, wood-frame house where seven-year-old John Conlon was "awakened from a sound sleep" by his bed and house quaking. His father, a fire department battalion chief, rushed into John's room, grabbed him and his younger brother, and herded them "into a doorway for protection."

Stronger shockwaves rolled through block after block of two- and three-story homes. Violent convulsions sent church steeples crashing onto streets and sidewalks and brick chimneys like wrecking balls into bedrooms and neighbors' homes. In her home near the park Panhandle (a newer neighborhood soon known as Haight-Ashbury), a young girl who was not frightened by the initial tremors "thought it was time to get up" once the vibrations grew. As she reached her door, the chimney smashed through her ceiling and into her bedroom in a pile of bricks and mortar. With the house shaking and morning light shining through the jagged hole of ripped shingles and snapped roof joists and trusses, she climbed over brick piles with bare feet to escape.

But many residents were caught in their beds, still asleep as falling chimneys bored through their ceilings. Twenty-four-year-old William Carr was crushed to death in his bed by a falling chimney, and another fractured the skull of twenty-one-year-old Henry Magill, who was rushed by his father to a nearby house for treatment but died within hours. The chimney of a three-floor residence crashed through the ceiling of sixty-year-old maid Annie Whelan's top-floor bedroom and crushed her in her bed. She was found by the family who employed her after they climbed up from their second-floor bedrooms. Annie's only obituary was a brief mention in the listing of known victims in the next day's paper reporting she was "killed while asleep."

A few blocks away, twelve-year-old Marion Baldwin slept through the first few tremors. Her parents had returned late from their Palace Hotel dinner and let her sleep. Now she dreamed she was on a boat and "could hear the creaking and the roaring and the noise of waves as they bounced around and bounced around, and then something hit us!" She opened her eyes and realized the jolt in her dream was her dresser hitting her bed. Her senses were overtaken by violent jerks and ominous sounds. Her room was "going from side to side" and the house filled with "the noise of things falling and flapping." After "more jerks," she "thought it was the end of the world."

Surface waves reached Emma Burke as she tried to sleep in the bedroom of her fourth-floor flat. Her husband was in the kitchen lighting the gas stove to heat water for coffee. "The shock came" and tossed Emma's bed against the wall. She jumped up and grabbed her bed's jumping footboard, trying to keep her balance to reach the door in the darkness as a din of "rumbles, crackling noises, and falling objects" filled the air. The apartment building torqued and twisted and the door wedged shut. Emma pulled on the doorknob with all her weight, yelling, and from the other side her husband pushed, and the door yanked open only as intensifying shocks twisted the walls back. They braced together in the doorframe: "It grew constantly worse, the noise deafening, the crash of dishes, falling pictures, the rattle of the flat tin roof, bookcases being overturned, the piano hurled across the parlor, the groaning and straining of the building itself." A large, 125-pound framed painting smashed to the floor of their flat. So too did the chimney through their ceiling. They noticed neither as they gripped the doorframe, hoping their building would stand.

The earthquake caught most residents throughout the city asleep. People not crushed or trapped awoke to a violent assault on all their senses: unfamiliar sounds of cracking walls and crumbling bricks, sights of streets opening and homes falling, the smell of burning gas, the taste of thick dust and soot, the pain of broken glass on bare feet or the agony of a shin bone broken by a wooden beam. For some the shock alone was too much to survive. Forty-four-year-old Margaret Bullard died in her Lombard Street home of heart failure soon after the earthquake hit. So too did young fifteen-year-old Ottilie Kettner, who reportedly rushed into her father's room when the awful shock came and shouted: "'Oh papa, I am dying,'" then "fell dead in [her] father's arms."

Surface waves rolling into the Mission District caught eight-year-old Dewitt Baldwin up early for his piano lesson in his parents' third-floor flat on Dolores Street. "I had gotten as far as sitting up with my feet over the side of the bed when totally unexpectedly the house began to shake violently." He heard dishes break and watched furniture move. He had felt earthquakes before, but this was "a more destructive one than [I] had known." A few blocks away, another eight-year-old, Gregory Lighthouse, was also awake and sitting up in bed "when the house started rocking." Still feeling guilty for staying out past his curfew the night before, he thought God was punishing him. "I tried to pray, but could not." His father rushed into his room: "I don't remember what he said, but I will never forget the terror and frightful expression."

Shockwaves slowed and strengthened as they pulsated into the soft fill land beneath the Valencia Hotel, bouncing off bedrock and back again through the loose soil, doubling and tripling the shaking of the foundation just as police lieutenant Henry Powell stepped out the hotel's front door onto the sidewalk.

The vibrations made him "hurry [his] paces" toward the street out from under the three floors of iron fire escapes and wooden bay windows above him. Secondary waves then bounced and whipped the street as if it were the surface of a shaking bowl of gelatin, dancing and rolling "in waves like a rough sea in a squall." Two sets of cable car rails "lifted themselves out of the pavement, and bent and snapped."

Powell found it "impossible" to keep his balance as he ran from the hotel. Wood-frame houses around him "were cracking and bending and breaking the same as the street itself and the car tracks." Sinkholes that were swallowing the street and sidewalk crept nearer to the hotel. Still running away, Powell "heard the hotel creak and roar and crash," and he turned back to see the night clerk sprinting out the front door with one of the men who had been playing cards in the cafe seconds before. Powell glanced up at the four-story face of bay windows and fire escapes, which "lurched forward as if the foundation were dragged backward from under it, and crumpled down" over the pavement.

There was no cloud of destruction or pile of debris: "It did not fall to pieces and spray itself all over the place, but telescoped down on itself like a concertina." The fourth floor and roof, seemingly undamaged, settled on a forward tilt at street level. The bottom three floors—filled with at least fifty people—had simply vanished, sunk deep into an underground void or smashed to flattened oblivion.

The earthquake reached Van Ness Avenue, a residential north-south thoroughfare running between the Western Addition's neighborhoods and the older city to the east—Nob Hill, Russian Hill, North Beach, Chinatown, and the banking and harbor districts. Among the homes of the wealthy lining the wide boulevard was the three-story Victorian home of seventy-five-year-old James Stetson, president of the California Street Cable Railroad. The "very severe shock" woke him up and grew "so violent that it nearly threw [him] out of bed." A large bookcase and china cabinet in his room were both thrown to the floor, and plaster chunked onto the mantel and tables. A widower with two housemaids, James made for the door, carefully aiming his steps on a shaking floor covered with shards of shattered glass and jagged pieces of broken china.

Two blocks away, a twelve-year-old boy woke up to the shaking on his third-floor bedroom and buried his head in the pillow. "[I]t felt like this was the end of the world. I really did some praying." Violent convulsions yanked the house side to side, slinging the top floor in concussive jerks that wrenched the wooden frame apart and snapped load-bearing beams. An outer wall collapsed and pulled his bedroom wall away in an explosion of cracked plaster and splintered siding. "It opened up the side of the house, and here I was, looking up in the sky."

Two blocks east of Van Ness, *Examiner* reporter Fred Hewitt was walking on a sidewalk past the sprawling columned wings and domed top of City Hall when the shock came. He was "thrown prone" into the street on his back "and the pavement pulsated like a living thing." Tall buildings all around him "wobbled and veered" as "[c]rash following crash resounded on all sides" and "terrified humanity streamed out into the open in [an] agony of despair." Lying in the street, Fred caught a blurry image of his friends running and yelled, "Keep in the middle of the street, Mac!"

When leading tremors rolled beneath City Hall, Officers Edward Plume and Jeremiah Dwyer were each working the desk shift on the first floor in the City Hall Police Station. At first, Officer Plume felt only "a slight trembling," but in a few seconds it strengthened. Officer Dwyer said, "That's an earthquake!" and Plume "was thrown clear out of the chair." Both were at the mercy of the massive building torquing violently above and on all sides. The power went out. Chunks of masonry crashed down the flue, tossing burning wood and cinders from the fireplace and filling the dark room with smoke and soot.

Seismic convulsions rippled up through City Hall's structure to the top of its towering dome 330 feet above the city where the *Goddess of Progress* statue teetered in creaks, side to side. The rumble in the ground below grew to a deafening roar, and vibrations intensified to violent shaking, surpassing the building's structural limits. With insufficient cross supports, the massive dome's steel frame rippled and bent, and its one- and two-ton masses of masonry and tall columns cracked free and peeled off in chunks. Immense sixty-foot-tall decorative pillars of the outer colonnade fractured, sending cornices and eaves from the façade crashing to the ground.

Down in the first-floor police office, Officer Plume grabbed at things in the dark to steady himself while "the noise from the outside became deafening." Pillars cracked "with reports like cannon, then falling with crashes like thunder." Outside the office doors, "[h]uge stones and lumps of masonry came crashing down," and the chandelier in the grand lobby crashed to the ground. Plume felt like he was riding a ship in a heavy storm, "expecting every moment to be buried under a mass of ruins." He shouted to Officer Dwyer to "get out." They both rushed for the door, "stumbling over chairs and desks and other litter" before making it out onto Larkin Street.

* * *

Leading tremors ripped up the steep incline of Nob Hill. A police sergeant who lay awake with his wife in the darkness of their bedroom in their Broadway Street flat noticed the air was unusually "stuffy" and "oppressive" and asked her if the windows were open. They were. He looked out and noticed "a peculiarly beautiful pink sky." At that moment, the apartment building "began to jump and twist and crackle with a noise that sounded as if somebody was trying to crash a giant cigar box under a giant heel." His wife grabbed him: "My God! What's that?" As the wooden beams and walls of their flat shook and twisted, they rushed to grab their two young daughters.

A few blocks away in his Sutter Street home, photographer Arnold Genthe "had scarcely been asleep" since his late-night walk home from the opera when the "terrifying sound" of his Chinese porcelain shattering on the floor awakened him. His "whole house was creaking and shaking," and his chandelier swung "like a pendulum." Plaster crumbled from the ceiling, and he covered his head, telling himself to "accept what comes."

A block up the steep incline in an apartment house, Sarah Phillips and her roommate Lillian Simpson were both awakened by the shock. Lillian saw "pictures falling" and "the walls apparently caving in." Sarah jumped out of her bed and "caught the china cabinet as it was about to fall." Lillian rushed to help her, "glad to have it to hold, as if not we could not stand on our feet."

Another block up the hill, Ada Higgins and her husband, Jack, held each other in bed. The earthquake shook them "like rats in a trap," and Ada felt certain they "would be buried in the crash." Convulsions tossed the rooftop water tank off the apartment building, and on its fall it took out the back stairs, damaged support beams, and crashed into the corner of their bedroom. The room filled with the sounds of neighbors' screams and Ada's screams and "crushing timbers, falling tile, dishes, and glasses crashing and breaking, pictures falling."

Vibrations sent rooftop chimneys tearing into living spaces and smashing onto streets all up and down Nob Hill. Thirty-six-year-old Sarah Corbus was killed in her second-floor bedroom of her father's Jones Street home when the chimney slammed directly onto her bed "in an avalanche of brick." One more block up Jones, school principal Jean Parker was killed in her bed when the chimney of her two-story home fell through her ceiling and crushed her. "Miss Jean Parker" was later eulogized as "one of the best-known teachers ever taught in S.F. schools."

Surface waves rippled along the peak of California Street, shaking iron fences and the opulent woodwork of mansions built for Crocker and Colton and Stanford and Hopkins and Flood. Bells atop Grace Church clanged with discordant notes. Stone garden urns tipped and brick gateposts toppled and statues fell and chandeliers crashed. In the Stanford mansion, the earthquake awakened Chinese butler Ah Wing, who "could not stand steadily" during the shaking and, through his upstairs window, could see the chimneys of nearby homes "tumbling down." But through Nob Hill's firm ground of sandstone and shale, seismic waves traveled faster without intensifying, and most of the hill's mansions stood largely undamaged. The Stanford walls stood "unhurt," and even its chimneys "stood the quake well."

But down in the crowded working-class streets South of Market, where construction was not so sound and much of the ground unstable, the experience was starkly different. Seismic waves rolled into the soft fill beneath streets and buildings, the vibrations slowing and amplifying, bouncing back and forth through the clay and mud and exaggerating even initial minor tremors into the most violent jolting. Even stronger shocks followed, liquefying fill land and jerking the brittle shell beyond its breaking point. The effect on old, closely built, wood-frame apartment buildings and hotels was devastating.

Seven-year-old Peter Mullins awoke to his "house in motion," and even though his parents "remained cool," he could hear frightened neighbors running into the street. Surface waves crossed 11th Street and rocked the tightly wedged rows of two-story apartment flats along an alleyway where Edward and Anna Butler slept in their second-floor bedroom. Large chunks of brick masonry from the three-story brick factory next door to them bored down through their building. Both suffered serious wounds, and Anna's were mortal—she would die the next day, along with their neighbor Mary Donovan, also hit in her bed by masonry from the same wall.

Leading tremors crossed 10th Street and woke up thirty-eight-year-old liquor merchant Hermann Meyer, who had been sleeping in the front room of his Mission Street home. He was rushing to go check on his wife, Julia, and their five-year-old daughter when "a chimney crashed through the roof and buried him." Newspapers would report Hermann "was conveyed to a hospital and died the next night." But no report of what it was like for Julia to find her husband so broken, of whether they were able to speak with each other as she pulled the bricks off his wounded body, or what must have gone through their young daughter's mind in the sad final hours of her father's life.

Vibrations ripped eastward across 9th Street, then 8th, then 7th. Through block after block South of the Slot, the scene repeated itself: sleeping families falling victim to the force of an earthquake turning the ground beneath them to jelly and reducing their rickety, wooden apartment houses to matchsticks. These "cheap mantraps," writer Mary Austin observed, "folded in like paste-board." And death came in different ways. Fifteen-year-old Myrtle Muge died of suffocation beneath a fallen support beam. Twenty-four-year-old Cecilia O'Toole also suffocated when the large picture over her bed fell and crushed her face. Adolph Schwinn, a grocer, was killed when a falling wall fractured his skull. And John Judge, a locomotive engineer, died of a heart attack while fighting to open a jammed door to free his family from their shaking apartment.

In no other part of San Francisco was the destruction from the earthquake so complete or deaths so numerous as South of Market, and the area surrounding 6th and Howard Streets was ground zero. Once a swampy wetland where subterranean lakes were covered with a crust of peat moss, when the first piles were driven into the muck to construct Mission Street one block north, they reached a depth of eighty feet without hitting bedrock. Timbers were stacked and sand was poured until leveled and paved at official grade, and on this fill land were crowded blocks divided by narrow, thirty-foot-wide alleyways lined with cheap two- and three-story wood-frame tenements. The deepest, most unstable fill lay beneath the northwest corner of 6th and Howard Streets, where taller lodging houses stood side by side by side like dominos. On the corner at Howard Street was the four-story Brunswick House, then beside it the three-story Ohio House, then the three-story Lormor, then the four-story Nevada on the alley corner. The four buildings were home to 120 people or more at the moment of impact.

Among them was eighteen-year-old Edna Ketring, asleep in her room on the second floor of the Brunswick. She was one week away from her wedding day, and her fiancé, Thomas Bowes, was two rooms down. She leapt to her feet when the building began shaking: "The walls were cracking open, the plaster was falling in showers, the furniture was being tossed about." She rushed into the hallway filling with dozens of other guests, and she caught sight of Thomas running out of his room to find her.

On the floor above them, another guest, James Jacobs, "jumped out of bed and made a grab for [his] clothes," and when the stronger shockwaves hit, they felt to him like a "second quake." Through the thin walls of his small room, James heard the "shrieks" of other boarders and the ominous sounds of structural failure—the "noises of cracking, and rending."

Three buildings away on the fourth floor of the Nevada House, the violent shaking of William Stehr's bed and noise of creaking timbers jarred him from sleep. He ran and opened his window overlooking the roofs of the Lormor and Ohio Houses. With the shaking so violent, he was about "to jump out of the window on to the roof" of the Lormor below him when the Lormor itself "collapsed with a deafening roar and spilled down in a cloud of dust." Through his open window, William could hear "agonizing screams" of the people inside the Lormor as it fell. Its debris cloud rose and "choked" him and he backed away from the window, then heard another "crash." Through the dust he saw the Ohio collapse and beyond it, the Brunswick "tumbling into a heap of ruins in a smother of dust."

Inside the Brunswick, engaged couple Edna and Thomas had fought their way through the crowded hallway and were just three feet apart and reaching for each other when the ceiling caved in and everything went "intensely dark." In his room on the floor above, James Jacobs felt the building break apart around him and "felt paralyzed as the building crackled downward and outward with a noise [he could not] describe." He was "suffocated with the lime and dust," and the space around him "was dark as a dungeon." The Lormor and Ohio Houses had toppled sideways like dominos onto the Brunswick, and it split into three pieces: the south side fell onto Howard Street, the front pitched into 6th, and, as James described it, "the northwest corner of the building, diagonally back from the street corner, remained standing," its broken rooms exposed like an open dollhouse.

Back up on the top floor of the Nevada House—the only one still standing—William Stehr threw clothes on to flee his own swaying building but could not escape his room: his door was jammed. And stronger jerking jammed it "faster and tighter." His floor tilted and sank and he knew the building was falling. He "hung on instinctively to the door handle while the whole floor dropped." On his room's grinding slide down, William felt "three distinct bumps" as each floor beneath him flattened, and "[w]ith each bump came a frightful crash and cracking of timbers and glass and the cries of other people in the house."

All four buildings had "collapsed like card houses." And even stronger seismic shocks followed. One block away, the four-story wood-frame Corona House also sank into the fill, trapping or crushing at least three dozen boarders. Another block away, the newly built, three-story, timber-joisted masonry Kingsbury House toppled and crushed the wood-frame Girard House beside it, killing or entombing untold more. A police officer who responded later said the Girard was crushed "flat," and guessed "some fifty or sixty people were killed at this spot."

* * *

A few blocks away on Market Street, a world removed from the crowded, "cheap mantraps" south of its expanse, tremors reached the Palace Hotel as *Chronicle* newspaperman Frank Ames stared through its large windows at the palm trees and "bright and inviting" lights of its Grand Court. He saw the palms start to sway and thought it was an optical illusion, but then "the ground felt as if it were sinking under [his] feet." Frank likened the sensation to riding "in a swiftly descending elevator." He turned to see the Chronicle Building wavering and the Call Building rocking. Bricks and cornices smashed on the sidewalk around him, and horses broke free from a nearby carriage and ran past him, their eyes "big with terror." By the time he reached an alcove for safety, the pavement was moving "in waves under [his] feet" and "the cobblestones of Market Street seemed alive."

Five floors up, Enrico Caruso's bed rocked him awake. He felt like he was "in a ship on the ocean" and thought he was dreaming of "crossing the water" back to Italy. But as the rocking intensified and chandeliers jangled and marble rattled, he went to the window, raised the shade, and saw "buildings toppling over, big pieces of masonry falling, and from the street below the cries and screams of men and women and children."

Most guests in the hotel were jerked from sleep by the shock, awakening to plaster falling and lights crashing. Some stayed in bed gripping their blankets; many sprung to their feet to escape; and some were thrown to the floor. A man on the sixth floor was tossed from bed "and halfway across the room," and a woman one story above him who woke up on the floor felt that the entire hotel had "turned on its axis." Another said the building swayed "like the top of a tree in a heavy windstorm."

One of the first shocks cut the building's electricity, sending frightened, half-asleep guests stumbling into dark, crowded corridors as the shaking grew even stronger. Ominous, foreign sounds, "tremendous and indescribable," filled their ears, "the roaring and cracking of falling timbers" and "breaking glass" and "the rumbling of the earth." Young maids and bellboys ran through hallways "as if they were mad," and guests wandered unclothed, aimless. A salesman from Detroit raced to the elevator shaft in his nightshirt and considered sliding down the cables but, worrying of fire, he ran through the shattered hallway window and descended the swinging fire escape in bare feet bloodied by broken glass. On the second floor, Caruso's opera company manager, Ernest Goerlitz, held his wife in bed while chunks of the ceiling fell on the blanket he pulled up over their heads.

The scene was similar three blocks away in the taller St. Francis Hotel, where

Melissa Carnahan awoke feeling she was "on a ship in a gale pounding against the rocks." She woke up her husband, Will, who felt they were on a train "coming to a sudden halt or stop with grinding noises, twistings and jarrings, ending in a vicious bump." Guests in the top floors feared the building would fall. On the tenth floor, St. Louis brewing millionaire August Busch felt the building swaying "from south to north like a tall poplar in a storm." A physician visiting from Pasadena feared the hotel "would tip over," and after running to the window to view the city, he "saw the big buildings waving like stalks in the wind." Down on the second floor, a guest awoke to the sensation of his bed being lifted and dropped and lifted and dropped and worried "that the ten stories above us would fall, not allowing us to escape alive."

The structure twisted, cracking walls and jamming doors. A man on the top floor trying to escape with his wife later remembered that their room door "required all my strength to open it." In the dark hallway they found men "shouting and women screaming hysterically." Without power, no elevators were running, and people "fell and rolled down the narrow stairway" even as the shaking continued.

Leading tremors rolled into Chinatown, sending bricks slicing through laundry lines and filling narrow alleyways with crashing balconies and smashed awnings. A thick dust cloud of grinded masonry and rafter dust from the initial tremors snuffed out the morning light on Commercial Street where a police officer felt the stronger secondary shockwaves hit: "Then the big twist came and the whole place seemed to rise up and sink down." He yelled to his partner that he expected a tsunami from the bay. "The buildings began to give way and the crashes of falling cornices, walls and chimneys joined in the uproar."

Seven-year-old Lily Soo-Hoo and her older sisters were all "woken up very rudely" in their parents' third-floor apartment, and fifteen-year-old Hugh Kwong Liang and his cousins awoke in their second-floor room to their beds tossing and plaster falling. Police officers and early-rising merchants escaped the falling brick buildings of Sullivan and Baker Alleys to the safer, wider breadth of Jackson and Washington Streets, which soon filled with frightened, half-naked residents in full sprint for the open space of Portsmouth Square.

Up in the third-floor fire alarm office overlooking the square, James Kelly stood at the window watching the morning light—still twenty minutes from sunrise—cast across the stone of the Hall of Justice opposite him and spill over the grass and walkways below when the first tremors reached his building. He ran to the wall clock to time the earthquake's duration, but the secondary shockwaves "became so severe" he feared a "danger of the walls and ceiling of the building falling" and could not count past nineteen seconds before running underneath the wide frame of a front window for safety. Across Portsmouth Square, James saw large, jagged pieces of the outer walls of the Hall of Justice's bell tower shaken to the street, leaving higher sections clinging precariously to the frame.

The fire alarm office fell dark as gas lamps and electric lights went out. In the back room, shelves of glass-encased wet-cell batteries that powered the circuits were shaken into "a mass of glass"—the batteries were ruined, and all the "circuits were broken and disconnected." Before the jerking even stopped, all fire department communications were severed and any street alarms with wires not already cut were rendered useless.

Convulsions ripped down Washington Street through Sergeant Jesse Cook's harbor district beat, where the noise startled one of Cook's officers, Harry Schmidt, as he grabbed a drink of water between stacked orange crates in the back of a wholesale fruit warehouse. "It sounded like thunder outside," and around him "was a creaking and snapping of beams, and the rush of falling plaster, and all sorts of other jarring noises." Schmidt rushed to the front of the building, "looking which way to dash" while hurtling orange crates fell into his path. He halted when he reached the front doorway, seeing men across the street waving for him to stay back. He heard "the pattering of bricks on the awning" above the sidewalk in front of him, "jumped back into the arch of the doorway," and braced his hands over his face and head. The building's upper front wall fell forward; it "crushed through the awning as if it were paper" into a pile on the sidewalk and through the doorway where he stood. His feet were covered by "dust and debris," and the "wall of ruin and rubbish" blocked the entrance in front of him as high as his neck.

One block away, Sergeant Jesse Cook watched the surface shockwaves roll down Washington Street "like the waves of an ocean coming down the hill" before he took refuge in a doorway. He saw forty-four-year-old Frank Bodwell and his clerk crushed to death by a falling wall, the same wall he thought also killed his friend fruit merchant Tom Burns. But in the cloud of dust and chaos, Cook could not see Burns's narrow escape: a short, heavy man, Burns had somehow managed to leap through a tight opening between walls of stacked wooden fruit boxes and onto the street clear of the raining brick. A chunk of masonry hit his heel and he twisted his ankle as he bolted for the open street where he collided with a stampede of panicked horses. Dazed,

Burns ran toward the far side of the street until he saw a wall falling toward him, then ran for his life: "At that moment I believe I was beating every world's record running against time, and running every way at once." As he ran, the shaking pavement "opened and shut."

In no section of the city were there more people awake and working when the earthquake hit than in the streets near the waterfront, where fruit sellers and produce merchants had been working for an hour or more. And in the fish market along Merchant Street, inside old, heavy, timber-joisted masonry stores on fill land, fishermen and fishmongers had been up even longer, weighing and cleaning and cutting and wrapping inside open-air brick stores. Handcarts of seafood and wagonloads of shad and bass and salmon crammed curbs outside. Eighteen-year-old Alex Paladini, working for his father's business, Achille Paladini Fish Company, was helping unload a wagon when the shaking began. Immigrant workers and fishermen began running into the street, but Alex, accustomed to tremors, yelled for them to return: "It'll be over in a minute!" Then secondary shockwaves hit, and the ground beneath the pavement liquefied and "Merchant Street began waving in billows, houses began to waggle and topple, horses screamed as the masonry crashed down on them and the wagons." Alex "dropped the fish, quit business, and ran for shelter."

Directly across the street, the three-story brick building of Enea Fish Company "fell outward on top of the men and horses." Alex stopped in his tracks and retreated into his father's store, a newer building that "stood solid." But the Enea building's "whole front fell across the street as if it had been pushed out." And "the dust of the masonry" of the Enea building's collapse "blew across" the street into Paladini's building, and stores neighboring both sides of it also "collapsed and crumbled," burying workers inside and deliverymen and horses on the sidewalk. Relentless shockwaves hit with stronger jolts and shook more bricks loose and kept survivors in huddled groups inside doorways and under wagons. But already the carnage on just that single block was complete: dozens of men crushed or trapped, dead or dying.

South of Market, tremors reached the brittle shell of 1st Street where Thomas Chase fast-walked to work. Pulsations of primary waves arrived as "a low distant rumble" and stopped him mid-stride. He stepped off the sidewalk and turned his head to listen as the deep, approaching sound grew "louder and louder." At once, the stronger secondary waves hit, thrusting the ground sideways and jerking it back and then over again and each time faster and harder.

Slung side to side, Thomas struggled to stay on his feet, jumping out into the open street.

The fill land liquefied, and the paved surface of cobblestone and concrete began cracking. Thomas noticed that buildings "crumbled like card houses" the length of 1st Street. Overhead, power lines and streetcar wires "snapped like threads" and whipped loose onto the street "writhing and hissing like reptiles." He jumped back to avoid the sparking electric lines, but the shaking grew stronger, knocking him flat on the street. On all sides, glass pieces and bricks crashed onto cobblestones, which "danced like corn in a popper." He worried that the two-hundred-foot-tall brick shot tower above him would fall, but it stood even as the flag at its top "whipped and snapped like the popping of a whip."

Tremors reached the eastern waterfront and rippled up through the Ferry Building, bending the flagpole above its clock tower and dislodging the gears of its giant clock, freezing the hour and minute hands a few seconds past 5:15—three minutes fast to the end. It had taken less than three seconds for the first seismic waves from the break in the fault to span the entire city. And the Pacific Plate was still ripping loose from the North American Plate along the fault northwest and southeast at the speed of about three miles per second in both directions, splitting and crushing bedrock that had been locked at depth with the rock mass of each plate tearing free from its strained position, then springing back into place. And as the fault fracture lengthened, the increased surface friction and violent releases of accumulated energy with each elastic rebound of bedrock produced a range of seismic convulsions that propagated new shockwaves to smash through the city, one after another after another, second after second after second.

For all its strength, it was the sounds of the earthquake that would be forever stamped on the memories of survivors. One man likened the noise that rolled through the ground beneath him to "distant thunder" that grew in volume "much as it does when a train approaches one through a tunnel." A musician related it to "a thousand violins playing off key." Punctuating the roar was the clatter of destruction, "the sound of groaning lumber, the creaking of nails and spikes being drawn, the snapping of painted woodwork," the loud report of "cracking bricks," and "the rattle and jar of everything loose." Above it all were the awful screams of human pain, the "crying of the children," and "a horrible chorus of human cries of agony." Thirty-nine-year-old art gallery owner Henry Atkins later wrote the "indescribable sound" was one "you feel rather than hear."

And the shock of the earthquake reached far beyond San Francisco. Primary seismic waves rolled eastward through the bay, followed through the ground by secondary shockwaves that smashed into east Bay Area communities. In Oakland, Agnes Ehrenberg "huddled up in bed," afraid her parents' house would collapse, and the next day wrote it felt "much jerkier" than riding "in a small boat on a stormy sea." Frank Leach, superintendent of the San Francisco Mint, awoke to his Oakland home "jumping up and down a good part of a foot at every jump" and "terrifying noises, the cracking and creaking of timber" and the "thumping of falling bricks coursing down the roof sides from the chimney tops." In Berkeley, twenty-two-year-old Ivan Rankin awoke "feeling something shaking me like a dog does a rat in its jaws." His house, only two years old, "groaned, creaked, and cracked," and out his window Ivan could see "the chimney come tumbling down" off his neighbor's house. Also in Berkeley, Gertrude Atherton "sprang out of bed and opened the door" before it jammed, and as the "earth danced, and leaped, and plunged, and roared," she worried everyone in her hotel was "going to the bottom of the Pacific."

The shock rolled northward to Sausalito, where William Hancock was admiring the "rosy dawn" of the "lovely morning" from his window in the top floor of a boardinghouse. He "felt a slight trembling of the room" followed by a "crash"—part of his ceiling was pulled away as the cupola of the house collapsed down three stories into the lobby and chimneys fell outward. Further north in San Rafael, the shock struck US Ninth Circuit Judge William Morrow's home "like a cyclone." Vases were thrown to the floor and the house twisted "as though it was in the grip of a demon." Even further north in Glen Ellen—forty miles from San Francisco—writer Charmian London awoke to the shaking in the upstairs bedroom she shared with her husband, Jack. Through the window, she endured the "sickening onrush of motion" while "watching the tree-tops thrash crazily" through "the longest half-minute I ever lived through."

Tremors ripped southward down the peninsula to Stanford University where twenty-two-year-old Laurence Klauber—only a few hours into sleep after a late-night return from the opera up in the city—was awakened by "the noise of the falling buildings." The jerking motion was so strong, he noted, that "you couldn't fall, because when you started to, you were jerked in another direction." And further south in San Jose, Anna Poston felt her end of the hotel where she was staying "lift clear off the ground, and then the other." She did not try to get out of bed because she "would have been unable to stand." Even there the shaking "seemed like hours."

The great earthquake was felt as far north as Oregon, as far east as Nevada, and south beyond Los Angeles. Across the country, the pen of the seismograph machine at the weather bureau in Washington, DC, registered the "violent agitation." The Pacific and North American Plates had displaced in some places more than twenty feet horizontally and six feet vertically, and the rupture in the San Andreas Fault stretched from near Cape Mendocino to San Juan Bautista, a distance of 296 miles.

The final vibrations rolled through San Francisco as Mary Ashe Miller, up in a home on Telegraph Hill, found herself asking, "Will it never stop? Will it never stop?" Finally, mercifully, it did stop. Precisely how long San Francisco was shaken is impossible to pinpoint. For those who endured the great earthquake's dragging seconds, it seemed eternal. Reporter James Hopper wrote that it lasted a "hideous minute and a quarter," and *Examiner* newspaperman Jack Barrett wrote, "It seemed a quarter of an hour before it stopped," but edited that to "about three minutes." There were some who thought it lasted "not more than 25 seconds," or "about 30 seconds," others who felt that it "kept up without stop for three or four minutes," and even a few who recorded that it "seemed five or six minutes," or even longer.

Because primary and secondary waves travel at different speeds, people further from the epicenter sensed the shaking for longer than those nearer, just as those in homes on soft fill land endured much stronger vibrations than those on bedrock. The duration—as with the intensity—varied by location. Professor Alexander McAdie of the city's weather bureau, who was so intent on keeping accurate earthquake data that he kept a watch, open notebook, pencil, and electric flashlight on his bedside table, estimated it took him at least six seconds to wake up and begin timing, and by his watch the shaking lasted "about forty seconds duration" from that point. Sometime the next morning, a clerk in the city's circuit court noted in the court minutes "a most violent earthquake shock, lasting for 48 seconds." The next day's newspaper would also declare "the shock lasted forty-eight seconds," a duration adopted by many eyewitnesses who later recounted the great earthquake, even if a few added the context of human experience to the sterile number: "I am told that the shake only lasted 48 seconds," one man wrote, "but it seemed to me nearer 48 minutes."

After interviewing hundreds of witnesses and collecting data "from every damaged area as well as from records from seismograph stations throughout the world," the State Earthquake Investigation Commission published a report on the disaster two years later concluding that "the sensible duration of the shock was about one minute." Today, the US Geological Survey reaffirms that assessment, estimating that a foreshock was followed twenty to twenty-five seconds later by "strong shaking" that lasted forty-five to sixty seconds.

No matter the earthquake's precise duration, James Hopper felt "incredulity at the mere length of the thing, the fearful stubbornness of it." Thousands of eyewitness accounts survive as monuments to small, private impressions of those slow ticks of the clock, each person's attempt to convey their own longest minute of indescribable devastation and fear and confusion through colorless words on flat paper. Of them all, perhaps Walter Scott, a young salesman shaken awake in his downtown lodging house, found a way to describe the time best in a letter to his aunt: "how long it lasted God alone knows—it seemed eternity."

4. Fire and No Water

THEN I NOTED the great silence." From his third-floor hotel room, James Hopper observed "when the roar of crumbling buildings was over and only a brick was falling here and there like the trickle of a spent rain, this silence continued, and it was an awful thing." He looked through the hole in the wall where his window had been just a minute before. In that minute, he had felt "like a fish in a frying pan" in his bed and watched the window jerked from its frame and the back wall of his hotel fall onto "little wooden houses in the alley below," the bricks smashing through their roofs "like tissue paper." Now after the awful "snarl" of the violent shaking, he heard only the "awful" silence. Hopper bounded down two flights of stairs to the street that was already "full of people, half-clad, disheveled, but silent, absolutely silent."

Two blocks away, photographer Arnold Genthe also noticed an "ominous quiet." His frightened Japanese valet, Hamada, gathered a basket of food and headed for the door, saying, "Master, very bad earthquake—many days nothing to eat—I go, yes," then bounded down the stairs. Out the window, Genthe saw "a number of men and women, half-dressed, rushing to the middle of the street for safety." The same silence filled the air down in the Mission, where eight-year-old Gregory Lighthouse followed his parents and little sister outside and "noticed the quietness that people stood in groups and only seemed to whisper."

A few people awakened by the earthquake fell back to sleep. James Warren and his friend Sam Mack, both visiting from Sacramento and staying in the St. Francis Hotel, were "shaken up pretty lively with the shock," but feeling their building was safe, they returned to sleep. In his Mission District home, eight-year-old William Dunne was in bed with his parents, and although all three awoke during the shaking—his father covering his mother and him and saying, "It's an earthquake"—all three "dropped off to sleep again." Even the violent shaking and deafening racket was not enough to wake some residents from their deep slumber. Seven-year-old Alex Young was "sound asleep until awakened by [his] father's touch, feeling only the last few vibrations of the quake." And five-year-old Anna Meakin "did not even feel the earthquake." Her first memory of that morning "was the comfortable sensation of being dressed while waking up. . . . Everyone seemed disturbed about something."

In their home on Lower Nob Hill, police sergeant William Ross and his wife, Permelia, were both awake and about to head outside but wondered about the silence from her uncle David's room. William ran upstairs and traversed "the fallen furniture and debris" in the room and found the Murphy bed folded upright—it had "shut up like a jack knife" with David inside. William wrenched the bed open and found David "nearly dead from fright and suffocation." A few blocks away in Hayes Valley, the guests in Charlotte and Hiram Daniels's home went to check on their hosts, who were asleep in a folding bed in another room, having given them use of their own bed. As in the Ross home, the bed was folded up against the wall. When the guests pulled it down, Charlotte gasped for air, having nearly suffocated, but her husband beside her was dead—he had sat up when the first tremors hit, and the subsequent shaking had sprung the bed up, breaking his neck. He was sixty-six. Charlotte, also sixty-six, was now a widow after forty-eight years of marriage.

South of Market, Thomas Chase picked himself up off 1st Street's cracked pavement and surveyed the damage around him: holes and depressions where there should be pavement, bent streetcar rails, and a half-collapsed apartment house with its rooms exposed "like a dollhouse." People had run or been thrown onto the sidewalk "in their night clothes and barefoot, moaning and wringing their hands." A man in a third-floor flat ran to his window "and saw that the streets were full of people, who looked like frenzied ants whose home had been stirred up with a stick." Another man ran to his fourth-floor hotel window and "raised the shades, and looked out" to see people "running out of the houses helter-skelter in all sorts of attires, yelling, gesticulating, talking excitedly and many could only gasp." But a nurse who made it outside noticed the "quietness of everyone" in her neighborhood and guessed they "were evidently struck dumb with awe."

"I did not think there were so many people in our street until the morning of the quake," one man noted with surprise of the scores of neighbors he had never before met and who now "swarmed out of their houses like bees out of a hive." As a woman on Nob Hill observed, they "seemed to grow in the street like magic—all of them keeping well in the middle of the road." Sidewalks and yards and streets throughout the city filled with people of all ages and all classes shocked and dazed and wide-eyed, most wearing only what they wore to bed or were able to grab on their rush to escape their houses, flats, and hotel rooms. "The streets presented a weird appearance," Arnold Genthe observed, "mother and children in their nightgowns, men in pajamas and dinner coat, women scantily dressed with evening wraps hastily thrown over them." South of Market, six-year-old Etta Siegel's father took her and her brother and sister outside; her siblings did not have "a stitch of clothes on," and she was wearing "just an old top shirt." Out near Golden Gate Park, Emma Burke looked from her fourth-floor apartment and saw a neighbor rush into the street "in her nightclothes," carrying her baby. Emma yelled down that she should cover herself, and the neighbor replied that her husband was getting something for her.

As people cast their vision beyond the damage to their bedrooms or living spaces, they were confronted with a tragedy incomprehensible in scope: their city broken in every direction as far as the eye could see. Many were silent as they huddled in the middle of streets—away from buildings in case of aftershocks—scanning the scene and absorbing the ruin to their homes and neighborhoods. Once the cloud of white dust on Van Ness Avenue settled, it revealed the fallen chimneys and wreckage of carved woodwork on the Spreckels mansion and fallen stonework of St. Luke's Episcopal Church, which was, as one resident would describe, "piled up on the sidewalk and against the sides of the church for a depth of 8 or 10 feet."

Throughout the city, electric poles were bent over sidewalks or thrown flat into streets, their wires draped over fallen bricks and overturned wagons. Sidewalks were buckled and raised, cable car slots were bowed and rails misshapen, and in some places, pavement had sunk five or six feet or was pushed up and cracked open with broken mains gushing water. Yards were filled with chunks of smashed chimneys and broken glass, with front stone steps split open and wooden stairs splintered. One man walking through downtown to check on his business wrote days later, "I do not remember a single chimney

standing anywhere." Buildings "were badly cracked" and stood at strange angles, in some cases "laying over against another." One witness described the
leaning houses across the street from her: "You know when you build a deck of
cards and you touch it and all the cards fall?"

Many found the devastation even within the limited view of their street or
city block overwhelming. Former mayor James Phelan threw on a suit and hat,
turned off the gas, ordered his staff not to cook, and walked out of his Valencia
Street home. As soon as he made it through the gate, he was confronted by
excited neighbors pointing to the ruins of the Valencia Hotel a block away,
saying, "Everyone is killed!" He rushed there to see only the top floor of the
four-story building visible, at street level, leaning forward with the bottom
three stories gone, and deep inside were "men and women imprisoned by the
fallen timbers." Their moans and cries were audible. A small crowd, including
police lieutenant Henry Powell and residents of the top floor who had stepped
out to the sidewalk through broken windows, was trying to rescue the dozens
trapped. Both nearby water mains had broken—one sixteen inches in diameter
and the other twenty-two inches—and "the street was like a river," with water
flowing into the buried hotel, adding urgency to the rescue. Phelan ran home,
gathered his house employees, and drove his two-horse carriage back to "the
hotel disaster" with axes and saws.

On the streets of Lower Nob Hill, police officer James Welch was walking
patrol when the earthquake hit. He saw the chimney and upper portion of the
brick wall of the eight-story California Hotel "shake off and topple over" and
smash through the roof of the three-story firehouse beside it, directly into the
third-floor apartment of Chief Sullivan and his wife. When the jerking ended,
Officer Welch managed to "find [his] feet again" and ran into the firehouse. It
was lit only faintly by predawn light through its broken windows and the jagged
holes in the roof and ceilings above. Firemen "were barefooted and in their un-
derclothes," disoriented, pulling beams and rubble off their engine and checking on their horses in a "smother of darkness and debris and choking dust." The
chimney and wall of the hotel had bored through both upper floors and crashed
onto the ground-floor fire engine, hose wagon, and the chief's buggy.

Dust settled and word spread through the house that the Sullivans were
buried beneath the debris on the first floor. Officer Welch jumped in to help.
The rest of the company rushed down the stairs from their quarters to pitch
in. Hot spray from a cracked radiator hissed from the pile. The men pulled
the wreckage back and could see the chief's bloodied head and bared shoulders being burned into blisters by the scalding steam. They heaved beams off

him high enough to pull their chief out. Two men lifted his arms over their shoulders and carried him to a buggy at the stable next door to rush him to a hospital. Chief Sullivan's skull was cracked, his ribs were broken, his lung was punctured, and the burns to his skin were second- and third-degree, but he was conscious and, according to one witness, "in full possession of his senses, and his first words were to ask the men to look for his wife."

The first tremors had awakened the chief, asleep in the guest room just a couple of hours after returning from the cannery fire. Reportedly, after hearing Margaret's "cries," he was "instantly alarmed" and ran into Margaret's room, but in the darkness he could not see that the floor was gone—the wall and roof of the California Hotel had smashed through it and the floor below and taken Margaret in her bed with it. He stepped blindly into the void and fell two stories onto the concrete floor, not far from Margaret and directly beside the cracked radiator. Joists and furniture and debris rained down on top of them through holes in both floors "as through a funnel," trapping them. Now that the chief had been rescued, the men dug for Margaret, buried deeper, and extracted her and sent her to a hospital as well. Protected by mattresses and bedding, she was not as seriously injured.

In firehouses throughout the city, men awoke to the clamor and confusion and leapt into action. In their 6th Street house South of Market, the firefighters of Engine 6 ran down the dark stairs to find their horses gone—the earthquake had shaken the large wooden doors wide open, and morning light shined in through settling dust. The stone floor was cracked down the middle, and toward the back of the house the floor was crumbled and the walls were torqued and broken at angles where the whole back wall had sunk down at least three feet. The firemen were still throwing on their uniforms and caps as they walked out onto 6th Street to survey the damage on their block.

The three-story wood-frame building beside them was "completely wrecked." The soft fill land beneath it had liquefied, causing second- and third-floor dwellings to pancake onto the first-floor liquor store, leaving a flattened pile of snapped beams and joists. Someone spotted a tiny bare foot in the debris, prompting a scramble of men to heave timbers and broken window frames up to rescue the child. With axes they cut into the rest of the pile, pulling two more children and five adults from the wreckage. And on the other side of their house was a "partly caved-in" two-story building in danger of collapse. Without a moment to spare, the firefighters cut through the collapsed front to free five more adults and three more children.

Cries of "fire!" carried up and down 6th Street while the men of Engine 6 rescued survivors. "Turning our eyes from our work," their captain, thirty-three-year-old Charles Cullen, reported, "we beheld threatening flames rising from different directions." He and his men returned to their firehouse, where the alarm panel was dark and silent. Wasting no time and without horses, the firemen strained to pull their three-ton engine by hand over the cracked house floor and onto the brick street. Captain Cullen sent five men to haul the engine up a block to the nearest fire, and he kept five at work clearing crashed buildings of survivors.

Up in the fire alarm office at Portsmouth Square, as soon as the shaking stopped, the floor caught on fire. As with nearly every building in the city, the earthquake had knocked the chimney off the roof. Bricks and mortar had plunged down the flue and hurled flaming embers onto the office floor. Switchboard operator James Kelly ran to the sink to draw water, but there was no pressure. Water from broken wet-cell battery cases in the adjoining power room streamed in and snuffed out the fire. But the dual omen of fire and no water pressure lingered as Kelly went to the window and "saw the smoke of an apparently large fire begin to rise" above Market Street. His coworker Charles Daley looked out the other window a few moments later and saw "three columns of smoke," and within minutes, Kelly could see "five additional fires starting" across the district. Alarms were being pulled throughout the city, but in the office there was only silence—no phone rings, no ticking of the ticker-tape machine with incoming alarms, and no way to send messages to fire companies—all lines were severed and communication broken.

One of these first columns of smoke coiled upward from a single-floor wood-frame laundry house on Howard Street, South of Market. The earthquake had shaken the roof down and a falling ceiling joist had knocked over the furnace used to heat irons, spilling burning coals. The small building "blazed up like tinder." William Dove, a carpenter and habitual early riser, was standing on the corner of 3rd and Howard Streets when the shock hit and saw the roof collapse and fire ignite. He "could see the flames" through the front windows of the laundry and worried for his friend who owned and lived in the saddlery shop directly next door. He broke into the saddlery shop, "found [his] way through the smoke," and rushed his friend out to the safety of the street.

Thick black smoke poured from the laundry house. Inside the dry, wooden structure, wool, cotton, and silk laundry in stacked piles on tables or jammed in linen bags fueled the flames' spread until flashover—the point where every combustible substance in the building was aflame—which produced deadly carbon monoxide and even deadlier hydrogen cyanide. Heat shattered storefront windows and flames shot out the top, licking up the wood siding of the taller buildings on either side. Directly across Howard Street was the Engine 4 firehouse, where Captain Charles Murray and his men had spent the minutes since the earthquake pulling bricks of a collapsed wall off the limp body of fireman James O'Neil, "crushed and instantly killed" while serving as night watchman. Captain Murray "ran out into the street," saw the fire in the laundry, and gathered his men—still "bewildered" by the death of one of their own—who rolled their steam engine out to the street by hand (like Engine 6, the shaking had flung the doors open and their horses had disappeared in a stampede). A hoseman ran a spanner wrench to the hydrant in front of the firehouse, twisted the cap off, wrenched the back stem nut to open the water flow, and, in a portent that would repeat through the coming hours and days, he yelled back, "No water." He ran to the other corner hydrant: no water. And the further corner hydrant: no water.

Unable to send a message to the fire alarm office for support, Captain Murray sent one of his men running around the corner to Chemical Engine 1's firehouse on 2nd Street. Hearing "yelling" from inside the flaming laundry, Murray "grabbed an axe off the wagon," chopped an opening through the wall, held a full chest of breath behind pressed lips, and rushed into the wall of smoke to save the trapped workers. But the blaze was beyond control, and the men pulled their captain out before he was incapacitated by the lethal fumes and just a few seconds before the burning structure collapsed. Within minutes, Chemical Engine 1 rolled up behind its horse team, its firefighters having dug their way through the collapsed brick front of their firehouse to respond. Chemical Engine 1's firemen hooked up a line to their tank and put a stream of water on the blaze, but the fire was too large, having already turned the three-story boardinghouse next door into "one mass of flames." Engine 4's firefighters, still trying to find water, dropped a suction hose through the manhole of a nearby cistern, but what little they were able to pump from inside "was of no use whatever." As one frustrated hoseman reported of the blaze, "[I]t soon got away from us."

Three blocks away, smoke from another fire rose from the five-story Mack & Company Drug Wholesaler on Fremont Street just south of Market. Like most of downtown's older buildings of timber-joisted masonry construction, its floor framing and girders and floor trusses and interior support columns and ceiling joists were all wooden. Interior columns were plastered for fire resistance, but there was no fireproofing for the rest of the wood and timber supports, as none was required. The store carried "drugs, chemicals, and fancy goods," and its combustible inventory—most stored in glass jars on high shelves—included alcohol, kerosene, the highly volatile diethyl ether and glycerol, oxidizers like copper oxide and peroxide (which release oxygen when heated), and ammonia, prone to explode at high temperatures. Next door, the three-story corner office of the Oceanic Steamship and Western Sugar Refining Companies, owned by the Spreckels family, fronted Market Street, and next door to that on Market was the five-story Montague Company, a stove and range wholesaler. The back walls of Spreckels's office and Montague's adjoined the side wall of Mack's, and each business employed night watchmen and private security guards.

When the shaking stopped, the night watchman for Montague's rushed from a coffeehouse across Market Street and into his store. In the back he could feel intense heat through the rear wall and "heard several explosions" from Mack's drugstore on the far side. He unrolled the emergency fire hose but "discovered that we had no water." He ran back outside onto Market Street where the security guard for Spreckels's office had just tried pulling a street fire alarm with no response. When they ran around the corner onto Fremont Street, the front of Mack's "began smoking and banging in a series of explosions." A police officer arrived and held them and other onlookers back as the drugstore went up like fireworks, its inventory "going off like artillery discharges and shooting lighted beams and brands all over both sides of Fremont Street." The night watchman rushed back around the corner and into Montague's and saw flames burning through the back wall.

Mack's drugstore was a "mass of flames" by the time the first fire engine rolled up. The captain had noticed the smoke from the company firehouse three blocks away, hitched up his horse to his buggy, and ordered the men of his engine company to follow. When they arrived and jumped off their hose wagon to hook their stoked engine to the nearest hydrant at the corner, they could get no water. The captain sent them down one block to the next hydrant on Fremont Street: no water. They doubled back to the next one a block down on Market Street. The captain grabbed a wrench and ran "from one street to another to find some water." On Fremont, all five stories of Mack's drugstore were "burning fiercely." Inside the brick shell, flames consumed the wood and timber skeleton while ceilings collapsed and floors pancaked one onto another. Firefighters pulled the steam engine and hose wagon back from the heat just before another explosion blew the entire front wall out into the street. And still the yells kept coming: "No water!"

At last, a hoseman found a working hydrant a block down Market at Beale Street, and the captain ordered the line connected and ran back to the engine at the corner of Fremont. By then, Mack's drugstore was engulfed, and flames had spread to Spreckels's corner office. Firemen "threw a stream" on the office and on Montague's next door, but with the blaze growing on the inside in the rear of both buildings (where the fire from Mack's had burned through), the effort was futile. Hoping to keep the fire from jumping blocks, the captain ordered his men to shift the single line of water they had onto the buildings on the opposite side of Fremont Street.

Another engine company arrived and was directed a block and a half down Fremont Street past Mack's where the Martel Power Company was ablaze. The four-story structure was a combustible mix under a single roof: the power company occupied the first floor with engines and generators; the second floor was a silk factory; and the third and fourth floors housed a tamale factory, with multiple ranges and steam kettles. It is unknown where the spark ignited the powder keg, but a saloonkeeper across the street looked out his apartment window "immediately after the earthquake" and noticed the building already on fire, and within a minute it was fully engulfed. Firefighters worked their way through hydrants along the block with no luck, and the power company blaze spread to the machine shops and hardware stores to its left and right.

Countless small fires started with the earthquake, and in different ways: open flames or electric sparks ignited leaking gas, broken chimneys tossed burning embers from fireplaces, space heaters and ovens overturned and spilled flaming contents, kerosene and oil lamps fell and cracked, lit candles tipped. One man awoke to the chandelier falling in his bedroom, leaking gas. On his way to turn it off at the meter, he stomped out a flame where some matches had fallen and ignited. Every fire started small, and most were like this, in a home or apartment or, as in the fire alarm office, a workplace where someone was able to douse the initial flames immediately.

But in a sea of dry wooden buildings bunched in clusters on streets with almost no water, any unattended small fire could burn down not just the building or block but also its neighborhood and district beyond. There was no main fire or first fire, but in every district there were a few that ignited in unoccupied spaces—mostly commercial—and enough of these spread so rapidly that their smoke climbed high enough to be seen by many—as the men observed up in the fire alarm office—as soon as the earth stopped jolting. "Immediately after the quake," a man in the Western Addition saw smoke rising "in half a dozen places." It was "within five seconds of the end of the shock" that the British consul general, Sir Courtenay Bennett, saw from his hotel room "twenty or thirty fires [that] broke out all over the lower parts of the city." When the ground finally stilled near the top of Sacramento Street in Chinatown, a woman looking out her window noticed the "columns of smoke," which she later likened to "signals of alarm."

In the absence of working building alarms or street boxes and with no telegraph communications, bells and gongs of firehouses sat eerily silent, forcing captains and battalion chiefs out to streets or to the roofs of their houses to spot the "signals of alarm" lifting above the broken city, and they then aimed their engines to the nearest one. Just as the first smoke pillars South of Market pointed fire companies to Mack's drugstore and the Martel Power Company and the Howard Street laundry house, out in the Western Addition the first smoke rose from the corner of Hayes and Laguna Streets in the Hayes Valley neighborhood. Firefighters of a truck and engine company two streets away saw the "large columns of smoke" and "left at once." So did crews of two other nearby engine companies, where men saw the same smoke and responded. A local physician could see the same fire "growing larger" and "heard the fire engines rattling over the streets on their way" past his house.

Five blocks from the fire, the Ellis Street home of fifty-three-year-old Patrick Shaughnessy, the second assistant chief of the fire department, was equipped with a bell and telegraph connected with the fire alarm office. Both had sat silent since the last of the alarms transmitted for the North Beach cannery fire before 4:00 a.m. As he dressed in the moments following the earthquake, Shaughnessy did not know Chief Sullivan had been gravely wounded or that he was now the department's acting assistant chief. His operator pulled up to his house in his buggy within ten minutes to alert him of—and take him to—the fires in Hayes Valley.

On the corner of Hayes and Laguna Streets, flames were consuming a two-story wood-frame drugstore, and three fire engines had already arrived. No sooner had firemen started pumping from a corner hydrant than the water pressure faded to a trickle and "gave out after a few minutes." As elsewhere, they checked hydrant after hydrant without luck. Another company of firemen arrived and joined in the hunt for water, having worked their way two blocks down from a bottling company blaze that had already consumed half of its block and was still spreading.

"After a long search" for water, firefighters found "a good supply" in a single hydrant a block west at the corner of Hayes and Buchanan Streets. Tapping this valuable source, an engine pumped the water through a hose back up the street to another engine, where crews applied a line of water on the drugstore fire. And through two more engines positioned block by block connected one with another by eight-hundred-foot-long hoses, water was pumped to the bottling company fire. With water scarce, improvisation played an outsized role, and these "engines in tandem" managed to stretch the reach of water from a single hydrant across five blocks to keep both Hayes Valley fires from spreading further to surrounding homes and apartments.

While his crews fought both fires, Acting Assistant Chief Shaughnessy looked to the east and saw "several columns of smoke rising perpendicularly in the air" and "several fires South of Market." He hopped on his buggy to find an automobile "for the purpose of going from fire to fire," still unaware Chief Sullivan was in the hospital, leaving him second-in-command. Four blocks behind him and on higher ground was the city's fire marshal, fifty-six-year-old Charles Towe, who had ventured in his buggy to the top of the Hayes Street hill, reined his horse, stood up in his buggy, and squinted into the eastern sky where the sun was just breaking above the horizon and the morning's blue was shrouded by "smoke or fire arising from different parts of the city." Charles saw smoke at the lower end of Market Street, and along the waterfront, and South of Market, and "in several places" in the Mission. "I should judge I counted from 15 to 20 columns of smoke."

At the base of each of these smoldering columns were other battles being fought: another axe-wielding fireman hacking his way into a burning structure, another police officer keeping curious crowds back, another parked engine puffing steam with an engineer feeding coal to keep its boiler fire stoked, another driver walking blanketed horse teams further away from the spreading flames, another frustrated battalion chief sending runners off with urgent requests for support, and another hoseman lugging a wrench in a flat sprint from hydrant to hydrant searching for water without luck. "The lack of water," one man later declared, "was perhaps the worst feature of the calamity."

In the minutes following 5:12 a.m., running water throughout San Francisco was, with very few specific exceptions, cut off. In many places, as with James Kelly up in the fire alarm office, nothing trickled from faucets after the earthquake. In others, a small amount could be dripped from pipes but was soon exhausted. One man wrote that he and his family filled "every receptacle we had with water," and soon after, "it ceased running." Another woman, still "speech-less" from the shock of the earthquake but thinking quickly, "set to work filling the three tubs, washtub, and every pot and pan or anything that could hold water." Still another, unable to get any from the dry tap, "went about and took all the flowers out of the vases to save the water that was left." A twelve-year-old girl, instructed by her father to fill the bathtub as soon as she dressed, watched water fill the tub slowly "and then it just stopped by itself."

Water in bathtubs and sinks and hydrants stopped running because the earthquake caused an almost total failure of the Spring Valley Water Company's distribution system. Although all three of the company's reservoirs and both dams in San Mateo County withstood the earthquake, as did eight of its nine reservoirs in San Francisco County, almost nothing else went right. The forty-four-inch pipe that carried water up the peninsula from the largest reservoir, Crystal Springs, which supplied the waterfront area and entire South of Market district, broke in seven places south of the city where the wooden trestle that lifted its pipes over swamps and marshland collapsed (nearly a mile of the pipe was torn and scattered, and an entire five-hundred-foot-long section was "thrown from its trestle onto the mud flats"). The San Andreas reservoir pipeline, which supplied the Mission and much of the city north of Market Street, "was badly fractured," and the thirty-inch pipeline from the Pilarcitos reservoir, the source for most of the western portion of the city, "was so badly damaged" that company engineers "decided to abandon it." In the city, fill and made land was turned into what an engineer described as a "bowl of mud," and transmission and distribution mains telescoped into iron ribbons or tore apart. More than three hundred street mains cracked, and more than twenty-three thousand breaks were later found in service pipes, which delivered water from mains into buildings and homes.

Although no water was flowing into the city, in many places there was a small amount of water left in pipes, sufficient for a short supply of drinking water. In a few hotels and apartment buildings with rooftop tanks, tenants and guests still had pressure where wall service pipes had not cracked. And the eighty million gallons of water sitting in distribution reservoirs in the city—more than enough to fight even a citywide fire—was either emptying into subsoil or could not be accessed because mains were broken. A handful of street distribution main sections and at least one long section of the transmission main from the Laguna Honda Reservoir held, and within these small pockets there was a continuous supply of water. But these isolated supplies were limited and scarce, and of the city's 4,213 hydrants, fewer than four dozen were found to connect with working mains. Even if fire crews located each of them—as with the Hayes and Buchanan Streets hydrant near the fire in Hayes Valley—and stretched each supply to reach the nearest blazes, it would not be enough. By sunrise at 5:31 a.m., more than fifty fires were burning and spreading, and the fate of most of the city was already sealed.

This "Daguerreotype of 1850" shows downtown streets lined with buildings of wood-frame and timber-joisted brick masonry constructed in the wake of recent fires. A thicket of masts marks where hundreds of ships logjam the shallow water of Yerba Buena Cove, soon to be filled in to expand the city six blocks out from Montgomery Street. *San Francisco History Center, San Francisco Public Library*

This 1851 city survey of San Francisco shows the streets and blocks of landfill-"made" ground extended from the original waterfront. *Bancroft Library*

TOP LEFT: Dennis Sullivan, Chief Engineer of the San Francisco Fire Department. *Bancroft Library*

TOP RIGHT: San Francisco Mayor Eugene Schmitz. *San Francisco History Center, San Francisco Public Library*

BOTTOM: A view of the city in 1905 looking northeastward on Market Street from an upper floor of the Call Building. The Ferry Building and its distinctive clock tower stand at the foot of Market Street on the waterfront, and Yerba Buena Island (then called Goat Island) is visible out in the Bay. *Bancroft Library*

TOP LEFT: Sergeant Jesse Cook of the San Francisco Police Department, pictured before the disaster. Cook served as the city's police chief from 1908 to 1910, then as police commissioner for the next twenty years. *Jesse B. Cook Scrapbook, Bancroft Library*

TOP RIGHT: Seismic shockwaves liquefied the fill-land South of Market, as seen by its effects on these paving stones and bent streetcar rails at 6th and Howard Streets within the first hour following the earthquake before fires destroyed every building in the area. *Bancroft Library*

BOTTOM: Hundreds help rescue survivors from the top floor of what was the four-story Valencia Street Hotel before it sunk into the fill-land of Valencia Street between 17th and 18th Streets. Dozens were crushed or trapped, and those who did not drown in water flooding from the broken street main died in the fire that followed. *San Francisco History Center, San Francisco Public Library*

TOP: Among the earliest and most devastating fires South of Market was the Howard Street Laundry House Fire, captured here in a photograph looking west on Howard Street around 6:00 a.m. *Bancroft Library*

BOTTOM: The Spreckels office building on Market Street at Fremont is fully engulfed around 7:00 a.m. after flames burned through its rear wall from Mack's drugstore. Note the wood scaffolding to the right, a portion of which would soon ignite and spread the fire up Market Street toward the Palace Hotel. *San Francisco History Center, San Francisco Public Library*

FIFTH ST. 6 A.M. APRIL 18, 1906.

Copyright 1906
by W.E. Worden

ABOVE: Refugees carry belongings toward Market Street along 5th Street early the first morning as the South of Market fire approaches the Mint where employees would spend the hours until sundown fighting off the flames surrounding them with water from the building's well. Their efforts saved the nation's western gold reserve leaving the Mint as the lone financial institution in San Francisco in the days following the fire. *Bancroft Library*

AT LEFT: The scene in the banking district around nine o'clock the first morning at California and Sansome Streets. Offices within the nine-story Mutual Life Insurance Company burn as firefighters of Engine Company 31 receive water from another engine a block back (out of frame.) *San Francisco History Center, San Francisco Public Library*

ABOVE: Army Brigadier General Frederick Funston, seen here at the division commander's quarters at Fort Mason. *San Francisco History Center, San Francisco Public Library*

AT LEFT: Navy Lieutenant Frederick Freeman. *Mare Island Museum*

BELOW: The view Lieutenant Freeman and his sailors had as they glided near the waterfront that first morning: smoke and flames consuming downtown and threatening the Ferry Building and the wharf, wooden slips, and piers. *Bancroft Library*

TOP: Shortly after nine o'clock the first morning, residents watch the first flames of the Hayes Valley Fire. Although newspapers blamed "a woman cooking ham and eggs for breakfast," the fire initiated within structures inhabited mostly by men, and most likely within a first-floor business. The caption on this photograph claims the Posner Cigar Store on the first floor in 377 Hayes was "credited with starting Ham and Eggs fire." *Bancroft Library*

BOTTOM: In the eleven o'clock hour, residents offer wagons to evacuate hundreds of wounded patients from Mechanics' Pavilion as the Hayes Valley Fire threatens. All patients were safely evacuated, and by noon the building was consumed by fire. *San Francisco History Center, San Francisco Public Library*

AT LEFT: The Call Building burns late the first morning. Market Street has been cleared of most onlookers, and hoses stretching back (out of frame to the left) to an engine pumping from a Palace Hotel hydrant are laid out near Lotta's Fountain (bottom center). *San Francisco History Center, San Francisco Public Library*

BELOW: The South of Market fire (left) eats toward the foot of Market Street the first morning as onlookers watch firefighters use water pumped from the Bay to soak the Hotel Terminus (right). Their efforts slowed but could not stop the fire before it spread north of Market (to the right) and consumed every building visible here. *Edward J. Torney Sr. Collection*

5. Indescribable Confusion

MANY OF THE first South of Market fires were in businesses unoccupied at the moment of impact. But flames did not have to spread far to reach highly congested residential buildings, mostly wooden and all in a district quickly running out of the last small amounts of water firefighters could pump from trickling hydrants or half-empty cisterns. On Howard Street, the laundry house fire ate to both ends of the block within the first hour—west to 3rd Street and east to 2nd—and then jumped to the north side of Howard. Firemen of Chemical Engine 1 watered down buildings at the end of the block where Howard met 2nd "to check it from going easterly," and when forced back by the heat they shifted and applied their engine's last drops of water from its tanks onto buildings on the east side of 2nd Street to keep them from catching. But tall orange flames shot burning chunks of awning and wood more than eighty feet across the street, and another block ignited, this one mostly residential.

Seeing this, fireman Frank Tracy left the engine and ran down the east side of 2nd Street past the growing flames to evacuate the neighborhood. He ran down the next block of Howard Street shouting for people to get out. He ran down alleyways between boardinghouses, yelling up at open windows that the fire was coming. He jumped fences and kept shouting his warning. "I had to run as fast as I could," he later reported. When he saw more smoke ahead from the fires at Mack's drugstore and Martel Power on Fremont Street, he worried the two blazes could merge, and he ran up and down more blocks "and ordered the people out." The earthquake had awakened most residents, and many had spilled into the street driven by curiosity or worry of aftershocks. And his warnings coaxed more out of apartments and hotels who might otherwise have stayed.

But many were trapped, and rescues were slow going. Deep in the wreckage of the Brunswick House on 6th Street, Edna Ketring awoke ("I guess I must have fainted") pinned in total darkness. She could hear "excited people" crying out around her. Reaching with her free arms, she "found on all sides timbers and plaster" but sensed an open space. She wrested herself free and began crawling through the dark void; she smelled smoke and heard "crackling of burning timbers," and she scrambled toward daylight. By the time she emerged from the pile, flames were "raging furiously." Bruised and covered with blood, she wrapped herself in a comforter she found, and her eyes darted over each face in the crowd gathered around the flaming ruins, but she could not find her fiancé, Thomas.

From the smashed space of his own room, James Jacobs "burrowed toward the daylight." On his way, he helped another roomer loose from between timbers, and both emerged "on part of the roof that had pitched over into Sixth Street." As they stepped from the shattered rooftop onto the street, "the whole mass of ruins seemed to be blazing into flames." A crowd of volunteers gathered, but the woodpile "burned like tinder" and the few who attempted rescue were driven back by the heat. Arriving firefighters pushed into the burning pile toward screaming voices while onlookers "held up blankets and comfortables [sic] to protect the workers from the heat." They rescued two people before "the heap of wreckage was a mass of flame." From the flames could be heard moans, pleas, screams, and what one witness described as "a terrible, low, heart-rending cry of utter resignation."

Dozens of people were still trapped in the wreckage of the Brunswick. Among them were the proprietor, Frank Keefe, his wife, Florence, and their twelve-year-old son, Leo. And Abraham Lichtenstein, who lived behind the shop he ran on the first floor, along with his wife, Johanna, their twenty-year-old son, Moses, and their fourteen-year-old daughter, Esther. And sisters Maud Johnson and Mary Irwin. And Edna Ketring's fiancé, Thomas. Lodgers included widows, families between homes, nomadic blue-collar workers passing through town, recently evicted single mothers, and immigrant laborers working odd jobs. Most had no family to notice their later absence and the records of their stay at the Brunswick burned with them.

Months later, the night clerk who had managed to escape before the collapse strained his memory for names of those staying that last night, his mind running through flashes of faces never to be seen again. Some he remembered in groups, like the "Wilson sisters" or the "Cummings (2)"; of a few he could only remember last names, like "Murray, Randoff, Jones, and Woodward"; and without any specific number, he remembered the "children."

The same world of employers and lodgers was lost in the Ohio House next door. And in the Lormor House the next door down. And in the Nevada House at the corner, where the proprietor's son later remembered prying himself from the heap, one of only thirteen to escape before the flames came. Still trapped were his mother, father, and eighteen-year-old sister. And twenty others he knew as neighbors. Single mothers, like forty-year-old Emma Greiner who lived with her eighteen-year-old daughter, Edna. And Alma Harris with her three-year-old daughter, Virginia. Laborers like Joseph Cook, a barber; Fred Espinola, a lather; James Reilly, a plumber; and Joseph Murray, a tile setter. A fortune-teller he knew as Mrs. Francis and a dressmaker, Mrs. Jones. All were trapped and all died in the flames. The four lodging houses, collapsed and burning, became the final, unmarked resting place for countless souls, their final moments unrecorded and lives unremembered.

A dozen blocks away in the Mission, a squad of policemen and at least fifty volunteers—including former mayor Phelan and his house staff—"were working with rageful energy at the tangle of wall and rafters" of another lodging house, the wood-frame Valencia Hotel. The street "was split open about six to eight feet," allowing the growing throngs to look down into the mud of the old Mission swamp. Water gushed from the broken twenty-two-inch-wide transmission main (from the College Hill Reservoir) and poured "like a river" into the chasm filled with hotel wreckage and trapped survivors. With axes and saws and pry bars and rope pulled from their own houses or nearby hardware stores, rescuers cut and lifted and peeled away layers of bent siding and split beams toward the sounds of moans and cries and rushing water. A truck company of firefighters rolled up on the way to another fire, reined their horse teams, jumped off, and joined the rescue. "[B]y pulling up floors and sawing away the joists," people were pulled out of the top of the sunken structure one by one. Some were awake and talking, others were limp, wounded, and moaning, a few were unconscious, and the rest were dead.

"The sights there were very distressing," Lieutenant Powell later related, "even for a man as well trained in casualties as a policeman has to be." Eight of the dead were pulled out and "placed in the alley at the rear of the hotel." Among them were lone boarders like Annie Conway, a twenty-seven-year-old widow;

Patrick Broderick, a fifty-nine-year-old laborer; Lorenze Goetz, a sixty-four-year-old carpenter; and William Krone, forty, also a carpenter. And laid out side by side were the Johnson family, thirty-two-year-old Nathan; his wife, thirty-one-year-old May; their little son, two-year-old Harold; and Nathan's older brother, Edward. Their daughter, six-year-old Virginia, was pulled out alive. She would be taken in by her uncle days later, after he identified the bodies of the family, including those of his two brothers.

Approximately seventy-five people had been inside the Valencia at the moment of impact, including the manager and his family, upward of fifty boarders and guests, and hotel employees including a clerk, a cook, a bedmaker, a waitress, a dishwasher, and a chambermaid. Only two—the night clerk and a guest—managed to sprint out the front door in the seconds that followed before the earth swallowed three of the hotel's four floors. Many in rooms on the fourth floor were able to climb out of their shattered windows onto the street, but fewer than a dozen were rescued from the ruins of the bottom three floors in the minutes and hours that followed. The wounded were carried on doors and large boards to a nearby house for treatment, and later to one of the few hospitals not in the path of the spreading fire. At least two of those rescued would later die.

Among those pulled out alive were Annie Bock, fifty-seven, unhurt, and her son, Albert, twenty, with a broken shoulder. Annie begged rescuers to find her husband, fifty-one-year-old William, who was the hotel manager, and her older son, William Henry, twenty-three, both still trapped. Whether William and William Henry were dead already or whether they would drown in the flooding or whether they were fated to die in the fire that would eventually reach them is unknown. Nor is there any way of knowing when or how death came to the rest of those still trapped, and most of their bodies were never recovered.

Downtown in the moments after the shaking stopped, a "cloud of deep dust hung tenaciously around City Hall," reporter Fred Hewitt noticed as he picked himself up from Larkin Street, which was littered with large pieces of columns and chunks of masonry. Together with onlookers filling the streets around the civic plaza—many in underwear and nightclothes—Fred stared at the debris cloud, spellbound. "As the wind carried the dust away and uncovered the ruins there stood a mountain sheared of all its crowning glory." The towering dome, stripped of its outer shell, now "appeared like a huge birdcage against the morning dawn." One man noted the "dome was stripped clean off and only the uprights were supporting what was left of the dome," and a teenage boy likened it to "a huge skeleton."

The dome's top and statue balanced atop iron supports, bent and exposed. Walls and pillared colonnades had disintegrated like plaster, and massive columns that had once appeared so solid lay broken across street pavement, their soft insides exposed by cracked eggshell façades. "Earthquakes uncover strange secrets," a magazine editor who saw it that morning articulated, adding that its expensive, ruined edifice "cried to heaven the shame of the men who built it." As a passing nurse perceived, it "stood now like a lie exposed."

Among onlookers on Larkin Street were Officers Plume and Dwyer, smacking dust from their uniforms and winded from their sprint out of the City Hall Police Station. Dwyer walked with a limp after almost breaking his leg falling on a streetcar rail where the paving stones had been removed for the line's conversion from cable to electric traction. Mindful of their lieutenant and three arrestees still trapped inside, both officers ran back into the settling debris cloud, climbed stacks of rubble into the darkness of an inner hallway, and made their way back into the station. Joined by their lieutenant, they felt their way deeper inside to the holding cells "in perfect darkness." The male arrestee "was shaking his cell door and howling to be let out." Held only for a misdemeanor, he was released. In the other cell, the two women—sisters—were quiet, found "lying on the floor senseless." The officers carried them out, revived them with a wet towel, and "after the terrible fright and punishment they had been through," released them also.

Also trapped were the staff and patients of the city's Central Emergency Hospital occupying much of City Hall's ground floor and basement. "It was black dark and smothering" inside, and the officer on duty, "choking" on plaster and mortar and "suffocating dust," could not "see his hand in front of his face." Exits were blocked with rubble stacked to their tops, and slivers of morning light sliced through settling mortar clouds. Joined by a nurse and the physician on duty, the officer pulled fallen bricks and ceiling slabs from the entrance to the mental health detention ward to release patients held on involuntary commitments, and amid their "yelling and shrieking" ushered them over debris and upstairs into the light where a group of officers had "managed to effect an entrance" from the outside by digging away piled rubble and tearing iron bars from the loose grout around windows, allowing the staff to carry and escort the patients out onto Larkin Street.

Another of the hospital's physicians hurried to the scene and, with a police captain, rushed across Larkin Street to Mechanics' Pavilion, "forcibly opened" its large front doors, and found the superintendent, who then opened the enormous wood-frame building "as a temporary hospital." Inside was a vast open space normally used for roller-skating, prizefights, balls, revival meetings, presidential speeches, and annual fairs. The night before, the pavilion was host to a "masked carnival" on roller skates, where prizes from season tickets to diamond rings were awarded for the fastest skater and best costume. Streamers and decorations from the event still hung from the sixty-foot-high arched ceiling, and two rows of windows stretched its length, casting morning light on more than 92,000 square feet of open floor—nearly the size of two football fields.

Patients walking under their own strength entered and sat on the floor. Others were carried in and laid on mattresses rushed over from the hospital. A chain of nurses and physicians and police officers formed across Larkin Street to the ruins of the hospital, passing "operating tables, cots, medicine chests, instruments, and every other accessory we could carry out of the place," some hauled on gurneys and in handcarts, all into the pavilion. Nurses unfolded cots, and surgeons established operating spaces. Two police officers loaded a patrol wagon with "bandages, cotton, lint, and other necessary medical supplies" from a nearby pharmacy and grabbed beds and blankets from hotels and rooming houses and returned. Soon the hall was transformed into "a serviceable semblance of a real hospital," ready for the countless injured incoming from all corners of the city.

As in the Mission and South of Market Districts, rescue work north of Market Street was feverish. After the fish market collapse, Merchant Street was in a "terrible state of ruin," blocked entirely by piled bricks and masonry. Horse teams and wagons and the dead and wounded were "littered all about" beneath fallen brick walls. A police officer noted "the spectacle was pitiable." He helped workers and arriving fire crews "dig and drag from the ruins" bodies. "Legs and arms were sticking out here and there to guide us." At least nine were dead and two dozen injured. Alex Paladini helped his father dig from the rubble a man with a broken leg, then loaded him on their fish wagon and took him to the waterfront's Harbor Emergency Hospital.

Across the street from the Tivoli Opera House a block north of Market Street, the sidewalk in front of the Orienta Bar and Café was choked with heaped remains of the eight-story front wall of the Hotel Orienta. A crowd of bystanders watched a police officer and volunteers lift the body of a dead young woman off the top of the pile. She had fallen from five stories up. Still in her nightclothes, without a mark or bruise on her, she "looked as calm as if she were asleep." Word passed through the onlookers that a police officer was buried beneath the rubble, possibly alive. A second officer rushed up to help the gathered crowd heave chunks of mortar and slabs of brick walls, and they reached the officer, thirty-eight-year-old Max Fenner. Tall and muscular, Max had been a boxer and wrestler before joining the force and was known as the "Hercules of the police department." During the earthquake, he had reportedly seen a woman run out of a building beneath a tottering wall, and when he started across the street to warn her back inside, the wall of the hotel smashed on him. He was found beneath the rubble lying on the sidewalk with his eyes open, still breathing, looking "terribly crushed and battered." Officers loaded him on a commandeered wagon and jumped on to ride the seven blocks to Central Emergency Hospital, where they were redirected to Mechanics' Pavilion.

In the wrecked firehouse on Lower Nob Hill where Chief Sullivan had already been carried away with serious injuries, the firemen of Chemical Engine 3 pulled Mrs. Sullivan from beneath the wreckage and ushered her next door into the lobby of the California Hotel where she was checked by a doctor. There Battalion Chief Walter Cook received reports that a local physician, Dr. J. C. Stinson, was trapped in his room on the hotel's top floor by a portion of the brick wall that had smashed through the firehouse. Finding the hotel elevator had "crashed down the shaft," Cook and a couple of his men ran up the stairs to the eighth floor and found the room "full of bricks and the floor badly caved in from the heavy weight." The ceiling and a portion of the outer wall were gone, a breeze filled the room with the sounds from outside, and instead of a bed there was a mound of bricks. "Thinking that he might be alive we dug for him and found him, but he was dead."

From down at street level with a view blocked by tall buildings, Battalion Chief Cook had not seen smoke rising from other parts of the city. But now from the commanding vista of the eighth floor, he looked out and "saw fires in every direction." And word passed to him there was no water in the hotel. If hydrants were also dry, the water in the pressured tanks of their chemical engine would be crucial. Cook directed his firemen to gather volunteers to clear the debris from their firehouse and "get the horses and chemical engine out." The engine was broken in two, but after rigging it together with a large bolt, they hitched it to horses and headed to fires on Davis Street near the waterfront.

As with Chemical Engine 3, most fire crews north of Market Street, in firehouses from Chinatown to Nob Hill and up to North Beach, were "tired and worn out," having spent most of the night at the cannery fire. After hours fighting the blaze, most had not returned until after 3:00 a.m. By the time the earthquake hit, some had managed to grab one or two hours of sleep, but at least a couple of men in each house had spent that time cleaning out their engines and still had not slept at all. Now they would each be called to draw from their already drained reserves and give battle at fire after fire, for what would be days without rest.

Inside the Palace Hotel, morning light shined through the shattered window-panes of the expansive skylight above the Grand Court and spilled through its encircling balconies and down darkened corridors. Shielded from the devastation outside, hotel guests still in nightshirts and sleeping gowns were "standing in their doorways in a state of shock." Many who had run into hallways during the shaking now retreated into their rooms to get dressed as panic turned to bewilderment. Chairs had danced to room centers, dressers and bookshelves had overturned, and broken glass and ceiling plaster covered carpeted floors, but the hotel had withstood the earthquake without serious structural damage. As one visitor observed, "The proud boast that the Palace was earthquake-proof had been vindicated."

After dressing, a physician from Chicago found his room door jammed, so he and his wife climbed with their luggage out the window to the balcony overlooking the court and descended the stairs. Elevators were not running; their shafts were "blocked two floors deep with plaster and other debris." The lobby was filling with people, most calm and quiet, unsure whether to leave or stay. "Women and children with blanched faces stood as if dazed." At the check-in counter "by the glimmer of a tallow candle," clerks shuffled room cards and squinted at registries helping guests settle their bills and check out.

The dining room was not scheduled to be open at that hour, but a cook was "preparing coffee and rolls for the help," and a few guests grabbed handfuls. Soon the doors were thrown open, and employees brought out stacks of plates and cups and milk and rolls and butter from the kitchen. Couples and lone boarders helped themselves to "delicious dishes of coffee and hot rolls," which they enjoyed at empty tables in the Palm Court while employees in white shirts "calmly" swept up broken glass and dusted plaster from the furniture.

Enrico Caruso, who had reportedly spent the minutes after the earthquake "in a frantic state" running up and down the hallways "in the scantiest of attire, shouting excitedly and twirling at his moustache with unconscious nervousness," was now back in his room. He dressed, grabbed a signed photograph of President Roosevelt—personalized "To Enrico Caruso"—for identification and safe passage, left his valet packing his trunks, and descended five flights of stairs to the street. On the second floor, opera company manager Ernest Goerlitz "tried to wash, but only an ink like fluid flowed from the faucets." He and his wife dressed, walked downstairs to the court, and, after hearing that Caruso and other members of his company were heading to the St. Francis Hotel, decided to follow them. Outside, he would finally confront the "enormity of the damage done by the earthquake."

Men in derbies and pressed suits and women in waist jackets with elbow-length sleeves and train skirts and feathered hats emerged from the sheltered confines of the Palace Hotel into the turbulence of the morning, exhibiting a shock of realization like first-class passengers on a sinking ship joining lines for lifeboats across a listing deck. People in every manner of dress clogged the width of Market Street "like herds of sheep," dodging wandering horses and frightened livestock, and sidestepping large fallen chunks of ornamental cornices. Many were "stunned speechless," and others craned their necks to see smoke rising above jagged rooftops. Wagons and automobiles edged through the crowds, as did fire engines chugging black smoke from boilers and heading to fires South of Market. Power lines lay across sidewalks, "spitting blue flames and writhing like snakes." Even the air itself carried a "peculiar smell," alternating between the foul odor of leaking gas and the creosote of railroad ties, and tinted "sort of a bluish yellow."

Terry Owens, the Denver fire chief, exited the Grand Hotel beside the Palace with his wife and little boy and encountered a scene "of indescribable confusion" on Market Street: "Wires were down, naked and half naked men and women were running along the streets, cattle and horses were mixed up with the nude." Owens saw fire two blocks away where the blaze from Mack's drugstore had spread to Montague's and Spreckels's office building on Market, and he watched as an engine hitched to a hydrant but then "seemed to be doing nothing." He ran closer, asked the engineer what was wrong with the engine, and the answer was "no water." As Owens later shared, "I saw enough in those minutes to convince me the city was doomed."

Ernest Goerlitz and his wife crossed Market Street from the Palace in the direction of the St. Francis Hotel through streets "strewn with debris." They walked four blocks, forced into the middle of the street for fear of bricks and cornices "still falling" from the tall buildings on either side, several of which had "collapsed in themselves." Another man visiting from Detroit walked the same route among "automobiles, wagons, vehicles of all kinds rushing through the streets that were passable." He could "see and hear strong men and helpless women crying." Looking back and seeing "the smoke and flames" then growing south and east of the Palace, he "felt sure that the world had come to an end."

The twelve-story St. Francis, like the Palace, had withstood the earthquake without serious structural damage. Aesthetic cracks ran through the outer walls, and the steel frame of a new third wing under construction stood strong. Inside, a few broken pieces of stucco and marble wainscoting littered floors and the elevators were jammed inoperable. The lobby, like that of the Palace at that hour, was "filled with an excited throng." Some were still in robes while many had descended from their rooms "gorgeously dressed and bespangled with jewels." Wealthy guests sat in large lobby chairs "amongst their luggage waiting to escape," and around them, groups of women and children "were dazed and did not know which way to turn."

Melissa Carnahan and her husband, Will, felt "no occasion for hurry" and "leisurely dressed" before walking downstairs to the lobby. They entered the dining room where cool morning air gusted in through the shattered front window as staff served coffee and leftover rolls to "the chilly and excited crowd." Will found a comfortable chair in the library facing a large window where Melissa sat and surveyed Union Square, already "crowded with more or less frantic people who were in ludicrous stages of attire."

The square's green lawn and walkways were stirring with men, women, and children, some sitting on benches or lying on the grass. They had walked from the St. Francis and other hotels and apartment buildings facing Union Square, like the Savoy and the Geary, both with collapsed floors. One man noticed the park at that early hour was "filled with people—hardly a square foot unoccupied." Another saw families congregated "in a state of terror—children and women crying and carrying on or huddling on bundles of clothing and valuables." James Hopper passed through and saw "a man in pink pajamas, a pink bathrobe, carrying a pink comforter under his arms, walking barefooted upon the gravel." In the center of the square, he saw an elderly man "with great concentration of purpose deciphering the inscription" at the foot of the Dewey Monument, oblivious the lenses had fallen out of his glasses. Most in the crowd were silent, but when a man in the square yelled, "Look!" Hopper and others turned their gaze to where the man was pointing and saw smoke rising through the top of the Geary Hotel.

The Geary was a three-story wood-frame lodging house facing Union

Square sandwiched between a seven-story furniture company and a nine-story-tall steel frame of a new dry goods store under construction. The earthquake had shaken an upper portion of the furniture company's brick wall onto the Geary, crushing its roof "like an eggshell" and driving portions of all three floors into the cellar. The front wall stood "like cardboard scenery," and portions of each floor still dangled in place. At the sight of smoke, the sidewalk out front began "swarming with rescuers." A fire engine company arrived, and many of its firemen threw on coats and leather helmets and rushed into the smoke while hosemen tried the hydrants on both nearby corners without success.

The cries of trapped men and women could be heard, but the structure "was very rickety and dangerous," making rescue work difficult. Firemen were joined by two police officers and a few eager volunteers, including James Hopper. They ascended the partially dislodged stairs gingerly, climbing "over piles of plaster and laths" and hugging the wall. In one room they found a young woman "still alive, a little," and carried her down. They found another woman pacing a small portion of hallway floor still connected to the side wall, repeating that her husband was dead, pointing into a room filled with "a mound of bricks with the end of a bed-post emerging."

Smoke lifting over the wreckage added urgency to the already frantic efforts. The second-floor hallway "had been broken away from one wall, and was slanting at a heavy angle, threatening to drop at any moment," but the men rushed through it, one at a time, toward audible cries. A little boy was found dead, his mother carried out with internal injuries, and his father with a broken arm. "A stairway gave out" beneath the fire captain as he carried a woman to safety, dislocating the bones in his foot and spraining his ankle. Each person carried from the tottering frame brought applause from the watching crowd out in Union Square. Two survivors were placed in a fish wagon, a third in a furniture delivery wagon from next door, a fourth in an automobile, and all were taken to Mechanics' Pavilion for treatment. The fifth, forty-eight-year-old Ida Heaslip, died minutes after being carried from the ruins. At least two more bodies were removed, but no one else was rescued. And even without water, firemen were able to isolate the "incipient blaze" in a back corner of the wreckage against the rear brick wall of Delmonico's Restaurant behind the hotel and get the fire "entirely subdued" before it spread further.

Mechanics' Pavilion was "chaotic" and quickly becoming "a ghastly sight." Its massive floor was "strewn with mattresses" and cots "filled with dead, dying, and injured," and "its vaulted ceiling echoed their cries and groans." At each entrance with large barn doors propped open, new patients arrived by the minute in automobiles and delivery wagons and handcarts, "carried in on the doors or shutters or whatever other apologies for stretchers on which they arrived and were laid on the floor." The injuries of those crushed by falling walls and collapsed buildings were horrendous, with arms and legs "horribly mangled," often with "broken bones protruding through the flesh." Others were brought in with collapsed lungs and deep gashes from glass and second- and third-degree burns, most from South of Market.

Dr. Charles Miller, chief surgeon of Central Emergency Hospital, took charge with four physicians and two surgeons. The pavilion was used "much as a field dressing station is used in war," as one doctor explained. "Each patient was dressed and patched up as well as could be done without recourse to major surgery." Bandages for burn victims were fashioned from torn bedsheets, and splints for broken limbs were improvised "from packing cases or anything else that came in handy."

When nurse Lucy Fisher, who had walked from her home to offer her services, entered, she was surprised at how "well-equipped" the makeshift hospital was, with operating tables, dressings, instruments, enamel pans and basins, and hot and cold sterilized water. She removed her hat and wrap, pinned a pillowcase to her waist to carry dressings, and "hurried around among the quickly strewn mattresses with an extra blanket and a hot water bag or cup of hot coffee for those with feeble pulses and blue lips." She encountered "heart-rending scenes," as when she knelt to hold the hand of a crying woman who had lost her three children, giving Lucy a sense "of a grief that made physical injuries seem slight in comparison."

When local physician Dr. Margaret Mahoney entered to offer her own help, the first thing she saw was "a dead body [being] carried out in a wicker basket coffin." Priests and a rabbi walked among the mattresses and cots, kneeling to minister or pray with the injured, or, in a few cases, offer last rites. Bodies of the dead were laid under sheets behind folding chairs on either side of the floor "so as not to distress the injured." Among these was police officer Max Fenner, who was dead on arrival. By some reports, dead bodies within the pavilion would number sixteen within the first hour, and by morning's end, sixty were "piled in the corner to make room."

6. The Whole City Will Burn

BRIGADIER GENERAL FREDERICK Funston was the commander of the Army's Department of California headquartered in San Francisco, and he lived with his wife, Eda, and two sons, four-year-old Arthur and two-year-old Fred Jr., in a Washington Street home on Nob Hill. He had grown up in Kansas, attended college, and, with the help of his congressman father, got a job with the Department of the Interior where he was paid to venture on naturalist expeditions into the heat of Death Valley and the cold of the Alaska territory. During the Cuban War of Independence with Spain, Funston journeyed to Cuba where he spent eighteen months as an artillery officer for the Cuban army and a war correspondent for *Harper's Weekly* and he returned after a bout with malaria and with a limp caused by his horse falling and crushing his thigh. Back in Kansas, newspaper accounts of his overseas adventures—most of which he wrote himself—combined with his father's political influence to wrangle an officer's commission from the governor to command a regiment of state volunteers deploying to the Philippines, where the United States was replacing Spain as colonial occupier.

While in San Francisco before deploying in the fall of 1898, Funston married Bay Area native Eda Bankart, then shipped to the Philippines for two tours of duty, during which he was awarded the Medal of Honor for fording a river while under fire and won acclaim for capturing the Filipino revolutionary leader by dressing in costume as a prisoner of war. Despite credible and corroborated reports of his employment of violence on civilians and the execution of detainees by soldiers in his regiment, he returned from the Philippines a revered war veteran. In 1901, at just thirty-five, with less than three years of military experience and not a single day of active service as a "regular" (active-duty Army soldier), Funston was commissioned a brigadier general in the US Army and within a year was handed command of the Army's Department of California. Thick-necked with closely cropped hair and a pointed goatee, Funston stood five feet, three inches at his most upright, walked with a noticeable limp, and was uninhibited by military standards with which most men under his command had more experience.

The Army's newest and youngest general officer repeatedly made national headlines with his unbridled tongue, loudly asserting his low regard of the Filipino people and publicly belittling public officials who disagreed. Funston's imperialist worldview brought the rebuke of prominent Americans like Mark Twain, and his reckless speech even earned him a reprimand from President Roosevelt for his "entirely improper" remarks and an order from the Secretary of War "to cease further public discussion of the situation in the Philippines." Funston bided his time in San Francisco, working in the shadow of his division commander, Major General Adolphus Greely, awaiting the day his own star could once again shine. When the earthquake struck, with General Greely out of town on his way to a family wedding and Funston the Army's ranking officer in the city and acting commander of the Pacific Division, Funston's day had come.

Like so many others throughout the city, Frederick and Eda Funston were both shaken awake by the shock. Frederick donned a suit, stepped out of their home into the "beautiful clear morning," and limped his way two blocks along Jones Street for a better vantage point to survey the damage. "The streets were filled with people with anxious faces," and what struck him most was "the strange and unearthly silence." He descended the hill to California Street, where a view of the city unfolded. Funston saw a "dozen or more columns of thick black smoke rising from the densely populated region south of Market Street." Shocked crowds gathered, silently absorbing the scene, and Funston noticed "no talking, no apparent excitement." Even from the downtown below "there came not a single sound, no shrieking of whistles, no clanging of bells."

Seeing smoke rising near the waterfront, Funston fast-walked eight blocks down the California Street hill where a fire was spreading through a block of three-story brick offices. Watching frustrated fire crews trying hydrant after hydrant without luck and seeing even more smoke filling the sky South of Market, Funston "realized then that a great conflagration was inevitable." In that moment, as he later recorded, he decided "to order out" every soldier from the Presidio and Fort Mason to guard federal buildings and assist the police and fire departments. He flagged down a police officer and told him to inform his chief that "all available troops" were coming, then he hobbled at a run-walk back up California Street's steep incline over the crest of Nob Hill to the Army stables, a distance of more than a mile.

Funston arrived at the stable sweating, panting, limping, and in such a "serious condition" that he "could scarcely stand." He ripped a page from a notebook, scribbled orders to the colonel at the Presidio to report with every soldier on post to the police chief at the Hall of Justice, and handed it to his carriage driver, who saddled a horse. As the driver took off at a gallop, Funston yelled additional directions to swing by Fort Mason and order the captain there to report with his troops as well, and "fully armed." With the extraordinary plans in motion for the entire garrisons of Fort Mason and the Presidio—seven companies of coast artillery, three batteries of field artillery, three troops of cavalry, two companies of engineers, and a company of medics—to march into San Francisco, General Funston walked home to get a cup of coffee and check on his family.

Nearly two miles away out in Pacific Heights, a car raced up to the corner of Vallejo and Fillmore Streets, braked hard, and two men with the city attorney's office jumped out and hurried down the steep Fillmore Street sidewalk and up the front steps of the two-story Victorian home of Mayor Eugene Schmitz, who answered the door, surprised by their urgency. A few minutes earlier after the shaking stopped, the mayor had "immediately got up and dressed," walked out onto the street to assess the scene, noticed only a few chimneys down on his block, and returned inside. Now confronted with the men's account of the damage downtown, and the fire, and the devastation to City Hall, Schmitz told his wife and children, "I must go at once." He donned his hat and followed the men out the door and up the steep sidewalk to pile onto the bench seats of the parked car.

With the steady coughing of an engine revving at full throttle, the open touring car carrying the three men sped along Vallejo Street toward downtown. By the time the car turned onto Van Ness Avenue, the overwhelming sight of smoke rising across the city—from the Mission District to South of Market to the harbor district near the waterfront—was visible. The driver slowed as they neared a long column of uniformed soldiers marching with shouldered rifles. Schmitz asked the driver to pull up to the officer leading the column and identified himself as the mayor and asked where his men were heading. "City Hall," the captain replied. He was leading two companies of engineers from Fort Mason on General Funston's orders. Mayor Schmitz explained that City Hall was "destroyed" and redirected the captain to "the Hall of Justice where you will receive orders what to do."

The car raced toward the Hall of Justice, slowing only when passing the ruins of City Hall, where one of the men noticed "the Mayor was deeply grieved" at the sad sight. They pulled up to the "badly damaged" Hall of Justice, where Schmitz jumped out and "immediately took charge of the situation." He rushed inside and found the police chief, who ushered Schmitz down into the basement for safety as the building's damaged tower appeared close to falling.

Chairs and tables were squeaked across the floor, and by the light of oil lamps and street-level windows near the low basement ceiling, a temporary city headquarters was established. Schmitz told the police chief to detail his officers to commandeer "every automobile and wagon possible" to help transport the wounded. He informed the chief that soldiers were on their way: "As soon as they arrive, send fifty men into the banking district, put ten men on every block in Market Street and a guard for City Hall." And he asked the chief about prisoners in the jail up on the top floor, to which the chief replied, "I am rather afraid for them." Schmitz ordered all "drunks" released and the rest ushered downstairs, and within minutes jailers escorted the line of shackled prisoners into the basement. To those held on nonviolent misdemeanors, Schmitz "administered a severe lecture," releasing them with a warning they would be "shot down" if "caught in any overt act." He also lectured and released three female arrestees. The remaining seventy-seven prisoners held on serious charges and felonies were brought down and locked in the old basement holding cells.

Eight blocks away at the six-story flatiron-style Phelan Building where O'Farrell Street angles into Market, General Funston arrived, having made the fifteen-minute walk from his home after giving "a few hasty instructions" to his wife about packing and evacuating with their two sons to the Presidio. Across Market, rolling smoke filled the sky behind the endangered Call and Examiner Buildings and the Palace Hotel, one and two blocks away. Funston noticed the streets were "full of excited, anxious people watching the progress of the various fires now being merged into one great conflagration."

Funston climbed the stairs to the fourth-floor office of the Pacific Division headquarters and sat, still wearing the suit he had thrown on earlier, exhausted by his morning walking tour. Around him gathered several uniformed officers of his staff and General Greely's staff, all awaiting instructions. Orderlies and runners scurried to collect files and records in crates, planning for evacuation. Funston informed the staff that garrisons from the Presidio and Fort Mason were on their way, then ordered the chief signal officer to Fort Miley—a small Army post out past the Presidio near Ocean Beach—to send both companies of coast artillery to report to him at the Phelan Building. And Funston scratched out a handwritten order to be taken to the captain of the Army steamer *General McDowell,* docked at the Presidio, who was to ferry the order to the commander of Fort McDowell on Angel Island to embark with all the soldiers of his infantry regiment, dock at the Ferry Building, and march to the Phelan Building and report for duty.

The Army's engine was now gunned to deploy more than 1,700 soldiers into San Francisco. The move was not unprecedented. Since General Andrew Jackson had deployed military troops into the streets of New Orleans in 1814, two other Army generals had ordered soldiers into American cities, once during the Civil War and another during a deadly riot. Thirteen governors had also done so, during war, riots, labor disputes, and natural disasters. Two mayors had gone so far as declaring martial law—the displacement of local civil authority by the military—the mayor of Chicago after the fire of 1871 and the mayor of Galveston after the hurricane of 1900.

The Posse Comitatus Act of 1878 prohibits the federal government from using the US Army to "execute the laws" on American soil without congressional approval. When the mayor of Galveston imposed martial law in 1900, it was after requesting relief and military support from the Texas governor, and the temporary laws—curfews, bans on firearm possession, and travel restrictions—were enforced by troops of the state guard and militia. The only other legal authority for the use of federal forces on American soil was when ordered by the president at the request of a governor or state legislature to suppress lawlessness and rebellion under the Insurrection Act of 1807. San Francisco had already been the focus of such a request a half century earlier in 1856 when armed vigilantes carried out summary punishments and executions in defiance of state law, the city charter, and court orders. In that case, the governor urged the commander of the Army's Pacific Division and the commander of the naval forces at Mare Island to send troops into the city, but both referred him to President Pierce, who declined to intervene.

General Funston lacked the legal authority to order federal troops into San Francisco, something he likely understood but disregarded. Of all the oral and written orders he issued that morning, he had sent no messages to higher command, no requests for guidance, not even a report of the situation to the president, or the war secretary, or the governor, or his direct superior, General Greely. War Secretary Taft sent three telegrams to Funston requesting information, each with increasing impatience "waiting for particulars" of measures taken, and "under what authority," and finally imploring him: "Wire as soon as possible."

Although there were operational telegraph offices in San Francisco through midafternoon—and at least one Army officer successfully sent a dispatch from the city that morning after 10:00 a.m. to the quartermaster general in Washington—Funston later claimed after hearing phone communications were "paralyzed," he doubted wires could carry his message and made his decisions believing he was cut off from higher command. It was not until later that evening that Funston finally dictated to his staff a telegram to be sent to the War Department in Washington.

But while Funston's orders surpassed his lawful authority, they did not *yet* amount to martial law, as he ordered his soldiers to report to the chief of police, specified their role was "to aid the police and fire departments" and placed them at the police chief's "disposal." Although city newspapers would misreport that San Francisco was under "martial law," Funston that first morning did not replace civilian authority with military control; he assigned soldiers under his command to the control of city officials to augment and assist the city's seven hundred police officers and five hundred firefighters. As he soon wrote, he "marched the troops into the city, merely to aid the municipal authorities and not to supersede them."

For his part, Mayor Schmitz as the elected chief executive of the city and county of San Francisco possessed the emergency powers inherent to the head of every sovereign government and was specifically required by the city charter to "take all proper measures for the preservation of public order." For this he was authorized to "use and command the police force," and in the event the police force should prove "insufficient" during an emergency, the charter required him to "call upon the Governor for military aid in the manner provided by law."

Schmitz had not yet requested any military assistance from the governor, nor had he asked General Funston to send troops—Schmitz did not even know of Funston's orders until encountering the columns of soldiers on Van

Ness Avenue. The mayor used the troops placed at his disposal, as he would state under oath a few months later, because he believed it "necessary to augment the police force, and also those who were doing the fire fighting."

The soldiers would add desperately needed manpower to assist police and firemen at the front lines, but no law permitted a general to unilaterally order Army soldiers onto the streets of an American city or granted a mayor authority to command federal troops. The orders had been given in the unconstrained urgency of the moment, an urgency growing as the disaster spread. And any limits on rules of engagement wielded by battalions of armed soldiers now being unleashed onto San Francisco's streets would depend entirely on the pronouncements of a general and a mayor, neither of whom had yet demonstrated any capacity for restraint.

Every fire south of Market continued to spread. The Mack's drugstore blaze had burned through from the back of the Spreckels office building on the corner of Market Street. Flames devoured wooden desks and stacked paper files and upholstered chairs, spreading through the office building rapidly until combustibles filling all three floors were aflame. Windows fronting Market Street shattered from the heat, and through the openings erupted orange surges as flames reacted with fresh oxygen from outside air. Montague's store next door—filled mostly with metals, stoves, and ranges—burned even faster through all five of its floors, and with no water to douse it, flames spread through a shared wall into the warehouse next door.

Around 6:20 a.m., in an avalanche of orange sparks, the five stories of Mack's drugstore collapsed into a red-hot pile of flaming timbers. By this time—just more than an hour after the fire started—the structures lining that entire side of Fremont Street from Market down to Mission Street were ablaze, hurling cinders and firebrands onto the walls, awnings, and roofs of buildings facing them across the street. Firemen had drained the single working hydrant up on the corner to a trickle, and they pulled their engine a block down to a cistern in the Mission Street intersection. The manhole was already laid off to the side, with another fire company's engine pumping from it to fight the Martel Power Company blaze a block further down, which was growing past their reach to both ends of its own block. The men positioned their steam engine alongside the other, dropped in their suction hose, and when their engineer opened the release valve, the lines stiffened and hosemen soaked the storefronts across Fremont Street to keep them from igniting.

Their hoses focused on the brick walls of the five-story Whittier Coburn

Co., directly across the street from Mack's. But within ten minutes—around 6:30 a.m.—both lines limped to sputtering trickles as the cistern ran dry just as thirty-five-year-old Bill Whittier reached his business after fast-walking two dozen blocks from his Western Addition home toward the growing smoke columns. By the time he arrived, Mack's "had practically burned itself out," with flames lifting from its basement up through its smoldering ruins and eating through structures on either side. His own business, undamaged by the earthquake and dripping with the final sprays of water, was protected now only by the eighty-two-foot width of the street. Whittier Coburn sold paints, oils, and canned grease, and Bill—whose father, William, was a founding partner—was vice president. Bill unlocked the front door just as employees began to appear—the bookkeeper, night watchman, salesmen—out of breath from their own walks in and squinting in the face of hellish temperatures radiating from the blaze across the street. After a few minutes, the company president, Clarence Coburn, fifty-four, and his son Clarence Jr., twenty-five, arrived after an even longer walk from their Pacific Heights home. They entered the back office, retrieved cash and valuable papers from the safe and desks, then hurried back out to the street.

The fire by that time, 7:00 a.m., "had gutted the buildings" facing Whittier Coburn's employees, even the Spreckels office building: "Some short pieces of walls were standing but the main building was gutted." Above them firebrands and cinders bounced off Whittier Coburn's brick walls. A few hit the large wooden sign three floors up, and it caught fire. Mr. Coburn said, "If one of the boys would go up there and try to get it out it might save the building." A stocker and the night watchman ran inside and up the stairs to the fourth floor, unstrapped a brass fire extinguisher from the wall ("[I]t is the kind which you turn upside down and pump it down and it comes out," the stocker explained), ran to the windows, leaned out, and extinguished the flames on the sign.

Drawn by the pillars of smoke churning from so many parts of the district, business owners and workers flooded the streets South of Market in the minutes and hours following the earthquake. Coppersmiths and grocers and druggists and barbers and bartenders and carpenters and blacksmiths rushed from their homes and flats and boardinghouse rooms by foot and horse-drawn buggies to their own livelihood's small corner of the city, a single-story wood-frame saddlery shop or a third-floor bookkeeping office or a five-story brick warehouse. Some rushed inside and retrieved valuables while others tried to make a stand against fires they still believed could be stopped. Most who turned valves on their folded emergency hoses found no water pressure in their building service pipes. A few were armed with extinguishers. Harry Myers, a cook, climbed up to his restaurant roof and, with buckets of water, doused flames started by cinders floating from the blaze across the street. And workers in the Wieland Brewery's Hawthorne Street side "got the best of it" by dumping water from the tanks on their third-floor roof onto flames spreading through buildings across the narrow street to keep the fire from reaching them. At least for a few minutes.

But in the seven o'clock hour, there were at least eight large fires South of Market that had consumed their blocks and grown strong enough to jump wide streets and spread beyond control. A wooden lodging house near the waterfront "was blazing furiously" and spread westward across the street where it devoured a flour warehouse and lumberyard. Three blocks west, the blazes that began in Mack's drugstore and in the Martel Power Company a block south had incinerated every structure between them, merged, and were spreading to surrounding blocks. Three more blocks west, the fire that consumed the Howard Street laundry house ignited buildings across the street—including the firehouse of the men who responded to the blaze—and spread eastward through structures down both sides of Howard, jumping an alley, then across 2nd Street. And spreading westward, the fire turned the boardinghouse on the corner of 3rd Street into "one mass of flames" and was threatening the next block. Firemen were still at work there temporarily slowing the fire's westward progress with water pumped through two engines from a cistern two blocks distant (and when that cistern ran dry, another engine company found water in a cistern a block beyond that and pumped to refill the one being used, and so they continued until both ran dry). Another fire in a three-story wooden house near 4th Street had already spread through the wooden homes to its left and right and behind, and it took little time for the flames to leap the narrow, thirty-five-foot-wide street in front and spread further.

And the fire that began as smoke and flames within the ruins of the four collapsed lodging houses on 6th Street was now "only the base of one great flame that rose to heaven with a single twist." There were no more screams from inside. The fire company that had attempted rescue was forced to retreat from flames "raging around" their engine, and the men—"with wet sacks" wrapped around their blackened faces, panting, dripping with sweat—pulled their engine by hand away from the march of the blaze, finding cisterns in their path "dry or filled with mud." When they finally located one with water, flames reached them and destroyed their hose. And blazes in a wooden lodging house on 7th Street and in a drugstore beneath a lodging house on 12th

Street had devoured each of their own blocks and were also spreading. As one man observed, "[T]he fire had ceased to be just a rumor. It was very real." Observing the "swath" it was cutting South of Market, he wondered, "[H]ow far will it go?"

North of Market Street, a handful of fires had already been successfully extinguished. With water as scarce as South of Market, these small successes required ingenuity, as with the engine company whose firemen filled pails with sand from a nearby construction site to douse a blaze in a drugstore. Others demanded five and six times the manpower to stop what would ordinarily be single-alarm fires, as up in North Beach, where it took sixty firemen with a chemical engine and five steam engines connecting with "several lines from different directions" to reach a hydrant with water and get a single blaze in a lumberyard—caused by a chimney falling and smashing open brick kilns at a neighboring brick company—"under control." But the blazes that had started in the harbor district near the waterfront were, despite the best efforts of fire crews, spreading almost unchecked.

When the ground had finally stilled earlier that morning, police sergeant Jesse Cook stepped out of the large doorway—his shelter through the earthquake—and the moment he hit the street he "noticed that smoke was coming out of the windows" of a wholesale grocery at the end of the block. He tried the corner alarm box, then ran to the nearest firehouse where firemen were dragging their hose wagon and equipment out into the street from beneath a fallen wall. "As soon as I gave the alarm," Cook reported, "the firemen hooked up the teams and started off." But they couldn't reach the grocery fire, stopping on the way at a blaze burning through a packing company. And after finding the hydrants at each corner dry, "[T]hey could do little to stop the flames."

By 6:30 a.m. at least five separate fires in the harbor district had burned through the buildings in which they started and were spreading west into the banking district toward Montgomery Street, south toward Market, and east toward the waterfront. Curious crowds filled the streets in stunned silence, watching the fire devour the city's largest, strongest buildings—the ten-story Scandinavian-American Savings Bank and the nine-story Mutual Life Insurance Company and the six-story Anglo Californian Bank.

James Stetson, the seventy-five-year-old president of the California Street Cable Railroad, made it on foot from his home on Van Ness to his downtown office building by 7:00 a.m. By then, "fire and smoke filled the street," and the crowds had backed a block away. With his head ducked and his arm raised to cover his face, James cut through the crowd and could feel the heat of the flames as he sprinted to his building. In the lobby he met the janitor, who warned him he could not make it upstairs. But James went anyway, climbing stairs in a sprint to his fifth-floor office where he grabbed a few files of papers, clicked through the combination on his safe, grabbed gold coins from inside, then resealed it. Breathing heavily, he paused for a moment to open his window blinds for a last look from his office. On the street below he could see flames rising "fully 50 feet high." James ran to the stairs, leapt down two steps at a time with his arms full of papers, and by the time he made it back out the door of the building, "the air was a mass of sparks and smoke." Worried his papers would ignite from the intense heat, he tucked them under his buttoned suit jacket, pulled his hat over his eyes, and with his head down in a full sprint, "virtually drove through it" back up the middle of the street.

Fueled by combustibles and stoked by a steady breeze from the bay, fires on separate blocks in the banking district grew considerably until the flames were large enough to cross streets and coalesce into a single inferno. Like James Stetson, other frantic businesspeople—insurance agents, bankers, attorneys—elbowed through crowds in foolhardy sprints through heat and smoke, "carrying out books and other articles" and running to stack them on sidewalks a block or two away, salvaging what little they could before the unstoppable march of the flames reduced desks and pictures and irreplaceable records of life's works to floating flakes of hot ash. Firemen found enough water in a cistern to pump through their engine into a single stream on storefronts across the street from one of the blazes. But the crews of other engine companies, unable to find any water in any hydrants in the district, could only evacuate buildings and hold onlookers back.

The fire department's first assistant chief, John Dougherty, arrived in his buggy with his driver. Dougherty had turned sixty the day before. He was a former plumber, had served as a state senator, was a thirty-year veteran of the fire department, had been first assistant chief throughout Chief Sullivan's tenure, and was only two months away from retirement. Like Acting Assistant Chief Shaughnessy then touring the fires in his automobile, Dougherty had not yet learned that Chief Sullivan was gravely wounded, making him the acting chief. On his ride in from his South of Market quarters, he noticed "big cracks" in the streets, many of which "were opened," forcing his driver to guide the horse around fallen poles and slowly over downed wires as they crossed Market Street and entered the banking district. His driver reined the horse as they encountered firemen, and when Dougherty asked why they were "not at work," they explained, "No water." He cussed his exasperation, was told about City Hall and that Mayor Schmitz was at the Hall of Justice, and it was likely here that he learned Chief Sullivan was in the hospital. With the weight of the department on his shoulders and assessing at a glance that without water, only firebreaks could save the city, Dougherty sent a messenger to the Presidio requesting "all available explosives, with a detail to handle them" be sent to the Hall of Justice. And he ordered his driver to take him to the Spring Valley Water Company's maintenance yard to demand answers and action.

By that point, as one man observed, "The whole of the lower portion of the city then seemed to be on fire." A woman on Russian Hill viewing the blazes spreading throughout downtown heard someone nearby remark, "Look at the fires; the whole city will burn."

"Why, what nonsense," she responded. "The whole city can't burn."

In the basement of the Hall of Justice came word that help was needed to deal with the bodies arriving at the city morgue next door. A police officer sent up to assist saw "an endless cavalcade" of "wagons and trucks" pressed into service as hearses, most coming from the fish market collapse. The officer helped carry sheet-covered stretchers into the dark morgue and laid bodies on slabs, sometimes two or three at a time. "The saddest thing I saw while there," he recalled twenty years later, "was a case where three bodies were brought in all clinging together . . . a young man, his wife, and their baby, all crushed and stone dead." The three were laid on two slabs pulled together, "with the baby between the mother and the father." The bodies kept arriving, and after running out of slabs they were laid on the tile floor "until the morgue was full and could hold no more." The officer ran next door to the Hall of Justice to tell them the morgue was "filled to overflowing with the bodies of victims." The basement shooting range was made available for overflow, and soon bodies of the dead were carried downstairs, past the lamp-lit headquarters of Mayor Schmitz and the police chief, and "laid out on benches."

It was later reported that rumors spread of dead bodies "being rifled of valuables" by "ghouls and thieves that came along pretending to be anxious to identify their own dead," and even a variation of ancient lore was added: that down in the Mission a woman's body had been found with the ring finger amputated, "evidently by some thief." But the only report of crime reaching the Hall of Justice by that early hour was of some "rowdies" breaking into saloons and helping themselves to liquor. Mayor Schmitz told the police chief, "Close up every saloon at once." He ordered the closing of all places where liquor was sold, discontinued all liquor sales, and if any should disobey, "the liquor in his place should be confiscated and spilled into the street."

An executive from United Railroads arrived in the basement and told the mayor that his company had "2,000 men in uniform [with badges] and no cars running," and offered them for "patrol work" or "in any other work you may desire." Mayor Schmitz accepted, explaining, "We are afraid of looting, and if they patrol in the Mission District their uniforms will pass them as policemen." The railroad executive left to notify his employees—gripmen, operators, conductors, and maintenance workers—who were sent in their uniforms with their badges from their carbarns into the Mission to patrol unarmed. For even more manpower, Schmitz directed that someone "[h]unt up" the sheriff and "have him swear in two hundred deputies." And he issued a written directive to the police chief: "As it has come to my notice that thieves are taking advantage of the present deplorable conditions and are plying their nefarious vocations among the ruins in our city, all peace officers are ordered to instantly kill anyone caught looting or committing any other serious crimes."

The mayor's written order demanding summary executions for looting and "any other serious crimes" was passed from the police chief down to the captains and lieutenants with directives to relay to their sergeants and officers who were then scattered throughout the city. Presumably this was also to be communicated to deputies and the two hundred special deputies Schmitz had ordered the sheriff to add to his force.

Despite later attempts to justify the order with claims of widespread lawlessness, this order was not based on any reports of theft or looting, as Mayor Schmitz himself soon admitted: "The proclamation was issued with a view of anticipating the possibility of looting under the conditions that existed at that time," but he added, "I had no reason to anticipate that possibility." Schmitz had read in the past of looting and lawlessness in other cities "under like conditions," so, as he liked to say, he "took time by the forelock" and acted. But when pressed a few months later under oath whether any conditions in the city justified deadly force, he answered simply: "None."

The mayor's suspension of due process and authorization of summary executions for suspected thieves—and suspects of other unlisted and undefined "serious crimes," which presumably were whatever an officer or deputy or special deputy decided—exceeded his authority even in an emergency and was manifestly illegal. A police captain defended the order's necessity because officers "were busy conveying the wounded" in commandeered automobiles and wagons and "had no time to arrest thieves" and "no place to incarcerate them if arrested," revealing a disturbing preference for execution as a solution to shortages in manpower and detention space.

Given the large number of officers occupied with transporting injured residents for medical care, it is unknown how many received the mayor's initial order in its original wording or how much was lost in word-of-mouth transmission. One of the officers guarding bodies of the dead in the morgue later reported they "had no time to arrest" people they caught or suspected of stealing. It is unclear what version of the mayor's order he and the other officers heard, but he saw no suspects shot: "We just kicked and clubbed them out."

An hour and a half past dawn, the sun's dim circle gave little light through thick shrouds of billowing smoke, appearing to onlookers as "red as blood." As the writer Mary Austin described, "[T]he sun showed bloodshot through it as the eye of disaster." Outside the Hall of Justice, the red morning light stretched shadows of buildings across the grass plaza of Portsmouth Square, which was "literally packed with hundreds of Chinese, of all ages, sexes, and conditions of apparel." They had fled the confines of Chinatown following the shock and, as James Kelly saw from up in the fire alarm office, filled the square with a "suddenness," thrust out of the familiar haven of their neighborhood and into the square they knew as *fah yuan gok* ("corner of the flower garden") and which for them was the entrance to a larger, unwelcoming, hostile world. They huddled in groups, crowds of male workers and families with rarely seen wives—many with bound feet, for whom even the short walk had been a challenge—and children still in bedclothes, worried for their homes and stores, conversing while a few were animated with "excited terror."

Through a canyon of buildings leading to Portsmouth Square echoed the march of boots in cadence on pavement, and along the street bordering the plaza appeared two columns of soldiers in tan, wide-brimmed campaign hats and fixed-bayonet rifles on their shoulders and khaki cartridge belts over blue tunics with boots dusty from the two-and-a-half-mile march. These were the two companies of Army engineers ordered from Fort Mason by General Funston, reporting as directed by Mayor Schmitz when he had encountered them on his ride in. They halted on Kearny Street in front of the Hall of Justice amid rubble from the bell tower and beneath twisted power lines and wooden poles bent broken over the street. Their captain reported in the basement to Mayor Schmitz, who sent them to guard downtown banks to prevent looting, and any looters were to be shot.

One company was assigned to stand guard along Montgomery Street in the banking district, a few soldiers per block, and the other was assigned to Market Street, which "was full of excited, anxious people watching the progress of the various fires now being merged into one great conflagration." When the first troops on Market Street reached the Phelan Building, General Funston noted that "[t]hey were greeted with evident good-will by the crowd and made a fine impression with their full cartridge-belts and fixed bayonets." They had been sent, as he would later report, "with instructions to shoot instantly any person caught looting or committing any serious misdemeanor."

It is unknown whether General Funston knew his soldiers would be sent into San Francisco's streets with shoot-to-kill orders, though he likely foresaw it as he specifically ordered for them to report "fully armed." And there is no evidence that he questioned the loose rules of engagement given by the mayor. Conversely, in a strong sign of his endorsement, when the soldiers from the Presidio arrived at the Phelan Building around 7:30 a.m.—two troops of cavalry and three batteries of field artillery mounted on their horses and seven companies of coast artillery on foot, "armed and equipped as infantry"— Funston sent them to report to Mayor Schmitz at the Hall of Justice for similar duty under the same orders.

By 8:00 a.m. the Presidio troops had arrived at the Hall of Justice, and Mayor Schmitz told their colonel to send details to guard the US Mint and the main post office and to distribute the rest of his men "over the city" to "drive the people back from the burning houses and keep them away from the ruins of houses that had collapsed or been burned." And Schmitz repeated that the colonel and his soldiers should "let the news be widely spread that anyone caught looting should not be arrested but should be shot." The colonel pressed the mayor: "Do you really stand for shooting looters and thieves?" To which Schmitz replied, "I certainly do," qualifying "not to be too quick" to execute based on suspicion, "but if they are positive that a person is looting or stealing, then shoot to kill." The colonel responded, "Your orders shall be carried out."

Back in division headquarters on the Phelan Building's fourth floor, now two blocks from the growing South of Market fire, General Funston's staff ran records from desks and file cabinets downstairs and out to a wagon to be hauled to Fort Mason. Former mayor Phelan rolled up in his carriage, and although he had earlier helped with the rescue at the Valencia Hotel collapse, he did not "realize the magnitude of the calamity" until his ride in when he saw the wreckage of City Hall, which he likened to "the ruins of the Temple of the Dioscuri in the Forum in Rome." Now in the flatiron-style building his late father had built twenty-five years earlier, Phelan encountered the troops shuttling files past him as he climbed the stairs to his fifth-floor office and found it mostly undamaged, with books thrown to the floor covered by "a mantle of snow" (fallen plaster). Outside, billowing smoke lifted from growing fires just beyond the far side of Market Street.

The Phelan Building was filled with art the former mayor and his father had collected—prized oil paintings and sculptures by Rodin—and in his office were his mayoral papers and family records dating to 1849, stored in wooden cabinets. His staff began removing paintings—including his father's portrait—and brought sculptures and boxes down the stairs to his carriage. And just as General Funston limped into Phelan's office to check how things were up on his floor, the building began to shake.

The men paused for a long moment, jolted by quaking and side-to-side jerking and upward bumping. Plaster fell in crumbles. The deep, loudening roar from the early morning returned and from outside the high pitch of screams could be heard and above it all again was the dissonant clanging of church bells. Funston staggered out of Phelan's office and down the trembling stairwell, arms stretched outward, working to stay upright as the building swayed and torqued.

Panic shot through the crowds outside. A man climbing Nob Hill saw "the people below darting into the middle of the streets," and another saw "the tops of the buildings on lower California Street appeared almost to come together." A police officer in the banking district "did not know which way to run" as he saw "cornices and masonry that had been loosened by the big shake" earlier now come "tumbling into the street." The "jerky, ugly shock" sent a woman on a street in the Western Addition hurrying "in the center of the street" away from tall homes on either side, and she heard someone warn her, "Lady, be careful of electric wires overhead." A woman on Telegraph Hill later wrote the "violent shock" sent her halfway down her stairs and arrived "with a sound like an explosion, and that particularly finished everyone's nerves."

This aftershock struck at 8:14 a.m. Three hours earlier during the 5:12 a.m. earthquake—the mainshock—the edges of the Pacific and North American Plates had torn apart and moved past each other for a considerable distance—in some places more than twenty feet—causing massive stress changes in the adjacent crust. During the hours and days that followed, the land along the fault readjusted in fits and jerks as aftershocks released energy and sent out seismic waves just as the mainshock had, and a few of these were violent enough to be felt and cause new damage. Professor McAdie of the US Weather Bureau recorded fourteen aftershocks that first morning before 9:00 a.m., but he noted the one at 8:14 a.m. to be "of particular severity, a sharp twister," which he timed at five seconds long. As an art student on Nob Hill estimated, this "heavy shock" was "equally violent" to the first, even if it did not last nearly as long.

The sensation especially unnerved those who had slept through much of the violent shaking three hours before. Melissa Carnahan was still seated in the lobby of the St. Francis Hotel when she noticed the aftershock "startled afresh the excited crowd." Guests who had returned to their rooms in the upper floors scrambled for the stairs. One woman grabbed her "jewels and small bag of necessaries" and rushed to the lobby. Down in the Mission District, an eight-year-old boy watching the ongoing rescue at the Valencia Hotel later remembered how the shock "terrorized" him with "a fear that I never again hope to feel." It "caused a panic" in the crowd of onlookers and rescuers, "and in the mad rush to get away many people were trampled upon and many others almost crushed to death in the seething mass of humanity."

After five long seconds the trembling stopped. The aftershock was "so severe," General Funston worried the Phelan Building could fall and relieved his staff of hauling further records from the Army's fourth-floor offices, "not deeming them of sufficient importance to risk the lives of a dozen men." But with confidence in the building's construction and the solid ground beneath it, James Phelan and his staff continued filling his carriage parked on the street below with selected works from his art collection and personal valuables, records, and papers.

In Mechanics' Pavilion where at least two hundred of the city's injured were being treated, the aftershock had swayed the wooden structure and creaked the rafters in the tall ceiling, sending panic sweeping through patients and caregivers alike. Nurse Lucy Fisher later wrote that people "started to run out of the building," but to avoid a stampede, policemen at the doors stopped them, and a doctor yelled out, "Stay where you are!" A few minutes later, Lucy heard a physician ask another for the time, and when the answer came as "half past eight," the physician exclaimed, "Great heavens, I thought it was at least twelve o'clock."

7. Black Powder and Dynamite

T HE EARTHQUAKE HAD caused an electric power outage through most of the city, disabling communications and leaving hotel guests and apartment tenants in the dark. It had been twenty-seven years since a light company in San Francisco had built the first electric power–generating station in the nation for distribution to the public, giving unprecedented competition to the San Francisco Gas Light Company and setting the city yet again on the vanguard of progress. Soon electric lights brightened hotels, theaters, restaurants, and streets, and within a few years, electricity lifted elevators and powered streetcars and connected first responders through an intricate alarm system. By 1903, many competing gas and electric providers were merged into the San Francisco Gas and Electric Company, and its nine generating stations sent power to substations that delivered electricity to customers in every district through underground cables and overhead lines. While most businesses in the city had electricity, most homes still did not—only newer houses were built with conduits inside walls while older homes and lodging houses strung wires along walls and up stairwells through porcelain knobs secured with tie wires, adding to the city's long list of fire hazards.

Much like the devastation to Spring Valley Water Company's water mains and service pipes, the effect of the morning's earthquake on the power delivery system of the San Francisco Gas and Electric Company was, in the words of an electrical inspector, "one of utter demoralization" rendering it "unfit for performing any service of any nature whatever." Seven of its nine generating stations were disabled. South of Market, Station C was destroyed when its smokestack collapsed, rupturing the boiler of the station's steam engine and killing twenty-one-year-old employee Gerald Kirkpatrick. Underground iron conduits cracked or telescoped, and cables pulled apart. According to one of the company's assistant engineers, "cables on 7th between Mission and Folsom were practically destroyed for two blocks." The twelve-inch-wide concrete walls of subterranean junction stations (where workers inspected and maintained cable connections between conduit ends) were "cracked and shattered," and many of the manholes covering them were bent or in pieces. Overhead lines too were broken on nearly every block, especially where chimneys sliced through them or where poles toppled or snapped. A police officer reported "the trolley wires, the telephone, electric light and other electric lines were hanging in festoons all over the place." Trolley lines, he noticed, "hung so low that the people were lifting them up so as to pass underneath them." Providentially, the lines carried no live current.

As with water and electricity, so it was with gas. 590 miles of gas pipes ran beneath San Francisco, and the damage suffered was, in the words of the San Francisco Gas and Electric Company's superintendent of distribution for gas, "quite extensive." In some places, "pipes telescoped," and others broke "up and down, like waves." Gas mains fractured in more than four hundred places and service pipes in more than six hundred. Gas hissed through each fracture and crack, filling cavities beneath street paving stones, in some cases detonating with explosive force when ignited by sparks of downed power lines—there were at least twenty-one of these subterranean explosions by 7:00 a.m. One man saw "several huge holes in various streets due to the blowing up of the gas mains." A police captain saw a "manhole cover [that] blew straight up in [the] air fully 100 feet with a report like a cannon," and a teenage boy on 10th Street after the earthquake witnessed another gas main explosion: "the cobblestones on the street blew very high, and many people were hurt." One of the injured was sixty-three-year-old Marie Paris, whose skull was fractured by a paving stone hurled by the explosion of the 10th Street gas main after evacuating her home. She was rushed to the City & County Hospital in the Mission where she lingered five days before dying.

The principal gas hazard was inside tens of thousands of kitchens where residents ignited stovetops to heat coffee and breakfast. To eliminate the threat, the gas and electricity company's chief engineer traveled up to the North Beach facility and turned off the main valves of undamaged tanks, then went to the other plant at Potrero Point and did the same, cutting off all gas throughout the city by 7:30 a.m. He reported this to Mayor Schmitz, who directed the shutdown of both gas and electricity to continue until he ordered otherwise. One woman cooking a meal on her gas stove that morning later wrote, "I burned all that was in the pipes and then there was no more." The handful of gas lights still connected to the few intact lines flickered off, burning the last wisps of gas in San Francisco for the next twenty-three days.

Breakfast for some that morning was almost normal. After checking on his opera company members in Union Square, Ernest Goerlitz returned to the Palace Hotel where he and two dozen members of the company "had plenty of coffee, milk, rolls, butter, cups, and plates" in the Grand Court. Guests in the Occidental Hotel had breakfast served as on any other morning. "[T]he dining room of the hotel had been cleared, the tables set, and hot coffee, buns and butter was being served," as a guest would write his mother in a letter a few days later, adding a simple declarative sentence about what would soon be a memory of something no longer possible: "We went into the dining room and were served."

Guests at the St. Francis Hotel had similar ease finding breakfast, albeit with coffee and rolls. Same with members of the nearby Bohemian Club. Before going to Mechanics' Pavilion to help treat the wounded, Dr. Margaret Mahoney breakfasted in a Market Street restaurant "where they served hot coffee and where the electric lights were still burning." And a woman in North Beach "found comfort" at Luna's, a Mexican restaurant where the chimney was one of the few in the city still intact. She and her friends enjoyed bacon and eggs and coffee, which, as she would soon write, was "the last comfortably cooked and served meal we had for many a day."

But for most people in the city, finding food was a challenge. At the Occidental Mission Home for Girls on Sacramento Street, they "secured a large basket of bread from the nearby bakery" just after the earthquake, and a neighbor brought them "some apples and a kettle of tea," all to feed approximately fifty girls. Some went without—as a man wrote his father later that first day, "crackers was my first meal of the day about noon." A man on Nob Hill rushed to his nearby grocery and found it "about sold out," able only to get "some canned oysters and cream and some canned meats," and another man could find only "crackers, sardines, malted milk" at his. No food could be bought at a grocery store on Fillmore Street as the earthquake had so devastated its interior; as one passerby described it: "glass show-windows broken, and everything off the shelves in a beautiful omelet or pie on the floor; olive oil, vinegar, wine, milk, whiskey, etc., pouring out the front door." Twelve-year-old Marion Baldwin walked with her father to the nearest food store, which was just as damaged: "I saw everything on the floor: the eggs; the soda barrel had tipped over and another barrel of flour or something, and then the great big pickle barrel had tipped over," forming "a kind of goo on the floor." Her father found "a big chunk of yellow cheese" and some "packages of hard chocolate" and paid the owner, who was on the floor, cleaning up and repeating aloud, "I'm ruined! I'm ruined!"

With water distribution mains and service pipes broken throughout the city, fresh drinking water was even scarcer than food. And for those without any saved in sinks or bathtubs, desperation grew. A man visiting from Detroit saw "a small muddy stream of water spurting up through the pavement" on a street corner, "and there many were drinking but I could not bring myself to drink it." He found a grocery store with broken front windows and stood in line with "a large number of people" to pay $1 (equal to approximately $33 in 2023) for some crackers and water. Water quickly became a hot commodity, and many businesses took advantage. A thirteen-year-old girl remembered paying 10 cents per cup, and later that morning, 25 cents. The Palace Hotel—which had its own water supply—began charging 20 cents per cup for coffee and restricted water to its paying guests. In the St. Francis, bottles of Apollinaris were sold at a premium from the lobby bar, but in the Bohemian Club, the only water available for its members was what the staff had saved in pitchers early that morning from the little left in pipes. A laundryman who ducked into a coffee shop was able to get two eggs, but no coffee because there was no water, "so I drank milk."

As soon as sixteen-year-old Howard Livingston returned home from exploring the damage to his Cow Hollow neighborhood, his mom—with no water or gas in the taps—sent him rushing to the bakery with money. Although the shop "was crowded," he found what was on her list ("it was the last bread we would be able to buy for some days"), and he carried it home where she cooked breakfast on the woodstove, "the last time she would be able to use it for some days." Cooking inside homes, most of which had damaged chimneys, was the leading cause of fires that morning in the hours following the earthquake. When the shockwaves tossed chimneys from rooftops, falling bricks and mortar chunks punched holes in the tiled interior of flues. If a fire was started in a fireplace or a stove venting to a broken chimney, breaks and cracks in the flue gave smoke and superheated gases and flaming embers a pathway to ignite upper-floor living spaces or attics. After fire crews extinguished yet another blaze caused by a resident "lighting a fire in a defective chimney," the local battalion chief ordered his engine companies to walk through the neighborhoods and "warn everybody not to light fires in their stoves, as all chimneys were down."

Some residents needed no warnings and improvised to cook outside. "We took a few bricks and built a fire between them in the middle of the street," one woman recounted, "and ate our breakfast on the steps of our home." A cook in a Pacific Heights home knew not to use the stove because "the brick chimney had fallen off the house" and prepared breakfast for his employers on a fire he built in the backyard. A thirteen-year-old boy in Cow Hollow helped his parents construct "a crude stove at the curb with the loose bricks as other neighbors were doing." Twelve-year-old Marion Baldwin noticed a neighbor "having his children collect all the bricks that had fallen around his house," and after they cleaned them, he was using them to build a stove for his morning coffee.

At nine o'clock, firemen were fighting two blazes in Hayes Valley with water pumped through four steam engines from a single hydrant. They had cut off the bottling company's fire at the block's end and were keeping the drugstore fire "confined to the building," as would be reported, even if the store was "completely gutted." A few blocks away, the spark of a single flame would add its own chapter to the disaster. Along the 300 block of Hayes Street, lined with wood-frame, slanted-bay-window Italianate Victorians, the temblor had toppled nearly every chimney but otherwise caused little damage. On the south side of the street, businesses occupied ground floors and above them were second- and third-floor residential flats housing families or retirees or unmarried male workers splitting rent. Inside one of these spaces, a fire broke out that would burn through more blocks and destroy more of the city than any other in the disaster.

How the fire started or who started it is unknown. It started inside and burned out through the roof, first visible atop the three-story building fourth from the corner. "I saw it when it first began to burn," one man reported, describing it as "just a tiny flame that shot up from the roof" that "looked to me as if a little bucket of water would subdue it." But there was nobody with a bucket or a hose to douse the "tiny flame," and it spread, first across the flat roof, then down the cornice and ornate wooden-panel moldings, brackets, and friezes. And it licked up the higher mansard roof of the building beside it and ate away at the wood siding as smoke puffed from open windows of the upper and lower floors. Residents helplessly watched as flames "made remarkable progress" until every structure on the south side of the block was ablaze.

It had only taken minutes. Columns of dark billows churning into the sky from the spreading Hayes Street fire dwarfed the smoke lifting from the other two neighborhood fires and caught the attention of residents in other districts. South of Market, James Hopper saw "heavy volumes of smoke" rising above Hayes Valley that "announced another conflagration." But by this time, as would be reported, "The fire department was all engaged, and no concerted action to stop it was possible." The district's battalion chief, then South of Market, noticed the smoke and ordered an engine company to drop their efforts on 6th Street and rush to the Hayes Valley blaze.

First on the scene were firemen of the truck company who had been extricating the dead from the collapsed Valencia Hotel down in the Mission District for the past two hours, and on their arrival, they assisted in evacuation and rescue. Flames raced down the line of Victorian row houses, consuming first-floor businesses and the flats above them and catching the wooden apartment houses behind them like matchwood. And the blaze jumped the sixty-eight-foot-wide expanse of Hayes Street and ignited the row of narrow, two-story, wood-frame houses on the north side, eating into the line of wooden flats behind them and the brick shirt factory mid-block.

Behind horse teams at a full gallop, the puffing steam engine and hose wagon of the engine company arrived from South of Market to find two blocks engulfed. Hosemen jumped off and "tried to obtain water from the hydrant on the southeast corner but were not successful." They heaved up the manhole and found the sewer dry. And as elsewhere, they ran up a block and over a block and down a block and found every hydrant dry. An onlooker noticed the firemen standing as near as they could to the raging blaze "with lines of hose, patiently waiting for the water that never came." The battalion chief arrived, redirected the engine company two blocks west to hook with the fire engines then pumping from the single working hydrant at Hayes and Buchanan Streets, to keep the fire from spreading further west. But there was no water to keep it from spreading east, further into the city. And although Acting Chief Dougherty eventually sent more engine companies to the scene, the firemen could do little against the growing inferno because, as their captain reported, they "were unable to obtain any water."

Within five weeks, the San Francisco *Examiner* concocted a legend by dubbing it the "Ham and Egg Fire" with a headline blaming "[a] woman cooking ham and eggs for breakfast on a stove connected with a defective chimney." But within the same article, the *Examiner* reported, "It has been impossible for any person to locate the exact origin of the blaze," able only to narrow its location based on eyewitness accounts of Hayes Valley residents who "almost to a man" were "certain" it started in one of the five structures nearest the corner of Hayes and Gough Streets. The people listed as residing in those addresses and their family members totaled fourteen men and five women, and while the first visible flames began on the roof of the fourth building at 383/385 Hayes Street, home to five male tenants, another contemporaneous account pinpoints the fire's initiation to a ground-floor cigar shop in the fifth building at 377/379 Hayes, also home to five male tenants.

It is unknown which tenants or guests were present in the nine o'clock hour or whether the fire began in one of the two first-floor stores or an upstairs apartment. But the legend of a woman starting a "ham-and-egg" fire spread with the same speed as that of "Mrs. O'Leary's cow" in Chicago thirty-five years earlier. Finally dismantling the myth, it is only certain the Hayes Valley fire started inside one of the structures on the south side of the 300 block of Hayes Street sometime after 9:00 a.m., and it grew into one of the most destructive blazes of the disaster.

As fires spread that morning, streets filled with the curious and the newly homeless. Many had returned indoors after the earthquake and even stayed through the aftershock, but flames eating through tenement houses South of Market forced tenants and families from their homes and living spaces. A man in a boardinghouse noticed the panic of other boarders caused by the approaching fire as if "all remembrance of the earthquake seemed to disappear." Firemen on the street below yelled up to him through an open window to "pull all curtains and blinds down" because they were flammable. He did so and noticed walls outside the window "were quite warm, caused by the heat of the approaching fire," still a half block away. Once the blaze reached three doors down, he grabbed a few things and ran downstairs for the last time. Two blocks away a young girl saw flames marching toward the building where her family lived and nearer her father's tailor shop at the corner: "It was a terrible sight, the streets caved in and, oh, the fire was coming." Her father told them they had to all leave immediately and "go away from it as far as we can." She and her brothers left only with "what they wore," and all her mother had time to grab "was her bedding."

Ten-year-old Bernadette McKittrick and her sister watched the blaze of the collapsed Brunswick House a block away spreading toward them. The front stairs of their building had collapsed, and their father helped their mother and them and their dog Prince down the back stairs, and stairstep by stairstep their father heaved the sewing machine their mother had begged him to save. There was no time to save anything else. The sidewalk was broken and the street wet from a broken water main. They crossed with neighbors to Columbia Park, where "we sat and watched the fire burning and come closer and closer to our house." The flames reached the building and devoured it. Bernadette's father tried to console her mother: "It was an awful sight for our poor mother to see all her belongings that she had accumulated since her marriage go up in smoke."

Time was running short for residents facing the impossible task of reducing a lifetime's possessions down to what could fit into a car or a wagon or be carried by hand. Some had only seconds to escape, where the value of material things distilled into fleeting moments of grabbing a family Bible or leaving a grandmother's ring. Even for those with more time, the decisions were no less daunting: food or family pictures, work clothes or wedding dress. "I took what money and jewelry I had with me," one woman noted, able only to grab "a change of underwear," no other clothes, just "the usual things one would take for a night's stay—brushes, a toothbrush, nail files and the like." Another woman and her husband and son packed suitcases with their new Easter clothes, but "it proved more than we were able or had strength for." The three fled their home all with "both hands full"—her husband "had the suitcase strapped on his back, a huge bundle in one hand and framed pictures and other oddments in the other," their son pedaled his prized bicycle, and she carried a large napkin bundling food and knives and forks in one hand and her Easter hat in the other. One boy later remembered his older brother getting "the smart idea that we may need something to get money to live on, so he had all of my mother's flat silverware packed up." With no time to grab more, "We didn't take anything else but the silverware."

Some people buried their valuables. One girl saw her neighbors "digging vast holes in the yard" and "thought they had lost their minds when I saw them bury their expensive piano, silver, and I don't know what else." Another girl's father dug a deep hole in the garden behind their home while she helped her mother fill a trunk "with our silver, cut glass, fine china that escaped being broken, family album, all records and deeds, everything that could not be replaced and we buried in the trunk." One man sent his servant into the backyard to dig "deep trenches into which we threw the silver and bronzes."

People were desperate to haul large items from homes and businesses in the path of the fire, but available wagons and cars were scarce. A man trying to save the trunks from the hotel room where he and his mother were staying walked to the nearest livery stable but "found that every available horse and vehicle had long since been hired by people." Neighbors bid against neighbors for a wagon or even some open space in a car, and prices skyrocketed. Reporter James Hopper hired a car for the rest of the day for $50 (roughly $1,660 in 2023). Many drivers and draymen charged that amount for a one-way trip, and as one resident observed, "[N]ot one man in one thousand had $50.00 in cash in the house when he retired Tuesday night." Especially not in the working-class streets South of Market. Tenants in one lodging house were lucky their landlady arranged to have a few of the wagons of her husband's delivery company lined up to carry her boarders' things away. A boarder who volunteered to drive one of the wagons described them as "filled up pretty well with trunks, bedding and blankets, furniture." As he steered the horse pulling his wagon from the inferno, he heard a "crashing and smashing noise" behind him and in quick glances over his shoulder, he saw flames "rushing at a fast and furious pace" in his direction. Crowding him on both sides "were so many vehicles of different descriptions on the street going the same way" that it was difficult for him to keep up with his wagon caravan.

Negotiating broken streets during the maddest rush in the city's history was arduous. Hooves clopped and engines coughed and wagon wheels grinded over worn paving stones of jammed streets between tall buildings forming brick-walled canyons echoing yells of draymen and wheezing car horns. "Ambulances, patrol wagons, fire-engines are flying in all directions," a man wrote that day. A pastor walking up Market Street noticed "vehicles of all sorts were cluttering up the streets, soldiers, policemen, rushing ambulances, all mingling in the mass." Another resident described wagons piled high with people and belongings pulled by horses "struggling over the earthquake-torn street." Pavement cracks swallowed car wheels, and some sinkholes were so large that horses fell in and "wagons were overturned." In the melee, thirty-one-year-old Frank Nunan, a boarder from the Mission District fleeing with his things on the back of a brewery wagon, was thrown onto the street and run over. Although rushed by onlookers to City & County Hospital, he died of internal injuries within hours.

San Francisco had become a city of refugees in flight, and most were on foot. They carried bundles and dragged trunks and hauled valuables piled on anything with wheels—wagons, baby carriages, wheelbarrows, bicycles. "Every possible contrivance was used for getting baggage along the streets," a man wrote days later. He saw "one man who had mounted his trunk on a pair of roller skates" and "an old lady dragging along by a rope a small round table with two or three dresses perched on the top." People placed stuff on boards set across the tops of two bicycles. Others loaded chairs and pulled them over their backs with ropes or strapped large trunks atop lawn cutters. Elderly family members and invalids were laid on sofas with casters and rolled, or set upon mattresses and dragged along. Eleanor Perry was only two and a half when, as she remembered years later, "I was suddenly snatched from my crib and laid not too gently into a clothes basket with my little brother and sister," which her parents dragged along the sidewalk behind them. One couple balanced their things on a long wooden ladder on rollers—as it passed over each roller, the man would hold the ladder in place while the woman moved a roller from the back to the front and he rolled it forward a little more. And so on.

"Even pianos were being pulled and pushed along," a laundryman noticed. "All had their burdens—old and young, rich and poor, sick and well, all in a mad scramble to save something." The things they carried or stacked or balanced or dragged laid bare inventories of their life's treasures, many holding a singular value incomprehensible to others. Families bore necessities like clothes and blankets and utensils or oddities like pots of calla lilies, mantel clocks, parrot cages, ornate vases, and electric phonographs. Photographer Arnold Genthe saw "an old lady carrying a large bird cage with four kittens inside, while the original occupant, the parrot, perched on her hand" and "a scrub woman, in one hand a new broom and in the other a large black hat with ostrich plumes." One man noticed "a great many comical sights such as a woman carrying ironing boards and an iron," and another saw "a young lady on a bicycle with a bird cage fastened to the handle bars with the canary singing as though nothing had happened." Even a seven-year-old boy noticed "the odd articles the refugees would carry," such as "large oil paintings with huge gold frames." And the most common thing pulled by exhausted evacuees was trunks. They were "dragged along with a kind of fury," producing a "grating, squeaking sound." One man was able to summon the noise from his memory six decades later: "The constant rasping of trunks dragging over cement sidewalks or cobblestone pavements is a sound still fresh in my ears."

Acting Chief Dougherty's plan to blow firebreaks was the first attempt at a coordinated strategy to stop what was growing into a citywide firestorm. More than five hundred firefighters were throwing whatever water they could find on blazes burning through five separate districts. This removed heat, which with oxygen and fuel, forms the "fire triangle" necessary to keep a fire burning. Removal of any of the three will stop a blaze. Firebreaks would remove fuel by eliminating flammable structures and combustible material from the path of the fires and stop their spread. San Francisco's streets acted as natural firebreaks, but the flames devouring large structures and whole blocks were generating heat at temperatures high enough (in places more than 2,000 degrees Fahrenheit) to easily radiate across narrow twenty-eight-foot-wide alleys and forty-foot-wide streets and ignite wooden structures (fuel) on the far sides. And the morning's breeze and wind were not only feeding blazes with more oxygen but were also carrying flaming embers and superheated air across wider eighty-two-foot-wide streets and threatening to cross even the city's widest paved thoroughfares, 120-foot-wide Market Street and 125-foot-wide Van Ness Avenue. With fires spreading so rapidly, firebreaks would require the swift demolition of swaths of buildings in the path of shifting fires, thus Dougherty's plan to use explosives.

At the Presidio, when Acting Chief Dougherty's messenger arrived requesting explosives, the only immediately available on post was black powder. And as a handful of soldiers heaved forty-eight barrels of black powder and spools of wire and fuses onto horse-drawn artillery caissons, the officer selected to lead the detail, twenty-seven-year-old Lieutenant Raymond Briggs, harbored reservations. As an artillery officer in his ninth year of service, Briggs had experience handling black powder as a blank cartridge charge in gunnery training and knew of its dangers, especially when employed for building demolition. Highly flammable and volatile, black powder is a low explosive prone to igniting by impact, friction, smoke, or open flame. It requires a tight, confined space for its detonation to have enough destructive effect to bring down a structure—as with boreholes drilled into rock for mining. And among explosives, black powder has the longest-lasting flame, making it more likely to set a building on fire than to demolish it. "The use of this powder was naturally not desired," Lieutenant Briggs later explained, "if stick dynamite could be procured." And since it could not—at least not yet—Briggs and his soldiers convoyed their barrels of black powder carefully through the city to the Hall of Justice and reported to Mayor Schmitz by 9:00 a.m.

Acting Chief Dougherty had already met with Mayor Schmitz and the police chief and shared his plans to blow firebreaks and his request for explosives from the Presidio. Schmitz asked around the room where dynamite could be obtained, and when someone answered they "could get all they wanted at the Judson Powder Works at Pinole," he ordered "a police officer and a military man of some kind to get a tug and proceed to Point Pinole and bring down all the dynamite that the tug would carry."

From there, word spread of the mayor's call for dynamite, and in a city with roots sprawling through decades of mining, companies answered the call. The first load arrived in granular form by wagon from California Powder Works just after Lieutenant Briggs arrived. But the company president who brought it was "so far under the influence of liquor as to be of no service." And granular dynamite was, as Briggs knew, nearly as dangerous as black powder as "any building destroyed by it would, in addition, be set on fire."

In the basement of the Hall of Justice, Lieutenant Briggs found himself in a discussion of where and how firebreaks should be blown. A fire commissioner and battalion chief discussed the how, and political boss Abe Ruef—who owned property in the banking district—focused on the where. Possibly Briggs shared the need to use stick dynamite for demolition, the hazards of using the black powder he brought, and the need to blow breaks far enough ahead of fires to effectively stop them. Or possibly the young lieutenant hesitated to interject at such a gathering. When he emerged on the street, more artillery soldiers from the Presidio had arrived with wagons loaded with three hundred pounds of stick dynamite acquired from a civilian employee of the post engineering department. Along with the granular dynamite, it was unloaded under a tent on a grass corner of Portsmouth Square.

Schmitz ordered the first firebreak to be blown at the nearest leading edge of where flames had reached into the city's banking district, at the time only two blocks away. And he ordered only structures already in contact with fire could be demolished and not to extend demolition to other streets without his permission. Roiling smoke columns crept nearer and nearer the Hall of Justice and Portsmouth Square, and time was critical. Lieutenant Briggs and his team of soldiers left the black powder, grabbed a few cases of stick dynamite, and headed toward the fire.

The caissons of black powder from the Presidio—left where Briggs had parked them—were driven by soldiers toward the South of Market fires under the direction of a police captain. Horse teams pulled the caissons through Market Street crowds, then turned at 6th Street and halted. Flames were a half block away, eating toward Market, nearing Jessie Alley where a platoon of soldiers kept crowds back from the approaching fire. The police captain approached the Army officer in charge, twenty-nine-year-old Lieutenant

Charles Pulis, and "asked if there was not some way that some buildings could be blown down." Pulis, an artilleryman with the same reservations about black powder as Lieutenant Briggs, had little time to demur before an Army major appeared and ordered him to demolish any buildings the police captain designated.

Lieutenant Pulis and a few of his soldiers followed the police captain to one of the parked caissons, heaved a barrel of black powder, and lugged it into a corner saloon on Jessie Alley. It was a two-story wood-frame building, and while soldiers carried the barrel down into the basement, Pulis sent one of his men through the upstairs to evacuate anyone left. Lieutenant Pulis only had experience handling black powder as a cartridge charge in artillery, not in building demolition. For a fuse, his men dribbled a "train" of powder from the barrel to the front door, lit it at the end, then ran back a safe distance. But nothing happened. The men uncovered their ears and opened their eyes. The building was still and silent, and flames were licking at its far end. Pulis and the fire captain ran back to the front door, Pulis knelt to relight the powder, and in a sparking, booming flash the building exploded.

The police captain was flung out into the street and Pulis was buried beneath a heap of splintered wood and shattered glass. The captain, struggling to his feet and "blinded by the blood that was flowing from wounds all over his head and face," pushed soldiers attending to him away, gestured to where Pulis was buried, and yelled, "Go get him!" Beneath the debris, Charles Pulis was found unconscious and covered in blood flowing from deep gashes. Soldiers bandaged and rushed him to Mechanics' Pavilion, where he was treated for serious lacerations, a skull fracture, broken bones, and internal injuries.

Initially it was reported that Pulis was "probably fatally injured" and "will not recover," but owing to the efforts of surgeons and physicians and nurses in the makeshift emergency space, he did. The police captain was also taken to the pavilion where large shards of wood and glass were removed by a surgeon. He was so "full of splinters," the last one was not pulled from his scalp until two years later. And in a scene that would repeat many times on many streets in the coming hours and days, the amateur demolition crew had propelled burning fragments across the narrow, thirty-five-foot-wide alleyway, igniting another block and threatening Market Street.

Six blocks away, the Mack's drugstore fire now consumed most of its block. Directly across the street from Mack's blazing ruins, the defenders of Whittier Coburn Co.—the Whittiers and the Coburns and many of their employees—tried to douse every flame ignited by sparks and firebrands land-ing on their five-story building's wood trim or sign or roof, but the furnace-like heat forced them to retreat a half block to the open space of Market Street where they panted gasps of fresh air and looked back to watch the inevitable. They stood beside a protective wood scaffolding shrouding the sidewalk wrap-ping around the corner brick Lachman Building.

"The sparks were flying," a barber in the watching crowd observed. And it only took a few seconds for the wood scaffolding to ignite, forcing the on-lookers back to the middle of Market Street. "The outside portion of the scaf-folding caught fire first," a security guard noted, and a woodworker described flames starting from "falling embers striking and remaining on it." An orange flicker on a beam fluttered into a flame that spread along the top and ate down the supports and through the woodwork of the doors and window frames of the first-floor storefront. Helpless spectators backed away further from the hot flames. In a familiar scene, glass shattered from the heat, combustibles inside the first floor ignited, and in little time orange flames were surging from windows of all five floors. The fight to save the block was lost. The blaze spread deeper down Fremont Street through a paper box factory and then Whittier Coburn Co., destroying the decades-old family business in minutes. And the fire crept up Market Street to the five-story Sheldon Building at the corner of 1st Street, only a block and a half from the Palace Hotel.

Beyond its sturdy construction, which had proven itself during the morning's earthquake and aftershock, the Palace was also built to be fireproof. Beneath the central Grand Court was a 368,000-gallon reservoir from which seven steam engines in a building on the south side of Jessie Alley pumped water up to six iron rooftop tanks with capacity for 750,000 gallons. Emergency water pipes ran down through the building—fourteen inside and twenty-four on outside walls near fire escapes—with connections on each floor for six emer-gency hoses ranging from 100 to 250 feet long and able to reach every square foot of the hotel's inside and outer walls. At street level, a dozen hydrants on sidewalks also linked with the rooftop tank supply, allowing firemen to connect in the event of insufficient city pressure. The Palace Hotel had been designed to stand against every possible disaster, even this one.

Behind the Palace, the inferno spreading from the Howard Street laundry house fire had "leaped from block to block as though through dry grass," as one man described it. Flames had crossed Mission Street from behind the ho-tel and were marching up 3rd Street on its side. Bellboys and cooks unspooled emergency hoses and ran them down corridors through windows and onto fire escapes where they leaned out against thin metal railings and shot water onto the hotel's enormous façade of ornate bay windows to keep it from catching fire. Remaining guests were told to grab their belongings and exit to Market Street—the only safe way left—where they were waved across the wide street by soldiers forming a fire line.

From the far side of the "cordon of police and soldiers," James Byrne rushed back toward the Palace to retrieve trunks and valuables from the suite he and his mother had shared after attending the opera the night before. He was passed through the fire line after a *Chronicle* reporter vouched for him, and he ran into the dark, empty lobby and up six flights of stairs to the room where he threw his mother's jewelry case in his coat pocket, locked the trunks, then looked out the window and saw flames consuming buildings lining the narrow alley along the hotel's south side, including its water-pumping station. The "fire brigade of bellboys" on spindly fire escapes covered the outer wall with water left in the rooftop tanks. Water flowed down the exterior and dripped from bay windows, steaming from the heat of the threatening fire with temperatures topping 2,000 degrees Fahrenheit. Rippling heat waves distorted vision and hellish air "at times terrific" forced workers "to hold an arm up to protect their faces while trying to manage the hose with only one hand."

A physician and his wife left the hotel through the Market Street doors and to their right saw an inferno, which, as he would later describe, "was now assuming alarming proportions," eating through buildings toward the Palace. They turned and walked the opposite direction up Market. At each street crossing they stole glances to their left to see the South of Market fire burning along Mission Street—running parallel one block south—"so rapidly, consuming wooden buildings, as to keep pace with us." They were on foot, "for not a vehicle could be had for love or money." Worried the blaze would cross over and cut them off, "we forged on as best we could, and outran the flames."

In their fast walk up Market Street, one building they rushed past—possibly without noticing—was the California Academy of Sciences. Beside the massive Emporium department store between 5th and 6th Streets, the academy's seven floors housed a library, museum, thousands of bird and insect specimens, sediment sections, and gems and minerals collected by geologists. And on the sixth floor was an herbarium with botanical collections and thousands of plant specimens, many of which had been collected by forty-seven-year-old Alice Eastwood, curator of the botany department. In her fifteen years with the academy, she had covered the Pacific Northwest on foot and horseback up steep hills and through deep canyons collecting and discovering previously undocumented plant types from the plains to the coast. These she painstakingly preserved and documented, bundling each into individual boxes, alphabetized by type.

After the earthquake awoke her that morning, Alice worried about the department's collection. She grabbed her Zeiss lens (an optical magnifier to study specimens), left her Taylor Street home and her other possessions, and walked thirteen blocks to the academy. Finding the front door padlocked, she entered through the Emporium's side access door into the academy's dark lobby. "It was necessary to climb over a lot of fallen bricks to reach the staircase," she wrote a few days later. She found sections of the stairs and connecting landings gone and returned to the street to find help; she encountered a friend who accompanied her back into the building where the museum director, the librarian, and her own assistant had arrived. Together they "had to climb up the staircase to the sixth floor mainly by the iron banisters which seemed to be firm." Alice found the case holding the boxed specimens "thrown down on its face" and the boxes "scattered." She quickly organized the boxes, instructed her friend to tie them with string, and devised a way to lower them "down by string doubled to the floor of the museum six stories below" where she stood to receive each one. It was a time-consuming process, and out in front of the museum, she could see soldiers keeping people on the far side of Market Street and knew flames must be close.

By 10:00 a.m. South of Market was a firestorm. It was "no longer 'only a fire,'" as one woman at this hour described it, "but a terrible, raging, uncontrollable, sheet of flames swallowing up building after building." A man passing Mission Street noticed, "The street was like looking in the door of a furnace," and the inferno pulled superheated air up and sucked fresh air in from surrounding blocks with such force that it generated its own wind, "rolling up the street with a roar, then up hundreds of feet." Flames rushed up streets and down alleys so quickly some people could barely outrun them. A drayman on a delivery wagon felt the speeding fire catching up to him, so he steered into the curb, unhitched the horse, and abandoned his wagon to the "raging inferno." A visitor from Sausalito heard "the crackling and roar . . . as it swallowed up lines of houses from two to four stories high," and he saw "flames bursting from all the windows and then the whole line falling backwards, just like houses of cards."

Inside many of these burning houses were trapped tenants, helplessly holding last lungfuls of air beneath descending curtains of thick, black smoke. For some, the end was agonizingly slow. Evacuees heard a man screaming "For God's sake help me" from a basement apartment beneath a collapsed floor of a burning lodging house on Mission Street. For others, mercy came only in the form of unconsciousness after just a few breaths of smoke filled with hydrogen cyanide, not awake when they burned or asphyxiated, whichever came first. In some places, charred remains of couples and whole families were found together, like the Hansen family—Daniel, twenty-seven; Sarah, twenty-three; and their son, William, only one—and the Stamblers—Louis, thirty-five; Celia, thirty; their daughter, Rosie, ten; and their niece Fannie Weiner, twenty-three—prompting devastating thoughts of how many parents stayed with trapped children, or children with parents, or how many babies or toddlers of dead parents died in the flames without a hand to guide them to safety. If the coroner's causes of death for forty-six-year-old Michele Canepa ("killed by falling building") and his wife, forty-one-year-old Maddalena ("burnt to death"), were correct, it seems she died while choosing to stay at her husband's side.

Still standing a block south of Market Street in the middle of the firestorm was the US Mint. The three-story federal bank and coining foundry was one of only four mints throughout the United States, and in a time still thirty years from the construction of a national gold depository at Fort Knox, the San Francisco Mint was effectively the era's western Fort Knox, housing more than a third of the nation's gold reserve. As such it was a fortress, built with walls of masonry and sandstone more than three feet thick with iron doors and shutters that locked from within. A squad of ten armed soldiers now stood guard on the twenty-one steps leading to its iron doors facing 5th Street even as flames along Mission Street blackened the sandstone of its side wall. Behind its closed, iron shutters were fifty employees who had shown up in the hours since the earthquake "to do their best to help save the property of the government," as the superintendent later reported, with a "sense of loyalty to duty [that] had not been modified by fear of earthquake or the horror of being penned up in a big building surrounded by fire."

The mint had its own emergency water supply, if a bit more modest than that of the Palace Hotel: water from a reservoir beneath the cement courtyard pumped to two rooftop tanks feeding standpipes running down through the building with connections on each floor for emergency inch-wide hoses on reels to connect and reach every wing of the two upper levels, the basement, and the central courtyard. Joe Hammill, a basement refinery worker, had arrived when the laundry house fire to the east and lodging house fires to the west were not yet threatening the mint, and he was pleased to find the structure had "escaped serious damage" with only some chimneys toppled and "furniture overturned." But now blazes approached from three sides: flames from the black powder fire started by the improvised demolition crew in the corner saloon less than a block away were spreading along Jessie Alley into the back side of the mint and nearing its rear wall, and fire was sweeping up Mission Street along its side and 5th Street along its front where Hammill saw blazing structures sending "great bursts of flame two or three hundred feet into the air."

From his rented car riding along the outer limits of the firestorm, James Hopper noticed the mint with its iron shutters sealed, untouched by flame, "unmoved, inscrutable as a sphinx" and standing "like a rock in the flaming sea." All around it, the "heaving red sea" of flames devoured the district "in a swath four blocks wide," between Market and Folsom Streets from 2nd Street to 8th, "and with a roar it was rushing on, its advance billow curling like a monstrous comber above a flotsam of fleeing humanity." To a constant din of squeaking chair casters and humming wagon wheels and trunks grinding along pavement, the mass exodus of evacuees had reached full tide and would not subside for days. "At every cross-street, streams of people from South of Market came, staggering under the weight of the burden of their loads," magazine editor Mary Edith Griswold saw from Market Street. To James Hopper they seemed "miserable and crushed," trudging along sidewalks and streets with "heads bowed, eyes dead, silent and stupefied." They streamed westward toward Golden Gate Park, southward down the peninsula, and many aimed for the only other escape from the city, the largest gateway still open to the outside world—the waterfront.

8. Saving the Waterfront

WHEN TICKET CLERK Thomas Chase reached the Ferry Building that morning after the earthquake had thrown him to the street on his walk in, he found one outer wall had crumbled and some stone and brick from upper parts of the tower had fallen, but otherwise the gray-painted Colusa sandstone appeared undamaged and the steel-framed structure was matching its indestructible reputation. Ferries and tugs "had all backed out into the clear" during the shaking but were returning to their slips, and he noticed "waves were lazily lapping at the pilings as if nothing had happened."

Thomas walked inside through lines of passengers filling the grand nave and into his small ticket office, where he "found the counters and floor covered with plaster" and everything wet from the broken pipes, but, like the docks outside, the office was still functional. The weekday morning rush of commuters in the six o'clock hour, always busy, was more congested than ever. Urgent voices of a growing, panicked crowd echoed off the high ceiling of the commodious grand nave where janitors swept shards of glass from broken skylights into piles on the marble mosaic floor among long lines of evacuees hopeful for a ticket to escape the city. Thomas's boss and coworker had not yet arrived, but a ferry captain walked in, "sized up the situation," and as Thomas later wrote, "We decided to get busy and busy it was."

Thomas issued tickets as quickly as he could. Knowing space would be limited, vessel crews instructed passengers to drop larger belongings and trunks outside on the cobblestone of East Street. "This pile grew until it was like a hay stack," Thomas noticed, and "after leaving their bundles they apparently gave no further thought to them." Clutching tickets, the "dazed or stunned" crowd in all types of hurried dress flowed through covered walkways out to the docks and onto bobbing ferries, where they were directed by gatekeepers to cram onto benches and into the standing room of top cabin decks and even bottom freight decks, some reaching double capacity. "The crush was tremendous and I thought the ferry would be swamped with so many people crowding on board," described Josephine Jacoby, a member of the opera company who made it from the St. Francis Hotel. Another young man and his coworker managed to grab two spots on the Oakland ferry with "a mass of refugees," even though they knew nobody over there. Like many others aboard, they were "just getting out of what seemed a doomed city, going they knew not where."

The first ferry loaded with evacuees was underway by 6:20 a.m., "only 20 minutes late," Thomas Chase reported proudly, "then we resumed normal schedule." But that morning the waterfront and wharf and crowd sizes and traffic were anything but "normal." Massive wooden freight sheds along the six-hundred-foot-long piers lining the shore north and south of the ferry slips had "fallen flat," some into the water, some onto the wharf, and some onto vessels berthed alongside. The steamship *City of Pueblo* was nearly cut in half by a shipyard crane that fell across the vessel amidships—she "began to take water and in a short time she filled and went to the bottom." A letter carrier arriving for work at the Ferry Building noticed pieces of the south wall had fallen through the heavy planking and foot-thick wooden girders "as though they were but matchwood," and he saw "several large pieces of stone had fallen from the masonry of the tower and lay near the turntable" where cable cars of five lines were normally lined up, most of which were still back in their carbarns, unable to run for damaged powerhouses, dislodged cables, and bent rails.

By 7:00 a.m. throngs of people fleeing the South of Market fires "were pressing down to the ferries" into a human crush at the foot of Market Street and forcing policemen to stretch downed telephone lines across either side of the street "as a sort of a barrier" to keep the crowds safe "from live wires, fires, and collapsing walls." Among the officers working crowd control was Sergeant Jesse Cook, and in the multitudes streaming to the Ferry Building, Cook noticed "an old Italian" who was "staggering along under the weight of a rolled-up mattress" which "seemed so heavy and the man seemed so eagerly careful about it." Three young children were huddled with him, and when Sergeant Cook asked the man what was in the mattress, the man's daughter—

who could speak English—answered, "He has my mother in the mattress." She explained her mother was killed in the earthquake, which also destroyed their home. Her father was trying to save his children and late wife's remains from the fires. Sergeant Cook escorted them through the lines to a steamship and convinced the crew to allow them aboard. "So there I left them," Cook wrote many years later of the moment: "I don't know what their names were or what became of them afterwards, because I never saw or heard of them again."

By the nine o'clock hour, the fires in the harbor and banking districts were a single inferno. Crowds, held back at a safe distance by armed soldiers, stared up at the dispiriting sight of tall steel-framed skyscrapers of brick and stone wrapped with orange flames. They "burned by rooms, as it were in compartments," Reverend William Nichols described. He watched flames devour the nine-story Mutual Life Insurance Company building—which "though tall and of brick, was of wood in the interior"—from the inside out, like "a big chimney, with one solid mass of flame working up through it." Superheated wind blew down streets, igniting stacks of books and boxed items left by employees forced to sprint from blistering heat, and firemen pulled back to save their hoses and soak buildings lining Sansome Street to keep the blaze from spreading west. They had found no working hydrants, so their engine was getting water from another engine a block up on California Street where it was pumping to them from a 35,000-gallon cistern. When that ran low, the men of another engine company found water in a cistern two blocks further up California Street, which they pumped back down to refill the first cistern, which was then pumped to firemen making the stand at Sansome Street where breezes fed the flames and blew spray from their stream sideways.

Photographer Arnold Genthe returned to his Sutter Street apartment—still blocks from the blaze—to retrieve his camera. "The one thought uppermost in my mind," he later wrote, was "to make photographs of the scenes I had been witnessing." Finding his cameras damaged by fallen debris and useless, he walked seven blocks to the Montgomery Street store of his camera dealer who told him, "Take anything you want. This place is going to burn up anyway." Arnold grabbed "the best small camera"—likely a No. 3A, B2, Folding Pocket Kodak—and stuffed his pockets with film and set off to document the disaster in real time with an artist's eye.

From his 24th Avenue home nearly five miles away, Ernest Adams had seen the sky above downtown filled with smoke just after the earthquake and ran the distance to his silver flatware store on Kearny Street. By the time he arrived, sweating beneath his hat and breathing heavy from the run, he saw flames two blocks away and firemen scrambling without any nearby cisterns. He unlocked the door, "waded through plaster," and found most of his boxed inventory thrown from shelves onto the floor but undamaged. With little time left he exited, locked the store, and spent a long hour navigating through the "pandemonium" in the streets before finding a wagon driver he hired for $50 to haul his sterling from the fire. He and the wagon and his stock of silverware made it out just as soldiers cordoned off the street.

William Alexander also made it to his downtown office before soldiers blocked his way, and while gathering bankbooks and stock records and cash from his desk, through the window he saw the fire "raging" only a block away. He escaped down on the street with both arms full and watched "the advance of the terrible fire as it devoured one by one San Francisco's finest buildings" and saw firemen directing other people loaded with contents from stores and offices away from the flames. Two young men kicked through the door of a Kearny Street pet shop as the blaze threatened, releasing the animals—including several monkeys. "It was a gesture of kindness," a witness observed, "but a foolish one; I am certain they all perished in the raging inferno."

A black pall of smoke filled the sky and to those in the city, the sun looked like "a blood red ball," and as one man described, "what with the gloom, the falling ashes and the people fleeing, it was a picture of the last days of Pompeii." By 10:00 a.m. the inferno was within one block of East Street and the crowded wharf that was more combustible than the downtown structures already ablaze. North of the Ferry Building's slips a series of six-hundred-foot-long wood piers jutted out into the bay, and along this section of East Street ran the State Belt Railroad, used for hauling freight among the docks and up around North Beach to the new Fisherman's Wharf. South of the Ferry Building were twenty more piers extending down to South of Market's Southern Pacific Railroad's passenger depot, the only other safe passage for refugees escaping the city (and soon to be a critical artery for relief supplies). Each pier was a planked wood surface built on wood supports and wood pilings. Much of the wharf was planked wood. The freight sheds and storage sheds and coal bunkers lining the docks were wood, as was the Ferry Station Post Office. With no pressure in pier hydrants connected to city mains, if the fire reached East Street there would be nothing to save the waterfront.

Twenty-five miles from San Francisco across the waters of San Francisco Bay and San Pablo Bay, the USS *Perry*, a six-year-old torpedo boat destroyer undergoing repairs after recent target practice off the Mexican coast south of

California, was docked alongside a pier at the Mare Island Naval Shipyard across a narrow strait from Vallejo. The skipper, thirty-year-old Lieutenant Frederick Freeman, and his engineer, twenty-one-year-old Midshipman John Pond, had both been awakened in their cabin by the earthquake, which they felt as "an intense vibration of the whole vessel." They stepped into slippers and reached the deck before the trembling stopped. Water lapped up between the *Perry* and the quay wall, "presenting the appearance of tide rips," and the vessel was vibrating as if backing up at full speed. Pond glanced across the water and saw "people running out of the houses" into the streets of Vallejo.

Most of the crew of seventy-five were on liberty in Vallejo, due back by 8:00 a.m. Sailors returned with rumors that San Francisco was "demolished and in flames, with terrific loss of life." Lieutenant Freeman and Ensign Pond were eating breakfast when the radioman brought a wireless message also peppered with unsubstantiated rumors: "San Francisco. Nearly demolished city. Call Building is down and Palace Hotel, both telegraph offices. Wells Fargo Building. All water pipes burst. City fire department helpless. City is in flames." Then after "another shock" shook the vessel—the 8:14 a.m. aftershock—an orderly arrived with a message from the admiral at Mare Island directing Freeman to "report immediately." Freeman went ashore and returned with orders to take "all available surgeons and nurses" from the naval yard to San Francisco aboard the *Perry*'s sister ship, the USS *Preble*, docked nearby (and, unlike his own vessel with dismantled engines under repair, seaworthy).

Frederick Freeman was thin, medium height, and clean-shaven. Born and raised on the outskirts of Fort Wayne, Indiana, as the youngest of six children to a traveling salesman, the midwesterner had trained to serve on the sea since entering the Naval Academy at the young age of fifteen, where his classmates called him "The Kid." Since his 1895 graduation he had served as a junior officer on training ships and torpedo boats and had now captained the *Perry* for six months. His engineer, Midshipman John Pond, a recent Naval Academy graduate and the son of a Navy commander, had spent the past several months under Freeman's command and knew him as "a born leader of men, a skipper whose men would go to Hell and back for him." Most importantly, Freeman was a leader of initiative and improvisation, "not a man who would wait for instructions before taking action in an emergency."

The only instruction given to Freeman that morning was to transport medical personnel to San Francisco aboard the *Preble*. To that end he sent two of his crew to scour the yard and training station for nurses and doctors and medical supplies. But he also calculated from a distance that city firefighters would need water pumped from the bay, considering the "All water pipes burst" message. So he expanded his single-vessel medical mission to a firefighting flotilla and added the *Leslie*, a seventy-five-foot-long wooden Navy fireboat, and the *Active*, a 107-foot-long Navy steam tug (like the fireboat, with high-capacity pumping capability), and he assembled his crew at quarters and asked for volunteers to man the *Leslie*. "Of course everyone wanted to go," Pond noted, and those "grumbling" at missing the cut "went on the jump" when Freeman asked for more to man the *Active*. The rest joined Freeman aboard the *Preble* to augment its skeleton crew.

The fireboat *Leslie* shoved off just after 9:00 a.m. and chugged down the channel and into the open water of San Pablo Bay with a dozen sailors under a chief petty officer. A few minutes later, after grabbing his pistol, ammunition, and waterfront chart from his cabin and waiting for a detachment of marines he was to transport to the city, Pond got the tug *Active* underway. "The trip down the bay was an exciting race," he later recounted. The fireboat had a head start, but his steam tug was faster. When he overtook the *Leslie*, his small crew "passed her a tow line without even slowing down" and towed her toward the city. Back at Mare Island, after coaling the *Preble* and getting the boilers of her engines up to pressure, Lieutenant Freeman and his sailors and medical teams were underway before 9:30 a.m.

The dark olive steel hull of the *Preble* cut through the whitecaps of San Pablo Bay and San Francisco Bay "under full boiler power." It did not take long to overtake the *Active* and *Leslie*. Freeman manned the bridge, bearing for the churning base of the giant smoke clouds blacking out the morning sky above the city. Down on the ship's deck behind him were sailors and a team of nurses and doctors and orderlies from the naval yard's hospital. Dark smoke puffed from the vessel's four short stacks and flattened out as a dark trail on the water behind them, obscuring the rolling figures of the steam tug *Active* and fireboat *Leslie*, both still connected by a tow rope, chugging and straining to keep up speed. Strong tailwinds helped the *Preble* make the twenty-five-mile race to San Francisco in just more than an hour, arriving at 10:30 a.m.

The *Preble*'s engines throttled down as it neared the waterfront. Freeman maneuvered alongside another Navy tug, the *Sotoyomo*, skippered by a lieutenant commander who told Freeman he was going to get fresh water and to await his return from Goat Island (present-day Yerba Buena Island). But as the tug sped away, Freeman could see time was pressing. Smoke clouds of black and gray and white churned from one end of the city to the other and blotted out the blue sky. Long, bent roofs of flattened freight sheds draped broken over piers. Freeman maneuvered nearer the waterfront, where the wall of smoke roiled just behind the buildings nearest the wharf, and orange flames could be seen down streets and alleys by the crew as the *Preble* glided closer. Freeman dropped anchor, raised the hospital flag, and sent his medical team ashore in the service boat along with a crewmember to ask fire department officials where they needed the tug and fireboat to berth. The sailor returned with word they were needed South of Market and to tie them at Pier 8 at the end of Howard Street, four piers south of the Ferry Building.

Still towing the fireboat *Leslie*, the *Active* chugged into view with smoke puffing from its single tall stack and young Midshipman Pond in the wheelhouse. "As we approached the waterfront we were appalled by the immensity of the holocaust," he later wrote. "The city was burning in several places," and he could see flames eating toward the waterfront where, with several large structures collapsed and the pole atop the Ferry Building bent sideways, "everything seemed askew." Overwhelmed by the scene, Pond and the sailors and detachment of marines aboard the tugboat "began to realize our insignificance compared to the task lying before us." Amid the mayhem, he saw the *Preble* anchored near the end of the Howard Street pier, and Freeman—having "already sized up the situation"—signaled for both vessels to tie up alongside as he jumped onto the wooden pier. In his tailored service blues with high collar and white officer's cap he cut a commanding figure as he rushed across the East Street wharf and up Howard Street near the edge of the South of Market fire and found a battalion chief who shook Freeman's hand and "expressed his appreciation of the assistance offered." The chief pointed to a lumberyard, warehouse, and power company along Spear Street and the south side of Howard "where he needed streams of water." Firemen with hoses followed Freeman back to the pier, where he ordered the crews of the *Active* and *Leslie* to connect the lines and begin pumping. And Freeman sent word to engine companies to bring over their steam engines—which could pump salt water but needed fresh water for their boilers now running dry—and they refilled their boilers via a bucket brigade from freshwater tanks of the tugs. By 11:00 a.m., as Midshipman Pond later reported, they "had several lines of hose laid out" snaking from the fireboat and tug along the pier and across the wharf and up Howard Street, and from that minute the sailors fought the blaze "shoulder to shoulder with the city's firemen."

Lieutenant Freeman noticed ferries returning from Oakland filled with "sightseers," who after landing "scattered through the city" and, as he would report, "increased the difficulties we had to contend with a thousandfold." Pond also vented about the crowds of "able-bodied men" who refused to lend a hand while they "stood about and got in our way." Seeing no police or soldiers in the district, Freeman employed the platoon of marines to enforce fire lines across the wharf. And he sent a runner to the Ferry Building with orders directing ferry companies not to admit anyone onto a vessel bound for San Francisco without a pass from either General Funston or himself.

From this hour on, Freeman "assumed complete control of the entire waterfront district," as Pond would later note. "His orders were instantly obeyed and his authority was recognized without questions by all, officials and civilians alike." Even the admiral and General Funston let him be and "gave him a free hand, recognizing him as the man for the job."

One of many arriving at that hour in a ferry from Oakland was fifty-nine-year-old Frank Leach, superintendent of the San Francisco Mint. Leach had been brought to California by his parents from New York in 1852 when he was only five, the same year the government established the first mint on the West Coast in San Francisco to process miners' gold into coins. After school he worked as a newspaper publisher in Vallejo and served in the legislature and then acquired a newspaper in Oakland where he lived with his wife and four sons. In the eight years since his appointment as mint superintendent, Leach had electrified its refineries and improved its efficiency and, with increasing amounts of gold arriving from deposits discovered up in the Yukon, oversaw the minting of more than $1 billion in gold coins, an output during that span which eclipsed the mints in New Orleans and even the nation's oldest and largest in Philadelphia.

From his breakfast in his Oakland home after the earthquake, Leach had seen "that the heavens above the city were filling with the black smoke of a great fire." Worried that flames might reach the mint and its vaults, filled with more than $300 million in gold bullion, he rushed from his house and secured one of the last available seats on a train headed for the Oakland Mole ("It seemed as if all of Oakland's population was bound for San Francisco"), then grabbed one of the last spots on a ferry. On the crossing, he pushed his way forward through the crowd to the front railing of the upper deck to absorb the "terrible sight" of the city as it neared: "Flames were leaping high in the air from places scattered all the way across the front part of the city" and "clouds of black smoke filled the sky and hid the rays of the sun."

After landing, Leach walked against the tide of "hundreds of refugees racing for the Ferry Building" and snaked through the harbor and banking districts, avoiding the fires that seemed to be everywhere. "How far the fire had extended I could not make out," he later wrote, and this "uncertainty increased my anxiety to reach the building." Each block he tried to wind his way down to Market Street and cross, but at each crossing he faced soldiers wielding loaded rifles enforcing fire lines with shoves and the sharp ends of bayonets. He later reported troops "pushed me back" in many of his several attempts to cross toward the mint. Finally, with the help of a policeman who recognized him, Leach was escorted across Market Street's wide expanse, now eerily quiet, mostly empty, and under a smoky, late-morning twilight, where the sun could not reach and where the city's grandest and tallest buildings in their final moments awaited their inescapable fate.

Six blocks away, the Hayes Valley fire had grown into an inferno covering two city blocks. The blaze was spreading east toward Van Ness Avenue, and "in less time than it takes to tell the story," as a witness noted, flames reached the tops of the two two-hundred-foot-tall ornate wooden spires above St. Ignatius Church and College, which occupied an entire city block on the west side of Van Ness. "A shower of burning embers rained upon the nearest tower, setting [it] on fire," Friar John Frieden, the college president, later recounted. "A few minutes more and the other tower was wrapped in flames." As the blaze ate down the towers to the roof and into the church and rooms of the attached four-story dormitory, priests and students rushed the Blessed Sacrament (bread and wine of Communion) to safety, and wagons were secured to haul away vestments and altar furniture.

Fire companies in Hayes Valley kept the flames from spreading west by relaying water through three engines from their single source at the Hayes and Buchanan hydrant. But the only thing keeping the fire from spreading east—where Mechanics' Pavilion sat just a block away and City Hall a block past that—was the 125-foot width of Van Ness Avenue, wider even than Market Street and a natural firebreak to halt the spread of most ordinary fires. But as with South of Market, the scale of the Hayes Valley fire had now grown into a firestorm, and glowing embers floated through roasting air rippling across the avenue, igniting walls and rooftops of two-story apartments on the east side.

Inside Mechanics' Pavilion just after 11:00 a.m., word came to a priest in a "subdued but startling whisper" that the fire was "only a short distance off and sweeping this way" and all patients—nearing four hundred at that hour—"must instantly be moved to a place of safety." For the past five and a half hours, every available ambulance and wagon and automobile and conveyance had been employed bringing in the injured. Most had been treated but were unable to walk, and only with great care could they be moved again. The task of evacuation would be mammoth, but time was critical. Two police officers and the pavilion superintendent climbed access stairs to the roof and found the "shingles were smoking in several places, and sparks from adjacent fires were continually dropping on the roof." The superintendent carried buckets of water up to "try to quench the sparks when they caught the shingles" but "the roof was very big and very dry," and as one of the officers noted, "[I]t was only a matter of time when the whole building would be burnt." Small flames caught near the eave and bloomed across the dry roof, and one of the officers rushed back down the stairs to begin evacuation.

Nurse Lucy Fisher was walking among patients on floor mattresses with a pot of coffee and pieces of bread when another nurse approached and "in a low excited voice" told her, "The building is on fire; the patients are to be re-moved as quickly as possible at the rear entrance." Throughout the large pavil-ion Lucy could see the news passing in hand-covered whispers among doctors and nurses and volunteers. Smoke began wafting through the rafters of the vaulted ceiling high above. A surgeon whispered to Dr. Margaret Mahoney with urgency, "The place is afire, we must get them out at once." Nurses and physicians and pastors and other volunteers began pulling patients on their mattresses across the floor or carrying them on cots or stretchers to the exits. The first few were placed in ward ambulance wagons backed up at the doors, but the process was "too slow," as Dr. Mahoney noted. "Four men took each mattress and carried the sufferers out" where "they were put into autos and every manner of vehicle" and transported to hospitals at Golden Gate Park and the Presidio.

Hundreds of patients lay on the massive open floor awaiting evacuation, and outside the blaze was nearing three sides of the wooden pavilion. "Fires were by this time alight all around us," a police officer still up on the roof noticed, "and it was a hard job for us to keep the Pavilion roof from breaking into flames before all the patients could be taken from the building." Seeing the only safe exits were those on the Polk Street side, Dr. Margaret Mahoney helped organize the exodus. Patients in lines at other exits were shifted, and evacuation was quick, efficient, and orderly. As a priest noted: "Never in my experience have I witnessed coolness and intelligence, and readiness of expe-dient" as during those moments. And all were calm. When the fire ate through part of the roof and showed orange flame near the skylight, a patient staring up at it asked the priest, "Do you think you will get us all out?" He responded "most confidently" that they would. Of the hundreds of patients, "some hobbled with help, some had to be carried, cots were pushed, mattresses with their unconscious burdens lifted." They were lined up by staff and volunteers and one by one placed "into the waiting automobiles, wagons, etc., as speedily as possible."

By the time the side wall along Hayes Street caught fire after 11:30 a.m., all 354 patients had been removed. The chief surgeon and his staff carried the last of the operating equipment out as the superintendent and police officer climbed down the inside skylight and rafters and down the stairs. "I believe I was the last person to leave the Pavilion by way of the front door," the officer later reported, "and I know that when I left there was nobody in the front end of the building." Contrary to later rumor, every patient had been safely evacuated, and the bodies of the dead had all been removed. A volunteer driver of the Central Emergency Hospital ambulance truck was the last to leave the Polk Street exit, and he saw the last two bodies—including that of fallen police officer Max Fenner—placed into a laundry wagon for removal to a temporary morgue. The pavilion's demise was swift once it caught fire. A minister who helped escort patients to safety likened the evacuation to "a wild retreat after a lost battle," and he noted, "Hardly had we gotten away when the whole building stood in flames, and in 10 minutes was completely leveled."

In the eleven o'clock hour, the Grand Opera House on Mission Street—where Caruso had been captivating a full house just hours earlier—was "burning with explosive violence," as James Hopper described, taking with it the opera company's scenery, sets, props, costumes, and sheet music for nineteen different operas. And the South of Market firestorm had eaten through to Market Street where it threatened the city's tallest, the Call Building. Flames consuming the structure beside it licked up the skyscraper's granite and sandstone walls and entered the broken windows of an upper floor. Once inside, flames burned through office furniture and fed on oxygen sucked through open transom windows and spread down long hallways and through remaining offices in minutes. Firemen on the far corner of 3rd and Market Streets could see smoke puffing from high office windows and moved their engine to pump from an alley hydrant connected to the Palace Hotel's water supply, and with the assistance of soldiers—one hundred of them, by Assistant Chief Shaughnessy's later account—they "took the line of hose up" the stairs to reach the fire, "but when we got to the second floor the water gave out."

Elevator shafts worked like chimney flues, and flames spread to the baroque domed roof and down to lower floors quickly, forcing firefighters and soldiers to evacuate. A man on a rooftop two blocks away saw the Call Building "burst into flame gradually beginning at the top apparently." Another man on the far side of Market Street—where the fire line was being enforced by soldiers—could see "the whole interior alight, flames pouring from every window." Hopper wrote the skyscraper "was glowing like a phosphorescent worm." And the rest of newspaper row would soon follow.

Across 3rd Street was the eight-story Examiner Building where the earthquake had sent heavy linotype machines on the top floor crashing through seven floors to the basement and threw presses out of gear both there and in the Call Building. Before any worry of fire reached them, employees from both papers ventured across Market Street to the Chronicle Building to discuss issuing a joint extra edition on the disaster. Now within minutes of the Call Building catching fire, the Examiner Building suffered the same fate and was reportedly a "seething bonfire" by noon. And flames spread through the clothing factory and stables and press offices behind it and the adjacent ten-story Monadnock Building, still under construction, leaving only the thirty-eight-foot width of Annie Alley between the blaze and the Palace Hotel, now endangered from two sides.

Inside the Palace, bellboys and cooks soaking the south exterior walls climbed back inside and ran their hose lines up hallways to west-end windows and climbed out onto shaky fire escapes in the face of flames licking from across the narrow alley and leaned their weight out against railings scalding to the touch. Oven-like heat steamed water from the façade as quickly as it was sprayed. Pressure in their hoses weakened noticeably by the fire engine pumping from the hotel's alley hydrant, but it was still strong enough to keep drenching the walls. But out on the hotel's front sidewalk at Market Street, where the fire-escape battle on the far sides could not be seen, an engine company hooked to another of the Palace hydrants and began pumping to a fire engine across Market fighting to contain the blaze in the banking district. In that instant, streams of water jetting from hoses on the hotel's upper floors sagged to drips as the pressure dropped almost to zero.

Workers climbed inside from fire escapes, resigned in disbelief to the hotel's fate. A guest saw a bellboy "weeping bitterly because he and his colleagues now found themselves powerless, and he knew that all their work of the morning had been wasted effort." A few minutes past noon, flames caught wood-frame bay windows on the hotel's back side. James Hopper saw the Palace "was smoking but was still making a magnificent fight." But with no water there was no fight left, and all seven stories of oak floors and redwood paneling and carpeting and rugs and tapestries and paintings and furniture blazed like tinder. As one witness later recalled, "It became in fifteen minutes a volcano of flame."

Two blocks up Market Street in the Academy of Sciences building, Alice Eastwood was still pulling box after box of specimens off strings lowered from six floors up. The Emporium next door had caught fire from the rear and the air in the academy's lobby was growing hotter. Her friend descended the stairs by using the iron banisters as steps and handholds, and Alice grabbed one of the boxes and ran it outside. By that time, flames were emanating from the Emporium's windows next door, and Alice ran across Market Street—empty and guarded by soldiers—to a bank seeking a safe place to deposit the boxes, but "there was a line of men half a block long who were there for their money and it was hopeless." So she turned back, convinced a soldier to let her pass across, and she and her friend and the assistant and the librarian and the museum director carried every box across Market Street. Alice was the only one in the group with cash and hailed a man with a wagon to haul the boxes to a safe place. "I asked how much would the cost be to take the stuff to where I lived," she later wrote, and he responded with "a big price." She worried as she had only $14. "But he charged only three and I was so grateful I gave him four."

At the next block up Market on the far side of 6th Street, Superintendent Frank Leach made it to the roof of the mint around 1:00 p.m. to survey the "uncontrollable demon of a blaze" surrounding him and fifty employees and ten soldiers sealed inside the three-story fortress. To the east, the Lincoln School across 5th Street was engulfed and the fire was eating through the Emporium. To the south across Mission Street, the four-story Cosmopolitan Hotel was ablaze, as were the blocks beyond it and to the southeast. And to the west and north, wood-frame and brick lodgings fronting Market Street and across Mint Avenue and Jessie Alley were all on fire. Leach felt his position was, with understatement, "rather perilous," and that from his vantage point, "[i]t did not seem probable that the structure could withstand that terrific mass of flames that was sweeping down upon us from Market Street."

Blazing wood-frame buildings sixty feet across Mint Avenue radiated "a fierce heat that was hard to stand against." The "whirlwind" of fire blew glowing cinders onto the roof, and refinery worker Joe Hammill and two employees ran a hose up from the third floor. Water pressure from the tanks was sufficient "to force a good stream to any part of the roof" even as "flames leaped 200 feet" against the mint's north wall. Burning buildings collapsed, launching fountains of yellow and orange sparks and flames with a "roaring" sound that was "awful." On all sides, the mint's outer walls burst with reports "like shells exploding" as the oven-like heat expanded moisture trapped in sandstone walls and caused explosive spalling. Down below, workers and soldiers along the outer perimeter of each floor filled buckets with water and readied hoses for a long battle.

Up in the banking district, Lieutenant Raymond Briggs and his soldiers and cases of dynamite pushed east from Portsmouth Square toward the flames, past the fire line, one block then two, past Montgomery Street and toward Sansome until the wall of oven-like heat stopped them. The street rippled with heat waves carrying floating ash and glowing embers, and sidewalks were lined with valuables and inventory from businesses—cash registers and safes and stacked paper bags and large spools of twine and printing presses, too heavy to carry and left behind when no wagons could be found before soldiers cleared the block.

Soot-smeared fire crews in their seventh hour of work stood on Sansome Street fighting the fire with water pumped through one line from a cistern and through another from the Palace Hotel's tanks. But the inferno turned both lines of water into steam, the Palace supply gave out, and flames jumped Sansome and spread through buildings toward Lieutenant Briggs and his soldiers and their dynamite. To stop the blaze's westward march, Briggs and his men took a crate of stick dynamite and a roll of electric wire into a three-story brick building on an alley corner, entering through a ground-floor diner. They could feel the heat from burning buildings across the narrow alleyway and smoke drifted into broken street-front windows of the empty diner. A couple of men ascended to clear the second- and third-floor offices of people and the rest found the basement access and descended stairs into the darkness where they worked by the light of a battery-powered portable flashlight. They tied sticks of dynamite to support beams, rigged them with blasting caps, unspooled lines of wire back upstairs and across the smoky diner floor and out the alley to the far side of the street. There Briggs wrapped the copper ends of the wires around the two posts of the wooden box detonator, and, with firemen and artillerymen around him in protective hunches with hands over ears, he pushed the plunger handle down.

A booming flash blew up a fountain of glass and chunks of masonry and splintered wood, and its shockwave shattered windows up and down the street. The concussion hit the men's ears like a punch and the blast made everything still and hushed and for a few seconds there was a hollow ringing. When the smoke and dust cloud thinned and blew clear of the pile of crumbled brick walls and broken timbers, a new fire crackled in the two-story wood-frame building beside the flaming wreckage.

Like a fighting retreat in the face of an advancing enemy, Lieutenant Briggs and his soldiers and firemen backpedaled to Montgomery Street—now just one block from City Hall—and tried to widen the street's sixty-two-foot width into a firebreak by demolishing more buildings. They brought down the three-story bank on the corner, but the force blew sparks and burning chunks of wood across Montgomery Street and started a new fire in the ground floor of a corner building, setting another block ablaze.

Still under orders not to demolish any buildings not already in contact with fire—or along any new streets without the mayor's permission—Lieutenant Briggs sent a runner back to the Hall of Justice, now less than a block from the fire, to get permission to dynamite buildings along the next block to Kearny Street. And another crew of men under a fire department battalion chief carried dynamite down to Sacramento Street to try to stop the westward march of flames there. Per Mayor Schmitz's orders, they chose buildings already in contact with fire, which only spread flames and made their work more perilous. As an Army officer would later describe, "[T]he charges often had to be laid in buildings already on fire" and dynamite was "carried by hand through showers of sparks." Often after running wires to a detonator a safe distance away, a neighboring explosion would sever or cause a short in the lines, forcing men to run tools near flames to splice and reconnect or climb leaning poles to cut down street wires to use. And by dynamiting buildings near the blaze, as would be reported, their work "accelerated rather than retarded the march of the flames."

Crates of both stick and granular dynamite—typically stored at Goat Island or out on remote Point Pinole safely away from the city—were raced toward Portsmouth Square in speeding automobiles and rattling wagons over broken city streets, answering the mayor's call. Some came from Fort Mason and the Presidio, others from waterfront piers, delivered by tugs from Point Pinole storehouses. And some came up the peninsula from near the San Mateo County line where contractors were working on a new Southern Pacific Railroad route, hauled up into the city in a commandeered automobile "at a speed that was often in excess of fifty miles an hour, over streets that in places were molded into bumpy waves by the earthquake, and were littered with broken masonry and other debris, not to mention nails and splintered glass," as the car company's owner later described. "Such racing in cars that were loaded with dynamite, percussion caps and fuses was a risky pastime."

In Portsmouth Square, John Davis, an Army master electrician who had accompanied the first dynamite from the Presidio that morning, was in charge of supplying demolition crews with explosives. From his tent surrounded by stacked crates of dynamite and powder, he "gave out high explosives to at least a dozen different parties." From there, makeshift teams of firemen and police officers and soldiers—all with orders to attempt firebreaks only in structures already aflame—began scattering with stick dynamite to fires South of Market, in the Western Addition, and the banking district.

By the one o'clock hour, dynamite blasts, jarring even among the already shocking sounds of the day, sounded throughout the city "like the report of heavy cannonading" or "thunder." An Army officer at the Presidio could hear "the sound of explosions" from the banking district, which to his ears "suggested a battle going on three miles away." Residents still indoors and refugees trudging toward the ferries could hear and feel the detonations that boomed with increasing frequency from that hour forward for three days. "At first we did not know what it was," one girl remembered years later. "There would be a fearful commotion, a rumble, then severe shaking which was terribly frightening." She found the concussive demolitions "terrifying and so hard on the nerves." An artillery officer later recounted that "every time they set off a blast a shower of glass, brick, stone, etc., loosened by the earthquake would come tumbling down in the street," and even he was unnerved: "I began to wish I were somewhere else."

In the Ferry Building's ticket office, Thomas Chase's two coworkers arrived late, one after a five-mile walk from his home where he had been hit by pieces of his fallen chimney. They spent the morning distributing ferry tickets to all comers "in order to keep the crowds moving as the fire was spreading fast." By the noon hour, crowds had "thinned out" due to Thomas's work and the quick work of captains and crews of ferries and steamers evacuating the crowds and the efforts of police officers and soldiers in guiding people safely around fire lines and the exhaustive battles fought by firemen to keep blazes from reaching the wharf with bay water thanks to Lieutenant Freeman's initiative and coordination. And casualties were arriving from throughout the city and from the evacuation of Mechanics' Pavilion. "Some had heads, arms, hands, legs and feet bandaged," Thomas noted. They were attended by physicians who had spent the morning working in the pavilion and by medical personnel Lieutenant Freeman had brought, and "very soon," as one physician reported, "a naval boat came over from Goat Island, where there was a naval hospital, and removed the whole group."

When the fire reached East Street, the pile of luggage "ignited and in a short time that was a pile of ashes," as Thomas Chase observed. Flames of South of Market's firestorm jumped Market Street's wide expanse, showing first as "a little wisp of smoke" in a window of the Hotel Terminus on the street's north side; then orange flames flickered and glass shattered and flammable interiors crackled and smoke churned from upper floors and adjoining buildings went the same way. "Within a half-hour's time Market Street was going good," Thomas observed, adding, "It was not long until all avenues of escape were cut off from the Ferry Building." Fire hoses snaked from the Navy tug *Sotoyomo* and the Italian bark *Elisa* across the wharf and through propped-open doors of the Ferry Building to fire engines on East Street where firemen battled the blaze that had jumped Market Street and converged with the harbor district fire. But "[t]he water just went up in steam and they had to give up," Thomas Chase observed. "A bucket of water would have done as much good." Heat could be felt within the Ferry Building, and Thomas and his coworkers "momentarily expected the wharves and the Ferry Building to ignite." They ceased ticket sales, locked money in vaults, "closed up shop," and "opened the gates to what was left of the crowd" to give them free passage "to safety and the boats."

The firestorm South of Market was four blocks deep in most places along its length, but nearer the waterfront it had only reached two blocks to Howard Street, where a battle was being fought by workers to keep fires from spreading to their offices and warehouses and lumber and coal yards. On the south side of Howard, the new five-story J.A. Folger & Co. headquarters, barely a year old and built soundly of brick over steel frame above wood pilings driven deep into soft fill, had withstood the earthquake without structural cracks or crumbles or even broken glass (a broken flywheel on its roaster steam engine was the only reported damage). Inside, James Folger II, forty-one-year-old son of the late founder, and "as many of his men as could be gathered" were keeping cinders and flaming chunks of the Howard Street fire from entering the building. Without water, their only defense was keeping the building's windows—lacking wire frames—from breaking in the intense heat. With rolls of packing paper from the fourth-floor packaging room and labels and glue from the second-floor label room, as would be reported, they "pasted them wet upon the panes of glass to keep them from cracking, and thus [held] out the heat and the fire." Their resourcefulness kept the building sealed even as heat inside spiked and conditions outside disintegrated. Salvation came in the form of firemen soaking the building's outer walls with salt water from the bay through long hoses laid out along Howard Street from Lieutenant Freeman's vessels at the pier, the *Active* and *Leslie*.

At the Howard Street pier, the Army harbor tug *Slocum* arrived from Fort Mason, connected to a fire engine, and started pumping. Noticing the local battalion chief "was completely exhausted," Freeman "assumed control" of all fire crews in the neighborhood. He ordered more hose wagons to be brought up and directed firefighters and sailors to unroll lengths of hose to connect— some at a distance of one thousand feet and more—and joined with the lines connected to the strong pumps of the Navy and Army tugs. As Midshipman John Pond would recount, Freeman rushed to cheer on crews manning each hose line with yells of "Sock it to 'em!" By midafternoon they had kept the fire on the north side of Howard Street and the west side of Main Street, saving five blocks of businesses, including the Folger Coffee Company Building, the Mutual Light & Electric Company, a lumberyard, and the four-story, two-hundred-room Sailors' Home. But it was only one end of a firestorm burning wider and faster through South of Market, just as others had burned through the harbor and banking districts and Hayes Valley and toward City Hall and Chinatown and Nob Hill. And throughout the city, firemen of more than sixty separate companies fought to coordinate a strategy to cover longer fire lines around a growing disaster zone with communication limited to yelled voices and messages run from one burning block to another.

9. A Great City Vanishing in Flame

WHEN US NINTH Circuit Judge William Morrow picked up the phone in his San Rafael home early that morning after the earthquake and called "Central" to inquire about how things looked down in San Francisco, the operator told him wires into the city were not working. In San Francisco, Jacob Levison picked up his telephone to call his brother but was met only with the silence of a dead line and concluded "the telephone wires were broken." With wires and lines twisted in knots around downed poles and torn apart, telephone and telegraph communications throughout the city, as the Army would report, "were completely destroyed."

Communication lines to and from the city were effectively severed. There was no mail delivery, and the last newspapers to roll off that morning's presses carried yesterday's news—now a time forgotten. At most telegraph offices, multi-cell main batteries were either broken or disconnected, cutting the current so no messages could be transmitted through the insulated, galvanized iron wires of underwater telegraph cables crossing the bay or the Pacific, cutting San Francisco off almost entirely from the outside world. Almost.

The Navy had recently established wireless stations in the area, and before 6:00 a.m., a wireless message was sent from Goat Island up to Mare Island (the message relayed to Lieutenant Freeman by his radioman during breakfast aboard the *Perry*). This was followed by a shorter plea for help from San Francisco: "Earthquake. Town on fire. Send marines and tugs." The same was relayed south, reaching the DeForest wireless station in San Diego and vessels of the Pacific Squadron—the cruisers *Chicago* and *Boston* and the gunboat *Princeton*—all then underway to Long Beach. When squadron commander-in-chief Admiral Goodrich received the message aboard his flagship *Chicago* and confirmed the news with the San Diego wireless station, he ordered the *Chicago* to San Francisco "at full speed" and ordered "fires started under all boilers" of all other available squadron vessels—the *Boston* and *Princeton*, the cruiser *Marblehead*, and the destroyer *Paul Jones*—to follow.

In San Francisco, many people rushed to the telegraph offices after finding telephone lines dead. Before 6:00 a.m., Sarah Phillips and her roommate went "directly" to the nearest Western Union office, which, although "a wreck," was already crowded with "hundreds," but when they "worked [their] way through the debris to the desk" piled with "telegrams waiting to be sent," they were told "the wires were all down." Within a half hour of the earthquake, George Way walked from the Palace Hotel to the Postal Telegraph Office across Market Street and wrote out a message for his family in Detroit: "Lost everything, am safe. Thank God." But George's message went in the stack waiting to be sent, since the one machine on which operators were trying to transmit messages, as he later complained, "was monopolized by the press."

But even the press struggled to get anything sent. The night editor and operator at the Associated Press office in the banking district were at their desks when the earthquake hit and broke their telegraph line. They wrote a brief bulletin and carried it upstairs to the Western Union office in their building and filed it to be sent in case lines were restored. When their boss, the AP's western superintendent, arrived at the office "after a rapid sprint" from his home, he wrote a bulletin: "A terrific earthquake struck San Francisco and vicinity today. The entire business district is demolished; all wires are down. City is now on fire." He rushed it down to the Postal Telegraph Office on Market Street where he "stood over" the operator who "tested and manipulated" the machine working on "a feeble" connection with the Chicago office. "Finally," as the superintendent would later recount, "there was a hopeful click and away went the news to Chicago." The time was roughly 6:40 a.m.

Up in the AP office, the day editor and stenographer arrived and, in the superintendent's words, "the story of the earthquake was being written as rapidly as the typewriters could work." They ran the two-block distance between their office and the Postal Telegraph Office, where they were given a second line that had been restored after its main battery was reconnected. Their "news commenced to go out," the superintendent later noted, but "[j]ust after a fair start the wire failed, and we danced up and down with impatience." At Postal Telegraph Offices in Chicago and New York, operators huddled over incoming ticker-tape messages, reading them aloud as AP reporters transcribed in violent haste until the tapes stopped again "almost immediately."

From there news of the disaster zoomed eastward through wires from city to city, then circled back westward where it finally reached the state capital in Sacramento via "a great circuit" of thousands of miles. Governor George Pardee sent a telegram to Mayor Schmitz: "Am appalled and overwhelmed by the great calamity to San Francisco, only meager details of which have reached me. I extend sympathy and assurance of my earnest desire to help those in distress in any manner in which I am able." And word reached Washington, DC, where President Roosevelt dictated a telegram to Governor Pardee that he had received "rumors of great disaster," was frustrated to "know nothing of the real facts," and offered "any assistance I can render." Pardee responded, echoing similar frustration with "the interruption of telegraph communications" and admitting the "extent of disaster [is] not well known here." And the president also cabled Mayor Schmitz extending his "most earnest sympathy" and assuring him, "If there is anything the Federal Government can do to aid you it will be done."

But it would take hours for those messages to reach San Francisco. For at least three long hours that morning, no messages made it into the city by wire, and in the city's Western Union offices, outgoing messages piled up. In telegraph offices in other cities, notices were posted that any messages filed to San Francisco were "subject to indefinite delay." Only a handful (including those first AP bulletins) made it out of the city over feeble connections from the Postal Telegraph Office. One official message, a handwritten plea by Mayor Schmitz to the Oakland mayor for help, was tapped out by the Postal Telegraph's assistant manager around 8:00 a.m. and received across the bay in Oakland: "Mayor Mott, Oakland. Send fire engines, hose, also dynamite immediately. E.E. Schmitz, Mayor."

San Francisco's chief operator for Western Union, Harry Jeffs, lived in Oakland, and after the earthquake he left his home and rode the train out to the Oakland Long Wharf, where the cables linking San Francisco with telegraph stations to the east emerged from the bay and ran into tangles and knots around insulators on wooden crossarms twisted atop poles. Looking for any line with a signal, Jeffs grabbed a pocket relay sounder from the pier telegraph office and "climbed the telegraph poles at intervals," connecting the device to test each wire looking for a response. Finding each line dead, he would run down to climb another pole and repeat. Finally at 8:30 a.m. atop a pole near the water's edge in West Oakland, Jeffs found a "tangle in the mass of wires," straightened it out, then connected with each one until he "received a response from Sacramento," as it would be reported. On his handheld relay, he then tapped out "the first story of the disaster to go out over the Western Union wires." Jeffs then connected that line with a long wire reaching back to the pier to restore telegraph communication between San Francisco and Oakland—effectively reconnecting the city with the world. At least for a while.

With a working wire, telegraph operators began transmitting messages, copy from AP reporters, messages from public officials or military to Sacramento and Washington, DC, and reassuring notes of survival ("All well and safe" or "Lost Everything. Am Safe. Thank God") from residents to friends and family. As author Philip Fradkin later described them, they read "like hurried missives desperately flung from a dying civilization, or firsthand accounts transmitted from a sinking passenger liner."

By that time in the morning, two offices of the Postal Telegraph and two of the Western Union were already destroyed by fire along with stacks of messages never sent, and more offices followed—in the Palace Hotel, the Emporium, South of Market, and in the banking and harbor districts. But in a shrinking pocket of safety on the north side of Market Street, operator George Parsons stayed at his desk in the Postal Telegraph Office all morning in the midst of "a total wreck" of damage and worked by window light sending real-time news bulletins over the working wire even as the flames reached the south side of Market Street and spread in both directions and the banking district fire threatened from the office's north and east. "The Call Building is in full blaze now," he sent at 10:30 a.m., "and it is only question of minutes for us in Postal here." Thirty-five minutes later, after Parsons wired that he was visited by police officers warning him of the blaze's proximity and ordering the AP reporters to leave, the following wire darted through other cities: "San Francisco says fire within few doors now. They are going to move out right now."

Newspaper reporters in cities and towns throughout the country hung on every AP bulletin from San Francisco and began writing articles about the calamity to be printed in extras or evening editions. Headlines broadcast the first news residents in other states would read of the disaster: "EARTHQUAKE AND FIRE WRECK AND RUIN THE CITY OF SAN FRANCISCO" and "SAN FRANCISCO IS VISITED BY AN APPALLING EARTHQUAKE AND FIRE." Articles filled every page announcing, "Flames rage unchecked," "All the water pressure is gone," "Fire department is practically helpless," and "buildings being blown up," along with shocking news that "The city is now under martial law" and "Soldiers will shoot on sight anybody found stealing." Articles included devastating numbers of casualties, reporting thousands injured and hundreds dead, with a few papers claiming inaccurately that "5,000 dead have been found," and others repeating outlandish reports that the "dead will probably number 20,000."

Desperate for an eyewitness account of the disaster, *Collier's* sent a telegram to writer Jack London up at his home on his Glen Ellen ranch offering to pay him as a special correspondent to travel into San Francisco and write the story of what he saw, with the price to be negotiated later. Writer and editor Charmian London accompanied her husband for the journey, starting on horseback across heights of their ranch where from forty miles distant, as she would describe, "a mighty column of smoke in the direction of San Francisco" was visible. They rode to the nearest train station and caught a train to Santa Rosa with the hope of catching another train down, then riding a ferry to San Francisco to report from the scene.

But even within the city, accurate news was difficult to get. People knew only what they saw—the damage to their own home or business or street or district or along the streets that they trudged with belongings. And they imagined what was happening at the foot of smoke columns billowing from behind building tops framing their limited view. With no local phones or means of gathering updated news, rumor and misinformation spread faster than the fires. In a letter marked "10:30 a.m." a witness wrote, "The Ferry Building toppled over in the Bay." Another resident heard that "[t]he Cliff House had fallen into the ocean." Even wild fiction about other cities spread through ranks of San Franciscans watching their own city burn. One woman heard that "Chicago had been levelled to the earth" and a "Tidal wave had engulfed New York." Another heard that "Chicago was under seven feet of water, Salt Lake City was prostrate, Kansas City was burning up, Seattle and Portland were both under water, Los Angeles had been shaken by the earthquake and was on fire."

Rumors gained traction inside San Francisco partly because local news outlets were paralyzed. By afternoon, the Call Building was gutted by fire and the Examiner Building was still burning. Many of their employees had moved to the Chronicle Building, where editors and reporters and typesetters from all three papers now worked on an extra edition even as the Palace Hotel blazed directly across Market Street and the banking district fire threatened from two directions. The city editor had arrived early that morning just after the earthquake and found the building still had power and was "not seriously hurt." He was early enough to take the elevator to the ninth-floor stereotyping room before the power was turned off. Others who followed climbed the stairs. Printing in that era was a five-step process, requiring type to be set, then a thick, soft sheet of paper-mache was hammered over the metal type to get a clear impression of every line and letter, then it was placed into a semicylindrical mold into which molten metal was poured to create an impression of the page, which could then be rolled through ink and printed onto newspaper.

When the employees reached the stereotyping room that morning they found "three or four tons of molten metal" had been thrown out of the metal heating pot and "splashed over and completely covered the machinery," and a portion of the outside wall had crashed in over the cutting machinery, leaving the room "open to the heavens," as machine operator Fred Ewald later recounted. But even without power and no water for the boilers, reporters scratched out articles describing the developing catastrophe, and typesetters and machine operators "tore out the doors and broke up the furniture, getting all the wood or anything else that would serve as fuel" to melt enough metal in the pot to print a two-page extra.

"I don't believe a single man in the outfit went up those stairs for the purpose of earning a day's wages," Ewald later explained. "We went up because . . . we had to do something to try and quiet the people who were so terribly upset and frightened by false reports." But with no power they would be unable to get the papers through the presses in the basement. And seeing the fire closing in on them from three sides, they knew hope for an extra edition that day was lost. From there, as the city editor later noted, the editors and staff of the three newspapers "agreed to try to publish a one-for-all paper somehow and somewhere Thursday morning."

Against all odds, one newspaper covering the earthquake and fire would be issued that day from inside the city. The San Francisco *Daily News* was a small upstart paper in its third year of business. With short, one-cent daily issues sold primarily in working-class neighborhoods of the Mission and South of Market, the "penny paper" had the smallest circulation of the city's newspapers and would earn a reputation as "the littlest, scrappiest newspaper in San Francisco." With no power to run the press at the paper's small South of Market office, its editor decided to move two blocks west to a smaller printing office with manual presses. With one page of news written, linotype operators returned "to the old-time plan of setting type by hand" onto two presses, as the editor would later explain. One flat press was "manipulated by foot power" and the cylindrical press was spun "by means of a monkey wrench fastened to the fly wheel." The work was strenuous, and each employee took turns printing "several thousand copies" of the single-page extra, which they distributed for free.

Beneath a headline "HUNDREDS DEAD!" was a list of the "Known Dead" so far, including policeman Max Fenner, and a list of "Other Dead" and "Injured," including those still at Mechanics' Pavilion that morning. And it reported fires in multiple buildings, difficulties faced by the fire department, the collapse of the Valencia Hotel, and the wreck of the Majestic Theatre and City Hall. The information packed into the single page—proven mostly accurate even after more than a century of archival corroboration—was a valuable injection of factual news for those it reached that day.

In another small printing office down in the Mission a dozen blocks south of where the *Daily News* extra edition was being printed, a press was spinning out copies of a different document at an even faster rate. Sometime after first issuing his "shoot to kill" order that morning, Mayor Schmitz asked an attorney to draft a public proclamation. Schmitz approved the wording, and from there it was carried to the printing office and by noon, as would be reported, "soldiers outside the shop stopped passers-by and compelled them to take turns at the treadle of the press." Five thousand six-by-nine-inch circulars were printed and "sent out by couriers in automobiles as fast as printed and posted on lamp posts and telegraph poles all over the city." Each read as follows:

> The Federal Troops, the members of the Regular Police Force and all Special Police Officers have been authorized by me to KILL any and all persons found engaged in Looting or in the Commission of Any Other Crime.
>
> I have directed all the Gas and Electric Lighting Co.'s not to turn on Gas or Electricity until I order them to do so. You may therefore expect the city to remain in darkness for an indefinite time.
>
> I request all citizens to remain at home from darkness until daylight every night until order is restored.
>
> I WARN all Citizens of the danger of fire from Damaged or Destroyed Chimneys, Broken or Leaking Gas Pipes or Fixtures, or any like cause.
>
> E. E. SCHMITZ, Mayor

By the time these hit the streets, at least 1,500 armed soldiers were patrolling the city. A physician who helped evacuate Mechanics' Pavilion noticed on his journey through downtown that "the streets were policed by soldiers, sailors and marines armed with rifles." Out in the Western Addition, a man noted just after breakfast his neighborhood was "already patrolled by the soldiers from the Presidio," and a woman up on Nob Hill saw passing her "at full gallop a company of United States Cavalry," and concluded, "The city was under martial law."

It was not. But even though city government was not displaced and military units within the city were temporarily acting under the orders of the mayor, to residents and refugees throughout the city facing rifle-wielding troops patrolling streets and sidewalks and entering homes and businesses, the distinction made little difference. And it meant even less after the noon hour when thousands of freshly printed, tan-colored notices began appearing on telegraph poles and lampposts and trees with the eye-catching "PROCLAMATION" followed by five sentences from the mayor, with two words capitalized: "WARN" and "KILL."

From early that morning, soldiers were the blunt end of Mayor Schmitz's orders, the first of which was shutting down liquor sales. A police officer who accompanied an Army sergeant sent "to clean out and close all the saloons" toward the waterfront South of Market before the fire had reached there later recounted, "We went into every place that was open, drove out all the men that were in them, and raked down all the bottles from the shelves with a big stick." After telling patrons it was the mayor's orders, "there was little or no trouble."

The city directory listed nearly 1,900 licensed liquor dealers, though it was known that the unofficial number was higher. Soldiers and police went to many—bars, saloons, taverns, dance halls—and ordered all liquor sales stopped. If any business was later found in violation, as a police captain reported, "every ounce of liquor in the establishment was turned into the sewer." In many places, soldiers did not issue warnings or wait for a violation. Sarah Phillips soon wrote that after the mayor ordered saloons closed, "the soldiers entered each one & broke every bottle and barrel head & the liquor ran out in the gutters." And in some neighborhoods, soldiers went beyond the order and punished mere *possession* of alcohol: "Liquor of any kind found on anyone was taken away and destroyed," noted thirty-year-old Charles Leithead of enforcement out in the Western Addition. "Men with suspiciously bulging pockets were searched," and after forced searches, "soldiers broke bottle after bottle."

The mayor had also ordered troops to maintain order and kill looters. Troops in the city that first morning and afternoon were all active-duty "regulars." Army soldiers and, by midday, sailors and marines were also stationed nearer the waterfront. Troops who happened to be stationed on military posts in or near San Francisco were from all over the country. They lacked the local familiarity and community trust policemen like Sergeant Jesse Cook had worked daily to build. Some were still in their teens and early twenties fresh from training, and a few were in their thirties or forties with combat experience on foreign soil, but almost none were trained for policing the residents and neighborhoods of an American city; all were armed with live ammunition. Many heard the mayor give the shoot-to-kill order and they all heard their officers and NCOs repeat it. And they saw it in bold print on the bulletins they'd posted.

Most soldiers encountering looters exercised restraint despite the mayor's order. One man later wrote (anonymously) of going "into a place where they were ransacking a store . . . to see what I could get." Seeing little was left to take, he began to leave when "two soldiers emerged from the rear" and yelled, "Get out of here," and at that, "Everybody made for the door." The stampede was too large for the front door, and with so many pressed against the big show window, it crashed out onto the sidewalk. "That piece of excitement," he admitted, "frightened me about ten times more than the earthquake."

While nobody was shot in that melee, it was inevitable a soldier somewhere would shoot rather than yell a warning. And that day it happened on a street corner a block from Union Square where, according to a police captain, a man "was caught while he was making an attempt to burglarize" Shreve & Company, where watches, diamonds, jewelry, and silverware were sold. The suspected thief "was turned over to a soldier who killed him and left his body to be consumed by the fire." Two days later, Arnold Genthe took a photograph of the charred, blackened corpse facedown on the street, and later another photographer took a shot of the same body.

The shooting happened at a location (Post and Grant Streets) where the few state guardsmen in the city were not yet patrolling, contradicting General Funston's later claim that "there is no well-authenticated case of a <u>single person having been killed by regular troops,</u>" a point he found necessary to underline in his report. Many tall tales would circulate that insinuated summary executions by the military were widespread during the disaster, and their number and severity would grow with each retelling. But this well-authenticated case corroborated by witnesses and evidence was not the only one that day, and there would be more in the days to come.

Many soldiers ordered to guard certain buildings—the mint, main Post Office, Custom House, City Hall—pitched in to assist employees or firemen in dousing flames. And around the expanding fire they enforced fire lines, where they stood side by side across streets with rifles and held crowds back with the tips of bayonets, leading to occasional tension. Near the north end of the Hayes Valley fire that afternoon, an exhausted fireman ran up to the fire line at Gough Street near Golden Gate Avenue and yelled for volunteers from the crowd of onlookers, but "so thoroughly cowed were the citizens by the soldiers that no one responded," an attorney in the crowd later recounted. He stepped forward to volunteer "and was stopped by a soldier who ordered me back," and only after a "prolonged argument" was he allowed through to help. When he reached the hose line, the fireman asked why more did not volunteer, and the man explained many were willing but "were afraid of the soldiers." So the fireman ran back to the fire line and urged soldiers to let volunteers pass through.

But in other places where troops worked to keep people at a safe distance from fires, there was little tension. "The crowd was most orderly and we had no trouble," an Army officer reported, adding that only when "we had to move them back a block to get them out of the way of the fire department and dynamite squad" did a few protest they needed to grab things from their homes or businesses. "We passed most of them with some slight identification," the officer explained, "and so far as possible allowed them to remove their stuff."

Of all the challenges thrown on the military during the disaster, the job of relief—providing food and water, rendering medical assistance, reestablishing communications, and providing emergency shelter and sanitation—was the largest and the one for which it was best equipped. During that first day, the most immediate need for residents and refugees was finding food and fresh water, by afternoon a crisis as pressing as the spreading fires. Tens of thousands displaced from their homes had only what food they thought to grab as they left. Laundryman Thomas Angove, in a park with other refugees, "ate soda crackers and cured ham" for his afternoon meal and "begg[ed] coffee from a good-natured woman" nearby. In Union Square, thirsty refugees lined up for a drink from a "sprinkling cart." Many had no food and those with change in their pockets bought food at any store they could find still open. One man walked from Union Square to a grocery and scrounged "twenty cents worth of cookies and ten cents worth of cheese." Another managed to get "two loaves of bread, crackers, cakes, canned goods, meats, butter" from a store at noon. But he could see even then that "[a]ll groceries were going up rapidly in price and it was apparent that there would be a scarcity soon."

After noon, many grocery stores not already cleaned out of inventory raised prices to oppressive levels. One resident wrote of stores "selling at ruinous prices," such as 5 cents for a dozen crackers or 25 cents for a loaf of bread. Another wrote of leaving a breadline at one store because "a woman said she had bought the last loaf for .50" and another complained "a loaf had cost her a dollar." When soldiers caught a grocer on California Street charging a dollar for a loaf and $1.50 for a dozen eggs, they "immediately took possession of the store and made the clerks sell everything at old prices," as one witness noted. In other places, soldiers put a stop to price gouging by ordering provisions be given away for free. "[T]he stores were all thrown open," a boy in Noe Valley later recounted. "People could go in and help themselves." Out in the Western Addition, soldiers stationed at the doors of the California Baking Company coordinated free bread distribution throughout the day. Troops also gave away food from stores in the path of the fire, as one witness saw soldiers enter a grocery near the flames and "shove the contents into the street for people to pick up."

Sergeant Jesse Cook had been on his feet since midnight, and in the hours since the earthquake, he and his officers had helped maintain fire lines and assisted thousands of evacuees in escaping the burning city. But he worried about his wife and daughter and the condition of his house. By the time he approached his captain at two o'clock to get permission to go home, he had been on duty for fourteen hours and fire was threatening the station itself. His captain sent him home to his family with the order, "If they are all right, come back, but if they are not, stay with them." Cook also obtained permission for one of his officers, Harry Schmidt, to check on his own home and family.

Cook ordinarily made the daily commute back to his Ashbury Heights home by riding a red Market/Haight line cable car for free—a courtesy extended to police officers—and hopping off within a block of his Delmar Street house. But with no cars running, he walked the three miles home on foot.

Officer Schmidt managed to catch a ride on a passing wagon down to his apartment in the Mission where he was relieved to see his neighborhood was not on fire and his house—with a broken chimney—was "standing all right." He caught sight of his wife and two daughters returning from a neighbor's home, who "were glad to see me," an understatement considering the dire rumors they had heard all day, fearing he "might have been killed."

Jesse Cook finished his long walk to find his wife and daughter fine and "not a dollar's worth of damage had been caused to our home." Hungry, he and his family fashioned an oven in the street and cooked a meal, joining neighbors doing the same. But with the crisis throughout his beat and his city worsening and fires spreading at a faster rate, Sergeant Cook bid his family farewell and began the long walk back to his station where more long hours awaited him.

By midafternoon, the Palace Hotel "was well on fire" with flames incinerating every elegant feature. In the Call Building "every window from top to bottom sent out flames the full size of the window." An orange inferno enveloped the melting frame of Mechanics' Pavilion. And the insides of City Hall's crumbled ruins were now "blazing." Rather than evacuate to the west or escape by ferry, a good number of refugees climbed hills to higher ground north of the growing inferno and gazed from rooftops or stood on sidewalks to watch the spectacle of San Francisco burning. One witness on Telegraph Hill "where already hundreds of homeless people had congregated with their few possessions" watched what he described as a "furnace destroying our dear old City."

On Nob Hill, ten-year-old Helen Huntington went with her family to watch the progress of the fire from atop the roof of the nearly completed, nine-story Fairmont Hotel where her father was to be the general manager on its grand opening a few weeks away. Looking over the rooftop's low parapet at the overwhelming panorama of the burning city below, Helen saw "gigantic fires" that were "sending smoke and fire billowing miles into the sky," and as she later recalled, "It was a frightening scene." Also on Nob Hill, a woman noticed "the smoke was almost obscuring the scene by this time and it made everything look ghastly—the fire was traveling almost a block an hour by now."

In the same hour, a man wrote, "Solid blocks along Market Street are burning now," and "nearly every large building on the South side of Market Street is burning or is in a heap of debris." Still monitoring the firestorm from a car, James Hopper described downtown streets that afternoon "as those of a barricaded city in the throes of its last assault," with "one great flame" from the waterfront to a dozen blocks up Market still spreading and "the blocks literally melting before its advance."

Afternoon sun was directly overhead in a cloudless sky, but even to people standing on the highest points of Nob Hill, its light was "almost invisible through the smoke." What had been a "dense, spreading white cloud," as one woman described it, "became black and smoky." An eight-year-old boy would later remember, "Toward mid-day the sky became darker and darker and at times seemed of a reddish hue." The air was hot even to people far away from the fires with mercury nearing eighty degrees, and as the inferno continued to spread, the "close and humid" air nearer the flames became, as one resident would understate, "very smoky and too warm." There was "a fine ash carried by the wind"—a "spanking breeze," as James Hopper described it—and residents still inside homes near the fire's edge noticed ashes "sifting in through doors and windows."

Over in the Panhandle of Golden Gate Park across from her parents' Fell Street home, twelve-year-old Marion Baldwin was sitting atop a haystack watching the fires when a man on a buggy rode up. While his dray horse "nibbled a little bit on the hay," the man asked Marion to get her father, Edward Baldwin, owner of the Ferry Drug Company. When her father stepped from the house, the man handed him a letter inviting him downtown for "a meeting of citizens, and to get there as fast as he could." Edward rushed inside, "put on his city clothes and his derby hat," then emerged and hopped on Marion's new bicycle to race downtown, looking "kind of funny" with his coattails flapping as he pedaled away.

The meeting was set for 3:00 p.m. in the basement of the Hall of Justice. Mayor Schmitz had acted on an idea hatched by two men—one a capitalist and the other an attorney, neither a public official but both with the mayor's ear—to form a committee of San Francisco citizens "to solve the problems" confronting the city, and he sent messengers summoning the "men of the community" he deemed "best equipped" for that purpose.

The chosen men began appearing at the Hall of Justice, summoned from their homes or businesses by delivery drivers or soldiers, and were directed downstairs into one end of the basement where long tables had been arranged. They were attorneys, real estate investors, a former judge, an opera house manager, railway executives, a former city attorney. Former mayor Phelan was present. Abe Ruef, giving directions to dynamite squads, was not. Citizens "best fitted for the task" had been selected, according to Schmitz, "irrespective of their politics or their social standing." And those he deemed "best fitted" included no South of Market residents, no residents of Chinatown, no representatives of North Beach's Italian American community, no Black residents, and no women.

Even as the invitees gathered, fires outside crept closer. Sixteen-year-old Howard Livingston had walked along California Street from his parents' Western Addition home to "see the flames for the first time." He followed it over Nob Hill and into the banking district to the intersection of Kearny Street, where he was halted by police keeping people back from the fire. "I watched the burning buildings and was impressed by the intensity and swiftness of flames" as they "seemed to start at street level and soon envelope the entire building." He looked further down California Street beyond the fire line and "could hardly see past the first building, as flames completely filled the street between tall buildings." The firestorm in the banking district had, like the one South of Market, reached temperatures above the autoignition level for dry wood surfaces, and as hellish air blew through street canyons lined with tall buildings, flames blossomed in waves.

A few blocks away, Charles Kendrick walked down Montgomery Street and saw the far side of Market—where he had walked two hours earlier—was "now a veritable inferno." Charles and two friends stood on Montgomery and watched the Palace and Grand Hotels burn. In the roasting air of the Postal Telegraph Office in the building beside them, telegraph operators dripping with sweat were forced out by soldiers. "City practically ruined by fire," read the last wire tapped out at 2:20 p.m. "No water. It's awful. There is no communication anywhere and entire phone system is busted. I want to get out of here or be blown up."

The operators grabbed every instrument they could carry—"typewriters and all," as one of them later recounted—and loaded them in a Cowell Cement Company wagon "and rode to the ferry landing to go to Oakland." The heat also forced Charles Kendrick and his two friends to run back up Montgomery Street away from Market ("[T]he three of us took off our coats and held them before our faces as a shield against the heat") just as the buildings beside them "exploded into flame." The men broke into a sprint as "clouds of black smoke billowed down upon us until it was dark as midnight and we lost contact with one another." In the smoky space around him Charles saw "chimneys and sheet iron from the rooftops" tossed by "a cyclone-like vacuum" onto the pavement. He turned from Montgomery, dropped to his knees and crawled down another street "on all fours" to another block "where, emerging from the vacuum, I was able to stand up."

Four blocks away, more than fifty men in the Hall of Justice basement crowded around long tables beneath the low ceiling, fanning themselves with their hats. The air was dank and still and hot. Mayor Schmitz and the police chief and an Army captain and a few staffers entered at 3:00 p.m. Schmitz declared to the gathering—what the next morning's newspapers would call a committee of "50 representative citizens of San Francisco"—that he had ceased liquor sales and ordered all policemen and military troops in the city to use lethal force "without hesitation in the cases of any and all miscreants who may seek to take advantage of the city's awful misfortune," and he announced "three men have already been shot down without mercy for looting." While this was not the case, word had in fact been passed to him that "three boys had looted a store," as he would state under oath months later. Schmitz did not seek advice or feedback (reportedly announcing his shoot-to-kill order to the committee with "Let it also be understood . . ."), but he later proudly recounted they "endorsed the action I had taken."

To the weighty topic of relief, Mayor Schmitz announced that 2,400 tents supplied by the Army were being erected on the grounds of Jefferson Square, Golden Gate Park, and the Presidio. He explained that wagons and automobiles had been commandeered that morning to transport the injured for medical treatment, and more would be needed for relief efforts. To this, someone interjected that expressmen were charging evacuees as much as $30 to haul items (many were actually charging as much as $50), which "provoked great indignation" from the gathering. In response, Schmitz turned to the police chief: "Tell your men to seize the wagons of all such would-be extortionists, and make use of them for the public good."

Dynamite detonations on the streets above sent sharp shocks through the basement, rattling windows. Men held down the table tensely and looked up at the ceiling as thuds from crashing buildings followed. The meeting continued with more urgency. A Finance Committee was formed to address the threshold question of funding. More committees would be formed and led by men from this group—for water, food, sanitation, temporary shelter, medical supplies, transportation—but they could wait for a later meeting in a safer place. Demolition teams were getting closer, and when one nearby explosion "brought glass and cornice work in the Hall of Justice crashing down," two men urged Mayor Schmitz to evacuate the building: "Your life is too valuable, Mayor, at this dreadful juncture for any unnecessary risk to be taken." The meeting was removed to Portsmouth Square with a plan to resume at 8:00 p.m. in the Fairmont Hotel on Nob Hill.

Eleven blocks away in the South of Market firestorm, the battle to save the mint was in its sixth hour. Superintendent Frank Leach and a handful of his employees ran their hose line from one end of the "shaky roof" to another, extinguishing any flames that caught. The blaze was especially close on the north side where buildings three, four, and five stories tall across Jessie Alley were fully aflame. Winds would shift suddenly and send flames taller than the building sweeping in across the rooftop and forcing the men back.

Worried the fire might enter the mint through fourth-floor windows below the roofline, refinery worker Joe Hammill hurried back downstairs to run the building's second hose line into the fourth floor. Although the windows were still holding, the heat on the floor was tremendous. A few of the deep interior wood window frames ignited, and, with two of his refinery workers, Hammill sprayed "the blazing woodwork." The alley looked like a furnace through glass panes that bent from the heat, then "melted down like butter." Instantly "the flames leaped in and the smoke nearly choked us," as Hammill recorded. "[W]e were ordered downstairs, for it was supposed that the mint was doomed."

Frank Leach and the others on the roof ran their hose back downstairs to the refinery through floors now "almost dark as night by a mass of black smoke sweeping in" through melted-away windows. Mint workers ran buckets of water up the stairs into the "veritable furnaces" of the second and third floors, then held their breath in sprints toward window openings where flames were shooting in. After dousing any furniture or walls or ceiling that ignited, they sprinted back to catch their breath and refill their buckets. Soldiers had retreated into the building and stood at the large main doors, "nearly strangling" from smoke pouring in as any breathable air turned hotter and hotter. As Joe Hammill later wrote of those long hours trapped in a stifling fortress surrounded by fire, no longer was the "preservation in shape of over $300,000,000 in the vaults" the driving force behind their efforts—it was survival: "we were prisoners and fighting for our lives."

The mint's center courtyard was open to the sky and surrounded by four interior walls with windows on each floor. As the blaze around the building intensified, what had been a light shower of glowing firebrands turned into a hailstorm of "sparks and cinders" and flaming debris, landing on the roof "in drifts nearly two feet deep" and raining into the courtyard where a soldier pulled a hose line to extinguish the embers. Frank Leach saw "a dozen little fires were starting at various places in the court," and he entered the courtyard to help the soldier with his hose line. By the time he ran back inside, his "clothes and hat were scorched by the falling cinders." Worried for the roof, he sent Joe Hammill and a few workers back upstairs with a hose. Each floor on the climb was hot and smoky, but the bucket brigades were keeping the interior from catching fire. On the roof, men kicked embers aside and Hammill sprayed "the red-hot copper surface" wherever he saw flames. "There we worked for an hour," he later wrote, "ripping up sheet copper and playing the water and using the hose where they would do the most good."

As the banking district blaze crept northward and reached Washington Street, a line of sweating soldiers kept pace to stay ahead of the flames and keep business owners from risking life for property. Thirty-one-year-old artist Maynard Dixon and his wife, Lillian, beat the approaching fire line and rushed up into his third-floor studio to save what they could from his years of illustrations and paintings of Western life. They grabbed all they could hold and tuck under arms and carry over shoulders—Western artifacts and a couple of rugs and many of his sketchbooks—and rushed back down into the smoky street. From there the couple walked north to beat the flames threatening his studio, library, prized Navajo rugs, and all his paintings.

The fire reached the south side of Washington Street across from the Appraisers' Building, the temporary location for the Custom House, which was where import taxes were collected on goods entering the port of San Francisco. In a time before a national income tax, when duty on incoming goods was a chief source of federal revenue, protecting the Custom House of the West Coast's primary port of entry was vital. Customs officials and Army soldiers and revenue cutter sailors[2] stood ready to fight flames on the roof and at each window "with wet cloths and improvised mops," as the deputy collector would later report. The revenue cutter sailors had been ordered from their vessel to safeguard the Custom House, and the soldiers had been assigned that morning to guard the federal offices within the building. Their captain had been ordered "to protect the Custom House[3] and any United States property," so he posted a squad on each side with instructions not "to leave the immediate vicinity of the building." The two-story commission houses across Washington Street were engulfed by flames filling the street with suffocating heat and forcing the soldiers inside the Custom House, where they joined customs officials and revenue cutter sailors to keep flames from entering. Using buckets of water from the building's artesian well, they kept windowsills and frames soaked and extinguished any flame "as soon as ignition occurred on the window casings or any exposed woodwork."

On Sansome Street alongside the building one block up from the fire line, Oakland firemen with a fire engine and hose wagon—one of the three engine companies sent by the mayor of Oakland answering Mayor Schmitz's early morning telegram requesting assistance—joined the battle against the blaze. After ferrying over that morning, they reported to a battalion chief who thanked them for coming and directed one of their engine companies a block from the Washington Street fire where they could get water from the hose of an engine pumping from a cistern another block further up. Oakland firemen

---

2 The US Revenue Cutter Service later merged with the US Life-Saving Service to form the US Coast Guard.

3 The Appraisers' Building as a temporary location for the Custom House is hereinafter referred to simply as the Custom House to avoid wordiness.

fresh to the fight unrolled a line from their hose wagon, hooked it to their engine, and, to avoid losing their hose to the flames creeping north toward them along Sansome, pulled their line sideways along Jackson Street and snaked it down through a narrow, twenty-two-foot-wide alley (present-day Hotaling Place) to Washington Street, and they joined a chemical engine company in hosing down burning buildings on the street's south side. The blaze had already consumed most of the structures along the street: a corner restaurant, fish market, shirt factories, and liquor stores. But directly across from them, the fifty-three-year-old, four-story Montgomery Block was still living up to its status as the city's oldest "fireproof" building.

As the flames had approached the previous hour, soldiers rolled up to dynamite the Montgomery Block, believing its demolition could create a sufficient firebreak. But the building manager, thirty-two-year-old Oliver Stidger, stopped them. An attorney whose office was one of the building's 160 rooms, Stidger blocked them from entering and argued to spare it from demolition because its fireproof structure would serve as its own firebreak. Convinced, the soldiers relented, and their captain yelled for fire companies to water it down so it wouldn't ignite.

Firefighters redirected their hose lines and played streams upon the Montgomery Block as flames from the adjacent two-story saloon licked up its side wall. "[W]hen the woodwork in the deep-set windows at the side began to smolder," as a witness would later recount, firemen aimed their lines at each window to quench each "incipient blaze" before it could spread, and the prospect of saving the building looked "hopeful." But as elsewhere, waves of heat carried glowing embers up to rooftops, and soon the cornice atop Montgomery Block began smoking. Hosemen aimed their nozzle up, but it was beyond the stream's reach, and "it seemed as though the building was doomed like its neighbors." A fireman grabbed an axe and ran inside. "Flames were then spurting from the cornice" by the time he reached the rooftop, crawled out to the edge, "and chopped off the burning cornice with his axe."

The building was saved for the moment, and with the cistern two blocks away running low, the men "used the water sparingly" to prevent the fire from catching the building or crossing to the north side of Washington Street. By the time the cistern ran dry at 4:00 p.m., the walls of Montgomery Block dripped and steamed, blackened but unburned. Every other building along its side of the street "was burned down." Like the untouched Custom House a block away, "the old stone structure of the Montgomery Block remained intact and dark," as a witness would describe it, "silhouetted against a background of blazing and toppling buildings and twisting wires, its deep-set windows reflecting the flames and the fire."

The battalion chief received a report that the Hall of Justice "was in immediate danger" and sent the engine companies to Portsmouth Square where flames were now within a block of the Hall of Justice. The mayor and police chief and dozens of men were gathered outside after emerging from their basement meeting, shocked to see the fires so close. Many of them stood on the grass in groups, discussing the meeting and watching the blaze move nearer. Mayor Schmitz ordered the prisoners evacuated from their basement cells, directed that all valuable records be removed from the building, and moved his headquarters outside to the Army's explosives-distribution tent at the far end of the square where he used a dynamite box for a chair and stood another on its end for a desk.

Firemen arrived and hooked a hose to an engine parked at the corner of Portsmouth Square and stretched the line along the street in front of the Hall of Justice and around the corner to soak the fire threatening the building's south side. With no pressure in nearby hydrants, their engine was fed water through a hose by two more engines pumping from cisterns one and two blocks up the street. Through this three-engine relay, water was flowing three blocks to reach the flames. And the single line was slowing but not stopping the blaze's spread.

City employees and policemen hurried back and forth between the Hall of Justice and Portsmouth Square lugging heavy boxes of files and records and stacking them on the grass. And under the guard of jailers and soldiers, seventy-seven shackled prisoners tramped out of the building single file over the hose line and across the street into the square. Huddled gatherings of Chinatown residents and men from the committee meeting cleared a wide space for them, and as a witness described, "There on the grass of the old square sat the hand-cuffed group." A judge from the meeting ordered them moved four blocks north to the county jail.

At the mayor's tent, the doctor in charge of the morgue entered and asked whether the bodies in the basement shooting gallery should be "left to their fate or removed elsewhere," and Schmitz told him to move the bodies outside to the square. The doctor and soldiers and police officers carried the bodies—thirty in all, wrapped in white sheets—out to the corner of the square and laid them out on the grass. Soon heat from the approaching fire "became too intense" and the bodies were moved across the lawn. Crowds kept their distance but stared at the sight of sheet-wrapped, stiffened forms, and when flaming embers floated into the square, canvas was unfolded and spread over the boxes of records, and Mayor Schmitz instructed the doctor "not to wait for any formality of law, but to bury the bodies immediately" and provide some means for later identification.

"That meant we had to dig trenches to bury them," a police sergeant later recounted, adding that since the graves were temporary, they did not dig deep. "There was only about two feet of earth on top of them." Wrapped with each body was a handwritten card linking the remains to a name, or a manner of death, or the place it was found, or just "unknown." Among the wrapped bodies were three who had died the day before, already in the morgue when the earthquake struck. The rest had been killed in the earthquake or died of their injuries. Like Rafaelo Paolinelli, a fruit merchant whose body Officer Harry Schmidt had pulled lifeless from beneath a pile of bricks on Washington Street just moments after the shaking stopped. And Ida Heaslip, who had died just after being rescued by firefighters from the Geary Hotel ruins. And John Day, also rescued from the Geary and taken to Mechanics' Pavilion, where he passed after his leg was amputated. Fifteen were "unknown," at least two from the fish market collapse. And there were smaller wrapped bodies of children. Like that of ten-year-old Nathan Kornfield, crushed to death in his bed by the collapse of his family's South of Market apartment. And little William Vail, who died in his parents' home in the Mission, just two weeks before his fourth birthday. One "Unknown Japanese," and two labeled "Unknown Chinaman."

Throughout the city, bodies of the day's dead were borne by wagons and automobiles away from the expanding blazes, and many were buried in parks and squares where ground could be broken. Along East Street near the waterfront, Sergeant Jesse Cook asked a man driving a wagon bearing a figure hidden under canvas, "What have you got there?" The man answered, "Dead man." Cook raised the canvas and "Sure enough it was a dead man."

Tom Burns, Sergeant Cook's friend who had narrowly escaped being crushed by a falling wall that morning, was giving rides to friends in his produce wagon that afternoon when he saw a parked wagon "full of human bodies" and beside it "a lot of men with picks and shovels who started digging trenches." A thirteen-year-old girl saw "a most pitiful sight" of dead being buried in a city park that day: "Picture if you can row upon row of the unfortunate ones who met death in the earthquake & all were being buried in one grave in a city park." A woman up in North Beach's Washington Square "saw the morgue and undertakers' wagons beginning to arrive" that afternoon, some bearing bodies from Mechanics' Pavilion. By the time she left late that afternoon, "twenty corpses lay on the grass across the street, covered with canvas, and more were coming all the time." A dozen were buried in Washington Square and more than thirty in an empty lot five blocks north at the corner of Bay and Powell Streets, including eight from the Valencia Hotel collapse.

But most of the dead would never be found. Despite rescue efforts at collapsed hotels and lodging houses, many trapped boarders could not be reached. And for every Valencia Hotel or Geary Hotel or Brunswick House or Wilcox House, there were small homes or tenements or walk-up apartments over commercial space or crowded basements in Chinatown crammed with cots and bunks where residents were dead or trapped by falling walls or stairwells or beams or jammed doors, but there was no rescue. Their voices were not heard, many of their last moments were alone, and, like the buildings in which they died, fire reduced their physical remains to ash.

Between Portsmouth Square and the Hall of Justice, firemen stood at intervals keeping their hose line stiffened with a steady flow of cistern water pumped through three engines. The line snaked around the corner where hosemen at the nozzle watered down buildings ahead of the flames eating westward along Clay Street and nearing the south side of the Hall of Justice, but the single stream was doing little to slow the blaze's progress. By 4:30 p.m. the air in Portsmouth Square "became so hot" from the approaching fire, Mayor Schmitz moved his headquarters four blocks up to the empty Fairmont Hotel on Nob Hill. And soldiers and policemen rushed to scoop the last piles of dirt over temporary graves and tamped the earth flat with backs of shovels.

Army Lieutenant Raymond Briggs and his demolition team appeared at the corner of the square eyeing the buildings just yards from the flames. This was the last chance to blow a firebreak to stop the blaze before it reached the Hall of Justice and Portsmouth Square, and then Chinatown and beyond. But Briggs and his team had used up all their stick dynamite, and when they rushed to the explosives tent, they found that Army electrician John Davis had distributed all the dynamite and could only offer them black powder. Briggs and soldiers and firemen ran a barrel of powder to a two-story corner building and inside the first-floor pharmacy (above which apartments overlooked the grass square). Firemen pulled their hose back a safe distance nearer their engine. Briggs and his men ran the fuse line out the front, lit it, and after a few long moments the building exploded.

Those watching from Portsmouth Square—John Davis and firemen and police officers and soldiers—felt the blast and were enveloped in smoke while chunks of masonry and jagged pieces of wood rained on the grass around them. The building was wrecked. Its broken edges and splintered ends were seething with orange flames. And the blast had propelled flaming mattresses and bedding from the second-floor apartments "across the street, setting fire to another lodging house on the opposite side," which, as a watching battalion chief later described, was soon "a roaring furnace." Rather than create a firebreak, black powder had again started a new blaze on a new block, sending fires westward up Clay Street toward Chinatown.

"The fire rapidly surrounded the square," a police captain later reported, and the police officers guarding the records "became prisoners." Fire crews backed up and hosed down the Hall of Justice while flaming cinders "were falling like hail" onto Portsmouth Square and "constantly igniting the canvas spread over the records." Initially they stomped out any flames that started, but eventually they used bottled beer from a nearby saloon to keep the canvas from igniting. By 5:00 p.m., as James Hopper would describe, the blaze marched toward Chinatown "with a rattle of eagerness." And that same hour, Charles Kendrick—who had crawled out of the vacuum of the fire when it had crossed Market and nearly overwhelmed him—walked up to the top of Nob Hill and stood with others on a sidewalk watching "the great and ghastly spectacle" of the city burning: "The whole scene was terrifying, yet majestic and awesome beyond the power of words—a great city vanishing in flame."

10. Night as Bright as Day

BUILDINGS AROUND THE mint were burned to the ground by 5:00 p.m. and billowing smoke replaced tall flames. Up on the mint's roof, Frank Leach and Joe Hammill and their workers and soldiers watered and stomped out the last few simmering flames. "The fight was won," Leach later proudly wrote of the moment. "The mint was saved." The five dozen men had spent seven hours barricaded within the structure fighting flames that would have otherwise gutted every floor, and their efforts spared the nation's largest gold depository the fate of thousands of buildings within its view, including the Call Building and the Palace Hotel, now hollowed-out shells still filled with flames feeding on every last discernible feature.

The mint's large front doors had been sealed that morning to a view of 5th Street's buildings threatened by fire, and when the doors were opened again, the buildings were gone. Frank Leach was shocked by "the change that had taken place there within a few short hours," and later wrote that "the view presented was one of utter ruin, desolation, and loneliness." Buildings "were piles of smoking and blazing ruins." 5th Street "was encumbered with fallen trolley poles and tangled wires." Most jarring was the stillness and complete absence of life. "Not a human being was to be seen," he noted. "It seemed as if all the people and buildings of the city but the mint and its defenders had been destroyed."

The soldiers stepped outside into "a most depressing scene of desolation" and lined up to guard the mint once again. Through their boot soles they could feel the heat of the scorched pavement. Mint employees began a late-afternoon journey to check on their homes and families. Frank Leach trekked toward the waterfront to catch a ferry, and "after dancing over the hot cobbles of Fifth Street for a block," he "looked back on the battle-scarred mint," its stately silhouette standing charred but unbroken against the jagged edges of South of Market's smoldering wasteland.

In the five o'clock hour north of Market Street, flames chewed through City Hall. The wealth of material inside its massive space—furniture and woodwork and art throughout its dozens of offices and lining its long corridors and tall chambers and multilevel circular galleries of its rotunda—fueled a ferocious blaze now threatening the east-wing Hall of Records. With the help of city employees and local citizens and commandeered wagons, police officers cleared bricks from stairways to reach the second-floor city recorder's office, and they threw typewriter covers stuffed with deed records and map books and important papers out a bathroom window to men who ran them across the grass to waiting wagons on McAllister Street. And they saved the large portrait of George Washington from the Board of Supervisors' chamber and carried it out over rubble-strewn stairs.

The sun's dim, red circle dropped low in the western sky, and dusk went almost unnoticed for the smoke. "Because of the pall of smoke blanketing the city," a man walking past City Hall's blazing shell noted, "nightfall came quickly; by six o'clock it was dark." A physician walking through the streets still a good distance from the fires saw refugees from the burned districts filling every block. They rested "in beds on the street or lawns, under wagons and in every conceivable place," and those not resting or camping were "fleeing to the hills, park, and Presidio with what they could carry, pull, or push."

Some stayed even as fires swept to the edge of grassy parks and squares where they camped. "It was disgustingly hot," one witness wrote of the empty lot across from their burning neighborhood, "oppressive from the fire, and cinders." Arthur Dangerfield hauled everything he could carry from his McAllister Street house to the crowded sanctuary of Jefferson Square as the Hayes Valley fire "was coming up the city by leaps and bounds," as he soon wrote in his journal. He and his friend "staked our claim out in the middle and settled down to camp," and from there, as the sun set, Arthur watched flames reduce his home to "a smoldering mass of ashes."

A flood of residents flowed toward the waterfront to flee the city by ferry, but their journey around the spreading inferno grew longer and more difficult through the afternoon and evening, forcing them to climb steep streets north of the banking and harbor district fires before joining the masses jamming East Street down toward the wharfs. Forty-six-year-old writer Bailey Millard, who joined the "rush of the grand army of refugees" through North Beach, likened the scene to "the flight from Pompeii." Bay Street was clogged with "a surging tide of humanity"—families on foot, women with "baskets on their heads," men who "strained under terrible burdens" jumping out of the way of wagons "loaded with furniture and swarming over with men, women, and children," and rushing automobiles "piled high with bedding and hastily snatched stores" that "tooted wild warnings amid the crowds." Among the faces in the throng Bailey saw artist Maynard Dixon "coatless, and sweating, tugging away at a little child's wagon on which was piled all that he had saved from his burnt studio," and Maynard's wife, Lillian, also "loaded down with luggage." On Telegraph Hill, Bailey passed a refugee campground patrolled by armed soldiers where families rested under "little tents of sheets and blankets, held up with sticks taken from collapsed buildings."

Bailey walked with the rush of people down East Street. On one side were "crazily leaning warehouses" and on the other "twisted" rails of the waterfront's State Belt Railroad were lined with freight cars, immobile, filled with produce and livestock, guarded by soldiers. He followed the slowly moving crowd past "smoking ruins of the lower business section" and a "line of silent fire engines" to the Ferry Building where Sergeant Jesse Cook, on his feet since starting his midnight shift more than eighteen hours earlier, had directed his officers to organize the throngs into orderly lines. In the building's grand nave, refugees "crushed into the waiting rooms," some of whom "had been waiting for hours for a chance to cross the ferry." Exhausted, hungry, thirsty residents filled benches or leaned against walls or sat on the floor in lines with their handfuls of ash-covered belongings. A young girl later remembered her father paying a wharf fruit vendor a dime for an orange: "Never have I tasted anything more refreshing." Their line creeped slowly along the pier as crowds ahead of them filled departing ferries and steamships, and when their ferry for Oakland finally arrived, as the young girl later described the moment, "The very sight of its lights—just ordinary electric lights—put heart into us."

A physician who got his family aboard a ferry bound for Tiburon looked back on San Francisco, a scene he would soon describe in a letter: "From the boat, the burning city was a grand but terrible spectacle; the sky reddened, cinders flying, and the smoke stifling made a picture never to be forgotten." A passenger crossing to Oakland "could see the ships, sailing and steam, laying at anchor, all over the bay outlines against the fire."

Crossing in the opposite direction bearing for the burning city were Charmian London and her husband, Jack, having traveled forty miles from their ranch via horseback and rail and water, eager to get to the scene and report. "I watched the vast conflagration from out on the bay," Jack wrote. "Not a flicker of wind stirred," but as the ferry neared the waterfront, onshore wind rushed in from behind him and, by his impression, from all directions into San Francisco. Rapidly rising intense heat from multiple fires pulled air skyward, leaving a street-level vacuum that sucked air from around the expanding inferno and created its own windstorm. "The heated air rising made an enormous suck," and as Jack described, the fire built "its own colossal chimney through the atmosphere." Another man on a ferry into the city to check on family later remembered a panorama of "walls of flame, extending the full breadth of the city," and "as we neared the shore, the explosions of dynamite, the falling walls and roaring furnaces of fire were absolutely deafening."

At 6:47 p.m. the sun set in the western sky and the gray dusk slipped to darkness. No lamplighters went out to ignite gas streetlamps, and with no power, electric streetlights—whether toppled or still standing—stayed dark. But the firestorm lit the city after the sun had slipped below the horizon, and as one man described, it was "light enough to read a book." The glow of the "flame lighted sky" was so bright it even spilled into homes out in the western reaches of the city far from the fires, as one young girl later recalled: "Ordinary blinds could not shut out the intense brightness." A policeman downtown noted, "[T]he flames lit up the place with a glare as bright as day." At his fire line the heat was "unbearable," and he was impressed by firemen nearer the flames who "were fighting the fire like maddened heroes."

Along the South of Market waterfront, the firestorm was still held north of Howard Street and west of Main by Lieutenant Freeman's sailors and firemen with water pumped from their fireboat and tugs. They were joined by the revenue cutter *Golden Gate*, which had steamed to the Folsom Street pier after disembarking men for guard duty up at the Custom House. Midshipman Pond noticed "a shift and slight increase in the breeze" driving flames southward and westward "at a terrific pace" toward the Rincon Hill neighborhood. Once home to the city's wealthy, many of its large hilltop homes were now boardinghouses subdivided into small flats for working-class tenants. Until this hour, the neighborhood was a safe distance from the fires, and most of its residents had stayed home.

Seeing the blaze speeding toward the neighborhood, Freeman sent Pond and a petty officer running up the hill "to warn the poverty-stricken residents of that section to get out." Even as the "fire was sweeping up the hill at such a rate that it seemed impossible that anyone on the hill could escape its path," the two men ran into boardinghouses and pounded on locked doors and yelled their warnings down hallways and up stairways. "Those who heeded our warning escaped to the waterfront," Pond later reported, "but many who delayed to gather personal belongings became panic-stricken when they found escape in one direction cut off by flames and smoke." Things were tossed from windows and valuables carried out front doors, but the speed and heat of the approaching blaze—"so intense" it reportedly caused "the cobbles of the streets to pop like popcorn"—forced many residents to drop everything and run. Pond saw elderly, bedridden people on mattresses "carried a little way and dropped, then picked up by someone else, carried a little further and dropped again." To him the scene "was heartrending."

With the fires marching away from his boats, Lieutenant Freeman maneuvered his improvised flotilla to rejoin the battle. He ordered hose lines disconnected and sent sailors back to crew the Navy vessels *Active* and *Leslie*, then sent them with the Army tug *Slocum* and revenue cutter *Golden Gate* to take up new positions in docks south of the advancing flames. And he directed fire crews to reconnect at piers five and six blocks south. Exhausted firemen dragged flattened hoses back to engines, where they pulled black leather helmets off their sweat-matted hair and unfastened throat straps and unsnapped rubber-lined coats and tossed them on hose wagons. Drivers fed handfuls of oats to horse teams, climbed onto benches, drove engines and hose wagons against a tide of people fleeing Rincon Hill, and arrived at piers at the foot of 1st Street where the Navy tug *Sotoyomo*—having just arrived with another freshwater supply from Goat Island—provided water for the men and horses and engine boilers before Freeman sent the tug back to Goat Island for more.

Flames atop Rincon Hill were threatening a lumberyard adjacent to the Pacific Mail Steamship Company's warehouse and piers, one of which was the terminus for the rail line connecting to the Southern Pacific passenger depot two blocks west. If the lumberyard caught, the rail line's wooden pier would follow, and it would close off one of the city's most important supply arteries— soon to be of critical importance during relief efforts.

Freeman coordinated with fire engine companies to reconnect with tugs alongside both of Pacific Mail's piers. A fire engine rolled up to the mail dock to meet the tugs "and doubled up with their lines," as the captain would report, "running a stream up several blocks to meet the fire." Sailors and hosemen pulled two hose lines into the lumberyard and "nozzle-men stood fearlessly at their stations on lumber piles" at the foot of the steep cliff of Rincon Hill's south side, "where their lives were in constant danger from flaming timbers and other debris falling from the burning houses along the edge of the cliff above them," Midshipman Pond noted. Flames ate through buildings beside the lumberyard, moving nearer the docks and trapping escaping residents.

The *Golden Gate* steamed up alongside the Pacific Mail pier where roasting temperatures singed the paint of its hull, and the crew—draped with wet blankets—ran hoses up the pier so near the flames their faces and hands blistered. While many of the crew fought to keep the blaze from consuming the wharfs, the rest helped take aboard their cutter roughly one hundred refugees, many of whom had to be carried because they were drunk after gulping down the doomed inventory of liquor stores in the path of the fires.

Two blocks west, the fight to save the Southern Pacific passenger depot at 3rd and Townsend Streets was underway. Railroad employees and volunteers had been stomping out fires in the rail yard since the afternoon hours, and with the blaze approaching Townsend Street, it was growing more difficult to extinguish flames on the walls and roofs of the wooden freight sheds, which "caught fire several times."

The skipper and crew of the freight steamer *Juliette*—trapped at its moorings by the lowered 4th Street drawbridge (unable to lift with no power) in the Mission Creek Channel a block south—ran up a hose from the vessel's pumps and with it "the sheds were kept drenched with salt water," as a railroad agent reported. And workers and volunteers dropped piles of sand "on the flowing oil, thus keeping the fire from getting to the sheds."

A fire engine company arrived, having spent their day fighting through the South of Market blaze with only what they could draft from sewers. A stench of sewage, urine, and waste hung on their clothes and equipment as they filled their engine's boiler with fresh water by the bucketful from the *Juliette*'s tanks, hooked to the steamer's line, and pumped the salt water through their engine strong enough to cover the north side of Townsend Street where flames were only eighty feet from the wood-frame passenger depot.

By 10:00 p.m. the fire engine's boiler ran dry and the *Juliette*'s freshwater tank was empty. The battalion chief ran word to Lieutenant Freeman that fresh water was needed urgently down at the Mission Creek Channel. With the threat to the mail docks nearly neutralized, Freeman disconnected the 1,500 feet of hose from his tug *Leslie*, piloted the tug down to the channel below the passenger depot, and ordered the *Sotoyomo*—just arriving with more fresh water from another voyage to Goat Island—to follow. Both tugs steamed into the channel and stopped at the lowered bridge on the far side of the *Juliette*. The fire was one block away on the far side of the rail line and passenger depot. Freeman jumped onto the wharf and started a bucket brigade running fresh water from the *Sotoyomo* to the fire engine's boiler.

The wharf was teeming with crowds and Army soldiers kept order among the refugees driven from their homes by fire. Freeman heard voices "piteously crying for water." His men filled a large barrel with two hundred gallons of fresh water from the *Sotoyomo* and set it on the bridge for the refugees. They transferred the rest of the five thousand gallons to the *Juliette*'s tank, and Freeman sent the *Sotoyomo* back to Goat Island on another voyage for more fresh water.

Hosemen sprinted sloshing buckets of water to the fire engine in the railroad yard, but fresh water in its boiler steamed out faster than they could resupply and "made it impossible to keep up the necessary steam pressure." As the battalion chief noted, "[I]t became impossible to continue any further." Firemen unhooked the hose from their engine and connected directly with the *Leslie*'s strong pumps, stretched it to Townsend Street, and, as Freeman dryly reported, "by its use the Southern Pacific freight sheds were all saved." So too was the passenger depot and rail line, and the lumberyard at the foot of Rincon Hill, and the Pacific Mail warehouse and piers.

Freeman and his sailors and firemen and volunteers beat the blaze back to 8th Street, and San Francisco's southern waterfront was saved. Firemen gathered hose lines and Midshipman Pond coordinated efforts to secure equipment and reassemble the sailors, the bulk of whom Lieutenant Freeman sent back to the *Active* to get some rest. And Freeman, resolute and tireless, returned to the *Leslie* to make "an inspection of the waterfront" back up to the Ferry Building and beyond.

Mint superintendent Frank Leach caught a ferry back to Oakland and landed after dark. On his walk home, he noticed "the flames from the burning buildings in San Francisco illuminated the western part of the heavens" so brightly, "the light reflected made the streets of Oakland like twilight." In Berkeley, a young man walked "to a vantage point on a little street" to gaze across the bay at the conflagration, "which now seemed to stretch a continuous fiery length of the entire waterfront." Up in Sausalito—at least five miles from the firestorm—a woman noted she "could see to read fine print by the glow, and the cinders and burnt papers carried so in the smoke that at times it sounded like rain in the trees." Further north that night in San Rafael, Judge William Morrow could see "the whole southern heavens were aglow with the light of the conflagration raging in San Francisco, and it seemed at the time that the city was doomed." South of the city, down the peninsula in Half Moon Bay, a young boy joined others in staring at "the flaming sky over the mountains to the northeast," and many of them "thought that the world had come to an end." Even further south, a man in a country home outside San Jose told his brother in a letter, "That night the north sky was lighted up through a gap in the mountains," adding that by 9:00 p.m., "the red glare of the flames could be seen larger than ever through the northern pass, and we knew that the very worst must be happening to poor San Francisco."

Up in the middle of the very worst, two dozen police officers and soldiers in Portsmouth Square dodged flying embers from fires nearing the grass plaza and held longneck bottles out over the canvas covering stacks of records, splashing beer on each flame that ignited. On the north side of the plaza, fire engine companies used cistern water to soak walls of the now-abandoned Hall of Justice, but with flames dancing along two sides, it was only a matter of time until it caught. Fire from the black powder demolition of the drugstore ate through buildings along the south side of the plaza, spreading westward along Clay Street toward Dupont into the heart of Chinatown. To cut the blaze off—or at least slow its progress—firemen at the cistern a block away connected a second hose line to their engine, led it down Dupont, and played water onto the leading flames, but too much worked against their single stream—strong winds, dry combustibles, and a fire now too far gone.

As the blaze threatened their neighborhood, "the grave, sad merchants of Chinatown gathered a few portable treasures into packs and long pole-swung baskets, and," as one woman observed, "poured out of their city into the unfamiliar reaches of North Beach." Policemen and soldiers ran ahead of the flames to clear residents from the tiny abodes of crammed boardinghouses above and below street-level storefronts. "We would let them sleep until the fire reached their block," a police sergeant noted, "[t]hen we would go and rout them out in time for them to pack up and save some things if they had anywhere to take them to."

Evacuations from city blocks and neighborhoods and districts had been going on since early morning, but it was different here. Women and children in Chinatown rarely ventured beyond the safety of their neighborhood into the city where only the men of their families would hazard to travel out of necessity or for work, returning often with the pain of ridicule and sometimes with scars of physical assault. Now armed soldiers and policemen were ordering them out, but even in the face of approaching flames, to vacate their community and lead their children into the hostile streets of the world beyond was a leap over a barrier of language and culture and across a wide chasm of distrust many could not voluntarily take.

A few of Chinatown's residents sought refuge in city homes where they worked. A resident of Washington Street soon wrote that the Chinese cook his family employed approached the front gate asking if he and his friends could seek shelter there. The man allowed them in and noticed, "Throngs of Chinese were now pouring out of Chinatown, like beetles from a burning log, and passing in procession up Washington Street, carrying what little they could in their hands, some of the poor women silently weeping." But even then, in "the general terror" of the night lit by firestorms, the urgency to leave "had not yet set in." Most left, but many stayed and had to be forced out, as policemen found in a lodging house on Dupont Street. A police sergeant and his squad entered the building through the storefront and sprinted upstairs only to find the floor jammed with residents, and "every man in that particular gang had packed his trunk and lashed himself to it with ropes." When the officers pointed to leave, the men tied to trunks objected, in broken English, "You take me; you take him too!" as the sergeant would later report. "'Him' was the trunk." The policemen cut the ropes and forced the protesting residents out to save them from the approaching fire.

Twenty-eight-year-old Lee Yoke Suey, his wife, their baby—one month old that day—and his elderly parents all saw the approaching flames from the flat they shared above their family's Commercial Street store. Soldiers and policemen were moving up their street ordering people to leave, and with little time left, the Lee family gathered jewels, food, and blankets. But "[d]espite the urgency of the evacuation," as a family member would later recall, Lee Yoke Suey's wife "paused for a symbolic, abbreviated observance of a 'red eggs and ginger' celebration" for their baby, Alice, a Chinese custom marking a child turning one month old, consisting of "snipping a lock of the baby's hair and rolling an egg over her little head." Then they left, joining the exodus of fellow countrymen reluctant to leave their community even as it faced destruction. The young mother struggled to walk on her bound feet, forcing them to stop for rest in a park, where Lee Yoke Suey comforted her, "I think Chinatown is still safe. We can go back soon."

But the flames had not been slowed by the water of single streams relayed from cisterns, and with soldiers assigned by Schmitz to try and save businesses in the banking district, the task of blasting a firebreak in Chinatown was left to the California Powder Works president, presumably still drunk. He and his demolition crew began blowing structures along Dupont Street. "It was here that I saw them dynamiting building after building," one witness passing through Chinatown soon wrote, "but they seemed to catch fire almost immediately." The crew used stick dynamite, but with no water to douse the resulting flames, they managed only to accelerate the spread of the Clay Street fire.

Looking on from a nearby park, Lee Yoke Suey and his family realized Chinatown was doomed to burn, and he found a wagon to carry them out to Golden Gate Park. Then he left them to save his birth certificate from the flames. "He was born in San Francisco and a merchant," as his granddaughter would later explain, "but without proof of his status, he could be detained or deported. It was worth the risk." Soldiers filled Chinatown's narrow, smoke-filled streets and alleys, many plundering items from bazaars and stores. Emboldened by the mayor's orders, they violently removed remaining inhabitants and barred entry to residents trying to return. Lee Yoke Suey sneaked back into his store and grabbed his birth certificate, but a soldier confronted him and forced him out, stabbing him in the side with his bayonet and leaving him for dead. Lee Yoke Suey lay motionless until the soldier left, then he held his wound to stop the bleeding and staggered back to his family, clutching his birth certificate, permanently scarred by the mayor's soldiers.

Mayor Schmitz had moved his headquarters into the completed but unopened Fairmont Hotel at the top of Nob Hill. At 8:00 p.m. he and the police chief and Army officers from Fort Mason and the Presidio and members of the "Citizens' Committee" all met in the hotel's dark ballroom, seated on packing cases and the stage. Schmitz still had faith a coordinated effort could save the yet-unburned parts of downtown, including the retail district and Union Square, as well as Nob Hill, North Beach, and Telegraph Hill. With virtually no water, he affirmed his confidence in dynamiting firebreaks and asked the Army and fire department and civilian explosives experts to work together. And he emphasized that soldiers would be patrolling neighborhood streets through the night to enforce his curfew and ensure no indoor fires were lit. Subcommittees were set up for relief (of hungry, of sick and wounded, of Chinese), for restoration (of water, of light and telephone, of fires in dwellings), and for resumption (of civil government, of transportation, of judiciary, of retail trade). Others were formed for sanitation, citizens' police, and housing the homeless. And to chair the important Finance Committee, the group nominated former mayor Phelan to be chairman, widely regarded as a fastidious steward of public funds. The meeting adjourned with plans to reconvene again in the Fairmont ballroom at 10:00 the next morning.

Up in General Greely's quarters at Fort Mason with his staff and the boxes of records saved from the downtown Phelan Building before evacuating, General Funston, still wearing the suit he had thrown on at his Nob Hill apartment, issued orders dividing the city into two: the streets west of Van Ness would be patrolled by soldiers under the command of a colonel (who fell under Funston's command, theoretically still acting under the mayor's orders), and to the east, soldiers would remain assigned to police and fire departments "in keeping order and in fighting the fire." And he finally dictated a message to be carried to Oakland where it could be wired to the War Department in Washington, DC.

Although Funston later wrote that he announced in his telegram that he had "turned out" troops into the city, his message only stated the Army was "doing all possible to aid residents." Possibly seeking retroactive approval for his deployment of soldiers into San Francisco, he asserted his "trust" in "the War Department to authorize any action I might have to take." And he concluded with urgency, "We need tents and rations for twenty thousand people. (Signed) Funston." By 8:40 p.m. a local telegraph line was restored by the Signal Corps, and Funston drafted another message for the War Department (which would arrive in Washington before his first message). In it he estimated 100,000 to be homeless and 1,000 dead, announced "troops all on duty assisting police," and requested "thousands of tents and all rations that can be sent."

The last request came directly from the Presidio where the gargantuan task of relief had begun. Seeing that San Francisco's population was, in the wake of the disaster, "returned to primitive conditions in regard to all necessities of life," the post quartermaster, Major Carroll Devol, began the day gathering all available supplies for distribution. After noon he learned the Army storage warehouses in the city had burned, and with them went $2.2 million worth of clothing, equipment, and supplies. Devol's staff opened the four storage warehouses on post, each fortunately "uninjured by the earthquake." With refugees already streaming into the post and Golden Gate Park, shelter was the immediate need. Soldiers gathered 3,000 tents, sent 2,400 of them into the city for distribution to parks and squares, and set up the remaining 600 in open spaces on post, starting with the parade grounds and the lawn in front of the Army General Hospital.

Lieutenant Colonel George Torney was a physician and commanding officer of the hospital, and shortly after the earthquake that morning and without waiting for orders, he had opened it—not badly damaged, though its brick ventilation shafts had crushed through the roof and there was no power or running water—to wounded civilians and dispatched a medical team into the city to render first aid and tell local authorities "that this hospital was open for the care of injured and sick." And he ordered his medical officers to "hold themselves in readiness for active work."

The hospital's chief nurse was twenty-nine-year-old Dora Thompson, a nurse for nine years and one of the first to join the newly formed Army Nurse Corps four years earlier. She and her team of forty nurses and Dr. Torney and his physicians had been working since daybreak, aided by volunteers including Eda Funston, who had evacuated with her two sons to the Presidio that morning. By 1:00 p.m. they had seventy-five patients under their care, including Fire Chief Dennis Sullivan. By that night the number reached 127, and more were coming.

So were more refugees. For all the thousands who fled the burning city by ferry, tens of thousands evacuated to the open grounds of the Presidio, Golden Gate Park, or park squares or vacant lots where they could park their saved possessions and find rest a safe distance from the fires. "Since the earthquake there had been moving crowds everywhere, but now the whole population of the city seemed to be in the streets," a witness on Washington Street noted. Families huddled on sidewalks and lawns, sitting on chairs brought outside "with blankets or rugs drawn up over their knees as though they were tucked into a sleigh." And they grabbed sleep wherever they could. "The sidewalks at night were covered with improvised beds upon which were men, women, and children & rocking chairs in which aged people of all conditions in life wrapped in blankets spent the night," one woman observed. Men slept in their suits on grass, hats over their faces. Women slept on "inverted four-posters"— tables topped with mattresses. Thomas Angove dozed in his laundry wagon under an overcoat with his horse tied to the wheel.

In neighborhoods still unburned, many slept indoors. Former mayor Phelan slept in his home in the Mission, but, worried about gas leaks, he kept windows open. His sister, more anxious, slept outside in the garden. A ten-year-old girl who had fled with her parents to her aunt's house later remembered spending that night with the windows open, and they "had to wake every once in a while and shake" off their blankets "because they were heavy with ashes." A pregnant woman and her husband had fled her mother's apartment to the Palace Hotel, then from there to the third floor of a family friend's home that night, but "no one could sleep under such circumstances," the mother noted, "with the glow of the flames enveloping every room, as well as outside scenes."

Botanist Alice Eastwood had been safeguarding her boxes of 1,497 plant specimens in the front hallway of her Taylor Street home all day since rescuing them from the Academy of Sciences. Now with downtown fires spreading, she "became uneasy and decided to take them to a friend's house four blocks away on Russian Hill, which seemed a safe place." Since cars and wagons were charging "a big sum down," she enlisted the help of neighbors, "and we carried them, making several trips." And the final block of each trek up Taylor Street to Vallejo Street was steep. When she returned home, even though the fires were not yet close, she "could not sleep." So after packing a few personal items, she walked back up Russian Hill to stay at her friend's home.

Many residents gave shelter to family and friends and even strangers fleeing the fires. A four-year-old girl later described how she and her parents and three siblings were wandering the streets by the glow of the flames when "a man asked my father if we wanted to sleep in his stable across the street." They accepted, and the man opened a bale of hay to make a bed for the six of them. Another girl noted her parents took in so many friends that "[t]here were now 14 of us in a small 5-room cottage built for two," and she added, "I have no recollection of how so many found available sleeping space." A woman wrote in a postcard that a stranger opened his home to her and her friends, "and thirteen of us stayed in one room" where they "used what bags they had for our heads and managed to get a little sleep." Edith Cook, only a child at the time, later remembered sleeping that night in a vacant house because, although her parents' home was a safe distance from the fire, her father worried about the tall apartment building next door to their home, "halfway off its foundations and leaning toward us." And Santa Fe Railway employee Michael Maher slept that night in a toolshed near the tracks.

Domingo Ghirardelli Jr., president of the chocolate company and son of the late founder, was at his warehouse ensuring all was safeguarded while his wife, Addie, welcomed refugees into their home. She gave guests "chocolate in unlimited quantities" to hand out to evacuees on the neighborhood sidewalks. "The city was now under military rule," one of her guests observed, who saw armed soldiers patrolling and heard them call out at the top of every hour through the night, "All's well on precinct," which was to her "a welcome sound." Also heard from soldiers throughout the hours of darkness was "Lights out," sometimes hollered as a reminder but often shouted at a specific home or flat. In a city with no power, any light showing through any window meant a burning flame of a candle or a lamp or stove. The mayor's proclamation warned residents of the dangers of broken chimneys but stopped short of ordering no indoor lights, and many did not know of the unwritten order until armed soldiers enforced it, sometimes with threats of violence.

A six-year-old boy noticed "the military would very threateningly call out 'LIGHTS OUT'" if they saw a light in a window, he recounted a few years later. "If one continued to leave the lights on or delayed too long or refused, then a warning shot might follow." A woman in the Richmond District wrote days later in a letter that if a resident did not obey lights-out orders, "the soldiers would shoot right through your window." A boy who was only eight carried the same impression in his memory into his adult years when he wrote of "the militia, which would shoot you on sight if they saw a light in your window, they'd shoot right through your window." One family using candlelight to feed their toddler was startled by a soldier on their doorstep yelling, "No lights to be lit!" For each feeding that followed, they covered their windows with towels or rags so no light showed.

Seven-year-old Alex Young lived with his parents and younger brother and baby sister in a Presidio Avenue home, and his mother lit an alcohol stove in a closet so his baby sister could have warm milk. But a soldier came to the front door and demanded "with bayonet" that she give him the stove, as Alex later remembered: "I never will forget the sight of that gun pointed at my mother."

Most could not find an indoor space to sleep, and many others, fearing aftershocks and further collapse, opted for the outdoors. "Those who were not afraid of the fire were scared to death of another earthquake," one soldier noticed, adding that the park he patrolled "was a seething mass of humanity scattered among every kind of household plunder from a grand piano to a toy rocking horse." Mailman Roland Roche and his family lay on mattresses in an empty lot a few blocks south of the Hayes Valley fire. "All night long the fire and flames glowed with a wild bright light." For him it was difficult to sleep for the "wild bright light" of the fire or its "cracking, buzzing sound," or the constant "explosion, sometimes in the distance, sometimes close at hand" of dynamite, or the stinging burns of "cinders, embers and paper ashes" showering them, or the worry that the firestorm would suddenly reach him and his family. "Every now and then someone would go out of the tent to view the fire and see if we were safe," a man camping on a grass lot down in the Mission wrote. "I didn't sleep very much."

In Pacific Heights two blocks west of Van Ness Avenue, Lafayette Park was, as one young man observed, "crowded with people and their belongings—most of them rolled up in blankets and asleep." A woman who left her stifling Buchanan Street home to get some air in the park found it "completely covered by mattresses, blankets, beds, tents, baggage, dogs, canary birds, soldiers, men, women, and children." The grass slope, crowded but elevated, afforded her a clear view of the city to the south and east. "For the first time I could see that awful fire," she soon wrote in a letter describing the "one great rising flame" that lit the sky. "It was horrible to look at:—I turned away."

Also in Lafayette Park was Mary Ashe Miller and her family. Worried for aftershocks, they had left their home with "steamer rags, blankets, and cushions and spread them out in a rather secluded bit of lawn." Although "the terrible glow of the fire was like a rosy dawn over the hill," they managed to rest for a few hours, even if Mary's rest was fitful: "Several times during the night I walked across the square and watched the progress of the fire eight or ten blocks away, and coming toward us with a roar and crackle that was so monotonously constant that it finally seemed as though we always had the sound in our ears since the first of life."

Further west, people filled the grass of Alta Plaza "by the thousands." Forty-three-year-old Jacob Levison had spent the day seeing smoke lifting from the eastern reaches of the city and watching "the stream of humanity pouring out to the Presidio" past his Pacific Avenue home. Now he and his sister walked to the hilltop park for their first clear view of the firestorm across the city "and what a sight met our eyes!" While staring at the "line of fire almost as far as we could see," Jacob later recalled telling his sister "that the pictures I had seen of Rome burning under Nero were bonfires in comparison." At their feet, the grass was thick with "men and women wrapped up in blankets, lying side by side and conversing as freely as if they were on a camping trip." Many had nothing stacked around them, no blankets or mattresses, only the clothes they were wearing. Jacob was overcome by the scene: "The glare of the flames—the roar of the fire—the heat—and the utter hopelessness and helplessness of it all—to these I cannot do justice."

In Jefferson Square, thousands who had fled the Hayes Valley fire through the day clung to their small plots of grass even as flames neared. "People crowded the sidewalks around the square, and many were sitting or lying on the grass," noticed sixteen-year-old Howard Livingston. He also saw people in the park "standing around a table, eating a meal." These were warm meals—very rare that night—prepared by a field kitchen set up by a local national guard company.

Although the California National Guard command was scattered and had not yet arrived, guardsmen who lived in the city acted independently that first day and, as a historian would later explain, "left burning homes and terrified families to assemble at their local armories for duty" that morning. Now from a tent headquarters in Jefferson Square they issued food and patrolled through the night to guard nearby stores and maintain order. One young guardsman in the park took a moment to write his mother "by the glare of the fire" to let her know he was "ok and still alive and kicking." And knowing he would be on duty for some time, he handed the letter to a man who promised to deliver it to his mom's address.

Fire crews of four engine companies were fighting to keep the Hayes Valley fire from spreading north to Jefferson Square and beyond, and, unlike most other parts of the city, here they were armed with water. Although the La-guna Honda Reservoir had suffered a cracked wall, its millions of gallons of water still flowed at full pressure through the unbroken twenty-two-inch-wide transmission main running up through the Western Addition, feeding hydrants along streets through a handful of unruptured six-inch-wide street distribution mains. One of these ran along Hayes Street far enough to deliver pressure at the hydrant at the corner of Buchanan Street, where firemen had been pumping since morning. And six blocks north, the Eddy Street main running along the north side of Jefferson Square was intact for a dozen blocks, feeding hydrants all the way to Van Ness Avenue.

Since early afternoon, engine companies had been pumping from two of these Eddy Street hydrants through long hose lines snaking south along streets on the east side of Jefferson Square, relayed through more engines and hose lines to reach the blaze. When they had started, the fire was three blocks south of Jefferson Square and water was pumped five blocks to reach it. Through the early evening, flames driving north forced firemen to roll engines and hoses back while keeping boilers filled and stoked. Now flames neared McAllister Street, just one block from the park.

Seeing the fires approaching his McAllister Street home, Arthur Danger-field dragged bedding and mattresses and what else he could carry to Jefferson Square, and as more neighbors forced from their homes sought refuge on the grass, "there wasn't hardly a square inch you could stand on." Soldiers went door-to-door ordering residents to leave. A man wrote his mother that a soldier knocked on his McAllister Street apartment door and announced to him and his roommates, "Time to get out, boys."

Hatted throngs in suits and dresses sat on trunks or lay on grass. Confused children clutched dolls or toy trains they had saved. Uniformed guardsmen walked patrol, stepping gingerly over sleeping figures on the grass and casting tall, flickering shadows across the sea of campers lit brightly in orange and yellow by the glow of the flames. "It was a strange scene that night," Arthur Dangerfield soon wrote his father, describing how difficult it was to get any rest with the fire only a block away. "We settled down to sleep but what with the cinders coming down like heavy rain, the roar of the fire, the crash of dynamite as they blew down whole blocks of buildings in front of the advancing fire and lastly a good strong earth tremor every few hours or two—no one did much sleeping."

There was little sleeping on the grass of downtown's Union Square either. Charmian and Jack London passed through in the eight o'clock hour during their circuitous walk through the city and Jack noticed the square "was packed with refugees. Thousands of them had gone to bed on the grass." The tall, windowed faces of the St. Francis Hotel's two rectangular twelve-story wings stood silent watch over a sea of people and trunks and blankets covering the grass and benches and steps surrounding the Dewey Monument. The space "resembled a battlefield," one man observed of the strewn possessions of poor evacuees and "wealthy guests of the St. Francis" who "fearing another earthquake were lying encamped in a state of abject terror." Magazine editor Mary Edith Griswold noticed "the crowd was perfectly quiet"—so quiet the "unearthly, unnatural calm" made her "afraid to speak."

Since morning, necks in the square had strained and stretched to get eyelines above painted advertisements topping tall buildings or through towering steel frames of new construction to monitor the progress of fires at the base of churning skies of smoke. Throngs had shifted through the afternoon for a view down the narrow canyon of Geary Street at the unbelievable sight of the Palace Hotel burning on the far side of Market Street. And since nightfall, an orange glow above rooftops signaled the firestorm was burning through Chinatown, just four blocks north.

Many who had begun the day in the square evacuated further from the fires, like Metropolitan Opera company manager Ernest Goerlitz, who accepted an invitation to stay in a friend's cousin's Clay Street home. Other company members—including Enrico Caruso—were wary of staying indoors and opted for the open ground of Jefferson Square or Golden Gate Park. And Melissa and Will Carnahan lucked into getting a $5 horse-drawn cab to take them from the St. Francis to her cousin's home in Pacific Heights.

By nine o'clock, crowds still in Union Square looking down Post Street could see flames shooting from the Crocker Building two and a half blocks away. The steel-frame flatiron was home to the Crocker-Woolworth National Bank and occupied the sharp corner where Post Street meets Market. Its eleven-story façade of stone and pressed brick had stood defiantly unburned all through the day and evening even as firestorms engulfed the Palace and Grand Hotels across Market Street and the ten-story Union Trust Bank Building and five-story Hobart Building (home to the Postal Telegraph Office) across Montgomery Street. The sight of flames engulfing the Crocker's tall form meant fire had crossed Montgomery Street on the near side of Market and now threatened the rest of downtown.

Within minutes another ominous sign appeared: a single but distinct column of smoke billowing from a roof behind the buildings facing Union Square. The fire had started on one of the five floors of Delmonico's Restaurant on the far side of the adjacent block, reportedly from "the carelessness of soldiers" who had started a fire to make coffee. The building's rear brick wall stopped the blaze from spreading through the back into the ruins of the Geary Hotel, where an earlier fire had been smothered and a few survivors rescued twelve hours before. But flames spread out the front and from both sides unchecked through the heart of the theater district, first to the adjoining five-story Alcazar Theatre, then into the Fischer Theatre and then into restaurants and offices.

The Crocker Building fire spread closer to the square along Post Street. In its path was the four-story Bohemian Club where Jerome Landfield, a professor from Berkeley, played dominos with the club president by firelight and drank water saved in pitchers. "The flames crept nearer and it was obvious that the club was doomed," Landfield later wrote. Earlier in the afternoon he had given a pillowcase stuffed with silverware and photographs to another club member with an automobile. Now he and the president grabbed blankets and valuables and retreated a block west to Union Square. But before the blaze reached the club, Landfield returned once more, used a pass he had earlier obtained from General Funston's staff to cross the fire line, and entered the dark club "to have a last look at the place where I had spent so many happy hours." In the stifling air of the darkened main parlor, he cut paintings and drawings from their frames with his pocketknife, rolled them up, and ran them back to Union Square.

On the corner of the square at Geary and Stockton the steel skeleton of an unfinished building acted as a small, temporary firebreak between the Delmonico's Restaurant blaze and the square. But the fire spreading along Post Street from the Crocker Building marched nearer, catching the roof of the Bohemian Club, and the picket line of soldiers enforcing the fire line reached the corner of the square. Looking down from a room on the tenth floor of the St. Francis, guest James Warren saw the fire was menacing the packed square from two directions, but he and his friend Sam decided it was still safe to stay for the night. By midnight the fires were so close, a man down at ground level observed that the square "was walled by flames, and blazing brands were dropping everywhere." At that point, James and Sam dragged their trunk down the stairs of the St. Francis, stacked it with a large pile of abandoned trunks on the sidewalk, and carried what they could in bags up the steep incline of Powell Street to Nob Hill.

In the same hour four blocks away, "Chinatown was catching everywhere," noticed a man who was watching the "awful and heart-rending sight" of residents "crying, cursing, yelling terribly, trying to save trunks, clothing, and other household goods." The blaze was now so fast, "in most instances all had to be abandoned to the fire." People escaping Chinatown and Union Square ascended Nob Hill from both directions where, breathing heavily from the climb, they sat on sidewalks to watch the firestorm below them consuming downtown, which compared to that day's burning "was now intensified a hundredfold." Tall buildings were "shooting flames high into the heavens," framing a scene that to many was "terrifying." One man wrote his mother he had to abandon their Clay Street home after 1:00 a.m. because the firestorm was "licking up block after block" toward him "at an uncomfortable speed." And in places still far from the edge of the growing blaze, red-hot cinders—some "the size of my hand," as one man noted—rained on fleeing residents.

The boom of dynamite explosions reverberated with more frequency and from more places near and far, unnervingly constant. "They sounded just like thunder," a man trying to sleep in a tent down in the Mission soon wrote. "After every detonation you could hear it echoing away in the hills for about half a minute." James Hopper likened it to "the pulse of the great city in its agony."

Following Mayor Schmitz's directive, demolition crews brought down only structures already on fire, and the detonations spread flames faster, often to unburned blocks. A Washington Street resident watched soldiers blow up a burning house a few doors down. "[S]uddenly a great shower of live embers and flaming tinder, in pieces as large as one's hand, fell upon the house and the street in front of it," and she noted it was "only by an extraordinary chance" that the roof of her own house did not ignite. Another resident wrote their home was dynamited because it was already "half burnt," but the explosion "spread the flames three houses to the northward." Three neighbors from the next block "implored the authorities to dynamite a block ahead" even though they owned a portion of it because it "was the only way to save property beyond, but their requests met with no response."

The Crocker Building fire spread north and south and "steeple-chased up Geary, Post, and Sutter Streets," as James Hopper would describe it, "melting before it the rich retail section and then the private hotel district." A Geary Street resident noticed his neighbors "out in the middle of the street watching the fire," and although he was exhausted and "tried to snatch some sleep on the lounge" inside his house, it was impossible: he would constantly "wake up and rush out to the street to see where the fire was." Art dealer Henry Atkins and one of his employees were filling a wagon with paintings and prints from Henry's Post Street art store—their third load of the night—when they "were cleared off the scene at bayonet point" by troops as the fire marched nearer. And demolition crews on Sutter Street tried again to get ahead of the flames. Photographer Arnold Genthe and his neighbors stood at a safe distance and "watched with others the dynamiting of the block of our homes." Between blasts, Genthe heard his neighbors quip with resignation, "Well, there it goes!" and "That's that!"

Charmian London's ears filled with these "muffled detonations of dynamite" as she and Jack walked downtown streets in the path of the fire. After 1:00 a.m. she noticed districts that had been filled with thick crowds just two hours earlier now were block after block of emptied stores and restaurants and clubs and hotels and theaters, an entire district "abandoned to destruction that could not be retarded."

Jack too noticed the change. "A rain of ashes was falling" on sidewalks and dark lampposts of empty streets lined with more of the city's finest buildings in their final hour. Night watchmen "were gone," police "withdrawn," no soldiers, "no firemen, no fire engines, no men fighting with dynamite." Muted emptiness awaited walls of approaching flames, distant but inevitable. Another man noted the eerie loneliness of downtown that night was "the most terrible sight in the burning city," streets "vacant, deserted, dreadful; empty of all human sound; lighted only by the hideous glare of oncoming horror." He likened the "awful silence" to "a cry of agony before impending doom."

Charmian would later remember Jack remarking to her in those moments of unfolding fate, "I'll never write a word about it. What use trying? One could only string big words together, and curse the futility of them."

11. Too Much for Sleep

CAPTAIN CHARLES CULLEN and his ten firemen of Engine 6 had begun their day nineteen hours earlier rescuing ten adults and six children from the collapsed ruins of apartments on either side of their damaged 6th Street firehouse South of Market. They dragged their engine by hand to meet the nearest fire at 5th Street, drafted water from a broken main, and saved two people pinned in the Corona House ruins. In the afternoon as the fires burned westward through streets with dry hydrants and emptied mains, they waged a fighting retreat, pumping wastewater from sewers and working so near the intense heat they draped wet towels over their heads and lost some of their hose to the flames. The blaze destroyed their firehouse and every one of their own flats and apartments. And as they worked to save what was left of their South of Market district, they gulped water from buckets and their only food was a few crackers or pieces of fruit handed to them by passing evacuees.

The firestorm had burned westward along a front seven blocks wide since sundown, forcing Cullen and his firemen back block by block, barely saving their engine from the flames more than once. Now at midnight on 11th Street, they again found hydrants with no pressure but searched for a building with an independent supply, finding one at the Standard Electric Company's substation. They hooked their engine to its building hydrant and ran their hose two blocks up and "succeeded in saving a few manufacturing plants located in this neighborhood," as Cullen would report, understating their success in cutting the blaze off along three separate blocks and narrowing the width of its front from seven blocks to four.

Ten blocks north, the Hayes Valley fire reached homes lining Golden Gate Avenue's south side, raining sparks and ash flakes on the helmets and backs of firefighters hosing down the wooden fronts of two- and three-story Victorians along the avenue's north side. Hoses snaked along brick pavement to two steam engines, their wheels jerking back and forth in fast rhythm with the clicking of steel pistons driven by steaming boilers, pumping water from Eddy Street hydrants two blocks away. The water supply held, and the fire crews' tactic of pumping it through seven hundred feet of hose to soak the line of unburned structures worked: every burning ember or flaming chunk of wood that floated on waves of heated wind onto rooftops and house fronts sizzled dead on the dripping exteriors. "The final stand was made at Golden Gate Ave.," a fire captain proudly reported. "[W]e saved the two blocks on the north side." On the west side of the blaze, firemen acting with the same ingenuity pumped water through two engines and one thousand feet of hose from the day's most reliable hydrant at Hayes and Buchanan and kept the flames from marching further west toward the Western Addition and the Panhandle of Golden Gate Park.

In a day and night filled with devastation and defeat, these small triumphs may not have shined as brightly as the flames or resonated as loudly as the dynamite, but to residents, local victories in their own small corner of the city were all that mattered. Every alleyway where engineers ran buckets of water to keep their engine at pressure and every neighborhood where hosemen pulled hose lines up steep streets to triple the normal reach of a distant cistern's water supply to stop flames from crossing a superheated avenue meant another home or business or school or church had been saved. But men of the fire department—strained already to the edge of their physical endurance, a third of whom were working on one or two hours of sleep since responding to the cannery fire the night before—simply could not contain what was growing into a citywide conflagration.

Intensifying and strengthening and fueled by nighttime gusts, the great fire continued expanding into unburned neighborhoods and districts. After midnight, the South of Market fire had narrowed to a four-block front but was rolling west and south through an area with no cisterns or working hydrants and threatening the Mission District. And the fire that had crossed Van Ness Avenue from Hayes Valley and leveled Mechanics' Pavilion and devoured the insides of City Hall's ruins now aimed north into the lodgings and theaters and saloons and brothels of the neighborhood at the foot of Nob Hill known as the Tenderloin.

In search of more small victories, Acting Assistant Chief Shaughnessy ordered engine companies from Hayes Valley to roll east and try to stop the fire in the Tenderloin from spreading further north. One engine company hooked to a hydrant at the corner of Van Ness Avenue and Eddy Street, which pulled water through the same unbroken six-inch main as the others along Eddy, among the few still getting a steady flow from the Laguna Honda Reservoir, which the water company had begun refilling with a repaired line and pumps that night. Firemen connected hose sections to extend their water supply three blocks to fight flames on Larkin Street where a resident noticed "Sparks and large cinders were blown our way, and I was afraid they might set fire to the house." And four more engine companies coupled their engines two by two along two streets to stretch another supply from a single hydrant down two blocks to keep the same blaze below Eddy Street.

Thousands of San Franciscans landed at the Oakland piers that night, where even from the far side of the bay "one could almost read by the light of the flames." In Oakland there was water, telephone, and electricity, and it was becoming the temporary home for most evacuees. As one of them would soon write, "[I]t has seemed a paradise after S.F." Parks were opened for campers, two hundred cots were set up in a downtown theater, and churches opened their doors with signs posted: "Shelter for Refugees." Relief stations were set up throughout downtown, and the lawn of City Hall became the resting place for more than five hundred refugees, some with blankets and bedding they brought with them, some in tents provided by the local Elks Lodge, but many "had only coats to cover them" as they slept on the grass.

Citizens also opened their homes. Fourteen-year-old Vera Imbruglia later recounted that her parents took in forty-two refugees, and "we had to take our mattresses off our beds and put them on the floor to let the younger kids sleep on them." It is estimated that Oakland's population—fewer than 100,000 on Wednesday morning—nearly doubled by the end of that first night and within a few more days nearly tripled, temporarily making it California's most populated city.

As the terminus for railroad lines and with operational telegraph wires, Oakland also became the early nerve center of relief efforts and the junction for most communications between San Francisco and the outside world.

Governor Pardee, an Oakland native and the city's former mayor, arrived in his hometown by train after 1:00 a.m. and set up temporary headquarters in the mayor's office. The governor had already mobilized the state's national guard troops, some of whom were soon on patrol in Oakland. He sent wires to cities throughout the state requesting food, clothing, and medical supplies for San Francisco and declared the next day a bank holiday. And given the state of San Francisco's wires, Pardee remained in Oakland—sleeping nights in the mayor's office—where he could maintain unbroken contact with the rest of the state and Washington, DC.

Oakland's telegraph offices were filled with refugees trying to send messages to friends and family. "I had to wait for more than an hour before my time came," one man remarked of the line he faced at Western Union. Mint superintendent Frank Leach convinced the operator to give his message to the US mint director in Washington, DC, official priority, finally sending news that the San Francisco Mint was saved: "It is the only building not destroyed for blocks." And a soldier breathing heavily from his hurried trek from Fort Mason arrived just before midnight clutching the message from General Funston for the War Department that was also given priority, sending Funston's initial request for tents and rations for twenty thousand people, already proven understated by the pace of events and misjudged by a factor of five.

At downtown's *Oakland Tribune* office, employees arrived to assist the six reporters representing San Francisco's three homeless papers, the *Call*, *Chronicle*, and *Examiner*. On arrival that evening by ferry, the reporters had telephoned the *Tribune*'s proprietor asking for his help in issuing a joint newspaper, and he opened his building to them and offered his equipment, paper, ink, and presses for the job and sent his employees to assist. By 1:00 a.m., the articles were stereotyped onto a four-page template and the presses began churning out forty thousand issues of the *Call-Chronicle-Examiner*, intended for free distribution to San Francisco residents scattered in Oakland and across the bay in parks and squares.

Departing the Oakland Mole that night bearing for San Francisco was a ferry filled with ROTC cadets from the University of California who had earlier been ordered "to go home and get plenty of food and water" before assembling in their khaki uniforms with rolled blankets at the campus armory where they were issued rifles. "Five cartridges were distributed to each cadet, and then we marched down and got aboard the train," one of the young men later recounted. Another cadet, just nineteen years old, noted, "That was the first time I think any of us had ammunition with our guns." The group was formed into three battalions, took a train down from Berkeley, and embarked on the ferry. "There was not much loud talking," one noticed on the crossing as they approached the burning city. "[A]ll seeming to be expecting hard work and preparing themselves for it."

The cadets were to join the Army patrolling residential streets in San Francisco's western districts, and after landing they walked through the streets of North Beach a safe distance around the fires where they "stumbled over cobblestones in the dim light." One of the cadets wrote that a few of the refugees camping in parks and sidewalks and yards alongside their journey "clapped as we passed." The young men, many unfamiliar with the city and all unaccustomed to policing a displaced population, arrived in Pacific Heights and were placed on four-hour shifts to walk neighborhood patrols, enforce the lights-out order, and "to destroy the stock of any liquor store found dispensing booze." Of looters, they were instructed "to shoot and shoot to kill." Cadets not assigned to the first patrol shift that night rested as many of the Army soldiers in the same district did, under their single blanket inside abandoned or commandeered homes.

Around 1:30 a.m. orange light flickered on the face of the St. Francis Hotel as tall flames consumed the other buildings surrounding Union Square. "The fire was then on three sides," noted a woman in a tent on the corner of the grass, and "the soldiers came along and drove everybody out of the square." Unable to carry her large box of saved possessions, she left it on the sidewalk. "It was frightfully hot," she noticed as she fled, "live coals and cinders were falling everywhere."

On a street beside the square, an elderly man on crutches stood near a wagon loaded high with trunks and suitcases he had been entrusted with safeguarding and tried paying anyone passing by cash for a team of horses to haul the wagon away from the flames. He offered as much as $1,000 before Jack London convinced him to leave the wagon and save himself. Within minutes, the wagonload was "burning merrily in the middle of the street," as were stacks of suitcases and chairs and tables and tents on the square's deserted grass.

The roof of the St. Francis Hotel began smoking, and windows showed the telltale orange glow from inside as floor after floor of luxurious trappings and grand adornments blazed into ashes from the top down. By 2:30 a.m. the two twelve-story wings were "flaming heavenward," adding another burning monument to the grim tally of the past twenty-one hours and, as an Army officer would later observe, proof "there is no such thing as a fireproof building."

Seven blocks north, firemen of two engine companies in their seventh hour of pumping water from a Washington Street cistern were fighting a losing battle against the blaze burning through Chinatown. With only one water source in the vicinity, a battalion chief sent the Oakland fire engine back across the bay and kept the hose wagon and three dozen Oakland firemen who continued working hand in hand with the local engine company, pulling hose lines back from burned streets and rerouting them along unburned blocks. The blaze spread so quickly they were "driven out," forced to pull back and barely saving their hoses. A man with a small group walking a street on the outskirts of the district, "in an attempt to get around the fire," sprinted to escape it: "I thought we were going to get cut off." The entire neighborhood "ignited like kindling wood," as another witness observed. In the two o'clock hour, a police sergeant protecting records in Portsmouth Square could see "Chinatown was all ablaze, and the last of its inhabitants that we could find had been cleared out."

With no water left to make any stand against the Chinatown inferno, fire engines and hose wagons were ordered back to the Montgomery Block, where the fire had again reached Washington Street. Once again the engines pumped from distant cisterns, soaking the exterior walls of the four-story structure. And once again it was saved, but with the blaze burning northward, officials emptied the sixty cells of Broadway Street's County Jail around 3:00 a.m. and evacuated the 176 prisoners—including the seventy-seven transferred the previous afternoon from the Hall of Justice—up to Fort Mason. Deputies and police officers, with the help of Army soldiers and national guardsmen and revenue cutter sailors who had helped save the Custom House, provided escort. "All the murderers and hard cases were handcuffed to a long chain so they were safe from escape" and "others were lined up between us fellows," one guardsman noted. "The order was given to load, fix bayonets and to shoot to kill in case any one of the prisoners attempted to break the line." By the flashing light of flames, the line of shackled inmates was conducted through the brick streets of North Beach under armed guard without incident.

From out on the water after 3:00 a.m. during his inspection of the waterfront, Lieutenant Freeman noticed tall flames "sweeping through Chinatown, up toward Nob Hill." The Fairmont Hotel and palatial mansions crowning the hill had earlier seemed a safe distance from the fires, but as the blazes from Chinatown and downtown converged and climbed the hill from two directions, residents on the lower hill who had begun their night believing their homes were safe now faced the worst.

"Mama was convinced that the fire would not reach our house," Dolly Brown wrote her fiancé of that night, "and the trunks were got packed after a very tearful pleading with her." She and her younger brother pulled "clothes and a few trifles in two trunks and baskets" up Bush Street away from the fire, but their widowed mother would not leave, "determined to see the house burn down." After a half hour, waiting on a sidewalk with the trunks and bags, there was still no sign of their mother, and with fire "roaring up the street," Dolly went back down through the wall of intense heat and back inside to find her. "I entered the house in the total darkness with the fire crackling in the rear of the house and looked in all the rooms, fearing that she had fainted or lost her mind," but the thick smoke and superheated air overwhelmed Dolly, and she "had to leave without her."

Dolly led her brother westward toward the home of a family friend out near the Panhandle of Golden Gate Park, and they joined the stream of people evacuating lower Nob Hill headed to Golden Gate Park or the Presidio. After seven blocks, Dolly "spread a blanket on the concrete sidewalk" to let her brother sleep for a while, then made it a few blocks further, rested again, and by 4:00 a.m. made it to the house and found nobody home. In a two-story firehouse across the street, the ten firemen of Engine 21 had just returned from fighting the Hayes Valley fire long enough to scarf down some food and gulp water and throw an extra hose on their wagon. They noticed Dolly and her brother stranded on the front steps of the locked house, took them in "bag and baggage," and gave them a bed in their upstairs quarters before rolling back to the front lines. Although comfortable in an empty firehouse a safe distance from the fires, Dolly "did not sleep one wink but only prayed that if anything had happened to mama, that the roof would cave in and kill us all."

All through the rest of the night on the street below and through every western neighborhood of the city, the steady stream of recently homeless trekked westward by the thousands. Most passed the jammed parks and squares of the Western Addition and Pacific Heights and aimed for the wide-open space of Golden Gate Park and its grass Panhandle. The hundreds of canvas Army tents quickly filled, and the open spaces between rows of staked rope tie-downs grew congested with trunks and suitcases and makeshift lean-tos of quilts and blankets.

Wary to sleep indoors for fear of another aftershock, many were from nearby homes, like Emma Burke and her husband and son, who walked one block from their Waller Street flat with a mattress and some bedding to sleep "under the protecting branches of some bushes" in the outdoor safety of "the Park, the Mecca of all the city." Most had journeyed far, like W. E. Alexander, who made it there with his wife and three sons from their apartment on the far side of Nob Hill, and who noticed so many around him from neighborhoods miles distant in the Mission or South of Market "carrying on their backs or dragging along on improvised sleds or toy express wagons all they had saved," adding "you can understand what strength and determination it took to reach [the park] and carry anything with you."

Twelve-year-old Marion Baldwin and her parents had been camping in the Panhandle across the street from their Fell Street home since the previous morning. Her father had returned from the downtown meeting at the Hall of Justice with a special badge and holstered pistol to serve as a neighborhood guard, and he "was so sad" from the sight of the destruction of his downtown drugstore that "he didn't want to talk." Now from mattresses on the grass, Marion and her parents watched the flames shooting high above the city in the eastern sky less than two miles away, lighting the night and reaching them with floating ash and flaming debris. "There was a breeze and it would bring all these cinders which were just like rain coming down," she later recalled. "Every once in a while great chunks of wood—not great ones but as big as your hand some of them," along with smaller embers all "still red hot," fell on them, stinging their skin and singeing clothes and blankets. Her dad ran to their house and brought back three umbrellas for them to sleep under that night.

Arnold Genthe also spent that night in Golden Gate Park and noticed a "cheerful spirit" in the crowd surrounding him, an atmosphere that "suggested more a camping out than refugees from a disaster." By the small hours of the morning a calm silence settled over the multitudes. They were "sleeping the sleep of exhaustion," Emma Burke observed while keeping warm in her long coat on the mattress beneath the bushes with her husband and son. The quiet was broken only by "the wail of a baby, the clang of an ambulance, and the incessant toll of wheels and tramp of feet." And in the hour before dawn, voices began calling out, "Bakers wanted! Bakers wanted!" And "Union telegraphers wanted."

Somewhere in the silent crowd that night was Dennis Grady, a horsekeeper who fell asleep in the park by his wife's side after an exhausting, stressful, shocking day and never woke up. "Mrs. Grady awoke," as a newspaper would report, "to find her husband dead beside her." He died of "exposure." The night also took Henry Mayer, a forty-five-year-old auctioneer who had been brought to a tent in the Panhandle for treatment after collapsing while escaping the

South of Market blaze. He was alive when he arrived but succumbed from "exhaustion resulting from effort to escape flames," as would be reported. By his side was his wife of sixteen years, Celia, forty-one, and his daughters, Clara, fourteen, and Henrietta, ten.

The tent where Henry died was part of the Park Emergency Hospital's temporary outdoor location established after the earthquake had shaken portions of the hospital's walls to the ground, exposing support beams and heaping mortar and bricks on the ambulance and blocking the main entrance. Physicians and staff had moved surgical tables and medical supplies into the tunnel beneath the Alvord Lake Bridge, and beds were set up in Army tents on the open ground beside the damaged hospital to treat patients. Nurse Lucy Fisher, on her feet since beginning the early morning in Mechanics' Pavilion, arrived at the park hospital that night to help treat the injured. "Lights were twinkling from many lanterns among the shrubbery" when she arrived. A group of doctors and nurses performed surgery in a tent by the light of hanging lanterns. She donned a long white smock and grabbed a pot of coffee and some hypodermic needles and morphine from the supply tent and found the doctor in charge to begin work.

"Patients were being brought in continually through the night and beds had to be made ready for them," Lucy noted. As the tents filled, mattresses were dragged out and laid under trees. She and other nurses "went from one patient to another"—there were broken arms, deep lacerations, third-degree burns, or limbs bandaged from amputations. And there were wounded firemen, one of whom "had a deep gash on his forehead and his hair was matted with blood." And a singer with the Tivoli Opera House, Bernice Holmes, suffering from two broken legs.

Lucy and the other nurses carried coffee and hot water in bottles to each patient. For those who needed pain relief, the doctor in charge prescribed morphine, but through the night as the number of patients became overwhelming, he told the nurses, "Use your own judgment." Lucy administered morphine through needles, and for those needing a stimulant, she would drip drops of bitter strychnia on their tongues. "The glow from the burning city almost turned night into day," she noted as she rushed among patients, so occupied that she quickly forgot she was working outside in the park. It was only in lone trips to and from the supply tent where she "would catch the odor of apple-blossoms from above my head or sweet-scented broom by my side."

Wounded patients also flooded the Presidio's Army General Hospital, where beds were filled to capacity. Dr. George Torney ordered the four barracks of the men's hospital corps to be "vacated and established as wards," opening more beds for the coming day, which would see the number of patients double yet again. And he directed that a large circus tent be erected on the grounds out front in which he and his staff organized a "tent emergency hospital" to meet the overwhelming need for first-aid treatment.

Most of the patients suffered wounds related to the earthquake or fires—broken limbs, burned hands and arms, internal injuries. And most had been transferred from other hospitals in the path of the fire. Army Lieutenant Charles Pulis had been brought from Mechanics' Pavilion, still unconscious, his head wrapped after surgery to his fractured skull from the black powder explosion that morning on 6th Street. Also brought from Mechanics' Pavilion was Edward Manville, a night steward on duty in the Central Emergency Hospital beneath City Hall at the time of the earthquake, who was injured by falling mortar.

Agnes Lawless had been recovering from surgery in Clara Barton Hospital on Lower Nob Hill when the earthquake struck, and her physician evacuated her first to another hospital on Sutter Street, then to the Presidio by nighttime. Her husband, Robert, a steamship captain, was in the South Seas, and on his return the next month he sang the praises of Dr. Torney and the medical staff: "If she'd been General Funston's wife she could have had no better care," he effused. "Attendants, nurses and doctors could not have been kinder to their own sister than they were to my wife and we will never forget it."

By the light and heat of thousands of acres of burning buildings, the city's most illuminated night passed into its haziest, smokiest dawn. People still in San Francisco had survived their city's longest day. Few had slept. "The noise of explosions, the heat, the wonder how far the Flame had now reached," one man explained, "were too much for sleep."

Beyond the noise and dangers of the night there was no end to the worry, anxiety, stress, uncertainty, fear, and sorrow. Tens of thousands of heads rested on ash-covered mattresses or dewy patches of grass, their first night in a place and time of no material permanence—homes, businesses, streets, lightposts, doorways, their own desk or bed, whole neighborhoods, the skyline many had known their entire life—gone. The accumulated treasures of a lifetime and the touchstones of daily routine had evaporated in the short space of hours or minutes or seconds.

Thousands stayed awake with worry for a missing spouse or child or parent or friend, and many unfortunate souls tried to sleep through tears, their minds flooding with the awful images of a son's broken body or the sound of a wife's last words. Only numbness or exhaustion could allow sleep to conquer the shock of what was seen and heard and felt the day before, or the worry of what more damage had been done through the night. Or what morning light might reveal. Or how much more the new day could bring. One four-year-old girl who found some fitful sleep on a bale of hay with her family in a stable noticed her older brother and younger sister slept, but her parents did not: they simply "watched for the new day with despair."

12. The Day of the End of the World

THE FIRST CABLE car line had been carrying passengers up Clay Street to Nob Hill for barely a year when railroad baron Mark Hopkins purchased a lot atop the hill in early 1875 to build a home. When he died three years later, the task of completing the home passed to his widow, Mary, who "had difficulty settling on one style," it would be reported, "so she instead tried to incorporate them all." The result was a four-story wooden monstrosity of cupolas and turrets and chimneys and porches of mostly Gothic style in brown and gray. In 1887, sixty-nine-year-old Mary wed forty-six-year-old Edward Searles, who would later say he married her for "both love and money." Mary died less than four years later as the richest woman in the United States, and after settlement of her contested will Searles got the mansion.

Driven as much by his desire to return to his home state of Massachusetts as by any philanthropic virtue, Searles gave the mansion to the University of California to be used as a school under the San Francisco Art Association for "instruction in and illustration of the fine arts, music and literature." A portion of the ground floor was converted into an art gallery and the two-story stables at the bottom corner of the lot were refitted into an art school. By 1906, the Mark Hopkins Institute of Art hosted as many as thirty thousand art students for day and evening classes annually, seasonal art exhibitions, and weekly music concerts, and its collections included paintings, drawings, and sculptures of international renown.

Like the Hopkins Institute of Art, the other four mansions lining California Street on the pinnacle of Nob Hill had been erected by the fortunes of men no longer alive, monuments of accumulated wealth still holding the city's high ground and casting long shadows on the wage-earning residents of Lower Nob Hill and the city's low ground of immigrant laborers in working-class tenements. These "preposterous palaces," as a visiting architect dubbed them, crowned the hill where "pretension rules the crest while poverty battens on the slopes," as a local newspaper observed.

And Wednesday morning's earthquake had left them mostly undamaged. The secretary and janitors of the Hopkins Institute of Art inspected the building and found it "intact and uninjured." In the Stanford mansion next door on the lower slope of the block, servant Ah Wing awoke to broken statues and vases but found its "walls uninjured," paintings "unhurt," and even the chimney "stood the quake well." Through the day, Ah Wing watched the fires growing and spreading through South of Market and downtown, and though he "could hear the bumps and blasting and dynamiting" and watched the various blazes "connecting," he stayed, believing the mansion was safe. The fires of Wednesday also did not concern staff in the Hopkins Institute of Art "because of their distance," but as night came, the secretary "took the precaution of extracting some of the more valuable pictures from their frames," ready if quick evacuation became necessary.

After midnight, Ah Wing saw the fire had reached Chinatown two blocks down the hill, and the wind "drove the fire toward us like a tiger." After 3:00 a.m. another servant saw the fires eating their way up California Street from Chinatown and up Powell from Union Square and urged Ah Wing to leave, but he stayed and asked the gardener and watchman to help him guard the Stanford mansion.

Seeing flames climbing the hill, art students and professors and volunteers flocked to the Hopkins Institute of Art and "spent the next couple of hours carrying paintings, statuary, bronzes, bric-a-brac and ceramics across the street to the Fairmont," as a witness reported, "and piled them on the floor of the lobby." A good number of paintings were also carried out the front and stacked on the lawn of the Flood mansion on the opposite block. Around five o'clock, Mayor Schmitz returned to Nob Hill in his car after a visit to his Pacific Heights home where he had grabbed a couple of hours of rest with his wife and children. By the time he arrived back at the Fairmont, "the fire had crept up on all sides of the hotel," burning just one block away on both its south and east sides.

Sparks and embers carried over streets and rained from two directions on the wooden walls of the Stanford mansion. The first flame caught on the second floor and the watchman managed to smother it. Another ignited on the porch above the front door and with buckets of water stored upstairs, as Ah Wing reported, "[i]t was put out in ten minutes."

But the blaze burned uphill along the far side of Pine Street. At the top of the block, a fire engine rolled to the corner of the Hopkins Institute of Art and firemen yanked up an iron manhole cover, dropped a suction hose into a cistern, and walked hose lines through the front gate and across the lawn to play two streams on the structure's slate roof and wooden walls. Revenue cutter sailors maintained a fire line and impressed nearby men to help with the hose and carry art from the institute. Firemen kept the art institute's buildings soaked, and when the cistern dried up they pulled the engine onto the grounds and hooked the hose to the basement and first-floor hydrants connected with the institute's reservoir in a desperate stand. Mayor Schmitz walked over from the Fairmont "to encourage us in our good work," the fire company's captain would later report, "and left orders to work our best in trying to save the institute."

The blaze spread through the three- and four- and five-story wood-frame apartments across one street and then another. "Houses seemed to melt away before your eyes to disappear like magic," a witness described. "A line of red would run along the eaves, there flames would issue from the roof and upper windows," which would turn into "a red mass."

And the blaze was not stopped by the sixty-nine-foot width of the streets. "The flames crossed the streets in great loops so that the burning buildings seemed to be lassoing those opposite." Scorching gusts of superheated air drove the volunteers and revenue cutter sailors back while the firemen at the foot of the Hopkins "continued working until the fire surrounded us in a very threatening manner," as their captain described. The rooftop nearest the flames "suddenly blazed at the turrets and cornice," as the institute's director reported, "and the destruction of the entire building quickly followed." Orange sheets of flame ate from the rooftop down the turrets and bay windows, and carved wood melted away. Firemen backed away with arms over their faces and heaved their engine up the driveway out the gate and up the street, barely saving it.

Down in the Stanford mansion, Ah Wing saw the Hopkins mansion "in flame," and with blazes on three sides of him, he knew the mansion where he had lived for nearly a quarter century, where he had served Mr. Stanford until his death and then Mrs. Stanford until hers, was doomed to burn. "Instantly, tears came to my eyes," he later wrote. He packed a few things and left. By habit he locked the door on his way out.

Ah Wing walked up California Street past the Fairmont and past the Flood mansion, "very sad and melancholy on the way, and unwilling to look back." When he reached Jones Street he looked back and saw "the Stanford house was in flame." He found a friend, Yee Ching Wo, and together they walked to a vegetable garden to rest, away from the fires. Also taken a safe distance from the fires were the paintings that had been rescued, transported in wagons out to Golden Gate Park and the Presidio.

Just one block away from the burning Hopkins Institute of Art, writers Jack and Charmian London awoke from a fitful rest on the cold stone steps of a two-story house on the corner opposite the Fairmont Hotel. The streets and sidewalks were thick with ash, and Jack noted "a sickly light was creeping over the face of things." Charmian looked across the street and saw flames spread from the Hopkins Institute of Art and invade the granite and terra-cotta walls of the Fairmont as its unfinished interiors began to burn. The sidewalk and steps below Jack and Charmian were clustered with sleeping refugees.

The homeowner returned from finding his downtown office burned, climbed quietly among the sleeping figures on his steps, and, as he unlocked the front door, he invited the Londons inside. "It was a luxurious interior, containing the treasures of years," Charmian noticed. He showed them through his home under the heavy, unspoken realization they were witnessing its final hour. When they passed his piano, the man asked Charmian if she would play. She lifted the fallboard but hesitated, feeling it a "cruel thing to do, with annihilation of his home so very near." But Jack whispered, "Do it for him—it's the last time he'll ever hear it." She sat and played. "The first few touches were enough and too much" for the man, who "made a restraining gesture," and she stopped.

Thursday morning's sun rose at 5:30 a.m. and its light cut through the smoke to lay bare the devastation of the last twenty-four hours. Only the scorched skeletons of skyscrapers and blackened carcasses of brick storefronts outlined where streets ran. The Call Building and St. Francis were flame-scarred shells, appearing taller for all the flattened buildings surrounding them. The gutted frame of the Palace remained, stripped of its ornate façade and unrecognizable. At the top of the charred birdcage of City Hall's wrecked dome the *Goddess of Progress* still stood, a witness to the past day and still viewing the city's slow death by fire. "Nob Hill, the Fairmont, the homes of the pioneer millionaires,

Mark Hopkins's, with its art treasures were aglow," James Hopper observed of the fire still raging at daybreak, "a ruby tiara upon the city."

"The sun came up bright but the smoke was so thick that it looked like the moon eclipsed," one man noted. People in the city that morning described the rising sun as appearing "red as wine" or "blood-red, and showing quarter its usual size." James Hopper likened it to "a red wafer behind clouds of smoke." Ash and dust hung like fog. Thick air carried a raw sting of smoke and the reek of burned garbage and roasted horses and cremated bodies. People walking through ruins of the burned district left tracks through "about an inch of ash" covering sidewalks and could feel the heat of the paving stones through their shoes. "The streets were filled with debris and almost impassable," one man noticed. "Towering walls, festooned with broken wires and bent and twisted steel framework, appeared ready to fall at the slightest touch." The Londons descended Nob Hill to walk downtown's "waste of smoking ruins," as Jack wrote, encountering a few other men and women wandering and trying like them to absorb the panorama: "It was like the meeting of the handful of survivors after the day of the end of the world."

Huddled families and lone refugees, most newly homeless, crowded the yards and sidewalks of unburned districts. A member of the opera company who had escaped Nob Hill during the night with her friends awoke atop a blanket on a North Beach lawn "chilled to the marrow in the night by the dew—which we could literally wring from the blankets." Even that far from the fires "the air was filled with falling soot and bits from the burning city."

And the cloud-filtered sunlight lured outside the lucky few who had spent the night indoors. Dolly Brown and her brother emerged from the firehouse where they had spent the night and were relieved to find their mother alive at their friend's home across the street. She had walked there "all but mad" and like Dolly had been awake with worry, but now she could find sleep and rest her mind knowing her children were safe.

Up in Pacific Heights, Melissa and Will Carnahan had spent the night inside her cousin's house after evacuating the St. Francis Hotel, and at daybreak saw "men, women and children on the front porches of the houses in the neighborhood." Most were near the end of a long trek from distant burned-out homes, heading for Golden Gate Park or the Presidio, and, in Melissa's estimation, "had from sheer exhaustion dropped in their tracks." Many were "lying down, their baggage serving as pillows," and those sitting up were "bracing themselves against the columns of the porches or the walls of the buildings."

Evacuees with sufficient reserves of energy continued walking past in a procession unbroken through the night and through the morning, most "in silence, features stony and eyes glazed," as Melissa later recounted of the "ghost-like" scene. One man dragging a trunk that morning was overheard quipping he had "lost faith in the story of Lot's wife" in the Bible turning to salt when turning to look back at Sodom and Gomorrah, because he was now convinced "she died of heart failure from dragging her trunk out of the doomed city."

Around the north side of the downtown area's fires and through the burned streets of the harbor district and South of Market, refugees flowed toward the waterfront. "In our walk from the west to the east of S.F. to reach the Oakland ferry boat we saw scenes which baffle description," a woman wrote in a letter, seeing "the earth yawning open for yards—the asphalt sidewalk in hills." Exhausted and shocked by what the morning sun revealed, multitudes aimed for the tower of the unburned Ferry Building, as frozen in time as the hands of its clockfaces, an enduring symbol of yesterday's city.

Enrico Caruso walked with another singer toward the waterfront, both in hats and frock coats and carrying alligator-skin personal bags. They offered a water company engineer cash for a ride in his wagon to the Oakland ferry, but he explained his work was too urgent, gave them directions, and, as he would later relate, "left them regretfully, two weary travelers anxious to put as much distance between them from the city that had so rudely awakened them by throwing them from their beds in the Palace Hotel the day before." Caruso eventually got a ride in a wagon his valet secured to carry him—along with his trunks—to the piers, and on the way he saw "buildings in ruins, and everywhere there seems to be smoke and dust."

A man who rode a two-horse wagon with his wife and another couple that morning to the waterfront (they had split the $20 charge) described the wharf and found "thousands of people were camped there in the hope of getting out as we had hoped to do." A woman who walked with her party from North Beach and whose feet "were almost blistered by the stones which had so recently been exposed to the ravaging heat of fire" made it to the Ferry Building. After a half-hour wait "that seemed an eternity," she "boarded the ferry which, smelly and awful as it was, seemed heaven." On the crossing to Oakland, she and her group went to the vessel's saloon where corned-beef hash and coffee were served: "One could eat little," she admitted, "although the hot coffee was life-giving." But the food was welcomed by most passengers. "While on the boat we got something to eat," one man described, "not much, but after twenty hours it tasted like 'quail' [a delicacy]."

ABOVE LEFT: Lee Yoke Suey was bayoneted by a soldier while rushing back into his family's upstairs flat to save this, his birth certificate, as fires reached Chinatown the first night. *Chinese Historical Society of America*

ABOVE RIGHT: Ng Poon Chew, the editor and owner of *Chung Sai Yat Po,* employed his newspaper to inform and mobilize residents and merchants of Chinatown to successfully resist post-disaster efforts to move their community out of San Francisco, and Chinatown was rebuilt in its original location in the heart of downtown. *History San Jose*

AT LEFT: Chinatown residents watch the fire move up Washington Street toward their homes and businesses midafternoon the first day. By the next morning, their entire neighborhood— including every building visible here—was destroyed. *Bancroft Library*

TOP: The view down California Street from the Mark Hopkins Institute of Art as flames climb Nob Hill the first afternoon. Visible on the near right is the Stanford Mansion at the bottom of the block, and to the left is the lower portion of the newly built Fairmont Hotel. *San Francisco History Center, San Francisco Public Library*

BOTTOM: Residents gathered in Lafayette Park watch their city burn at dusk the first night. *San Francisco History Center, San Francisco Public Library*

TOP: Residents flee by foot and wagon through Market Street's smoking ruins toward the Ferry Building while fires still burn in other parts of the city. *San Francisco History Center, San Francisco Public Library*

BOTTOM: Photo captioned "Body of looter shot by soldier and left to burn in fire. Man was allegedly looting Shreve & Co. Jewelers, Grant Ave. and Post St." *Bancroft Library*

ABOVE: View of the city's ruins looking eastward toward Nob Hill from Van Ness Avenue. *Bancroft Library*

MIDDLE: The remains of City Hall after the fire. *San Francisco History Center, San Francisco Public Library*

BOTTOM: The ruins of the Hall of Justice photographed from Portsmouth Square after the fire. *San Francisco History Center, San Francisco Public Library*

TOP: Two children view the remains of a few blocks of the Mission District. Note the houses still standing along the south side of 20th Street where the fire was stopped. *Bancroft Library*

BOTTOM: Refugees with the only surviving pieces of their former lives they could save before flames reached them. Approximately a quarter million residents were made homeless by the disaster, and they camped wherever they could find space in empty lots or parks or squares. *San Francisco History Center, San Francisco Public Library*

AT LEFT: With chimneys and flues broken by the earthquake and gas turned off throughout the city, no interior fires were allowed, and "street stoves" were commonplace for weeks following the disaster. *San Francisco History Center, San Francisco Public Library*

ABOVE: Breadline on Ellis Street April 21, 1906. *Bancroft Library*

AT LEFT: With many schools destroyed and most classes cancelled for six months, the relief fund employed many of the city's children—even of very young ages—in cleanup work. Here boys paid as street sweepers pose for a photograph. *Bancroft Library*

TOP: Refugees and their belongings fill Dolores Park one week after the fire. *San Francisco History Center, San Francisco Public Library*

BOTTOM: Camp cottages fill Dolores Park in 1907. The 5,610 cottages throughout the city were eventually moved from public parks to private lots at owners' expense. Today more than two dozen of these "earthquake shacks" survive in renovated, remodeled forms in the Bay Area. *Bancroft Library*

TOP: One week after the fires were extinguished and before rubble was cleared, United Railroads began running electric streetcars on Market Street, to and from the Ferry Building. Note the wood supports and cable wrapping the walls of the lower clocktower as temporary bracing for its cracked brick and sandstone exterior. *San Francisco History Center, San Francisco Public Library*

BOTTOM: Market Street as it appeared after one year of rebuilding, April 18, 1907. In the distance the Call Building's interior is being rebuilt as construction proceeds on the new Humboldt Bank Building (center) and the Pacific Building (bottom right). *San Francisco History Center, San Francisco Public Library*

"The greatest good fortune during the calamity undoubtedly lay in the preservation of the Southern Pacific ferry, which allowed us and probably another 150,000 people to escape to Oakland and vicinity," wrote opera company manager Ernest Goerlitz, who also crossed that morning. Ferry evacuations continued uninterrupted because the wharf and piers and Ferry Building had been spared from the flames by fire crews and Lieutenant Freeman and his sailors, who were by 6:00 a.m. underway in the tugs *Active* and *Leslie* bearing for Goat Island where the crew was given water and served breakfast on the docked receiving ship *Pensacola*.

Most vessels on the bay were still operating under Freeman's orders of not transporting individuals into San Francisco without a pass signed by himself or General Funston (crews also accepted passes issued by Mayor Schmitz or Oakland mayor Mott or Governor Pardee). But some transport companies shuttled anyone into the city who was willing to pay. Fifteen-year-old William McGillivray was wandering the wharf when tug company owner Thomas Crowley called him over and enlisted his help getting a fare-paying boatload over to Oakland, and after disembarking their passengers, they were approached by people wanting passage back to San Francisco. Crowley charged them $10 each, as William later declared, "Mr. Crowley was quite a businessman then, I guess." Once back in the city, Crowley said to William, "Say, kid, let's go back and get another load," as William would recall. They did, and though charging a premium per head again, "We could get all we could take aboard."

Another of Crowley's tugs was piloted by nineteen-year-old Willie Figari, who carried "big shots" across the bay who had paid extra to avoid riding the ferry. Once in Oakland, Willie too was approached by a group who offered "anything" for a ride over to the city. He charged them $1 each, which he thought was high (the usual fare was a nickel). "Then another bunch came," and they paid, and he "had about fifty or so on the boat," far over capacity. On his return, Willie gave the money to Mr. Crowley, who sent him back over to pick up more.

On one of his trips early Thursday morning, Willie transported issues of the combined newspaper *Call-Chronicle-Examiner* from Oakland to San Francisco. "There must have been fifty bundles of paper," he noticed. The newspaper employees escorting the bundles, exhausted from pulling an all-nighter, "didn't know how they were going to get rid of them," even for free. Forty thousand copies of the edition had been printed through the night. Twenty thousand were rushed off on outbound trains north to Vallejo and Santa Rosa, east to

Sacramento and Reno, and south to Fresno and Los Angeles. Ten thousand papers were kept in Oakland for distribution to refugees there, and after the tug bearing the rest arrived at the Ferry Building, policemen and soldiers impressed the service of wagons and automobiles to carry the remaining ten thousand to squares and parks to be handed out to camping residents.

Across the top of the front page was its title, *The Call-Chronicle-Examiner*. No weather forecast, no "Price Five Cents," no theater schedule. Just the city, the day, and the date: "San Francisco, Thursday, April 19, 1906." And the headline: "EARTHQUAKE AND FIRE: SAN FRANCISCO IN RUINS." The four-page edition was a combined effort of the city's three largest newspapers and the first and last of its kind in the city's history. "Death and destruction have been the fate of San Francisco," began the main article, which reported Wednesday morning's earthquake to have lasted forty-eight seconds and resulted in fires destroying the South of Market district and most of downtown. The paper confirmed the destruction of the Call Building and newspaper row, the Palace Hotel, the Emporium, St. Ignatius Church and College, and City Hall. Articles announced Mayor Schmitz's afternoon meeting with "50 representative citizens" in the Hall of Justice, reported dynamite was being used "to stay the progress of the flames," and misreported that President Roosevelt had placed the city under martial law. And with flames still raging, the paper struck no optimistic tone: "Everybody in San Francisco is prepared to leave the city, for the belief is firm that San Francisco will be totally destroyed."

Among the officials ferrying from Oakland with a pass was mint superintendent Frank Leach. After landing at the Ferry Building, he walked up Market Street past the jagged remnants of yesterday's tall buildings. His steps sounded softly on the layer of dust and ash, muffled by morning fog and lingering smoke, and "every now and then suffocating clouds of smoke enveloped me so closely I could hardly see or breathe." In places where burned rubble "filled the street from curb to curb, several feet deep," he could only proceed "on all fours." He passed a dead body lying on the street near the sidewalk: "The head had nearly all been burned off, though the clothes were scarcely scorched."

When Leach reached the mint he was inspired to see that workers had run a makeshift pole out the top of the front gable and hung a large American flag from it, its blue and red popping brightly against a cityscape of gray and black. "On the sidewalk around the building was an encampment made of all kinds of improvised shelters," Leach noticed, "occupied by several hundred people." Knowing drinking water was scarce and urgently needed, he arranged for pipes to be run from the mint's abundant supply out to the sidewalks where refugees lined up "awaiting their turn at the faucets."

"Water was now more precious than gold," a woman camping in Golden Gate Park declared, "and not a drop must be wasted." And on such a "dusty and hot" day with winds "showering us with ashes and stinging our eyes with smoke from the ever-increasing fire," the plea for hydration from the multitudes was widespread. Ninety-minute-long lines of parched and panting refugees formed in the park for a full pitcher each of drinking water from barrel faucets. More lines formed to get tin cups filled with boiling water for coffee from a large cauldron set up on a fireplace fashioned from stones of the collapsed park lodge. Bulletins circulated through unburned neighborhoods warning residents "not to drink any water which might come from faucets as it was contaminated." Those who had filled tubs and receptacles with water the previous morning rationed it for drinking as they had through the previous day and night. In Cow Hollow, sixteen-year-old Howard Livingston counted his family "extremely fortunate" to have a neighbor with a water tank in his backyard plant nursery who allowed Howard and his parents to carry buckets down the street to his "tank for water, and we were very careful with it."

Sprinkling carts of fresh water were ferried over from Oakland and set up on street corners where police and soldiers enforced one bucket per family or cup per person. On Russian Hill, a few residents pulled the manhole cover from a cistern and lowered buckets inside with ropes to draw water, as one of them later recalled, with "everybody being urged to be as sparing as possible lest this source of supply should give out." Down in the Mission District, a few homes and businesses had uncracked wells, and as one man later described, "at all times of the day one could see lines of people carrying pitchers and buckets of water from these wells to their homes." They scooped up water still gushing from broken mains, and the same man recounted seeing "an old man washing his feet in a trickling stream of water coming down the gutter from a broken main" and just a block down the same street, "people were dipping this water up and taking it into their houses" for drinking and cooking.

With thirst, Thursday also brought hunger, especially for those who had lugged heavy belongings across the city through the small hours of the morning. In a few places, the Army organized breadlines. "We lined up in single file, rich and poor alike, or, in reality, all poor, with an armed guard on either side, and each man received a very thick dirty piece of bread and half a cup of coffee," a man in Jefferson Square later recounted. "We appreciated it all the same." Likewise in Golden Gate Park, where soldiers distributed rations.

Lines also formed north of the Panhandle at the YMHA (Young Men's Hebrew Association), where "we were given hardtack," as a six-year-old recalled
many years later. The taste followed him into adulthood, and when he later
learned sailors confined to the brig were fed hardtack, he "determined then
never to join the Navy."

A woman on Russian Hill was surprised when her butcher appeared at
her doorstep that morning with eight pork chops she had ordered two days
before. He told her the fire was still a safe distance away, but for how long was
uncertain. Before turning to leave he asked if she might want six more chops,
"adding that it would probably be the last meat we should have for some time,"
and she accepted them "thankfully." But such a plentiful food supply was rare
on Thursday and the days following, and home delivery rarer still. Far more
common was the experience of a man who "set out on a foraging trip" with
a friend that morning to find food. They entered a corner grocery "where we
were welcomed and invited to help ourselves" and filled their pockets with "an
assortment of edibles consisting of crackers, cheese, sweet cakes, eggs, bacon
and bread."

In some grocery stores "bargains were offered, as the owners wanted to
be rid of their stock," as one woman later recalled, but in others, "prices had
advanced," continuing the price gouging into Thursday. "Bread was getting
scarce," another resident noted, "but we managed to get 2 or 3 loaves at 10 cts
a loaf that morning and by noon they were $1.00 a loaf." As with the previous
day, soldiers shut down the profiteering by forcing store owners to let food go
at regular prices or for free. Soldiers and police also forced free giveaways of
"the contents of all grocery stores which were in danger of being burned," as
a police captain later reported. One man ran from his camp in Alta Plaza to a
store he could see was "doomed" near the fire line. "After a while the soldiers
broke in the doors and we poured in to see what we could get." He made
off with cans of vegetables and corned beef and a bag of flour in the raid of
what he called "legitimate looting." Residents down in the Mission District
walked the railroad tracks a few blocks into the smoldering ruins of South of
Market and looted "fine hams and sides of bacon" from an unburned packing
warehouse—"Some had as many as they could carry," as one witness soon
wrote—until soldiers chased them out.

In every camp and neighborhood of unburned districts, soldiers patrolled
on horseback or foot, reminding residents and refugees that no cooking was
allowed indoors due to the fire hazard of cracked flues or broken chimneys.
"We cooked on the streets," a thirteen-year-old boy later remembered. "Dad

made kind of a wooden frame and we had a little stove out there burning coal and cooked on the street and everything." Families cooked on stoves, some lugged outside from kitchens and others homemade, fashioned the previous day from bricks of downed walls and chimneys. Most had coal in their homes for burning, and for those who did not, "Firewood was not difficult to secure from the buildings that had been partly damaged by falling chimneys," one man noted. A woman riding on a florist's wagon with her husband passed many of these makeshift street ovens: "Some were preparing pots of soup, some were frying pancakes, and others frying steaks."

Relief for hunger and thirst and shelter for those left in the city was still largely dependent on inventiveness and luck and means—what food had been saved by fellow campers or who had the cash to pay elevated prices or which wells had water or who had access to the homes of friends or friends of friends. While a few thousand tents had been set up and rations were being handed out by soldiers and charity groups and hot meals served from a field kitchen by national guardsmen, a comprehensive plan for the relief of hundreds of thousands of people was needed to address not just distribution of food and fresh water but also shelter, clothing, medicine, waste, and sanitation. And with almost no reliable running water in the city and a finite supply of food—much of which was destroyed by a fire still raging—all perishables and most supplies would have to come from elsewhere, requiring coordination of transportation by water and rail.

In Washington, DC, War Secretary Taft had responded to General Funston's telegrams (received there at 11:40 p.m. and 2:50 a.m. local time) with two wires: one at 4:00 a.m. (1:00 a.m. San Francisco time) reporting that 200,000 rations had been ordered from the Vancouver Barracks, inquiring if more troops were needed, and affirming the need to "do everything possible to assist in keeping order, in saving life and property, and in relieving hunger." And within the hour, Taft sent a second telegram reporting, "All available hospital, wall, and conical wall tents will be sent at once by express" from eight other posts, complaining again of "[l]ittle definite information" received of local conditions, and imploring Funston to "[w]ire details as comprehensively as possible."

In his temporary office in General Greely's waterfront quarters at Fort Mason, General Funston—having replaced yesterday's wrinkled suit with a khaki uniform sent by messenger from what his wife had taken to the Presidio—did not respond to Taft's inquiries for more than seven hours. He sent a telegram to Secretary Taft after 9:00 a.m. reporting the "City practically destroyed," repeating that troops were in the city "aiding police patrolling and maintaining order," and reiterating "[m]artial law has not been declared." Funston estimated 200,000 homeless, reported "[f]ood very scarce," and implored War Secretary Taft: "You cannot send too many tents or rations." In response, Taft directed the quartermaster general to send "all available canvas" in the Army's possession as well as an additional 200,000 rations to San Francisco, and the Army chief of staff wired Funston that the tents and rations were on their way.

The year 1906 was still seventy-three years from the establishment of FEMA and more than a quarter century from the first federal relief organization, and disaster response had been historically a local responsibility reliant on private generosity. Even without an existing mechanism to focus national resources to a distant area of urgent need, President Roosevelt was determined to steer further assistance for San Francisco from Washington. He sent Dr. Edward Devine, the head of the New York Charity Organization Society and leading social work expert, to San Francisco as a special Red Cross agent and appealed to Americans by proclamation "to express their sympathy and render their aid by contributions to the American National Red Cross." With this presidential sanction, Roosevelt added federal authority to the organization's role as the national leader of disaster relief. And he signed a congressional joint resolution appropriating $1 million to the "direction and discretion" of War Secretary Taft to procure and distribute needed supplies "to such destitute persons as have been rendered homeless or are in needy circumstances as a result of the earthquake which occurred April 18th and the attending conflagration."

Waiting for supplies to arrive, Presidio quartermaster Major Carroll Devol and his staff inventoried the remaining surplus in the post's four warehouses. They emptied storerooms of twenty thousand wool blankets and more than twenty-four thousand shirts, allowing campers with no changes of clothes to slip on clean, three-button, olive drab or khaki flannel uniform shirts. Finding more than eighty-four thousand pairs of boots that had been returned from units in the Philippines because the pattern was "obsolete," soldiers also began handing out ankle-high, lace-up, reddish-brown leather boots of all sizes to refugees who had escaped barefoot or in slippers. And hearing "that a large quantity of relief stores were enroute from all parts of the East, various Government depots and other sources," Major Devol met with the general manager of the Southern Pacific and they arranged for three "avenues of supply for the city," one where freight cars would initially arrive at the South of Market depot (spared from the fire the previous night), one at the Folsom Street pier (saved from fire the previous afternoon), and a third at the Presidio dock.

The fire in the Fairmont Hotel canceled the planned 10:00 a.m. meeting of the "Citizens' Committee"—or the "Committee of Fifty," as it would be dubbed—and forced Schmitz into new headquarters once again, this time the two-story Washington Street North End Police Station at the foot of Nob Hill. The fire in that hour was consuming Nob Hill, gutting the Flood mansion and the Fairmont, and devouring the heights of city fortune. Resident Louise Wall later wrote of the inferno's path since the previous morning, how it "rose humbly in a shabby wholesale quarter," then "climb[ed] gently toward the broking and banking center," after which it "hastily skirted Chinatown" and "climbed on to its culmination on Nob Hill." San Francisco's "rising and falling greatness," she concluded, "was that day lapped up and leveled to a gray uniformity in the democracy of ruin."

But for all the "gray uniformity" of ashes and blackened streets left in the firestorm's destructive wake, there was little "democracy" in the human experience or physical toll of the calamity. The earthquake had not flattened the city's social hierarchy and the fires had not erased economic fault lines. The disaster tore through neighborhoods filled with residents whose fate was largely predetermined by the quality of the buildings in which they slept and the strength of the ground under their floors. Five decades of city planning sidelining safety and ranking profit margins of developers above enforcement of building codes had engineered a wide gulf between San Francisco's wealthy and working-class districts.

And the distinctions were amplified at 5:12 a.m., Wednesday: a person's location in that moment determined the likelihood of injury and chance of survival. The same shockwaves that brought down crowded boardinghouses and liquefied "made" ground, entombing the city's poorest in cheap tenements, merely toppled chimneys on middle-class homes in western neighborhoods and left mansions on higher elevations standing with only fallen statues or broken chandeliers. The same flames that ignited in South of Market businesses and ate so quickly through shared wooden walls into cramped living spaces of residential flats, leaving low-income residents only seconds to escape, took another twenty hours to reach manor gates atop Nob Hill. The lack of "uniformity" was also apparent in the evacuation as the trunks of wealthy guests in the Palace Hotel were carried from danger by bellboys and chambermaids whose own apartments were burning. It was also seen in housefuls of belongings borne in wagons and automobiles owned or rented by middle- and upper-middle-class families who saved nearly everything while many of South of Market's poor were left to drag or carry what little they could salvage from toppled lodging houses or burning flats miles to safety. And the enduring class differences were obvious at the waterfront, where refugees exhausted from hauling burdens for miles waited hours for a seat on a crowded ferry while those with means paid for private charters on tugs after riding automobiles or hired cabs to the wharf.

Not even death was a leveler. Remains of many who died in hospitals or were buried in temporary graves in city squares would soon be borne in horse-drawn hearses with great care, destined for burials in Colma cemeteries[4] after graveside services attended by family and friends. But for untold hundreds of unnamed lives South of Market, their ashes mixed indistinguishable with the ashes of the tenements in their final moments, and for many there was nobody to note their absence or mourn their loss.

---

4 Due to high demand on limited space within San Francisco, new burials were prohibited after 1900, and bodies in existing cemeteries were moved down the peninsula to new cemeteries established in Colma. Today only two cemeteries remain in San Francisco (at Mission Dolores and the Presidio) and the remains of more than 1.5 million are interred in Colma, "The City of Souls."

13. Heroic Efforts

FORTY-THREE-YEAR-OLD ERNEST EDWARDS resided with his thirty-nine-year-old wife, Emma; their sons, Francis, four, and John, three; along with his sixty-three-year-old widowed mother, Ellen; and seventy-year-old aunt, Emily, in the Mission District. They shared a comfortably sized, two-story home on a narrow lot beside a line of row houses that ran up to the corner. Families lived here. The most recent census listed the occupants of the homes lined up beside Ernest as follows: a family of five, a family of three with two roomers, a widower and his two sons and their wives and four grandchildren, a family of five with a roomer, and a family of nine with two servants on the corner. Every adult on the block was of either German or Irish heritage. Within a three-block radius were four churches, three laundries, two schools, a grocer, a butcher, and a drugstore. It was only a two-block walk to the streetcar line. A Southern Pacific passenger depot was one block away, and the rails of its coast division main line ran within one hundred feet of Ernest's house.

If Guerrero Street between 25th and 26th was a microcosm of the Mission District, Ernest Edwards represented its demographic. He was born and raised in a South of Market flat until his father, an immigrant carpet importer, earned enough to move them to the Mission where families could establish deeper roots in sturdier, roomier apartments and houses on firmer ground. Unlike the district's deadliest earthquake scene, the Valencia Hotel collapse, there were far fewer lodging houses and fewer transient laborers and smaller pockets of fill land than South of Market. Most houses and apartment buildings here sat on firm ground and had survived the previous morning's earthquake with little damage, and Ernest's was no different. After the shaking stopped and he found his home undamaged, he donned his suit and hat, walked on foot past the bent-up rails and fallen wires of the streetcar line he customarily rode, journeyed around the expanding fire lines, helped salvage books and documents from the Hall of Records, rescued files and anything he could fit into his pockets from his downtown publishing office before it burned, and returned home. Ernest and his family spent the night in their beds, confident the South of Market fire would not reach the Mission District.

But at daybreak Thursday morning, residents and refugees throughout the district awoke to find the South of Market fire moving in their direction. Former mayor James Phelan walked out to the garden of his Valencia Street home, noticed the blaze creeping nearer, and decided to evacuate as much as he could save. He stuffed his pockets with his sister's jewelry and loaded trunks and bundles into a four-vehicle caravan—including a dog cart, two carriages, and a passing wagon he hired for $60—and relocated to Golden Gate Park. Down in his Guerrero Street home, Ernest Edwards awoke and saw the smoke above the north end of the district. Determined to help, he walked nine blocks toward the fire, entered a 16th Street firehouse, found a fire battalion chief, "and told him I was ready to go to work at anything he wanted me to do." Ernest was told to find Battalion Chief Conlon.

Firemen had kept the blaze from crossing 14th Street along Harrison Street and stopped it on Folsom Street just south of 14th earlier that morning, but flames had reached 15th Street along Mission, Capp, and Howard Streets. Ernest Edwards walked the fire line along 15th Street looking for Chief Conlon and encountered an engine company searching for a working hydrant. Ernest guided them to an old reserve cistern down on 16th, but when they cleared away debris and soil and lifted the manhole, they found it "filled with dirt." Chief Conlon and hosemen from four engine companies fanned out checking hydrants for water but "could not find any available supply." Ernest found Conlon and later recounted the tired battalion chief turned to him and declared, "Ernest, the Bible says the world shall be destroyed by fire," then pointed toward the flames along 15th Street and said, "Look at it!"

Army demolition crews arrived to blast a firebreak along 16th Street, and soldiers went house to house ordering families to evacuate. Around 10:00 a.m. a soldier bounded down Guerrero Street from 15th with "his scabbard rattling at his side," as a man would later recount, yelling at the houses, "You must all move on at once; these buildings will be dynamited within an hour." Most residents ordered to evacuate their homes trekked to "densely crowded" Dolores Park as dynamite detonations began. Blast after blast sent shockwaves through Mission District streets, shattering windows and sending dray horses into fits. And one by one, wooden buildings along both sides of Mission Street were blown to bits—saloon, drugstore, the two-story Mission Primary School and the three-story Mission Grammar School. And flames followed the soldiers down the block, methodically feeding on wood ruins left in the wake of each blast.

At the end of the block, soldiers saw an opportunity to blast a sizable firebreak by bringing down Pattosien's Furniture Company, which comprised several small, single-floor structures around the main two-story warehouse on a lot reaching from Mission to Capp Street, a demolition that would triple 16th Street's sixty-four-foot width of open space. But Pattosien's advertised goods read like a menu of flammables: "fine furniture, carpets, bedding, lace curtains, rugs." After soldiers rigged dynamite inside each structure and ran the wire back out, charges in the smaller buildings failed to detonate while the main store's insides were blown out into 16th Street "and almost immediately took fire." Flames spread with violent intensity through thrown piles of rolled carpeting and thickly stacked layers of upholstery. Strewn furniture "burned like powder," as Ernest Edwards observed. Temperatures climbed well above the autoignition level of dry wooden structures nearby, and blasts of heat from the failed demolition "quickly set fire to the buildings on the south side of Sixteenth Street, opposite," and a new block was on fire.

Flames ate their way through the mostly wooden, two- and three-story buildings along 16th Street, westward toward Valencia, with a steady wind driving the blaze and no water to stop it. Ernest Edwards mentioned to Chief Conlon he had seen "a good head of water" gushing from a busted main three blocks away down at 17th and Howard Streets, just "running to waste." Conlon sent two engine companies to check, and they found the cracked street filled with water still churning up from the broken twenty-inch transmission main beneath 17th Street. On the corner lot was a building under construction with piles of sand and cement. Ernest ran to a nearby coal yard and grabbed shovels and burlap sacks, and the firemen filled the sacks with sand and dirt and cement. Ernest joined them, as did police officers and a crowd of neighborhood volunteers eager to defend their homes.

Captain Cullen and his men of Engine 6 rolled up to join the effort from

South of Market, where the fire they had kept away from manufacturing plants and the rail line had finally run out of fuel. Together they "dammed the water that was running to waste," as Cullen reported, "making a cistern," as Battalion Chief Conlon described. The crowd filled and stacked sacks and rocks to pool every bit of water gushing from the street, and the makeshift cistern filled as quickly as its walls could be thrown up. Fire companies positioned engines at each block and the water saved from the broken main was pumped through four engines to reach the blaze.

Up on the western slope of Nob Hill, the two-story brick powerhouse and carbarn of the California Street Cable Railroad sat on the corner of California and Hyde Streets. Every morning, its double-ended cable cars coasted through the carbarn's wide doors onto either Hyde or California Street, then gripped onto cables running in the street slots to carry fare-paying passengers down to Market Street via O'Farrell and Jones Streets, up Hyde Street over Russian Hill, California Street eastward up and over the crest of Nob Hill and down to Market Street, or down California Street westward where its cables pulled cars out to Presidio Avenue and back at such speed—12.5 miles per hour—that round trips took less than an hour.

When company president James Stetson checked the building's condition Wednesday morning, he found the earthquake had damaged the structure and thrown the large smokestack "even with the roof." And even though the basement's three triple-expansion steam engines that powered the winding equipment that drove the cables were "apparently uninjured," with no water, boilers could not be brought up to pressure and the cables could not be run.

There was no apparent threat to the building or the fifty-two cars stored inside until Thursday morning when flames reached the top of Nob Hill a few blocks away. The superintendent James Harris and a few of his workers arrived early to try and save the cable cars from the blaze by moving individual cars from storage tracks over to the transfer table and coasting them down the incline from the carbarn to the street. Without running cables they tried using horses to pull the first car or two up the street but were unable. So they used gravity, coasting cars westward one by one down the California Street hill two blocks to the intersection with Polk where the street rose again.

When James Stetson arrived that morning and saw the cars lined up and down the street and the fire so near, he knew "nothing could be done but await the result" and walked back to his Van Ness Avenue home. Concussive dynamite blasts could be heard from up at the top of the hill where the wall of thick smoke had reached, and by 11:30 a.m. flames could be seen as the blaze crossed Jones Street and began descending the hill, eating its way westerly through more residential streets, just two blocks from the California Street Cable Railroad and four blocks from Van Ness Avenue.

Many of the residents of Nob Hill's western slope and the Tenderloin had spent the night in their own beds, confident flames would not reach them. A police sergeant who had returned to his Geary Street home to check on his family had fallen asleep seeing "no fire near us" and did not believe "it would ever come so far out our way." But when he awoke, he "saw that [the] conflagration was only a block and [a] half away, and I knew we had to become refugees just like the rest of the people." Another Geary Street resident wrote in his diary that morning that the "day dawned but the fire did not diminish. Little by little it came towards." His morning entries reflected the speed of the flames: "by 10 o'clock it was burning at Jones" and "[b]y noon it was raging from Sutter to Ellis." Resident Louise Wall later wrote, "The fire was swallowing a fresh block of houses every ten or fifteen minutes" through the morning. "The whole sky in that quarter was steam and smoke, torn by wallowing bursts of flame."

Firemen of three engine companies slowed the fire's westward path in the Tenderloin by hooking to hydrants at Van Ness Avenue fed with a steady flow of water from the last water left in the cracked Laguna Honda Reservoir through the same intact transmission and distribution mains that had saved the Western Addition the previous day. But hydrants along the streets of Nob Hill and northern blocks of Van Ness Avenue connected with the Clay Hill tank, ordinarily filled with water pumped uphill from the College Hill Reservoir down in South San Francisco. That reservoir's transmission main was severed down in the Mission District (where its dammed spillage was being used to fight the fire)—the pumping station could not operate without power, and most street mains connected with water left in the Clay Hill tank were broken. Flames that rolled down Nob Hill were driven more and more by winds from the south and east, and in their path the hydrants were dry. The only hope of saving the western half of the city from Thursday's fire would be a firebreak along the city's widest street, Van Ness Avenue.

At this hour, late in the morning on Thursday, roughly thirty hours into the citywide fire, there was still no uniform plan or prevailing strategy for stopping the fire or even a centralized command or guidance for the distinct groups of firefighters, soldiers, and volunteers still fighting the flames on multiple fronts. With no firebox communication possible, strategy was devised at each fire line, where engine companies coordinated with other companies on which hydrants worked or which cisterns had water. One of the only top-level decisions on battling the blaze had been the previous day's call for dynamiting firebreaks, but even then, Mayor Schmitz and Abe Ruef had limited demolitions to buildings already in contact with flames, all but eliminating the tactic's effectiveness. And it was unclear who was in charge of explosives or the crews handling them. In some places, firemen were ordered by civilians to join with soldiers in commandeered vehicles to haul explosives or destroy certain buildings. In other places, civilians were ordered by soldiers to drive explosives in their own automobiles or wagons or to evacuate a home selected for demolition. Mayor Schmitz would issue orders to blow certain streets or blocks based often on stale information, and by the time his orders were carried out, it was too late to make a difference. Fire battalion chiefs told soldiers where to haul dynamite, soldiers told firemen where to blow buildings, and firemen told soldiers where to backfire.

Even those in charge did not know who was in charge. Fire had forced General Funston to move his headquarters once, and Mayor Schmitz twice, and neither had yet met with the other personally. Soldiers had been ordered by General Funston the previous morning to act under the orders of the mayor or the police department or the fire department, but by nightfall he had placed soldiers west of Van Ness Avenue under a colonel's command and left those to the east assigned to police and fire departments "in keeping order and in fighting the fire." And added to these split forces were guardsmen and ROTC cadets and sailors and marines, most acting under the orders of whichever general or colonel or city official they had last encountered.

In his relocated headquarters in the North End Police Station on Washington Street, Mayor Schmitz acted in the belief that he had authority over all troops in the city, without differentiating—or perhaps without always grasping the distinction—between state national guardsmen ("militia") or active-duty soldiers ("regulars"). After deciding to try to stop the fire at Van Ness Avenue, he sent out an order through a national guard messenger to direct all available guardsmen to clear residents from the avenue and the blocks east and "all the regular troops that could be spared to take charge of the dynamiting" there. The messenger delivered the message up through the chain of command to his brigade commander, Brigadier General Koster, who had arrived the night before and set up headquarters in Jefferson Square, that "the Mayor desired" guardsmen be sent to Van Ness "to be utilized in clearing streets and buildings of people east of the avenue." Then the messenger found an active-duty Army captain with the Corps of Engineers from Fort Mason and told him "the Mayor desired all the regular troops that could be spared to take charge of the dynamiting of the buildings on Van Ness Avenue where a final stand would be made."

When the Army captain arrived at Schmitz's headquarters, he "found the Mayor and his cohorts without plans regarding the dynamiting" but was told a steamer bearing dynamite was due from Point Pinole by noon. And Schmitz and his staff seemed, in the captain's view, "tickled to death at the prospect of having a company of engineers to do the work for them." As the captain left, two police officers commandeered wagons to carry the explosives, but before he could send his soldiers with the wagons to meet the steamer and get the dynamite, a messenger galloped up on horseback with orders from General Funston for him and his men to return to Fort Mason.

In the same hour, General Koster ordered his national guard companies to report to Van Ness Avenue, then went personally to the mayor's police station headquarters, where Schmitz repeated the orders and added that "the necessary dynamite would be provided." By the time Koster made his way to Van Ness, the dynamite was brought up in a wagon, and a city employee from Schmitz's office instructed the soldiers hauling it to follow Koster's orders. Koster sent them down to the Sutter Street intersection with instructions "to remain at that point until further orders."

But at that same moment, Lieutenant Raymond Briggs—the Presidio artillery officer who had been dynamiting since the previous morning—was in search of stick dynamite, as his crew's supply had given out. When he located the wagon at Sutter Street, he ordered the soldiers—more accustomed to take orders from their own captain than a national guard general—to haul it up to the north end of the fire, where he and his crew were planning to continue demolition. As they drove the dynamite away from Van Ness Avenue, the plan to blow firebreaks along Van Ness was left without any dynamite.

Unlike the six blocks of Van Ness Avenue lined with wooden row houses and three-story flats and stables and churches and schools that had burned the previous day when the Hayes Valley fire swept across its wide pavement, the rest of Van Ness was still unburned, and much of it was a residential showcase for homes of the wealthy, separating the neighborhoods of the Western Addition from Russian and Nob Hills and the Tenderloin. While not occupied by the gaudy palaces like those burned earlier that morning atop Nob Hill, this stretch of Van Ness was home to the wealthy and upper middle class, with spacious two- and three-story homes lined up beside stately villas set back from the street behind large, fenced yards.

Among the finest homes on Van Ness was the three-story Victorian of James Stetson, where he returned that morning after checking on his company's California Street powerhouse and carbarn. "Matters about this time began to be rather wild," he would later write. With flames approaching the avenue on a broad front, his overnight guests had departed for the ferries, and he sent some of his things—"clothing, silverware, bedding"—in his son's automobile to a friend's home and his rugs out to the Presidio.

By late morning, Van Ness's asphalt pavement "was filled with people . . . loaded with bundles and dragging valises or trunks," having been ordered out by the national guardsmen. Seeing the panic in the street and the blaze so near, James arranged for his son to drive his daughter and grandchildren from their Pacific Avenue home out of the city and down the peninsula to Burlingame. Alone in his house, James stood at a large window in his parlor and watched the fire's progress through binoculars.

By noon, "the flames were continuous" and steamrolling steadily down the hill. Homes and businesses melted away in red and orange flames. As the blaze reached the California Street Cable Railroad's brick powerhouse and carbarn, the company superintendent scooped cash from the safes into a satchel and escaped just before the building caught. It raged like a furnace, a fire so hot it bent iron rods and cranks and pipes and melted Babbitt metal crankshafts and bearing liners. Outside, oven-like temperatures filled the street, expanding iron rails and warping street slots and cracking brick paving stones and, as would be reported, "the cable was subjected to such intense heat from the flames of the adjoining buildings that at one place the wire strands completely melted."

A few blocks south, twenty-two-year-old Edward de Laveaga sat watching the fire from the front steps of his father's Geary Street home two blocks west of Van Ness Avenue. He saw the blaze approaching from the far side of Van Ness—within two blocks of the avenue at noon and within one block by one o'clock. Neighbors began to congregate and yell for volunteers to help fight the fire and "about seventy men responded," Edward wrote in his diary, noting they brought axes and burlap bags and bottles of wine to wet the bags.

About two o'clock, two fire engine companies arrived on Van Ness and jumped from their hose wagons. They did not connect to hydrants or grab hoses; they spoke quickly with the national guardsmen, who proceeded to clear remaining residents out of houses and boardinghouses and hotels along the far side of Van Ness and order crowds further down the street. As residents left each house, firemen ran inside for no more than a minute or two and then left, one at a time. And one by one, roofs of homes began smoking and flames appeared in windows and firemen moved to the next houses. Although the dynamite was gone, Acting Assistant Chief Shaughnessy had decided they could wait no longer to act, and on his orders the firemen were to "back-fire"—starting a controlled burn of homes along the east side of Van Ness to remove the fuel of wooden frames and flammable contents from the path of the blaze.

Within minutes, the structures were engulfed, and winds blew flames sideways and carried burning pieces up over Van Ness Avenue. As a local attorney noticed, "[F]lames came roaring down, gaining in volume as they progressed, till soon the structures on the west side of Van Ness began to catch fire." It was the roof of Fletcher's corner drugstore that caught first. Still sitting on his father's front steps two blocks away and watching like every other resident on the western side of Van Ness for any flames on their side of the avenue, Edward de Laveaga saw the roof ignite, as did the assembled crowd of "volunteer fire fighters," who ran to the drugstore "cheered on by the onlookers." As down in the Mission District, residents armed with time and resources now fought to save their neighborhood. With ladders a few of them made it up onto the smoking roof "and with wet sacks and hatchets they beat out the sparks from the burning building across the street or chopped off the wood that had already caught fire," as Edward wrote in his diary.

From a few blocks north, James Stetson watched the "backfiring" through his binoculars as "house after house took fire along the line of the blaze." National guardsmen drove residents and crowds up Van Ness Avenue past his home, and by three o'clock, firemen and guardsmen were backfiring the houses across the street from him. Stetson watched them enter homes one at a time carrying bowls filled with some flammable substance. They "would climb to the second floor" and "go to the front window, open it, pull down the shade and curtain, and set fire to the contents of [the] dish, and in a short time the shades and the curtain would be in a blaze." They would then go to the next house and repeat the process while other firemen or guardsmen would "throw bricks and stones up to the windows to break the glass" and spread the fire faster.

After four o'clock, both churches and most of the houses along the east side of that section of Van Ness were on fire. An Army officer driving his automobile down that part of Van Ness Avenue at that hour "saw the flames leap the avenue opposite two churches whose tall frontage threw a maximum of heat across" and noticed the large homes engulfed in flames would "collapse, leaving their large chimneys looming up like spires." And behind the blazing row of backfired structures, the main fire was only a block away and still approaching.

Out on the city's eastern waterfront, Lieutenant Freeman was still acting without orders. After being sent to the city Wednesday morning by his admiral, his command decisions through the rest of the day and night were of his own initiative and had saved the waterfront and Southern Pacific passenger depot. Now after an early morning break at Goat Island with breakfast and fresh water and a brief rest for his crew, he was back in the city as the first shipment of food and provisions for relief arrived at the Folsom Street pier.

Noticing this and a temporary relief station being set up by a few soldiers and also approximately 150 freight cars filled with produce and live chickens parked on the State Belt Railroad tracks along the waterfront north of the Ferry Building with little visible security, Freeman wondered who was in charge. "[F]rom rumors which reached me I learned that the military was in control, and in the absence of police I assumed control of the waterfront with the handful of men I had," he later reported. He found the marine detachment he had disembarked at the waterfront the previous morning and ordered the lieutenant to patrol the waterfront with his men. With rifles and ammunition and belts he had secured at Goat Island, Freeman armed a number of his sailors and ordered them to patrol and assist with relief work. And noticing "the crying need was water" for thirsty refugees gathered at the makeshift relief station south of the Ferry Building, he obtained help from George Musson, the skipper of the SS *Henley*, a large British cargo steamship in port, who "rendered valuable assistance in starting his evaporators and distilling water for the thirsty." Musson also provided Freeman with water for the *Active*'s boiler, which, as Midshipman Pond noted, "was beginning to prime badly from the continued use of salt water in the make-up feed."

With armed sailors and marines patrolling city streets along the waterfront by his directives, and with ferries no longer bringing passengers into the city without a pass due to his earlier orders, Lieutenant Freeman took the tug *Active* to Fort Mason to report to General Funston, seeking guidance as well as endorsement for actions he had taken. Funston not only "approved" Freeman's order ceasing unauthorized passenger travel into the city, but also he sent him back with "an additional guard of marines." On his voyage back around the city's northern waterfront, Freeman saw the north and east ends of the downtown fire sweeping eastward from Nob Hill back toward the banking district's north end, pushing thousands more toward the wharves. Freeman glided alongside a pier adjacent to the State Belt Railroad tracks and deployed the marines to guard the freight cars of chickens and produce, which by mid-afternoon had attracted a hungry crowd.

The freight cars had arrived from Kansas City before the earthquake and sat idle on the tracks since. Armed marines lined up between the pressing crowds and the boxcars, joined by police sergeant Jesse Cook and his officers. After talking with a railroad official, a marine pulled open the doors of the livestock car containing the chickens, and with an explosion of cackling and clucking and bursts of feathers the rush was on. "[T]here must have been two or three thousand of them," Sergeant Cook later recounted, "and never before or since have I seen such a scramble for fowl as there was joined by soldiers and civilians." Cook grabbed four of them, keeping two and giving two to other officers. Alex Paladini, who had survived the previous morning's fish market collapse and was now bunking with at least forty other refugees on his father's ten-person fishing boat docked nearby, described how he and the others joined in the mad grab: "We caught four or five hundred of the chickens as they flew out, and we fed on chicken three times a day while they lasted."

Among those acting as waterfront security was thirty-nine-year-old Ernest Denicke, a civil engineer and retired national guard captain, who donned his old uniform, grabbed a loaded revolver, and posted himself among soldiers on the wharf. He saw a marine who was reportedly drunk—or "behaving in a drunken manner"—order a man to drop two chickens, and after dropping them, the man walked away. The marine pointed his rifle at the man and, while poking him in the back with the bayonet, said, "Come here, sir." The man—according to witnesses, "a man of large physique"—turned and grabbed the rifle and either carried it toward the waterfront or threw it on the ground. Denicke yelled "Halt!" then shot the man three times with his revolver. Denicke later claimed the man "turned toward me" with the rifle and "as a matter of self-defense I shot him." He also later claimed, believing the city was under martial law and a shoot-to-kill order in place, to have fired two warning shots yelling "Halt!" between each until finally shooting the man with a third shot. Refugees scattered at the gunfire, and the man, reportedly still "moaning but unconscious," lay in the street where he fell, bleeding and unattended, until he died. The next morning, an Army sergeant ordered the body weighed down with iron "and had it thrown in the bay."

Across the city, the mayor's headquarters had been forced by the fire to move yet again, this time to a Fillmore Street banquet hall in the Western Addition, and it was hoped this was far enough from the blaze to avoid a fourth move. Typewriters sat on the dining tables where city employees hammered out blank passes for the mayor's signature: "To all Civil and Military Authorities. Pass Bearer _____ through all lines to and from points beyond the limits of the City and County of San Francisco for the public good. Mayor." Staffers cut them into stacks near Mayor Schmitz, who "was in his shirt sleeves sweating," as one witness noted, surrounded by the police chief and other "prominent men" in a haze of cigar smoke while a line of citizens seeking an audience with him snaked out to the street. An assistant sat beside the mayor, watching for his signal to tap the date stamp in an ink pad to mark a pass for the mayor to sign and hand out. So did a stenographer, ready for the mayor to dictate the next special pass for a physician or pastor or relief worker.

Crowds cleared a path for a national guard officer who told the mayor their dynamite had been taken by some of Funston's soldiers and the firemen were reduced to backfiring the east side of Van Ness Avenue. Reportedly incensed, Schmitz turned to his stenographer and dictated an order "To the Officer in Charge of the Destruction of Buildings by Dynamite" instructing him "to immediately proceed" to destroy "the entire line of buildings" on the east side of Van Ness Avenue one block deep from Golden Gate Avenue up to Pacific—a distance of fifteen blocks. Then after hearing soldiers were dynamiting up at the north end of the fire six blocks from Van Ness, Schmitz dictated an even clearer order to the same officer: "You are hereby notified to take whatever dynamite you have and proceed immediately to Golden Gate Avenue and Van Ness Avenue where the destruction of the buildings in that locality will begin from that point." He also added, "This means that you will refrain from dynamiting buildings in your locality. MAYOR." As the messages went on their way, Mayor Schmitz jumped in his car and sped through Western Addition streets past clusters of refugees gathered around makeshift street stoves to Fort Mason for an overdue meeting with General Funston.

Schmitz removed his hat on entering the two-story residence of General Greely on Fort Mason's waterfront where Funston had made his headquarters. The handsome, goateed mayor stood a head taller than the short, stocky general, a contrast cast sharply in relief as they shook hands, worlds apart, surrounded by uniformed members of Funston's staff as well as the staff of General Greely, who was still steaming back to San Francisco by train. After pleasantries, Funston asked Schmitz if he "had enough troops," and as Schmitz would later recall from the conversation, "I told him that we needed all he could furnish." In front of the mayor, Funston ordered in troops from Alcatraz and Angel Islands and sent a telegram to Vancouver Barracks "to proceed to this city with the entire garrison of that post."

But Funston had ordered these troops from Alcatraz and Angel Islands the day before, and they had already arrived and been sent into the city to patrol under a colonel's command. Funston had done the same with soldiers from Fort Baker and marines from Mare Island. And Funston had placed the city's eastern waterfront and an additional guard of marines under the command of a Navy lieutenant. All of this was done without including the mayor or any city official, and there is no evidence any of it was agreed upon or even disclosed in the meeting. Funston lacked the authority to place federal troops under command of any municipal authority in the first place, and the troops he had ordered into the city at the "disposal" of the police chief and mayor were now back to taking orders from Funston and their own chain of command "in cooperation with" city authorities.

Blind to much of this shift toward military control—and martial law— Schmitz returned to the primary purpose for his visit: he wanted to clear up who exactly oversaw dynamite operations, and, perhaps worried the soldiers might ignore his instructions, he argued the fire department should have the final say in demolishing firebreaks, not the Army. The exact exchange was not recorded, but as a fire truck captain later reported, "it was finally settled that the fire chief was to take full command."

On Van Ness Avenue, the dynamite finally arrived. With the blaze just one block away, soldiers and firemen entered houses along the avenue's east side that had not already been backfired. The blasting began around 4:30 p.m., and with each boom, a home would explode in "upshoots of burning timbers and sparks," as a witness noted. For blocks around, windows shattered and bells of home burglar alarms clanged.

James Stetson was still watching from his window from across the avenue. "The explosions of dynamite were felt fearfully in my house," he later described, adding that each detonation "would jar and shake the house violently and break the windows." The concussive blasts also cracked his house walls. And within fifteen minutes, a soldier entered his home with a rifle and "not in a quiet manner" told Stetson, "Get out of this house." After an initial protest, Stetson relented and was marched outside "amid flames, smoke and explosions" and was marched two blocks up Clay Street away from Van Ness.

Another wagon of dynamite arrived, and soldiers ran the sticks and wires and charges into more homes and more slamming detonations followed—two minutes apart, then one minute, then every few seconds. One woman likened the blasts to "the booming of artillery fire," and another wrote they sounded "like tremendous bombs, as if the city were being bombarded by a hostile fleet." Flames and smoke churned from the wooden debris of flattened homes and burning pieces of paper floated above the wide avenue. Broken glass and charred wood shards blanketed roasting asphalt as firemen and soldiers, feeling the heat through their boots, fled in quick strides to the avenue's west side.

By 5:00 p.m., dynamiting and earlier backfiring had turned the east side of Van Ness Avenue into a wall of flame a dozen blocks long. Still at his father's Geary Street home two blocks west, Edward de Laveaga had seen the "heroic efforts" of neighborhood volunteers extinguish the drugstore fire on his side of Van Ness, but the flames on the far side of the avenue were now so massive "it looked as though the men on the corner could not hold the fire." As he soon wrote in his diary, "Even here two blocks away we could hardly stand the heat," and he imagined how "terrible" the scorching temperatures were "for those poor men on whose efforts so much depended." He and his father had gathered "the few things we wished to save by us on the steps"—a camera, a suitcase of clothes, and two shotguns—and guardsmen came by warning them to leave. But as the fight to save the drugstore seemed won and the fire on the far side of Van Ness started to wane, it seemed safe to stay. Then someone shouted, "Look at the Cathedral!" Every head within earshot turned and looked above the rooftops to see the 180-foot-tall steeple of St. Mary's Cathedral—on the near side of the avenue next door to the drugstore that had just been saved— "slowly but surely burning."

In the tower just below the shingled steeple, a man emerged from a small brick archway and leaned over the narrow perch above the belfry, more than one hundred feet above the street, and began lowering a rope over the side with a rake tied to the end. Edward and other residents kept their gazes fixed on the man and the flames above him as they walked over to O'Farrell Street to get a better view of the action. Down on the sidewalk at the foot of the tower, the parish priest held a hose connected to the building service pipe with pressure. He turned the nozzle to open the small stream, hooked the hose end to the rake, and the man atop the tower began pulling on the rope, lifting the rake carrying the hose, "twisting, spurting water all the while," as Edward noticed. "It was a grand sight and every one of us on the corner cheered." The man also pulled out an axe and chopped off flaming cornices and shingles.

From the street below, as would be reported, residents grabbed binoculars and craned their necks to watch "the brave man as he stood high above the street cutting away the blazing woodwork." He secured the hose and leaned out to spray the blazing shingles on each side of the steeple and, as Edward observed, "little by little the flames were extinguished." Resident volunteers had put out the fire in the drugstore and the cathedral, and "feeling now entirely safe," Edward returned to the front steps of his father's home, saved from the fire along with the rest of the neighborhood. And with fire still confined to the east side of Van Ness Avenue, the Western Addition was safe. For the moment.

14. The Second Night

THE BANK OF Italy was not yet eighteen months old but already a leading savings and lending institution for a growing base of North Beach customers. Its founder, thirty-five-year-old Amadeo Giannini, tall and charming with a neatly trimmed mustache, was the son of Italian immigrants. He had honed his business acumen as a produce broker, and after working in another local savings and loan, he opened his own bank to offer laborers and working-class immigrants the same services as the wealthy. The bank operated in the banking district's north end on a sharp corner at the five-point intersection where Montgomery Avenue (present-day Columbus) angled into Washington and Montgomery Streets. And its customers and shareholders were small businessmen—fish dealers, grocers, druggists, plumbers, barbers—"the little guys," as newspapers would report.

After the earthquake, the bank's clerk and assistant cashier had initially followed their usual morning routine and took a buggy from the North Beach flat they shared down to the Crocker-Woolworth National Bank on Market where the Bank of Italy's cash was kept overnight. There they retrieved three pouches filled with $80,000 (equivalent to more than $2.6 million in 2023) in cash, gold, and silver, and armed with revolvers they hauled it back to the Bank of Italy and opened for business. Giannini made his way up into the city from his San Mateo home—a five-hour journey by train and foot—and found his building not badly damaged. But worried about security and approaching fires, he closed the bank, secured two wagons and horse teams from his father-in-law's produce business, loaded both with trunks filled with the pouches of cash, gold, and silver, and covered them with crates of oranges. After darkness, disguised as produce freight, the two-wagon caravan rattled along cobblestone streets around the spreading fire on an all-night journey to Giannini's San Mateo home. They arrived after daybreak Thursday, and without a safe, Giannini stashed the cash, gold, and silver in canvas bags in his living room and his employees stood guard.

On Wednesday, the fire had three times reached within a block of the Bank of Italy—once spreading along the far side of the Hall of Justice and Portsmouth Square and twice more when flames threatened Montgomery Block across the intersection. Now on Thursday afternoon, the fire approached again as it marched down Washington Street from Nob Hill. Soldiers from Angel Island patrolled the district and their captain was in Portsmouth Square with dynamite, prepared to blow more firebreaks if the blaze came closer (still under orders to only blow buildings already on fire). A few of his soldiers wheeled dynamite toward the wall of the blaze and together with firemen they began demolishing building to building ahead of the flames. As the familiar booming of demolitions grew louder, nearer, windows in the empty Bank of Italy and other nearby businesses shattered. And inside many, store owners and workers prepared to stand their ground.

The employees of nearby Hotaling & Co., a whiskey dealer on the block adjacent to the Bank of Italy and the Montgomery Block, had been guarding their store and warehouse and its five thousand barrels of Old Kirk whiskey since the previous morning. Cashier and manager Edward Lind had taken the $2,000 in cash from the safe and ferried it to his parents' house in Oakland that morning and returned to help guard the warehouse. After spending Wednesday night at the business manager's home while other employees took shifts guarding the company, Lind had been back at the store since daybreak.

Worried Hotaling & Co. could be a target of dynamite teams, Lind and his manager walked to Portsmouth Square, and as attorney Oliver Stidger had done the previous day on behalf of Montgomery Block, they pled their case to the Army captain in charge of local demolition crews. They argued "the large stock of whisky in the warehouse" would turn any attempted demolition into an "immediate combustion of all this vast amount of highly inflammable spirit" that would "be virtually certain to destroy" the adjacent Custom House. The captain agreed and approved their proposal "to remove the stocks of whisky" from their warehouse into the burned district "where no further risk of fire existed" and authorized them to grab whatever supplies they needed from abandoned stores. They ran back to Hotaling and devised a plan to move five thousand barrels—each one weighing approximately five hundred pounds—the distance of two city blocks before the fire reached them.

Lind and his manager and employees "hurried to the waterfront" to find men to help move barrels, with the promise of $1 per hour pay (more than $33 per hour in 2023) for the work. They walked through crowds gathered around the boxcars—the same crowd that had just mobbed the poultry car in a grab for chickens—and returned with eighty men, "a mixed lot," Lind would later remember. "Some of them were good stout stevedores and sailor men; others were the scourings of the waterfront, thieves and all the rest of it." The men were ushered into the warehouse where employees lifted barrels off their racks with ropes and the hired hands rolled barrels—one at a time, two men to each—out over the bumpy cobblestones of Jones Street (present-day Hotaling Place) and Jackson Street down two blocks past the Custom House and into an empty lot, where the ground was still hot from yesterday's fire.

A few blocks north, Lieutenant Frederick Freeman stood on one of Telegraph Hill's steep streets where he had climbed to make "observations of the progress of the fire," which at that time was moving eastward from the foot of Nob Hill toward the unburned neighborhoods of North Beach. This district occupied the entire northeastern swath of the city, from the fish market and produce merchant houses of the harbor district's north end, along the delicatessens and hotels lining Montgomery Avenue, up the steep slopes of Telegraph Hill where Freeman now stood, and down through the warehouses and gasworks of waterfront streets around the seawall to Fisherman's Wharf. Much of the population was working class, and although the wood-frame tenements tucked between factories and perched on the hillsides were of flimsy construction, they stood on solid ground and most had survived the earthquake with minimal damage. Like the rows of rickety lodging houses South of Market, the dry, sunbaked wooden dwellings could turn a blaze into a firestorm. Unlike South of Market, the residents of North Beach had the benefit of time, and as in the Mission District and Western Addition, many stayed.

Freeman had positioned his tug *Active* and fireboat *Leslie* at the Union Street pier at the foot of Telegraph Hill where both would have the reach to defend North Beach. And seeing the fire creeping toward the Hall of Justice and Custom House, he "decided to lay a line of hose" from his fireboat *Leslie*—with "the most powerful available" pumps, as Midshipman Pond noted—"up over the side of Telegraph Hill" and down through the banking district's streets "and make a stand there." This would require a longer length of hose than they had yet attempted, and word was sent through engine companies to gather as many hose sections as possible for the job.

Sailors unrolled hose from their fireboat along the pier and across the tracks of the State Belt Railroad and up the steep streets climbing Telegraph Hill. There they met firemen who unrolled more sections, one from the Oakland hose wagon and another brought from the fire department's storage yard. Because Navy and fire department hoses were different sizes, coupling reducers (adaptors to connect hose sections of different diameters) were needed, and as Midshipman Pond later reported, "we had considerable difficulty in finding enough reducers to complete this line."

As the sun set red behind the smoke in the western sky, the sections were joined, snaking through streets up and over the hill and onto Broadway Street and turning onto Montgomery all the way down past Jackson Street—where Hotaling's hired helpers rolled whiskey barrels away from the approaching fire with greater urgency—and down to Washington Street where Midshipman Pond could see above the rooftops the flames consuming the Hall of Justice just a block away and watched "the skeleton of its cupola crumble and collapse." And the fire along Washington Street reached the Bank of Italy.

In the face of this "terrific heat from the blazing mass across the street," sailors and firemen and volunteers ran back up along Montgomery Street storefronts pulling curtains from windows and yanking down awnings and anything that could ignite. Embers and firebrands landed on rooftops, and sailors and volunteers and marines climbed stairs up to roofs to stomp out fires and chop off flaming cornices. And urgent yells carried along the cobbled-together hose, man to man, up the street and around the corner and over Telegraph Hill and down to the *Leslie*, the distance of a dozen blocks, to "start pumping."

There was considerable doubt that the fireboat's pumps would be strong enough to push the water up the hill and overcome the friction of nearly a mile of hose, but the pumps started and the line stiffened, and as Midshipman Pond later noted, "The first water coming through about 7:00 p.m. was the signal for spontaneous cheer." A fireman held the nozzle up and played a powerful stream on the unburned brick storefronts along Montgomery Street with sufficient flow to reach "a height of about two and a half stories," as Lieutenant Freeman reported.

But only a three-story brick boardinghouse on the west side of Montgomery Street separated firefighters and the block of buildings they were protecting from the blazing Bank of Italy. They aimed the hose stream at the boardinghouse's brick wall facing them to force an inward collapse (onto itself, rather than an outer collapse, which would spread the building's flaming contents across Montgomery Street and threaten to ignite another block). Sailors entered the building to remove flammables, "carrying out the lamps and tossing the bedding and furniture" out second- and third-floor windows into the street, and soldiers cleared the street as a potential collapse zone. The hoseman closed the nozzle and slung the line up to a marine on a second-story roof across the street who climbed it up to an adjacent third-story roof and opened the stream and continued soaking the wall.

The boardinghouse caught fire on the far side, and sailors and Hotaling employees helped pull the hose over the near side of the roof to keep the line from kinking and the flow at pressure. "Occasionally the stream would weaken when the hose sprang a new leak somewhere along its mile of splicing," Edward Lind, who was watching, would later explain. "Then he would close the nozzle until the power picked up again, and then he would renew the combat." For three hours the flames were fought back and the wall soaked with this single stream, the only water to reach that area that day and "the longest distance that any saltwater stream was taken from the waterfront," as Lieutenant Freeman would report. Finally, "after what seemed an interminable time," as Lind later remembered, "the wall fell inward, westward, with a crash, and the progress of the fire was thus stopped."

"The best work," Freeman later estimated, "of the crews under my command, was done at this point." Together with firemen and soldiers and marines and volunteers, they'd saved more than two city blocks, at least for the time being.

Over in the Western Addition, refugees in Lafayette Park were "awed by the almost incredible panorama" of the "semi-circle of furious flame," as one man later described, stretching the length of the city from the waterfront to Van Ness Avenue, just two blocks from them, and down to the Mission District two miles south. Most stood silently transfixed, stirred into startled jumps every time another dynamite detonation shook the ground as a spray of sparks and shingles and wood planks along the avenue signaled another hotel or apartment building or home demolished. "At this time," noted one resident of that night, crews "were dynamiting Van Ness and the noise was terrific. After each explosion the air would be filled with feathery cinders that fell on our clothes and covered our hats."

On the street in front of the park, James Stetson stood in his coat and hat with other residents who had been ordered from their Van Ness homes and marched up the Clay Street hill by soldiers. Stetson kept his gaze fixed on his house, two blocks down on the corner, silhouetted against the blazing far side of the avenue, "expecting every minute to see the flames coming out of it." Heat from the fire was "so intense" he noticed the soldiers had been forced away, and he resolved to sneak back to his house. He walked a block over, "quietly slipped down" to Van Ness, flipped up his coat collar, and, as he would later describe, "protecting the side of my face with my hat, I ran along Van Ness Avenue to my front door and quickly got into my house again."

The glow from across the avenue flickered orange and yellow on his walls and ceilings as Stetson watched the dynamiting through his tall bay windows, "so hot that I could not put my hand upon them." As far as he could see, the blaze had not spread to his side and "felt satisfied that it would not cross Van Ness Avenue." But two blocks down, the detonation of the First Presbyterian Church and adjoining three-story Knickerbocker Hotel blew sparks out more than 150 feet, igniting the front yard and wood siding and mansard roof of a three-story house on Stetson's side of the avenue, and with that, fire crossed to the Western Addition.

"We had no idea the fire would ever reach us," a young woman soon wrote, adding "we only had one hour to get out in and lost everything (but our skins)." Flames began marching up California Street toward Franklin Street—one block west and parallel with Van Ness—where shocked residents like John Walter began to pack. He had seen his family's carpet and upholstery business on Market Street burn the previous day, and this morning after seeing the blaze "sweeping down over the hill & approaching Van Ness," he did not believe "there was much chance for our house" so he hired three wagons (for prices ranging from $20 to $40 each) to haul books, bedding, chairs, clothes, and provisions out to a flat he had rented north of Golden Gate Park. Now with the fire on his side of Van Ness nearing his Franklin Street home, he grabbed what he could carry—"two valises of private papers, books, & the cash"—jumped on his bicycle, and wheeled westward up the hill.

Drivers slapped horse teams to pull fire engines and hose wagons up streets from Van Ness to get west of the fire and firemen fanned out into the Western Addition testing hydrants for pressure. The yell of "Water!" carried from a hoseman who found a working hydrant at the corner of Laguna and Bush Streets, and four engines maneuvered into a line, one per block, to relay from the hydrant and reach the fire. Three more engine companies began hooking up long sections of hose to reach each other and connect with a working hydrant four blocks south at Ellis and Van Ness, still drawing water from the intact distribution mains of Hayes Valley.

And the Army captain in charge of the dynamite requested and finally received authorization to demolish buildings "far enough ahead of the fire to avoid feeding the fire with flying embers and to effectually stop the fire for lack of fuel, by cutting a broad open belt ahead of the fire." This meant blowing up unburned homes along Franklin Street—a block west of Van Ness—and down cross streets where the fire had not yet reached, a significant departure from the previous practice of only dynamiting structures already burning. And the authorization for this descended from the Army colonel whom General Funston had placed in charge of all troops in the Western Addition, not from any fire department official, despite how "settled" Mayor Schmitz believed the fire chief's authority was after the conference with Funston at Fort Mason.

Exhausted hosemen with blistered faces and bloodshot eyes, sweating beneath singed helmets and panting in unbuttoned grime-smeared rubber coats with soot-blackened corduroy collars, took shifts on the nozzles keeping two streams of water—each pumped from four blocks distant—on the leading edge of flames climbing from Van Ness. And firemen ran from door to door evacuating residents ahead of the dynamite crew.

Edith Bonnell and her parents and uncle and brother "began to pack" as they saw the blaze marching toward their Gough Street home "at a terrifying rate." They dug holes in the yard to bury fine china and glassware, tied up mattresses and bedding, and stuffed clothes in baskets. The fire was more than a block away, but its radiated heat turned the air in their parlor so "oppressively warm" they "could hardly breath[e]." With a knock on their front door, a fireman ordered them out. And as Edith later described, "The fireman's face was puffed out with fire burn and his helmet scorched."

A horse team pulled the dynamite wagon up to Franklin Street where the captain directed soldiers to set the first house to blow, and before detonating they rigged the next house and then the house after and blew all three at once. Firemen ran the two hose lines over to water down the woodpiles before the blaze, climbing fast from Van Ness, could reach them. Then the captain pointed to the next three houses and the process repeated, with hosemen drenching the wreckage after each detonation. Flames climbing cross streets threatened to cut them off, but firemen redirected their streams and fought the flames back as the dynamite team continued. The captain later reported the blaze "outflanked my small party time and again." But the firebreak was blown successfully by bringing down a wide section of structures—large homes, row houses, stables, more than three dozen structures total—far enough from the blaze to cool down the wreckage and eliminate it as fuel. By "getting ahead of the fire on Franklin," as the captain concluded, "the fire was finally stopped." Or at least its westward progress was stopped.

No flames would again burn west of Van Ness, but onshore winds continued to feed the fires chewing northward up Russian Hill and from the banking and harbor districts up toward Telegraph Hill and the rest of North Beach. The inferno lit the night sky for a second night, appearing "just like a huge glowing volcano" to a refugee who had evacuated over to Berkeley and now could "hear all through the fire the thunder of the dynamiters" even from nine miles across the bay. A man in the Western Addition "watched the deep red glare and saw it advancing steadily northward" and noticed "the light was as bright as on the night before." And down among the campers in Jefferson Square, writer Mary Austin said to her friend, "Bob, it looks like the Day of Judgment!" He responded, "Aw! It looks like Hell!"

Desperate to escape this "Hell" on Thursday night were still more refugees at the Ferry Building. Most had wound their way through the burned city's hot, desolate streets from their homes where they spent the first night, each of which had seemed a safe distance from the fire until tonight. Many were shocked by the sights on their journey to the waterfront, through the ruins of a downtown they no longer recognized.

Melissa and Will Carnahan rode a hired wagon "over broad cracks and sunken places in the street caused by the earthquake" and through a stark scene of gutted buildings and smoldering ash piles of homes and businesses and the "blackened ruins of hundreds of warehouses." One resident trekking from the Western Addition on foot through South of Market soon described walking "over the hot pavement" and having "to dodge the dangling trolley wires." James Hopper likened his own walk down Market Street that night to a walk "through a dead city, not a city recently dead, but one overcome by some cataclysm ages past." Another man walking through "the smoking ruins" of the lower harbor district's almost indiscernible streets heading toward the familiar beacon of the Ferry Building's clock tower noticed, "One could hardly tell where Market Street had been."

Thousands filled the wharf as thousands had the previous night, waiting patiently for boats in "tiny tents made of rugs and blankets," many with "parrots in cages and pets of all kinds." One man noticed four "beautiful mastiff pups in a deep sleep on an old sack" and asked the young man sitting beside them if they were his, and he said no, the puppies "were the property of a rich man who had fled, leaving them behind." Evidence of relief efforts was already apparent at the waterfront. More sprinkling carts of drinking water had been ferried over from Oakland, and soldiers ensured everyone thirsty got a cupful and kept the line moving. Also brought over were milk cannisters, sweating from sitting on the crowded wharf, and soldiers converted a small supply shed into a milk distribution depot for women and young children. Large steamers were tied alongside piers from which deckhands debarked boxes of supplies "onto trucks well-guarded by soldiers," as one young man later described. He also noticed a handcart "loaded with oranges and candy and there were five soldiers on guard."

As ferries arrived and departed, the line slowly moved inside the nave where there was "crowding and pushing of people with too much baggage," as one person later described, adding that many "finally threw away their bedding to lighten their burden." Soldiers helped with baggage and encouraged men and women pulling large trunks to leave them to make space on ferries for passengers. "People packed like sardines into the waiting rooms and onto the boats, with bundles and bundles and bundles," a man taking a ferry to Alameda noted, "all going, fleeing, scared to death, from the holocaust." But some boarding the ferries "had nothing but the clothes on their backs." And ferry lines were still charging no fare. "No tickets had to be bought," a man who made it out on a boat that night with his wife later related. "We stepped on board, two among thousands, and started for Oakland."

From the bay, San Francisco on Thursday night was a glowing firestorm. "From the ferry toward the hills one saw but a sea of flames," one passenger noticed, and another later wrote, "The view of the burning city that night is beyond description." The Oakland pier was packed tight with evacuees—one witness likened them to "swarms of grasshoppers"—and passengers disembarked into a city teeming with frantic humanity. After the ordeal of the earthquake and fire and escape from the burning city, it all proved too much for sixty-eight-year-old Mary McIntyre, who "dropped dead of heart attack" as her husband, John, a bookbinder, was helping her off the ferry. Her body was carried through the crowd into town, and three days later, after a childhood in Ireland and a life in San Francisco, Mary was buried there in Oakland.

For evacuees walking into Oakland away from the crowded pier, the city itself presented a stark contrast to what they had escaped. "At Oakland it was hard to tell that anything had happened," one man noticed. "[T]he electric cars were running and business was being transacted much as usual." Refugees filled the lawns of churches and City Hall, and they stood in lines at relief stations and the train station, where the Southern Pacific had, as one of its managers would soon report, "been running relief trains since the earthquake" without pause, "taking destitute people free to all such points."

Southern Pacific officials received word by telegram from other towns down the line where refugees could be housed: from Fresno came offers to "accommodate 250 persons; from Selma 100; from Dixon 50." Among the thousands who evacuated that day by train were Ernest Goerlitz and the members of the Metropolitan Opera company, including tenor Enrico Caruso, who could "sleep very little" on the rail journey to New York, "for I can still feel the terrible rocking which made me sick." He promised he would never return to San Francisco, a promise he kept the rest of his days.

At least 300,000 residents and refugees remained in San Francisco, including thousands who were injured. At the Presidio's Army General Hospital, Dr. George Torney and his staff worked almost without rest, treating the 145 new patients admitted that day in addition to the 127 patients admitted the first day, filling the hospital ward and men's barracks.

Among those brought in that night was Dr. Clarence Edwards, who had been on Van Ness treating the wounds of a couple of soldiers injured by dynamiting when another blast shot "a long piece of wood" into "the inner corner of his right eye, passing through the bones into his nostril," as was reported. He had returned to helping the wounded after the wood was removed and his eye bandaged, and now he underwent painful surgery to remove the remaining splinters. Another patient, an ROTC cadet from the University of California who had been in the city providing security, had been shot in the thigh by a reportedly impaired soldier. "I was taken to the surgical ward, which was already filled to overflowing," he later recalled. "It held only forty-four beds, and I was patient No. 54." A doctor manipulated his leg, giving him "some of the most excruciating moments I ever endured." With a broken thigh bone, he was given chloroform and his leg rigged with a rope, pulley, and bricks to stretch and keep it at its proper length.

Refugees continued pouring into the post, many escaping spreading fires and many more relocating from the squares and parks of the previous night to an established camp. An Army major observed those who "drifted in the second day, after a night in the parks, with their hand-bags and what wraps they could carry." He and his wife offered the upstairs rooms of their quarters to refugee families, and "turned our parlor into a dormitory for ladies," as he would report, with "others camping on porch and lawn and reclining chairs in our living room."

Hundreds slept in tents on the parade grounds, including seventy-seven-year-old widow Omira Dodge, taken there that night in a wagon driven by her forty-year-old servant James Coombs after they were ordered from her Franklin Street home by soldiers. They had time to take mattresses, bedding, clothes packed in sheets, and "eatables" in baskets, so they "laid mattresses close together for comfort" in the tent, as she would write her son two days later, but found it "hard to sleep on the damp ground." Dr. Margaret Mahoney and her family and neighbors spent that night in Army tents on a fairway in the Presidio golf course, where she "slept in peace, wrapped in my blanket, with no bed save the ground."

Even more people paraded into Golden Gate Park, although the tents had all been claimed. "There were crowds of people all about, no one having any shelter except the trees, with maybe an old carpet, or a quilt, or a blanket tied or nailed to the trees for better shelter," noted a woman who had spent the previous night in a grass lot after evacuating Union Square. "We spread an old quilt we had carried and lay down on it for the night, not to sleep, but to shiver with cold from the fog and mist, and watch the flames of the burning city whose blaze shone far above the trees."

Among a sea of campers still wearing yesterday's clothes, the stench of body odor was pervasive, especially with water rationed for drinking and not for bathing or hygiene. One woman noted she "managed to keep, at least, a clean face by the use of my cold cream and violet water."

Also in the park that night was Dr. John Hollister, a visitor from Chicago who had witnessed his own city's inferno thirty-five years earlier. He and his wife had fled the Palace Hotel the previous morning to the home of friends in the Mission District, and from there soldiers had ordered them out to dynamite the house. Now joined in the park by their friends from the Mission, they rested on "mattresses spread upon the grassy lawn, canopied by beautiful shrubbery and stately trees," covered by open umbrellas for dew and floating ash. "The heavens were ablaze with the light of the burning city," Dr. Hollister described, "and the great forest trees that intervened seemed sharply silhouetted upon the sky." The city ablaze for a second straight night was a scene "never to be forgotten."

Down in the Mission District, refugees filled the grass of Dolores Park, which only recently had been expanded into two city blocks between 18th and 20th

Streets. After nightfall the fire was three blocks away and working its way closer. "During the early part of the night, burnt cinders began to fall on the tent like rain," one man later described, and "great thundering detonations" shook the ground. Many campers were South of Market residents who had evacuated the day before, and others had been driven from their Mission District homes that day by soldiers or the fire. And because transmission and distribution mains were unbroken south of 18th Street and fed from a reservoir to the south, campers here had drinking water carried in buckets and cups from a few local houses with unbroken service pipes.

Three blocks away, the battle against the fire and wind was still fought by firefighters and resident volunteers. Captain Cullen and his firemen of Engine 6 applied a hose stream on a row of two-story, wood-frame flats along Capp Street that had caught fire from the fire along 16th Street spread by the dynamiting of the furniture store. The hose line stretched a block and a half to the engine pumping from the busted main at 17th Street. They "had a very hard fight," as Cullen would report, "as the wind was blowing the intense heat of the fire in our direction." Flames jumped the sixty-foot-wide street and pushed southward against their water stream, and they were forced to backpedal, still "fighting every inch of the ground." But the water level in their makeshift cistern began to drop as the supply through the broken main diminished, and soon suction hoses of three more engines were sucking from shallow puddles in the broken pavement.

With no water to stop it, the fire spread southward past 17th Street, forcing more residents out. "It seemed to burn up a quarter of a block or more in about 15 or 20 minutes," one man noticed as it crossed 18th Street. It incinerated former mayor Phelan's home, then the ruins of the Valencia Hotel and burned its way down Valencia Street where "as far as I could see," an eight-year-old later recounted, "I watched the flames bursting on both sides meeting each other on the street."

Police officer Harry Schmidt and his wife and daughters had evacuated their 18th Street apartment earlier that evening, but he returned with a couple of neighbors to save his "new kitchen stove." Schmidt showed his badge to soldiers to get through the fire line, and he and his helpers climbed the stairs to his third-floor flat, disconnected the stove, and carried it to the street. Believing they had time, they returned for his family piano. They hitched some rope on the newel post of the stairwell banister, lowered the piano down the stairs, and rolled it on its casters out beside the stove on the street. By that time "the roof of the house was on fire," but a soldier who had climbed to Schmidt's flat to assist threw some furniture out the window and then ran out the front door as the apartment house filled with flames.

As they pulled his stove and piano away, the blaze was only a block from the refugees in the newly expanded part of Dolores Park where the ground was covered with manure spread by city workers to help grow new grass. Schmidt later recalled the "pitiable" sight of the campers in the park—many older and feeble, most newly homeless—that night "when the fire drew nearer and was sending showers of sparks and live cinders over them" and how they struggled "to protect their clothes and quilts and things by piling the damp manure over them."

Ernest Edwards was on 19th Street still assisting firemen when a police officer friend told him about the refugees in Dolores Park getting water from a house at Church and 20th Streets at the southwest corner—and highest point—of the park. Ernest grabbed a spanner wrench and ran uphill along Dolores Street, "opening every hydrant I passed on the way but finding no sign of water." As he reached 20th he turned and ran up toward Church where another friend of his told him "people were getting water from the house on the side of the hill."

They walked to the corner hydrant where Ernest twisted the cap off and "gave the hydrant about three turns, and the water shot clear across the street." Ernest wrenched the stream closed, left his friend to stand beside the hydrant, and, like a horseless Paul Revere, ran down the hill yelling and alerting anyone who could spread the news that "there was water in the hydrant" at the top of the hill. He told a man on horseback to take the message to a fire battalion chief, ran further and told a police officer, then a postal worker on a bicycle, and "Thus the news was spread."

When word reached the battalion chiefs, they ordered engine companies and hose wagons to the hydrant. A truck company gathered three wagons of hose to assist, and two University of California ROTC cadets brought a wagon loaded with hose they had found left in a street. When the first fire engine arrived at Church Street, Ernest Edwards noticed the horse teams "were too worn out to drag the engines up the hill." Neighborhood volunteers and campers from the park helped pull hose sections together and dragged the engine up the hill where it connected to the hydrant. Fed with the unbroken flow of water through a twelve-inch main, the hydrant fed the engine pumping two lines of water down the hill to two more engines through the long lines held by volunteers, the flow aided by gravity. Every inch of the hose was needed to reach the fires. Police officers pulled down a lamppost so the hose could cut a corner and reach the furthest edge of the blaze—2,200 feet from the hydrant—and the angle forced volunteers manning the line within just a few feet of the flames. Firemen at the nozzles applied two streams on buildings "from Dolores to Mission St.," as an engine company captain would report. "Doors were torn from houses," Ernest Edwards explained, "and held up as screens to protect the men on the hose lines."

The blazes along Valencia, Capp, Dolores, and Guerrero Streets were extinguished, and as the final fire ate along Mission Street toward 20th, two hose lines were played onto the roof and upper floors of the four-story, wood-frame boardinghouse at the corner, "drowning it with water," as one onlooker later described. When the fire reached the structure, it "burnt out at the bottom only," Ernest Edwards noted. "Then when it collapsed it fell inward, smothering its own ruins, and that spelled victory for the firefighters." As Captain Cullen of Engine 6 reported with understatement, "after fighting every inch of the ground we succeeded in getting it under control at 20th St."

The blaze they finally stopped halfway through the Mission District had begun two mornings before as single flames in quiet corners of South of Market businesses like Mack's drugstore and the Howard Street laundry house, individual fires that had merged into the great fire's southern flank, a firestorm that had burned through South of Market's warehouses, factories, foundries, and dwellings, the ruins of collapsed lodging houses, the finest hotels along Market Street—the Grand and the Palace—and office buildings, including the Examiner Building and the city's tallest, the Call Building. With few exceptions, the firestorm destroyed the entire district. And after burning its way further southward through the residential streets of the Mission District, it was the combined resourcefulness of firefighters and resident volunteers to extend the reach of water from a single working hydrant that finally stopped the inferno's onslaught in its forty-seventh hour. With the rest of the district saved in the dark hours of Friday morning, someone yelled, "Three cheers for the San Francisco Fire Department and Volunteers!" And the "great cheer" of residents in response was, as Ernest Edwards later noted, "the first really cheerful noise that had sounded in that part of the city for two days and nights."

15. The Third Day

IN THE SMALL hours of Friday morning, April 20, the north flank of the inferno burned northward through the city "like a grain field on fire" as one witness described. Its western half marched up Russian Hill and its eastern end in the banking district neared the streets of North Beach. When flames reached the intersection of Pacific and Kearny Streets—specifically political boss Abe Ruef's Commercial Hotel on the corner—Ruef himself appeared with a crew of soldiers and a wagon of dynamite, urging firemen and sailors "to do all they could" to save the block. But without water to soak debris, the dynamiting only spread the fire faster.

To head it off, Lieutenant Freeman and his sailors pulled their mile-long hose line back up Montgomery Street and laid it out along Broadway where they hosed down hotel walls and storefronts with salt water pumped from their fireboat *Leslie*. But the single stream was not enough and by midnight, flames jumped the street and began devouring North Beach's best ristorantes and hotels along the north side of Broadway, including the two-story New Buon Gusto Restaurant and its large "The Leading Italian Restaurant" sign above its broad, glass front windows. And the three-story New Toscano Hotel, known for its hospitality and good food and Petri family wine supplied by the owner, Raffaello Petri, who had emigrated with his family from Tuscany, and whose Filbert Street home a few blocks north would also soon be threatened.

Fires marched northward along Montgomery Avenue toward Vallejo Street, where Freeman and his sailors repositioned the hose to play on the St. Francis

Church, the oldest parish church in the city and home to North Beach's largest congregation. But "owing to the dilapidated condition of the hose at this time" and "the great pressure carried for two days" through its sections, as Freeman would explain, "numerous lengths became porous and a large stream could not be carried." Midshipman Pond watched the nozzle's stream get "smaller and smaller until it would barely reach second story windows." The firemen of at least one engine company were driven out by "the intense heat," and as their battalion chief reported, "[O]ur efforts were useless" as flames began "burning our hose."

Sailors ripped canvas from hampers found in a store, soaked the pieces in the water running through street gutters, and organized "relay teams" to hold up the wet canvas as shields for nozzlemen near the flames. Wearied sailors manning the line could barely stand. Pond found some rubber boots in a store on Broadway to replace his own, which had been "scorched the first night." Other sailors followed, kicking off war-battered, wood-soled leather shoes and throwing on fresh rubber boots to give their feet some relief. One sailor was so beat he lay on the ground in a vestibule and asked Pond to "awaken him when the flames reached the corner." The fire moved so quickly it had nearly reached him when Pond "happened to look back and to see those two big boots sticking out of the doorway." Beyond the fatigue of their men, it was obvious to Freeman and Pond "that we could not stop the fire here, but we kept on fighting it every inch of the way just the same, in the hope that some shift of wind or other favorable circumstance might come to our aid."

But circumstances did not improve and the wind did not shift. Lieutenant Freeman "decided to retreat and save the waterfront if possible," and soldiers and workers from a local milling company helped the sailors disconnect the hose sections and pull them back. And as the blaze moved eastward through the stores lining Broadway, Freeman yelled for volunteers to go find "as many wagons" as they could commandeer, which were then rolled to the street and "loaded with provisions from grocery stores and butcher shops" ahead of the flames and hauled down to the waterfront relief station.

As "a new fighting line was established," a second line of hose was brought up from the *Active* and a third from the steam tug *Pilot*, whose skipper—a former Navy man—volunteered his vessel's service and moored at the pier beside the *Leslie*. Now just three blocks from the waterfront, the flow through all three lines was strong, and they made a stand to save Telegraph Hill.

* * *

After 1:00 a.m., "the fire was spreading north unchecked on the east side of Van Ness Ave.," Acting Assistant Chief Shaughnessy reported. Hydrants lining the streets of Russian Hill were dry, and fire engine companies relaying streams from hydrants in the Western Addition or from a long hose pumped from an Army tug at the foot of Van Ness kept the fire from crossing the avenue. But they could not reach the heights of Russian Hill where the blaze was climbing toward the middle-class residential streets lined with gold rush–era homes of Gothic and early Craftsman style and newer Italianates and Victorians. With foundations anchored firmly on the hill's sandstone and shale bedrock, most houses here had suffered little earthquake damage. Ahead of the flames came the familiar sight of horse teams pulling dynamite wagons uphill and soldiers running door-to-door ordering residents to evacuate. But homeowners on a two-block residential section of Green and Vallejo Streets, neighbors who had stayed in their homes since the earthquake—many of whom had saved water in their bathtubs and boilers and wash bins—stood prepared and ready to defend their neighborhood.

Near the corner of Green and Leavenworth, eighty-year-old Louis Feusier lived with his wife and adult children and grandchildren in a home built forty-eight years earlier with walls of stone, sand, cement, and lime, and recently updated with a mansard roof and eight-sided cupola, giving it local fame as the "octagonal house." Louis had emigrated in 1851 from France, married, built a successful produce business in the city, and this was his forty-fifth year living in the home. When soldiers arrived to order the family out, Feusier's physician son-in-law told the soldiers they were not going to dynamite Mr. Feusier's home or any others on the block. In the face of his "firm resistance," as Feusier's son would later recount, "they made for the wooden stables out in back." Soldiers "planted three whole cases" of dynamite—324 sticks—"attached 100 feet of slow-burning fuse, lit it, and went away." In the "deafening" blast that followed, "the stables vanished," as Feusier's son described. And in the home—"unscathed" from the earthquake—"the explosion shattered every window, blew doors off their hinges, sent dishes crashing to the floor and completely terrified my family."

The Feusiers and their neighbors organized a makeshift force of volunteer firefighters. "Outbuildings and fences of all kinds were torn down" and firewood piles were removed to form a firebreak. As the blaze surrounded them—in places just across a street or as near as a neighboring house—residents positioned themselves on dry rooftops, and "with wet blankets and a small supply of water" they had saved, they kept their homes from igniting. Wind from the west blew flames across Leavenworth and turned homes along Vallejo into "seething furnaces," and residents formed a "bucket brigade" to keep the blaze away from homes along Green Street and stopped it from crossing Jones Street. Soldiers finally ceased their attempts to "demolish everything in sight" as residents stood in their way with "constant arguments and pleadings" and proof that the firefighting efforts were working. And "after several hours of the hottest work few men have ever been called upon to do," more than two and a half blocks of houses—including the one on Vallejo Street where botanist Alice Eastwood was safeguarding her rescued boxes of plant specimens—were spared from a blaze that continued rolling over the hill.

A similar battle was being fought in the same predawn hours by North Beach residents as the same winds blew fires "from the westward over Telegraph Hill," as Midshipman Pond described, "sweeping the wooden buildings on that eminence at the rate of a block every half hour." The streets of the hill—so steep they were marked on maps "Not Passable By [Horse] Teams"—were crowded with "huddled hundreds + thousands of miserable people," one man noted, adding that two passersby warned him, "This is no place for you, get off the hill it (the fire) may come up here."

But evacuation was difficult through narrow sixteen-foot-wide alleyways lined with narrow two- and three-story wooden apartment houses still jammed with tenant families. Soldiers and marines and Lieutenant Freeman's sailors ordered families from homes, and as one thirteen-year-old boy later recalled, "[A]ll we were permitted to take was a little clothing." Groups poured out of doorways in high numbers, like the Volpe family—seventy-year-old Mary, a widow; her daughter, Catherine, and sons, Domenico and Frank; her daughter-in-law; her granddaughter; and a boarder—all from a single flat of one of eighteen narrow apartment houses lining one alleyway.

The multitudes fled down the streets of the hill's east side to East Street, stepping over hose lines connected with the fireboat and two tugs. Hundreds were already camped along the streets near the seawall, and hundreds more trudged down toward the ferries. "One side was the water, on the other the flames of the already burned portion of the city which had been left unextinguished by the firemen who were needed worse in other parts of the city," one woman soon wrote in a letter. Of the night sky, she added, "Imagine—half the sky clear and starry—the other half masses of great flame-colored clouds. It was magnificently horrible."

With children and elderly household members safer near the seawall, and with Lieutenant Freeman and his sailors running hose lines up to protect the waterfront on the near (east) side of the hill, the Volpe brothers, twenty-five-year-old Domenico, a press feeder, and thirty-nine-year-old Frank, a box maker, climbed back up and over to their far (west) side of the hill to defend their street and their home. So too did Toby Irwin, a liquor store merchant and local prizefighter, and Tim O'Brien, a porter, and his roommate brother, Joseph, a stevedore. Together with a few dozen neighbors who had "hoarded a few buckets of water through the long days of fear and rumor" and others with "a barrel of cheap wine" in their cellar, as one resident would describe, they soaked their dry wooden homes and their neighbors' homes and their children's primary school with bucket brigades and with mops and blankets and suit coats dripping with wine.

Pushed by winds from the west, the leading flames of the blaze "swept up the slopes," as would be reported, "licking up cottages and tenements on its way." Dripping wood surfaces sizzled and steamed, slowing but not stopping the flames. Undeterred, the band of volunteers—their ranks swelling to hundreds—continued rolling wine barrels from cellars and chopping them open and dunking in wine any material they could grab—bedsheets, overcoats, curtains—which they "hung over the exposed portions of the cottages" and "drenched the shingles and sides of the houses with wine."

As the blaze marched uphill from the west, Lieutenant Freeman in "the lee of Telegraph Hill" (the east side, sheltered from the westerly winds) worried that the "large number of wooden shacks" on the hilltop would be "in danger of falling and setting fire to the large warehouses at the foot of the hill" if they caught fire. Freeman and his sailors and marines began a firebreak across the hill's crest, manually and without dynamite. And volunteers joined them— about three hundred in all—throwing ropes around tops of wooden structures and "pulling down fences, removing fuel, etc." and soon they "reduced the buildings . . . to ruins."

Sailors pulled the hose lines up, pumping from the fireboat *Leslie*, and "when the fire did get through," as Midshipman Pond reported, "it was easily extinguished with one stream of water." The east and north slopes of Telegraph Hill were saved, but the blaze burned through North Beach toward Fisherman's Wharf, and along the south side of the hill flames reached East Street, then fed southward on the only fuel remaining, the unburned blocks between there and the buildings saved a few hours earlier, including Hotaling's, the Montgomery Block, and the Custom House.

* * *

Back over on Russian Hill, Eleanor Briggs Putnam watched the fire from her third-floor flat: "It came on like a Fourth of July procession, with thunderous reports and flaunting streamers and fireworks, marching on, straight toward us, illuminating the whole house with its evil light." Her husband, Edward, was helping neighbors fight flames back. Their two-year-old son was in his bed, "completely dressed," and their bags were packed. Their neighborhood had turned into "empty rooms and furnished streets" with residents "sitting outside in hats and wraps, among their bags and bundles, ready for the signal to march."

But there were no soldiers, no firefighters, and no signal, just flames moving nearer with superheated air and showers of sparks. Eleanor grabbed her son—asleep as she carried him down the staircase until "the radiance of the fire" awakened him—and fled. She looked back at the three-story apartment house: "Is it really goodbye? Shall I never see it again?" she thought to herself, later recalling she looked up at her third-floor windows "without any emotion except that of unreality, and the house stared back at me like a strange face."

A couple of blocks away, a man in a Larkin Street home near the hill's highest point noticed "nothing effective was being done to arrest [the fire's] spread northward in our direction." He assembled neighbors as the blaze crept nearer and walked over to the corner grocery where the owner, standing guard at his storefront's broken windows, provided two barrels of vinegar to use against the flames. In the hours before dawn, fires jumped house to house, nearer and nearer, and winds swirling with flames brought waves of heat, then sparks and cinders, and residents got to work protecting their neighborhood. "A score of volunteers armed with blankets soaked in vinegar, extinguished flaming cinders on neighboring roofs," the man would later recount. On neighboring streets soldiers ordered people out as they dynamited, and onlookers warned, "Look out for bricks."

One of those evacuating down Russian Hill onto Van Ness Avenue was Eleanor Briggs Putnam, who noticed all around her "an endless procession of smaller makeshift vehicles" bearing possessions and dodging automobiles darting through pedestrians. "It was as tho' a colony of insects had been dislodged, and myriads of them were hurrying off into the darkness." She still carried her son, shielding his face with a handkerchief from "the cinders that fairly rained on us."

They joined the multitudes camping on the sand dunes near Fort Mason, on mattresses and unrolled bedding, near camps of Chinese families who had stayed together since evacuating Chinatown the previous night. At Fort Mason, soldiers who had spent the afternoon and evening setting up tents and digging latrines for refugees watched the fires crest Russian Hill, and a captain gathered ten men from his company and rigged explosives in a post warehouse should a firebreak prove necessary. "The post was nearly buried with ashes and we had to keep men on all the roofs with buckets of water," the captain noted. With his quarters filled with other officers and dependents who had given up their own barracks and quarters for refugees, the captain lay on his lawn and instructed his sergeant to awaken him should the blaze advance "near enough to threaten the post."

At 5:00 a.m. the sergeant shook his captain awake and pointed to the fire "coming over the hill toward us very rapidly." Magazine editor Mary Edith Griswold, who was camped at Fort Mason using an umbrella as a tent, described flames "coming up all sides of Russian Hill." Curious, she ventured toward the blaze for a better look where she saw "hundreds of huge roses glowing red in the light of the flames" and walked so near the blaze its heat made her "hair curl."

Out in the harbor near the piers of Fort Mason, the skipper of the cruiser *Chicago*, at anchor having arrived from San Diego after nightfall, noticed fire nearing the post as he prepared a relief force to send ashore at first light. "The air was filled with burning cinders which were blown by the wind far into the harbor," he reported, and as his vessel weighed anchor and glided in alongside the Fort Mason pier, the rain of sparks and embers was so heavy "all the awnings on board had to be furled and decks wet down to prevent fire." The waterfront was packed with "[t]housands of panic stricken, homeless and destitute people" awake and "eager to leave" but without transportation to evacuate them. The force of 189 sailors and marines landed and began helping soldiers "in demolishing outbuildings and fences" on the post's edge. The warehouse was not detonated, but wooden outbuildings and sheds and fencing were torn down as a firebreak and men were stationed on roofs of buildings with binoculars to watch for any flames on post.

The sun rose red again through the smoke above the city at 5:29 a.m. on Friday, April 20. There was no fog, but morning dew glued a film of gray ash to nearly every surface, and the air, already warm, would eventually climb above eighty degrees on what would be the hottest day of the year so far. "The morning awakening was to a scene of beauty," noted Dr. Margaret Mahoney, who awoke on a mattress on the Presidio golf course to "a blue sky and a fair day." Reverend William Nichols "had fairly good sleep and rest" in his Pacific

Heights home even though the "red glare of the burning city lighted up the windows around the curtains" through the night. As inside every house still standing there was no telephone, no power, no gas, no running water. And no indoor cooking or heating or lamps allowed. Outside no streetcars were running, no provision stores were open, "thickly posted sentinels" paced his street, and "the only running water available in our section" was "from a faucet several blocks off near Fillmore Street." All cooking was outdoors and with nearly every remaining wagon and automobile commandeered by authorities and many streets impassable for downed wires and split pavement, nearly all travel was on foot. Now forty-eight hours after the earthquake, even as fires still burned through the city, the greatest of all discomforts was hunger and thirst.

After waking up on mattresses in Golden Gate Park, Dr. John Hollister and his wife and friends from the Mission District ate breakfast prepared on "a little sheet-iron pocket cook stove" thanks to two men in their group who had once been prospectors. One of the men had lost his home to dynamite and his plumbing business to fire the day before, and his sister comforted him, "We are all here, and that is enough to be thankful for."

In unburned streets throughout the Western Addition and the Mission District, residents and their refugee guests huddled around homemade stoves cooking what little they could still forage from their pantries or the emptied shelves of nearby grocery stores. "What a sight on Dolores St.!" an eight-year-old in the Mission later described. "All the way down the middle of the street cooking stoves and supplies were lined one after the other." A man in a Green Street boardinghouse walked outside that morning with a metal bucket of water and the coffee grounds and eggs he had saved and enjoyed the "simple breakfast" he "cooked in a bucket in the gutter in front of the house, plus some bread." A woman on Gough Street wrote in a letter of hauling "water many blocks" back to cook breakfast with her family on their homemade stove of "bricks in the street." And an eight-year-old boy walked to a nearby grocery store "to get something to take to my folks," but with shelves mostly empty he filled his "pockets with bottles of extract" and rolled an unlabeled barrel three blocks back to his house, and "when I opened it I found that I had a barrel of nutmeg."

Even those charged with keeping the peace struggled to find sustenance. An ROTC cadet from Berkeley who had been pulling patrol shifts through two straight nights found himself out of rations by Friday morning and "set out on a tour to get something to eat," and his breakfast and lunch consisted of pretzels, cheese, sardines, and raisin cookies.

But signs began to show that such localized, stopgap measures were being supplanted by a citywide, uniform relief operation. Even as thousands continued evacuating by ferry and firefighters battled the blaze in North Beach, three waterfront piers near the Ferry Building were taken over by the Army for incoming relief shipments—one pier for tentage, one for forage, and the third for food supplies. Orders had been placed for provisions from neighboring military posts, and steamers would begin arriving that day with holds filled with blankets, bed sacks, boilers (for coffee and soup), cots, hats, kettles, mattresses, pans, pillows, ponchos, pots, cooking ranges, shoes, socks, trousers, undershirts, bunks, tents (conical, shelter, hospital, and storage), and tent accessories (poles, stakes, and stoves). In addition to the 400,000 rations already ordered by War Secretary Taft from Vancouver Barracks to be shipped with the "greatest urgency," the commissary general in Washington, DC, wired Seattle directing "immediate shipment of 300,000 rations" and authorized General Funston to send an officer to Los Angeles to purchase another 200,000 rations as well as coffee, sugar, soap, and candles.

The first shipments of these 900,000 rations began arriving overnight at the small Presidio dock, which post quartermaster Major Carroll Devol found to be "sadly inadequate to the amount of work demanded of it." Because pier space was "so limited that it became immediately congested if delivery was not taken from the dock as fast as consignments reached it," Devol posted a large number of soldiers to facilitate quick delivery from "boat to dock, dock to wagon, and from wagon to hands of the people." And the Southern Pacific Railroad—already running evacuees on passenger lines out of Oakland and South of Market's unburned passenger depot for free—began running freight relief shipments into the city free of charge.

Major Devol assisted the Subcommittee for Relief of the Hungry—a part of the Citizens' Committee—in establishing a system for broad distribution of food. Discontinued was yesterday's system of handing out on wharves or railroad yards whatever food had just arrived, and as rations and other food—cornmeal, flour, canned goods, potatoes—came in by water or rail, it was taken under guard by wagon or automobile—most commandeered—to each of a few dozen food stations that had been informally set up the previous day—at churches, in parks, squares, empty lots, the Young Men's Hebrew Association, at the Golden Gate Park Lodge, and the Presidio.

And long, hungry lines began to form. "We were somewhat early and there were only a few hundred ahead of us in the 'bread line,'" one man wrote in a letter describing the scene at the Presidio, where "the line behind us stretched out farther than we could see among the trees." The going was so slow he "dropped on the ground from fatigue" while waiting, and finally his turn came: "The soldiers who distributed the food were ranged in a circle, around which we passed, to receive a handful of tea from one, a can of meat from the next, rice, and mush, and canned fruit, and potatoes."

At other locations the selections were slimmer and the portions not so generous. Among those in line at a South of Market breadline after 9:00 a.m. that morning was Michael Maher, who had been burned out of his South of Market boardinghouse the first morning, slept in a railroad toolshed the past two nights, and not eaten since dinner Tuesday evening. When his turn came, he finally got a "cup of coffee and one thin slice of bread," breaking a sixty-three-hour fast, which he later wrote "was the longest period I ever fasted in my life."

One woman walked with her husband through downtown's smoking ash-covered ruins to a food station and "joined the line we saw forming" where they were handed precooked eggs and meat in a box: "We ate it from the box and thankful to have it." While walking back, they joined others sifting through the rubble of a burned-out china warehouse still "pretty warm in spots," and found a scorched but unbroken dinner plate, luncheon plate, and small dish: "What a find! Now we could pour out our dry food on a plate and feel more civilized."

Also distributed to camping residents that morning were newspapers. After the single-day joint issue, all three papers were separately printed in Oakland, the *Examiner* still from the presses of the *Oakland Tribune,* and the *Call* and *Chronicle* from the *Oakland Herald.* The city editor of the *Chronicle* counted, stacked, and tied his paper's seven thousand issues, loaded them on a wagon to the wharves, ferried them to San Francisco where an automobile was awaiting him, "and tore through what was left of the town, giving away papers from Noe Valley to the Presidio."

Residents and refugees, whether homeless in a park or crowded at home with displaced family and friends, craved updates on the state of their city. They knew for certain only what they had seen: a sky filled with smoke churning from a citywide inferno, lifting from different places every hour, for two days, and still going. Some had been rescued from the wreckage of collapsed apartment houses and sprinted through walls of flames to escape. Many had been evacuated ahead of the blaze and watched as their homes were dynamited or burned. They shared their experiences with others who had only seen the orange glow above hilltops. Most had not walked the burned sections of the city yet, nor had many ventured to high ground to absorb the new day's panorama of what was left of downtown, South of Market, Nob Hill, the banking and harbor districts, or the Mission.

So as an automobile chugged along the sides of parks and squares handing out newspapers, people starving for news flocked to grab one. "The people were crazy for them," the city editor noted, and with people jumping on the running boards and bumpers, the car had to keep driving for fear of getting swarmed. "If we had stopped anywhere we would have been stripped of our papers."

Beneath the headline "300,000 ARE HOMELESS, HUNGRY AND HELPLESS," the *Examiner* reported, "San Francisco is prostrate, but is not crushed," and highlighted the aid sent from all points: $85,000 pledged by Portland businessmen and $15,000 raised by that city's paper in a day; nearly $40,000 raised in Oakland; $75,000 in Sacramento—including $3,000 from its Chinese citizens; 3,500 tents sent from Philadelphia and a steamer with provisions from Stockton; $100,000 promised by John D. Rockefeller and the same amount pledged by the president of Postal Telegraph.

The *Chronicle* struck its own optimistic note, declaring "FLAMES COURSE AT LAST CHECKED," and crediting the "heroic work" of firemen and "the aid of dynamite" with stopping the fire at Van Ness. As of the hour their paper went to press, reporters were confident flames would "soon burn themselves out" down in the Mission, even though fire companies "were powerless to check their course toward North Beach," something apparent to readers that morning as smoke roiled from the northeastern swath of the city. James Hopper's article was included, the first comprehensive eyewitness account of the earthquake and fire available to the rest of the city and outside world. And optimistic reports followed, of the meeting of the "Relief and Restoration Committee," pledges of relief funds "from all sides," and Congress's $1 million appropriation for sufferers. And proclaiming, "The New City Begins Today," the newspaper's staff pledged to occupy its new building—already under construction and "practically undamaged" by the earthquake—"with all possible speed" once completed. Their example would "be followed by others as soon as the debris in the burned section can be cleared away," and the "new San Francisco will be the same old San Francisco in a more prosperous setting."

But the scope of the ongoing disaster—"wiping out at one sweep the physical progress of a half century"—was beyond written description. "The sight looked like the pictures of the ruined cities of the east, as pictured in books," noted a man who made his way past downtown's stark, smoking landscape that morning. Only the familiar shapes of the Fairmont, St. Francis, and Call Building—scorched and gutted but standing—"saved the city from becoming an unidentified and barren waste."

Edward de Laveaga returned to his father's Geary Street home, no longer in peril of dynamite or fire, and gazed from the familiar vantage point at an unfamiliar scene: "What was once the business part and swell part (Nob Hill) looked terrible," he noticed. "As far as you could see looking West of Van Ness was nothing but ruins."

Many were eager for not just a firsthand look at the damage in the city but a peek at the state of their home and livelihood, the harm to their own apartment or office or restaurant or store or warehouse. Two mornings earlier, Frederick Collins and his roommate and business partner Max Koenig had found their O'Farrell Street clothiers, Koenig & Collins, with only minimal damage, but as fires threatened they "locked the doors and left the swell store to its fate." They "hurriedly packed some useful clothing" and fled their downtown apartment to stay with a friend in the Western Addition. Now they returned to find the six-story brick building that once housed their store, a saloon, a bowling alley, and other businesses in ruins, and their cloaks and suits partnership "a complete 'wipe out,' wholesale and retail both." And they found "a pile of hot ashes and stone" where their apartment building once stood. "Sidewalk was even gone and a big deep hole with the contents of ten furnished floors," Frederick later described. Only a blackened, jagged shell of outer walls stood over twisted steel framing jumbled in a hot pit: "No chance of even finding a small piece of a glass bottle."

Amadeo Giannini rode a wagon back into the city from his San Mateo home and found his Bank of Italy building a scorched mound of rubble and its contents unrecognizable. James Stetson walked from his Van Ness Avenue home to the California Street Cable Railroad's engine house and "found it in ruins," still smoking and hot. "The form of everything was there, but rods, cranks, beams, and pipe were bent and burned."

Fruit merchant Tom Burns returned by wagon from his home near Golden Gate Park to his Washington Street business and found "our safe in the basement of what had been our fireproof store" of brick and iron shutters. "The building itself was destroyed." The man who had been looking to give Tom Burns a morning cigar when the earthquake struck, police sergeant Jesse Cook, was still keeping order among evacuees near the waterfront. He and another officer returned to the "relatively cooled" burned wreckage of their Harbor District Police Station to find their spare revolvers, climbing through the collapsed roof and digging through the ashes. "Both weapons were there, but only the metal work survived and it was fused in places." Cook returned to the wharves where Tom Burns—the man he believed was dead since seeing the building behind him collapse during the earthquake two mornings before—was picking up fruit from a freight car to run back out to refugees in Golden Gate Park. As Burns would later recount of Sergeant Cook's reaction, "when he recognized me, looked as if he was 'seeing things.'"

Through the morning, as fire crews battled the blazes on Russian Hill and in North Beach, firemen down in the Mission District extinguished the last sizzling embers along 20th Street and began returning to their firehouses. At least nine engine companies and two truck companies were finally relieved from the longest, hardest job any of them had ever faced or ever would again. At 4:00 a.m. the first company returned after forty-seven straight hours on duty. More followed at 6:00 a.m., 7:00 a.m., 8:00 a.m., 9:00 a.m., and 10:00 a.m. "We were finally ordered to our quarters at 11 a.m. April 20th, 1906, having been on duty 53 hours," reported the captain of one engine company. Another company returned "after having been on duty continuously for fifty-four hours." Firemen piled their singed coats and seared helmets on hose wagons and kicked off boots and tugged suspenders from shoulders and trudged up stairwells and peeled off sweat-soaked shirts and pants and collapsed on thin mattresses of firehouse beds.

But most firemen had no quarters left. Nineteen firehouses had been destroyed and two more were still in the path of the North Beach blaze. This left seventeen engine companies, five truck companies, and five chemical engine companies without a firehouse. Captain Charles Cullen and his ten firemen of South of Market's Engine 6 were finally relieved from duty at noon, nearly fifty-five hours after their longest shift began by rescuing adults and children from the collapsed apartments neighboring their 6th Street firehouse. Now the fire had destroyed their firehouse and each of their homes, from the Harrison Street flats of Captain Cullen and Lieutenant Edward Daunet to the 6th Street apartments of engineer Patrick Brandon and hoseman John Titus. The men were forced to find rest elsewhere, for many their only surviving material possessions being the grimy work clothes on their backs and tattered work shoes on their feet.

At least two-thirds of the city's firemen were still working. Most had not slept since the earthquake, and many had not slept since before the cannery fire the night before. An Army tug at the foot of Van Ness pumped salt water through two long hose lines to five engine companies "stationed at contiguous points" along the avenue, as one company's captain would report. He rotated his tired firemen in shifts at the engine and on the hose so they could grab "an hour or two of rest in the doorways" of buildings or on the asphalt beside their engine. His lieutenant and engineer collapsed from exhaustion and were carried by wagon up to the hospital at Fort Mason where they were given fluids and rest. After six hours, both returned to duty.

Their grueling work was showing results. The focused effort of the engine companies getting water from the bay combined with neighborhood volunteers to man hose lines and soak walls and roofs with water and wine and olive oil was working and most fires along Russian Hill were subsiding—"well in hand," as one resident assessed. A sixteen-year-old on Filbert Street noticed "a strong, cool sea breeze" from the west blowing "brands back over the burning area." He and others "could see that the fire east of Van Ness was burning itself out, and, for the first time, we felt some hope that the blaze might be brought under control." A man over on Russian Hill later recalled, "By eleven o'clock Friday morning we believed that the rest of our district was out of danger."

But with no regard for the waning blaze, dynamite crews under orders not rescinded and with explosives still unused worked like a runaway train, needlessly demolishing structures beside the dwindling fire with no water to douse resulting flames. "Suddenly I heard a dull explosion, followed by a cloud of dust and debris just below me," noticed a man standing on Van Ness. "Then came a burst of flame." It was the Viavi Building, a three-story wood-frame building on the avenue's east side. It was dynamited even though it was, as would be reported, "unharmed by the fire and no longer menaced by it." On the second and third floors above its first-floor offices, the company packaged liquid and capsule versions of its experimental "home treatment for mothers and daughters," and when the building was blown up, as one onlooker observed, the blast "ignited thousands of gallons of alcohol that were stored there." A police officer helping with volunteers and hose lines saw the insides of the Viavi Building "hurling skyward," shooting flaming debris and flammable chemicals onto wooden flats next door, "and ten minutes later the whole district was again in flames."

Temperatures topped eighty degrees and fires dashed through hot, dry, wooden apartment buildings and houses. The blaze "rose to something very like a cyclone in violence," described one witness who watched as "the unchecked fire roared up the hill, leaping from building to building, and reached Larkin Street" where occupants had abandoned a corner house to its fate: "The windows stood gaping open and long white curtains streamed out of them in horizontal lines sucking toward the advance of the fire."

Residents on Russian Hill's north slope got back to work along Greenwich and Lombard and Chestnut Streets, climbing to rooftops with wet blankets and buckets, soaking shingles and cornices, snuffing small flames before they could spread. And demolition crews persisted, prodding wary drivers of commandeered automobiles filled with dynamite to get ahead of the blaze by levering their throttles and sputtering up the Lombard Street hill to its peak at Hyde Street where soldiers ran fuses and percussion caps and boxes of dynamite down the next block of Lombard between Hyde and Leavenworth—a length of street so steep weeds grew along it for lack of regular traffic, still sixteen years from being reconfigured into what would famously (and inaccurately) be called the "Crookedest Street in the World"—and they blew up houses along its south side. Yet again with no water to soak the debris or surrounding structures, sparks and red embers shot in high arcs in all directions and started new fires.

Flickers of flames appeared on the rooftop of the corner house at the top of the hill, a Tudor and Mediterranean Revival built six years earlier by Fanny Stevenson, the widow of Robert Louis. "Two agile schoolboys with pails and cups climbed to the roof of the Robert Louis Stevenson house," observed a witness, "and saved the mansion by putting out sparks as they fell." By the same methods, residents up across the street saved the house, barn, and stables that had been the boyhood home of William Randolph Hearst, and on the corner opposite saved the gold rush–era "Humphreys' Castle," a southern plantation–style house with a long veranda crowned with an octagonal tower. Their efforts kept the blaze on the south side of Chestnut where, at the corner with Leavenworth, a man saved his house reportedly "with blanket and bucket and a little water from the tank on the roof" while the rest of his block burned.

The wall of fire rolled eastward down the hill, joining the blaze in North Beach where Abe Ruef was ensuring demolition crews spared his Lombard Street house. "Two streams of water were playing on Mr. Ruef's property," one witness observed of fire crews pumping water from a cistern a block distant trying to save Ruef's house. Along the rest of the street were locals defending their homes on their own: "carpets had been suspended from roofs of buildings" and "men and women worked might and main to prevent the fire from crossing the street" and "buckets of wine were poured from the roofs and with sacks dipped in wine they beat the walls." But no matter how each neighborhood's volunteers kept pace to beat the blaze, flames found undefended gaps and fires pushed northward. And the unburned streets of North Beach were shrinking by the hour, pushing more families to the waterfront and over to Fort Mason.

Down in one of the only unburned patches of the banking district, the racket of strained wooden staves and rattles and crunches of iron bilge hoops on cobblestones echoed down Jackson Street as a motley crew of hired hands rolled heavy barrels of whiskey in a noisy two-block procession from the Hotaling warehouse to an empty lot past the Custom House. 1,200 had been parked in the lot by daybreak, and through the morning fresh helpers were recruited and employees worked in shifts, carefully lowering each barrel from its rack, while others stood along the two-block route to point the way and, as company cashier and manager Edward Lind explained, "to egg on and spur into greater activity those who lagged in their barrel rolling." By noon, another one thousand had been added to the lot, guarded by hungry men kept on the job with "bottles of the best imported ale and stout." But time looked short as winds shifted and blew the fire back down toward them. "It curled along the foot of Telegraph Hill, and thence headed back, south, in our direction," Lind noticed, and by early afternoon "the fire was then sweeping down the hill and was menacing us from close at hand."

Lieutenant Freeman noticed this and sent Midshipman Pond and a crew with extra fire department hoses in the tug *Active* to the pier at the foot of Jackson Street to defend the Custom House again. "When we got the hose all laid out" and were about to start pumping, Midshipman Pond would later report, "we found to our dismay that we lacked a reducer with which to make the final connection." Pond ran back to the tug as "[a] strong wind was commencing to blow from the northwest and the fire was getting away from us again."

The fire was now within one block of the Hotaling warehouse, and the "barrel rollers were already becoming nervous and wanted to quit," Edward Lind noted. Hose lines snaked along pavement from the waterfront to the Custom House on the adjacent block where men stood ready at the nozzles, but no water was coming. Across the street "flames had eaten through the block from Pacific Street, and the buildings on the north side of Jackson Street were beginning to burn toward us." Down at the pier, Pond and his crew "searched frantically" for the adaptor, and "urgent messages came down to us to start the pump." But with no adaptor they could not connect. And with no water, Hotaling's defenders were almost helpless as "sparks and smoke" filled Jackson Street and the alley leading to the warehouse.

Lind and the others decided saving any more barrels would be too risky, "so we closed all the iron shutters, tore down the wooden signs of A.P. Hotaling & Company, and abandoned the property for the time being to what seemed its certain and fiery fate." Lind and the rest of the employees ran past the soldiers guarding the Custom House to the lot lined with their barrels. "The air was filling with live sparks and choking smoke, while numbers of government clerks and officials were removing important records" from the Custom House.

Beside the pier at the foot of Jackson Street, Lieutenant Freeman glided up in the *Leslie*, wondering about the delay in getting the stream going. "The look he gave me when I tried to explain the situation," Midshipman Pond later recalled, "showed plainly enough that he was not satisfied with my lack of foresight in not having a reducer available for this emergency." But the local blaze was no longer their priority as both officers could see the heavy wind "was sweeping the flames with great velocity around both sides of Telegraph Hill towards the waterfront." Freeman ordered Pond and his crew to "gather up the hose and take it back on board" and both the *Active* and *Leslie* were again underway to help the tug *Pilot* save the North Beach waterfront.

As they watched sailors roll up the hose line and walk it back down Jackson Street, Hotaling workers at the barrel-filled lot on Jackson Street noticed the wind lessen, "and instead of despairing," as Edward Lind would relate, "we all began to think of possible methods of salvage." They punched holes in two empty barrels, found two wine pumps in nearby warehouses, dropped them into sewers, and filled the barrels. And with the help of soldiers at the Custom House, they grabbed "buckets and tin pails" from a deserted grocery store "and a bucket brigade was formed" to carry sewage back up to the corner lodging house at the end of the block, which was then under a shower of sparks from the three-story restaurant—a fifty-three-year-old brick building built during the gold rush for the bank managed by William Tecumseh Sherman—"in full blaze" on the opposite corner.

Soldiers and employees and volunteers passed buckets up the lodging house stairway and "up a rickety ladder through a small man-hole to the roof" and splashed the putrid mix of urine and waste "on live sparks as they fell." The fire spread all along the length of the block until the north side of Jackson Street "was a roaring fury of flame, with walls toppling and smoke choking people." On the south side, soldiers on rooftops kept pace even as their skin blistered from the heat, passing buckets from rooftop to rooftop as shooting embers started flames on any dry surface. "Several times the block caught," an

Army captain reported. "I had men on the roofs who extinguished the flames during the afternoon and night and to protect it from flying sparks."

Edward Lind likened the lodging house rooftop at that hour to "a barbecue." Buckets were rushed up through the small opening and splashed on embers, and the sewage "made a steam that was suffocating as it evaporated on the roasting woodwork." The roof and top floor of the engulfed restaurant across the street "collapsed" and the "danger from that source was ended." Hotaling's workers helped soldiers defend the Custom House with their bucket brigade as the fires on Jackson Street's north side burned out. "Our side of the street was still unscathed," Lind would proudly recall, and as the Army captain later reported, "[I]t seemed likely that this block would be saved."

It was saved. Again. After fire threatened four separate times from all four directions over three days, soldiers and sailors and marines and firemen and store owners and employees and paid hands and volunteers had saved two and a half blocks of the banking district, including the Montgomery Block, Custom House, Hotaling's store and warehouse, and dozens of walk-up offices, including the art studio of Mexican American painter Xavier Martínez, who had evacuated the first day in such a rush he was able to grab only his brushes and easels, forced to leave all his paintings—including recent award winners—for what he believed would be their destruction. Now the paintings were spared along with the neighboring apartments and businesses of the lucky few tenants and owners of the small two-and-a-half-block section of the old city left standing amid a scorched, smoking landscape.

16. Extinguished

BY FRIDAY AFTERNOON, Fort Mason was congested with "herds of people," noted an Army captain who put his soldiers to work "cooking for the refugees" and issuing clothing, blankets, canned goods, coffee, soap, and more tents. With the help of sailors who had disembarked from the *Chicago*, the captain "rounded up all able-bodied men on the reservation, provided them with tools and made them build latrines." He sent wagons "to collect all rubbish and garbage" from campers and a detail of soldiers to clear people and items from roadways for supply trips. With the post's water supply "about exhausted," he arranged for the Navy to haul fresh water over from Mare Island. And with space dwindling and passage to the Ferry Building arduous for refugees trying to make it safely around the fires and dynamiters on foot, authorities also arranged for vessels to embark passengers directly from Fort Mason's pier.

"We are at the little dock below the fort waiting for a navy cutter to take us around to the Oakland ferry," wrote magazine editor Mary Edith Griswold from the Fort Mason wharf at 1:00 p.m. She had evacuated her Eddy Street home the previous day as fires on Van Ness were within two blocks—so close the "paint on the woodwork was blistering"—and camped at Fort Mason the previous night and now lamented, "My home will surely go." Also awaiting evacuation was Eleanor Briggs Putnam, who had carried her two-year-old son down from their camping spot on the nearby dunes, hoping for passage to her mother's home in Berkeley while her husband, Edward, stayed in the city. Some had been waiting for passage since morning, and the crowd swelled to standing room only with new arrivals, including wounded people bleeding and bandaged and those barely able to walk, "and it became extremely uncomfortable for us in the narrow space between the wharf and steep bank behind it," Eleanor noted. When the vessel appeared and glided to the pier, the multitudes "surged forward."

"This boat for Oakland. Women with babies and children and their escorts first!" yelled a deckhand as the boat tied alongside the pier. The response was an immediate uproar of protests from the crowd. "Oh, the babies! Always the women and their babies!" and "What business have the women and their babies here! Why don't they stay at home!" and "Do you think I've been standing here since ten o'clock [a.m.] to mind an order like that?" Eleanor, clutching her young son's hand, "could scarcely believe [her] ears" and looked around "to see what sort of folk these strange voices belonged to." From the crowd came self-serving attempts at boarding as if on the deck of a sinking ocean liner: "Can't I borrow that child?" and "Lady, will you let me be your escort?"

Eleanor made it aboard with her son and secured a spot on the lower deck for shade from the hot sun and near an open porthole for fresh air from the stuffy, crowded space. "There were no seats, but a large chest stood near the porthole, on which we placed the children." The vessel was almost overwhelmed with evacuees, and after repeated shouted orders from the captain and strenuous efforts of his crew to hold back the mob and prevent a panic, they untied and shoved off. After swinging out into the bay, Eleanor could see Russian and Telegraph Hills through her porthole, and "up and down and all around their slopes like torches, well developed fires were blazing, fanned by the fierce wind." As they glided past the wharves of North Beach, it was not "isolated fires" but rather "one continuous angry sea of flames." At the foot of Telegraph Hill she could see a tugboat "puffing and pumping away like a live thing" while "valiantly spraying the roofs and sides of the wharf with salt water."

This was likely the *Pilot*, which had been pumping alongside Lieutenant Freeman's fireboat and yard tug since the night before. Freeman had taken his vessels down near the threatened Custom House and left the tugboat alone at the Filbert Street pier early in the afternoon when he believed "that this whole section of the waterfront would be saved." But now the strong gales from the northwest whipped the flames up with new ferocity, overwhelming the sailors manning the *Pilot*'s hose line and nearing the wharf itself. "How inadequate!

How futile!" Eleanor thought as she passed the small tug fighting its lonely battle.

Freeman returned to aid the *Pilot* with the fireboat *Leslie* followed by the tug *Active*. At that hour, late-afternoon Friday, Freeman had been on his feet since landing in San Francisco Wednesday morning. "He looked all in," Midshipman Pond would later recall of his skipper in that moment, "with the sweat streaking down through the grime on his weather-beaten face onto the dirty white handkerchief he had tied around his neck, and he seemed discouraged at the unfavorable turn of events." Freeman stepped onto the pier to reconnect the hose lying where he had left it on the waterfront but its far end sat in the midst of flames, burning, and he was forced to cut it and the line leading from the *Pilot*, losing nearly two thousand feet of hose. "In order to save any part of the waterfront," he moved his firefighting flotilla a few blocks up to the Lombard Street pier at the north side of Telegraph Hill, where once again he would battle the blaze and "try to stop it from coming down the waterfront."

Out on the boat filled with evacuees from Fort Mason, an initial announcement that they were bound for Oakland and not the Ferry Building triggered the spread of rumors among passengers that the Ferry Building had been destroyed. But the vessel rounded North Beach and turned toward the city's eastern waterfront, and through her open porthole Eleanor Briggs Putnam could see "the tall watch tower of the Ferry Building, even if its flag staff was askew." Each pier along the waterfront was clogged with two or three vessels—barges filled with provisions or private charters evacuating residents. Boats were also serving as temporary, floating quarters for refugees. As with the *Marion*, a sixty-seven-year-old sloop-of-war state naval militia training ship that had taken on a few hundred people. And the *Hartfield*, a steamship from Liverpool whose captain gave food, clothes, and shelter to all who could fit aboard. And the *Henley*, a steamship from London, whose captain was not only housing hundreds of refugees—including a large number from Chinatown—but also had employed his evaporators to provide fresh water to the thirsty and keep boilers of fire engines and Lieutenant Freeman's Navy vessels at steam.

Because all ferry slips were occupied, Eleanor's boat pulled alongside the wharf and, with the rest of the disembarking evacuees, she helped her son up the steep gangplank. As she walked him toward the Ferry Building for passage to Oakland, she was "bewildered," as she later wrote, "for the oldest inhabitant would not have recognized his city." San Francisco's downtown was "a gray wilderness," and in the heat and the wind, her "eyes and lungs choked with smoke and cinders and a fine white dust which was the worst of all." They passed through the building's archway past a comforting sign that read, "Water for men. Milk for women and children." They boarded the ferry for Oakland, finding seats on the outside deck, and steamed away from the Ferry Building's clock tower, its hands still stopped where they had frozen three mornings before.

Oakland was thick with people. A man stepping off the ferry that day saw streets "crowded with thousands of refugees from San Francisco, and thousands of hungry and homeless men, women, and children were standing in line at the City Hall waiting for food from the local relief committee, who were giving away bread and canned goods." Another man went to the lawn of City Hall and heard a man yelling for "All who want a place to sleep" to line up. "More than a hundred of us fell in line in response to this summons," he noted. "We were marched to a gymnasium where had the floor to sleep on." Eleanor and her son stepped from the ferry and took a train to Berkeley, where her mother lived, and after arriving in town, Eleanor "felt as if we had passed into another world, such as the Bible speaks of, where there shall be 'no more pain, neither sorrow nor any crying, for the former things have passed away.'" The college town was, to her, "Paradise after the inferno." As Eleanor and her son arrived on the front lawn, her mother and sisters and niece "came running out and down through the grounds, with tears streaming down their faces, to meet us." They had heard "[t]errible reports" and "had been watching the smoke by day and the flames by night," worried Eleanor and her boy were "enduring cold and hunger, if not trapped in burning buildings." The worries evaporated, and Eleanor and her son "were kissed and hugged and cried over, and led into the house with great rejoicing."

The worry of those with family and friends in San Francisco worsened with each passing hour, most finally assuaged with the arrival of a letter or a telegram, always delayed and some taking many days or even weeks to arrive. There was no phone line to call for answers, and telegrams went unanswered. They could only watch the mailbox or pore over each line of the morning papers—especially extra editions—and jump at every knock on the door. A girl and her sisters who had been sent by their father on a ferry to Berkeley on Thursday had watched the fires from across the water for the past days, and now she worried for him and her brothers still in San Francisco: "from Thursday eve until Sunday we did not know how Pa & the boys were, dead or alive," she soon wrote in a letter. "The newspaper reports were terrible and all we could do was sit on Mrs. Hermann's west porch and watch the awful flames grow & leap heavenward."

People searching for loved ones posted notices "hurriedly scribbled in pencil on whatever scraps of paper could be found in such an emergency" in refugee camps and on fences and telegraph poles, as would be reported. "Lost. Paul E. Hoffes, nine years old, light complexioned, blue eyes. Please notify his mother, Panhandle, opposite Lyon street entrance," read one. "Harry Markowitz is looking for his Mother and Father. Can be found at the Denison News Co., Oakland Pier," read another. On the doorways of damaged houses or the nearest standing pole or fence post beside the ruins of burned or dynamited apartment buildings, displaced evacuees nailed directions where concerned family could find them. "Mother, Ray and Ethel E. Peck. We are at 631 Van Ness Ave. Mildred Peck if you see this come at once. We are O.K. Ethel E. Peck." And "A.C. Rass and family, formerly 1433 California st. are safe at 3632 Sacramento." And "Dr. Geo. H. Martin and wife please inform of whereabouts: we are safe and well. H.A.W. Piedmont." A man returning to his O'Farrell Street home found a strip of cardboard with a penciled message that he could find his "wife and all the folks in the Panhandle of the Park, Baker Street entrance."

Friday's newspapers provided some help, with the *Examiner* publishing the names of 141 known patients in the Army General Hospital at the Presidio, a "partial list" of those receiving care, including Army Lieutenant Charles Pulis, wounded in the first black powder demolition Wednesday morning, and Fire Chief Dennis Sullivan, reported as "seriously wounded, but will recover." And papers ran notices on behalf of people seeking family in the city: "A. Enkel, a prominent Los Angelan, is in Oakland diligently searching for his wife and children." After searching "every corner of the city," he had still not found her and asked "that she leave her address at the Owl Drug Company's Store in Oakland."

Most helpful was the city's postal service, which in one of the greatest feats of the disaster was back to collecting and delivering mail by Friday. The new main post office building had opened just six months before, a grand and ornate three-story beaux arts–style federal building made of brick faced with granite and an interior of imported marble. It stood at the corner of 7th Street (which had sunk more than one foot in the earthquake) and Mission Street (which had sunk more than three). Built on friction piles driven deep into the district's soft fill land, the building's granite exterior was badly cracked and interior mosaic and tiles shattered but, as an engineer later reported, "with-stood the earthquake surprisingly well."

Within an hour of the earthquake, postmaster secretary William Burke ar-rived to join more than forty employees who stayed past their morning shifts to protect the building from fire, which by late morning "was coming from all directions." They sealed the fireproof doors and, with four extinguishers and mail sacks dipped in water from boilers and a freight elevator tank, fought off flames invading window openings where glass had melted from the heat. As with their federal counterparts in the mint two blocks away, sweat-drenched postmen "worked like demons" and "fought in a perfect hell of fire," as their station superintendent would write, battling back the blaze like soldiers un-der siege, leaving the post office scarred but mostly unburned in the midst of South of Market's blackened rubble piles and gutted buildings.

The disaster had devastated the rest of the postal service system in San Francisco. Twenty-five of the city's local mail distribution stations had been destroyed in the fire and nearly 250 postal employees were homeless. Soldiers guarded the main post office on Thursday, and inside, William Burke and other employees worked through the day and night to get mail moving again. They righted upended mail racks and stamp registers and gathered and reorganized thousands of scattered letters and parcels. And they pickaxed a hole through the basement floor and dug a well in the soil below, and with its sand-gritty water got the basement boilers running again, restoring power to the building.

By Friday morning, the postmaster met with officials of the Inspection Di-vision and Railway Mail Service, their priority being outgoing mail. "Wagons and automobiles were impressed," Burke later recounted, and sent to stations to gather all mail that had piled up. And to set up service for refugees in camps, employees drove automobiles out to announce that letters would be collected that afternoon and "the Post Office would handle everything, stamped or un-stamped, as long as it had an address."

William Burke drove a commandeered auto to spread word through "the Presidio and Golden Gate Park and any intermediate gathering I could find." On the way he stopped at a carbarn and grabbed a "United States Mail" sign from a cable car that usually ran mail, and he fixed it to the front of his auto before entering the first refugee camp. "The effect was electrical," he later re-counted, and campers "cheered and shouted in a state bordering on hysteria." At the Presidio "there was almost a riot." As he told them to tell others where mail would be collected that afternoon, he saw it "as the first sign of rehabil-itation."

Friday afternoon, mail collection automobiles returned as promised. Excited people swarmed the auto Burke drove, dropping and throwing a "wonderful mass of communications" into mail pouches held by postmen in the back seat: "Bits of cardboard, cuffs, pieces of wrapping paper, bits of newspapers with an address on the margin, pages of books and sticks of wood all served as a means to let somebody in the outside world know that friends were alive and in need among the ruins."

"U.S. mail is carried in automobiles," wrote one resident, "and we are permitted to send letters without stamps as there are no stamps to be had and no money to buy it with." Another resident confided to his journal that he could mail a message on "any little scrap of paper" as long as he wrote at the top in place of a stamp "the all-powerful words 'from San Francisco.'" By nightfall Friday, autos and wagons returned with nearly one hundred pouches of "as curious mail as was ever handled," and along with nearly three hundred sacks of parcels saved from the fire, they were hauled to the Ferry Building and across the bay and dispatched on mail delivery trains to all points.

In a pouch on a train bound for a post office in Ohio was a folded scrap of paper from Karl Kneiss, a railroad worker living near the Panhandle, to his mother, Rosa: "S.F. Apr 20th Dear Mother: Up to now—5 PM—We are all well & safe. The fire is still burning hard but in the North part of town. I won't try to describe anything, as it is foolish to begin. There are no words." And he ended by assuring her, "Will write more when I can. With love to all, Karl."

The last time seven-year-old John Conlon Jr. had seen his father, fire department battalion chief John Conlon Sr., was Wednesday morning when John Sr. rode off toward the downtown fires in his polished red buggy behind his "beautiful, well-groomed" horse Prince. He had left John Jr. and his three-year-old brother, Gerald, in the care of the neighbors across the street until he returned, as their mother and sisters were out of town. Young John and younger Gerald had spent the three days exploring and walking to get a view of the fires and slept both nights along with the neighbors under blankets in Golden Gate Park just a block from their street.

Now after sunset on this warm Friday night, on their street lined with makeshift brick ovens, John's father arrived "tired and unshaven," riding "in his usually spotless buggy, now dust-covered and drawn by a shaggy-looking nag." His horse Prince, he reassured his son, was back in a livery stable "for a much-needed rest." And as much as Chief Conlon craved rest after more than sixty hours on duty, his wife and daughter would not make it back into the city until the following day, and his night was spent hosting a "deluge" of relatives, newly homeless "with only the clothes on their backs," who preferred a patch of hardwood floor or even cold basement concrete to the crowded parks and squares where they had spent the past two nights.

Throughout the city as the last North Beach fires burned to the waterfront, the lucky residents in homes unburned and undemolished took in friends, family, and even strangers, one or two here and a handful there, individual numbers of the quarter million dispossessed of homes and belongings by the grim lottery of fill land and fire and water pipes and dynamite. "We had fourteen people living in our house," an eight-year-old boy later recounted of that night. "All had been burned out." A six-year-old stayed with her parents in her grandmother's house in the Richmond District "filled to its capacity" with family and neighbors where "everyone was sleeping on mattresses on the floor with their clothing on. Only the oldest folks used beds or couches." On Russian Hill, residents sifting through hot, blackened chunks of their burned homes for anything salvageable past nightfall were offered shelter by neighbors in the small patch of saved houses along Green and Vallejo Streets.

Some who had been ordered from their homes for dynamite teams or approaching fires returned to find them standing but damaged. A man walking back to his Franklin Street home noticed all the yards along his block "covered with glass & debris" and was pleased to find his house still standing, albeit with windows shattered from the dynamiting of a neighboring business. James Stetson continued to stay in his Van Ness Avenue house even though its front was "very much blistered and blackened by the intense heat; the paint melted in a peculiar way, and over two of the windows it hung like drapery."

After two nights outside, Mary Ashe Miller slept that night with friends in a house near Lafayette Square. "No one went to bed," she noted, "but mattresses were spread on the floors in the drawing room, hall and dining room, and there every one lay, fully dressed, and got such sleep as they might." As in every home in the unburned sections of the city, their house was dark, and soldiers patrolled outside with shouts of "All lights out!" and "No lights permitted!" Mary and her temporary housemates suffered from hunger and strained nerves and "continuous stress and excitement" and throats parched from thirst and inhaled smoke and "no water for bathing" and no changes of clothes and limbs aching from miles of walking and ears ringing from days of dynamite blasts and shaking with fright at each aftershock. And the moon and stars were again shrouded by thick smoke from a fire still burning, though not enough to light the city as before. The night was one of "the blackest darkness" with "not a light in the city," and it was for Mary and doubtless others the lowest point: "Of all the time of the calamity nothing was more terrible than that night."

The early, dark hours of Saturday saw the final fight against the fire. Flames had devoured almost all of North Beach and were threatening warehouses and grain sheds along the waterfront between Telegraph Hill and Fisherman's Wharf. A woman taking refuge inside the Ghirardelli Factory saw "flames mounting in huge billows" and as winds increased, the blaze was "nearing rapidly our refuge." Lieutenant Freeman had moved his fireboat *Leslie* and tug *Active* to both ends of the long wooden grain sheds that stretched around four blocks of East Street at the seawall, and his sailors ran hoses to the hot cobblestones of East Street between the sheds and warehouses, but windblown flames swallowed their streams of salt water, and they were forced to retreat to their vessels. Freeman repositioned his fireboat and tug and aimed lines of water sideways, which bay winds carried onto the shed. Joined by the tugboat *Pilot* and state fireboat *Governor Irwin*, they pumped "large quantities of water" in long streams at angles against the wind where, as Midshipman Pond would describe, "this was carried as spray down the waterfront to the roofs over the piers acting as a blanket against the burning cinders."

But the fire was too much, and once flames caught one end of the sheds, they were soon engulfed up to their eaves. Undaunted and determined to save the piers and waterfront, Freeman redeployed his vessels to spray threatened wooden piers and a waterfront factory. But his sailors, most in their seventieth hour awake and their only meals a hurried breakfast Thursday morning and scraps of food found in grocery stores on Broadway Street that night, needed relief. "Our men were now on the verge of collapse and were approaching hysteria," Midshipman Pond later noted. "They were suffering terribly from blistered feet and were too weak to handle the hose." Freeman ordered Pond to take the *Active* to the USS *Chicago*, still berthed at Fort Mason, and request "relief crews." Pond got underway but was himself exhausted, and after boarding the cruiser, he was sent by the admiral's aide "below for refreshments and to bed."

The *Active* returned with a fresh crew, and a lieutenant commander arrived with men to relieve Lieutenant Freeman's crew of the *Leslie*, even as the fight to save the warehouses, factories, and piers along the waterfront continued. "The hardest fight we had during the fire was at this point," Freeman reported. "A sulfur works was burning, the wind was blowing a gale, and showers of cinders, some three or four inches square, made this spot a purgatory" for those manning hose lines from each of the vessels. Between 2:30 and 3:00 a.m., they "succeeded in gaining about ten feet on the fire" and that was the beginning of the end. "With these four lines," noted a fire captain, "we saved the ferry slip and stopped the fire on the south side of the grain sheds as it was working its way down the dock." The flames were stopped short of a brandy and wine warehouse, a cold-storage and ice company, and, as Freeman reported, "several others which I fail to remember." Also saved was "the whole line of piers from Lombard St. down," as well as the freight cars on the spur of the State Belt Railroad. And the Ghirardelli Factory. "When hope was almost gone the wind turned, the fire tugs brought water," a woman inside the factory noted, adding that "we were saved—the fire was checked."

By 7:00 a.m., more than seventy-three hours after it began, the fire was finally stopped. It had not burned itself out or run out of structures to feed on and no rain had fallen to save the day. It was stopped. The city's entire waterfront was saved by the leadership of Lieutenant Frederick Freeman and the indefatigable efforts of his sailors. And throughout the city, what began as small flames on shelves of drugstores or pressing rooms of laundry houses or kitchens of walk-up flats and spread into neighborhood-wide infernos and coalesced into a citywide firestorm were stopped by the ingenuity and toil of well-drilled firemen. They did not allow a lack of water to render them helpless, holding hose lines in alleyways as hot as furnaces to battle lodging house fires until cisterns ran dry, spraying the last trickles from busted mains to save schools, and relaying water from distant working hydrants to delay the spread of relentless blazes and give residents time to evacuate. Their feet bled and skin blistered while they fought battle after battle—losing some and winning others—against infernos in neighborhoods far from their own even as many of their own apartments and firehouses burned. Together with Lieutenant Freeman's sailors and resident volunteers and other uniformed servicemembers, San Francisco's firefighters refused to accept the odds against them and extinguished the Great Fire.

17. Wilderness of Ruins

ON SATURDAY MORNING, white smoke lifted from the last dying embers along the city's northern waterfront and a haze of gray feathered from the city's hot ruins. "When the sea of flames finally died down, some of the burned-over areas smoldered for weeks," one man later wrote, "and the wilderness of ruins was beyond words—thousands of blocks of complete desolation." The devastation was so extensive, he sensed the thousands still snaking toward the ferries "could see no hope and left the city vowing never to return." Another man wrote his sister a letter describing "the almost total absence of life" as he walked through what was once downtown's "great bustling thoroughfares, and now not a sound but the echo of one's own footsteps." Through his shoes he felt the heat of paving stones and "many of the ruins were so hot as to be unapproachable"; in the air he noticed "the smell of roasted bodies" carrying above what was apparently Market Street. "The smell of human flesh in the buildings on fourth and Howard is awful," a South of Market resident wrote that day. "I will not attempt to describe the horrors but I will say that newspapers do not exaggerate."

Many wide-eyed visitors found themselves disoriented by the spatial changes, where city blocks once topped with grand buildings now appeared as small, flattened, rubble-filled lots. "Walking down Market Street and looking right and left," a man noted he "now looked out on the open country, over a sea of smoldering ruins." A visitor from Oakland walking through Market Street's "most picturesque ruins" that day noticed that the landscape of shortened walls and chimneys where tall buildings had once stood "gave one the opportuning of seeing greater distances."

With the fire finally out, large numbers of newly homeless San Franciscans left their temporary shelters—homes of friends or family—and walked through streets choked with debris and tangled wires to the remnants of their homes to find something to save. A woman returned with neighbors to the site where their three-story apartment house once stood at 1007 Bush Street and tried to approximate where items would be. "We located the bureau and that was just beside the closet door," she wrote. Through ashes "a foot and a half deep" they were able to dig down to a concrete floor in the hope their coins and valuables had sunk through the ash, "but the heat must have melted the gold and silver coins very easily." A neighbor brought sandwiches and they "had lunch in 1007 for the last time." A woman named Mary returned to the empty lot where her house had once stood, and as she wrote her family, found only a doll's head and a vase before "an armed soldier ordered them off the place."

Uniformed troops were visible on every street. "The bugle-calls in the morning, the pacing sentries and galloping officers, told of our military occupation," wrote a woman of the scene in front of her Waller Street flat. More than two thousand federal "regulars" were in the city, and more from the Pacific Division were en route on Funston's orders. Two additional battalions of infantry from the Presidio of Monterey arrived that day, and more infantry companies and artillery batteries would arrive from Vancouver Barracks by Monday. The governor had mobilized every guardsman of one of California's two national guard brigades into the city by Saturday (guardsmen of the other brigade were on duty in Oakland, Berkeley, Alameda, San Jose, Santa Rosa, and Sacramento).

From his flagship *Chicago* now back at anchor near Fort Mason, Admiral Goodrich deployed sailors of his Pacific Squadron to take over waterfront security, and they were joined by Lieutenant Freeman and his men later in the afternoon after well-earned food, water, and rest. As Midshipman Pond would later recall, "[T]he entire waterfront from Fort Mason to the Pacific Mail dock at the foot of First Street, a distance of three miles, was patrolled by bluejackets, with a guard at every wharf."

With troops from every state and federal branch on duty in the city, ROTC cadets from the University of California were dismissed at noon and sent back to Berkeley. The young men had been pulling four-hour neighborhood-patrol shifts since arriving the first night, and they were, as one of them later noted, "Dead-tired when we reached [the] ferry."

Soldiers stood guard at the post office and the mint, two conspicuous survivors among the ruins. Troops guarded the portion of the five square miles of burned-out apartment houses and banks and mansions and hotels along Market Street and north (since most ruins South of Market were not deemed worth guarding), ensuring no salvageable property was stolen and keeping people clear of precariously balanced heat-weakened walls. Troops were posted at parks and squares to maintain order among the campers and along streets of surviving neighborhoods to enforce the curfew and see that no fires were ignited indoors. "The soldiers were parked about one to the block in our area, principally to look out for lights," noted a man staying in his sister's Webster Street home. "We often stopped to chat with them and ask for news." He felt "relief at sight of the military, not because of any fear of one's fellows, but because the soldiers constituted tangible evidence of guidance and control."

But in many corners, the overriding response of residents to armed soldiers was fear. "People have been shot right and left for disobeying the martial law, some for looting, others for refusing to work," Dolly Brown wrote her fiancé on Saturday. She described night patrols on Sacramento Street where she was staying with a family friend: "you are warned twice to put out the light, the third time you are shot." Frederick Collins, staying in the Western Addition, wrote his family that "they take a shot at you if you are out after 8:30 p.m." While there is no evidence that anyone was shot for violating curfew or keeping lights on, there are many accounts of soldiers threatening to do so. And the fear expressed by Dolly and Frederick was felt by many in the populace, an intimidation some soldiers employed to seize vehicles or property or in the recurring problem of forced labor.

"All the men that pass are grabbed by the soldiers and forced to go to work," a woman on Cole Street wrote. "So Pa and Mr. Sport are always very busy fixing bricks, sweeping the streets and taking our ash barrels out." A worker wrote to assure his employer he was trying to return to the city to check on the business, "but every man caught in town is placed at work cleaning the streets and they are kept at work until they drop." Men were ordered at the ends of bayonets by soldiers to clear heavy rubble from streets or dig privy holes for waste or trenches for bodies.

Almost anyone driving an automobile without a Relief Committee or Red Cross pass was stopped and forced to distribute provisions or haul away trash or, in a few instances, dead bodies. A man wrote his mother in England that the work of "cleaning debris, building conveniences" was mostly completed by "the first men passing" and "as the request was accompanied by a rifle pointed in your direction with a bayonet on the end it generally met with compliance." After a mountain of complaints reached his Fort Mason headquarters, General Funston ordered his officers that "this abuse of authority shall be stopped at once."

Forced labor largely proved unnecessary with tens of thousands of able-bodied residents displaced and out of work and eager to pitch in and help. When sixteen-year-old Howard Livingston walked to the food line at the Presidio Saturday morning, an officer called for fifty volunteers to help unload a barge of provisions. "I had an idea that it would be a good thing for me to volunteer for this detail," Howard wrote in a letter. He and others carried boxes from the wharf to horse-drawn wagons, then followed the wagons on foot to the post warehouse where they unloaded the boxes and organized the contents to be issued. "So many men were available that this took very little time," he noted. "As a reward, we were sent to the head of the line to receive our supplies."

With more residents running out of food in their pantries and the inventory of grocery stores all sold or distributed, food lines at relief stations on Saturday were even longer than Friday. Approximately 100,000 had been fed on Thursday, 150,000 on Friday, and at least 200,000 on Saturday. More volunteers with relief committees from other towns and cities arrived to assist, and more food stations were set up. "There was no starvation in the city for those who knew where to go," Howard Livingston explained, adding that the food he was given at the Presidio after helping the Army move supplies was more than the crackers of Friday, with flour, butter, sugar, and bread added. "Water is scarce, but food has been sent in large quantities and we manage to get enough to eat," noted a man staying with his brother in an empty lot near Fort Mason after both had been burned out of their apartment. "There isn't a store open so rich and poor of all nationalities stand in line, three times a day, and are given plenty to eat."

While rations, canned goods, and other nonperishables were arriving from all points, bakeries in unburned neighborhoods were reopened by soldiers for use by the Subcommittee for Relief of the Hungry, and a pleasant aroma wafted from repaired bakery chimneys as refugees from nearby camps were made bakers. A man camping in Dolores Park worked a two-hour shift in a neighborhood bakery, "putting the bread into the ovens, taking it out when baked, and packing it into big wooden trays." A guardsman in the Western Addition wrote his mother, "It is a great sight to see the people lining up to get bread at the California Bakery which turns out 3,000 loaves of bread an hour, if people haven't got the money they can have the bread anyway." At least thirty-five thousand loaves had been baked Friday and nearly fifty thousand on Saturday. Bakery owners would be compensated by the Finance Committee with either flour or payments per loaf and allowed to sell any surplus at no more than ten cents per loaf, five loaves per person.

Cooking for those at home was, as it would be for weeks to come, in the streets. "The neighbors helped build a brick stove finished with a tin plate on the top," one man noted. And construction was easy because "you could pick up bricks anywhere." A woman named Catherine wrote in a letter, "[W]e all have our stoves (they are mostly all laundry stoves) out on the edge of the street. Talk about fun, Jimmy, it's a picnic." She lived on Cole Street not far from Golden Gate Park, and one couple had started the trend along her block, then six or seven other families followed, then the whole neighborhood. "We all divide up our stock of provisions. And all our neighbors are simply lovely to each other." One family "had some chickens left in their cold storage place" and "they gave us two," and the man next door "gave us some elegant fillet of beef." Seven-year-old John Conlon Jr.'s fire battalion chief father "built an elaborate range from salvaged bricks and sheet iron on our front sidewalk and covered it with a lean-to roof" to cook for the houseful of relatives he was hosting. "I have seen few modern barbecue pits that surpassed our sidewalk kitchen," he opined more than seven decades later.

Still desperately needed was fresh water. Spring Valley Water Company chief engineer Hermann Schussler and his workers had been surveying the largest damage and repairing transmission and distribution mains where possible. They found the thirty-inch line from Lake Merced "gone beyond repair," as Schussler reported, and had routed water into pipes above the damage to start bringing six million gallons a day into the upper Western Addition. The transmission lines from Crystal Springs Reservoir, which supplied the Mission District, South of Market, much of downtown, and North Beach, as well as higher elevations through pumping stations, was "badly broken in hundreds, perhaps thousands of places, all of which will take a long time and a great deal of work to repair." While repairs were made, the company laid a temporary twenty-four-inch pipe through the Mission on top of Valencia Street's broken pavement to reconnect with mains along Market Street. And they had repaired the lines from the San Andreas reservoir to send ten million gallons to the College Hill Reservoir and bring some relief to the rest of the Western Addition.

But only when pipes were brought back up to pressure could the water company locate each leak and repair each crack or break in street mains and service pipes serving each business and residence. Until then, surviving with the limited supply already restored would depend on residents following Schussler's warning to be "exceedingly careful" with water use. To this end, Mayor Schmitz issued a proclamation published on Saturday for residents not to "use any water except for drinking and cooking purposes." There was to be no bathing, no clothes washing, and no use of "house closets (bathrooms) under any circumstances." People were to "dig earth closets in yards or vacant lots" and cover with any available disinfectant.

By Saturday, millions of dollars had been sent or pledged to San Francisco's relief from the federal government, foreign governments, business leaders, other states and communities, and the city's own business owners and citizens. But even in disaster, the municipal machinery so notoriously corrupted by Abe Ruef loyalists attracted contributions with strings attached. The owner of United Railroads had pledged $75,000 by telegram on Friday, but that was only the public portion of what would be a more expensive private bribe of city officials to finally approve overhead wires for electric streetcars along Market Street. Home Telephone Company was more blatant with its $75,000 pledge, openly conditioning payment upon city approval of its exclusive franchise.

But the money for San Francisco's relief was safeguarded by Finance Committee chairman James Phelan, whose "reputation for scrupulous honesty and the complete and exact discharge of public responsibilities placed him in the center of the relief matrix," in the words of his admiring biographers James Walsh and Timothy O'Keefe. The former mayor had been bitterly frustrated by his own inability to end Spring Valley Water Company's stranglehold on water by securing city ownership of a more reliable and affordable water service, efforts that had been recently blocked by Ruef's scheme to develop a separate private water system and bribe Schmitz and the Board of Supervisors to approve its purchase by the city at "a vastly inflated price." For this and a series of payoffs to City Hall by railroad companies and developers and gas and electric companies, Phelan had been publicly pursuing a criminal investigation of corruption in the Schmitz administration before the earthquake, and Schmitz's selection of the former mayor to chair the Finance Committee was seen as its own attempted form of patronage. But Phelan could not be bought. He was scrupulously depositing all relief funds in the well-guarded mint, and although his own house had burned down and the office building was all but destroyed, he personally contributed $10,000 to the fund. On Saturday afternoon he presided over the first of what would be daily meetings conspicuously separate from Schmitz's larger Citizens' Committee, gathering not in Franklin Hall but in a friend's home.

Other professionals joined Phelan in the critical task of administration and distribution of relief funds. Ninth Circuit Judge William Morrow—the same judge whose release of San Francisco resident Wong Kim Ark as a natural-born citizen was upheld by the Supreme Court eight years before—served as president of the California Red Cross, and since the earthquake he made daily trips into San Francisco from his San Rafael home. He had returned to his courtroom and chambers, part of the new post office on Mission Street, to formally postpone cases before the court for three weeks. And at the Ferry Building, he handed telegraph company messengers two prepaid telegrams to be carried to Oakland and wired to officers of the American National Red Cross, notifying them of the earthquake, the fire, the destruction, and of "[m]any thousands homeless." On his return to the city Saturday, three delayed telegrams awaited him at the Ferry Building, each from the Red Cross secretary in Washington announcing "special Red Cross agent" Dr. Edward Devine was on his way to the city by train with President Roosevelt's sanction.

With the fire extinguished, what Judge Morrow saw in San Francisco was "the immediate and pressing necessity for the administration of general organized relief." The most immediate needs of food, clothing, and shelter were being momentarily met, but with each passing day food lines were longer and unwashed clothes dirtier and the stench of unburied waste stronger. Crowded canvas tents and wooden lean-tos and tree cover would soon be untenable for shelter as sanitation deteriorated and the risk of sickness and disease escalated. And the crisis would be underscored that night by rain that fell too late for the fire and too soon for the homeless.

"In the night it poured," wrote Emma Burke, who walked with her husband and son from their tentless campsite at Golden Gate Park back to their "desolated" fourth-floor flat on Waller Street. The earthquake had broken both chimneys atop their apartment house, bending the tin roof down like a funnel just above their ceiling. "We heard an ominous drip, drip, and then a steady splash." They placed metal pots under the drips that "filled faster than we could empty them." A man staying in a friend's damaged house soon wrote his family, "We never closed our eyes that night and it began to rain and a cold mournful wind began to howl around open chimney holes and busted roofs."

And for tens of thousands of campers outside—parents, children, elderly, infirm—the night was worse. Families awoke beneath sopping-wet blankets and dragged half-soaked mattresses through mud to the nearest tree cover where others had crowded, shivering with cold. Canvas ceilings of tents darkened with rainwater and leaked, dripping then pouring in steady cascades. Privy holes and "earth closets" filled and overflowed and streams of urine and fecal chunks flowed through pathways between tents and camping spots. "Although I had seen plenty of misery during the day," one visitor to the city noted, "the distress I saw in the park was heart-breaking."

Sunday morning the clergy of the city's churches—many without sanctuaries—fanned out to at least nine different encampments to hold services for the homeless. At the Presidio, Fort Mason, Jefferson Square, Alamo Square, Dolores Park, Alta Plaza, the Panhandle, and Lafayette Square. An Episcopal priest held an 11:00 a.m. service in Golden Gate Park where the morning saw many shivering campers brought to Park Emergency Hospital. Serious cases needing fluids or showing symptoms of illness were taken by wagon to the Presidio's Army General Hospital where a captain was left in charge by Dr. George Torney, who had been ordered to take over "sanitary arrangements of the city" by General Funston at the request of the head of the city's health commission to address "the emergency problems of sanitation" in refugee camps.

Dr. Torney deployed Army surgeons and assistant surgeons into all encampments with soldiers to act as a "sanitary force," supplying tents, digging drainage, and distributing disinfectants. He established a medical supply depot and ordered more than two dozen medical dispensaries where medicine from the Army's supply was handed out for free. And he established a separate hospital for contagious diseases such as scarlet fever, measles, typhoid fever, and diphtheria with a two-hundred-patient capacity in a pavilion in nearby Harbor View Park where a steady water supply would allow washing of instruments, bedding, and clothes.

At the Army General Hospital, Dr. Torney's physicians and Dora Thompson and her forty nurses of the Army Nurse Corps were in their fifth day of working long shifts with little rest treating patients, now numbering upward of two hundred with overflow cases given beds in barracks or cots in the outdoor circus tent. Beds opened as fractured limbs were splinted or when bandaged burn victims stabilized. Or when another patient died. Six-year-old Emily Curran died that morning of "inhalation burns" suffered the first day of the fire. Her parents buried her down in Colma. Those who died in the hospital without known family were buried in the Presidio's San Francisco National Cemetery. Like Jens Sorenson, an eighty-six-year-old tailor who died after not regaining consciousness since she was carried in from her Larkin Street flat after the earthquake. And Holber Mansen, who died that Sunday morning having never recovered from multiple fractures in the collapse of his South of Market apartment.

Sunday morning in the Army General Hospital also saw the death of San Francisco fire chief Dennis Sullivan. It had been four mornings since he had been pulled by his firemen from the firehouse wreckage after falling through the collapsed floor of his third-story room. Eddie Graney, the fire department's horseshoer and the best friend of Sullivan since before he was chief, had been at his bedside since he was brought in. Sullivan had drifted in and out of consciousness and was reportedly never told of the fire his men were battling. While his wife, Margaret, was still recovering from her own injuries, Sullivan's funeral was held later that week in their 49th Avenue house where Chief Dougherty eulogized him before his body was temporarily placed in a vault at Calvary Cemetery (where the Anza Vista neighborhood sits today). One year later, in April 1907, thousands of San Franciscans turned out to line streets two and three deep to watch the coffin bearing his body borne through the city with full honors, his white fire helmet atop the horse-drawn hearse, escorted by his wife and police officers and firemen and followed by his horse Brownie pulling his empty red buggy in which he last rode the night of the cannery fire. He was eulogized in St. Mary's Cathedral, then buried in Holy Cross Catholic Cemetery down in Colma.

Then and today, many fret that more of the city could have been saved had Chief Sullivan not been mortally wounded in the first minute. Perhaps he would have attempted a different strategy, but he would have been hampered by the same challenges of communication and water as the battalion chiefs and acting chief. Perhaps his voice would have carried the weight to push back and force city and military leaders to execute firebreaks more effectively. As it happened, the resourcefulness of his firemen and the effectiveness of the equipment they pushed beyond their known limits all bore Chief Sullivan's imprint after years of his demands for constant training and advocacy to keep his department the best equipped. And his greatest contribution to San Francisco's future safety might have been the warnings its leaders ignored, warnings that outlived him and the disaster that proved him right.

That night soldiers and national guardsmen patrolled throughout San Francisco, and armed volunteer citizen guards manned traffic checkpoints in the Mission District, keeping sightseers from down the peninsula from entering the city. The guards had been issued badges by the local national guard colonel, who authorized lethal force if their orders were not followed. They manned intersections every two blocks along Guerrero Street, wielding rifles and pistols, checking every wagon or automobile heading northward into the city. No streetlights or streetlamps lit the pavement or sidewalks. Six of these citizen guards stood at the intersection of Guerrero and 22nd Street, and around midnight, they saw headlights appearing from the south, bearing on the intersection from four blocks away, then three. The men stepped out into the street to block its path.

At the wheel was thirty-five-year-old Heber Tilden, a member of the Red Cross who had volunteered his own automobile and those of his Mobile Carriage Company for relief use. He "had been working day and night since the outbreak of the fire," as would be later reported, taking invalids from the path of the fire and carrying wounded people to hospitals. He was presently returning from Menlo Park, where he had taken his wife and their three children. Sitting beside him was his escort, Lieutenant R. G. Seaman of the national guard, and in the back seat was Hugo Altschul, a coachman hitching a ride back into the city. Tilden wore a Red Cross badge. Seaman was in uniform with a Red Cross armband, and on the front hood was wired a Red Cross flag.

Tilden had driven through the first checkpoint at 26th Street slowly, approximately 15 miles per hour, without stopping. Lieutenant Seaman yelled "Red Cross!" and the citizen guards stepped aside and waved them through. The same happened at 24th Street. As the automobile crossed 23rd Street, Tilden accelerated to take the hill that followed 22nd. The headlights cast on the six guards standing in the approaching intersection. From behind the revving engine, Seaman once again yelled "Red Cross!" The guards in the roadway "opened to let us pass," as Seaman would later recount. But within a few more seconds a guard fired a shot into the air. As the automobile cruised through the intersection a crackle of four gunshots rang out like loud pops. As the car climbed the hill, from behind came eight more pops. "The shots came rapidly," Seaman noted, "as if three guns were being fired together." Behind the wheel, Tilden grabbed his upper chest and yelled, "My God, they've shot me! They got me!" The automobile lurched left as he let the wheel go. Single shots sounded from behind them. The coachman in the back seat ducked down. Seaman pulled his revolver, swung out on the sideboard, and fired five shots at the muzzle flash at the bottom of the hill. The automobile bounced against the curb and stopped. Tilden staggered from the driver's seat and collapsed on the sidewalk.

Seaman yelled down at the guards, "You've got one of us!" and called for help. Men ran up, one a physician who lived nearby. But Heber Tilden, unconscious, died within minutes there on the sidewalk. He had been shot through his back, and the bullet exited his chest. Lieutenant Seaman grabbed a lantern from the automobile to assist the doctor over Tilden's body. He then fainted and was found to be bleeding from his own back where the skin was split open around "a black and blue circle," aligned with where a bullet was found in the cushion of the automobile's front passenger seat where he had been sitting. The seatback had stopped the round before it entered his body. The coachman in the back suffered a burned cheek, probably grazed by a bullet. Two police officers on the scene within five minutes arrested three of the citizen guards, Edward Boynton, Malcomb Vance, and George Simmons. From them the police confiscated two rifles and a revolver, all "still warm." And from the automobile they removed at least two spent rounds. The men explained they were merely trying to stop the automobile after yelling and whistling for it to stop. They had not seen the Red Cross flag for the headlights and had been assigned to their posts with orders to "shoot to kill," orders still unchanged with armed soldiers and guardsmen and volunteer citizen guards throughout the city as a new week dawned.

Monday brought the first workweek in the new city. The sheriff, county clerk, and district attorney established temporary headquarters in Pacific Heights, the fire department headquarters were relocated to Fillmore Street, and the fire alarm office moved to Steiner Street. City Hall set up in a Hayes Valley opera house with the city morgue in a hastily thrown-up wooden shed on the street beside it. The burned-out California Supreme Court was allowed to use the courtroom of the Ninth Circuit in the post office. The Harbor District Police Station was established in the burned-out Hibernia Bank. Barbers set up open-air barbershops near camps. Members of bricklayers and mason unions followed building inspectors to repair broken chimneys. And the employees of Hotaling & Co., their "motley crew" of hired hands long gone, worked long hours rolling every barrel of whiskey back to their warehouse and lifting each by ropes up onto racks.

Signs were posted at empty lots of burned-out businesses and ads printed in newspapers announcing temporary offices set up in homes of unburned neighborhoods or over in Oakland or Berkeley. "Clerk, foremen and general employees will please report without delay at store of Henry Sutliff, Broadway, Oakland," read an ad from the John Bollman Company, dealers of cigarettes and tobacco. The Paraffine Paint Company announced its factory was "unin-jured" and orders could be "filled promptly," and with its South of Market of-fice burned down, it had established temporary offices in Oakland: "All office employees report to new address as promptly as possible." And employees of the Pacific Hardware & Steel Company, one of the warehouses firemen had managed to save South of Market, were told to "report at the store," as the company's inventory of iron, steel, and pipe would be in high demand.

Laundryman Thomas Angove wrote his parents, "My route is burned up," explaining his customers were almost all within the burned district. "Had the quake occurred a day later I would have been a good many dollars ahead for on Wed I usually collected my office & other weekly account." But he added he had $50 in his pocket, had secured enough oats and hay for his horse, and "grub is free." Sixteen-year-old Howard Livingston's employer Vulcan Iron Works had burned down, and he "knew I would have to find work where I could," as he later recalled. He responded to a placard announcing workers were "needed to clear the streets in the burned area," and when he reported to the downtown address and signed in, so many others had turned up he "waited all day without being called." Walking home he saw the task confront-ing work crews clearing streets. In downtown's burned wasteland, "some streets were clear enough to walk through, but others were impassable because walls had collapsed, dumping rubble into the streets." In the ruins, "piles of rubbish were smoldering, sill red hot." Through streets of Nob and Russian Hills, "the wooden buildings had disintegrated to beds of ashes within foundation walls" and "chimneys, or parts of them, stood like monuments in a long-abandoned cemetery." When he returned the next day, he found all the street-clearing jobs filled yet again.

The newspapers—5 cents each again—reported General Funston had is-sued orders "relaxing the rigidity of military rule," making it "no longer possi-ble to confiscate property or compel men to labor." Some of the men at work in the streets were United Railroads employees clearing rubble and debris from tracks. Others were workers for delivery and hauling companies, contracted by the Citizens' Committee with assurances they would be paid. Many others had lost their homes or workplaces and left their family in a tent to walk down-town in response to Mayor Schmitz's proclamation that "all who are regularly employed in the work of restoring the city will be paid for their services."

Also back in the streets were dynamite crews ordered from the Presidio to bring down "dangerous walls left standing in the thoroughfares of the city." A team of city inspectors had walked the length of Market Street to list where remaining walls of fire-gutted structures posed a danger and needed to be demolished "to open a safe artery from the outlying districts to the waterfront." Mint superintendent Frank Leach steered clear of these feeble walls on his daily walks to and from the mint. "They appeared as if the slightest earthquake shock or puff of wind would send them toppling." Fourteen-year-old Herman Schultz was killed when the wall he was sitting beside "fell and crushed every bone in his body." Many were tall—"some of them seven stories high"—and all were "in a tottering condition."

The list of buildings—or remnants of buildings—to be demolished bore sad testament to the impermanence of the city's once-imposing skyline and how daunting an undertaking it would be to rebuild. Just along Market Street, the Odd Fellows Building and its familiar clock tower were brought down with a single charge. The "pile of bricks and a wobbly wall" that was once the Donohoe Building was flattened. The walls of Prager's Department Store "would soon have fallen of their own weight" had they not been dynamited. "Three heavy blasts" were needed to bring down the shell of the Sterling Furniture Company across the street. The three-year-old Callahan Building "had almost disappeared" across from the Hibernia Bank. The Phelan Building, gutted and beyond repair, was dynamited. So was the Wiley B. Allen Building, the Pacific Mutual Building, the Columbia Building, the Pioneer Building, and the Academy of Sciences. But even multiple attempts could not bring down the seven-story frontage of the city's largest department store, the Emporium.

To clear streets where its lines ran, United Railroads paid its own employees and "as large a force of men as it might be possible to collect to repair the roadway." Out in the unburned Western Addition, hired hands worked up and down Fillmore Street for days clearing debris from the rails of its electric line and repairing wherever overhead wires had fallen or torn apart. Citywide power had not yet been restored for risk of electric arcing, and men with the Citizens' Subcommittee on Light, Power, and Telephone Service and the city's department of electricity walked the distance to ensure no current from the line could carry into dwellings and cause fires. By Saturday night they had cleared and repaired enough to test-run cars along eight blocks of Fillmore, now home to many new retail storefronts and already dubbed the city's "new Market Street." The familiar and welcome sight of cars running again "put new heart into the people" and "was greeted with cheers." The all-hands work would continue day and night to get United Railroads' Fillmore and 16th Street line running for passengers by week's end.

Monday marked the end of Brigadier General Funston's temporary command of the Pacific Division and the national press as Major General Adolphus Greely arrived back at his Fort Mason quarters after a long rail journey from Chicago. Through the five days Funston had been in charge, there had been no check on his power, not from Washington and not from Mayor Schmitz. Funston had been quick to act the first day, lawfully deploying federal troops at his disposal to guard federal property. And his unlawful decision to send soldiers to assist city authorities and first responders might be applauded if not undermined by his choice to allow his soldiers to be used as armed security against civilians, sent into neighborhoods with summary execution orders. Funston had sought no guidance or approval; he exploited the disaster's severance of communications with higher command by turning his temporary command into an island of sovereignty; and he spent every subsequent day of the disaster expanding his power within the city until General Greely's return.

Sixty-two-year-old Adolphus Greely had seen combat at Antietam and Fredericksburg, was in his forty-fifth year of Army service, and wore his uniform casually beneath a large white beard. After praising the "endeavor and accomplishment" of Funston and his soldiers, Greely began a deliberate process of returning the city to civilian control. He set up an office for Mayor Schmitz at his Fort Mason headquarters, and to ensure "no misunderstanding as to the status under which the United States Army operated in San Francisco," Greely was clear: his orders controlled only in "purely military" matters such as "the guarding of Federal buildings and property," but in all "nonmilitary duties" the Army was in the city solely "for the purpose of assisting the municipal authorities to maintain order, protect property, and especially to extend relief to the destitute and homeless." All his soldiers' actions would "be strictly confined" to the mayor's wishes "as necessary in the public interests." There would be no more property seizure or interference with business or personal liberty. And of greatest consequence, Greely granted authority to his troops "to arrest only persons guilty of assaults, robbery, looting, or other serious offenses," who were then "to be promptly turned over to the nearest police authority." With this order, Greely quietly but clearly ended Schmitz's shoot-to-kill order five days after it was given. There would be no more summary executions for theft or traffic checkpoints backed by lethal force.

Reports and rumors of varying reliability were swirling of shootings of civilians by soldiers, and Greely addressed only those that came to his desk as formal complaints or could be ascribed to another authority—national guardsmen, marines, police, or citizens deputized as "special police." He later reported "9 deaths by violence," five of which could be blamed on police or guardsmen or marines, and the remaining four "occurred at places not occupied by the Regular Army." But the man shot and left to burn in front of Shreve & Co. jewelers was shot by a soldier at a time and place where there were no guardsmen or marines. And newspapers had assigned more than a dozen shootings over those five days to soldiers, some with names and corroborated specificity. That very morning's *Examiner* reported two had been killed by "Presidio Soldier[s]," an Italian caught "prowling about in the darkness apparently intent on plundering" shot by Private Herman Philips, and a "Chinaman" under circumstances no soldiers wished to discuss.

The precise number of people shot and killed under shoot-to-kill orders of Schmitz and Funston is unknown. While far lower than the inflated numbers that grew with each exaggerated retelling, the number of active-duty soldiers who shot and killed citizens was certainly higher than either Funston's or Greely's claim of zero. That the number was not as high as legend purported is a tribute to the restraint of police officers and military personnel serving under an egregiously illegal order. It is unknown whether Greely would have stood for such an order had he been present during those five days, but ending it was one of his first actions on his return.

What General Greely considered the Army's "most important duty" was "administration of an adequate system of relief," and in that effort he and former mayor Phelan's Finance Committee and Schmitz's Citizens' Committee were joined by Dr. Edward Devine, who arrived on Tuesday from New York as representative of the American National Red Cross. President Roosevelt had pronounced the Red Cross would handle relief funds, inciting controversy that preceded Devine's arrival and made his welcome chilly. But in their first meeting, Devine and Phelan made the most important decision of post-disaster San Francisco and combined forces, forming the Finance Committee of Relief and Red Cross Funds. Into it went all money already given to the Red Cross for San Francisco sufferers and Relief Committee money Phelan had been safeguarding.

In their first meeting on Monday, Mayor Schmitz had asked if the Army could take over from the Citizens' Committee the work of food distribution, which Greely initially declined, as it would be "unwarranted by law." Now Greely was asked again, this time unanimously by all present, including Dr. Devine, because the "conditions were so urgent and desperate" that they had grown beyond the capability of the Citizens' Committee, making "it an imperative public duty for the Army to assume charge of the issue of food supplies." Greely agreed, and sixty-four officers and five hundred enlisted soldiers were supplying and staffing 177 relief stations within the week, feeding more than 300,000 the first day.

While the relief fund grew, cash and coin in city circulation was largely limited to what people had in pockets or had managed to grab from their desk or office safe. The hope of many lay inside strongboxes and safes they pulled from the ashes of their former office or store. "We have not yet gotten to our safe; it is being dug out today," Adolf Sinsheimer wrote on May 7. "I hope it is intact, as the loss of its contents would mean an almost impossible task."

While contents of air-proof safes and vaults within the burned district had been protected from fires, the only thing that had prevented the superheated interiors from igniting was lack of oxygen. After the 1904 Baltimore fire, many residents and bankers had lost valuables by opening safes before they had sufficiently cooled, and the same had happened to merchants in Italy after the recent Vesuvius eruption. For San Franciscans who did not know of or heed these warnings, hope for restarting was gone in a physical flash when they opened safes in the first two weeks and watched their cash and valuable papers combust. Newspapers printed warnings: "OWNERS OF SAFES ACT TOO HASTILY—OPEN THEM PREMATURELY AND SUSTAIN LOSS." The city tax assessor waited until May 2 to open the records vault in City Hall's wreckage, but "the contents burst into flames," destroying most property valuations. South of Market's American Hotel burned down but in its safe was up to $10,000 in cash and jewelry, and its former guests who had escaped grew impatient with the proprietor who made them wait until "all danger from combustion is passed." The post office waited until May 11 to open six safes from its burned branches, and its records, books, and stamps were preserved intact.

Because banks were in the burned district and their larger vaults would take even longer to sufficiently cool, Governor Pardee had extended the statewide bank holiday for one month to prevent a panic or run by depositors. San Francisco's banks had provided the building blocks for city commerce since the days of the gold rush, when bankers like Henry Wells and William Fargo provided money access and credit to residents and businesses, moving a frontier town from a messy barter system of foreign coins and gold dust to the heart of the West Coast's economy. And in 1906, San Francisco's banks were the largest in the state with depositors in all surrounding communities and commercial credit extended to businesses throughout the region. The effective freezing of so much capital would have carried devastating effects were it not for the $300 million in the vaults of the mint.

"There will be abundant money at once," declared mint superintendent Frank Leach in the *Call*. Leach wired the treasury secretary in Washington with the message, "Every bank in San Francisco Buried in ruins." With wire service finally restored to the city, Leach devised and the treasury secretary approved a system of "telegraphic transfer of funds," wherein an individual or business outside the city could transfer a specific sum of money to an individual or business within the city by depositing the amount in a local sub-treasury; the sub-treasury would then wire Leach's staff the amount deposited and the recipient's name and address; and the staff would send notices to recipients who could come to the mint to receive the money. In the first two weeks of this telegraphic transfer system, more than $40 million flowed into the city, as Leach reported, "in sums from $50 to over $1,000,000 each."

The city's banks met daily and with Frank Leach they developed an order system, wherein commercial depositors could secure a withdrawal order for an amount from their account (up to $500) at their bank's temporary location—many of which had set up in houses with large signs surrounding Lafayette Square, prompting campers to dub it "Banker's Row"—then take the order to the mint starting on May 1 to cash it. Individual depositors with savings banks still had to wait even for small emergency payments until vaults could be opened and books and accounts accessed, which for most would not be until mid-May.

But Amadeo Giannini was the exception. Not only had he cleverly safeguarded his Bank of Italy's $80,000 in cash, gold, and silver from the fire, but as his biographers Marquis James and Bessie James explained, "He knew every one of his distressed clients and, almost to the penny, their balances before disaster struck." He returned to the city, opened a temporary office in his brother's home on Van Ness Avenue, and down on the Washington Street wharf where most of his North Beach customers were back at work, he set up a branch that "consisted of a plank counter and a bag of money." Giannini knew his customers, their businesses, and understood his loan limits. After two weeks, *L'Italia* declared the Banca d'Italia was working "in *floridissime condizioni*" (in very prosperous conditions). Within three weeks he was banking out of the first floor of the Montgomery Block, and within six weeks his deposits exceeded his withdrawals. Giannini accepted insurance policies as collateral to extend loans to restart burned-out businesses and extended credit to many working-class residents of North Beach to rebuild their homes. Two years after the disaster, Giannini's institution moved into a new eight-story downtown headquarters, and from there Bank of Italy continued to finance much of the new city's construction. In the coming years, Amadeo Giannini extended the bank's reach into other towns and cities and pioneered branch banking, spreading his vision for local banking throughout California and the nation. Within twenty-five years, his boundless vision would expand Bank of Italy into Bank of America.

"We are quite fully insured," John Walter wrote his parents in late April, "but it is doubtful if more than 75% will be paid." John's carpet and upholstery business had burned in the fire—its storefront and office on Market Street, and its warehouse with $200,000 in inventory near Telegraph Hill, which was "almost the last building to go under." John's worry was the same as many in the city with policies containing "earthquake clauses" exempting insurers from liability "for loss occasioned by or through" an earthquake, or loss "caused directly or indirectly by" an earthquake. 137 different insurance companies underwrote property in San Francisco. Some insurers were based locally, but many were on the East Coast or overseas. The policies of a few contained no clause, and they paid in full, often advertising the fact to gain goodwill. Other companies lost their own buildings and records but still paid out damages from reserves and shareholder contributions to keep customers and stay in business. And many, accountable to their own shareholders or investors, either denied claims or offered adjusted settlements. Carrie Mangels wrote a friend in July that her father had not yet received anything from his insurance company. "The Company sent for him last week and offered him 75c on a dollar, but he would not take it." He then received an offer for 80 cents per dollar. "It paid to wait," she wrote, noting in August he received 83 cents per dollar.

Beyond the civic reasons to avoid seeming earthquake-prone, San Francisco newspapers and city leaders and prominent citizens urged the disaster be referred to as "the great fire" to encourage payouts for damages, and papers published honor rolls of "Dollar-for-Dollar" companies to shame "welchers" who only offered "six-bit" offers or denied payments. Nearly half of insurers denied claims, often haggling over ash piles about what damage had occurred before the fire. "I represented The Emporium in its insurance settlement," noted an attorney, who had to "secure a photograph which was taken after the earthquake and before The Emporium was partially destroyed by fire" to prove the dome had not fallen during the earthquake. A few policyholders went to trial, prevailing before juries in state court but not always in federal court, and some overseas insurance companies who lost declined to pay judgments unless they were tried in their home country.

In the end, $235 million was paid to insured San Franciscans for damages they incurred, covering roughly 90 percent of damage to underwritten property. But since shareholders and investors of most paying companies "were chiefly from the East Coast and Europe," as attorney Robert James would later explain, "a form of geographic wealth transfer contributed to the renaissance of the city."

One week after the earthquake, mail from refugees in the city reached friends and family. "We just received your letter and you cannot imagine the joy that it brought," wrote Marie Muller in San Gabriel to her aunt Josie Sewall in San Francisco. Josie and her husband, David, and son, Earl, had evacuated their South of Market apartment the first morning before their home burned along with the cannery across the street where David worked. Marie's mother, Minnie—Josie's sister—had sent letters for the past week having "read the papers with tears in my eyes." After six days of sending telegrams and studying faces of refugees coming from San Francisco "by the thousands" and being consoled by neighbors, Minnie wrote, "Not hearing from any of you since the terrible disaster of S.F. I feel greatly worried over your well fare [sic]," closing with, "If we can get only a few lines from you, what a relief it will be to us." Now she felt she could breathe again and invited them "to come stay with us" for a while.

But still many were missing. "Leo Jacobs please let mamma know where you are," read one ad. "Wanted—To know whereabouts of Mrs. William A. Gilmore, invalid, and daughter Grace," read another. Some would never get a response or even know what happened. In the debris of the Kingsbury House on 7th Street, "hip bones and other charred bones" were found and placed in a washtub. A man reported to the coroner he believed them to be the remains of a young woman he tried to rescue the morning of the earthquake before flames reached her: "Her name was not known to me." When workers clearing the lot a few weeks later found the remains of two more, he was sure they were those of a woman and her son based on "their position in the ruins." But he knew of at least three others who burned to death there, and their remains were never found.

Bodies were exhumed from temporary graves in Portsmouth Square and a lot at the corner of Bay and Powell Streets. Families of those with identification buried with them were notified, and many arrived at the coroner's temporary office in the Western Addition for the grim job of identifying remains buried for five days or more. Many were unidentified, as with half of the dozen in

Washington Square, at least ten at Bay and Powell Streets, and fifteen in Portsmouth Square. In most cases it was determined by the coroner how and even where an individual died, but not who they were or where they were from. And it is unknown today whether each of them was buried, and if so, where.

Many who had escaped death or physical harm carried mental anguish, and for some it was all too much. Sixty-year-old Sarah Boyle, who had kept a lodging house in San Francisco, ferried over to Oakland the day of the earthquake and committed suicide by drowning the last day of the fire. Thirty-four-year-old Ethel Gross was brought to an emergency hospital by her husband a few days after the fire, and the next morning at sunrise jumped from the fourth floor of the building, reportedly "[c]razed by the experience through which she had gone." Down in Los Angeles, fifty-six-year-old Albert Smith turned the gas on in his lodging house room, reportedly two weeks after evacuating there to find work, "despondent over the deaths of his wife and son in the San Francisco earthquake," after telling his landlady before going to his room he did "not care to live another day."

18. Undefeated

O N FRIDAY, APRIL 27, at 10:40 a.m., with a clang of the gong, United Railroads streetcar 1377 trundled from a wide bay of the brick Turk/Fillmore carbarn onto Fillmore Street where crowds in their tenth day of traversing the city on foot were reportedly "drawn to the car as though it were a magnet." After rolling seven blocks drawing a steady current from its overhead lines, it stopped at Bush Street where Mayor Schmitz boarded, took the controls, and proceeded to the Broadway terminus, then, after the switch, rolled south back down Fillmore through cheering crowds.

Riding in the "Mayor's special" were members of the press and at least sixteen invited guests, including Abe Ruef and a United Railroads executive. The car passed "long lines of people awaiting their daily rations" who "cheered lustily," and from the controls Schmitz quipped "Take the next car" to approaching people wanting a ride. Four more streetcars followed at fifteen-minute increments, each "for the public use" at no fare, back to running the Fillmore/16th line on schedule, and by the end of the day "carried happy thousands." Sixteen-year-old Howard Livingston rode on a car that first day, as he later recounted: "I rode it to the end of the line, and I think that most of the other passengers felt as I did, that it was good to be doing something so normal as riding a streetcar."

The same day, United Railroads announced it was "practically ready to operate" six more trolley lines, including "Market Street, from end to end," something the public could see coming with work crews raising overhead lines along the thoroughfare, a sight to some almost as shocking as the devastation along its length. Such were the complaints and outcry, Schmitz felt compelled to announce in the papers that the permission given to United Railroads to run a trolley line on Market Street "is wholly temporary" and he retained "full power to revoke the permit whenever he shall see fit." But Ruef had agreed on a $200,000 bribe to ensure the permit was not revoked (with members of the Board of Supervisors agreeing to payoffs of $4,000 each for their approval). On Saturday, April 28, at 4:30 p.m. the first trolley car "invaded" Market Street, as the *Call* headlined. The car ran from 5th and Market to the Ferry Building with a United Railroads executive as motorman.

Repair work took longer for cable cars, but they returned on many of their former routes, especially those too steep for electric traction. After its cable slots were repaired and cables brought to tension and its powerhouse chimney repaired, the Geary Street, Park & Ocean Railroads began running cars on its Geary Street line on June 21. And after retrieving the ash-covered trucks and grips of its incinerated cars from California Street rails at the bottom of Nob Hill, the California Street Cable Railroad got to work repairing its gutted powerhouse and carbarn, straightened the bent main shaft of its winding machinery, and contracted with J. Hammond & Company (formerly California Car Works) to build twenty new cars. In the short space of ninety days, eleven were completed, and along with the sole surviving car began limited service on August 17, with James Stetson as a passenger on the first run. Twenty-seven cars of the Ferries & Cliff House Railway had been stored in an unburned carbarn and survived the fire. But its powerhouse and carbarn at Mason and Washington Streets had been damaged by dynamite and gutted by fire and partially crushed by the collapse of its tall smokestack. After being rebuilt to two stories instead of its original three, it would resume service along its Powell/Jackson, Powell/Mason, and Sacramento/Clay lines, a few shortened, by the next year.

One-tenth of the nation's military was committed to disaster response in San Francisco, to that point the largest federal relief effort in American history. In Washington, Congress increased its appropriation of funds to War Secretary Taft for San Francisco's relief to $2.5 million, most to fund the Army's and Navy's efforts. And beyond insurance payments and the mint's assistance to local banks, the largest infusion of capital into the city would come from the Finance Committee of Relief and Red Cross Funds. To this, the Red Cross remitted the $400,000 it had so far raised, and contributions flowed in from roughly 2,500 other cities and towns; other countries, including China, Japan, Mexico, Canada, England, and Germany; and more than $413,000 from San Franciscans. In addition to other independent relief funds and forms of assistance such as Southern Pacific carrying more than 300,000 passengers free of charge during the first week, surrounding Bay Area communities giving relief and shelter to refugees, or outside groups bringing their own forms of relief (as with the hot meal kitchen run through the first week by the Los Angeles Relief Committee), the relief fund would eventually raise $9,673,057.94 (more than $321 million in 2023).

Gas was turned back on in a few neighborhoods starting on May 11, and more people returned to their homes. And those with repaired and inspected chimneys pulled their stoves in from the streets. For more than fifty thousand remaining refugees, the relief fund, with former mayor Phelan as its chairman, would pay for temporary shelter and rehabilitation, including grants for restarting businesses or building a house. And the Army would run food and clothing distribution and sanitation, with the organization of refugees and camps coordinated by the Red Cross and assisted by Associated Charities.

More than one hundred separate refugee encampments were scattered throughout the city, some with fewer than a dozen campers and others with upward of two thousand (the Presidio had three separate camps, and Golden Gate Park had four). The Army and Red Cross designated and numbered twenty-six refugee camps in early May, and Mayor Schmitz declared city squares, small parks, and the Panhandle would be cleared and refugees ordered to one of the official camps. The Red Cross began registration of individuals and families in official camps and issued food cards (with the number of dependents, good for ten days and then reviewed at which point "able-bodied men, for whom by this time there was abundant opportunity of employment, could be cut off"). By mid-May by order of General Greely, individuals or families would have to present a Red Cross food card or pay 15 cents for a meal.

Officially labeled "Camp No. 3, Presidio, Ft. Winfield Scott," this refugee camp was designated "For Chinese." Since being driven from their sanctuary of Chinatown, the few hundred Chinese refugees who stayed in the city were ordered by soldiers to move and move again and move again, each time because nearby residents or refugees complained about their presence. They were moved from Fort Mason's waterfront to its dunes, then again within a week of the earthquake it was reported they "would be collected and placed in Fontana's warehouses, near Fort Mason." Then later, "All of the Chinese at present in the city will be gathered together in tents in the block bounded by Octavia, Franklin, Chestnut and Fort Mason streets." Then after a proposed move to the Presidio golf course, at the request of Presidio Heights residents, they were concentrated further out to Fort Winfield Scott on the windy western section of the Presidio, "as remote as possible from the Caucasian camps," as a newspaper would report.

Most of Chinatown's residents had, often with great difficulty, managed to escape the city on ferries, and most evacuees were now in Oakland. Most were herded into a segregated section of Adams Point on the north end of Lake Merritt. And a good number were staying on the grounds of the two-block Pacific Coast Canning Company at the invitation of Lew Hing, a Chinatown entrepreneur who had expanded his cannery business into Oakland two years before. He opened his warehouse doors to his fellow refugees and set up temporary housing in rows of tents and hired cooks to feed the homeless.

On the third day of the fire, seven-year-old Lily Soo-Hoo had also made it with her parents and siblings to Oakland, where the Red Cross "gave us each a cup of coffee with Carnation cream and sugar and each a doughnut." Before joining them, her older brother tried to return to their third-floor apartment in the city to retrieve their birth certificates, but by the time he got near Chinatown, he found the street being dynamited, and as Lily would later recall, "everything we had was burned up . . . there was nothing left."

"The big fire has obliterated Chinatown from San Francisco forever," declared the *Chronicle* on April 25, one week after the earthquake. The Empress Dowager in China personally pledged $75,000 to the American minister in Peking for disaster aid, but when it was declined with appreciation, she sent it to Chinese representatives in San Francisco for the use of Chinatown's homeless. And charitable organizations in Hong Kong pledged an additional $40,000, the first $10,000 of which was remitted in gold on April 26.

But members of the Citizens' Committee, unconcerned with the welfare of Chinese homeless in their city, focused instead on how to get rid of them. That same day, in a meeting of the Citizens' Committee, James Phelan emphatically pushed for all Chinese residents still in San Francisco to be moved "at once" to Hunters Point, two and a half miles south of Chinatown's ruins, and he joined Abe Ruef—united only in their racism—to decide "the question of the permanent location of the Chinese quarter."

With perfect timing on that very day, the first post-earthquake issue of the *Chung Sai Yat Po* rolled off hand-cranked presses in Oakland after the strenuous efforts of its editor and owner, Ng Poon Chew, to resume operations after he and his paper were burned out of Chinatown. The seven-year-old newspaper had the highest readership of any in Chinatown and was the first Chinese American daily paper published. It was the creation of Ng Poon Chew, who had emigrated from China when he was only fourteen, studied theology, been ordained a Presbyterian minister, and started the newspaper in San Francisco in 1899 after his home and Presbyterian Mission in Los Angeles were destroyed by fire. It had been a mammoth undertaking to get individual printing press block pieces for multiple copies of more than eleven thousand traditional Chinese characters shipped from Japan (China lacked the foundries to produce the pieces). But Ng Poon Chew succeeded, and his *Chung Sai Yat Po* kept Chinatown's non-English-speaking residents armed with the latest news, an information service now made even more vital by the destruction of their neighborhood and scattering of their community. The papers were mostly distributed to Chinatown refugees in Oakland and carried the latest news from San Francisco of relocation efforts by city leaders. On April 29 an editorial warned, "Westerners have suggested moving the Chinese people out of Chinatown [translated]," and suggested hiring "famous attorneys to represent us"; that Chinese landlords "should restore their buildings as soon as possible"; and that tenants should "speak with their landlords as soon as possible and ask them to rebuild and rent them the building," which by experience white landlords were inclined to do "because the rent in Chinatown is higher than elsewhere." A few days later, the paper printed reports that "Chinatown would eventually be sold to rich westerners."

Ng Poon Chew organized Chinatown merchants, retained a prominent bank attorney, and made their case with Chinatown's white property owners, who pledged they were committed to rebuild "as soon as they could get an assurance from the city officials that the Chinese, to whom they wished to rent buildings, were not to be removed." For political muscle, the Chinese consulate general of San Francisco—working out of a temporary office in Oakland— was joined by the first secretary of the Chinese Legation, who had arrived by train from Washington, and together they met with Governor Pardee to make clear their intention to rebuild their consulate on its former lot in Chinatown. And they declared that Chinese lessees and owners of land in Chinatown "cannot be deprived of the right to rebuild if they so desire." The property owners organized a Dupont Street Improvement Association, and after more meetings with Ng Poon Chew and the merchants—and convinced they could not afford to lose the rent and revenue of this "important business center"— they devised a plan to reconstruct Chinatown as "a model Oriental city," which would be "one of the great and picturesque features of the new San Francisco." And in words that would ring loudest with city leaders, it would "bring greater profits to the owners of the property."

The San Francisco Real Estate Board endorsed the plan for "the Chinese style of architecture"—a Westernized faux-Chinese style—which would be "attractive to tourists," thus employing stylistic stereotypes to secure their position. The Chinese Merchant Association and property owners retained designers to plan large bazaars lined with decorative dragons and topped with pagoda-like towers, aimed to "attract tourists to the Chinese section" but also to thwart further attempts to dislodge the Chinese community from the heart of the city.

Construction would follow quickly, and the following year would see completion of the iconic buildings that would flank the two northern corners of Dupont and California Streets—the Sing Fat Co. bazaar and the Sing Chong Co. Building. And on the ruins of "Old Chinatown" in the city's center, "New Chinatown" began to appear. The maneuvers of Phelan and Ruef had failed, and Chinatown was rebuilt in the heart of San Francisco, where it was before and where it would ever be.

"The appearance and condition of the city is much like that of a new mining camp except, thank God, that no liquor is sold and no poker chips rattle," wrote a resident on May 18, one month after the earthquake. "Thank goodness we have the gas today and at least can boil water and make tea," wrote Carrie Duncan five days later. "[I]t would seem good to have a square meal once more." She and her mom had evacuated to her sister's place out in the Richmond District after fire reached their Van Ness Avenue house, and had now found an Oak Street flat to rent. "I still go every other day and stand in line for bread but hope it will only be for a short time." They had the funds to purchase food but were still limited to what was available. "I tell you I have had corn beef so much that I am ashamed to look a cow in the face."

In late May more than forty thousand city residents still lived outside, more than half in "unofficial" camps. Thirty-three-year-old Halvor Berg, a Norwegian immigrant who had lost everything in his third-floor room when his boardinghouse burned, wrote, "I have not slept in bed yet since the fire." Most refugees were South of Market residents unable to afford the rent of middle- to upper-middle-class apartments in Hayes Valley, Cow Hollow, Pacific Heights, Richmond, the Sunset, or down in the Mission District. "The majority of these people are of the poorer class and only paid from about $7.00 to $15.00 rent," wrote one resident to her family, explaining that rent in the "fine flats and residences" of the unburned district ranged "from $25.00 to $50.00 and upwards," fretting "it will be sometime before they are housed."

Dr. Devine and James Phelan began applying money from the relief fund to their own version of rehabilitation. In mid-May, they began the Business Rehabilitation Grant program, wherein residents who had been "successful in trade, business, or profession" before the fire and were "so crippled by the fire" that they needed assistance to restart and had "no other way of supporting themselves or their families" could apply for a grant. The first $75 was granted for the restart of a shoe-repair shop. Then $100 was granted for a restaurant. In all, 2,032 people applied and 1,226 were granted business aid ranging between $50 and $500. A partial list of occupations boosted by grants showcases the life of the old city bringing life to the new: a tailor shop, drayman, seamstress, cigar stand, millinery shop, bakery, boot- and shoemaking and repair shop, boarding and rooming house, and "huckster or peddler."

Owners of businesses large and small were determined to stay in San Francisco. While John Walter waited for insurance to pay at least a portion of the losses from his destroyed store and warehouse, he got his carpeting and upholstery business restarted from his house. "We started the office going in Marian's study room, and things look business like [sic]," he wrote his parents. "Got hold of two typewriters, and things are going fast—putting the mail & affairs into shape." He noticed his neighborhood was now "lined with offices— Anglo-California next door, with Ignatz Steinhart (he burnt out). Haas Bros. down the street." He could feel a general sentiment "of great confidence in the future of the city, & that it will soon be upbuilt."

Eighteen-year-old Alex Paladini, who had survived the fish market collapse, was still bunking with his father on a fishing boat at the Filbert Street wharf: "Two weeks after the earthquake we re-started fishing." His father's fish market store was gone, but they had saved their boat and nets, opened a market on Pier 23, "and people at once began coming from all over the place to buy fresh fish again." They stayed there for more than a year until they could rebuild in their old spot and start back "regular business."

Photographer Arnold Genthe, whose home and studio and negatives were destroyed, was invited by friends to relocate in New York City, where there would be "a fully equipped studio waiting for you." He was tempted, he later admitted, but would not leave his city. "I wanted to stay, to see the new city which would rise out of the ruins. I felt that my place was there. I had something to contribute, even if only a small measure, to the rebuilding of the city."

Black San Franciscans, almost all of whom had lost their homes and churches and schools, stayed to rebuild their community. Parishioners of Third Baptist Church sold the Powell Street lot where the fire had reduced their two-story structure to ashes, and they used the proceeds and their own tithes to build a new sanctuary on the western slope of Nob Hill. And with the houses of worship for both the city's African Methodist Episcopal churches destroyed by the fire—the First A.M.E. Zion and Union Bethel A.M.E.—the congregation of First A.M.E. Zion was welcomed into Union Bethel's rebuilt sanctuary on Powell Street for afternoon worship until they were able to raise enough money to build their own in the Western Addition.

As rubble was hauled in trucks and wagons to waterfront barges and dumped in the bay and along new wharves at the foot of King Street, rebuilding was underway. "Small houses are springing up everywhere, one story frame buildings, and business is being conducted as usual," a physician wrote on May 27. He had been giving medical care and vaccinations to refugees, and as he went back to treating his own patients, there was a slow return to normalcy. "Electric cars are running and the debris has been thrown out of the streets," he noted. "Banks have resumed business, and we are gradually getting back to work."

With steel in high demand, sixteen-year-old Howard Livingston's employer Vulcan Iron Works got restarted and he went to work on the framing of new buildings. He later remembered hearing people say "that the new San Francisco would be a far finer city than the one which had been destroyed," and as a native San Franciscan, he added, "It is a city for which I feel great affection, and I have always been glad that I was able to have a small part in its rebuilding."

And with carpenters in highest demand, Australian immigrant Percy Gregory had plenty of work. He had recently left carpentry to work as a butcher to provide more for himself and his pregnant wife, Helen, but after the fire, he "turned carpenter again." He wrote his mother on May 29, "[H]ave lots of work ahead of me for months to come, at four and a half dollars a day. Have one four roomed house nearly completed. Another two roomed house to start on and three more houses after that." Determined to see his adopted city "build up greater than ever," he declared, "Am going to stay right here and help all I can."

"THE CALL GETS FIRST PERMIT TO REBUILD," declared the *Call* two days after the fire was extinguished, announcing that "repairing of the noble structure at Third and Market will be started this morning" with a permit from the Board of Public Works, the first "granted since the earthquake." Throughout downtown, steel workers and masons and bricklayers and carpenters were employed restoring or rebuilding the city's most familiar landmarks. The shell of the Palace Hotel would have to be brought down and the structure rebuilt, during which time a temporary hotel would be opened, staffing "every cook and attendant connected with the big dining rooms and grill in the old Palace." A temporary one-story hotel built in Union Square would accept St. Francis Hotel guests while work proceeded on the restoration of its gutted interior and completion of its third wing. The owner of the Fairmont Hotel announced its "walls and steel structure were not seriously damaged," and within two weeks of the fire, men were at work "cleaning the walls and removing all evidences of the fire." Work was also underway to inspect, refit, and restore Market Street's Flood Building, the Mutual Savings Bank Building, Hibernia Bank, and the Merchants' Exchange.

Rebuilding was the priority of developers and business leaders, and its scale and rapidity was the narrative they pushed to shift attention from the disaster. "Let the whole idea be that the main thing in connection with the event was the clearing of a pathway to a greater San Francisco and the awakening to an even greater California," wrote a Southern Pacific Railroad executive to a chamber of commerce east of the Bay Area, underscoring the need to emphasize the recovery and "the work of reconstruction." The railroad's *Sunset* magazine went to press with a "New San Francisco Emergency Edition" full of bright promises of "a finer and a greater city," which, when "clothed anew, will invite you within the gates of the new and greater metropolis of the Pacific." The publishers wrote glowing reports that "all class distinctions were leveled" and citizens "rose above all price of place and possessions," and included poetry rhyming with optimism about "A city more fair than their old / Already uprising." This "hyperbolic nonsense," as author Simon Winchester called it, was part of a public relations effort to avoid grappling with safety concerns and hide lingering dangers behind the façade of a grand, new skyline.

For city planners with short memories, a team of engineers was sent by the US Geological Survey to investigate the wreckage of buildings and streets and water and gas pipes both inside and outside the burned district "for the purpose of studying the effect of the earthquake and fire on structural materials." A thorough report was prepared with detailed findings on what specifically went wrong within certain buildings. In just one South of Market structure, the Jackson Brewing Company, which sat outside the burned district with a design approved the previous year, engineers found its brick walls were held together with "mortar of poor quality" and many of its steel beams "were bolted together with an insufficient number of bolts, the girders and beams resting upon the walls without any tie; the columns, girders, and beams were not fireproofed." After noting "several persons were killed" by its collapse, they concluded that "the design was bad and the material and workmanship were very poor." Throughout the city, the team found more of the same. "Flimsy and loosely built structures collapsed like houses of cards under the terrific wrenching and shaking," and when flames reached structures that had withstood the first test, they "failed" the second "by reason of inadequate fireproofing."

Engineers made a list of recommendations for a new building code, including stronger foundations for structures "on soft, marshy, or made ground" and emphasized "no reasonable expense should be spared" in fireproofing. The State Board of Architects made its own suggestions, stating taller buildings should be restricted to steel-frame or reinforced concrete instead of brick and underscoring the need for pile foundations of not less than forty-five feet into alluvial soil of made land: "In the earth's vibrations it rests as does a ship in water." And the Structural Engineers Association urged use of reinforced concrete rather than heavy, rigid brick masonry, which had proved brittle in its inability to absorb compressive shock and its weight fatal to occupants. And ordinance changes were urged by insurance underwriters to mandate more sprinklers, better fireproofing of interiors, and an expansion of the fire district of noncombustible structures.

But city leaders were eager to get rebuilding, and in the revision of building and fire codes, safety was optional but speed was imperative. The cityscape of dust and piled rubble presented an urban tabula rasa luring developers nationwide. By early May, permits for new steel structures had already been granted for two dozen tall buildings, and local builders were joined by at least "eight or ten of the largest Eastern contractors" to handle the "overflow," all just waiting for the new building ordinances.

After a few public hearings where more consideration was given to cement workers and bricklayers—who opposed the changes—than to the findings of engineers and scientists, new building laws were pushed through in early July. The new code expanded the fire limits to include more of Nob Hill and the banking district but left its South of Market boundaries almost unchanged, ignoring Fire Chief Shaughnessy's urging to expand it through more of South of Market and into the Western Addition. It added reinforced concrete as a load-bearing material and a required interior support for one class of structures, and also added requirements that certain businesses—theaters, hospitals, department stores—not be located within wood-frame buildings.

But the new code mostly loosened guidelines for new construction, permitting taller timber-joisted masonry structures and taller Class-B structures (which could still be walled with unreinforced masonry), and a 1907 amendment removed previous height restrictions for steel-frame Class-A buildings. It inexplicably lifted the requirement for firewalls in adjoining buildings, removing an important fireproofing safeguard in row house construction. And of twenty-three total fire ordinances, nineteen were left unchanged, including those governing electric wiring in buildings and automatic sprinklers. City leaders had again left safety of residents to market forces, dangling from the prudence of developers and landlords, no matter the civic public relations push.

As the Army officially withdrew from San Francisco at the end of June and handed over its portion of relief duties to the Red Cross and the relief fund, at least thirty thousand displaced residents still needed permanent shelter. For residents who found themselves owning a lot in the burned area covered with ashes of their former house, a "Bonus Plan" offered up to one-third "of the cost of a home to be built on the ground owned" by them to replace their destroyed house. Bonuses, capped at $500 each, aided homeowners who had been uninsured or whose insurance companies had offered partial settlements. Within the plan's first six months, 470 "bonus houses" had been built at a cost of just more than $200,000, and in the end, $423,288.17 helped 885 residents and families rebuild.

But most who had been displaced and made homeless by the earthquake and fire had paid affordable rent in small South of Market lodging house rooms from wages they earned working long shifts in nearby jobs, in foundries or warehouses or machine shops or as longshoremen on the waterfront. Now displaced to life under tents in camps, those lucky few with employers who had restarted now walked two miles or more each way for the same hard work and the same long hours and the same pay. There were no affordable rentals left, and they did not qualify for grants or bonuses limited to homeowners and business owners. And if they wanted to save up their weekly wages to find a way out of their tent, every ten days they had to stand before one of Dr. Devine's Red Cross workers and prove they were still "destitute" and actively working so they could be fed.

In the late summer, construction began on nineteen two-story, wood-frame "tenement houses" South of Market, each of which could house 650 occupants. And the plan for "Camp Cottages" was devised, small wooden shacks of two or three rooms each. Built by union laborers of five local construction companies, the walls were California redwood, the floors fir, and each was roofed with cedar shingles and painted green. To secure one, people signed a one-year "contract of purchase and sale" agreeing to pay rent of $4 per month for a two-room or $6 for a three-, and after one year the cottage was theirs, to be moved at their own expense to a lot they rented or owned.

A total of 5,610 "refugee cottages" were built side by side in Dolores Park, Camp Richmond, Precita Park, and Lobos Square where the relief fund had paid construction crews to build wood-planked walkways and paved sidewalks and installed water and gas connections and a sewage system allowing for flushing toilets in each unit. These original tiny houses became home to 16,448 residents. "My father was able to get into one of those places," Etta Siegel, only six at the time, later recalled. "We lived there for about eight months. . . . There was only two rooms, a kitchen and a bedroom. My folks were permitted to have two because he had two children."

Over the next two years, Associated Charities installed sinks and tubs in many, and paid to move cottages for residents of the most modest means. Other new owners paid to have their "earthquake shacks" moved to permanent lots. Moving companies typically charged $15 to move one shack and $25 for two, depending on the distance. Many landowners in the city's outer reaches subdivided their property into smaller lots to sell to cottage dwellers. An owner out in the Richmond District listed lots for "payments of $50 down and $10 per, only five left, get busy and move your cottage there instead of leasing." Another offered to lease lots in the same district for $5 per month. Many new cottage owners who could afford to set up in the city skirted their lots with picket fences and added porches and all levels of improvements. Most were forced by high prices to move their shacks out of the city, like Etta Siegel's parents, who moved with other cottage camp neighbors sixteen miles down Mission Street where hundreds of working-class refugees were able to afford their own piece of land on and surrounding John Daly's dairy farm, and together they helped establish the community that would become Daly City.

In the fall, children returned to schools. Thirty-seven temporary primary and grammar schools had been set up, some in quickly built wooden shacks and others in large, wood-floored tents. And the population influx in unburned neighborhoods was such that eight schools in the Western Addition and the

Mission District were so overcrowded on the first day of the term, the school board approved construction to double the size of each from six rooms to twelve. "About October 1st our April-October vacation was over," seven-year-old John Conlon Jr. later remembered of his return to the classroom. "May the children of San Francisco, or any place, never again enjoy such an experience as mine."

With the change in seasons also came a shift in public sentiment. In the days and weeks after the fire, local newspapers had praised the "prompt, determined action" of Mayor Schmitz, who "rose to the occasion when the city was in flames" and "proved himself a leader of courage and energy." But as word spread of lucrative payments and hefty bribes involving streetcar lines and water companies while citizens worked to recover and rebuild, opinion turned against Schmitz and Abe Ruef and the Board of Supervisors. At the end of October, the district attorney appointed a prosecutor to convene a grand jury and investigate corruption in City Hall, but on Ruef's advice the supervisors suspended the district attorney and appointed Ruef interim county prosecutor. A judge signed a restraining order reinstalling the district attorney, and on October 26, Ruef needed a police escort to make it safely through "the crowd of angry citizens" and into the temporary courtroom set up in the synagogue of Congregation Sherith Israel in Pacific Heights. On November 15, the grand jury indicted Abe Ruef and Eugene Schmitz for five counts of extortion each. Both were arraigned in December and their trial would follow in the new year.

But other trials would fill the fall and winter court calendar before year's end, forcing local judges and twelve-men juries to grapple with the legal effects of Mayor Schmitz's shoot-to-kill order. In the Superior Court room of Judge Carroll Cook, temporarily located in the basement of Calvary Church on Fillmore Street in Pacific Heights, a jury heard evidence in the joint murder trial of Malcolm Vance and George Simmons, two of the three accused of killing Red Cross driver Heber Tilden (the third, Edward Boynton, opted to be tried separately). Heber's widow attended each day with their three young sons. Eyewitnesses in the car and on the street testified, as did the physician and medical examiner and police officers. As well as the national guard colonel, who admitted to deputizing them as volunteer guards and authorizing lethal force. And both Vance and Simmons testified in their defense, swearing they could not see the Red Cross flag in the darkness behind the headlights, claiming they did not hear "Red Cross!" yelled from the automobile, and admitting that they had each fired several shots at the automobile but believed they were acting lawfully under orders they were given. Judge Cook admitted

Mayor Schmitz's printed proclamation into evidence at the defense's request and instructed the jury that "although martial law did not exist, it might have been the impression of the accused that it was in force" and could only find them guilty if they concluded the men were acting "with malice aforethought." After eighteen minutes of deliberation, the jury found both men not guilty.

In October, after the jury's verdict acquitting the first two defendants and an earlier jury verdict acquitting a national guardsman for another shooting, Judge Cook entered an order dismissing the murder charge against the third, Edward Boynton. "I doubt if there were ten men in San Francisco during the fire, and I make no exception of the judges, who did not believe that martial law was in effect," he stated, concluding, "Boynton believed that he had been empowered by martial law to carry arms and to use them in what he believed to be the performance of his duty." And while this legally negated criminal intent, the court added, "[I]t is a great misfortune that a man of the fine character of Tilden should have been sacrificed."

The only remaining shooting cases from the disaster were two cases of manslaughter. In November, Judge Cook presided over one of them, "the third of those brought for the reckless taking of human life by amateur soldiers during the fire," as the paper would report. It was the case of Ernest Denicke, the self-appointed guardian who on the second day of the fire had donned his old national guard uniform and shot and killed a man at the waterfront who had ignored his order to "Halt!" after dropping the chickens he had grabbed for food and taking a reportedly drunk marine's rifle after being provoked. Eyewitnesses testified they never heard Denicke give any warning before shooting the man in the back as he walked away, and when one of them—a State Belt Railroad foreman—asked Denicke if it was necessary to kill the man, Denicke responded, "I only did my duty." To which the foreman responded, "Did you have to shoot him full of holes to do your duty?"

That "duty" was in line with "the rule of the bullet" prevailing in the city during the disaster, as attorney Garret McEnerney—the author of Mayor Schmitz's infamous shoot-to-kill proclamation—testified. Taking the stand in his own defense, Ernest Denicke claimed the man was facing him, that he told the man to halt at least three times, that the man still had the marine's rifle, and shooting him was his "duty as a sentry." Again, the defense claimed he was acting under martial law. Again, Judge Cook admitted Mayor Schmitz's printed proclamation into evidence at the defense's request. And again, Judge Cook instructed the jury that while martial law "did not" exist in the city, if they concluded the defendant acted "under a misapprehension of facts" that martial law was in effect, then the accused was innocent if he acted without criminal motive. The jury deliberated through the afternoon and into the night, for six hours, before returning a verdict of not guilty. In light of the jury's decision, Judge Cook dismissed the only other pending shooting case, a manslaughter charge against a national guardsman who shot and killed a man who was fighting with another guardsman, "the last of the series of murder and manslaughter cases resulting from" what newspapers called "the abnormal conditions existing at the time of the fire."

San Francisco's people had lived for five days under these "abnormal conditions," or more accurately, the "rule of the bullet," started by Schmitz and fueled by Funston, from the morning of the earthquake until the following Monday when General Greely ended it. Evidence indicates at least a dozen people were shot and nine killed during that time, and quite possibly more. Only four of those shootings resulted in criminal charges, and not a single person was ever convicted or held responsible for any of the killings or the atmosphere that incited them.

By December, the city's waterfront ferries ran at their former schedule, and the Ferry Building's slips averaged an arrival and departure every fifteen minutes, bringing fewer sightseers and more commuters. Many were former residents working their old jobs in the city but still displaced by the lack of affordable housing, a scarcity the rebuilding was not aimed to cure. Even with the tenement houses set up by the relief fund, there was less than one-seventh of the lower-rent space of flats and lodging houses in the city after the fire. And the calamity's transformation of the city's makeup was not just structural. There were fewer florists, fewer photographers, fewer artists of all types, and fewer employment agencies. Before the fire, the city was home to twenty-seven libraries; now there were only ten, including the Mechanics' Library, set up in a temporary building on the site of the old Mechanics' Pavilion ("The only thing saved from the former library building was a bronze bust of James Lick, which adorns a wall of the shack," the *Chronicle* reported). And the Public Library, its main branch formerly in a wing of City Hall, was operating out of a temporary main branch after losing more than 143,000 of its 166,344 volumes to the fire. "The greatest loss to the city is the loss of all libraries and the scientific collections," wrote botanist Alice Eastwood a few days after sparing a scientific collection for posterity from the fire that destroyed her own home. "Buildings can be replaced but these never can be."

For amusement-starved San Franciscans there was still boxing out at

Dreamland Pavilion and family fun at the Chutes amusement park, where the Orpheum had been putting on shows in the theater while it rebuilt its playhouse on Ellis Street. And Italian opera returned to the city with the Lambardi Grand Opera's presentation of *Aida* on Christmas Day in the Central Theatre's temporary wood-sided canvas-roofed theater at 8th and Market Streets. And there were nearly as many breweries and distilleries as before the fire and just as many restaurants. The Hibernia Bank was restored and open for customers, and the Metropolis Trust and Savings Bank was still in a temporary branch on Van Ness near Post while its new "twelve-story Class A Building" was being built at Market and New Montgomery Street on the former site of the Grand Hotel, part of a citywide construction boom echoing—and in places outpacing—its gold rush–era expansion.

By the end of 1906, San Francisco had more architects, builders, cabinet-makers, carpenters, chimney builders, lumber dealers, plasterers, plumbers, real estate agents, and furniture dealers than at the year's beginning. And there were twice as many fireproofers and contractors and three times as many cement dealers, sellers of building materials, and roofers. And the 1907 city directory would add new sections to its business listings, including "Concrete Construction," "Concrete Reinforced," "Concrete Piles," "Contractors—Building," "Engineers—Construction," and "Engineers—Structural," all reflecting a city almost singularly focused on upbuilding.

Docks were jammed with freighters bearing steel and concrete and lumber-laden schooners. So high was demand for lumber in San Francisco, temporary wharves were built, and lumber companies purchased extra vessels for shipping. The Portland Lumber Company purchased two transport steamers, removed the passenger cabins, and converted both to lumber freighters. On average, three million feet of lumber arrived at the waterfront every day. On just a single day in December, more than eighteen million feet of lumber and four million shingles were reportedly being loaded on twenty separate steamers, schooners, and barks along piers in Olympia, Portland, Astoria, and San Pedro bound for San Francisco, and more than a million shingles and 3,430,000 feet of lumber arrived at the city's waterfront. Stevedores and long-shoremen unloaded the stacks of lumber—white pine, yellow fir, red fir, and the sought-after fire-resistant redwood—faster than horse teams clogging the wharf could haul it away.

Santa Fe Railway employee Michael Maher wrote that month, "You can stand up and look in any direction you please, but all you can see is work, work,

work: all trades and professions being vigorously applied to the enormous task of rebuilding this once grand city." Michael had been burned out of his South of Market apartment and spent the next few nights sleeping in a toolshed before securing a room in a waterfront lodging house saved by Lieutenant Freeman's sailors. "In the burned section (down in the business district) there is nothing but dust and noise," he noted. Despite the passage of more than seven months and a fair amount of recent rainfall, ash and dust still hung everywhere, constantly stirred and lifted by streetcars and automobiles and wagons and long in settling. "During a windy day it is nothing to have to submit to the disgusting operation of having both eyes filled choke-full [*sic*] of dust," requiring an hour for him to wash it from his hands and face and hair and slap it from his hat and layers of clothes after being downtown.

December 31, 1906, was a Monday, a new workweek signifying a year ending with work just beginning. Sunday night's rain had settled the dust and left wet clumps of mortar powder and sawdust between paving stones and streaking down sidewalks to corner puddles. In the footprints of 28,188 buildings sat crumbled pieces of the former city, some beneath new foundations of new buildings going up but most still in forgotten heaps, scooped over months before with rubble and debris from streets and sidewalks, disregarded spaces waiting for their turn at whatever newer and better building might stand in their place. Downtown's noise was constant again. Wheelmen whistled and automobiles coughed and wagons rattled over repaired streets, more now carrying lumber or concrete than ever before. Through the air carried a constant racket of hammering and sawing and sanding and a rattle of chains bearing steel beams from swinging derricks atop rising structures. And down on Market Street, electric streetcars rolled in rhythmic click-clacks beneath metallic trundling of trolley poles along overhead wires, sounds workday crowds no longer noticed and a familiarity they would never lose.

In the late afternoon, under wooden shelters below steel skeletons of coming buildings, Market Street's sidewalks filled with rushing workers who cut out before the five o'clock hour to beat other commuters to the Ferry Building. One or two slowed in their walk, their attention fixed on the clock tower. A few more slowed and looked, then more still, and as a newspaper would report, "the rushing crowd instantly stopped." The minute hand on the clock was moving, "trying to knock off the figure nine with a succession of upper cuts." For 257 days the clock's face had loomed from the tower frozen in time, a persistent reminder of a single minute the city was still trying to escape. Now for the first time since 5:12 a.m. on April 18, the clock moved, "determined to tick the old year out and the new year in."

That night, from the smoke-filled air of rebuilt saloons to the parlors of refurbished homes along Van Ness Avenue to the new double-maple dancing floor of the new Paris Tea Garden on Washington Street or a society dinner at Tait's Café on Eddy Street where the "elaborately decorated" tables had been booked weeks in advance, San Franciscans rang out 1906. Stands along Fillmore Street sold "chopped-up, multi-colored paper" (confetti) thrown by partiers blowing fish horns and jangling cowbells until streets resembled "a kaleidoscopic snowstorm." Police officers on horseback tried to keep crowds on sidewalks; boys in fake beards and women in masks and men in evening dress were flaunting noisemakers. Morning newspapers would report the city celebrated "as if every citizen recognized that the year was the beginning of the city's true growth and prosperity," and the farewell to the year's passing was the "most joyous in the history of the city."

The great unspoken lingered just beneath the merriment and no further than a glance at the skyline, trauma each survivor carried the rest of their life and scars the city wears to this day. The folly and greed of men entrusted with the public good had ignited a firestorm more violent than the earthquake and a disaster that outlasted the flames. Their failures had nearly toppled the city's achievements, their crimes went beyond condemnation, and the suffering they caused reached deeper than sorrow.

But among the material destruction and against the grimmest of odds, there were hundreds of thousands of survivors. And what they had endured through the moments of shaking and days of fire and hunger and thirst and weeks and months of shock and loss and homelessness and stress and uncertainty never left them. It came back to them in the rumble of thunder or in the crash of a falling lamp or the jingling of crystals on a chandelier. Or the whiff of smoke from a stove or the sound of a fire engine responding to a neighborhood alarm. Or the sight of a soldier on horseback at the Presidio or a simple walk through a grass square.

For us the full story can only come in pieces, in a scribbled journal entry or a few typed words on a death certificate or a list of names and ages on a Red Cross registration card for a family of six still homeless three months after the fire. "It was all like this—broken bits of human tragedy, curiously unrelated, inconsequential, disrupted by the temblor, impossible to this day to gather up and compose into a proper picture," the writer Mary Austin, a survivor, later wrote. "The largeness of the event had the effect of reducing private sorrow to a mere pinprick and a point of time."

A glimpse of San Francisco as it was on December 31, 1906, is a look back at a city looking forward. San Francisco's new life was replacing its old, street by street and building by building. But The City was its people. Hundreds of thousands of residents had survived countless "broken bits of human tragedy," and many still were fighting inner battles for their own survival and some would forevermore. The City was nurses who had witnessed horrific injuries still volunteering services to refugees and teachers working to educate displaced children in tent classrooms. It was machinists and ironworkers and longshoremen and coppersmiths now commuting from other Bay Area towns to labor in the place they still called home but could no longer afford to live in. It was firemen who had lost their own homes while working to the edge of collapse fighting the largest firestorm any had ever faced, still drilling daily with their horses and maintaining their engines to be first to the next job. It was Black residents tithing their wages to rebuild their houses of worship before their own homes were rebuilt. It was Chinatown residents and merchants in segregated camps fighting to return to the neighborhood they were working daily to rebuild. And it was bakers and furniture upholsterers and seamstresses and milliners who lost their homes and their stores but stayed where they were to restart against all odds. The City was its people, and The City was undefeated.

Afterword

FOURTEEN MONTHS AFTER the disaster, in the second week of June 1907, throngs of reporters and city officials and business owners and curious residents jammed the seats and aisles of a makeshift court-room in the Bush Street Temple to see a jury of twelve find Mayor Schmitz guilty of extortion. The felony conviction automatically stripped him of the office of mayor, and the judge ordered him held in the County Jail. Three weeks later, after proclaiming "no man, no matter how exalted his station or how strong and powerful the social and financial influences which surround him, is above the law," the judge sentenced Schmitz to five years in San Quentin.

The municipal and judicial spectacle filling the next eighteen months of "graft prosecutions" played out like implausible fiction. Abe Ruef, by that time facing seventy-five indictments for bribing supervisors and accepting bribes from telephone franchises, United Railroads, and French restaurants in the Tenderloin, had signed a limited immunity agreement and testified against Schmitz. Based on the testimony of police officers and elected supervisors also granted immunity, other men were indicted in the scandal, including the former attorney general of California, lobbyists, boxing promoters, and executives with local telephone and railroad franchises. The city's police chief resigned after be-ing indicted for perjury. A witness's house was dynamited, and the witness—not home at the time—fled to Canada to avoid testifying. A man removed from one of the juries for having an undisclosed felony conviction—and accused of accepting a bribe from Ruef for an acquittal vote—returned to the courtroom and shot the prosecutor during a recess. The prosecutor survived, but the former juror later died of a gunshot to the head while in his city prison cell, in a scene pointing to—or possibly staged as—suicide. The new police chief—himself accused of being on the take from Ruef—was blamed for allowing the juror's death on his watch, and then disappeared from a boat during a bay crossing, a death ruled "accidental." Some of the graft/extortion trials ended in deadlocked juries and most in acquittals. Mayor Schmitz, held in the County Jail during his appeal, was released after seven months when his conviction was set aside by the Court of Appeals, a ruling affirmed by the state's Supreme Court. But luck ran out for Abe Ruef in December 1908 when a jury convicted him of bribery, and he was sentenced to fourteen years in San Quentin.

In 1912, Eugene Schmitz was brought to court again on the remaining twenty-seven indictments for bribery. Abe Ruef, brought from San Quentin under subpoena, refused to testify, and Schmitz's attorneys moved to dismiss the charges for insufficient evidence. In announcing his ruling granting Schmitz's attorneys' motion and dismissing the last "graft" cases arising from the "wholesale debauchery of the government of the city," the judge concluded, "It will remain a source of shame to San Francisco that where the showing of grave crime was so formidable the vindication of the law fell so far short of what was needed in the way of example."

In 1915, Abe Ruef was granted parole after four years and nine months in prison. Disbarred from the practice of law, he opened an office on the top floor of the Sentinel Building (later Columbus Tower) advertising services in "ideas, investments, real estate." And Schmitz, working in real estate, ran for mayor to, in his words, "redeem his good name" and "bring back the good old times" before the office was "stolen" from him in 1907. He was decisively rejected by voters who reelected by a wide margin the popular incumbent mayor James "Sunny Jim" Rolph.

Schmitz ran successfully for supervisor in 1917, was defeated by Mayor Rolph for mayor yet again in 1919 in what the *Examiner* characterized as a "K.O." in "1 round," was elected supervisor again in 1921, but defeated in 1923. He retired from politics, shaved his familiar beard and pompadour, returned to playing the violin, reportedly lost heavily investing in real estate and mines, and died of a heart attack in 1928. And Abe Ruef never did regain his former broker status in city politics, nor did his "ideas" ever take off again. He died in 1936, seventy-one years old and bankrupt.

*   *   *

Death came, as it must to all, to Frederick Funston at the age of fifty-one in early 1917, just before America entered the First World War. In the days and weeks following the earthquake and fire, largely based on the self-congratulatory account he wrote for *Cosmopolitan* magazine, the press hailed him as a hero and credited him with saving the city. He was also praised by Congress—especially members of California's delegation—even though his actions were, they admitted, "wholly and undeniably unconstitutional." When a San Francisco attorney dared dissent from the acclamations filling newspapers and published a letter critical of Funston's unlawful actions, the thin-skinned Funston—ever sensitive to his image in the press—responded with an open letter belittling the writer as "cowardly" and "ignorant." Funston continued his career in the Army, worked as commandant of Command and General Staff College at Fort Leavenworth—a school for professional Army officers he never attended himself—then was posted in the Philippines and Hawaii. After promotion to major general, Funston commanded the Army's Southern Department during the Punitive Expedition into Mexico chasing the revolutionary leader Francisco "Pancho" Villa. He died of a heart attack six weeks before America declared war on Germany, and he was buried in San Francisco National Cemetery in the Presidio after lying in state in San Francisco's new City Hall, the first individual to be honored so.

Most other military leaders who found themselves serving in San Francisco during those critical days received little credit in their time or historical note since. Raymond Briggs, the young artillery lieutenant who, acting under the misguided limitations placed on him, supervised demolition crews in safer employment of dynamite and prevented a wider use of black powder, continued his service in the Army and was promoted through the ranks. When the US entered the First World War he served as a colonel on General Pershing's staff, and on the Western Front he commanded a field artillery regiment and—after promotion to brigadier general—a field artillery brigade. Briggs served on General MacArthur's staff in the Philippines as America entered the Second World War, and he was kept on active service to command the VII Corps Area until 1944. He retired to San Diego and passed of a heart attack at the age of eighty-one on Christmas Eve 1959. He was eulogized not just as a veteran of the Spanish-American War and both World Wars, but also "for fighting the great San Francisco fire in 1906."

Dora Thompson, who led her team of nurses in treating all the patients inundating the Army General Hospital, continued her service as chief nurse in the Philippines and then as superintendent of the Army Nurse Corps through the First World War, for which she was awarded the Distinguished Service Medal for "her accuracy, good judgment" and "her splendid management of the Army Nurse Corps during the emergency." In 1932, after more than thirty years of service in the Army, Captain Thompson retired to San Francisco, where she lived until her death at seventy-seven in 1954. Her obituaries in city newspapers did not mention her role in helping so many in the disaster or her decorated service during the First World War, only that she was retired from the Army Nurse Corps. She is buried in Arlington National Cemetery in Washington, DC.

Lieutenant Colonel George Torney, who had ensured his hospital and staff could treat unprecedented numbers of wounded and succeeded as the sanitation officer in preventing disease outbreaks, was promoted twice more to brigadier general and appointed the Surgeon General of the Army in Washington, DC. He died of pneumonia at sixty-three years old and was buried with honors in the West Point Cemetery, but few today know his name or how much sickness and death he prevented in the disaster's aftermath. "Histories of the Army's role in 1906 concentrate on how soldiers dynamited buildings to stop the fire and on rumors that they shot looters," *Chronicle* reporter and columnist Carl Nolte observed in 2020. "But they did not write about what did not happen: The disaster was not followed by an outbreak of disease."

Also largely forgotten today is the man who saved San Francisco's waterfront, the Ferry Building, the Southern Pacific rail line and depot South of Market, the Custom House and surrounding businesses, and a good portion of North Beach and Fisherman's Wharf. Frederick Freeman was credited in letters from business owners to the admiral for saving their buildings and was cited by both the Army and Navy for his leadership and initiative averting greater disaster. Freeman was promoted to lieutenant commander, where he led a reserve torpedo flotilla, and after promotion to commander, he skippered the cruiser *San Diego* and a task force of destroyers. His star was still rising when he captained an admiral's flagship on an Atlantic crossing of torpedo boats during the First World War. But after losing merchant vessels to German U-boats on convoys he was escorting in 1918, mental depression forced Commander Freeman into a Philadelphia hospital for treatment. Reportedly so "[o]vercome by grief," Freeman fled the hospital, went absent without leave, was apprehended, and was dishonorably discharged from the Navy twenty-seven years after reporting to the Naval Academy at the age of fifteen.

Freeman went to live with his sister in Kentucky, then moved to San Mateo, California, where he struggled with alcoholism—resulting in a 1929 arrest for driving while intoxicated—and probably also suffered from untreated depression and post-traumatic stress disorder. He lived his final years in a hotel room in Soledad, where he was tracked down in 1940 by the man who served at his side through all three days of the fire, John Pond. The son of a rear admiral and a retired commander, Pond used his contacts in the Navy Department to clear his former boss's name, and in January 1941, President Roosevelt granted Freeman a full pardon. The very next month, as Pond worked to have Freeman's name added to the list of honorably retired officers, Frederick Freeman died at sixty-five.

Freeman was remembered in Bay Area newspapers as the "Navy Man Who Saved Piers in 1906" and the "Hero of '06 Quake." Survived only by a distant nephew and two nieces all out of state, Freeman's memory survived through John Pond, who sent obituary notices to local papers and scattered Freeman's ashes in the San Francisco Bay, reuniting him with the water thirty-four years after he saved the waterfront and so much of the city. It was only nine months later that John Pond died at his home in Berkeley, sealing forever the living memory of his lieutenant leading him and his sailors through the most exhausting and consequential seventy hours of their lives. Pond was buried with honors in Golden Gate National Cemetery in San Bruno.

Two months after the fire, Acting Chief John Dougherty of the fire department was officially offered the chief job by the fire commissioners, but he turned it down, opting after thirty years of service to retire as he had planned to his Webster Street home in the Fillmore District, where he passed four years later at sixty-four. Acting Assistant Chief Patrick Shaughnessy was appointed chief, and over the next four years he oversaw the start of construction of the Auxiliary Water Supply System, the project pushed for for years by the late Chief Dennis Sullivan and proven so critical in 1906 and still in use today. Water from a 10.5-million-gallon tank built atop Twin Peaks feeds tanks in Ashbury Heights and Nob Hill, and the three reservoirs supply water at high pressure to nearly two thousand oversized hydrants throughout the city. The AWSS was, in the words of the fire department's superintendent of engineering and water supply, "dedicated to the principle that the City will never again be destroyed by fire." And before his retirement in 1910, Chief Shaughnessy augmented the system with two fireboats, one of which was named *Dennis T. Sullivan*. Shaughnessy died in 1925, eulogized as a "fire hero, chief of fire fighters during the disaster of 1906, and builder of the existing system for prevention."

In 1919, as a stark reminder of the dangers faced by firefighters at all levels of the department, Assistant Chief John Conlon—who had returned home to his young sons after three straight days of work as a battalion chief in 1906—died of asphyxiation supervising the response to a basement fire in a Post Street apartment building. He was the nineteenth firefighter to die in the line of duty since the earthquake and fire, and his name is inscribed on the San Francisco Fire Department's Memorial Wall, displayed at the department's 2nd Street headquarters with the names of 148 other firefighters killed in the line of duty since 1851.

Addressing the heart of the water deficiency so starkly unmasked by the earthquake and fire, voters in 1910 approved a bond to construct a dam on the Tuolumne River more than 150 miles east of San Francisco and convert the Hetch Hetchy Valley into a reservoir to provide ample water and power for the city and the Bay Area. And in 1930, San Francisco purchased the Spring Valley Water Company, finally realizing the goals of the ex-Mayor Phelan and the late Chief Sullivan to free the public water supply from private hands. A few months later, James Phelan died at sixty-nine.

Phelan had continued his oversight of the relief fund after the disaster, supported the graft prosecutions to remove corruption from City Hall, and continued his successful battle for damming the Hetch Hetchy Valley as a better water source. He was elected to the US Senate in 1914—the first in which the senator was selected by voters and not the state legislature—and in Washington, DC, he continued his fight for public ownership of water and power and persisted in his anti-Chinese and anti-Japanese campaigns for immigration restrictions and discriminatory laws at the city, state, and federal levels. He campaigned for reelection in 1920 to pass stricter quotas on Asian immigration and "Keep California White," but he was defeated at the polls and returned to a very public life in San Francisco where he continued his generosity as a public benefactor, playing the critical role in extension of the civic center and creation of the War Memorial Opera House. And Phelan continued blaming societal ills on Chinese and Japanese residents, urging voters and civic organizations to "save our country from the yellow menace," public sentiment culminating in the 1924 passage of the Asian Exclusion Act. When Phelan died in 1930, flags statewide were lowered to half-staff and he was eulogized as a pioneer, a "great leader of California," and a "name linked with city growth" who "led fire relief," an outsized legacy forever stained by his bigoted, degrading policies and use of his prominent pulpit to dehumanize so many of his fellow San Franciscans.

*   *   *

Less prominent are the legacies of so many city residents who worked as a force for the greater good through the earthquake and fire. Lucy Fisher, the forty-three-year-old nurse who walked from her home the morning of the earthquake to offer her services to help the wounded in Mechanics' Pavilion, was also the associate editor of the *Nurses' Journal of the Pacific Coast* and already known for the work she did on behalf of tuberculosis patients. But she suffered from heart disease, and her exhaustive work for patients and refugees in 1906 reportedly "weakened her and she never fully recovered her former strength." Knowing her time was short, she handwrote a will in September 1910 noting she had "nothing of intrinsic value" but left her few earthly items to her sister and people "whose friendships have been my most precious possession." Declaring, "I believe in the immortality of the soul," she quoted the poem "Life" by Anna Lætitia Barbauld: "Say not Good night, but in some brighter clime / Bid me Good morning." Lucy passed away two months later at the age of forty-seven and was laid to rest in Mountain View Cemetery in Oakland.

Dr. Margaret Mahoney, the forty-eight-year-old physician who had spent the morning of the earthquake treating patients in Mechanics' Pavilion and had helped organize their safe evacuation when the fire reached the building, continued her medical practice, taught night classes, served as president of the San Francisco Teachers' Federation, and was an active leader of the Society for the Advancement of Women in Medicine. "We were not disheartened," she wrote after the disaster. "We old Californians are the children of pioneer fathers and not afraid of hardship." Margaret had been one of ten children born in the city to Irish immigrant forty-niner parents, graduated from the University of California and Cooper Medical College, and used her position as one of the early woman physicians of the West Coast to work to establish a women's hospital with a staff of female physicians and to help organize for women's suffrage, which was achieved in California in 1911, nine years before the Nineteenth Amendment enshrined it nationwide. In 1931, in her seventy-fourth year, Dr. Mahoney suffered a broken hip from a fall and died a few days later from her injuries. She was eulogized in Bay Area newspapers as a "pioneer physician," was memorialized by the Native Daughters of the Golden West, and was laid to rest in Holy Cross Catholic Cemetery in Colma.

The year 1931 marked twenty-five years since the earthquake and fire. San Francisco's population numbered just more than 634,000, roughly half that of Los Angeles, which was now California's largest city after more than doubling in size in the previous decade. Chinatown's thirty-thousand-plus residents lived in cramped tenements still owned by white landlords, and their streets were still patrolled by officers of the police department's Chinatown squad. War had come to their ancestral country that year when Japan invaded Manchuria, and in the previous quarter century of rebuilding their neighborhood, most had been denied or stripped of citizenship by the United States, the land where they lived and worked and made their home. That same year, one of the individuals most responsible for the survival of Chinatown as a San Francisco community, Ng Poon Chew, died of a heart attack the day before his sixty-fifth birthday. The minister, lecturer, editor, and essayist had traveled America speaking and writing on behalf of Chinese Americans about the degrading immorality of exclusion laws and worked tirelessly as the managing editor of his newspaper *Chung Sai Yat Po* until the end. He was survived by his widow and five children.

After staying in Oakland for some time following the disaster, seven-year-old Lily Soo-Hoo's parents decided to relocate her and her ten siblings to San Rafael, where her minister father began a new mission and wrote articles for *Chung Sai Yat Po* and where, as she would later recall, "there was not as much racial discrimination and prejudice." Lily's birth certificate was destroyed in the fire, but her father was able to get her a new one, and she was educated at the University of California and Oberlin College in Ohio where she met and married William Sung, a fellow student visiting from China. Under US law at the time, her marriage to William, a Chinese citizen, stripped her of her American citizenship, and she moved with her new husband to Shanghai, where he taught at a university and they raised four children, staying even through the occupation of Japan, finally returning to California after World War II and regaining her citizenship. They lived in Berkeley until William's passing in 1967, after which Lily Sung settled in Palo Alto. There she was interviewed in 1980 about the earthquake and fire and vividly remembered being "too frightened" and her mother and father calming her and her older sister, walking her from the flames for two days and nights ("We could feel the fire on our faces, even several blocks away") before finally escaping on a ferry. "And when I smell hot coffee now," she noted, it still brought back to her the feeling of relief she had felt as a seven-year-old when Red Cross workers greeted her family in Oakland, finally safe from the "burning city." Lily suffered a stroke in 1987 and passed in 1993.

Lee Yoke Suey, still bearing the scar of a guardsman's bayonet inflicted when retrieving his birth certificate before the flames destroyed his home, brought his family back to the new Chinatown where he worked again as an export merchant for Levi Strauss and the Haas Brothers. Lee Yoke Suey took his wife,

Lee Wong Shee, and their six children back to visit her family in China, but on a return trip without them to the city for business in 1922, he died of liver cancer during the crossing. When his family returned after him, the children were allowed entry but Wong Shee was detained—as a widow born in China she had no legal status. She was jailed on Angel Island, a "victim of technicalities of the immigration laws," as a newspaper would report. An attorney for the Haas Brothers was able to stop her deportation, but her detention appeal took more than a year, where she was separated from her young children who were taken in and cared for by families in Chinatown, able only to see their mother during occasional fifteen-minute visits. After fifteen and a half months, Wong Shee was released and reunited with her children in Chinatown.

Legal walls to immigrants from China were not torn down in San Francisco or the United States until 1943, and then only because China was an ally against Japan, war years that also saw the illegal detention and forced relocation of Japanese Americans into "internment camps" for three years, including more than five thousand from San Francisco's neighborhood of Japantown, which formed soon after the earthquake and fire. It was not until the Immigration and Nationality Act of 1965 that legal quotas on immigration from Asia were finally lifted, even though discrimination continued against Chinese and Japanese residents of the city, and anti-Asian violence continues to this day. More than seventy thousand current residents of San Francisco's Chinatown live and work in the same heart of the city where Lee Yoke Suey and Lily Soo-Hoo were born and where Lew Hing ran his cannery and Ng Poon Chew printed his newspaper, a physical neighborhood entirely rebuilt after the fire, but a strong community unbroken for more than a century and a half.

Many writers and photographers who observed the earthquake and fire and made it possible for others in distant places or later times to also see lived to cover other grand places, historic figures, and pivotal events, but their names would forever be linked to 1906. Photographer Arnold Genthe at first resisted the calls of friends in the East to relocate, signing a five-year lease on a Clay Street cottage near the Presidio—attracted more by the "fine old scrub-oak" in the garden than the space itself—which he refitted as a studio for portrait work. But when his lease expired in 1911, he moved to New York City and established a portrait studio on Fifth Avenue where he became one of the most sought-after portrait photographers of his time with subjects including President Wilson, former president Roosevelt, John D. Rockefeller, dancer and choreographer Isadora Duncan and her troupe, and the actress Greta Garbo.

He traveled and photographed throughout South America and Europe and published a memoir, *As I Remember*. Genthe returned to the city—his adopted hometown—in 1937 and told the *Chronicle* he had been hospitalized with a serious illness in recent months, but "[s]ince breathing San Francisco air I have improved more in a single week than in all the months they worked over me." But his health worsened, and while visiting friends in Connecticut in 1942, he died of a coronary occlusion at the age of seventy-three.

Charmian and Jack London continued their adventurous life and literary partnership, traveling the South Seas on their yacht and taking a sailboat around Cape Horn. Jack published more books edited by Charmian, and Charmian published short stories and books documenting their travels. In 1910 Charmian gave birth to their daughter, who died of birthing complications within two days; her subsequent pregnancies ended in miscarriages. Their custom-built dream house on their Glen Ellen ranch also burned down just before they could move in. Jack's drinking grew heavier, his health declined, and he died of kidney failure in 1916. For all his literary accomplishments—including the acclaimed novel *The Call of the Wild*—he was paid more for his 2,500-word article on the 1906 earthquake and fire than any other work. Charmian lived another thirty-nine years, continued to write—including a biography of Jack London—and was ever a vigilant guardian of his legacy. After a stroke and a broken hip resulting from a fall, she passed at eighty-three in 1955 in their home on the Glen Ellen ranch. Charmian Kittredge London was, in the words of her biographer, "a woman ahead of her time, not afraid to break the rules set for women in her day."

The very next year, James Hopper also passed. He and his wife had left San Francisco in 1907 for the literary colony in Carmel-by-the-Sea, where friends of his had recently settled, including George Sterling, Mary Austin, and Sinclair Lewis. From there he wrote short stories for *McClure's Magazine* and *Sunset* and published four novels. As he had in the Philippines, Hopper worked during the First World War as a correspondent on the front lines, reporting for *Collier's* from the trenches of the Western Front where American soldiers remembered him as the man who had told the story of the Great San Francisco Earthquake, and when he joined them in their first attack on German lines across no-man's-land under fire, according to George C. Marshall, then a young staff officer, a group of German soldiers surrendered to Hopper who was "embarrassed" because he had only "a pencil with which to receive them." Hopper returned to Carmel after the war, continued writing—articles, short stories, and another novel—raised a son and three daughters with his wife, and served as a local director of the WPA Federal Writers' Project. When Hopper passed in Carmel at the age of eighty in 1956, he was remembered as a "lawyer, war correspondent, football coach and teacher," as a "quarterback of the famous California football team which beat Stanford by the score of 52–0 in 1898" (the margin of victory having grown over the years from the actual score of 22–0), and as one of "California's authentically great men" who "contributed largely to California's reputation as a home and an inspiration to famous writers."

On April 18 of that year, San Francisco kicked off a five-day "Festival of Progress" to mark the fiftieth anniversary of the disaster, acclaiming the city's "rise from the ashes" with a ceremony at Lotta's Fountain, a twenty-four-foot-tall, gold-brown-painted cast-iron drinking fountain and a downtown connection to the city's first life. It stood then roughly where it does today and has for the past 147 years, on a Market Street pedestrian island across from the Palace Hotel where Kearny and Geary Streets intersect. The fountain was a gift to San Francisco from resident and nationally renowned actress Charlotte "Lotta" Crabtree in 1875 "to the use and benefit of inhabitants of San Francisco, henceforth and for all time." In its early years it saw the West Coast's first skyscrapers—the de Young Chronicle Building and the Spreckels Call Building—ascend beside it and across the street. It witnessed the destruction of the city all around it and the rebuilding that followed. It became a rendezvous point for friends and the host for commemorations, protests, political speeches, Days of '49 celebrations, liberty loan rallies during the First World War, and war bond rallies during the Second. When visitors during the 1915 Panama–Pacific International Exposition asked where one could find a drink of water in the city, the *Chronicle* answered, "Lotta's Fountain!" And when world-famous Italian opera soprano Luisa Tetrazzini was in a contract dispute with Oscar Hammerstein, she gave a free public concert on Christmas Eve 1910 from a stage beside the fountain to a crowd of San Franciscans that reportedly numbered a quarter million.

And at 5:12 a.m. on April 18, 1956, Lotta's Fountain was again the center of ceremony as a wreath was "placed on the fountain in memory of those who lost their lives" by the South of Market Boys—an organization of men who had grown up in pre-1906 South of Market and had begun formal April 18 commemorations first in 1926 for the twentieth anniversary, then again in 1931 for the twenty-fifth, both at the Civic Auditorium. They subsequently turned these formal events into an annual April 18 gathering and wreath laying at Lotta's Fountain, a tradition that endures to this day.

And the occasion was not just a look back at the disaster or salute to the city's resilience but a forward-looking gaze at the dangers attendant to the next big earthquake. A half century of advances in seismology—of elastic rebound and propagation of seismic waves and continental drift theory soon to develop into a fuller understanding of plate tectonics—armed scientists and engineers and city planners with a greater understanding of the threat, and the physical reminders of its inevitability were frequent. Tremors intermittently rolled through the ground beneath San Francisco from earthquakes centered far up north or down south, sensations almost commonplace to residents. As a newspaper reported on the eve of the anniversary, "Californians long ago learned to live with such disturbances." But the length of the San Andreas Fault that had ripped apart and unleashed so much devastation in 1906 sat eerily quiet for a half century, even as the Pacific and North American Plates continued to move past one another as before, loading the rock masses along the fault with increasing amounts of strain, and experts knew a fracture was inevitable. The California Office of Civil Defense spent the April 18 anniversary hosting an all-day conference on "California's Next Earthquake." Dr. Charles Richter himself said "California may go 10 years or more without a San Andreas quake—but one could come tomorrow."

Tomorrow came less than a year later in March 1957 when a magnitude-5.3 earthquake struck near Daly City where the San Andreas Fault straightens from a slight bend. While the fault is mostly straight where it runs alongside San Francisco, down south as it runs north-northwestward up toward the west side of the Bay Area, it steps left gradually in a restraining bend about sixty miles south of San Francisco, causing the faster-moving Pacific Plate on the left to collide diagonally with the slower North American Plate to the right, resulting in a compression strike-slip fault (where rock masses on each side are both running into and moving past each other), pressure that has over millions of years thrust up the Santa Cruz Mountains. And around Daly City, the fault sidesteps back to the right in a releasing bend where the two plates slowly pull apart as they move past each other. It was there where the fault fractured, collapsing a roadway along Lake Merced, killing one person and injuring forty. The shaking was strong enough in San Francisco to stop the clock on the Ferry Building "for the first time since April 18, 1906," as the *Examiner* would report, but although some older residents reportedly said, "[T]he shock seemed just as violent" as 1906, a seismologist studying data from the seismograph station in Berkeley declared it "a far cry from the 1906 San Francisco earthquake."

And the relatively mild shock was quickly forgotten. The clock was repaired within hours and the Ferry Building stood undamaged, still an enduring landmark of the city's past and an affirming symbol of resilience even as progress dethroned it as the West Coast's busiest transit terminal. In 1958, twenty-one years after the opening of the San Francisco–Oakland Bay Bridge and twenty after the opening of the Golden Gate Bridge, 108 years of ferry service officially ended. The Ferry Building was converted into commercial space, its grand nave subdivided into offices. And with bus and rail service replacing ferries and an explosion in automobile traffic, the state's first double-decked freeway—the Cypress Freeway—was opened on the far side of the Bay Bridge in Oakland. And the double-decked Embarcadero Freeway was built in San Francisco, running from the Bay Bridge up the Embarcadero (former East Street) to Broadway (with plans to connect to the Golden Gate Bridge in a future phase). It blocked the iconic Ferry Building, cut off views of the bay from much of downtown, and was—as the *Chronicle* complained the year it went up—a "hideous monstrosity."

As the San Francisco skyline changed, progress altered or toppled much of what 1906 had not. The Call Building, the tallest of the former city, was by 1907 restored to its former glory, once again "the handsomest office building in the world." And with height restrictions on steel-framed structures removed, developers raced to buy more of the sky. By 1922, the Standard Oil Building became the city's tallest, rising twenty-two stories above Bush Street. In 1925, the Pacific Telephone & Telegraph Company Building rose twenty-six stories. Then in 1927, the Russ Building topped them all with thirty-one. In 1937, with more space needed, the shrinking Call Building was "modernized" with an art deco façade and its four-story dome was removed and replaced with seven new floors. As *Architectural Digest* proclaimed of its unrecognizable new visage, "Economic forces prove stronger than earthquakes."

In 1955, the 103-year-old Montgomery Block—a century since it was the tallest in the old city—was dedicated as a state historical landmark, and a plaque was affixed to its outer wall: "This, San Francisco's first fireproof building, erected in 1853 by Henry Wager Halleck, was the headquarters for many outstanding lawyers, financiers, writers, actors, and artists," closing with "Escaping destruction in the fire of 1906, the building is preserved in memory of those who lived and worked in it." The plaque was unveiled by eighty-four-year-old Oliver Stidger, still a tenant forty-nine years after he convinced soldiers to spare the building from demolition. But four years later, both met their end—Mr. Stidger to illness and the building to a wrecking ball. A parking lot sat in its place for a decade until the "construction of a towering pyramid of commercial offices for modern day pharaohs of finance and industry," the Transamerica Pyramid, opened in 1971 as the city's tallest, a place it would hold for nearly a half century. Two years later, the original plaque from the Montgomery Block was placed in the Transamerica lobby, where it can still be seen today.

Ever wary of the danger constantly building in the earth's crust beneath the city, hundreds of emergency officials from more than two dozen federal, state, and local agencies in the Bay Area ran "a practice drill" in August 1989, streamlining communications and logistics in a simulation of "shattered hospitals, wrecked neighborhoods, blocked roads, out-of-commission phone systems and raging fires." The practice sessions were, in the words of the local FEMA associate director, "the biggest of their kind ever held," and they modeled scenarios possible with the reality of "a great earthquake," which experts gave a fifty-fifty chance of striking on either the Hayward or the San Andreas Fault within the next thirty years. And reality took only sixty days to arrive.

It was 5:04 p.m. on Tuesday, October 17, and the Army's Honor Guard from the Presidio was on the field of Candlestick Park to present the flag for the national anthem to begin Game 3 of the World Series between the Oakland A's and the San Francisco Giants. "There was a loud noise and we looked up to see the plane going overhead," a sergeant in the Honor Guard described, and "it was like the plane was causing the shaking—but no, that's not the plane." The ground started shaking violently. ABC's live coverage was interrupted as broadcaster Al Michaels exclaimed, "I tell you what, we're having an earth—" With a loud roar like a freight train, shockwaves rolled beneath the stadium. The Army sergeant "looked down on the ground to see whether or not there was a crack between my feet that's how strong it felt."

The earth's crust had ruptured sixty miles south of San Francisco where the San Andreas Fault bends gradually through the Santa Cruz Mountains. The epicenter of the magnitude-6.9 earthquake was near the range's highest peak—Loma Prieta—and surface waves shot through the ground northward up the peninsula through San Francisco for approximately fifteen seconds. The brick wall of a four-story apartment building on 6th Street—along the same South of Market block where so many lodging houses had collapsed eighty-three years before—peeled away and fell, crushing five people to death in their cars and on the sidewalk. Residential buildings in the Marina District—built on made ground of bay mud and clay backfilled in preparation for the 1915 Panama–Pacific International Exposition—sank, and as if echoing the past, gas pipes and water mains fractured in the liquefaction. Firefighters rescued survivors from ruins and evacuated residents in range of gas leaks, and when fires erupted, water pressure from even AWSS hydrants was lacking. As goes the quote often attributed to Mark Twain: "History does not repeat itself, but it rhymes."

There was no repeat of 1906, and the rhyming was lessened by eighty years of preventive measures. The fireboat *Phoenix* supplied firefighters with sufficient water to keep the blaze in the Marina District contained to a single block. And the Central Fire Alarm Station's generator power kept more than two thousand fire alarm boxes operating. City Water Department workers closed, isolated, and began repair on valves to broken mains even through a 5.2-magnitude aftershock. And after power to hydropneumatic pumping stations was restored, AWSS operators were able to pump salt water to the Jones Street tank to restore high-pressure water supply to the Marina District within four hours. And while more than fifty people were arrested for looting, the district attorney said he would "ask for the maximum bail and the maximum sentences," promising due process instead of summary executions.

3,757 people were injured and sixty-three were killed—one motorist after the collapse of a section of the Bay Bridge's upper lanes (only a week before a scheduled retrofitting) and forty-two over in Oakland, where nearly a mile-long stretch of the Cypress Freeway's upper deck pancaked onto the lower, crushing more than two dozen cars and their occupants. Damages were measured in the billions of dollars—roughly half in San Francisco. Sixty buildings in the Marina District were destroyed or deemed uninhabitable, and residents were given only fifteen minutes to return and retrieve belongings. And the Embarcadero Freeway was so badly damaged it was eventually demolished, clearing the concrete monstrosity from the downtown landscape, freeing neighborhood streets from its ramps and connecting the city with the Ferry Building and waterfront once again.

Compared by magnitude to 1906, the Loma Prieta earthquake of 1989 was one-tenth the size and one-thirtieth the strength in energy released. And the rupture was twenty-five miles long, roughly one-twelfth the length of the 1906 rupture. Aside from that relatively short portion—and the even shorter portion that had produced the 1956 Daly City earthquake—the 296-mile stretch of the San Andreas Fault that had torn apart and unleashed so much devastation in 1906 was still locked, with strain on each side still building.

* * *

Six months and a day later, a handful of the "dwindling band of survivors" of 1906 again gathered with other San Franciscans at Lotta's Fountain to remember the Big One and what they were now calling the previous year's earthquake, the "Pretty Big One." Among them was eighty-nine-year-old Cora Luchetti, whose father, Rafaelo Paolinelli, was the fruit merchant Officer Harry Schmidt saw crushed by the falling brick wall in the first moments of the earthquake. Cora had been only five at the time, at home with her mother and brothers, and she recounted for a reporter the moment she found out her father had been killed: "When his horse and buggy came back, somebody else was driving it," she noted. "My mother knew then that he was dead."

On April 18, 1996, Cora was among twenty-five survivors to make it back for the ninetieth anniversary. Also attending was Helen Huntington Perrin, one hundred years old, who still carried vivid memories of her late father, Pliny Huntington, taking her and her mother and brother up to the roof of the Fairmont Hotel ninety years before to watch the fires. Because the fire gutted the Fairmont a few hours later, ownership changed, and it denied her father the opportunity to serve as the hotel manager and dashed her dream of staying in the Fairmont (something she later said she could never afford even as an adult). In 1994, the Fairmont Hotel fulfilled her childhood dream by inviting her and her family to celebrate her ninety-ninth birthday in the dining room and stay overnight in a suite at 1907 rates ($10 for the suite, 30 cents for breakfast, 45 cents for lunch, and $1.30 for dinner). In 1997, the Fairmont extended the same courtesy for her 102nd birthday. Helen passed away in 2002 at the age of 106. Cora Luchetti passed at the age of 100 in 2000, just months after attending her last 1906 ceremony at Lotta's Fountain—an event her family said she never missed. By the centennial ceremony in 2006, only five survivors were present, ranging in age from 101 to 109, and brought to the event by police escort.

With the arrival of April 2006, San Francisco contended with its own incomplete record of the disaster, a century of discounting lives lost and ignoring the ashes it buried beneath its rebuilding. The Board of Supervisors unanimously voted to "set aside the death toll of 478" and amend it to a more accurate number. The resolution was coauthored by Gladys Hansen, who had spent nearly half a century as a librarian and two decades as the city's archivist with the San Francisco Public Library combing through newspaper archives and voter registration lists and records of the health department, coroner's office, and funeral homes to count the uncounted dead. By creating a three-by-five card for every name, she had compiled a list of those who died and its total soon passed the original "official" count. She sent bulletins out to historical and genealogical societies throughout the country requesting members who lost family in San Francisco in 1906 to contact her, resulting in "what seemed like thousands of letters." By 1985, she had reportedly collected "the names of 1,500 persons" who perished in the earthquake and fire, and eventually by her own count the number exceeded three thousand.

After her 1992 retirement, Gladys Hansen worked as curator of her Virtual Museum of the City of San Francisco and continued to build on the data she had typed and written onto the hundreds of index cards at the public library, compiling a "1906 List of Dead & Survivors." Armed with Hansen's claim to have "tallied more than 3,400 fatalities," the Board of Supervisors, in setting aside the original death toll, invited "interested members of the public" to "use the resources of the San Francisco History Center of the Public Library, as well as other local history repositories, to establish a certified death count, with the names of all the victims." And the board requested a "certified death count and list of names be presented to the Board of Supervisors for a vote on amending the toll" prior to April 18, 2006.

But that count and list was never presented. And Gladys sadly passed away in 2017. The index cards completed with such care by her still fill drawers at the San Francisco Public Library, containing more than 600 names and 185 unknowns ("John/Jane Doe"). And her Virtual Museum's "Integrated List All Deaths" of 1906—last updated in 2010—contains 992 names and 75 unknowns, although—as with the index cards at the library—many are listed multiple times under alternate spellings, and several names are included of individuals who committed suicide, died of natural causes weeks or months after the disaster, or were later determined to have survived. Given the untold numbers of undocumented deaths—especially South of Market and in Chinatown—the exact number of people killed in those three days in San Francisco in 1906 can never be known. To this day there is no "certified death count," but thanks to Gladys Hansen's work, the historical record of 1906 is far more complete.

Also part of the city's commemoration of the 100th anniversary in 2006 were events in earthquake preparedness planning, the largest of which was a three-day conference organized by the Earthquake Engineering Research Institute, Seismological Society of America, and California Governor's Office of Emergency Services, and attended by more than 2,500 scientists, engineers, and local, state, and federal emergency response planners. "When the Big One Strikes Again," a study presented at the conference, predicted that a repeat of a magnitude-7.9 earthquake striking the Bay Area—with a more than tenfold increase in population since 1906—would cause an estimated 800 to 3,400 fatalities and more than $100 billion in damages through four counties. Focused on "seismically vulnerable" buildings as the "primary risk to life safety" in an earthquake, the study recommended more seismic retrofitting of older buildings. "The Bay Area is probably better prepared than most urban areas for a natural disaster," the conference chairman concluded, "but it's not prepared enough."

As certain as tides and irregular as weather, earthquakes shake the ground of California nearly every day, even if most are imperceptible. Since 1906, more than thirty major earthquakes with epicenters in the state have occurred with a moment magnitude of 6.0 or greater, and at least eight of 7.0 or greater. Most of these have struck up north near Cape Mendocino, where the Pacific Plate meets the smaller Gorda Plate as it collides with (or slides beneath) the North American Plate, forming the Mendocino Fracture Zone. Or down south in the "creeping section" of the San Andreas Fault, an eighty-mile stretch from San Juan Bautista down to Parkfield, where the rock masses continuously release the strain between the plates by rupturing at intermittent intervals to accommodate movement averaging nearly one inch per year. But the length of the San Andreas Fault running alongside San Francisco has not ruptured since 1906. And to the east, the seventy-four-mile-long Hayward Fault—which runs through Oakland and Berkeley and crosses five highways, railroads, BART's Berkeley Hills Tunnel, and cuts directly through the middle of California Memorial Stadium—has not ruptured since 1868, and scientists warn "a large quake there is inevitable." For well more than a century, the Pacific and North American Plates have continued to move, loading the rock masses on both sides of both faults with increasing amounts of strain. That another big earthquake will strike the Bay Area again is not a question but a certainty.

Since 1868 and 1906 and 1989, San Francisco leaders have grappled with the tension between the benefit and expense of seismic safeguards, or, as one city official put it, the balance between "life safety and socioeconomic impact." Since 1989, the city has passed ordinances requiring seismic retrofitting of "soft-story" buildings and unreinforced masonry in structures and approved bond issues for landlords and property owners to obtain low-cost loans for retrofit expenses. The soft-story ordinance, as the *Chronicle* reported in 2019, "has since become a model for other earthquake-prone cities," such as Oakland, which passed its own in 2018.

To address an aging water main infrastructure and minimize breaks in water transmission and distribution mains in the event of an earthquake, engineers with the San Francisco Public Utility Commission have worked to replace old, brittle cast-iron pipes with ductile iron, which has more tensile strength, and sections are now connected with flexible joints. Additionally, the ninety-million-gallon Sunset Reservoir underwent a seismic upgrade, thirty new emergency water cisterns were added throughout the city, and miles of pipes were added to its AWSS, connected with the Sunset Reservoir, to supply western neighborhoods—the Richmond and Sunset Districts—with an emergency high-pressure water supply for fire suppression and drinking water.

And on October 17, 2019—the thirtieth anniversary of the Loma Prieta earthquake—a public earthquake early warning system was launched for California after nearly two decades of development. A network of ground motion sensors throughout the state can detect an earthquake's initial primary waves and transmit data to an earthquake alert center where the location and size of the shock are calculated and an alert is sent through the wireless emergency alert system and the ShakeAlert® app to users' devices: "Earthquake. Drop, cover, hold on. Shaking expected." Oregon and Washington were added by 2021, giving the entire West Coast access to advance warning of incoming earthquakes. While predicting where and when an earthquake will strike is impossible, even a few seconds of advance warning can, as was reported on the system's launch, "grant people enough time to slow down public transit, discontinue surgeries, open firehouse doors, stop elevators, or drop and cover."

The annual remembrances of 1906 continued every April 18, attended by mayors, fire chiefs, and the shrinking ranks of 1906 survivors who showed up and told their stories until the last one attended in 2013 and the last one passed in 2016, leaving the city itself as the lone survivor. And parts of its skyline still echo the past. The tall letters "Palace Hotel" shine over Market Street atop the corner of the grand nine-story beaux arts–style hotel, which since rebuilt and reopened in 1909 has occupied the same footprint over the past 113 years as the original Palace did for 31. The Fairmont—its gutted interior restored in time to open on the first anniversary of the earthquake—still stands atop Nob Hill across the street from the only surviving mansion, the James C. Flood Mansion, now home to an elite social club. And the St. Francis with its completed third wing still looms over Union Square and the Dewey Monument. The "Old Mint," which has not operated as a US mint since 1937 and still stands on 6th and Mission Streets, is both a California and National Historic Landmark now owned by the city. And the Old Post Office on 7th and

Mission, restored after 1906 and again after the 1989 earthquake, is still the grand home of the US Court of Appeals for the Ninth Circuit.

Beneath the shade of century-old trees atop Russian Hill are a few of the houses saved by residents from dynamite and fire; three of them stand side by side on Green Street between Leavenworth and Jones. One at 1045 Green, another at 1055 Green (built in 1860 but redesigned in 1916). And the third at 1067 Green near Leavenworth, where the unmistakable eight-sided roof rises behind a plaque informing visitors they are seeing the "Feusier Octagon House, Built by George Kenney, Circa 1852, Occupied by the Feusier Family for Over 80 Years." Louis died in the home in 1917 at the age of ninety-one, and his son, Clarence, still lived in it in the summer of 1949 when a *Chronicle* reporter approached the seventy-eight-year-old and found him tending the garden, more than happy to speak about his family home and the fight to save it back in 1906: "'The house may not have suffered from the earthquake,' [Clarence] concluded with a wry shake of his head, 'but it certainly got an awful shake from that dynamite.'" Clarence died two years later, as his father had, in the home, and his family's five-generation, eighty-year occupancy ended after his funeral services in "the high-ceilinged front room which overlooks Green Street."

Fires reached every block of what was rebuilt into the present-day Financial District, and almost none of its buildings predate 1906. Almost. Near where the Transamerica Pyramid ascends to mark the footprint of the old Montgomery Block, a few battered survivors still stand in Jackson Square as monuments to the repeated, three-day fight to save that two-and-a-half-square block of the old city against fires from all four directions. The Ganella Building at 728 Montgomery, built in 1853, still stands, as does the Golden Era Building at 732, built in 1852 on the site of one of the buildings destroyed by the 1851 fire. The Belli Building at 722 Montgomery was built next door the same year, originally serving as a tobacco warehouse, then later as a theater where Lotta Crabtree performed, and eventually it became famed attorney Melvin Belli's office.

Hotaling & Co. survived the earthquake and fire but not Prohibition, and its old warehouse, the Hotaling Building, still stands on Jackson Street beside the alleyway renamed Hotaling Place. In 1992, a historic marker was dedicated on the outside wall proclaiming the building and its liquor were spared "due to a mile long fire hose laid from Fisherman's Wharf over Telegraph Hill by the U.S. Navy." The marker closes with the most popular passage to arise in the disaster's aftermath, a poem still recited by many San Franciscans:

If, as they say, God spanked the town
For being over frisky,
Why did he burn the churches down
And save Hotaling's whisky?

It was not yet 4:30 a.m. on April 18, 2022, when I arrived at Lotta's Fountain for the commemoration of the 116th anniversary of the earthquake and fire, the long-standing annual tradition broken only recently by the COVID-19 pandemic, which had caused the cancellation of the 2020 ceremony and forced a more subdued 2021 event with fewer attendees. When I arrived, the fountain looked as if it was the center of a movie set. Workers stood on stepladders training the bright beams of spotlights atop tall poles onto the fountain, and before it a microphone atop a stand was wired to speakers. Parked along the Market Street side were two SFFD engines and a ladder truck. Police officers with reflective safety vests over their uniforms redirected the occasional car as a growing crowd gathered around the curbed island from all sides, reporters and city officials, chiefs of the fire department and police department in their dress uniforms, and quite a few spectators in 1906-era costume: bustle dresses and feathered hats and folded parasols and corsets and bow ties and top hats and tails and vintage leather firefighter helmets and police custodian helmets.

Within a few minutes, the crowd was at least twelve deep on all sides. A few wore pins with pictures and names on their jackets, honoring relatives or loved ones who were 1906 survivors. Many wore whatever they could throw on at that early hour—sweatshirts, flannels, Giants jackets—and a good number were in formal wear. The lady standing beside me was dressed in a long coat and feathered hat, her hair and makeup were impeccable, and her gloved hand clutched the leash of her small dog beside her. "I never miss this," she told me. "Glad it's back this year." A man on the other side of me in a sweater and jeans had brought his young son: "Woke him up early so he could experience this before school."

At 4:45 a.m. the master of ceremonies—former 49ers stadium announcer Bob Sarlatte, wearing a SFFD helmet—grabbed the microphone and proclaimed, "Once again you hearty, crazy folks have come together at this ungodly hour to remember and honor the memories of those hearty San Franciscans who survived being tossed from their beds one hundred and sixteen years ago this morning." After reciting a timeline of events for the three days of the earthquake and fire, he recognized the special guests, including ninety-three-year-old Joe McCaughey, the grandnephew of Eugene Schmitz. And Sarlatte introduced each speaker, including former mayor Willie Brown, the police chief, the sheriff, the executive director of emergency management, and Fire Chief Jeanine Nicholson, who assured the crowd, "We are resilient, and the San Francisco Fire Department is ready for anything that comes our way, whether it be fires, medical calls, or earthquakes." The last speaker was Mayor London Breed, the city's forty-fifth mayor, dressed for the event in an Edwardian dress and coat and feathered hat, who spoke about how the people of the city came together during the recent COVID-19 shutdown, and "although we may not have anyone still alive from the 1906 earthquake, this is a city that will still remember, remember the past and what makes San Francisco so extraordinary."

At 5:12 a.m. the crowd observed a moment of silence "to remember those who perished and those who survived to rebuild San Francisco." After a few seconds of still, solemn quiet, the siren of a fire truck sounded to mark the moment of the earthquake's impact. The microphone was then handed to Donna Huggins, dressed and in character as Lillie Hitchcock Coit—an early patron of the city's volunteer firefighters and namesake and benefactor of Coit Tower—and as she has at every annual ceremony since 1976, Huggins led the crowd in singing "San Francisco" from the 1936 film of the same name. And a flowered wreath was tied to the fountain to mark the 116th commemoration of 1906.

From there it was announced that the morning's tradition of commemorations would move down to 20th and Church Streets in a half hour for "the annual gilding of the fire hydrant that saved the Mission District." I rode BART from the Montgomery Street Station down to the stop at 16th and Mission and took the remaining eight blocks through the Mission District on foot—south along Valencia Street past the former site of the Valencia Hotel rescue and then along 18th Street where hoses had once been stretched by firefighters and volunteers to save their neighborhood. Every bit of ground I covered by foot and rail from Lotta's Fountain to that point had all once burned, just eighteen of more than five hundred blocks of the massive "burned district." I ascended Dolores Street a block, then took a pathway through Dolores Park to Church Street and uphill another block toward the crowd already assembled around the golden hydrant, the "Little Giant," the hydrant Ernest Edwards had led firefighters to on the third morning of the fire, the hydrant that helped save the Mission District.

Donna Huggins, still in period costume as Lillie Hitchcock Coit, emceed at the microphone, and with a can of gold spray paint in hand, invited people to step onto the sidewalk and gild the hydrant. One by one people stepped from the crowd, took the can and microphone, and dedicated their own moment at the hydrant to specific people. Some spoke in memory of relatives, of recently passed friends "who never missed this event," or "in thanks for all the first responders who still keep us safe." One of the fire chiefs stepped forward, Chief of Operations Robert Postel, a fourth-generation firefighter, and he gilded the hydrant on behalf of his father, the former chief of the fire department, both of his grandfathers, and his great-grandfather, who survived the earthquake and fire as a child and died in the line of duty in 1937. And another man walked forward and said, "This is for my great-grandfather Rafaelo Paolinelli, a fruit merchant who was killed when a wall collapsed on him the morning of the earthquake."

After he stepped back to the street, I met him. Tony was his name, and he introduced me to his brother Terry, who also helped gild the hydrant. They were eager to tell me about their great-grandfather Rafaelo Paolinelli and Rafaelo's children, including "Babe" Pinelli ("[T]hey shortened the longer Italian name to Pinelli," one of them explained), who was a Major League Baseball umpire who called Don Larsen's perfect game in the 1956 World Series. And they told me of Rafaelo's daughter—their grandmother—Cora Luchetti. They shared how she told them she was awoken by the earthquake and knew her father had died when his horse and wagon came home driven by someone else. And here on the 116th anniversary of their great-grandfather's death, Tony and Terry were carrying on their grandmother's tradition of never missing an April 18 anniversary.

Behind the crowd and parked against the inclined Church Street curb was a large SFFD fire engine, capable of reaching an alarm three times as fast as the fire engines of 1906, and able to pump with four times the power and battle a blaze with more water in less time. Gathered beside it were a handful of young firefighters, the living heirs of their 1906 predecessors, armed now with far better communications and equipment and technology. As a wreath was placed on the hydrant, shiny with its newest coat of gold paint, the young firefighters stood beside their engine, bareheaded in heavy turnout coats, a few watching the remembrance of the past but all fully ready in the present for the next alarm, prepared to play their part ensuring no firestorm ever again visits the city, no other hydrant is honored as a district's sole source of water in any future fire, and memorial wreaths laid by future generations of San Franciscans bear no year beyond 1906.

Acknowledgments

FROM MY EARLIEST study of source materials on the San Francisco earthquake and fire of 1906, it was clear this was not a story about houses or tall buildings but of the lives lived in them and lost in too many. Although I began with the goal of chronicling a natural disaster, even my early research highlighted causes for devastation reaching deeper than a study of science or geology or tectonic plates or movements along faults could explain, a loss of human life and property taken not by a natural event but by the actions or inaction of men in charge after too many dire warnings. Thousands of pages of archival materials mapped the narrative back through decades of decisions by individual men—to act, to forget, to neglect, to profit, to warn, to ignore—through destructive earthquakes and six devastating fires until one earth-shattering minute exposed fault lines engineered by city leaders between the favored and the forgotten. And after years of grappling with a growing list of names of the fallen and causes of death or details of their final moments, I scrapped my efforts to estimate a number. Because no matter how many people were killed, they died one by one. Their names matter, the number does not.

My first call was to Gladys Hansen, retired librarian and city archivist. She was most gracious with her time to speak with me, and after each topic we covered, she returned to the man she credited most with saving not just the waterfront but the lives of many evacuees and the city, Lieutenant Frederick

Freeman. After her passing, her son Richard Hansen was very kind to speak with me on numerous occasions and helpful in sharing materials and information from the Virtual Museum of the City of San Francisco he still maintains. As with anyone who conducts research on 1906, I stood on the shoulders of Gladys Hansen's work and am thankful for the history she gathered and preserved. I am grateful to both Richard and his late mother, Gladys, and I am hopeful the latest, most complete list of names of the 1906 dead compiled by both will one day be made public.

It was an honor to be assisted by the late Charles Fracchia, historian and author and teacher and founder of the San Francisco Historical Society. He told me early on that the story of the earthquake and fire "is a tricky one" to tackle, and his writings and knowledge and guidance and advice and encouragement were essential in not only gaining a fuller understanding of the disaster but also of San Francisco's lightning-paced half century of history from the gold rush to 1906. I was one of the last of a long line of fortunate individuals who learned from him, and thanks to the work he left us, the learning continues.

My research visits to the city never felt like work, not only for its fascinating history and bottomless opportunities for exploration but especially because of the people. Among those who made my time productive and research rewarding was Susan Goldstein, city archivist at the San Francisco Public Library. Her work in collecting and preserving so much diverse San Francisco history in the library's San Francisco History Center is monumental, and I am humbled by her personal assistance and guidance. I thank Christina Moretta, photo curator, for making so many unscanned photographs from the library's 1906 collection available for me, and I also thank the scanning department manager Lisa Palella for scanning them.

Working from the East Coast presents a logistical challenge when most research material is on the West Coast, and between research trips to the city I relied greatly on the assistance of Marisa Louie Lee, a San Francisco researcher who specializes in Asian American history and immigration and naturalization records. I could not have completed the research in the time I did without her help, and I am also grateful to her for sharing with me wonderful publications and sources covering the history of Chinatown.

I thank Frances Kaplan, reference and outreach librarian for the California Historical Society, for assisting me with my many requests for materials and for making my visits there so productive. I also thank Debra Kaufman, the society's rights and reproductions coordinator, for her assistance. I am grateful to Brienne Wong and Palma You of the Chinese Historical Society of America for being so patient in answering my questions and assisting me with their collections. I thank Lauren Menzies of the Society of California Pioneers for her assistance. And I am grateful to Stephanie Bayless, director of the National Archives at San Francisco in San Bruno, and her staff for their hard work, especially Charles Miller, research archivist, who was able to locate documents I requested even with his reduced staff during the COVID-19 shutdown, and John Seamans, archives technician, whose assistance scanning documents and sending them while the building was still closed to the public helped me immensely.

The 1906 earthquake and fire was an intersectional event of geology and physics and emergency response and city planning and engineering, and its full story cannot be understood or told without consulting with experts and professionals in many diverse fields. I first thank Dr. David Russ, geologist and former regional executive for the US Geological Survey, for allowing me to interview him and taking the time to very patiently answer my many questions about tectonic plates and strike-slip faults and compression faults and subduction zones and elastic rebound and primary waves and secondary waves and surface waves and seismic creep and moment magnitude. And I thank him for reviewing portions of the manuscript and correcting my many mistakes. He was and is a deep source of knowledge, and for me his expertise was matched by his patience as a teacher. I also thank geologist Tim Elam for giving me a walking tour of streets and sidewalks on fill land in South of Market and the Financial District. I appreciate him explaining so much about the propagation of seismic waves through alluvial soil and old bay clay, and especially for answering my many questions about the soil or mud or clay or bedrock beneath each building we visited.

I am very grateful to Bill Koenig, who retired from the San Francisco Fire Department as a lieutenant after thirty years of service, including service during the 1989 Loma Prieta earthquake. I have never worked as a firefighter and had no previous understanding of anything involved in firefighting—I did not know how a fire engine works, how hydrants work, had no grasp of pressure or gallons per minute or friction through hose lines, and I certainly knew nothing about turn-of-the-century steam pump engines. So I appreciate Bill sharing his knowledge gained from a career of experience and from his many years of gathering and writing so much of the department's history. I thank him for his patience in my many interviews and answering hundreds of questions by phone and email. And I thank the volunteers at the SFFD Museum and Guardians of the City Museum, including retired captain James Lee. I also thank Lieutenant Jonathan Baxter, the department's public information officer, for connecting me with other members of the department.

I appreciate the courtesy extended to me by Dr. Stephen Tobriner, architectural engineer and professor of architectural history at the University of California. When I read his exceptionally detailed book *Bracing for Disaster*, I discovered just how little I knew about the materials and construction methods in use between 1850 and 1906, and I appreciate him taking the time to speak with me and answer my many questions and review the manuscript. His expertise in structural engineering and knowledge of architectural history are bottomless, and his comments and guidance were indispensable.

While I am a lifelong fan of trains, something I inherited from my grandfather and passed on to one of my two sons, I knew very little about cable cars or electric streetcars. So I appreciate Emiliano Echeverria, the San Francisco (and world) expert on cable cars and author of many books on the city's cable car history, which were invaluable sources, for taking the time to answer my many questions. I also thank Joe Thompson, the "cable car guy," for sharing so much of his knowledge with me and for the vast amount of information on his webpage.

I thank Anne Evers Hitz, whose books on the Ferry Building and the Emporium were wonderful sources of information, for sharing so much history with me about the Ferry Building. I thank antique clock repairman Dorian Clair, who maintains the Ferry Building clock, for answering my questions about the tower's original 1898 clock, which he restored to working condition. I am thankful for the valuable input of Nick Wright, creator and administrator of very informative San Francisco history Facebook groups, who has collected thousands of digital images of the city and assembled digital panoramas from the earliest gold rush years to 1906, and through his years of work has managed to build a database of the history of individual buildings and houses on specific streets. I am grateful to Joyce Kurtz of San Francisco City Guides, Cate Mills of History San José Research Library, and Joe Adkins of the Board of Supervisors Clerk's Office.

Researching an event from more than a century ago can be a lonely endeavor, and the company I kept was voices of the past. The story is not mine to tell; it is theirs, and I have worked to build the narrative with their words. Reading letters and diaries and interviews and testimony and reports and memoirs connected me with the personalities of individuals far beyond the physical reach of the present. So the most rewarding contacts were with members of their families. Richard Torney, great-grandson of Dr. George Torney, was most kind to share information about his great-grandfather as well as photographs taken by Richard's grandfather—Dr. Torney's son, Ned—on his drive through the city the first day of the earthquake and the days following. And Grant Gildroy was very gracious to speak with me about his family's history in the city, their connection with Hotaling & Co., and show me his family photographs of Hotaling's whiskey being saved in barrels rolled from the warehouse. I thank them both immensely.

I thank Robert Postel, SFFD chief of operations and fourth-generation San Francisco firefighter, for taking the time to share with me about his great-grandfathers', two grandfathers', and father's service, as well as his own reasons for becoming a firefighter ("I grew up in firehouses in the city and from as long as I can remember it was the only profession I ever considered"). And I thank Terry and Tony Bosque, whom I met at the gilding of the hydrant in the Mission on April 18, 2022, for sharing their family's stories of their great-grandfather Rafaelo Paolinelli, as well as their own memories of their grandmother Cora Luchetti. And I thank Donna Huggins, whom I met the same morning while she was in character as Lillie Hitchcock Coit, for allowing me to assist in gilding the hydrant. It was an honor I will carry with me always.

I thank Jennifer Allen and her sister Melissa Gunderson for sharing the 1906 letters of their great-grandparents David Henry and Josephine "Josie" Seawall. And I thank Nancy Cedeño for sharing information about her family and the death of her great-grandfather Hiram Daniels. I also thank the following individuals for taking the time to respond to my messages about their family members: Lynda Briggs, whose late father-in-law was the son of Raymond Briggs; Carolyn Walton, the grandniece of James Stetson; and Sarah Finkenstaedt, second great-granddaughter of Grace Roberts Moore.

Historic recognition is owed to mankind's earliest inhabitants of the land that became Yerba Buena and San Francisco. To that end, I acknowledge that the research and outlining and writing and editing of this book was completed on the traditional homelands of indigenous peoples and nations, including the Ramaytush Ohlone, Muwekma Ohlone, Miwok, Munsee Lenape, Lumbee, Skaruhreh/Tuscarora, and Pamlico peoples, who stewarded through generations the lands and waterways of what are now portions of Northern California, New York City, and Eastern North Carolina.

I am grateful to my agent, Sam Fleishman of Literary Artists Representatives, for believing in this project from the first time I suggested it to him, for using his enthusiasm to help it find a home, and for always giving sound advice rooted in a confidence far more unwavering than my own. I thank Daniel Huffman for his work using period Corps of Engineering maps of San Francisco to render a map of the city as it was in 1906. And I thank my editor, Pete Wolverton, who saw the potential in the telling of this true story from the first time I mentioned it to him in New York City in 2016. His faith in the importance of a nonfiction work like this was matched with a critical eye and literary judgment that guided my work continuously along the way to translate the early idea into reality.

I owe a special thanks to my high school friend Eric Holwell, who lives with his family in the Bay Area and has highlighted each of my visits with great local beer and greater company. And I extend my deepest gratitude for family. I thank my parents for encouraging me with this book as they did with the first, and for instilling within me an interest in the past and an unwavering attention to detail. I am grateful to my brother-in-law, Blair Ross, as wise a student of history as I have ever had the good fortune to know, for his own guidance and advice in countless conversations over smooth bourbon and delicious Scotch.

And of course my greatest debt is owed to my sons, Watson and Keegan, and my wife, Jessica. In the spirit of saving the best for last, they are the best and the last.

Notes

ABBREVIATIONS USED
To Cite Select Sources

MANUSCRIPT COLLECTIONS

BL	Bancroft Library, University of California, Berkeley
CHS	California Historical Society, San Francisco
CHSA	Chinese Historical Society of America, San Francisco
CSL	California State Library, Sacramento
LOC	Library of Congress, Manuscripts Division, Washington, DC
NA	National Archives, Washington, DC
NA-SF	National Archives at San Francisco, San Bruno, California
RSS	Recollections of the San Francisco 1906 Earthquake by Stratton Students, Bancroft Library
SCP	Society of California Pioneers, San Francisco
SFPL	San Francisco History Center, San Francisco Public Library, San Francisco
SGC	Selections from Growing Up in the Cities: Oral History Transcripts of Tape-Recorded Interviews, Bancroft Library

MANUSCRIPTS AND PAPERS

Allen	Experiences of Captain (SFFD) R. Allen, Engine 34, Bancroft Library
Angove	Thomas R. Angove, letter to parents, April 22, 1906, San Francisco Public Library

Baldwin   Marion Baldwin Hale, "The 1906 Earthquake and Fire," Oral History Transcript 1975, Bancroft Library

Bauer   William F. Bauer, interviewed by Frederick M. Wirt, July 26, 1977, Selections from Growing Up in the Cities: Oral History Transcripts of Tape-Recorded Interviews, Bancroft Library

Bennett   Sir Courtenay Walter Bennett, Official Dispatch from British Consul General in San Francisco to the Foreign Office in London, April 25, 1906, California Historical Society

Boden   Experiences of Captain M. Boden, Engine 21, Station 1152 Oak St., Bancroft Library

Carew   Experiences of Captain (SFFD) William Carew, Truck 7, Station 3050 17th St., Bancroft Library

Conlon   Experiences of J. J. Conlon, Battalion Chief (SFFD) District 9, Stationed with Engine 30, Station Waller Near Stanyan Sts., Bancroft Library

ConlonJr   John J. Conlon Jr., "April 18, 1906," Selection from "Tale of a San Franciscan," compiled around 1977, Bancroft Library

Conniff   Experiences of Captain (SFFD) J. Conniff and his men from April 18th to April 20th, Engine 26, Station 327 2nd Ave., Bancroft Library

Cullen   Experiences of Captain (SFFD) C. J. Cullen, Engine 6, and his men, Station 62 South St., Bancroft Library

DBrown   Dolly Brown, letter to Henry Anderson, April 21, 1906, California Historical Society

Dryer   Experiences of Captain (SFFD) J. F. Dryer, Truck 6, and his men, Station 1152 Oak St., Bancroft Library

Dunne   William Dunne, interviewed August 1977, Selections from Growing Up in the Cities: Oral History Transcripts of Tape-Recorded Interviews, Bancroft Library

Einstein   Lesley Einstein, An Eyewitness Account of the San Francisco Earthquake and Fire, California Historical Society

Fay   Experiences of Captain (SFFD) John Fay, Engine 22, and his men, Station 1348 10th Ave., Bancroft Library

Freeman   Report of Lieutenant Frederick Freeman Commanding USTBD Perry on his unit's activities during the earthquake and fire in San Francisco April 18–23, 1906, dated April 30, 1906, Department of the Navy, Twelfth Naval District, Office of the Commandant, National Archives San Francisco, Record Group 181

GBrown   Experiences of Captain (SFFD) G. F. Brown, Engine 2, and his men, Station Pine near Larkin, Bancroft Library

Goerlitz   Ernest Goerlitz, "Story of the San Francisco Earthquake and Con-
flagration as far as it Affected the Conreid Metropolitan Opera
Company April 18th, 19th, and 20th, 1906," California Historical
Society

JCook1   Jesse B. Cook, Account of the April 1906 Earthquake and Fire,
March 1, 1935, Society of California Pioneers

JKelly   Report of fire alarm operator James C. Kelly to Chief Hewitt of
the Department of Electricity in regard to matters related to the
fire alarm system on April 18, 1906, May 14, 1906, San Francisco
Public Library

Kindelon   Report of Chief Special Agent Patrick J. Kindelon of Southern
Pacific to Southern Pacific Superintendent, June 22, 1906, San
Francisco Public Library

Lafler   Henry Anderson Lafler, "How the Army Worked to Save San
Francisco: Being of a supplementary nature to 'How the army
worked to save San Francisco, personal narrative of the acute and
active commanding officer, by Frederick Funston, Brig.-Gen.
U.S.A.' in the *Cosmopolitan* magazine for July," Bancroft Library

Landfield   Jerome Barker Landfield, "Operation Kaleidoscope: A Melange
of Personal Recollections," A City in Ruins, Chapter 28, Bancroft
Library

Laveaga   Diary of E. I. de Laveaga, California Historical Society

Leithead   Charles Leithead, Account of the 1906 Earthquake and Fire, May
2, 1906, California Historical Society

Mahoney   Dr. Margaret Mahoney, "The Earthquake, the Fire, the Relief," July
28, 1906, Bancroft Library

McCluskey   Experiences of Battalion Chief (SFFD) J. McCluskey, District 1,
(Temporary) Station, Stockton & Broadway, Bancroft Library

Mitchell   Experiences of Captain (SFFD) H. Mitchell, Engine 20, Bancroft
Library

Moore   Grace Roberts Moore, "Biography of Grace Roberts Moore: and
related papers: Autobiography," Bancroft Library

Morrow   Hon. William W. Morrow, "The Earthquake of April 18, 1906, and
the Great Fire in San Francisco on That and Succeeding Days—
Personal Experiences, Inauguration of Red Cross and General
Relief Work," Bancroft Library

Murphy   Experiences of Captain (SFFD) T. J. Murphy, Engine 29. and his
men, Station 11th & Bryant Sts., Bancroft Library

Nankervis   Elizabeth Maud Johnston Nankervis, "One Woman's Experience,"
ms (with typed transcript), 1959, Bancroft Library

Newell   Experiences of Captain (SFFD) Daniel Newell, Engine 13, 1458 Valencia St., Bancroft Library

Nichols   Experiences of Captain (SFFD) F. Nichols, Truck 4, 1648 Pacific St., Bancroft Library

Perrin   Helen Huntington Perrin, "Early Years in San Francisco," Bancroft Library

Putnam   Eleanor Briggs Putnam, "Earthquake and Fire Days San Francisco 1906," Hooker Family Papers, 1783–1951: Lessons of the Great Fire, Bancroft Library

Radford   Experiences of Captain (SFFD) J. Radford, Engine 25, Bancroft Library

Russell   Experiences of Captain (SFFD) S. D. Russell, Engine 27, Bancroft Library

Schmidt   Experiences of Captain (SFFD) Schmidt, Engine 28, Station Stockton & San Francisco Sts., Bancroft Library

Siegel   Etta Siegel, interviewed by Frederick M. Wirt, July 18, 1977, Selections from Growing Up in the Cities: Oral History Transcripts of Tape-Recorded Interviews, Bancroft Library

Sinsheimer   Letter from Adolf Sinsheimer to Max, May 7, 1906, ALS with photocopy and transcript, California Historical Society

Stetson1   James B. Stetson, Statement of James B. Stetson, Esq., Member of Firm of Holbrooks, Merrill, & Stetson, President of the California Street Cable Railroad Company, June 22, 1906, Bancroft Library

Waters   Experiences of Battalion Chief (SFFD) W. D. Waters, District 7, Bancroft Library

WCook   Experiences of Battalion Chief (SFFD) W. A. Cook, Stationed Ferry Building, Bancroft Library

Welch   Experiences of Captain (SFFD) A. Welch, Engine 7, Bancroft Library

Wing   Ah Wing, Handwritten Eyewitness Account of Earthquake Damage to the Stanford and Hopkins houses in San Francisco by Ah Wing, Employee of the Stanford Family (in Chinese with an English Translation), Stanford Libraries, Department of Special Collections, Manuscripts Division, Stanford University, Stanford, California

COURT TRANSCRIPTS

CWAvCU   *California Wine Association v. Commercial Union Fire Insurance Co. of N.Y.* (S.F. Superior Court, April 1908), Bancroft Library

LSvTF   *Levi Strauss Realty Co. v. Transatlantic Fire Insurance Co. of Hamburg* (N.D. Cal., Sept. 1906), National Archives at San Francisco

WCvAL   *Whittier-Coburn Co. v. Alliance Co. Ltd. of London* (N.D. Cal., Sept. 1907), National Archives at San Francisco

NEWSPAPERS & PERIODICALS

Arg.   *The Argonaut*
BE   *The Buffalo Enquirer*
CCE   *Call-Chronicle-Examiner* (single issue April 19, 1906)
CT   *Chicago Tribune*
EB   *The Evening Bee* (Sacramento)
KCS   *The Kansas City Star*
LAH   *Los Angeles Herald*
LAT   *Los Angeles Times*
LI   *L'Italia* (San Francisco)
NYT   *The New York Times*
OH   *Oakland Herald*
OT   *Oakland Tribune*
PM   *The Pacific Monthly*
SB   *The Sacramento Bee*
SFB   *The Bulletin* (San Francisco)
SFC   *The San Francisco Call*
SFCh   *San Francisco Chronicle*
SFE   *The San Francisco Examiner*
SLT   *Salt Lake Telegram*

PUBLISHED PRIMARY SOURCES

Atherton   Gertrude Atherton, *Adventures of a Novelist* (London: Jonathan Cape, 1932)

Austin   Mary Hunter Austin, "The Tremblor: A Personal Narration," *The California Earthquake of 1906*, edited by David Starr Jordan (San Francisco: A. M. Robertson, 1907)

Bacigalupi   Peter Bacigalupi, "Mr. Bacigalupi's Own Story," *Edison Phonograph Monthly*, July 1906

Burke   Emma M. Burke, "Comprehending the Calamity," *Overlook Magazine*, June 2, 1906

Carnahan   Melissa Stewart McKee Carnahan, *Personal Experiences of the San Francisco Earthquake of April, 1906* (Pittsburgh: Melissa Stewart McKee Carnahan, 1908)

Caruso   Enrico Caruso, "Caruso on the Earthquake," *The Theater*, vol. VI, no. 65, July 1, 1906

CLondon   Charmian London, *The Book of Jack London*, Vol. II (New York: The Century Co., 1921)

Duke   Thomas S. Duke, Captain of SFPD, History of the Great Earth-
                quake and Fire From Police and Municipal Records, *Celebrated
                Criminal Cases of America*, Published With Approval of the
                Honorable Board of Police Commissioners of San Francisco (San
                Francisco: 1910)

Eastwood   Dr. Alice Eastwood, "The Earthquake and the California Academy
                of Sciences," *Torreya*, vol. 6, no. 6, pp. 120–123 (Torrey Botanical
                Society, June 1906)

Fisher   Lucy B. Fisher, "A Nurse's Earthquake Experience," *American Jour-
                nal of Nursing*, vol. VII, issue 2, November 1906

Funston   Brig. Gen. Frederick Funston (US Army), "How the Army Worked
                to Save San Francisco," *Cosmopolitan*, vol. XLI, no. 3, July 1906

Genthe   Arnold Genthe, *As I Remember . . . the Autobiography of Arnold Gen-
                the* (New York: Reynal & Hitchcock, 1936)

Hewitt   Fred J. Hewitt, "Wreck of City's Buildings Awful," *The San Fran-
                cisco Examiner*, April 20, 1906, p. 8

Hollister   John Hamilcar Hollister, *Memories of Eighty Years: Autosketches,
                Random Notes, and Reminiscences* (Chicago: privately printed, 1912)

Hopper   James Hopper, "Our San Francisco," *Everybody's Magazine*, June
                1906

JCook2   Account of Jesse Cook, "The Great Fire of 1906," *Arg.*, May 1, 1926

JLondon   Jack London, "The Story of an Eyewitness," *Collier's*, May 5, 1906

Kendrick   Charles Kendrick, *Memoirs of Charles Kendrick* (San Francisco:
                Grabhorn Press, 1972)

Leach   Frank A. Leach, "Fight to Save the United States Mint," *Recollec-
                tions of a Newspaperman: A Record of Life and Events in California*
                (San Francisco: S. Levinson, 1917)

Millard   Bailey Millard, "Thousands Flee From Blazing City," *The San Fran-
                cisco Examiner*, April 21, 1906

Miller   Mary Ashe Miller, "My Own Story," *The Pacific Monthly*, August
                1906

Phillips-Jones Dorothy Fowler, *A Most Dreadful Earthquake: A First-Hand Account
                of the 1906 San Francisco Earthquake and Fire, with Glimpses into
                the Lives of the Phillips-Jones Letter Writers* (Oakland: California
                Genealogical Society, 2006)

Pond   Commander John E. Pond, US Navy (retired), "The United States
                Navy and the San Francisco Fire," *US Naval Institute Proceedings*,
                September 1952

Soulé   Frank Soulé, John H. Gihon, and James Nisbet, *The Annals of San
                Francisco* (New York: D. Appleton, 1855)

Stetson2   James B. Stetson, *San Francisco During the Eventful Days of April, 1906, Personal Recollections of James B. Stetson* (San Francisco: The Murdoch Press, 1906)

Way   George P. Way, *Story of Earthquake As Experienced In San Francisco On April 18, 1906* (Detroit: Mr. Geo. P. Way, 1907)

OFFICIAL REPORTS & PUBLICATIONS

Briggs   Report of Raymond W. Briggs, First Lieutenant, Artillery Corps, Presidio of San Francisco, May 10, 1906, *Special Report on the Relief Operations Conducted by the Military Authorities of the United States at San Francisco and Other Points*, with Accompanying Documents (Washington: Government Printing Office, 1906), Exhibit F, pp. 228–229

Devol1   Reports of Maj. Carroll A. Devol, Quartermaster, USA, Presidio of San Francisco, May 16, 1906, *Special Report on the Relief Operations Conducted by the Military Authorities of the United States at San Francisco and Other Points*, with Accompanying Documents (Washington: Government Printing Office, 1906), pp. 176–183

Devol2   Major Carroll A. Devol, Quartermaster, US Army, "The Army in the San Francisco Disaster," *Journal of the US Infantry Association*, vol. IV, no. 1 (July 1907)

Greely   Maj. Gen. Adolphus W. Greely, US Army, Earthquake in California, April 18, 1906. Special Report of Maj. Gen. Adolphus W. Greely, USA, Commanding the Pacific Division, *Special Report on the Relief Operations Conducted by the Military Authorities of the United States at San Francisco and Other Points*, with Accompanying Documents (Washington: Government Printing Office, 1906), Appendix A, pp. 85–134

ReliefSurvey   "The Organization and Methods of Relief Used After the Earthquake and Fire of April 18, 1906," *San Francisco Relief Survey* (New York: Survey Associates, Inc., 1913)

ReportNBNYC   *Report of National Board of Fire Underwriters: By Its Committee of Twenty on the City of New York, N.Y., Brooklyn and Queens* (New York: The Board, 1906)

ReportNBSF   *Report of National Board of Fire Underwriters: By Its Committee of Twenty on the City of San Francisco, Calif.* (New York: The Board, 1905)

ReportSEIC   *The California Earthquake of April 18, 1906, Report of the State Earthquake Investigation Commission*, in Two Volumes and Atlas (Washington: Carnegie Institute, 1908)

SanAndreas   Robert E. Wallace, ed., *The San Andreas Fault System, California*, US Geological Survey Paper 1515 (Washington, DC: Government Printing Office, 1990)

SanbornMap   *Insurance Maps: San Francisco, California*, in Six Volumes (New York: Sanborn-Perris Map Co., 1899–1900) with Annotated Corrections to Sept. 1905

SFDirectory   *San Francisco Crocker-Langley Directory for the Year Commencing May 1905* (San Francisco: H.S. Crocker Company, 1905)

Structures   Grove Karl Gilbert and Joseph Holmes, *The San Francisco Earthquake and Fire of April 18, 1906, and Their Effects on Structures and Structural Materials*, USGS (Washington: Government Printing Office, 1907)

Taft   William H. Taft, a letter of the Secretary of War, with accompanying documents, April 21, 1906, H.R. No. 714, 59th Cong., 1st Session; *59th Congress: 1st Session, December 4, 1905–June 30, 1906; House Documents*, vol. 49 (Washington: Government Printing Office, 1906)

Torney   Report of Lieut. Col. George H. Torney, Medical Department, United States Army Hospital, Presidio of San Francisco, May 14, 1906, *Special Report on the Relief Operations Conducted by the Military Authorities of the United States at San Francisco and Other Points*, with Accompanying Documents (Washington: Government Printing Office, 1906), pp. 209–210

WaterSupply   Hermann Schussler, Chief Engineer, *The Water Supply of San Francisco, California, Before, During and After the Earthquake of April 18th, 1906: and the Subsequent Conflagration* (San Francisco: Spring Valley Water Company, 1906)

DIGITAL AND ONLINE SOURCES

Cameron   Donaldina Cameron, Account of the Flight from Chinatown, Virtual Museum of the City of San Francisco, https://www.sfmuseum.org/1906/ew15.html

Chase   Account of Thomas Jefferson Chase, Virtual Museum of the City of San Francisco, https://www.sfmuseum.org/1906/ew1.html

DeathIndex   *California Death Index 1905–1929*, State of California Department of Public Health Bureau of Vital Statistics and Data Processing, www.ancestry.com (Provo, UT: Ancestry.com Operations, Inc., 2013)

Hammill   Letter from Joe Hammill to brother, May 11, 1906, Virtual Museum of the City of San Francisco, https://www.sfmuseum.org/1906/ew9.html

Livingston	Howard Livingston, "Memories of the San Francisco Earthquake and Fire of 1906," Virtual Museum of the City of San Francisco, https://www.sfmuseum.org/1906/ew20.html
Perry	Victor Elmo Perry, Assistant Superintendent of the Spring Valley Water Company, "Pass Bearer Through Lines," April 18, 1956, Virtual Museum of the City of San Francisco, https://www.sfmuseum.org/hist3/perry.html
VMSF	Virtual Museum of the City of San Francisco, https://www.sfmuseum.org
1900Census	*1900 US Federal Census*, https://www.ancestry.com (Provo, UT: Ancestry.com Operations, Inc., 2013)

Prologue

1 **Temperatures had reached seventy degrees . . . :** The highest temperature reported in city newspapers between January 1, 1906, and April 17, 1906, was 68 degrees on April 14, "The Coast Record," *SFC*, April 15, 1906, p. 29. Five inches of rain fell in March, per daily reports in *SFC*, and Professor McAdie of the Weather Bureau quoted in "Better Weather Promised," *SFC*, April 1, 1906, p. 39. In that same issue, .48 inches of rain were reported for the previous day, March 31, 1906, "The Coast Report," *SFC*, April 1, 1906, p. 55, and .01 inches were reported for April 1, 1906, *SFE*, April 2, 1906, p. 15. Every subsequent issue reported ".00" inches of rain for San Francisco through April 18, 1906.

1 **"One nickel" . . . :** Weekday issues of *SFC*, *SFCh*, and *SFE* cost 5 cents each.

1 **"enough money to get a bed" . . . :** Quoted from a report of an unhoused man being arrested after entering a Market Street business and saying, "I want enough money to get a bed" with a threat of violence before being arrested. *SFE*, February 27, 1905, p. 16.

1 **thirteen hundred lodging houses . . . :** *SFDirectory*, pp. 2177–2184.

2 **"snappiest hat of the season" . . . :** Lyndstrom's Hat Parlors ad, "Get One for Easter," *SFC*, April 14, 1906, p. 2.

2 **custodian helmets . . . :** In 1895, SFPD began requiring patrol officers to wear "Monitor helmets" like those worn at the time by the NYPD, which were a type of custodian (or bobby) helmet. "The Police Force Will Soon Wear New Caps and Helmets," *SFE*, May 5, 1895, p. 12.

2 **Postal Telegraph or Western Union . . . :** *SFDirectory*, p. 2290.

2 **fifty banks . . . :** *Ibid.*, p. 2015.

2 **"amusements" . . . :** "Amusements," *SFCh*, April 16, 1906, p. 7; *SFC*, April 18, 1906, p. 9.

2 **sixty-six foundries . . . :** "Brass Founders," *SFDirectory*, p. 2032; "Iron Foundries," *SFDirectory*, pp. 2153–2154.

2 **Recreation Park . . . :** *SFC*, April 18, 1906, p. 9.

2 **"Queen City of the Pacific" . . . :** "German-Americans Sound Praises of Crocker," *SFCh*, October 29, 1903, p. 9; "Fraternal Woe Touches Court," *SFC*, January 26, 1905, p. 7. Another nickname for the city was "Paris of the Pacific." *SFC*, October 5, 1905, p. 1; *SFC*, November 21, 1905, p. 5; *Evening Bulletin* (Honolulu, Hawaii), December 12, 1901, p. 8.

3 **twice the size . . . :** The respective populations of Los Angeles and San Francisco in the 1900 federal census were 102,479 and 342,780. *Twelfth Census of the United States Taken in the Year 1900*, Vol. I (Washington: Government Printing Office, 1901) pp. 430, 432. In 1906, the population

of San Francisco was estimated at above 400,000 while that of Los Angeles was estimated to have doubled to roughly 230,000. "Population is Past 230,000," *LAH,* April 15, 1906, p. 5. By the 1910 federal census, the population of Los Angeles had increased to 319,198 while San Francisco—due in large part to the 1906 disaster—was 416,912. *Thirteenth Census of the United States Taken in the Year 1910,* Vol. II (Washington: Government Printing Office, 1913), p. 139.

3 **"[f]ire and earthquake proof"** . . . : The Palace Hotel was advertised as "Fire and earthquake proof." *SFE,* January 30, 1890, p. 4.

3 **eighty-six carriage and wagon sellers** . . . : "Carriage and Wagon Makers," *SFDirectory,* pp. 2050–2051.

3 **twenty-six dealers** . . . : "Automobiles," *ibid.,* p. 2011.

3 **5-cent cigars** . . . : United Cigar Stores advertised "a 5-cent cigar that every cigar smoker in the United States is bound to recognize as a matchless-value." *SFE,* April 8, 1906, p. 68.

3 **two dimes, one for the beer** . . . : Willie Figari, a young tug pilot in 1906, later recalled the dance halls of the Barbary Coast before the earthquake and fire, specifically Purcell's on Pacific Street (current-day Pacific Avenue), where a beer cost 20 cents—"the house would get 10 and girl dancing would get 10." "William Figari: San Francisco Bay and Waterfront," interview by Ruth Teiser in 1968, Oral History Center, BL.

3 **"cribs"** . . . : The small rooms of sex workers within brothels were commonly referred to as "cribs." *See e.g.,* "Supreme Court Kills Pon Injunction," *SFCh,* July 11, 1905, p. 14, reporting litigation over the "thirty-three 'cribs'" of a Dupont Street brothel, or "Police Are Closely Shadowed," *SFCh,* January 20, 1905, p. 16, reporting about police paybacks to protect "over 100 cribs" of the brothel at 620 Jackson Street.

4 **Double-decker steam ferries** . . . : Passenger ferries with regular Ferry Building service at the time were double-ended, double-decker, coal-burning, and paddle-wheel-propelled. Some carried train cars on the main deck and passengers on the cabin deck. Ferries for the Southern Pacific Railroad, South Pacific Coast Railroad, California Northwestern Railway, Santa Fe Railway, North Shore Railroad, Oakland Harbor, and Mt. Tamalpais Railway arrived and departed the Ferry Building's seven slips daily, with hours only differing on Sundays. "Railway Travel," *SFC,* April 2, 1906, p. 4.

4 **nine-hundred-pound swinging weight** . . . : Author interview with clock master Dorian Clair, who has been maintaining the Ferry Building's clock since 2000, on January 29, 2021, and February 3, 2021.

4 **police sergeant Jesse Cook** . . . : Biographical information about Jesse Cook and details of his experiences on April 18, 1906, were obtained primarily from "Jesse Brown Cook Scrapbooks Documenting San Francisco History and Law Enforcement, ca. 1895–1936," BL, and his own recollections in JCook1, JCook2.

4 **harbor district** . . . : The "harbor district" was a downtown district designated by the police department as Battery Street east to the waterfront. It is part of what is currently the city's larger Financial District, which includes what was then known as the banking district and the harbor district. *See e.g.,* "Harbor District is Enlarged," *SFC,* July 2, 1902.

5 **"fill-land"** . . . : Details about where Yerba Buena Cove was filled and when were obtained primarily from Soulé; Maps of San Francisco, Calif., 1847 and 1853, Yale University Library; and Charles A. Fracchia, *When the Water Came Up to Montgomery Street* (Virginia: The Donning Company sponsored by San Francisco Museum and Historical Society, 2009).

5 **"was all filled in land . . ."**: JCook1.

5 **"What's the matter with your . . ."**: . . . JCook1.

6 **"The whole street was undulating"** . . . : JCook2, p. 4.

6 **eight-inch iron water main . . . :** Dimensions and locations of water transmission mains and distribution mains throughout the city were obtained from *WaterSupply* and *SanbornMap.*

6 **"gaping trench" . . . :** JCook2, p. 4.

6 **"felt like it was slipping . . .":** JCook1.

6 **a few seconds past 5:12 a.m. . . . :** Bruce A. Bolt, *Earthquakes, Fifth Edition* (New York: W.H. Freeman & Company, 2003), p. 4; Philip L. Fradkin, *The Great Earthquake and Firestorms of 1906* (Berkeley: University of California Press, 2005), p. 52; Emmet Condon and Gladys Hansen, *Denial of Disaster* (San Francisco: Cameron + Company, 1989), p. 13.

7 **"Extra!" editions . . . :** By 1:00 p.m. San Francisco time, newspapers in other cities were sharing details of the earthquake and fire. The four o'clock edition of *The Standard Union* in Brooklyn, NY, headlined "EARTHQUAKE WRECKS SAN FRANCISCO; FLAMES SWEEPING CITY; MANY DEAD," with news of "No water to fight the conflagration" and "Troops on Guard." Four O'Clock Edition, *The Standard Union,* April 18, 1906, p. 1. The five o'clock edition of *The Buffalo Enquirer* in Buffalo, NY, headlined "SAN FRANCISCO IS VIS-ITED BY AN APPALLING EARTHQUAKE AND FIRE!" Five O'Clock Edition, *The Buffalo Enquirer,* April 18, 1906, p. 1. An afternoon extra edition of *The Oklahoma City Times-Journal* headlined "LATE REPORTS GROW WORSE" with news of "Thousands Killed—The Entire City of San Francisco in Flames—Terror Striken [sic] Inhabitants Flee in Terror." Extra Edition, *The Oklahoma City Times-Journal,* April 18, 1906, p. 1. The disaster also monopolized all evening editions in other towns and cities. *See e.g., The Evening Star* (Washington, DC), April 18, 1906, p. 1; *EB,* April 18, 1906, p. 1; and *Boston Evening Transcript* (Boston, MA), April 18, 1906, p. 1.

7 **city filled with professional photographers . . . :** For further reading on photography in the city during and following the disaster, see *Among the Ruins: Arnold Genthe's Photographs of the 1906 San Francisco Earthquake and Firestorm* (Fine Arts Museums of San Francisco: Cameron + Company, 2021) by Victoria Binder, James A. Ganz, Carolin Görgen, Colleen Terry, Richard Misrach, and Karin Breuer (editor).

8 **all three cathedrals . . . :** These were St. Mary's Cathedral, Holy Trinity Orthodox Cathedral, and Cathedral Mission of the Good Samaritan (Episcopal). *SFDirectory,* pp. 42–45.

8 **five of the seven synagogues . . . :** These were the synagogues for the Congregation Beth-Israel, Congregation Chebra Thilim, Congregation Emanu-El, Congregation Keneseth Israel, and Congregation Shaari Zedek. The sanctuary for Congregation Sherith Israel on the corner of California and Webster Streets, completed in 1905, survived with little damage and is still the congregation's sanctuary today (and as an unreinforced masonry structure, underwent a required seismic retrofit completed in 2017). And the synagogue for the Congregation Ohabai Shalome on the south side of Bush Street between Octavia and Laguna survived and still stands today as a State Landmark, the Bush Street Temple at 1881 Bush Street, an assisted living home as of 2023. *SFDirectory,* p. 43; *SanbornMap.*

8 **four lodging houses . . . :** These were the Brunswick House at 148 6th Street, Ohio House at 142 6th Street, Lormor House at 136 6th Street, and Nevada House at 132 6th Street, discussed in greater detail in Chapter 3. *SFDirectory, SanbornMap.*

8 **"GREAT BUILDINGS ARE TO RISE . . .":** *SFCh,* April 25, 1906, p. 1.

8 **478 . . . :** In 1907, the Board of Supervisors adopted a "General History of the San Francisco Earthquake and Fire of 1906" and ordered it published in the municipal reports. It declared, "The loss of life attending the great disaster is officially recorded at 478." *San Francisco Municipal Reports for the Fiscal Year 1905–6, Ending June 30, 1906, and Fiscal Year 1906–7, Ending June 30, 1907* (San Francisco: Neal Publishing, 1908), p. 703.

9 **"SAN FRANCISCO WILL CELEBRATE . . .":** *SFCh,* April 18, 1907, p. 1.

9 **"SAN FRANCISCO'S REBUILDING . . .":** *SFE,* April 18, 1908, p. 1.

9 **"HOME AGAIN AFTER THREE YEARS" . . . :** *SFC,* April 18, 1909, p. 1.

9 **"the rebuilding which has obliterated . . .":** "San Francisco Celebrating," *Long Beach Daily Telegram,* April 17, 1915.

9 **its last known member . . . :** This was William Del Monte, who was three months old on April 18, 1906, and passed in January 2016, eleven days before his 110th birthday. "WA. Del Monte, 109, 1906 Quake Survivor," *NYT,* January 13, 2016, Section B, p. 13.

9 **296 miles . . . :** Data regarding the April 18, 1906, earthquake was primarily obtained from *ReportSEIC; SanAndreas;* and "The Great 1906 San Francisco Earthquake," *USGS,* US Department of the Interior, earthquake.usgs.gov/earthquakes/events/1906calif/18april/.

9 **estimated moment magnitude of 7.9 . . . :** The moment magnitude (expressed as Mw), the current and most reliable quantitative measure of an earthquake's relative size, was developed in 1979 and differs from the Richter scale (expressed as ML) devised in 1935. And both of these logarithmic scales differ from the linear Rossi-Forel scale (I-X) and Modified Mercalli scale (I-XII) in use in 1906. The intensity was estimated to range between VIII and IX on the Modified Mercalli scale. Schultz, S., and R. Wallace, *The San Andreas Fault,* USGS (Washington, DC: Government Printing Office, 1989), p. 5. Using the Rossi-Forel scale, Dr. Harry O. Wood, a seismologist with the State Earthquake Investigation Commission, determined the intensity in San Francisco between VII on solid ground to X on alluvial fill land. *ReportSEIC,* p. 340. The magnitude on the Richter scale was estimated as high as 8.25 or 8.3. *SanAndreas,* p. 161; "1–2 Jolt Worst in Valley Since 1906," *SFE,* April 10, 1961, p.1; "A Big Quake on the Calaveras," *SFE,* August 12, 1979, p. 5; "Relationship Between Earthquake Magnitude and Energy," *SFE,* April 25, 1977, p. 8. These have been determined an overestimate, and the moment magnitude has been widely estimated at 7.9 Mw. Wald, D. J., Kanamori, H., Helmbeger, D. V., and Heaton, T. H., *Source Study of the 1906 San Francisco Earthquake,* Bulletin of the Seismological Society of America, vol. 83 (4), 1993, p. 989.

10 **more than twenty-eight thousand structures . . . :** The number of structures destroyed was counted as 28,188 covering 4.7 square miles. "The Story of Statistics," *SFE,* April 19, 1906. 490 blocks were completely destroyed and 32 blocks partially destroyed, totaling 2,593 acres. *Structures,* p. 61.

10 **Approximately a quarter million residents . . . :** The number of SF residents rendered homeless by the disaster has been commonly estimated between 225,000 and 300,000 people. *See* Point Paper—US Army Activities in the 1906 Earthquake and Fire, SFPL, estimating the total at 300,000; "Preparing to House the City's Homeless," *SFC,* June 17, 1906, p. 5, reporting on housing for the remainders of "the 225,000 rendered homeless by the fire"; "Great Fire Stopped at City Front," *SFC,* April 22, 1906, p. 1, reporting "over 250,000 people homeless"; *A Study of Earthquake Losses in the San Francisco Bay Area—Data and Analysis,* NOAA, US Department of Commerce, A Report Prepared For The Office Of Emergency Preparedness, 1972, p. 205, calculating "225,000 left homeless"; and "Civic Rites to Mark Anniversary Today of City's Destruction," *SFE,* April 18, 1956, p. 2, estimating "265,000 homeless."

10 **more than three thousand people . . . :** The death total estimated by Gladys Hansen is discussed in greater detail in the afterword.

11 **thirty-six-year-old Sarah Corbus . . . :** Sarah "Sadie" Corbus was killed in her residence at the corner of Jackson and Jones Streets by bricks from a falling chimney. *SFC,* April 29, 1906; *Arg.,* April 21, 1906 (listed as "Sarah Corbett"). She lived at 1511 Jones Street (near the corner of Jackson St.) and was born February 1870 per the 1900 census. She died at thirty-six on April 18, 1906. *Death Index,* p. 2197.

11 **forty-year-old Margaret Fundenberg . . . :** Margaret E. Fundenberg's card in Gladys

Hansen's Death Records in SFPL lists her cause of death as "burned to death," citing Coroner's Book C, p. 116. She died at 38 and he died at 14, both on April 18, 1906. *DeathIndex*, p. 3710.

11 **"three persons"** . . . : "Substantiates 'Examiner's Report," *SFE*, May 21, 1906, p. 13.

1.

13 **the Yelamu** . . . : Malcolm Margolin, *The Ohlone Way: Indian Life in the San Francisco–Monterey Bay Area* (Berkeley: Heyday Books, 1978); Charles Wollenberg, *Golden Gate Metropolis: Perspectives on Bay Area History* (Berkeley, CA: Institute of Governmental Studies, University of California, 1985); John Alioto, *Before the Gold: A History of San Francisco Before the Gold Rush, 1769–1847* (San Francisco: Norfolk Press, 2020); and the Association of Ramaytush Ohlone website, ramaytush.org.

13 **"proselytize"** . . . : Alioto, *Before the Gold*, p. 22.

13 **"civilize"** . . . : *Ibid.*, p. 27.

14 **barely two hundred residents** . . . : H. W. Brands, *The Age of Gold: The California Gold Rush and the New American Dream* (New York: Anchor Books, 2003), p. 249.

14 **Yerba Buena was renamed** . . . : Information about the early history of Yerba Buena and San Francisco was obtained primarily from Soulé; Fracchia, *When the Water Came Up to Montgomery Street*; and Brands, *The Age of Gold*.

14 **"abundance of gold in that territory . . ."**: James K. Polk, *James K. Polk Papers: Series 5: Messages and Speeches, 1833–1849; 1848; Dec. 5, fourth annual message; 2 of 6*, Manuscript/Mixed Material retrieved from LOC, https://www.loc.gov/item/mss365090107/.

14 **fewer than two thousand residents** . . . : Estimates of population increase in the city during 1849 were obtained from Soulé, pp. 243–244; and Rand Richards, *Historic San Francisco* (San Francisco: Heritage House Publishers, 2011), p. 62.

15 **Martin Roberts** . . . : Moore.

15 **"San Francisco seemed to have . . ."**: Bayard Taylor, *El Dorado, or, Adventures in the Path of Empire: Comprising a Voyage to California, Via Panama; Life in San Francisco and Monterey; Pictures of the Gold Region, and Experiences of Mexican Travel*, Vol. II (New York: George P. Putnam, 1850), p. 38.

15 **On Christmas Eve 1849** . . . : Facts about the six major fires in the city between 1849–51 were gathered primarily from Soulé, pp. 241–347; John S. Hittell, *A history of the city of San Francisco and incidentally of the state of California* (San Francisco: A. L. Bancroft & Co., 1878), pp. 133–170; "Appalling and Destructive Conflagration!!" *Tri-Weekly Alta California*, December 26, 1849; and Rev. Albert Williams, *A Pioneer Pastorate and Times, Embodying Contemporary Local Transactions and Events* (San Francisco: Wallace & Hassett, 1879), Pdf retrieved from LOC, https://www.loc.gov/item/06038070/.

16 **City leaders called a special** . . . : Establishment of a fire department began informally in December 1849 and was formally approved in the summer of 1850 after elections under the new city charter. "Fire Department," *Tri-Weekly Alta California*, December 28, 1849; Soulé, pp. 616–617.

16 **"Scarcely were the ashes cold . . ."**: Soulé, pp. 241–242.

16 **"These, like those that had . . ."**: *Ibid.*, p. 242.

16 **"over one thousand homes enveloped . . ."**: Letter from Benjamin Cowell to his wife, May 7, 1851, BL.

16 **"worked all night"** . . . : Moore.

17 **Montgomery Block . . . :** Soulé, p. 483.

17 **new city building code . . . :** Stephen Tobriner, *Bracing for Disaster* (Berkeley: University of California, 2006), pp. 31–33.

17 **Martin Roberts, busy working . . . :** Moore.

17 **"A copper coin was a strange sight" . . . :** Soulé, p. 253.

17 **"thoroughly fireproof" . . . :** *Ibid.,* p. 526.

18 **"You are the oldest native Californian . . .":** Moore.

18 **Domenico "Domingo" Ghirardelli . . . :** Alex Bevk, "Tracing the Totally Sweet History of the Ghirardelli Empire," *Curbed SF,* October 28, 2014; "About Ghirardelli," https://www
.ghirardelli.com/about-ghirardelli.

18 **James Folger . . . :** Ruth Waldo Newhall, *The Folger Way—Coffee Pioneering Since 1850* (San Francisco: J.A. Folger & Company, 1970).

18 **Levi Strauss . . . :** Lynn Downey, *Levi Strauss: A Short Biography* (Levi Strauss & Co., 2008); Levi Strauss & Co.—Company History, https://www.levistrauss.com/levis-history/.

19 **topping 100,000 residents . . . :** San Francisco's population was 56,802 in the 1860 federal census and increased swiftly during the Civil War, likely topping 100,000 in the first two years of the war. The city's population was 149,473 by the 1870 federal census. Population by Counties, Table II—State of California, *Ninth Census—Volume I, The Statistics of the Population of the United States* (Washington, DC: Government Printing Office, 1872), p. 15.

19 **Spring Valley Water Works . . . :** Information about the Spring Valley Water Works Company was obtained primarily from *WaterSupply*; Testimony of Hermann Schussler, *WCvAL*; and Hermann Schussler, *The Past, Present and Future Water Supply of San Francisco* (San Francisco: C.A. Murdoch & Co., 1908).

19 **After the fires of 1849–51 . . . :** Order 1752-To Define the Fire Limits of the City and County of San Francisco, and Making Regulations Concerning the Erection and Use of Buildings in Said City and County, *General Orders of the Board of Supervisors Providing Regulations for the Government of the City and County of San Francisco* (San Francisco: B.J. Thomas, Printer, 1884), pp. 120–169.

20 **In 1866 . . . :** Assembly Bill No. 182 in the California House of Representatives provided for a "paid fire department for the city and county of San Francisco.""Letter from the Capital," *SFE,* February 12, 1866, p. 3. It was passed after amendments in the Senate. "Letter from the Capital," *SFE,* March 6, 1866, p. 3.

20 **"endless-chain, stationary-engine, uphill railroad" . . . :** "Subsidy Hallidie," *SFCh,* August 30, 1873.

20 **"aristocratic thoroughfare" . . . :** "On California Street," *SFE,* December 30, 1889, p. 6.

20 **"nabobs of Nob Hill" . . . :** "Views on the Convention," *SFE,* April 18, 1878.

20 **The cable car transformed . . . :** Information about the cable car was obtained primarily from *San Francisco's Powell Street Cable Cars* and *San Francisco's California Street Cable Cars,* both by Walter Rice and Emiliano Echeverria; the Cable Car Museum in San Francisco; and author interviews with Joe Thompson (writer and administrator of "The Cable Car Guy," www
.cable-car-guy.com) and with author and cable car historian Emiliano Echeverria.

21 **"metropolis of California" . . . :** *SB,* September 25, 1872.

21 **At noon on February 22, 1872 . . . :** "The Corner-Stone," *SFE,* February 22, 1872, p. 3.

21 **"municipal palace" . . . :** "Washington's Birthday," *SFCh,* February 22, 1872, p. 3.

21 **In 1874, a new US Mint . . . :** "Mint Statistics," *SFE,* October 5, 1874, p. 1.

21 **755 guest rooms . . . :** "The Great Caravansary of the Western World," *Frank Leslie's Illustrated Newspaper,* October 9, 1875.

21 **233,959 . . . :** Table V: Population by Race and by Counties; *Statistics of the Population of the United States at the 10th Census* (Washington, DC: Government Printing Office, 1882), p. 382.

21 **"Latin Quarter" . . . :** The Latin Quarter was also referred to as the "Italian Quarter" and the "Italian residence quarter." "In the Latin Quarter," *SFE,* March 9, 1889, p. 4; "Shrove Tuesday Observed in the Latin Quarter," *SFCh,* March 6, 1889, p. 5.

21 **"Little Italy" . . . :** "A Cosmopolitan Thoroughfare," *SFC,* March 15, 1996, p. 17; *see also* "Italian Life at North Beach," proclaiming "Every one knows that Telegraph Hill and North Beach form in many respects a little Italy." *SFC,* August 13, 1893, p. 17; and "Little Italy, a Typical Colony of Altruria in Our Midst," *SFC,* September 9, 1903, p. 21.

21 **"Colored" . . . :** Table IV, Population by Race, Sex, and Nativity and by States and Territories, *Statistics of the Population of the United States at the Tenth Census (June 1, 1880)*(Washington, DC: Government Printing Office, 1882).

21 **William Leidesdorff . . . :** Rudolph M. Lapp, *Blacks in Gold Rush California* (New Haven and London: Yale University Press, 1977), pp. 9–11; Jan Batiste Adkins, *African Americans of San Francisco* (Charleston, SC: Arcadia Publishing, 2012), p. 10.

22 **"the town has lost its most valuable resident" . . . :** Obituary, *The California Star,* May 20, 1848, p. 3.

22 **When gold fever spread . . . :** Lapp, *Blacks in Gold Rush California*; Adkins, *African Americans of San Francisco.*

23 **1,176 . . . :** This and the 1,330, 1,628, and 21,790 numbers following were obtained from Table V: Population by Race and by Counties: 1880, 1870, 1860, *Statistics of the Population of the United States at the Tenth Census (June 1, 1880)*(Washington, DC: Government Printing Office, 1882), p. 382.

23 **"There were hordes of long . . .":** Soulé, p. 257.

23 **"the Chinese problem" . . . :** *See e.g.,* "California's Blight—The Great Chinese Problem and Its Solution," *SFCh,* June 16, 1873, p. 3; "The Chinese Problem," *SFE,* June 17, 1873, p. 2; "A Solution of the Chinese Problem," *SFE,* June 7, 1873, p. 2. For information on the legal exclusion and violent treatment of Chinese Americans in California during this period, I relied heavily on Jean Pfaelzer's book *Driven Out: The Forgotten War against Chinese Americans* (Berkeley: University of California Press, 2007); and Erika Lee's book *At America's Gates: Chinese Immigration during the Exclusion Era, 1882–1943* (Chapel Hill: University of North Carolina Press, 2003).

23 **"The Chinese Must Go!" . . . :** *SFCh,* January 11, 1878.

23 **Workingmen's Party . . . :** Stephanie S. Pincetl, *Transforming California: A Political History of Land Use and Development* (Baltimore: The Johns Hopkins University Press, 1999).

24 **"*provided,* no native of China . . .":** Article II, Section 1 of the Constitution of the State of California, ratified May 7, 1879, *Statutes of California passed at the Twenty-Third Session of the Legislature, 1880* (Sacramento: State Office, J. D. Young, Supt. State Printing, 1880), p. xxiv.

24 **"any Chinese or Mongolian" . . . :** Article XIX, Section 2, *ibid.,* p. xii.

24 **"includes the children born, within . . .":** *United States v. Wong Kim Ark,* 169 US 649 (1898) at 693.

25 **"scared to death of them" . . . :** Siegel.

25 **approached 300,000 . . . :** San Francisco's population totaled 298,997 in the 1890 census, per comparative tables in *1900 Census,* p. 139.

26 **"municipal purposes" . . . :** When George Ensign's corporation was formed by the

California Legislature in 1853 with the exclusive right to provide pure, fresh water to the city and county of San Francisco, this included "furnishing to the city, free of charge, water for all municipal purposes." The California Supreme Court ruled, after interpreting the enabling act and subsequent transferred duties of the competing San Francisco City Water Works, this was limited to cases "of fire or other great necessity." *The City and County of San Francisco v. The Spring Valley Water Works*, 48 Cal. 493 (Cal. 1874).

26 **"extortionate"** . . . : "Down With Gas And Water Rates" and "The Examiner Petitions," *SFE*, January 29, 1897, p. 9.

26 **"handicapped by the lack of water . . ."**: "Bigger Mains Demanded—Chief Sullivan's Scathing Report on the City's Lack of Water," *SFC*, July 10, 1895, p. 9.

26 **"the lengthened shadow of one man"** . . . : Ralph Waldo Emerson, "Self-Reliance," *Essays: First Series* (New York: John B. Alden, 1886), p. 17.

26 **"wonderful physique"** . . . : Blake Evarts, ed., *San Francisco and its Municipal Administration 1902* (San Francisco: Pacific Publishing Company, 1902), p. 210.

26 **"extraordinary adaptability to the work"** . . . : Sullivan had been selected as the first assistant chief on the passing of the previous chief engineer, even though Sullivan was the youngest of the three considered. When Chief Scannell passed, Sullivan, although younger than District Engineer Dougherty, was appointed chief engineer. "The Two White Hats—Sullivan for Chief and Dougherty for Assistant," *SFE*, April 4, 1893, p. 4.

26 **"Chief Sullivan arrived in less . . ."**: "A Great Blaze," *SFC*, February 27, 1894, p. 10.

26 **"scarcity of hydrants"** . . . : "After the Fire," *SFC*, February 28, 1894, p. 3.

27 **"hydrants were too far away . . ."**: "Died On Duty," *SFCh*, June 8, 1893, p. 5. In December, the *Examiner* editorial staff reported "hydrants are so few that it is a common occurrence for buildings to burn to the ground for want of water" and urged supervisors to not "close their eyes" to the problem, especially in light of Chief Sullivan's repeated protests. "No Excuse For The Neglect," *SFE*, December 26, 1893.

27 **"weak streams"** . . . : "Bigger Mains Demanded," *SFC*, July 10, 1895, p. 9.

27 **"alarming increase in the number . . ."**: "The Fire Department. Recommendations of Chief Sullivan to the Supervisors," *SFC*, August 29, 1893, p. 3.

27 **"scathing report on the city's lack of water"** . . . : "Bigger Mains Demanded," *SFC*, July 10, 1895, p. 9.

27 **especially true South of Market** . . . : *SanbornMap*; *WaterSupply*.

28 **James Phelan** . . . : Information about James Phelan was obtained primarily through contemporaneous reporting of Bay Area newspapers and *Legacy of a Native Son—James Duval Phelan & Villa Montalvo* (New Mexico: Forbes Mill Press, 1993) by James P. Walsh and Timothy J. O'Keefe.

28 **"He was immune to the temptations . . ."**: Bean, *Boss Ruef's San Francisco*, p. 8.

28 **"full paid" professional fire department** . . . : *SFC*, July 22, 1898, p. 9.

28 **"large sums collected . . ."**: *SFC*, January 23, 1898.

29 **rusting ironwork and falling** . . . : *SFC*, January 19, 1899.

29 **"a dark and dismal pile . . ."**: *SFC*, March 28, 1899.

29 **more than $5.7 million** . . . : *SFC*, April 18, 1909.

29 **The threat of earthquakes** . . . : Information on tectonic plates and the geology of the portion of the San Andreas Fault running through and alongside northern and central California and specific data on earthquakes there, including 1906, was obtained from Bruce Bolt's book

Earthquakes (Fifth Edition) (New York: W. H. Freeman & Co., 2004); Robert S. Yeats, Kerry Sieh, and Clarence R. Allen, *The Geology of Earthquakes* (New York: Oxford University Press, 1997); D. J. Wald, H. Kanamori, D. V. Helmbeger, and T. H. Heaton, *Source Study of the 1906 San Francisco Earthquake*, Bulletin of the Seismological Society of America, vol. 83, no. 4 (1993); *SanAndreas*; and author interviews with Dr. David P. Russ, former regional director for the Northeast Region for the US Geological Survey (USGS) and former deputy chief of the Office of Earthquakes, Volcanoes, and Engineering in Reston, VA.

30 **"slight" to "violent"** . . . : "Slight" shocks occurred on May 17, 1851, January 9, 1854, January 2, 1855, October 18, 1856, September 24, 1859, November 19, 1859, December 6, 1859, etc. And a "violent" earthquake struck on November 26, 1858. San Francisco Earthquake History 1769–1879, 1880–1914, VMSF. The *Examiner* reported the 1868 Hayward earthquake as "a violent shock," *SFE*, October 27, 1868, p. 1.

30 **"the heaviest earthquake shock"** . . . : Mark Twain, "Earthquake at San Francisco," *Montana Post*, October 1865.

30 **"Never was a solemn solitude . . ."**: Mark Twain, *Roughing It* (Hartford, Conn.: American Publishing Co., 1891), p. 434.

30 **"big"** . . . : Putnam.

30 **"the great earthquake"** . . . : "The Earthquake," *SFCh*, October 22, 1868, p. 2; "Great Earthquake in San Francisco," *The Guardian* (San Bernardino, Cali.), October 31, 1868, p. 1; "The Earthquake," *Santa Cruz Weekly Sentinel*, October 31, 1868, p. 1. Even in 1905, it was still referred to as "the great earthquake of 1868." *SFC*, January 26, 1905, p. 8.

30 **"totally demolished"** . . . : *SFC*, October 22, 1868.

30 **six in the city** . . . : *SFE*, October 23, 1868.

30 **"providing against the effects . . ."**: *SFCh*, December 9, 1868.

30 **Even without a public report** . . . : In his book *Bracing for Disaster*, Dr. Stephen Tobriner makes the point that the report might not have been fully completed, and whether it was completed and subsequently not published made little difference because "the message had penetrated public consciousness" and builders and planners "had a new awareness of seismic danger and of earthquake-resistant retrofit and design." Tobriner, *Bracing for Disaster*, pp. 57–58.

31 **"earthquake proof"** . . . : The Palace Hotel was advertised as "Fire and earthquake proof" in *SFE*, January 30, 1890, p. 4.

31 **"long rolling"** . . . : Gladys Hansen, Richard Hansen, and Dr. William Blaisdell, *Earthquake, Fire, and Epidemic—Personal Accounts of the 1906 Disaster* (Untreed Reads Publishing, 2013), p. 7. This was the description by seismologist George Davidson referring to a March 26, 1872, earthquake.

31 **"sharp, undulating shock"** . . . : *Ibid*. This was George Davidson's description of an April 19, 1892, earthquake, which the *Call* reported was "the severest one felt here since the big earthquake of 1868." "The Earth Swayed," *SFC*, April 20, 1892, p. 8.

31 **"like the snapping of a whip"** . . . : This was a description of an April 1898 earthquake: "Tall buildings shook like the snapping of a whip and drove tourists out into the streets in their night clothes." Hansen, *Earthquake, Fire, and Epidemic*, p. 19.

32 **"the company declines"** . . . : Hermann Schussler, in a March 4, 1901, letter responding to another of Chief Sullivan's recommendations for additional hydrants—by that point the list had grown to 498—wrote it would result in an added expense. "Therefore, in reference to your communication, we beg to say that the Spring Valley Water Works positively declines this proposition, not only because the general allowances are entirely inadequate, but also as an approval by the Spring Valley Water Works of the above contingent offer might be construed as an acceptance

of the ordinance, which the company declines." *San Francisco Municipal Reports for the Fiscal Year 1900–1901* (San Francisco: The Hinton Printing Co., 1901), pp. 178–179.

32 **"to ensure a sufficient supply . . ."**: D. T. Sullivan, 1903 Recommendations of the Chief, SFFD Fire Museum, guardiansofthecity.org/sffd/chiefs/dt_sullivan_yearly_recommendations .html. Note: this is corrected from the original spelling "to insure . . ."

32 **"light-draught, high-power"** . . . : D. T. Sullivan, 1904 Recommendations of the Chief, SFFD Fire Museum, guardiansofthecity.org/sffd/chiefs/dt_sullivan_yearly_recommendations .html. Note that Chief Sullivan began requesting this in his 1897 Recommendations of the Chief.

32 **"the small and inadequate"** . . . : D. T. Sullivan, 1905 Recommendations of the Chief, SFFD Fire Museum, guardiansofthecity.org/sffd/chiefs/dt_sullivan_yearly_recommendations.html.

32 **political boss Abe Ruef** . . . : Walton Bean, "Boss Ruef, the Union Labor Party, and the Graft Prosecution in San Francisco, 1901–1911," *Pacific Historical Review*, vol. 17, no. 4 (November 1948); Walton Bean, *Boss Ruef's San Francisco—The Story of the Union Labor Party, Big Business, and the Graft Prosecution* (Berkeley: University of California Press, 1952); "Hon. A. Ruef, Attorney for the Mayor's Office," in *San Francisco and its Municipal Administration 1902*, ed. Blake Evarts (San Francisco: Pacific Publishing Company, 1902), pp. 32–33; Abraham Ruef, "The Road I Traveled: An Autobiographic Account of My Career from University to Prison, With an Intimate Recital of the Corrupt Alliance between Big Business and Politics in San Francisco," *San Francisco Bulletin*, May 21, 1912–September 5, 1912.

32 **"the power behind the throne"** . . . : Dunne, p. 12. Ruef himself wrote, "Behind that throne, I saw myself its power, local, state—national . . ." Ruef, "The Road I Traveled," *SFB*, May 21, 1912; *Boss Ruef's San Francisco*, p. 27.

32 **"a commanding figure of a man"** . . . : *Boss Ruef's San Francisco*, p. 20.

33 **"legal advisor"** . . . : Blake Evarts, ed., *San Francisco and its Municipal Administration 1902* (San Francisco: Pacific Publishing Company, 1902), p. 29.

33 **"attorney's fees"** . . . : *Boss Ruef's San Francisco*, p. 30.

33 **"for advice in matters of municipal law"** . . . : *Ibid.*, p. 29.

33 **"share his fees"** . . . : Bean, "Boss Ruef, the Union Labor Party, and the Graft Prosecution in San Francisco, 1901–1911," *Pacific Historical Review*, vol. 17, no. 4 (November 1948): p. 446.

33 **"Ruef-Schmitz"** . . . : *OT*, October 1, 1904; *EB*, October 5, 1904; *SFCh*, July 31, 1904; *LAH*, September 28, 1905; *SFC*, November 4, 1905.

33 **93 percent of its structures** . . . : As of 1901, there were 3,881 brick structures and 50,494 frame structures in San Francisco, according to the 1901 Report of the Board of Fire Commissioners, *San Francisco Municipal Reports for the Fiscal Year 1900–1901* (San Francisco: The Hinton Printing Co., 1901), p. 124.

33 **"very little frame construction"** . . . : *Report of National Board of Fire Underwriters: By Its Committee Of Twenty on the City of New York, N.Y., Brooklyn and Queens* (New York City: The Board, 1906), p. 69.

33 **44 percent wooden** . . . : 1901 Report of the Board of Fire Commissioners, *San Francisco Municipal Reports for the Fiscal Year 1900–1901, Ending June 30, 1901* (San Francisco: The Hinton Printing Co., 1901), p. 124.

33 **updated building ordinance in 1903** . . . : Bill No. 465, Ordinance No. 645, *Building Ordinances—City and County of San Francisco, Adopted February 6th, 1903* (San Francisco: Daily Pacific Builder, 1903), pp. 6–84.

34 **584 full-time firefighters** . . . : "Report of the Fire Department," *San Francisco Municipal Reports for the Fiscal Year 1905–6, Ending June 30, 1906, and Fiscal Year 1906–7, Ending June 30, 1907* (San Francisco: Neal Publishing, 1908), p. 719.

34 **"light"** . . . : *Report of National Board of Fire Underwriters: By Its Committee Of Twenty on the City of New York, N.Y., Brooklyn and Queens* (New York City: The Board, 1906), p. 209.

34 **"alarmingly severe"** . . . : Grove Karl Gilbert, Joseph Holmes, John Sewell, and Frank Soulé, *The San Francisco Earthquake and Fire of April 18, 1906, and Their Effects on Structures and Structural Materials* (Washington, DC: Government Printing Office, 1907), p. 64.

34 **2.2 percent of buildings** . . . : In the "fire limits," the board found water pressure "too low for automatic sprinkler equipments, standpipes, etc.," and the "fire hydrants were of an old style, and many water mains were too small." They also found "the building laws were not enforced thoroughly and impartially." Within the "congested-value" portion (.49 square miles) of the "fire limits" (1.6 square miles total), the board found 29.5 percent of its 2,086 buildings were wood-frame, 68.3 percent were wood-joisted brick, and only 2.2 percent were fireproof. *Ibid.*, p. 139.

34 **"unmanageable from a fire-fighting standpoint"** . . . : *Ibid.*, p. 51.

35 **"San Francisco has violated all . . ."**: *Ibid.*, p. 140.

2.

37 **Eight-year-old William Dunne** . . . : William J. Dunne (12/09/1897–12/25/1980) grew up on 22nd and Guerrero Streets. His Irish immigrant father, William, worked as a salesman for a liquor distribution company until 1905 and then as a gardener in Golden Gate Park. His mother, Florence, a California native, was a practical nurse. Most information on William's life and experiences in San Francisco before, during, and after the earthquake and fire was obtained from Dunne, *SFDirectory*, and census and voter registration records on Ancestry.com.

37 **"pride and identity"** . . . : Dunne.

38 **"new city"** . . . : Resident photographer Arnold Genthe later wrote, "I wanted to stay, to see the new city which would rise out of the ruins," in Genthe, p. 97; another resident, Sylvan Lisberger, wrote "a new city was to rise on the ashes of the old" in Chapter VI: 1906–1915 of his memoir "The Family," BL; the *Chronicle* headlined "THE NEW CITY BEGINS TODAY" on page 1 of its April 20, 1906, issue; and the *Call* headlined "NEW CITY TO DEFY FLAMES" on page 1 of its April 4, 1906, issue.

38 **morning issue of *L'Italia*** . . . : Page 1 of the April 18, 1906, issue headlined "*PENSATE ALLE VITTIME DEL VESUVIO*" ("THINK ABOUT THE VICTIMS OF VESUVIUS"), and donors and amounts raised were listed on page 4.

38 **"cleated like the gangplanks . . ."**: "Little Italy, a Typical Colony of Altruria in Our Midst," *SFC*, September 9, 1903, p. 21.

38 **forty-three-year-old Melissa Carnahan** . . . : Carnahan.

38 **"tired, but well"** . . . : "Long-Overdue Ship Elisa in the Harbor After Months of Gales in the South Seas," *SFCh*, April 18, 1906, p. 15; "Italian Ship Has Close Call," *SFC*, April 18, 1906, p. 11.

39 **"confronted by a confusion of tracks"** . . . : "Demands Market Street for Trolley," *SFCh*, April 15, 1906, p. 53.

39 **"unsightly"** . . . : The petition circulated among Market Street business owners read, in part, "We believe the construction of an overhead trolley system to be unsightly, dangerous and not in keeping with the endeavors of the citizens of San Francisco," as reported in "Poles Favored By New Body," *SFC*, April 6, 1906, p. 9.

39 **"many wooden blocks"** . . . : "High Praise for the Fire Department of this City," *SFC*, April 18, 1906, p. 9.

40 **twelve-year-old Marion Baldwin** . . . : Baldwin.

40 **In Chinatown . . . :** Details about life in Chinatown during that period were obtained primarily from John Kuo Wei Tchen (selections and text), Arnold Genthe (photographs), *Genthe's Photographs of San Francisco's Old Chinatown* (New York: Dover Publications, 1984); Philip P. Choy, *San Francisco Chinatown: A Guide to Its History & Architecture* (San Francisco: City Lights Books, 2012); Lee, *At America's Gates: Chinese Immigration during the Exclusion Era, 1882–1943*; Pfaelzer, *Driven Out: The Forgotten War against Chinese Americans*; and Yung and the Chinese Historical Society of America, *San Francisco's Chinatown.*

41 **Melissa and William Carnahan . . . :** Carnahan.

41 **"BRILLIANT ASSEMBLAGE CROWDS GRAND . . .":** *SFC,* April 17, 1906, p. 1.

41 **Tickets for balcony seats . . . :** Dennis Smith, *San Francisco Is Burning—The Untold Story of the 1906 Earthquake and Fires* (New York: Viking, 2005), p. 12.

41 **"the dresses seemed more beautiful . . .":** "Brilliant Audience Greets New Carmen," *SFCh,* April 18, 1906, p. 5.

42 **"[A]ll of San Francisco and . . .":** John Barrymore, *Confessions of an Actor* (Indianapolis: The Bobbs-Merrill Company, 1926), p. 55.

42 **"ringing tenor woke up the . . .":** "Caruso Superb in Role of Don Jose," *SFCh,* April 18, 1906, p. 5.

42 **"a brilliant company" . . . :** Philip Fradkin, *The Great Earthquake and Firestorms of 1906* (Berkeley: University of California Press, 2005), p. 46.

42 **"the goods" . . . :** Letter from Laurence M. Klauber to his sister Alice, May 1, 1906, CHS.

42 **"Surely, what I have felt . . .":** Hopper.

42 **"string of carriages" . . . :** Letter from Laurence M. Klauber to his sister Alice, May 1, 1906, CHS.

42 **"with the music of *Carmen* . . .":** Genthe, p. 87.

42 **"ashamed and guilty" . . . :** Baldwin.

42 **Hugh Kwong Liang . . . :** *The Unshakable—Rebirth of Chinatown in 1906* (Brisbane, CA: Sing Tao Newspaper Ltd., 2006), p. 18.

43 **Lily Soo-Hoo . . . :** Interview of Lily Sung, by Connie Young Yu, at Lily's Palo Alto home, March 27, 1980; taped recording transcribed by Yu, January 26, 2006; *The Unshakable— Rebirth of Chinatown in 1906*, p. 16.

43 **"delightful" . . . :** Account of Gregory Lighthouse, 1919, RSS.

43 **"Mission boy" . . . :** Dunne.

43 **switchboard operator James Kelly . . . :** JKelly.

43 **"a man could stand on . . .":** Testimony of Charles F. Daley, *WCvAL.*

43 **"FIRE ALARM STATION" . . . :** A 1906-era firebox is on display at the SFFD Fire Museum on Presidio Avenue.

43 **handle of any street box . . . :** Information about the fire alarm system and procedures of the switchboard operators and the 10–1, 10–2, and 10–3 signals for first, second, and third alarms was obtained primarily from JKelly and the sworn testimony of Charles F. Daley, *WCvAL.*

44 **burning at the Central California Canneries warehouse . . . :** *SFC,* April 18, 1906, p. 2.

44 **When the bell rang on . . . :** GBrown. Information about the training and procedures of the San Francisco Fire Department's engine, chemical, and truck companies to a first, second, or third alarm was obtained from author interviews with Bill Koenig, retired SFFD lieutenant and founding member of Guardians of the City; his book, *Everything Took Time—The Actions of the San Francisco Fire Department During the 1906 Great Earthquake and Fire* (Evansville, IN: M. T.

Publishing Company, 2020); the History of SFFD series by Battalion Chief Frederick J. Bowlen, which ran in *SFCh* in 1939; and the SFFD Fire Museum.

44 **"12 seconds"** . . . : "Hoses Hitched, Set in 7½ Seconds," *SFCh*, June 10, 1939, p. 7.

45 **tapped out the second alarm** . . . : JKelly.

46 **"big and bulging"** . . . : Charles Keeler, *San Francisco and Thereabout* (San Francisco: The Stanley-Taylor Co., 1902), p. 45.

46 **"basket-work of iron enclosed in brick"** . . . : "The Work Goes Bravely On," *SFE*, November 23, 1874, p. 3.

46 **"happy"** . . . : Caruso.

46 **"as particularly peaceful"** . . . : Hopper.

47 **around 3:00 a.m.** . . . : GBrown, JKelly.

47 **$50,000 in damages** . . . : "Almost Lose Life in Fire," *SFC*, April 18, 1906, p. 2.

47 **Charles Daley tapped out a signal** . . . : Testimony of Charles F. Daley, *WCvAL*.

47 **"spread its brightness on the . . ."**: Charles Morris, *The San Francisco Calamity by Earthquake and Fire* (Washington, DC: W. E. Scull, 1906), p. 67.

48 **"bright and inviting"** . . . : Account of Frank Louis Ames, *Arg.*, November 6, 1926.

48 **"within a stone's throw"** . . . : Hewitt.

48 **police officer Harry Schmidt spoke** . . . : Account of Harry C. Schmidt, *Arg.*, May 1, 1906.

48 **Sergeant Jesse Cook spoke with** . . . : JCook1, JCook2.

3.

49 **Thomas Chase's morning walk** . . . : Chase.

49 **"North of the slot were . . ."**: Jack London, "South of the Slot," *Saturday Evening Post*, May 22, 1909.

49 **"clear and bright"** . . . : Chase.

49 **thick sedimentary layer of old bay clay** . . . : This "old bay clay" consists of glacial deposits from millions of years ago and reaches great depths particularly in the South of Market district. Beginning in 2013, foundation piles for the Salesforce Tower were driven through the fill land and clay to depths of more than 250 feet in some places to reach bedrock. *See e.g.*, Ron Klemencic, Michael T. Valley, and John D. Hooper, "Salesforce Tower: New Benchmarks in High-Rise Seismic Safety," *Structure* (magazine), June 2017, pp. 44–48. *See also* any story on the leaning Millennium Tower high-rise in South of Market, constructed in the same alluvial soil and clay on friction piles not driven to bedrock.

50 **Hillenbrand Hotel** . . . : The Hillenbrand, the original name of the four-story wood-frame hotel at 718, 719, and 720 Valencia Street, was sold at auction in October 1890. *See* "Notice of Sale," *SFE*, October 20, 1890, p. 7; *SFCh*, October 27, 1890, p. 5.

50 **"[e]verything was peaceful and orderly"** . . . : Account of Lt. H. N. Powell, *Arg.*, October 9, 1926.

50 **At that moment, seven miles** . . . : Information about the earthquake of April 18, 1906, including its timing, focus, epicenter, and magnitude, was obtained primarily from *Report-SEIC;* "The Great 1906 San Francisco Earthquake," US Geological Survey, earthquake.usgs.gov /earthquakes/events/1906calif/18april/; and D. J. Wald, H. Kanamori, D. V. Helmbeger, and T. H. Heaton, *Source Study of the 1906 San Francisco Earthquake*, Bulletin of the Seismological Society of America, vol. 83, no. 4 (1993).

51 **Clarence Judson, a thirty-six-year-old . . . :** *1900Census, SFDirectory,* and *DeathIndex.*

51 **"a breaker larger than usual . . .":** Hansen, *Denial of Disaster,* pp. 29–30.

52 **"dashed to the ground" . . . :** Letter from Ernest H. Adams to Messrs. Reed & Barton, April 23, 1906, VMSF.

52 **"bed sliding about on its castors" . . . :** Letter from William Stephenson, Maj., US Army, May 31, 1906, BL.

52 **"unwonted stir" . . . :** Eugenia C. Murrell Poston, Personal Experiences from Apr. 18 to June 10, 1906: signed and amended typescript, BL.

53 **"awakened from a sound sleep" . . . :** ConlonJr.

53 **"thought it was time to get up" . . . :** Letter from Catherine to Elise, April 22, 1906, Nine Miscellaneous Letters from Unidentified Eyewitnesses to the San Francisco Earthquake and Fire, 1906, CHS.

53 **Twenty-four-year-old William Carr . . . :** William Carr died April 18, 1906, at his residence, 1547 Ellis Street, by asphyxiation by suffocation, was buried temporarily in a lot at Bay and Powell Streets, was disinterred on April 24, 1906, and was reburied in Laurel Hill Cemetery. *SFB,* April 25, 1906; Gladys Hansen Death Index, SFPL. The April 19, 1906, issue of the *Houston Post* reported his death, under the name Willie Carr. *DeathIndex* lists the death of only one William Carr, 24, in May 1906, in Surnames A-E, p. 1648.

53 **twenty-one-year-old Henry Magill . . . :** Henry Magill Jr. was born in 1885 in New Zealand and died April 18, 1906, at 1021 Van Ness Avenue of a fracture of the skull from a falling chimney. Coroner's Book C, p. 42, Gladys Hansen Death Index, SFPL; *1900Census.* The *SFDirectory* lists him as a clerk living at 422 Post Street. *DeathIndex* lists his death at twenty-one years old on April 18, 1906, and he is buried in Holy Cross Catholic Cemetery in Colma, CA, under the same headstone as his father, who passed in 1922.

53 **sixty-year-old maid Annie Whelan's . . . :** Annie Whelan died at sixty years old on April 18, 1906, at 2722 Sacramento Street by asphyxia by suffocation. Coroner's Book A, p. 44, Gladys Hansen Death Index, SFPL; *DeathIndex*; *SFE,* April 25, 1906, p. 2. She was killed in her bed according to the *Houston Post,* April 19, 1906, p. 1.

53 **"killed while asleep" . . . :** Annie was reportedly "killed while asleep, at 2782 Sacramento Street, by fall of chimney." *The Boston Post,* April 19, 1906, p. 1.

53 **"could hear the creaking and the roaring . . .":** Baldwin.

53 **"The shock came" . . . :** Burke.

54 **Forty-four-year-old Margaret Bullard . . . :** Margaret J. Bullard of 1836 Lombard Street died of heart failure on April 18, 1906. *SFC,* May 18, 1906; *SFE,* May 19, 1906; Coroner's Book C, p. 43, Gladys Hansen Death Index, SFPL; *SFDirectory.* She was buried in Olivet Memorial Park.

54 **fifteen-year-old Ottilie Kettner . . . :** Ottilie Kettner was born 1891 in California to George Kettner and Caroline Winsdorfer and died at fifteen on April 18, 1906, at 3034 Pierce Street of "Shock caused by earthquake." Coroner's Book C, p. 80, Gladys Hansen Death Index, SFPL; W. P. Peterson & Co. Funeral Records, San Francisco; *1900Census*; *DeathIndex.*

54 **" 'Oh papa, I am dying'" . . . :** The April 19, 1906, issue of *The Pueblo Chieftain* (Pueblo, CO) reported "Otto Setner, 16 years old, 324 Pierce St, rushed into the room of his father when the awful shock came and shouted: 'Oh papa, I am dying.' The child fell dead in his father's arms." This is listed under "Setter, Otto" in Gladys Hansen Death Index, SFPL, but is referring to Ottilie Kettner.

54 **"I had gotten as far as . . .":** Dewitt Baldwin, "Memories of the Earthquake," as related to Ana Maria P. de Jesus, September 19, 1988, VMSF.

54 **"when the house started rocking"** . . . : Account of Gregory Lighthouse, 1919, RSS.

55 **"hurry [his] paces"** . . . : Account of Lt. H. N. Powell, *Arg.*, October 9, 1926.

55 **"very severe shock"** . . . : Stetson1.

55 **"[I]t felt like this was . . ."**: Harold L. Zellerbach, excerpt from "Art, Business and Public Life in San Francisco," Oral History Transcript, BL.

56 **"thrown prone"** . . . : Hewitt.

56 **"a slight trembling"** . . . : Account of Edward J. Plume, *Arg.*, September 18, 1926.

57 **"stuffy" and "oppressive"** . . . : Account of Sgt. Stephen V. Bunner, *Arg.*, August 14, 1926.

57 **"had scarcely been asleep"** . . . : Genthe, p. 87.

57 **"pictures falling"** . . . : Letter from L. M. Simpson to George, April 27, 1906, Phillips-Jones.

57 **"caught the china cabinet as . . ."**: Letter from Sarah Phillips to George, April 18, 1906, *ibid.*

57 **"glad to have it to hold . . ."**: Letter from L. M. Simpson to George, April 27, 1906, *ibid.*

57 **"like rats in a trap"** . . . : Letter from Ada Higgins, April 1906, SFPL.

57 **Thirty-six-year-old Sarah Corbus** . . . : Sarah "Sadie" Corbus was thirty-six years old and lived at 1511 Jones Street (near Jackson). She was listed at this address in the 1903 San Francisco City Directory, and listed as residing at this address with her father, Andrew T. Corbus, in *1900 Census*. She was killed from shock due to injuries from falling bricks in the earthquake, according to the Gladys Hansen Death Index, SFPL, and the April 29, 1906, issue of *SFC*. Note the April 21, 1906, issue of *Argonaut* reported a Mrs. Corbett, her young child, and her Japanese servant, all living at the corner of Jones/Jackson, killed by a brick chimney falling into their bedrooms. This was likely a misspelling of Corbus, as no record of any Corbett living near Jones/Jackson Streets or dying on this day can be found. Sarah is listed as two separate people in VMSF's Register of Dead: "Miss Sadie Corbus" and "Sarah C. Corbus." *See also* note for Sarah Corbus from prologue, *supra*.

57 **"in an avalanche of brick"** . . . : *SFC*, April 29, 1906.

57 **school principal Jean Parker** . . . : Jean Parker resided at 1320 Jones Street and was the principal of S.F. State Normal School. Gladys Hansen Death Index, SFPL.

57 **"Miss Jean Parker"** . . . : "Miss Jean Parker, one of the best-known teachers ever taught in S.F. schools, was killed at her home on Jones Street near Jackson." *SFB*, April 26, 1906, p. 2.

58 **"could not stand steadily"** . . . : Wing.

58 **"house in motion"** . . . : Account of Peter J. Mullins, RSS.

58 **Edward and Anna Butler** . . . : Anna (Mrs. Edward Butler) was a Salvation Army officer who died April 19, 1906, at 913 Natoma Street of injuries from falling at her home. *OH*, April 27, 1906. According to Coroner's Book C, p. 143 rear fly leaf, she died at Dr. Simon's Sanitarium at 2344 Sutter Street, and her husband, Edward, was injured. Gladys Hansen Death Index, SFPL. *DeathIndex* only lists one Anna N. Butler, dying May 1906, in Surnames A-E, p. 1456.

58 **Mary Donovan** . . . : Mary resided at 915 Natoma Street and died at fifty-five years old on April 19, 1906, of internal injuries sustained from a falling building. *SFDirectory*, *DeathIndex*; *SFC* and *SFCh*, April 24, 1906.

58 **Hermann Meyer** . . . : Hermann M. Meyer was thirty-eight years old, injured at 1422 Mission Street, and died at Mount Zion Hospital from shock following injuries to his head, chest, and right leg. Coroner's Book C, p. 81, Gladys Hansen Death Index, SFPL; *DeathIndex*; and *SF-Directory*. Note: Hermann is listed in a duplicate as Meyer Hermann in the Gladys Hansen Death Index, SFPL.

58 **"a chimney crashed through the . . ."**: "Mr. Meyer, who was sleeping in a front room, got up and rushed to see if his wife was safe . . . a chimney crashed through the roof and buried him beneath falling brick. . . . He was conveyed to a hospital and died the next night." *SFC*, p. 7.

59 **"cheap mantraps"** . . . : Roger W. Lotchin, ed., *Narratives of the San Francisco Earthquake and Fire of 1906* (Allentown, PA: The Lakeside Press, R.R. Donnelley & Sons Co., 2011), p. 251.

59 **Fifteen-year-old Myrtle Muge** . . . : Myrtle Muge died at fifteen years old on April 18, 1906, at 158 Langston Street from asphyxiation by suffocation. Gladys Hansen Death Index, SFPL; *DeathIndex*; *SFCh*, April 27, 1906; *OH*, April 27, 1906, p. 3.

59 **Twenty-four-year-old Cecilia O'Toole** . . . : The coroner's office received a Cecil A. O'Toole, who was listed as being crushed by a falling building on 9th Street between Bryant and Brannan. SFFD Captain J. T. Murphy of Engine 29 reported, "We received word that a building situated on 9th between Bryant & Brannan, had also been shaken down and on our arrival we rescued a family named O'Toole." Murphy. And *DeathIndex* lists a Cecil A. O'Toole dying April 18, 1906, at twenty-four years old. This was later determined to be Cecilia O'Toole, the wife of Michael O'Toole, confirmed by a December 15, 1984, letter from Barbara E. Huth: "I lost an aunt in the quake . . . she was killed because a large picture over the bed fell on her breaking or crushing her nose and she suffocated. My uncle dragged her body around for several days before she was finally buried." Cecilia was buried in Holy Cross Catholic Cemetery in Colma, CA. Coroner's Book C, p. 69, Gladys Hansen Death Index, SFPL.

59 **Adolph Schwinn, a grocer** . . . : Adolph Schwinn died at thirty-one years old on April 18, 1906, at 1741 Howard Street, crushed by the collapse of a building. Coroner's Book A, p. 48, Gladys Hansen Death Index, SFPL; *DeathIndex*. His wife, Emily, twenty-nine, died with him. Coroner's Book A, p. 49, Gladys Hansen Death Index, SFPL; *DeathIndex*. They are buried together in Mountain View, CA.

59 **John Judge, a locomotive engineer** . . . : John Judge died at thirty-four years old April 18, 1906, from heart trouble aggravated by the overexertion of kicking down a door of his home to rescue family members during the earthquake. *Oakland Enquirer*, April 18, 1906, extra edition, p. 1; *DeathIndex*. He is buried in St. Mary's Cemetery in Oakland, and his headstone bears a date of death of April 21, 1906.

59 **eighteen-year-old Edna Ketring** . . . : Edna was born July 1887, per *1900Census* when she lived with her parents in San Bernardino. Her account of surviving the earthquake in the Brunswick Hotel and losing her fiancé, Thomas Bowes, was reported in the April 24, 1906, issues of *LAH* and the *Los Angeles Sun* and the May 3, 1906, issue of *SFCh*. There was a Thomas Bowes in the *SFDirectory*, listed as a sash maker living on Clara Street, and he does not appear in the 1907 city directory.

59 **"The walls were cracking open . . ."**: *Los Angeles Sun*, April 24, 1906.

59 **"jumped out of bed and . . ."**: James Madison Jacobs was in his eighth day staying in room 56 on the third floor of the Brunswick Hotel, and his account was published in *Arg.*, October 9, 1926.

60 **"to jump out of the . . ."**: William F. Stehr was a baker at Vienna Model Bakery at 222 Sutter Street and was staying on the top floor of the Nevada Hotel. He got off work around 1:00 a.m., got in bed around 2:00 a.m., and was awakened by the earthquake. His account was published in *Arg.*, October 2, 1926, and October 9, 1926.

60 **"intensely dark"** . . . : *Los Angeles Sun*, April 24, 1906.

60 **"felt paralyzed as the building . . ."**: Account of James Jacobs, *Arg.*, October 9, 1926.

60 **"faster and tighter"** . . . : Account of William Stehr, *Arg.*, October 9, 1926.

60 **"collapsed like card houses"** . . . : Account of William Stehr, *Arg.*, October 2, 1926.

60 **"flat"** . . . : *Denial of Disaster,* p. 24.

61 **"bright and inviting"** . . . : Account of Frank Louis Ames, *Arg.,* November 6, 1926.

61 **"in a ship on the ocean"** . . . : Caruso.

61 **"and halfway across the room"** . . . : Recollection of Egbert Gould, *Denial of Disaster,* p. 28.

61 **"turned on its axis"** . . . : Recollection of Cora Older, wife of *Bulletin* editor Fremont Older, *ibid.,* p. 27.

61 **"like the top of a tree . . ."**: Way.

61 **"tremendous and indescribable"** . . . : James W. Byrne, *Recollections of the Fire—San Francisco's 1906 Earthquake and Fire* (San Francisco: privately printed, 1927), p. 11.

61 **"the roaring and cracking of . . ."**: Way.

61 **"breaking glass"** . . . : Recollection of Henry Hahn, visiting from Portland, *Denial of Disaster,* pp. 27–28.

61 **"the rumbling of the earth"** . . . : Goerlitz.

61 **"as if they were mad"** . . . : This was Egbert H. Gould, *Denial of Disaster,* p. 28.

61 **A salesman from Detroit** . . . : This was George P. Way, founding owner of Artificial Eardrum Company in Detroit, MI, staying in room 612 of the Palace Hotel. His story was told in several articles in the *Detroit Free Press* (in the April 19, 24, 25, and 27, 1906, issues) and *The Evening Record* (Windsor, Ontario) (in the April 27, 1906, issue).

62 **"on a ship in a gale . . ."**: Carnahan.

62 **"from south to north like . . ."**: "BUSCH DESCRIBES IT ALL; The St. Louis Brewer Tells of His Adventures in San Francisco," *NYT,* April 21, 1906, p. 2.

62 **"would tip over"** . . . : Recollection of Dr. W. Edward Hibbard, *Denial of Disaster,* p. 33.

62 **"that the ten stories above . . ."**: Recollection of J. C. Gill, *ibid.*

62 **"required all my strength to . . ."**: Recollection of W. R. Harriman, *ibid.*

62 **"Then the big twist came . . ."**: Account of Edward J. Wiskotchill, *Arg.,* June 5, 1926.

62 **"woken up very rudely"** . . . : Interview of Lily Sung, by Connie Young Yu at Lily's Palo Alto home, March 27, 1980; taped recording transcribed by Yu, January 26, 2006, *The Unshakable—Rebirth of Chinatown in 1906,* p. 16.

63 **"became so severe"** . . . : JKelly.

63 **"a mass of glass"** . . . : Charles F. Daley, *WCvAL.*

63 **"It sounded like thunder outside"** . . . : Account of Harry C. Schmidt, *Arg.,* May 1, 1906.

63 **"like the waves of an ocean . . ."**: JCook1.

64 **"At that moment I believe . . ."**: Account of Thomas Burns, *Arg.,* May 22, 1926.

64 **"It'll be over in a minute!"** . . . : Account of Alex Paladini, *Arg.,* August 7, 1926.

64 **"a low distant rumble"** . . . : Chase.

65 **"distant thunder"** . . . : Joseph Harper, Observations of the San Francisco Earthquake, delivered before the Montana Society of Engineers, January 11, 1908, VMSF.

65 **"a thousand violins playing off key"** . . . : *Denial of Disaster,* p. 36.

65 **"cracking bricks"** . . . : Dr. Wilber M. Swett, letter, May 27, 1906, BL.

65 **"crying of the children"** . . . : Letter from Charles to Flora, May 8, 1906, SFPL.

65 **"a horrible chorus of human . . ."**: Morris, *The San Francisco Calamity by Earthquake and Fire,* p. 68.

66 **"indescribable sound"** . . . : Letter from Henry Atkins to art dealership partner Frederic Cheever Torrey, April 26, 1906, BL.

66 **"huddled up in bed"** . . . : Letter from Agnes Ehrenberg, April 19, 1906, CHS.

66 **"jumping up and down a . . ."**: Leach, p. 313.

66 **"feeling something shaking me like . . ."**: Ivan S. Rankin, Recollections of the Earthquake and Fire in San Francisco, April 18, 19, 20, and 21, 1906, CHS.

66 **"sprang out of bed and . . ."**: Atherton, p. 394.

66 **"rosy dawn"** . . . : Letter from William Hancock to his sister Mary, May 29, 1906, CHS.

66 **"like a cyclone"** . . . : Morrow.

66 **"sickening onrush of motion"** . . . : CLondon, p. 100.

66 **"the noise of the falling buildings"** . . . : Letter from Laurence M. Klauber to his sister Alice, May 1, 1906, CHS.

66 **"lift clear off the ground, and then the other"** . . . : Letter from Anna Poston to Papa, April 20, 1906, Nine Miscellaneous Letters from Unidentified Eyewitnesses to the San Francisco Earthquake and Fire, 1906, CHS.

67 **"violent agitation"** . . . : *KCS*, April 18, 1906.

67 **"Will it never stop? . . ."**: Miller.

67 **"hideous minute and a quarter"** . . . : Hopper.

67 **"It seemed a quarter of an hour . . ."**: Morris, *The San Francisco Calamity by Earthquake and Fire*, p. 67.

67 **"not more than 25 seconds"** . . . : Letter from Silas W. Mack to Clara W. Mack, April 20, 1906, the Gilder Lehrman Collection, the Gilder Lehrman Institute of American History.

67 **"about 30 seconds"** . . . : Einstein.

67 **"kept up without stop for . . ."**: Letter from Tom Davis to mother in England, 1906, CHS.

67 **"seemed five or six minutes"** . . . : DBrown.

67 **"about forty seconds duration"** . . . : Testimony of Professor Alexander G. McAdie, *WCvAL*.

67 **"a most violent earthquake shock . . ."**: Morrow.

67 **"the shock lasted forty-eight seconds"** . . . : *CCE*.

67 **"I am told that the shake . . ."**: W. E. Alexander, Account of the 1906 San Francisco Earthquake and Fire, CHS.

67 **"from every damaged area as . . ."**: *ReportSEIC*.

68 **"strong shaking"** . . . : US Geological Survey, "The Great 1906 San Francisco Earthquake," earthquake.usgs.gov/earthquakes/events/1906calif/18april/.

68 **"incredulity at the mere length . . ."**: Hopper.

68 **"how long it lasted God . . ."**: Walter C. Scott, letter to his aunt, April 20, 1906, CHS.

4.

69 **"Then I noted the great silence"** . . . : Hopper.

69 **"ominous quiet"** . . . : Genthe, p. 87.

69 **"noticed the quietness that people . . ."**: Account of Gregory Lighthouse, 1919, RSS.

70 **"shaken up pretty lively with . . ."**: Letter from James Warren to his son Pete, April 21, 1906, CHS.

70 **"It's an earthquake" . . .** : Dunne.

70 **"sound asleep until awakened by . . ."**: Account of Alex J. Young, December 6, 1919, RSS.

70 **"did not even feel the earthquake" . . .** : Account of Anna Meakin, RSS.

70 **"the fallen furniture and debris" . . .** : Account of William M. Ross, *Arg.*, May 15, 1906.

70 **Hiram Daniels's . . .** : Hiram M. Daniels, born June 10, 1839, in Vermont, died April 18, 1906, at his residence, 519 McAllister Street, when the earthquake caused the folding bed to close and break his neck. Coroner's Book C, p. 78, Gladys Hansen Death Index, SFPL; *SFC*, May 18 and 19, 1906; *SFE*, May 19, 1906. He was sixty-six years old, was buried in Cloverdale Cemetery, and his spouse was Charlotte, who was in the Murphy bed with him and nearly suffocated before their houseguests lowered it. Author interview with their great-granddaughter Nancy Cedeño (the granddaughter of Hiram and Charlotte's youngest daughter—of nine children—Nellie), July 27 and August 4, 2019.

70 **"like a dollhouse" . . .** : Chase.

70 **"and saw that the streets . . ."**: W. E. Alexander, Account of the 1906 San Francisco Earthquake and Fire, CHS.

70 **"raised the shades, and looked out" . . .** : Sinsheimer.

71 **"quietness of everyone" . . .** : Fisher, p. 86.

71 **"I did not think there . . ."**: Account of Michael Maher, December 1, 1906, SFPL.

71 **"seemed to grow in the street . . ."**: Letter from "Aunt Bertha" to Elsa Ellerbeck, May 13, 1906, BL.

71 **"The streets presented a weird . . ."**: Genthe, p. 88.

71 **"a stitch of clothes on" . . .** : Siegel.

71 **"in her nightclothes" . . .** : Burke.

71 **"piled up on the sidewalk . . ."**: Stetson1.

71 **"I do not remember a . . ."**: Leithead.

72 **"You know when you build . . ."**: Siegel.

72 **"Everyone is killed!" . . .** : Walsh and O'Keefe, *Legacy of a Native Son*, p. 94.

72 **"the street was like a river" . . .** : Diary of Mary Murphy, 1898–1909, BL.

72 **"shake off and topple over" . . .** : Accounts of James R. Welch and Frank J. Tautenberg, *Arg.*, September 11, 1926.

73 **Reportedly, after hearing Margaret's "cries" . . .** : *Ibid.* and WCook.

73 **"completely wrecked" . . .** : Cullen.

74 **"saw the smoke of an . . ."**: JKelly.

74 **"three columns of smoke" . . .** : Testimony of Charles Daley, *WCvAL*.

74 **"five additional fires starting" . . .** : JKelly.

74 **"blazed up like tinder" . . .** : *Arg.*, August 6, 1927.

75 **"crushed and instantly killed" . . .** : "Tremendous Battle Against 1906 Fire Told," by Frederick J. Bowlen, then SFFD battalion chief and former member of Engine 4, *SFCh*, June 28, 1939, p. 26.

75 **"ran out into the street" . . .** : Letter from Jean Ramsey Voigts, March 12, 1970, CHS.

75 **Hearing "yelling" from inside** . . . : Testimony of Charles R. Murray, *WCvAL*.

75 **"[I]t soon got away from us"** . . . : *SFCh*, June 28, 1939, p. 26.

76 **"drugs, chemicals, and fancy goods"** . . . : Testimony of Adolph Mack, owner and proprietor of Mack & Company Drug Wholesaler, *WCvAL*.

76 **"heard several explosions"** . . . : Testimony of George Kessack, *WCvAL*.

76 **"began smoking and banging . . ."**: Account of Harry F. Walsh, *Arg.*, May 15, 1926.

76 **"mass of flames"** . . . : Testimony of Jeremiah Sullivan, *WCvAL*.

77 **"immediately after the earthquake"** . . . : Testimony of Henry Muller, *WCvAL*.

78 **"Immediately after the quake"** . . . : Leithead.

78 **"within five seconds of the . . ."**: Bennett.

78 **"columns of smoke"** . . . : Cameron.

78 **"large columns of smoke"** . . . : Dryer.

78 **"growing larger"** . . . : Letter from Dr. Wilber M. Swett, May 27, 1906, BL.

78 **fifty-three-year-old Patrick Shaughnessy** . . . : Testimony of Patrick H. Shaughnessy, *WCvAL*.

78 **"gave out after a few minutes"** . . . : Report of Second Assistant Chief Patrick H. Shaughnessy, September 13, 1906, SFFD Fire Museum, Guardians of the City, https://www .guardiansofthecity.org/sffd/fires/great_fires/1906/Shaughnessy.html.

79 **"After a long search"** . . . : Boden.

79 **"several columns of smoke rising . . ."**: Testimony of Patrick H. Shaughnessy, *WCvAL*.

79 **"smoke or fire arising from . . ."**: Testimony of Charles Towe, *WCvAL*.

79 **"The lack of water"** . . . : Goerlitz.

79 **"every receptacle we had with water"** . . . : Untitled Earthquake Narrative, Hooker Family Papers 1783–1951, BL.

80 **"speechless"** . . . : Letter from Rose Barreda to nephew Frederick Barreda, May 15, 1906, with cover letter by Frederick, October 1963, CHS.

80 **"went about and took all . . ."**: Austin, p. 344.

80 **"and then it just stopped by itself"** . . . : Baldwin.

80 **almost total failure** . . . : *WaterSupply*; Testimony of Hermann Schussler, *WCvAL*.

80 **"thrown from its trestle onto . . ."**: Perry.

80 **"bowl of mud"** . . . : Testimony of Hermann Schussler, *WCvAL*.

80 **More than three hundred street mains** . . . : Spring Valley Water Company chief engineer Hermann Schussler testified in 1907: "I made an accurate count of the repaired breaks in the main pipe system . . . and they amounted to a little over 300. . . . In the service pipes, the pipes that supplies the houses, we had by that time found in the neighborhood of 23,200 breaks." Testimony of Hermann Schussler, *ibid.*

80 **4,213 hydrants** . . . : *WaterSupply*.

5.

---

83 **"to check it from going easterly"** . . . : Testimony of Frank Tracy, *WCvAL*.

84 **"I guess I must have fainted"** . . . : "Miss Edna Ketring," *The San Bernardino County Sun*, April 24, 1906, p. 6.

84 **"burrowed toward the daylight"** . . . : Account of James M. Jacobs, *Arg.,* October 9, 1926.

84 **"held up blankets and comfortables** . . .": Mahoney.

84 **Frank Keefe** . . . : Frank Keefe, aged forty-six, and his wife, Florence Keefe, aged thirty-seven, and their son, Leo Keefe, aged twelve, all died on April 18, 1906, in the collapse of the Brunswick Hotel. *SFB,* May 24, 1906, p. 8; Gladys Hansen Death Index, SFPL.

84 **Abraham Lichtenstein** . . . : Abraham Lichtenstein "burned to death" April 18, 1906, at Brunswick House. Coroner's Book C, p. 115, Gladys Hansen Death Index, SFPL. He was born February 1854 in Russia and is buried in Salem Memorial Park and Garden. His wife, Johanna (born July 1860); daughter, Esther (born July 1891); and son, Morris (born July 1885), all died with him. *1900Census*; *SFC,* June 6, 1906, p. 11.

84 **Maud Johnson and Mary Irwin** . . . : Letter from Mrs. D. McDonald to Coroner Walsh, May 28, 1906. *SFE,* May 30, 1906, p. 14.

85 **"Wilson sisters"** . . . : "Brunswick Hotel Death List," *SFC,* June 26, 1906, p. 12.

85 **And in the Nevada House** . . . : Frank Lee, son of the Nevada House proprietor, told the reporter "that but thirteen out of thirty-six lodgers were brought from the ruins alive." *SFC,* May 11, 1906, p. 8.

85 **"were working with rageful energy . . .":** Hopper.

85 **"was split open about six to eight feet"** . . . : Perry.

85 **"like a river"** . . . : Diary of Mary Murphy, 1898–1909, BL.

85 **"[B]y pulling up floors and . . .":** *Arg.,* October 26, 1906.

85 **"The sights there were very distressing"** . . . : Account of Henry Powell, *ibid.*

85 **Annie Conway** . . . : Annie L. Conway died at twenty-seven years old on April 18, 1906, in the Valencia Hotel collapse. Coroner's Book C, p. 72, Gladys Hansen Death Index, SFPL; *SFC,* April 24, 1906; *SFE,* May 4, 1906; *DeathIndex,* Surnames A-E, p. 2147.

86 **Patrick Broderick** . . . : Patrick Broderick died at fifty-nine years old on April 18, 1906, by "asphyxiation by suffocation" in the Valencia Hotel collapse. Coroner's Book A, p. 58, Gladys Hansen Death Index, SFPL; *SFCh,* April 30, 1906; *SFC,* May 18, 1906; *DeathIndex,* Surnames A-E, p. 1216.

86 **Lorenze Goetz** . . . : Lorenze Goetz died at sixty-four years old on April 18, 1906, at St. Francis Hospital after being fatally injured in the Valencia Hotel collapse. *DeathIndex,* Gladys Hansen Death Index, SFPL.

86 **William Krone** . . . : William R. Krone died at forty on April 18, 1906, in the Valencia Hotel collapse. Department of Public Health death registry, SFPL; *DeathIndex,* Surnames A-E, p. 5950; Gladys Hansen Death Index, SFPL. He was listed as "Crone" in the *SFDirectory* as a carpenter living at 2222 Grove Street, but it says "See Krone." Note there is a separate card in the Gladys Hansen Death Index for "William R. Crone," but they are the same individual.

86 **the Johnson family** . . . : Nathan, thirty-two; May, thirty-one; and Harold, two, along with Nathan's brother, Edward, forty-three, were all killed in the Valencia Hotel collapse on April 18, 1906. *DeathIndex,* Surnames F-L, p. 5439. Nathan died of a skull fracture. Coroner's Book A, p. 62. May died of hemorrhage, shock, and a compound fracture of both legs. Coroner's Book A, p. 63. Harold of asphyxiation by suffocation. Coroner's Book A, p. 64. Edward died of a skull fracture. Coroner's Book A, p. 65. They were buried in temporary graves in a lot at Bay and Powell Streets, disinterred on April 24, 1906, and reburied in Cypress Lawn in Colma, CA. *SFB,* April 25, 1906; Gladys Hansen Death Index, SFPL.

86 **Annie Bock** . . . : William P. Bock and his son, William H. Bock, died April 18, 1906,

in the collapse of the Valencia Hotel. *SFC*, April 24, 1906; Coroner's Book C, p. 74; *Arg.*, October 16, 1926; and *DeathIndex*, p. 972. They are buried side by side in Cypress Memorial Park in Colma, CA. Annie died in 1915 and is buried with them.

86 **"cloud of deep dust hung . . ."**: Hewitt.

86 **"dome was stripped clean off . . ."**: Leithead.

87 **"Earthquakes uncover strange secrets"** . . . : Mary Edith Griswold, quoted in *Narratives of the San Francisco Earthquake and Fire of 1906*, edited by Roger W. Lotchin (The Lakeside Press, R.R. Donnelley & Sons Co., 2011), p. 74.

87 **"stood now like a lie exposed"** . . . : Fisher, p. 88.

87 **"in perfect darkness"** . . . : Account of Officer Plume, *Arg.*, September 18, 1926.

87 **"It was black dark and smothering"** . . . : Account of Officer E. F. Parquet, *Arg.*, September 25, 1926.

88 **"forcibly opened"** . . . : Account of Dr. Tilton E. Tillman, *Arg.*, October 2, 1926.

88 **"masked carnival"** . . . : The April 16, 1906, issue of *SFCh* and signs on the Larkin Street sidewalk of Mechanics' Pavilion (still visible on the morning of April 18, 1906) advertised the "masked carnival."

88 **"operating tables, cots, medicine chests . . ."**: Account of Officer Ed F. Parquet, *Arg.*, October 2, 1926.

88 **"terrible state of ruin"** . . . : Account of Sgt. Stephen V. Bunner, *Arg.*, August 14, 1926.

88 **"littered all about"** . . . : Account of Officer Wiskotchill, *Arg.*, June 12, 1926.

89 **"looked as calm as if . . ."**: Account of Officer Behan, *Arg.*, June 19, 1926.

89 **"Hercules of the police department"** . . . : Duke, p. 168.

89 **"terribly crushed and battered"** . . . : Account of Officer Behan, *supra*.

89 **"crashed down the shaft"** . . . : *SFCh*, April 28, 1906, p. 4.

89 **"saw fires in every direction"** . . . : WCook.

90 **"tired and worn out"** . . . : Nichols.

90 **"standing in their doorways in . . ."**: Recollections of Cora and Fremont Older, *Denial of Disaster*, p. 28.

90 **"The proud boast that the Palace . . ."**: Griswold, quoted in *Narratives of the San Francisco Earthquake and Fire of 1906*, p. 72.

90 **"blocked two floors deep with . . ."**: Account of William Cushing, *Arg.*, November 6, 1926.

90 **"preparing coffee and rolls for the help"** . . . : Account of James W. Byrne, *Arg.*, November 27, 1926.

90 **"delicious dishes of coffee and hot rolls"** . . . : Hollister, p. 156.

90 **"in a frantic state"** . . . : Account of Josephine Jacoby, *Arg.*, November 13, 1926.

91 **"To Enrico Caruso"** . . . : Caruso.

91 **"tried to wash, but only . . ."**: Goerlitz.

91 **"like herds of sheep"** . . . : Recollection of Zebedee R. Winslow, *Denial of Disaster*, p. 29.

91 **"spitting blue flames and writhing . . ."**: Account of Frank Louis Ames, *Arg.*, November 6, 1926.

91 **"peculiar smell"** . . . : Letter from John to Lucy R. Schaeffer, May 15, 1906, SFPL.

91 **"sort of a bluish yellow"** . . . : "Eyewitnesses Tell of Frisco Horrors," *Fort Worth Star-Telegram,* April 21, 1906, p. 8.

91 **"strewn with debris"** . . . : Goerlitz.

92 **"automobiles, wagons, vehicles of all . . ."**: Way.

92 **"filled with an excited throng"** . . . : Recollection of Ella Ransom, *Denial of Disaster,* p. 33.

92 **"gorgeously dressed and bespangled with jewels"** . . . : Letter from William Hancock to his sister Mary, May 29, 1906, CHS.

92 **"no occasion for hurry"** . . . : Carnahan.

92 **"filled with people—hardly a . . ."**: Sinsheimer.

92 **"in a state of terror—children . . ."**: Letter from Dr. Wilber M. Swett, May 27, 1906, BL.

92 **"a man in pink pajamas . . ."**: Hopper.

93 **"like an eggshell"** . . . : Recollection of Arthur C. Poore, *Arg.,* Spring 1990.

93 **"swarming with rescuers"** . . . : Hopper.

93 **"was very rickety and dangerous"** . . . : Recollection of Officer E. W. Meredith, *Arg.,* July 3, 1926.

93 **"over piles of plaster and laths"** . . . : Hopper.

93 **"a mound of bricks with . . ."**: *Ibid.* Note: this may have been Jane Burge, whose husband, Frank J. Burge, died at seventy-six on April 18, 1906, at 239 Geary with Jane, proprietor for the Geary Hotel. *SFDirectory; DeathIndex,* Surnames A-E, p. 1386.

93 **"had been broken away from . . ."**: Account of Officer E. W. Meredith, *Arg.,* July 3, 1926.

93 **"A stairway gave out"** . . . : GBrown.

93 **Ida Heaslip** . . . : Ida O. Heaslip (born 11/19/1857 per *1900Census*) died April 18, 1906, at 239 Geary Street from falling walls and asphyxiation by suffocation. *DeathIndex; Houston Post,* April 19, 1906. Her body was temporarily buried in Portsmouth Square and was disinterred on April 25, 1906, identified by her son, and shipped to Live Oak Cemetery in Harrison County, Mississippi, for burial. *SFCh,* April 26, 1906, p. 2. Her son, Francis Jr., died in 1914 and is buried beside her.

93 **"incipient blaze"** . . . : GBrown.

93 **"chaotic"** . . . : Account of Dr. Tilton E. Tillman, *Arg.,* October 2, 1926.

93 **"a ghastly sight"** . . . : Arthur Dangerfield, Journal of the Quake, April 24, 1906, BL.

93 **"strewn with mattresses"** . . . : Fisher, p. 87.

93 **"filled with dead, dying, and injured"** . . . : *CCE.*

94 **"carried in on the doors or shutters . . ."**: Account of Dr. Tilton E. Tillman, *Arg.,* October 2, 1926.

94 **"horribly mangled"** . . . : *CCE.*

94 **"much as a field dressing . . ."**: Account of Dr. Tilton E. Tillman, *Arg.,* October 2, 1926.

94 **"well-equipped"** . . . : Fisher, p. 87.

94 **"a dead body [being] carried . . ."**: Mahoney.

94 **"so as not to distress the injured"** . . . : Account of Dr. Tilton E. Tillman, *Arg.,* October 2, 1926.

94 **"piled in the corner to make room"** . . . : Letter from Charles to Flora, May 8, 1906, SFPL.

6.

96 **"entirely improper"** . . . : "Roosevelt Tells Funston to Quit Talking So Much," *St. Louis Republic*, April 24, 1902.

96 **"beautiful clear morning"** . . . : Funston.

97 **"fully armed"** . . . : Cpt. Kelly, US Army Corps of Engineers, Ft. Mason, to family in Boston, "Earthquake and Fire at San Francisco, Cal., April 18-May 19th," BL.

97 **two men with the city attorney's** . . . : Myrtile Cerf and John T. Williams, *Arg.*, January 15, 1927. The route taken by their car was obtained from Testimony of Eugene Schmitz, *LSvTF.*

97 **"immediately got up and dressed"** . . . : Account of Eugene Schmitz, *Arg.*, January 15, 1927.

97 **"I must go at once"** . . . : Account of John T. Williams, *supra.*

98 **"City Hall"** . . . : Account of Eugene Schmitz, *supra.*

98 **"the Mayor was deeply grieved"** . . . : Account of John T. Williams, *supra.*

98 **seventy-seven prisoners** . . . : *San Francisco Municipal Reports for the Fiscal Year 1905–6, Ending June 30, 1906, and Fiscal Year 1906–7, Ending June 30, 1907* (San Francisco: Neal Publishing, 1908), p. 52.

98 **"a few hasty instructions"** . . . : Funston.

99 **"execute the laws"** . . . : 18 U.S.C. § 1385 (1878).

100 **"waiting for particulars"** . . . : Telegram from Taft to Funston, April 18, 1906, Box 87, Record Group 107: Records of the Office of the Secretary of War, NA.

100 **officer successfully sent a dispatch** . . . : This was Major Carroll Devol, who sent a telegram to the quartermaster general requesting relief. Erwin N. Thompson, *Defender of the Gate: Presidio of San Francisco, CA 1900–1904* (Denver, CO: National Park Service, 1997).

100 **"paralyzed"** . . . : Account of Frederick Funston, *Arg.*, February 12, 1927.

100 **"to aid the police and . . ."**: Funston.

100 **"martial law"** . . . : *CCE.*

100 **"marched the troops into the . . ."**: Letter from Gen. Funston, Presidio of San Francisco, Cal., July 2, 1906, *Arg.*, July 7, 1906.

100 **"take all proper measures for . . ."**: Charter of the City and County of San Francisco, 1900, Article IV, Chapter I, Sec. 2.

101 **"necessary to augment the police . . ."**: Testimony of Eugene Schmitz, *LSvTF.*

102 **"had practically burned itself out"** . . . : Testimony of William R. Whittier, *WCvAL.*

102 **"had gutted the buildings"** . . . : Testimony of Clarence W. Coburn, *WCvAL.*

102 **"If one of the boys . . ."**: Testimony of August Fahlberg, *WCvAL.*

103 **"got the best of it"** . . . : Account of M.T. Lestrange, *Arg.*, August 28, 1926.

103 **"was blazing furiously"** . . . : Account of Cpt. Gillig, *Arg.*, July 30, 1927.

103 **"only the base of one . . ."**: Hopper.

103 **"raging around"** . . . : Cullen.

104 **"[T]he fire had ceased to . . ."**: Reminiscences of Charles de Y. Elkus of the 1906 Earthquake and Fire (dictated some time in 1956), CHS.

104 **"several lines from different directions"** . . . : Schmidt.

104 **"noticed that smoke was coming . . ."**: JCook2.

104 **"fire and smoke filled the street"** . . . : Testimony of James Stetson, *WCvAL*.

105 **"carrying out books and other articles"** . . . : Account of F. Ernest Edward, *Arg.*, October 23, 1926.

105 **"big cracks"** . . . : Testimony of John Dougherty, *WCvAL*.

106 **"all available explosives, with a . . ."**: Account of Frederick Funston, *Arg.*, February 5, 1927; Report to the Adjutant, Presidio of San Francisco, May 2, 1906, VMSF; and Devol2, p. 63.

106 **"The whole of the lower . . ."**: Account of F. Ernest Edward, *supra*.

106 **"Look at the fires; the . . ."**: Miller.

106 **"an endless cavalcade"** . . . : Account of Officer Wiskotchill, *Arg.*, June 12, 1926.

106 **"laid out on benches"** . . . : *Arg.*, August 14, 1926.

106 **"being rifled of valuables"** . . . : Account of Officer Wiskotchill, *supra*.

106 **"evidently by some thief"** . . . : Duke, p. 165.

106 **"Close up every saloon at once"** . . . : Account of John T. Williams, *supra*.

107 **"2,000 men in uniform [with badges] . . ."**: Account of Thornwell Mullally, *Arg.*, August 28, 1926.

107 **"[h]unt up"** . . . : Account of John T. Williams, *supra*.

107 **"As it has come to my . . ."**: Duke, p. 165.

107 **"The proclamation was issued with . . ."**: Testimony of Eugene Schmitz, *LSvTF*.

107 **"were busy conveying the wounded"** . . . : Duke, p. 165.

107 **"had no time to arrest thieves"** . . . : Account of Officer Wiskotchill, *supra*.

108 **"red as blood"** . . . : Way.

108 **"[T]he sun showed bloodshot through . . ."**: Austin, p. 250.

108 **"literally packed with hundreds of . . ."**: JKelly.

109 **"was full of excited, anxious . . ."**: Funston.

109 **"over the city"** . . . : Account of Eugene Schmitz, *Arg.*, January 15, 1927.

109 **"Do you really stand for . . ."**: This was Colonel Morris, quoted by Schmitz, *ibid*.

109 **"realize the magnitude of the calamity"** . . . : *Legacy of a Native Son*, p. 95.

110 **"the people below darting into . . ."**: Letter from Charles Fisk to his mother in England, April 22, 1906, CHS.

110 **"the tops of the buildings . . ."**: J. B. Levison, "Memories for my Family," BL.

110 **"did not know which way . . ."**: Account of Harry C. Schmidt, *Arg.*, May 8, 1926.

110 **"jerky, ugly shock"** . . . : Letter from Rose Barreda to her nephew Frederick Barreda, May 15, 1906, with cover letter by Frederick, October 1963, CHS.

110 **"violent shock"** . . . : Miller.

110 **This aftershock struck at 8:14 a.m.** . . . : Information about the 8:14 a.m. aftershock was obtained from Testimony of Professor McAdie of the US Weather Bureau, *LSvT*; *ReportSEIC*, p. 410; Aron J. Meltzner and David J. Wald, "Felt Reports and Intensity Assignments for Aftershocks and Triggered Events of the Great 1906 California Earthquake" (Department of the Interior, USGS, 2002), Table 1, p. 12.

111 **"of particular severity, a sharp twister"** . . . : Testimony of Professor McAdie, *WCvAL*.

111 **"heavy shock"** . . . : Myrtle Robertson, "An Eye Witness—Miss Myrtle Robertson's Eye-witness Account Given Substantially in Her Own Words," CHS.

111 **"startled afresh the excited crowd"** . . . : Carnahan.

111 **"jewels and small bag of necessaries"** . . . : Emma Eames, *Some Memories and Reflections* (New York: Appleton & Company, 1927), pp. 259–260.

111 **"terrorized" him with "a fear . . ."**: Account of George R. Douglas, RSS.

111 **"so severe"** . . . : Funston.

111 **"started to run out of the building"** . . . : Fisher, p. 90.

7.

113 **It had been twenty-seven years** . . . : This was the California Electric Light Company. Although an exhibition of battery-powered electric lights was held on the roof of St. Ignatius College in 1874 and at Mechanics' Pavilion and on Market Street after that (Katie Dowd, "140 years ago, the lights were turned on in San Francisco for the first time," *SFGate*, July 4, 2016), the first to furnish electric lighting to customers was the California Electric Light Company, which formed in San Francisco in June 1879. *See* the February 8, 1890, issue of *Western Electrician*, vol. 6, p. 73.

113 **"one of utter demoralization"** . . . : Testimony of George P. Low, *WCvAL*.

114 **Gerald Kirkpatrick** . . . : Gerald Stanley Kirkpatrick, twenty-one, died at Station C on Jessie Street of a skull fracture. Coroner's Book A, p. 120; *SFCh*, May 1, 1906, p. 9; *DeathIndex*.

114 **"cables on 7th between Mission . . ."**: Testimony of Louis E. Reynolds, *WCvAL*.

114 **"the trolley wires, the telephone . . ."**: Account of Harry C. Schmidt, *Arg.*, May 8, 1906.

114 **"quite extensive"** . . . : Testimony of John J. Kelley, *WCvAL*.

114 **more than four hundred places** . . . : Specific data on damage and repairs to the city's gas system was obtained from the 1907 testimony of John J. Kelley, superintendent of distribution of gas for the San Francisco Gas and Electric Company, *WCvAL*.

114 **"several huge holes in various . . ."**: Arthur Dangerfield, Journal of the Quake, April 24, 1906, BL.

114 **"manhole cover [that] blew straight up . . ."**: Cpt. Kelly, US Army Corps of Engineers, Ft. Mason, to family in Boston, "Earthquake and Fire at San Francisco, Cal., April 18-May 19th," BL.

114 **"the cobblestones on the street . . ."**: Recollection of James J. O'Brien, *Denial of Disaster*, p. 31.

114 **Marie Paris** . . . : Marie Paris, a widow, died at sixty-two on April 23, 1906, at City & County Hospital from a skull fracture suffered during a gas explosion. Gantner Brothers Funeral Home Records, Provo, UT, www.ancestry.com; *DeathIndex*; *SFB*, April 24, 1906, p. 9, and April 25, 1906, p. 5.

115 **"I burned all that was in . . ."**: Nankervis.

115 **"had plenty of coffee, milk . . ."**: Goerlitz.

115 **"[T]he dining room of the . . ."**: Letter from James R. Tapscott to his mother, Mrs. I. J. Tapscott, April 22, 1906, BL.

115 **"where they served hot coffee . . ."**: Mahoney.

115 **"secured a large basket of bread . . ."**: Cameron.

115 **"crackers was my first meal . . ."**: Letter from John Walter to his parents, April 18, 1906, published in *To His Parents* (San Francisco: privately printed, 1935), BL.

115 **"about sold out"** . . . : Letter from Ada Higgins, April 1906, SFPL.

115 **"crackers, sardines, malted milk"** . . . : J. B. Levison, "Memories for my Family," BL. This was at Goldberg, Bowen & Co. on the southwest corner of Haight and Masonic Avenues.

115 **"glass show-windows broken . . ."**: Letter from Dr. Wilber M. Swett, May 27, 1906, BL.

116 **"I saw everything on the floor . . ."**: Baldwin.

116 **"a small muddy stream of water . . ."**: Way. This was probably at Powell and Market Streets, where a crowd was observed drinking from a muddy pool formed by water gushing up through the paving stones.

116 **thirteen-year-old girl** . . . : This was Florence de Andreis (Kenney) of 6 Vandewater Street, who wrote she and her family of five "were compelled to buy some at the very exorbitant price of ten and even twenty-five cents a glass." Florence de Andreis, Account of the April 1906 Earthquake and Fire, written July 1909, SCP.

116 **"so I drank milk"** . . . : Angove.

116 **"was crowded"** . . . : Livingston.

117 **"lighting a fire in a defective . . ."**: Conlon.

117 **"warn everybody not to light . . ."**: Conniff.

117 **"We took a few bricks . . ."**: Burke.

117 **"the brick chimney had fallen . . ."**: Charles de Y. Elkus, Reminiscences of the 1906 Earthquake and Fire (dictated sometime in 1956), CHS.

117 **"a crude stove at the curb . . ."**: Herbert F. Bauer, Reminiscences of the 1906 San Francisco Earthquake and Fire, CHS.

117 **"having his children collect all . . ."**: Baldwin. The neighbor was Angelo E. Bruni, a shirtmaker who lived at 1856 McAllister Street.

117 **"confined to the building"** . . . : "Blaze Started 399 Hayes Street," *SFE*, May 23, 1906, p. 3.

118 **"heavy volumes of smoke"** . . . : Hopper.

118 **"The fire department was all . . ."**: Laurence Joseph Kennedy, *The Progress of the Fire in San Francisco, April 18th to 21st, as Shown by an Analysis of Original Documents* (master's thesis, University of California, Berkeley, 1908), BL.

118 **"tried to obtain water from . . ."**: Cullen.

118 **"with lines of hose, patiently . . ."**: Account of Paul Springer, *Santa Cruz Sentinel,* May 9, 1906.

118 **"were unable to obtain . . ."**: Boden.

118 **"Ham and Egg Fire"** . . . : "HAM AND EGGS FIRE WAS NOT CAUSED BY TEMBLOR," *SFE,* May 23, 1906, p. 3.

119 **fourteen men and five women** . . . : According to *SFDirectory* and census and voter records of household members: In the corner liquor store at 399 Hayes was Charles Bechtel and his wife, Elizabeth, and above them in 397 Hayes was the Reich family—Henry; his wife, Clara; and their fourteen-year-old twin daughters, Alma and Irene. Clara's mother, Johanna Doncks, was listed as living with them but passed away in October 1905. Next door at 393 Hayes was a barbershop owned by Julius Heilfronn, and Levi T. Snow was listed as a resident. Upstairs in 391 Hayes was California L. Lee, a widow. Next door in 387 Hayes was a picture-framing business owned by Charles Brunke, who resided either there or in the upstairs flat. In the next building—which was three stories tall—downstairs in the back was a candy store owned by John D. Tryforos, who lived there, and in the front of 383 Hayes was a barbershop owned by George Stump, who lived upstairs

in the second- and third-floor flat of 385 Hayes with Charles Pomeroy, William T. Goines, and Carlos Caine. And in the fifth building from the corner, a cigar shop occupied 377 Hayes, where brothers Philip Posner, Joseph Posner, and Benjamin Posner resided. And upstairs in the second- and third-floor flat at 379 Hayes lived Jesse Johnson and Emil Scheinert (or Schiner).

119 **another contemporaneous account . . . :** A photograph of a young boy standing among men watching the start of the fire on the rooftops of 377–379 and 383–385 Hayes Street is captioned: "Posner, Philip. [Boy facing camera] Posner Cigar Store, 377 Hayes St. (basement), building on fire. Credited with started Ham and Eggs Fire, 1906. Donor, Mrs. Paul Gottlieb, reports, 1955, that the fire started in the building next door at right in photograph." [Call Number: FN-01078], BL. This was also mentioned by eyewitness Charles Levy ("Some say that it started in Posner's cigar store") in "Blaze Started 399 Hayes Street," *SFE,* May 23, 1906, p. 3.

119 **"all remembrance of the earthquake . . .":** Anonymous man, account of the earthquake and fire, April 25, 1906, SFPL.

119 **"It was a terrible sight . . .":** Amelia M. Peretz, interviewed by Frederick M. Wirt, August 1, 1977, SGC.

120 **"we sat and watched the . . .":** Bernadette McKittrick and Tessie Dowd, Told at Open House for Senior Citizens Mission Neighborhood Centers, Inc., Mission Adult Center, 1966, CHS.

120 **"I took what money and . . .":** Miller.

120 **"it proved more than we . . .":** Nankervis.

120 **"the smart idea that we . . .":** Harold L. Zellerbach, excerpt from "Art, Business and Public Life in San Francisco," Oral History Transcript, BL.

120 **"digging vast holes in the yard"** . . . : Nankervis.

120 **"with our silver, cut glass . . .":** Luzerne Smith Dean, Selection from "San Francisco, the City I Love," typescript 1956, BL.

120 **"deep trenches into which we . . .":** Letter from Charles Page to his son, a student at MIT in MA, April 21, 1906, CHS.

121 **"found that every available horse . . .":** James W. Byrne, *Recollections of the Fire—San Francisco's 1906 Earthquake and Fire* (San Francisco: privately printed, 1927), p. 22.

121 **"[N]ot one man in one thousand . . .":** W. E. Alexander, Account of the 1906 San Francisco Earthquake and Fire, CHS.

121 **"filled up pretty well with trunks . . .":** Anonymous man, account of the earthquake and fire, April 25, 1906, SFPL.

121 **"Ambulances, patrol wagons, fire-engines . . .":** Letter from Bert Tuttle to Mary Butler, 1:00 p.m. April 18, 1906, SFPL.

121 **"vehicles of all sorts were . . .":** William F. Nichols, "The Story" from *A Father's Story of the Earthquake and Fire in San Francisco, April 18, 19, 20, 1906* (privately printed, 1923).

121 **Frank Nunan . . . :** Frank P. Nunan (bookkeeper at Hibernia Brewery residing at 422 Oak St. per the 1903 city directory) died April 18, 1906, at City & County Hospital at thirty-one from internal injuries after being thrown from and run over by a brewery wagon. Gladys Hansen Death Index, SFPL; *DeathIndex.*

122 **"Every possible contrivance was used . . .":** Arthur Dangerfield, Journal of the Quake, April 24, 1906, BL.

122 **"I was suddenly snatched from . . .":** Account of Eleanor Perry, 1919, RSS.

122 **"Even pianos were being pulled . . .":** Angove.

122 **"an old lady carrying a . . .":** Genthe, p. 88.

122 **"a great many comical sights . . ."**: Bacigalupi.

122 **"a young lady on a bicycle . . ."**: Perry.

122 **"the odd articles the refugees . . ."**: Account of Alex Young, RSS.

122 **"dragged along with a kind . . ."**: Untitled Earthquake Narrative, Hooker Family Papers 1783–1951, BL.

122 **"The constant rasping of trunks . . ."**: Ivan S. Rankin, Recollections of the Earthquake and Fire in San Francisco, April 18, 19, 20, and 21, 1906, CHS.

123 **"The use of this powder . . ."**: Briggs, p. 229.

124 **"could get all they wanted . . ."**: Account of Jeremiah Deneen, *Arg.*, February 5, 1927.

124 **"so far under the influence . . ."**: Report of Cpt. Le Vert Coleman, US Army Artillery Corps, to the Adjutant at the Presidio, May 2, 1906, VMSF.

124 **Schmitz ordered . . .** : Information on the movements of dynamite under Lt. Briggs and the caissons of powder sent to eventually fall under the control of Lt. Pulis was obtained from Briggs and Testimony of Charles Pulis and John F. Davis, *LSvTF.*

125 **"asked if there was not . . ."**: Testimony of Charles Pulis, *LSvTF.*

125 **dribbled a "train" . . .** : Account of Sgt. John Lainsbury, *Arg.*, August 13, 1927.

125 **"blinded by the blood that . . ."**: *Ibid.*

125 **"probably fatally injured" . . .** : *Buffalo Times,* April 19, 1906, and *Detroit Journal,* April 19, 1906. Pulis survived, continued to serve in the Army, was promoted to the rank of colonel during the First World War, passed of pneumonia March 14, 1919, and is buried in San Francisco National Cemetery at the Presidio. Note: although he survived, Charles Pulis is listed as an earthquake and fire death in the Gladys Hansen Death Index, SFPL.

125 **"full of splinters" . . .** : Account of Dr. Tilton E. Tillman, *Arg.*, October 2, 1926.

126 **"The sparks were flying" . . .** : Testimony of Alfred Goddard, *Arg.*, July 10, 1926.

126 **"The outside portion of the . . ."**: Account of A. W. King, *Arg.*, November 6, 1926.

126 **Beyond its sturdy construction . . .** : Specific data on the 1875–1906 Palace Hotel was gathered from *SanbornMap* and "The Great Caravansary of the Western World," *Frank Leslie's Illustrated Newspaper,* October 9, 1875.

126 **"leaped from block to block . . ."**: Hammill.

127 **"cordon of police and soldiers" . . .** : Byrne, *Recollections of the Fire—San Francisco's 1906 Earthquake and Fire,* p. 22.

127 **"fire brigade of bellboys" . . .** : *Ibid.,* p. 23.

127 **"at times terrific" . . .** : *Ibid.,* p. 26.

127 **"was now assuming alarming proportions" . . .** : Hollister, p. 156.

128 **"It was necessary to climb . . ."**: Eastwood.

128 **"no longer 'only a fire'" . . .** : Letter from Amy Kahn to Mr. Coop, April 23–24, 1906, BL.

128 **"The street was like looking . . ."**: Chase.

128 **"the crackling and roar . . ."**: Letter from William Hancock to his sister Mary, May 29, 1906, CHS.

128 **"For God's sake help me" . . .** : This was Frank Corali, buried beneath the basement floor of the burning lodging house, according to *Daily News: Extra Edition,* April 18, 1906.

129 **the Hansen family . . .** : Daniel Clifford Hansen, twenty-seven, was a boatswain with the US Navy (and, per *1900Census,* was stationed as quartermaster aboard the USS *Paragua* in

the Philippines) and the son of Danish immigrants; his wife, Sarah, twenty-three, and their son, William C., one, all died ("burned to death") at 7th and Natoma Streets on April 18, 1906. *DeathIndex*; *U.S. Navy and Marine Corps Registries, 1814–1992*, vol. 2, 1906, p. 84. "Bodies of Daniel Clifford Hansen and his wife, Sarah Hansen, and his son, William Hansen, were found at Seventh & Howard Sts." All three were buried in the Naval Cemetery at Yerba Buena. *SFCh*, April 27, 1906, p. 7.

129 **the Stamblers . . .** : Louis Stambler, thirty-five; his wife, Celia, thirty; and daughter, Rosie, ten, all died April 18, 1906. H. F. Suhr & Funeral Co. records, Gladys Hansen Death Index, SFPL. Louis "burnt to death" per Coroner's Book C, p. 138, which added: "Human bones supposed to be Louis Stambler" were found by his sister Sadie Stambler of Los Angeles, who "searched ruins for some time . . . and this afternoon, May 29, came across bones which she says are those of her relatives." The *Eau Claire Leader* (Wisconsin) reported on May 31, 1906: "Five bodies were taken out of the ruins of the Kingsbury House. The first four were those of Louis Stambler, a tailor, thirty-four years of age, his wife Celia, their daughter Rosie, ten years of age, and Stambler's niece, Miss Fannie Weiner, twenty-three years of age . . ." Fannie Weiner, their niece, twenty-three, died with them, "burnt to death." Coroner's Book C, p. 139; *SFC*, May 30, 1906, p. 3; *SFCh*, May 30, 1906, p. 2.

129 **Michele Canepa . . .** : Michele died on April 18, 1906, at forty-six, killed by the falling of the building. Coroner's Book C, p. 131, Gladys Hansen Death Index, SFPL; *DeathIndex*, Surnames A-E, p. 1574. His wife, Maddalena, died the same day at the same address, "burnt to death." Department of Public Health Records, SFPL; Gladys Hansen Death Index, SFPL; *DeathIndex*, Surnames A-E, p. 1574.

129 **"to do their best to help . . ."**: Hammill.

130 **"unmoved, inscrutable as a sphinx" . . .** : Hopper.

130 **"At every cross-street, streams of people . . ."**: Griswold, quoted in *Narratives of the San Francisco Earthquake and Fire of 1906*, p. 73.

130 **"miserable and crushed" . . .** : Hopper.

8.

131 **"had all backed out into the clear" . . .** : Chase.

132 **"began to take water and in . . ."**: *The Independent* (Santa Barbara, CA), April 25, 1906, p. 1.

132 **"as though they were but matchwood" . . .** : Account of Roland M. Roche, *Arg.*, January 1, 1927.

132 **"were pressing down to the ferries" . . .** : *Arg.*, May 8, 1906.

132 **"as a sort of a barrier" . . .** : Account of Harry Walsh, *Arg.*, May 15, 1926.

132 **"an old Italian" . . .** : JCook2.

133 **"burned by rooms, as it . . ."**: Nichols, "The Story," *supra*.

133 **"The one thought uppermost in my mind" . . .** : Genthe, p. 89.

133 **No. 3A, B2, Folding Pocket Kodak . . .** : Genthe later wrote he grabbed "a 3A Kodak Special," *ibid.*, but as Victoria Binder notes in her essay, "Arnold Genthe and his Camera" in *Among the Ruins*, "This is chronologically impossible, as the No. 3A Kodak Special was not available until 1910. It is more likely that Genthe chose the model No. 3A, B2, Folding Pocket Kodak, manufactured between 1904 and 1906." *Among the Ruins*, p. 49.

134 **"waded through plaster" . . .** : Letter from Ernest H. Adams to Messrs. Reed and Barton, April 23, 1906, VMSF.

134 **"raging"** . . . : W. E. Alexander, Account of the 1906 San Francisco Earthquake and Fire, CHS.

134 **"It was a gesture of kindness"** . . . : Kendrick.

134 **"a blood red ball"** . . . : Letter from William Hancock to his sister Mary, May 29, 1906, CHS.

135 **"an intense vibration of the whole vessel"** . . . : Pond.

135 **"all available surgeons and nurses"** . . . : Freeman; Pond.

135 **"The Kid"** . . . : *Army and Navy Journal,* vol. XXXII 1894–1895 (New York: Publication Office Bennett Building, 1895), p. 603; US Naval Academy Alumni Association, *The United States Naval Academy Graduates' Association* (Baltimore: The Lord Baltimore Press, 1904), p. 132.

135 **"a born leader of men . . ."**: Pond.

136 **"under full boiler power"** . . . : Freeman.

137 **"As we approached the waterfront . . ."**: Pond.

137 **"expressed his appreciation of the . . ."**: Freeman.

137 **"had several lines of hose laid out"** . . . : Pond.

137 **"sightseers"** . . . : Freeman.

138 **"able-bodied men"** . . . : Pond.

138 **"that the heavens above the . . ."**: Leach.

139 **"in less time than it takes . . ."**: "Ham and Eggs Fire Was Not Caused by Tremblor," *SFE,* May 23, 1906, p. 3.

139 **"A shower of burning embers . . ."**: Friar John Frieden, "Some Personal Reminiscences of the Earthquake of San Francisco," ca. 1910, Manuscript Collection, University of San Francisco.

139 **"subdued but startling whisper"** . . . : Nichols, "The Story," *supra.*

140 **"shingles were smoking in several . . ."**: Account of E. J. Plume, *Arg.,* September 25, 1926.

140 **"in a low excited voice"** . . . : Fisher.

140 **"The place is afire, we . . ."**: Mahoney.

140 **"Fires were by this time . . ."**: Account of E. J. Plume, *supra.*

140 **"Never in my experience have . . ."**: Nichols, "The Story," *supra.*

141 **"I believe I was the last . . ."**: Account of E. J. Plume, *Arg.,* September 25, 1926.

141 **"a wild retreat after a lost battle"** . . . : Nichols, "The Story," *supra.*

141 **"burning with explosive violence"** . . . : Hopper.

141 **nineteen different operas** . . . : Goerlitz.

141 **"took the line of hose up"** . . . : Account of Patrick Shaughnessy, *Arg.,* January 15, 1927.

142 **"burst into flame gradually beginning . . ."**: Letter from Henry Atkins to art dealership partner Frederic Cheever Torrey, April 26, 1906, BL.

142 **"the whole interior alight, flames . . ."**: Letter from Tom Davis to his mother in England, 1906, CHS.

142 **"was glowing like a phosphorescent worm"** . . . : Hopper.

142 **"seething bonfire"** . . . : *Arg.,* April 30, 1927.

142 **"weeping bitterly because he and . . ."**: Byrne, *Recollections of the Fire—San Francisco's 1906 Earthquake and Fire,* p. 29.

142 **"was smoking but was still . . ."**: Hopper.

143 **"It became in fifteen minutes . . ."**: *Arg.,* December 11, 1926.

143 **"there was a line of men . . ."**: Eastwood.

143 **"uncontrollable demon of a blaze"** . . . : Leach.

143 **"a fierce heat that was . . ."**: Hammill.

145 **"[T]he charges often had to be . . ."**: Report of Cpt. Le Vert Coleman, US Army Artillery Corps, to the Adjutant at the Presidio, May 2, 1906, VMSF.

145 **"accelerated rather than retarded . . ."**: *Arg.,* August 13, 1927.

145 **"at a speed that was . . ."**: Account of William Harvey, *Arg.,* March 12, 1927.

146 **"gave out high explosives to . . ."**: Testimony of John F. Davis, *LSvT.*

146 **"like the report of heavy . . ."**: Letter from Charles to Flora, May 8, 1906, SFPL.

146 **"the sound of explosions"** . . . : Letter from Major William Stephenson, US Army, May 31, 1906, BL.

146 **"At first we did not . . ."**: Nankervis.

146 **"every time they set off . . ."**: Cpt. Kelly, US Army Corps of Engineers, Ft. Mason, to family in Boston, "Earthquake and Fire at San Francisco, Cal., April 18-May 19th," BL.

146 **"in order to keep the . . ."**: Chase.

146 **"very soon"** . . . : Dr. George Blumer's Eyewitness Account of the Disaster, VMSF.

147 **"ignited and in a short . . ."**: Chase.

147 **"as many of his men . . ."**: *Arg.,* August 13, 1927.

148 **"was completely exhausted"** . . . : Freeman.

148 **"Sock it to 'em!"** . . . : Pond.

9.

149 **"Central"** . . . : Morrow.

149 **"the telephone wires were broken"** . . . : J. B. Levison, "Memories for my Family," BL.

149 **"were completely destroyed"** . . . : Col. Milton B. Halsey Jr., "Point Paper: U.S. Army Activities in the 1906 Earthquakes and Fire," SFPL.

149 **The Navy had recently established** . . . : "Wireless Comes of Age on the West Coast," *AWA Review,* vol. 24 (2011): pp. 242–250.

149 **"Earthquake. Town on fire. Send . . ."**: Marshall Everett, *Complete Story of the San Francisco Earthquake* (Chicago: Henry Neil, 1906), p. 78.

150 **"at full speed"** . . . : Commander Charles J. Badger, US Navy, "Services Performed by the Flagship *Chicago* During Conflagration in San Francisco, California, And Operations of the Navy in Control of the Sixth District (Water Front) of the City," April 19 to May 10, 1906, NA, Record Group 45.

150 **"directly"** . . . : Letter from Sarah Phillips to George, April 27, 1906, Phillips-Jones.

150 **"Lost everything, am safe. Thank God"** . . . : Way.

150 **"after a rapid sprint"** . . . : Account of Paul Dowles, *Arg.,* April 9, 1927.

150 **"A terrific earthquake struck . . ."**: *Chicago Live Stock World,* April 18, 1906.

150 **The time was roughly 6:40 a.m.** . . . : While Chicago papers reported they received the first bulletins around 9:00 a.m. (CST, which would be 7:00 a.m. San Francisco time), there were

more specific reports from New York that Postal Telegraph had communication with its San Francisco office briefly at 9:40 a.m. EST (6:40 a.m. San Francisco time) "but lost the connection again almost immediately." *SLT,* April 18, 1906.

150 **"the story of the earthquake . . .":** Account of Paul Dowles, *Arg.,* April 9, 1927.

151 **"almost immediately"** . . . : *SLT,* April 18, 1906.

151 **"Am appalled and overwhelmed by . . .":** *CCE.*

151 **"rumors of great disaster"** . . . : "President Roosevelt Offers Aid," *Boston Evening Transcript,* April 19, 1906, p. 3.

151 **"subject to indefinite delay"** . . . : *BE,* April 18, 1906.

151 **"Mayor Mott, Oakland. Send fire engines . . .":** This telegram was first reported found by Judge Tyrell among his papers in Oakland on page 10 of the *Oakland Tribune,* April 19, 1949. He said it was received in Oakland around 8:00 a.m. It was confirmed authentic by William A. Galvin, who was the assistant manager of Postal Telegraph on April 18, 1906, and confirmed he sent it that morning after arriving at the office that first morning after 7:00 a.m. in article "Telegrapher of 1906 Disaster Gives Interesting Details" in the May 1, 1949, issue of *SFE.*

151 **"climbed the telegraph poles at intervals"** . . . : Account of Harry J. Jeffs, *Arg.,* April 9, 1927.

152 **"All well and safe"** . . . : Telegram from Isabelle Prentiss to Miss M. Prentiss, April 26, 1906, BL.

152 **"Lost everything, am safe. Thank God"** . . . : Way.

152 **"like hurried missives desperately flung . . .":** Fradkin, *The Great Earthquake and Firestorms of 1906,* p. 84.

152 **"a total wreck"** . . . : *EB,* April 18, 1906.

152 **"EARTHQUAKE AND FIRE WRECK . . .":** *Ibid.*

152 **"SAN FRANCISCO IS VISITED BY . . .":** *BE,* April 18, 1906.

152 **"Flames rage unchecked"** . . . : *KCS,* April 18, 1906.

152 **"All the water pressure is gone"** . . . : *Ibid.*

152 **"Fire department is practically helpless"** . . . : *Fort Worth Star-Telegram* (TX), April 18, 1906.

153 **"buildings being blown up"** . . . : 10:15 a.m. byline, *Daily Hanford Journal* (CA), April 18, 1906, p. 1.

153 **"The city is now under martial law"** . . . : 10:45 a.m. byline in "Extra!! Third Edition" of *Reno Gazette-Journal,* April 18, 1906, p. 5.

153 **"Soldiers will shoot on sight . . .":** 4:30 o'clock in Last Edition of *The Sacramento Bee,* April 18, 1906, p. 1.

153 **"5,000 dead have been found"** . . . : *Pine Bluff Daily Graphic* (Pine Bluff, AK), April 18, 1906. Sacramento's *Evening Bee* that afternoon declared, "Loss of life so far estimated to be at least 5,000 human beings." Not to be outdone, the same day's late issue of *The Neodesha Daily Sun* (Neodesha, KS) claimed, "5,000 dead bodies had already been gathered and placed in temporary morgues."

153 **"dead will probably number 20,000"** . . . : *Lawrence Daily World* (Lawrence, KS), April 18, 1906. The same day's late issue of *The Neodesha Daily Sun* also declared, after claiming 5,000 bodies had been taken to the morgue, that "a rough estimate places the dead at no less than 20,000."

153 **"a mighty column of smoke . . .":** CLondon, pp. 100–101.

153 **"10:30 a.m."** . . . : Letter from Nellie to Pa, April 18, 1906, One of Nine Miscellaneous Letters from Unidentified Witnesses to the San Francisco Earthquake and Fire, 1906, CHS.

153 **"[t]he Cliff House had fallen . . ."**: Myrtle Robertson, "An Eye Witness—Miss Myrtle Robertson's Eyewitness Account Given Substantially in Her Own Words," CHS.

153 **"Chicago had been levelled . . ."**: Letter from Mary A. Briggs to Rhoda, Anna, Mary, and Minnie, April 23, 1906, BL.

153 **"Chicago was under seven feet . . ."**: Myrtle Robertson, "An Eye Witness—Miss Myrtle Robertson's Eyewitness Account Given Substantially in Her Own Words," CHS.

153 **"not seriously hurt"** . . . : Account of Ernest Simpson, *Arg.*, April 23, 1927.

154 **"three or four tons of . . ."**: Account of Fred Ewald, *Arg.*, April 23, 1927.

154 **"agreed to try to publish . . ."**: Account of Ernest Simpson, *supra.*

154 **"penny paper"** . . . : Milly Bennett, *On Her Own: Journalistic Adventures from San Francisco to the Chinese Revolution, 1917–1927* (Armonk, New York: M. E. Sharpe, 1993), p. 13.

154 **"the littlest, scrappiest newspaper . . ."**: *Ibid.*

154 **"to the old-time plan of . . ."**: Account of William B. Wasson, *Arg.*, April 16, 1927.

155 **"HUNDREDS DEAD!"** . . . : *San Francisco Daily News,* April 18, 1906.

155 **Schmitz asked an attorney** . . . : This was Garrett W. McEnerney, a prominent San Francisco attorney who testified under oath on November 27, 1906, that he drafted the mayor's proclamation. *SFC,* November 28, 1906.

155 **"soldiers outside the shop stopped . . ."**: *Sunset: The Magazine of the Pacific and of all the Far West,* vol. XVII, May to October 1906, p. 204.

155 **"The Federal Troops, the members . . ."**: Proclamation of Mayor E. E. Schmitz, CHS.

156 **"the streets were policed by . . ."**: Dr. George Blumer's Eyewitness Account of the Disaster, VMSF.

156 **"already patrolled by the soldiers . . ."**: Leithead.

156 **"at full gallop a company . . ."**: Cameron.

156 **"to clean out and close . . ."**: Account of Harry C. Schmidt, *Arg.*, May 8, 1906.

156 **"every ounce of liquor in . . ."**: Duke, p. 168.

156 **"the soldiers entered each one . . ."**: Letter from Sarah Phillips to George, May 1, 1906, Phillips-Jones.

156 **"Liquor of any kind found . . ."**: Leithead.

157 **"into a place where they . . ."**: Anonymous man, account of the earthquake and fire, April 25, 1906, SFPL.

157 **"was caught while he was . . ."**: Duke, p. 166.

157 **"there is no well-authenticated case . . ."**: Funston.

158 **"so thoroughly cowed were the . . ."**: Account of Frank Hittell, *Arg.*, March 19, 1927.

158 **"The crowd was most orderly . . ."**: Cpt. Kelly, US Army Corps of Engineers, Ft. Mason, to family in Boston, "Earthquake and Fire at San Francisco, Cal., April 18–May 19th," BL.

158 **"ate soda crackers and cured ham"** . . . : Angove.

158 **"sprinkling cart"** . . . : Account of De Witt J. Lipe, *Arg.*, July 10, 1926. Laurence Klauber also mentioned these in typed annotations on transcript of his 1906 letter, CHS: "I think we got such water as we had from sprinkling carts that were parked at different corners."

158 **"twenty cents worth of cookies . . ."**: Account of De Witt J. Lipe, *ibid.*

159 "[T]he stores were all thrown open" . . . : Bauer.

159 "shove the contents into the street . . .": Sinsheimer.

159 "If they are all right, come back . . .": JCook1.

159 "standing all right" . . . : Account of Harry C. Schmidt, *Arg.,* May 8, 1906.

159 "not a dollar's worth of damage . . .": JCook2.

160 "was well on fire" . . . : Stetson1.

160 "every window from top to bottom . . .": Letter from James R. Tapscott to his mother, Mrs. I. J. Tapscott, April 22, 1906, BL.

160 "where already hundreds of homeless . . .": Unidentified Account in letter, filed in Putnam.

160 "gigantic fires" . . . : Perrin, p. 29.

160 "the smoke was almost obscuring . . .": Letter from Ada Higgins, April 1906, SFPL.

160 "Solid blocks along Market Street . . .": Letter from Bert Tuttle to Mary Butler, 1:00 p.m. April 18, 1906, SFPL.

160 "as those of a barricaded . . .": Hopper.

160 "almost invisible through the smoke" . . . : Letter from "Aunt Bertha" to Elsa Billerbeck, May 13, 1906, BL.

160 "dense, spreading white cloud" . . . : Letter from Rose Barreda to nephew Frederick Barreda, May 15, 1906, with cover letter by Frederick, October 1963, CHS.

160 "Toward mid-day the sky became . . .": Account of Kaufman L. Coney, RSS.

160 "close and humid" . . . : Nankervis.

160 "spanking breeze" . . . : Hopper.

161 "sifting in through doors and windows" . . . : Nankervis.

161 "nibbled a little bit on the hay" . . . : Baldwin.

161 "to solve the problems" . . . : Account of Eugene Schmitz, *Arg.,* January 15, 1927.

161 "see the flames for the first time" . . . : Livingston.

162 "now a veritable inferno" . . . : Kendrick.

162 "City practically ruined by fire" . . . : Anderson, "The Story of the Bulletins," *The Pacific Monthly,* vol. XV, p. 744; *SFE,* April 19, 1964.

162 "typewriters and all" . . . : *SFE,* May 1, 1949.

162 "[T]he three of us took . . .": Kendrick.

162 "50 representative citizens . . .": CCE.

162 "three boys had looted a store" . . . : Testimony of Eugene Schmitz, *LSvT.*

163 "Let it also be understood . . .": CCE.

163 "endorsed the action I had taken" . . . : Account of Eugene Schmitz, *Arg.,* January 22, 1927.

163 "provoked great indignation" . . . : CCE.

163 "shaky roof" . . . : Hammill.

164 "almost dark as night by . . .": Leach.

164 "preservation in shape of over . . .": Hammill.

164 "sparks and cinders" . . . : Leach.

164 **"the red-hot copper surface"** . . . : Hammill.

165 **revenue cutter sailors** . . . : Information on the work of the US Revenue Cutter Service in the earthquake and fire was obtained from "Always ready—the Revenue Cutter Service and the great San Francisco earthquake," *The Northern Mariner/Le marin du nord*, vol. XVII, no. 4, (October 2007): pp. 22–39.

165 **"with wet cloths and improvised mops"** . . . : Rand Careaga, *The United States Customhouse in San Francisco, An Illustrated History* (Washington, DC: General Services Administration, 2011), p. 15.

165 **"to protect the Custom House . . ."**: Testimony of Cpt. Orrin R. Wolfe, US Army, during hearings by the Inspector General, February 2, 1907, VMSF.

165 **"as soon as ignition occurred . . ."**: *The United States Customhouse in San Francisco, supra.*

166 **narrow, twenty-two-foot-wide alley** . . . : This was Jones Alley, and acting under the orders of SFFD Battalion Chief McCluskey were SFFD Engine 20 and Oakland FD Engines 1 and 4.

166 **"[W]hen the woodwork in the . . ."**: Account of Edward Lind, *Arg.*, July 17, 1926.

166 **"used the water sparingly"** . . . : McCluskey.

166 **"the old stone structure of . . ."**: Account of Edward Lind, *supra.*

167 **"was in immediate danger"** . . . : McCluskey.

167 **"There on the grass of . . ."**: Untitled Earthquake Narrative, Hooker Family Papers 1783–1951, BL.

167 **"left to their fate or . . ."**: Account of Eugene Schmitz, *supra.*

167 **"became too intense"** . . . : *Arg.*, June 26, 1926.

168 **"not to wait for any . . ."**: Account of Eugene Schmitz, *Arg.*, January 22, 1927.

168 **"That meant we had to dig . . ."**: Account of Sgt. Maurice Behan, *Arg.*, June 9, 1926.

168 **Rafaelo Paolinelli** . . . : Rafaelo Paolinelli died at forty-four at the produce market at Washington and Front Streets, killed by a falling wall on April 18, 1906, *DeathIndex*. He was an Italian immigrant, married to Ermida, and was father to four children: Orlando, Rinaldo, Cora, and Fiori.

168 **Ida Heaslip** . . . : Ida O. Heaslip (born 11/19/1857 per *1900Census*) died April 18, 1906, at 239 Geary Street from falling walls and asphyxiation by suffocation. See further biographical information in note for p. 93, *supra.*

168 **John Day** . . . : John Day was thirty-five, injured at 235 Geary Street, and died that same day of a leg amputation. *DeathIndex*, p. 2576; Coroner's Book A, p. 134. He was buried in Portsmouth Square. *SFE*, April 22, 1906. His body was disinterred on April 25, 1906. *SFCh*, April 26, 1906.

168 **Nathan Kornfield** . . . : Nathan Kornfield died at 939½ Folsom Street of asphyxiation by suffocation. Death certificate for "John Doe Kornfield," www.ancestry.com; Gladys Hansen Death Index, SFPL. He was the son of Hungarian immigrants Adolf and Giza, the second of four children, and was eleven. *1900Census.*

168 **William Vail** . . . : William Cameron Vail was the son of William Henry Vail and Emma Vail and died at three years old on April 18, 1906, at his home, 260 Stevenson Street. Coroner's Book A, p. 138. He was buried in a temporary grave in Portsmouth Square and disinterred on April 25 after his body was identified by his father. *SFCh*, April 26, 1906. He was buried in Olivet Cemetery in Colma, CA. His father was buried beside him in 1912.

168 **"Unknown Japanese"** . . . : Record of Interments in Laurel Hill Cemetery, removed "fro. Portsmouth Square," reburied in Laurel Hill on April 25, 1906, p. 88, BL.

168 "Unknown Chinaman" . . . : *Ibid.*, pp. 88–89.

168 "What have you got there?" . . . : JCook2.

168 "full of human bodies" . . . : Account of Thomas A. Burns, *Arg.*, May 29, 1926.

168 "a most pitiful sight" . . . : Florence de Andreis, Account of the April 1906 Earthquake and Fire, written July 1909, SCP.

168 "saw the morgue and undertakers' . . .": Miller.

169 "became so hot" . . . : Account of Eugene Schmitz, *Arg.*, January 22, 1927.

170 "across the street, setting fire . . .": Account of Battalion Chief O'Brien, *Arg.*, February 5, 1927.

170 "The fire rapidly surrounded the square" . . . : Duke, p. 168.

170 "with a rattle of eagerness" . . . : Hopper.

170 "the great and ghastly spectacle" . . . : Kendrick.

10.

171 "The fight was won" . . . : Leach.

171 "the change that had taken . . .": *Ibid.*

171 "a most depressing scene of . . .": *Ibid.*

172 "Because of the pall of . . .": Kendrick.

172 "in beds on the street . . .": Letter from Dr. Wilber M. Swett, May 27, 1906, BL.

172 "It was disgustingly hot" . . . : Letter from member of Armer Family, 5:00 p.m., April 20, 1906, SFPL.

172 "was coming up the city . . .": Arthur Dangerfield, Journal of the Quake, April 24, 1906, BL.

173 "rush of the grand army . . .": Millard.

173 "Never have I tasted anything . . .": Letter from Amy Kahn to Mr. Coop, April 23–24, 1906, BL.

173 "From the boat, the burning . . .": Letter from Dr. Wilber M. Swett, May 27, 1906, BL.

173 "could see the ships, sailing . . .": Letter from John to Lucy R. Schaeffer, May 14, 1906, SFPL.

174 "I watched the vast conflagration . . ." : JLondon.

174 "walls of flame, extending the . . .": Account of J. C. Havely, *Arg.*, April 2, 1927.

174 "light enough to read a book" . . . : Dr. George Blumer's Eyewitness Account of the Disaster, VMSF.

174 "flame lighted sky" . . . : Irene Jensen Stark, excerpt from "Come Walk With Me in My Beautiful Garden of Memory," 1979–1980, BL.

174 "[T]he flames lit up the place . . .": Account of Sgt. James Cottle, *Arg.*, August 21, 1926.

174 "a shift and slight increase . . .": Pond.

175 "and doubled up with their lines" . . . : Conniff.

176 "nozzle-men stood fearlessly at . . .": Pond.

176 "caught fire several times" . . . : Kindelon.

177 "piteously crying for water" . . . : Freeman.

177 "made it impossible to keep . . .": Murphy.

177 **"by its use the Southern Pacific . . ."**: Freeman.

177 **"the flames from the burning . . ."**: Leach.

177 **"to a vantage point on . . ."**: Ivan S. Rankin, Recollections of the Earthquake and Fire in San Francisco, April 18, 19, 20, and 21, 1906, CHS.

177 **"could see to read fine print . . ."**: Letter from Kate C. Woods to Nance Kynaston, April 22, 1906, CHS.

178 **"the whole southern heavens were . . ."**: Morrow.

178 **"the flaming sky over the mountains . . ."**: Ellsworth Francis Quinlan, Selection from "Under the Artichoke Bush: Reminiscence About Half Moon Bay, California," BL.

178 **"That night the north sky . . ."**: Letter from Herman C. Grunsky to his brother C. Ewald Grunsky, May 5, 1906, BL.

178 **"the grave, sad merchants of . . ."**: Louise Herrick Wall, quoted in *Narratives of the San Francisco Earthquake and Fire of 1906*, edited by Roger W. Lotchin (The Lakeside Press, R.R. Donnelley & Sons Co., 2011), p. 272.

178 **"We would let them sleep . . ."**: Account of Sgt. Maurice Behan, *Arg.*, June 19, 1926.

179 **"Throngs of Chinese were now . . ."**: Untitled Earthquake Narrative, Hooker Family Papers 1783–1951, BL.

179 **"every man in that particular . . ."**: Stephen V. Bunner, *Arg.*, August 14, 1926.

179 **Lee Yoke Suey . . .**: "Chinatown, 1906: The End and the Beginning," by Connie Young Yu, *The Unshakable—Rebirth of Chinatown in 1906*, pp. 14–15.

179 **"[d]espite the urgency of the evacuation"** . . . : *Ibid.*, p. 14.

180 **"It was here that I saw . . ."**: Letter from John to Lucy R. Schaeffer, May 14, 1906, SFPL.

180 **"He was born in San Francisco . . ."**: "Chinatown, 1906: The End and the Beginning," by Connie Young Yu, *The Unshakable—Rebirth of Chinatown in 1906*, p. 15.

181 **"in keeping order and in . . ."**: Account of Frederick Funston, *Arg.*, February 5, 1927.

181 **"doing all possible to . . ."**: This telegram was "Received 2:50 a.m." from Oakland, the first one drafted but the second received. Taft, p. 5.

181 **estimated 100,000 to be homeless . . .**: This telegram was "Received 11:40 p.m." at the War Department in Washington, DC. *Ibid.*

181 **"returned to primitive conditions"** . . . : Devol1, p. 176.

182 **"that this hospital was open . . ."**: Torney, p. 209.

182 **By 1:00 p.m. they had seventy-five . . .**: *Ibid.*

182 **"Since the earthquake there had . . ."**: Untitled Earthquake Narrative, Hooker Family Papers 1783–1951, BL.

182 **"The sidewalks at night were . . ."**: Letter from Mary A. Briggs to Rhoda, Anna, Mary, and Minnie, April 23, 1906, BL.

182 **"inverted four-posters"** . . . : Herrick Wall, quoted in *Narratives of the San Francisco Earthquake and Fire of 1906*, p. 278.

182 **"had to wake every once . . ."**: Winifred S. Thompson, interviewed by Frederick M. Wirt, August 16, 1977, Selections from Growing Up in the Cities: Oral History Transcripts of Tape-Recorded Interviews, BL.

183 **"no one could sleep under . . ."**: Moore.

183 **"became uneasy and decided to . . ."**: Eastwood.

183 **"a man asked my father if . . ."**: Account of Lillian Peacock, December 5, 1919, RSS.

183 **"[t]here were now 14 of us . . ."**: Perrin.

183 **"and thirteen of us stayed . . ."**: Postcard from Jane to Robert H. Grant, April 20, 1906, SCP.

183 **"halfway off its foundations and . . ."**: Account of Edith Cook, RSS.

183 **"chocolate in unlimited quantities"** . . . : Eugenia C. Murrell Poston, Personal Experiences from Apr. 18 to June 10, 1906: signed and amended typescript, BL.

184 **"the military would very threateningly . . ."**: Letter from Lloyd R. Burns to California Historical Society, May 1978, CHS.

184 **"the soldiers would shoot right . . ."**: Letter from Mrs. Thomas J. (Hulda) Blight, April 24, 1906, CHS.

184 **"the militia, which would shoot . . ."**: Herbert F. Bauer, Reminiscences of the 1906 San Francisco Earthquake and Fire, CHS.

184 **"No lights to be lit!"** . . . : Dora Landgrebe, 1966 Interview at Open House for Senior Citizens, Mission Neighborhood Centers, Mission Adult Center, BL.

184 **"with bayonet"** . . . : Account of Alex J. Young, December 6, 1919, RSS.

184 **"Those who were not afraid . . ."**: Cpt. Kelly, US Army Corps of Engineers, Ft. Mason, to family in Boston, "Earthquake and Fire at San Francisco, Cal., April 18-May 19th," BL.

184 **"All night long the fire . . ."**: Account of Roland M. Roche, *Arg.,* January 8, 1927.

185 **"crowded with people and their . . ."**: Letter from Laurence M. Klauber to his sister Alice, May 1, 1906, CHS.

185 **"completely covered by mattresses, blankets . . ."**: Letter from Rose Barreda to her nephew Frederick Barreda, May 15, 1906, with cover letter by Frederick, October 1963, CHS.

185 **"steamer rags, blankets, and cushions . . ."**: Miller.

185 **"by the thousands"** . . . : J. B. Levison, "Memories for my Family," BL.

185 **"People crowded the sidewalks around . . ."**: Livingston.

186 **"left burning homes and terrified . . ."**: James J. Hudson, "The California National Guard: In the San Francisco Earthquake and Fire of 1906," *California Historical Quarterly,* vol. 55, no. 2 (Summer 1976): p. 138.

186 **"by the glare of the fire"** . . . : Letter from Elmer Enewold to his father in Omaha, May 3, 1906, CHS.

186 **"there wasn't hardly a square inch . . ."**: Arthur Dangerfield, Journal of the Quake, April 24, 1906, BL.

187 **"Time to get out, boys"** . . . : Letter from Charles Fisk to his mother in England, April 22, 1906, CHS.

187 **"It was a strange scene . . ."**: Arthur Dangerfield, Journal of the Quake, April 24, 1906, BL.

187 **"was packed with refugees . . ."**: JLondon.

187 **"resembled a battlefield"** . . . : Letter from William Hancock to his sister Mary, May 29, 1906, CHS.

187 **"the crowd was perfectly quiet"** . . . : Griswold, quoted in *Narratives of the San Francisco Earthquake and Fire of 1906,* p. 76.

188 **"the carelessness of soldiers"** . . . : *38th Annual Report of the Insurance Commissioner for the State of California* (Sacramento: W. W. Shannon, Superintendent State Printing, 1907), p. 14.

188 "The flames crept nearer and . . .": Landfield, p. 3.

189 "was walled by flames, and . . .": Letter from Henry Atkins to his art dealership partner Frederic Cheever Torrey, April 26, 1906, BL.

189 "Chinatown was catching everywhere" . . . : Letter from John to Lucy R. Schaeffer, May 14, 1906, SFPL.

189 "was now intensified a hundredfold" . . . : Letter from Tom Davis to his mother in England, 1906, CHS.

189 "the size of my hand" . . . : Letter from Dr. Charles Cross to his brother in Texas, *Dallas Morning News,* May 1, 1906.

189 "They sounded just like thunder" . . . : Anonymous man, account of the earthquake and fire, April 25, 1906, SFPL.

189 "the pulse of the great city in its agony" . . . : Hopper.

190 "[S]uddenly a great shower of live . . .": Untitled Earthquake Narrative, Hooker Family Papers 1783–1951, BL.

190 "half burnt" . . . : Unidentified Account in letter, filed in Putnam.

190 "steeple-chased up Geary, Post . . .": Hopper.

190 "out in the middle of the . . .": Laveaga.

190 "were cleared off the scene . . .": Letter from Henry Atkins to his art dealership partner Frederic Cheever Torrey, April 26, 1906, BL.

190 "watched with others the dynamiting . . .": Genthe, p. 92.

190 "muffled detonations of dynamite" . . . : CLondon, p. 102.

190 "A rain of ashes was falling" . . . : JLondon.

190 "the most terrible sight in . . .": Lafler, p. 8.

191 "I'll never write a word . . .": CLondon, p. 102.

11.

193 "succeeded in saving a few . . .": Cullen.

194 "The final stand was made . . .": Russell.

195 "Sparks and large cinders were . . .": Putnam.

195 "one could almost read by . . .": Letter from John to Lucy R. Schaeffer, May 14, 1906, SFPL.

195 "[I]t has seemed a paradise . . .": Letter from Henry Atkins to his art dealership partner Frederic Cheever Torrey, April 26, 1906, BL.

195 "Shelter for Refugees" . . . : Letter from Charles Fisk to his mother in England, April 22, 1906, CHS.

195 "had only coats to cover them" . . . : "People Sleeping in City Plaza," *OT,* April 19, 1906.

195 "we had to take our mattresses . . .": Vera Votta, interviewed June 27, 1977, Growing Up in the Cities: Oral History Transcripts of Tape-Recorded Interviews, BL.

196 "I had to wait for more . . .": Letter from Charles Fisk to his mother in England, April 22, 1906, CHS.

196 "It is the only building . . .": Leach.

196 "to go home and get . . .": Einstein.

196 "That was the first time . . .": Account of Michael Maher, December 1, 1906, SFPL.

197 **"There was not much loud . . ."**: Einstein.

197 **"stumbled over cobblestones in . . ."**: Letter from Ernest Winton Cleary to Irene Neasham, April 14, 1971, CHS.

197 **"clapped as we passed" . . .** : Einstein.

197 **"to destroy the stock of any . . ."**: Letter from Ernest Winton Cleary to Irene Neasham, April 14, 1971, CHS.

197 **"The fire was then on . . ."**: Account of Anna Holshouser, *Arg.*, May 14, 1927.

197 **"burning merrily in the middle . . ."**: JLondon.

197 **"there is no such thing . . ."**: Devol2, p. 64.

198 **"driven out" . . .** : Mitchell.

198 **"in an attempt to get . . ."**: Letter from John to Lucy R. Schaeffer, May 14, 1906, SFPL.

198 **"ignited like kindling wood" . . .** : Myrtle Robertson, "An Eye Witness—Miss Myrtle Robertson's Eyewitness Account Given Substantially in Her Own Words," CHS.

198 **"Chinatown was all ablaze, and . . ."**: Account of Sgt. Maurice Behan, *Arg.*, June 19, 1926.

198 **"All the murderers and hard . . ."**: Letter from Elmer Enewold to his father in Omaha, May 3, 1906, CHS.

198 **"sweeping through Chinatown, up . . ."**: Freeman.

199 **"Mama was convinced that the . . ."**: DBrown.

200 **"under the protecting branches . . ."**: Burke.

200 **"carrying on their backs or . . ."**: W. E. Alexander, Account of the 1906 San Francisco Earthquake and Fire, CHS.

200 **"was so sad" . . .** : Baldwin.

200 **"cheerful spirit" . . .** : Genthe, p. 92.

200 **"sleeping the sleep of exhaustion" . . .** : Burke.

200 **Dennis Grady . . .** : Dennis Grady, a hostler, died of exposure in Golden Gate Park on the night of April 18–19, 1906. Gladys Hansen Death Index, SFPL; *OH,* April 25, 1906.

200 **"Mrs. Grady awoke" . . .** : *OH,* April 25, 1906.

200 **Henry Mayer . . .** : Forty-five-year-old Henry Mayer, husband of Celia, father of Claire and Etta, died the night of April 18–19, 1906, from exhaustion. Gladys Hansen Death Index, SFPL; *SFC,* April 21, 1906; *SFC,* May 4, 1906, p. 7.

201 **"exhaustion resulting from effort . . ."**: "VAST CAMP IN GOLDEN GATE PARK," *SFC,* April 21, 1906, p. 5.

201 **"Lights were twinkling from many . . ."**: Fisher, p. 93.

201 **"Patients were being brought in . . ."**: *Ibid.,* p. 94.

201 **"had a deep gash on . . ."**: *Ibid.,* p. 95.

201 **Bernice Holmes . . .** : "Bernice Holmes Victim," *LAH,* April 21, 1906.

201 **"Use your own judgment" . . .** : Fisher, p. 94.

202 **"vacated and established as wards" . . .** : Torney.

202 **Edward Manville . . .** : *SFCh,* April 24, 1906. Note: the newspaper lists him as a steward and by his last name. He is listed in the 1905 city directory as Edward H. Manville, assistant steward, Emergency Hospital.

202 **Agnes Lawless . . .** : *SFC,* May 21, 1906, p. 8. Note: the paper referenced Captain Lawless and Mrs. Lawless. Robert T. Lawless was listed in *1900Census* as a sea captain living

with his wife, Agnes Lawless, both residents of Alameda. *SFDirectory* lists him as still residing in Alameda.

202 **"If she'd been General Funston's . . ."**: "Says Patients At Presidio Were All Well Treated," *SFC*, May 21, 1906, p. 8.

202 **"The noise of explosions, the . . ."**: Letters from employer of William Duggan, April 24, 1906, and May 5, 1906, SFPL.

203 **"watched for the new day . . ."**: Account of Lillian Peacock, December 5, 1919, RSS.

12.

205 **Mark Hopkins purchased a lot . . .** : Hopkins purchased the lot at the northeast corner of Pine and Mason Streets for $45,000, *SFE*, January 18, 1875.

205 **"had difficulty settling on one style" . . .** : "The Tacky Robber Baron Palaces of Nob Hill," *SFGate*, April 17, 2016.

205 **"both love and money" . . .** : In the September 23, 1891, article "A FIGHT FOR MILLIONS—Remarkable Testimony of Mr. Searles," the *SFCh* reported, "In reply to a question, [the] witness said he married Mrs. Hopkins for all she had, both love and money, but should never have married her for money alone." *SFCh*, September 23, 1891, p. 1.

205 **"instruction in and illustration of . . ."**: Historical marker for "Site of the Mark Hopkins Institute of Art," California Registered Historical Landmark No. 754.

206 **"preposterous palaces" . . .** : "A Critic of Architecture," *SFC*, October 4, 1905, p. 8.

206 **"pretension rules the crest while . . ."**: "The City of St. Francis," *SFE*, January 28, 1894, p. 60.

206 **"intact and uninjured" . . .** : Report from the director of the Mark Hopkins Institute of Art to the president and board of directors on the destruction of the Mark Hopkins mansion, May 10, 1906, published in "The Mark Hopkins Mansion" by Becky Alexander, *Obits of Known and Unknown Objects* (University of California, Berkeley Art Museum—Pacific Film Archive), p. 19.

206 **"walls uninjured" . . .** : Wing.

206 **"because of their distance" . . .** : Report from the director of the Mark Hopkins Art Institute, May 10, 1906, *supra*.

206 **"drove the fire toward us . . ."**: Wing.

206 **"spent the next couple of . . ."**: Kendrick.

206 **"the fire had crept up . . ."**: Account of Eugene Schmitz, *Arg.*, January 22, 1927.

207 **"[i]t was put out in . . ."**: Wing.

207 **"to encourage us in our . . ."**: Cpt. Thomas Magner, Engine 3, quoted in Laurence Joseph Kennedy, *The Progress of the Fire in San Francisco, April 18th to 21st, as Shown by an Analysis of Original Documents* (master's thesis, University of California, Berkeley, 1908), BL.

207 **"Houses seemed to melt away . . ."**: Unsigned manuscript letter addressed to Uncle Wales (Wales L. Knox), BL.

207 **"continued working until the fire . . ."**: Cpt. Thomas Magner, Engine 3, quoted in Kennedy, *The Progress of the Fire in San Francisco, April 18th to 21st, as Shown by an Analysis of Original Documents*.

207 **"suddenly blazed at the turrets . . ."**: Report from the director of the Mark Hopkins Institute of Art to the president and board of directors on the destruction of the Mark Hopkins mansion, May 10, 1906, published in "The Mark Hopkins Mansion" by Becky Alexander, *Obits of Known and Unknown Objects*, p. 19.

207 **"in flame"** . . . : Wing.

208 **a two-story house on the corner** . . . : 1100 Sacramento Street, the home of George Per-ine, five blocks from his business, Renters' Loan & Trust Company, located in the Safe Deposit Building at the corner of California and Montgomery Streets.

208 **"a sickly light was creeping . . ."**: JLondon.

208 **"It was a luxurious interior . . ."**: CLondon, p. 103.

208 **"Nob Hill, the Fairmont, the . . ."**: Hopper.

209 **"The sun came up bright . . ."**: Letter from James R. Tapscott to his mother, Mrs. I. J. Tapscott, April 22, 1906, BL.

209 **"red as wine"** . . . : Griswold, quoted in *Narratives of the San Francisco Earthquake and Fire of 1906*, p. 78.

209 **"blood-red, and showing quarter . . ."**: JLondon.

209 **"a red wafer behind clouds . . ."**: Hopper.

209 **"about an inch of ash"** . . . : Bauer.

209 **"The streets were filled with . . ."**: Morrow.

209 **"waste of smoking ruins"** . . . : JLondon.

209 **"chilled to the marrow in . . ."**: Emma Eames, *Some Memories and Reflections* (New York: Appleton & Company, 1927), p. 270.

209 **"all but mad"** . . . : DBrown.

209 **"men, women and children on . . ."**: Carnahan.

210 **"lost faith in the story . . ."**: Miller.

210 **"In our walk from the . . ."**: Letter from Sara Tomlinson to her aunt, April 18, 1906, CHS.

210 **"left them regretfully, two weary . . ."**: Perry.

210 **"buildings in ruins, and everywhere . . ."**: Caruso.

210 **"thousands of people were camped . . ."**: Letter from James R. Tapscott to his mother, Mrs. I. J. Tapscott, April 22, 1906, BL.

210 **"were almost blistered by the . . ."**: Eames, *Some Memories and Reflections*, p. 270.

210 **"While on the boat we . . ."**: Letter from James A. Warren to his son Pete, April 21, 1906, CHS.

211 **"The greatest good fortune during . . ."**: Goerlitz.

211 **"Mr. Crowley was quite a . . ."**: "William J. McGillivray: Tugboats and Boatmen of Cal-ifornia 1906–1970," interview by Ruth Teiser in 1969 and 1970, Oral History Center, BL.

211 **"big shots"** . . . : "William Figari: San Francisco Bay and Waterfront," interview by Ruth Teiser in 1968, Oral History Center, BL.

212 **"San Francisco, Thursday . . ."**: *CCE*.

212 **"every now and then suffocating . . ."**: Leach.

213 **"Water was now more precious . . ."**: Burke.

213 **"not to drink any water . . ."**: Livingston.

213 **"everybody being urged to be . . ."**: Untitled Earthquake Narrative, Hooker Family Pa-pers 1783–1951, BL.

213 **"at all times of the day . . ."**: Kendrick.

213 **"We lined up in single file . . ."**: Arthur Dangerfield, Journal of the Quake, April 24, 1906, BL.

214 **"we were given hardtack" . . .**: Letter from Lloyd R. Burns to California Historical Society, May 1978, CHS.

214 **"adding that it would probably . . ."**: Putnam.

214 **"set out on a foraging trip" . . .**: Letter from William D. Alexander to his sister Mary C. Alexander, May 16, 1906, BL.

214 **"bargains were offered, as the . . ."**: Putnam.

214 **"Bread was getting scarce" . . .**: Letter from "Aunt Bertha" to Elsa Billerbeck, May 13, 1906, BL.

214 **"the contents of all grocery . . ."**: Duke, p. 167.

214 **"doomed" . . .**: Letter from Tom Davis to his mother in England, 1906, CHS.

214 **"fine hams and sides of bacon" . . .**: Anonymous man, account of the earthquake and fire, April 25, 1906, SFPL.

214 **"We cooked on the streets" . . .**: Jessie Stewart Harris, interviewed by Suzanne B. Reiss, January 10, 1978, "Selections from Memories of Girlhood and the University," Oral History Transcript and related materials, BL.

215 **"Firewood was not difficult to . . ."**: Laurence Klauber, typed annotations on transcript of his 1906 letter, 1958, CHS.

215 **"Some were preparing pots of . . ."**: Letter from Ada Higgins, April 1906, SFPL.

215 **"do everything possible to assist . . ."**: Telegram sent 4:00 a.m., April 19, 1906, Washington, DC, Taft, p. 5.

215 **"All available hospital, wall, and . . ."**: Telegram sent 4:55 a.m., April 19, 1906, Washington, DC, Taft, p. 5.

216 **"City practically destroyed" . . .**: Telegram sent 9:11 a.m., April 19, 1906, San Francisco, Taft, p. 7.

216 **"all available canvas" . . .**: Telegram sent April 19, 1906, Taft, p. 7.

216 **"to express their sympathy and . . ."**: "The Appeal Issued by the President," *Washington Post*, April 20, 1906, p. 2.

216 **"direction and discretion" . . .**: S.J.R. 18, Joint Resolution for the relief of sufferers from earthquake and conflagration on the Pacific Coast, *Statutes at Large of the United States of America from December, 1905, to March, 1907,* Part 1 (Washington, DC: Government Printing Office, 1907), p. 827.

216 **"obsolete" . . .**: Devol1, p. 176.

216 **"that a large quantity of . . ."**: Ibid., p. 177.

217 **"Committee of Fifty" . . .**: The "citizens' committee," or "Committee of Fifty" as it came to be known, eventually had nearly one hundred members in twenty-two subcommittees. There were eighty-nine members reported present on April 26, 1906. *Arg.,* January 22, 1927.

217 **"rose humbly in a shabby . . ."**: Herrick Wall, quoted in *Narratives of the San Francisco Earthquake and Fire of 1906,* p. 276.

13.

219 **Forty-three-year-old Ernest Edwards . . .**: Francis Ernest Edwards was born September 20, 1862, and lived at 1326 Guerrero Street with his mother, Ellen, and aunt Emily. *1900Cen-*

sus. Ernest and Emma were married in 1901; their sons, Francis C. and John E., were born in 1902 and 1903, per the 1910 census; and they resided at 1326 Guerrero Street in 1905 and 1906. *SFDirectory,* p. 637; and his account in the October 23, 1926, issue of the *Argonaut.*

220 **"and told him I was ready . . ."**: Account of F. Ernest Edwards, *Arg.,* October 23, 1926.

220 **"filled with dirt" . . .** : Account of F. Ernest Edwards, *Arg.,* October 30, 1926.

220 **"could not find any available supply" . . .** : Conlon.

220 **"Ernest, the Bible says the . . ."**: Account of F. Ernest Edwards, *Arg.,* October 30, 1926.

220 **"his scabbard rattling at his side" . . .** : Hollister, p. 157. Note: this was Dr. John Hollister, who evacuated first to the home of George Eastman at 532 Valencia Street but moved to the home of George's brother Edward at 456 Guerrero Street in the middle of the night.

221 **"densely crowded" . . .** : *Ibid.,* p. 158.

221 **"fine furniture, carpets, bedding, lace . . ."**: "Pattosien Company," *SFDirectory,* p. 1462.

221 **"and almost immediately took fire" . . .** : Account of F. Ernest Edwards, *Arg.,* October 30, 1926.

222 **"dammed the water that was . . ."**: Cullen.

222 **"making a cistern" . . .** : Conlon.

222 **California Street Cable Railroad . . .** : Information about the California Street Cable Railroad was obtained primarily from *San Francisco's California Street Cable Cars* by Walter Rice and Emiliano Echeverria, with Michael Dolgushkin; Stetson1; Stetson2; and author interviews with Joe Thompson and Emiliano Echeverria.

222 **"even with the roof" . . .** : Stetson1.

223 **"no fire near us" . . .** : Account of Sgt. William M. Ross, *Arg.,* May 22, 1926.

223 **"day dawned but the fire . . ."**: Laveaga.

223 **"The fire was swallowing a . . ."**: Herrick Wall, quoted in *Narratives of the San Francisco Earthquake and Fire of 1906,* p. 269.

224 **"in keeping order and in . . ."**: Devol2.

224 **"all the regular troops that . . ."**: Cpt. Kelly, US Army Corps of Engineers, Ft. Mason, to family in Boston, "Earthquake and Fire at San Francisco, Cal., April 18–May 19th," BL.

224 **"the Mayor desired" . . .** : *Annual Report of the Adjutant General of the State of California for the Fiscal Year Ending June 30, 1906* (Sacramento: W. W. Shannon, Superintendent State Printing, 1907), p. 44.

225 **"the Mayor desired all the . . ."**: Cpt. Kelly, US Army Corps of Engineers, Ft. Mason, to family in Boston, "Earthquake and Fire at San Francisco, Cal., April 18–May 19th," BL.

225 **"the necessary dynamite would be provided" . . .** : *Annual Report of the Adjutant General of the State of California for the Fiscal Year Ending June 30, 1906,* p. 44.

226 **"Matters about this time began . . ."**: Stetson1.

226 **"was filled with people . . ."**: Stetson2, p. 14.

226 **"the flames were continuous" . . .** : Stetson1.

226 **"the cable was subjected to . . ."**: *SFCh,* June 15, 1906.

226 **"about seventy men responded" . . .** : Laveaga.

227 **"back-fire" . . .** : Report of Lt. William F. Otto, Truck 5, Stationed 1819 Post Street, BL.

227 **"[F]lames came roaring down, gaining . . ."**: Account of Frank Hittell, *Arg.,* March 19, 1927.

227 **"volunteer fire fighters"** . . . : Laveaga.

227 **"house after house took fire . . ."**: Stetson1.

227 **"saw the flames leap the . . ."**: Letter from Major William Stephenson, US Army, May 31, 1906, BL.

228 **"[F]rom rumors which reached me . . ."**: Freeman.

228 **"was beginning to prime badly . . ."**: Pond.

228 **"approved"** . . . : Freeman.

229 **"[T]here must have been two . . ."**: Account of Frank Hittell, *supra*.

229 **"We caught four or five . . ."**: Account of Alex Paladini, *Arg.*, August 7, 1926.

229 **"behaving in a drunken manner"** . . . : Account of Andrea Sbarboro, *Arg.*, June 4, 1927.

229 **"a man of large physique"** . . . : Testimony of Andrea Sbarboro, "Denicke's Accuser Tells Dramatically of Tragedy, but Testimony Conflicts With Sbarboro's," *SFC*, July 16, 1906.

229 **"turned toward me"** . . . : Duke, p. 176.

229 **"moaning but unconscious"** . . . : *Arg.*, June 4, 1927.

229 **"and had it thrown in the bay"** . . . : This was Sgt. Charles Herring of the 22nd Infantry Regiment. *Ibid.*

230 **"To all Civil and Military . . ."**: Pass signed by Mayor Eugene Schmitz, April 22, 1906, SFPL.

230 **"was in his shirt sleeves sweating"** . . . : Letter from Dr. Charles V. Cross to his brother in Texas, *Dallas Morning News*, May 1, 1906.

230 **"To the Officer in Charge . . ."**: *Arg.*, January 29, 1927.

230 **"had enough troops"** . . . : Account of Mayor Eugene Schmitz, *Arg.*, February 5, 1927.

231 **"to proceed to this city . . ."**: Account of General Frederick Funston, *supra*.

231 **"disposal"** . . . : General Funston initially told the police chief and Mayor Schmitz the troops were being "placed at his disposal." *Arg.*, January 29, 1927.

231 **"it was finally settled that . . ."**: Nichols.

231 **"upshoots of burning timbers . . ."**: Nichols, "The Story," *supra*.

231 **"The explosions of dynamite were . . ."**: Stetson1.

232 **"the booming of artillery fire"** . . . : Griswold, quoted in *Narratives of the San Francisco Earthquake and Fire of 1906*, p. 81.

232 **"like tremendous bombs, as if . . ."**: Letter from May A. Briggs to Rhoda, Anna, Mary, and Minnie, April 23, 1906, BL.

232 **"heroic efforts"** . . . : Laveaga.

232 **"the brave man as he stood . . ."**: *SFC*, September 23, 1906, p. 37. The man was reportedly James Lang, a thirty-year-old resident volunteer, and the priest was Reverend Father Charles Ramm.

233 **"little by little the flames . . ."**: Laveaga.

14.

235 **The Bank of Italy . . .** : Information about A. P. Giannini, the Bank of Italy, and the subsequent Bank of America were obtained primarily from Marquis James and Bessie R. James, *Biography of a Bank—The Story of Bank of America, NT & SA* (New York: Harper & Row, 1954); and Francesca Valente, *A. P. Giannini—The People's Banker* (Temple City, CA: Barbera Foundation, 2017).

235 **three pouches filled with $80,000** . . . : *Biography of a Bank,* pp. 23–26.

236 **The employees of nearby Hotaling** . . . : Information in this paragraph obtained from account of Edward M. Lind, *Arg.,* July 17, 1926.

236 **"the large stock of whisky . . ."**: *Ibid.*

237 **"observations of the progress . . ."**: Freeman.

237 **"the most powerful available"** . . . : Pond, p. 989.

238 **"the skeleton of its cupola crumble . . ."**: *Ibid.,* p. 990.

238 **"terrific heat from the blazing mass . . ."**: *Ibid.,* p. 989.

238 **"a height of about two and . . ."**: Freeman.

239 **"carrying out the lamps . . ."**: Account of Edward M. Lind, *Arg.,* July 24, 1926.

239 **"the longest distance that any . . ."**: Freeman.

239 **"after what seemed an interminable time"** . . . : Account of Edward M. Lind, *supra.*

239 **"The best work"** . . . : Freeman.

239 **"awed by the almost incredible panorama"** . . . : Nichols, "The Story," *supra.*

239 **"At this time"** . . . : Unsigned manuscript letter addressed to Uncle Wales (Wales L. Knox), BL.

240 **"expecting every minute to see . . ."**: Stetson2, p. 18.

240 **"so hot that I could not . . ."**: Stetson1.

240 **"We had no idea the fire . . ."**: Letter from Carrie A. Duncan to Mrs. Noitchey, May 23, 1906, CHS.

240 **"sweeping down over the hill . . ."**: Letter from John Walter to his parents, April 26, 1906, published in John I. Walter, *To His Parents, April 18, 1906* (San Francisco: privately printed, 1935), BL.

241 **"far enough ahead of the fire . . ."**: Report of Cpt. Le Vert Coleman, US Army Artillery Corps, to the Adjutant at the Presidio, May 2, 1906, VMSF.

241 **"began to pack"** . . . : Letter from Edith Bonnell to Mabel Symmes, undated, CHS.

241 **"outflanked my small party time . . ."**: Report of Cpt. Le Vert Coleman, *supra.*

242 **"just like a huge glowing volcano"** . . . : Arthur Dangerfield, Journal of the Quake, April 24, 1906, BL.

242 **"watched the deep red glare . . ."**: Unsigned manuscript letter addressed to Uncle Wales (Wales L. Knox), BL.

242 **"Bob, it looks like the . . ."**: Austin, pp. 235–236.

242 **"over broad cracks and sunken . . ."**: Carnahan.

242 **"over the hot pavement"** . . . : Unidentified Account in letter, filed in Putnam.

242 **"through a dead city, not . . ."**: Hopper.

242 **"the smoking ruins"** . . . : Millard.

242 **"tiny tents made of rugs . . ."**: Letter from William Hancock to his sister Mary, May 31, 1906, CHS.

243 **"onto trucks well-guarded by soldiers"** . . . : Letter from Laurence M. Klauber to his sister Alice, May 1, 1906, CHS.

243 **"crowding and pushing of people . . ."**: Letter from a member of the Armer Family, 5:00 p.m., April 20, 1906, SFPL.

243 **"People packed like sardines into . . ."**: Sinsheimer.

243 **"No tickets had to be bought"** . . . : Letter from Charles Page to his son, a student at MIT, April 21, 1906, CHS.

243 **"From the ferry toward the . . ."**: Sinsheimer.

243 **"The view of the burning . . ."**: Letter from Charles Page to his son, *supra*.

243 **"swarms of grasshoppers"** . . . : Goerlitz.

243 **Mary McIntyre** . . . : Mary Dillon McIntyre was born in Ireland December 22, 1837, was married to John B. McIntyre, a bookbinder and book manufacturer, and died of a stroke aboard the *Newark* at the Southern Pacific Mole, on April 19, 1906. *1900Census*; *SFDirectory*; Gladys Hansen Death Index, SFPL; *DeathIndex*.

243 **"dropped dead of heart attack"** . . . : *Oakland Inquirer*, April 21, 1906, p. 2.

243 **"At Oakland it was hard . . ."**: Letter from Charles Fisk to his mother in England, April 22, 1906, CHS.

244 **"been running relief trains since . . ."**: Letter, Legislative Dept., City of Oakland, April 20, 1906, George C. Pardee Papers, BL.

244 **"sleep very little"** . . . : Caruso.

244 **145 new patients admitted** . . . : Torney, p. 209.

244 **"a long piece of wood"** . . . : "Brave Doctor Loses an Eye," *SFCh*, April 22, 1906, p. 1.

244 **"I was taken to the surgical . . ."**: Account of J. R. Aten, *Arg.*, March 26, 1927.

244 **"drifted in the second day . . ."**: Letter from William Stephenson, Maj., US Army, May 31, 1906, BL.

245 **"eatables" in baskets** . . . : Letter from Omira B. Dodge to her son, April 22, 1906, SFPL.

245 **"slept in peace, wrapped in . . ."**: Mahoney.

245 **"There were crowds of people . . ."**: Account of Anna Holshouser, *Arg.*, May 14, 1927.

245 **"managed to keep, at least . . ."**: Miller.

245 **"mattresses spread upon the grassy . . ."**: Hollister, p. 158.

246 **"During the early part of . . ."**: Anonymous man, account of the earthquake and fire, April 25, 1906, SFPL.

246 **"had a very hard fight"** . . . : Cullen.

246 **"It seemed to burn up . . ."**: Anonymous man, account of the earthquake and fire, April 25, 1906, SFPL.

246 **"as far as I could see"** . . . : Dewitt Baldwin, "Memories of the Earthquake," as related to Ana Maria P. de Jesus, September 19, 1988, VMSF.

246 **"new kitchen stove"** . . . : Account of H. C. Schmidt, *Arg.*, May 8, 1926.

247 **"opening every hydrant I passed . . ."**: Account of F. Ernest Edwards, *Arg.*, October 30, 1926.

248 **"from Dolores to Mission St."** . . . : Russell. Note: "st." in original corrected to "St."

248 **"Doors were torn from houses"** . . . : Account of F. Ernest Edwards, *Arg.*, November 6, 1926.

248 **"drowning it with water"** . . . : Anonymous man, account of the earthquake and fire, April 25, 1906, SFPL.

248 **"after fighting every inch of . . ."**: Cullen.

248 **"Three cheers for the San Francisco . . ."**: Account of F. Ernest Edwards, *Arg.*, November 6, 1926.

15.

249 **"like a grain field on fire"** . . . : Unidentified Account in letter, filed in Putnam.

249 **Commercial Hotel** . . . : Abe Ruef's properties were the subject of much discussion during his subsequent graft prosecution, and his interest in the Commercial Hotel was reported in the front-page story "RUEF SET FREE ON BAIL BONDS OF $1,560,000" in the July 7, 1908, issue of *SFC*.

249 **"to do all they could"** . . . : Account of Edward M. Lind, *Arg.*, July 24, 1926.

249 **"The Leading Italian Restaurant" sign** . . . : Catherine A. Accardi, *San Francisco's North Beach and Telegraph Hill* (Charleston, SC: Arcadia Publishing, 2010), p. 32.

250 **"owing to the dilapidated condition . . ."**: Freeman.

250 **"smaller and smaller until it . . ."**: Pond, p. 990.

250 **"the intense heat"** . . . : McCluskey.

250 **"relay teams"** . . . : Pond, p. 990.

250 **"decided to retreat and save . . ."**: Freeman.

251 **"the fire was spreading north . . ."**: Report of Second Assistant Chief Patrick H. Shaughnessy, September 13, 1906, SFFD Fire Museum, Guardians of the City, https://www.guardiansofthecity.org/sffd/fires/great_fires/1906/Shaughnessy.html.

251 **"octagonal house"** . . . : The house at 1051 Green Street was built in 1858, and an eight-sided octagonal cupola was added in 1900.

251 **Feusier's physician son-in-law** . . . : This was Dr. John Pincz, who resided in the home. Lewis Feusier's son, Clarence Feusier, in an interview many years later, credited his brother-in-law with stopping the dynamiters. "A Midsummer Story—Concluded," by Robert O'Brien, *SFCh*, August 3, 1949, p. 16.

251 **"firm resistance"** . . . : *Ibid.*

251 **"Outbuildings and fences of all . . ."**: "Block Saved on Russian Hill," *SFCh*, April 24, 1906, p. 1.

252 **"from the westward over Telegraph Hill"** . . . : Pond, p. 991; Freeman.

252 **"Not Passable By [Horse] Teams"** . . . : *SanbornMap.*

252 **"huddled hundreds + thousands . . ."**: Unidentified Account in letter, filed in Putnam.

252 **"[A]ll we were permitted to . . ."**: Florence de Andreis, Account of the April 1906 Earthquake and Fire, written July 1909, SCP.

252 **"One side was the water . . ."**: Letter from Amy Kahn to Mr. Coop, April 23–24, 1906, BL.

253 **"hoarded a few buckets of . . ."**: Lafler, p. 8.

253 **"swept up the slopes"** . . . : "Wine Used to Fight Flames," *SFCh*, April 22, 1906, p. 1.

253 **"the lee of Telegraph Hill"** . . . : Freeman.

254 **"It came on like a Fourth . . ."**: Putnam.

254 **"nothing effective was being done . . ."**: Landfield, p. 6.

254 **"Look out for bricks"** . . . : Letter from William D. Alexander to his sister Mary C. Alexander, May 16, 1906, BL.

254 **"an endless procession of smaller . . ."**: Putnam.

255 **"The post was nearly buried . . ."**: Cpt. Kelly, US Army Corps of Engineers, Ft. Mason, to family in Boston, "Earthquake and Fire at San Francisco, Cal., April 18-May 19th," BL.

255 **"coming up all sides of . . ."**: Griswold, quoted in *Narratives of the San Francisco Earthquake and Fire of 1906*, p. 80.

255 **"The air was filled with . . ."**: Report of Commander Charles J. Badger, US Navy, Commanding Flagship USS *Chicago*, to Commander-in-Chief of Pacific Squadron, May 31, 1906, NA, Record Group 45.

255 **"The morning awakening was to . . ."**: Mahoney.

255 **"had fairly good sleep and rest" . . .**: Nichols, "The Story," *supra*.

256 **"a little sheet-iron pocket . . ."**: Hollister, p. 158.

256 **"What a sight on Dolores St.!" . . .**: Dewitt Baldwin, "Memories of the Earthquake," as related to Ana Maria P. de Jesus, September 19, 1988, VMSF.

256 **"simple breakfast" . . .**: Dr. George Blumer's Eyewitness Account of the Disaster, VMSF.

256 **"water many blocks" . . .**: Letter from Edith Bonnel to Mabel Symmes, undated, CHS.

256 **"to get something to take . . ."**: Letter from Edith Bonnel to Mabel Symmes, undated, CHS.

256 **"set out on a tour to . . ."**: Einstein.

257 **"greatest urgency" . . .**: Telegram from Commissary-General Sharpe to Commissary, Vancouver Barracks, Wash., 1:00 a.m., April 19, 1906, Taft, p. 25.

257 **"immediate shipment of 300,000 rations" . . .**: Telegram from Commissary-General Sharpe to Commissary, Seattle, Wash., 11:00 p.m., April 19, 1906, Taft, p. 26.

257 **"sadly inadequate to the amount . . ."**: Devol1, p. 177.

257 **"We were somewhat early and . . ."**: Unsigned manuscript letter addressed to Uncle Wales (Wales L. Knox), BL.

258 **"cup of coffee and one . . ."**: Account of Michael Maher, December 1, 1906, SFPL.

258 **"joined the line we saw forming" . . .**: Nankervis.

258 **"and tore through what was . . ."**: Account of Ernest Simpson, city editor of *SFCh*, *Arg.*, April 23, 1927.

259 **"300,000 ARE HOMELESS, HUNGRY . . ."**: *SFE*, April 20, 1906, p. 1.

259 **"FLAMES COURSE AT LAST CHECKED" . . .**: *SFCh*, April 20, 1906, p. 1.

259 **"wiping out at one sweep . . ."**: *Ibid.*

259 **"The sight looked like the . . ."**: Letter from William D. Alexander to his sister Mary C. Alexander, May 16, 1906, BL.

260 **"What was once the business . . ."**: Laveaga.

260 **"locked the doors and left . . ."**: Letter from Frederick H. Collins to his family in Placerville, April 24, 1906, VMSF.

260 **"found it in ruins" . . .**: Stetson1.

260 **"our safe in the basement . . ."**: Account of Thomas A. Burns, *Arg.*, May 29, 1926.

260 **"relatively cooled" . . .**: JCook2.

261 **"when he recognized me, looked . . ."**: Account of Thomas A. Burns, *supra*.

261 **"We were finally ordered to . . ."**: Newell.

261 **"after having been on duty . . ."**: Boden.

261 **Now the fire had destroyed . . .**: All eleven members of Engine 6 lived either in the firehouse at 311 6th Street or within two blocks: Captain Charles J. Cullen at 925 Harrison Street,

Lieutenant Edward Daunet at 7½ Harrison Street, engineer Patrick H. Brandon at 340 6th Street, driver Joseph McDonald in the firehouse, stoker Charles Neil at 957 Harrison Street, hoseman John Titus at 309 6th Street, hoseman A. Swanberg at 297½ Clara, hoseman Edward McGrorey at 442½ Clementina, hoseman James C. Crowley in the firehouse, hoseman Edward McDermott in the firehouse (recently transferred from Engine 21), and hoseman John Doherty at 439 Clementina. *SFDirectory* and Bill Koenig, *Everything Took Time*, p. 36.

262 **"stationed at contiguous points"** . . . : GBrown.

262 **"well in hand"** . . . : J. B. Levison, "Memories for my Family," BL.

262 **"a strong, cool sea breeze"** . . . : Livingston.

262 **"By eleven o'clock Friday morning . . ."**: Landfield, p. 6.

262 **"unharmed by the fire and . . ."**: *Arg.*, August 20, 1927.

262 **"home treatment for mothers and daughters"** . . . : Ad in *SFC*, July 20, 1902. Medical journals reported testimony in lawsuits against the company, which used saleswomen to peddle its snake-oil home remedy with vague assurances to "cure the incurable." Its capsule form was inserted into the cervix and, as some lawsuits alleged, it could cause infection leading to sepsis. The "pharmaceutical" was marketed as a nonmedical alternative when surgery had been recommended by a physician. *Pharmaceutical Journal*, May 25, 1901, p. 688.

262 **"ignited thousands of gallons of . . ."**: Landfield, p. 6.

262 **"hurling skyward"** . . . : Account of Sgt. James E. Cottle, *Arg.*, August 21, 1926.

262 **"rose to something very like . . ."**: The Last Fire, Hooker Family Papers 1783–1951, BL.

263 **"Crookedest Street in the World"** . . . : Lombard Street between Hyde and Leavenworth Streets was a 27-degree grade at that time, and newspapers reported delivery drivers were unable to deliver loads to the top of "what is recognized as one of the steepest streets in the city," which one driver complained "is a billy goat proposition and not a truck one." *SFE*, August 15, 1920, p. 54. In 1922 the street's grade was reduced for that block by reconfiguring it into the series of switchbacks we know today, and until 1939 it was a two-way street. "Hairpin Insanity: San Francisco's Famous Lombard Street" by Karen Harris in *History Daily*, https://historydaily.org/hairpin-insanity-san-franciscos-famous-lombard-street. The "crookedest street" in San Francisco is Vermont Street between 20th and 22nd Streets in the Potrero Hill neighborhood.

263 **"Two agile schoolboys with pails . . ."**: Landfield, p. 6.

263 **"with blanket and bucket and . . ."**: Lafler, p. 11.

263 **"Two streams of water were . . ."**: Unidentified Account in letter, filed in Putnam. Note: the two were pumping from the cistern at Greenwich/Dupont, which was soon overrun by the blaze.

264 **"to egg on and spur . . ."**: Account of Edward Lind, *Arg.*, July 24, 1926.

264 **"When we got the hose . . ."**: Pond, p. 991.

264 **"barrel rollers were already becoming . . ."**: Account of Edward Lind, *supra*.

264 **"searched frantically"** . . . : Pond, p. 991.

265 **"so we closed all the . . ."**: Account of Edward Lind, *supra*.

265 **"The look he gave me . . ."**: Pond, p. 992.

265 **"and instead of despairing"** . . . : Account of Edward Lind, *supra*.

265 **"Several times the block caught"** . . . : Report of Cpt. Orrin R. Wolfe, 22nd Infantry Regt., US Army, May 24, 1906, VMSF.

266 **"a barbecue"** . . . : Account of Edward Lind, *supra*.

16.

267 **"herds of people"** . . . : Cpt. Kelly, US Army Corps of Engineers, Ft. Mason, to family in Boston, "Earthquake and Fire at San Francisco, Cal., April 18-May 19th," BL.

267 **"We are at the little . . ."**: Griswold, quoted in *Narratives of the San Francisco Earthquake and Fire of 1906*, p. 82.

268 **"and it became extremely . . ."**: Putnam.

268 **"that this whole section of . . ."**: Freeman.

268 **"How inadequate! How futile!"** . . . : Putnam.

269 **"He looked all in"** . . . : Pond, p. 992.

269 **"the tall watch tower of . . ."**: Putnam.

270 **"crowded with thousands of refugees . . ."**: Way.

270 **"All who want a place . . ."**: Account of De Witt J. Lipe, *Arg.*, July 10, 1926.

270 **"felt as if we had . . ."**: Putnam.

270 **"from Thursday eve until Sunday . . ."**: Letter from Mary, April 30, 1906, SFPL.

271 **"hurriedly scribbled in pencil on . . ."**: *Arg.*, April 2, 1927.

271 **"Lost. Paul E. Hoffes, nine . . ."**: *Ibid.*

271 **"Harry Markowitz is looking for . . ."**: *Ibid.*

271 **"Mother, Ray and Ethel E. Peck"** . . . : *Ibid.*

271 **"A.C. Rass and family, formerly . . ."**: *SFCh*, April 24, 1906, p. 5.

271 **"Dr. Geo. H. Martin and wife please inform . . ."**: *Ibid.*

271 **"wife and all the folks in the Panhandle . . ."**: *Arg.*, April 2, 1927.

271 **"partial list"** . . . : *SFE*, April 20, 1906.

271 **"A. Enkel, a prominent Los Angelan . . ."**: *Ibid.*

272 **"withstood the earthquake surprisingly well"** . . . : Recollection of Charles Derleth Jr., *Denial of Disaster*, p. 37.

272 **"was coming from all directions"** . . . : Account of William F. Burke, assistant postmaster, *Arg.*, December 25, 1926.

272 **"worked like demons"** . . . : Letter from Guy T. Gould, San Francisco postmaster, to his parents, April 23, 1906, SFPL.

272 **"Wagons and automobiles were impressed"** . . . : Account of William F. Burke, assistant postmaster, *supra*.

273 **"U.S. mail is carried in automobiles"** . . . : Letter from Annie Darbee, April 23, 1906, postmarked April 22, 1906, SFPL.

273 **"any little scrap of paper"** . . . : Arthur Dangerfield, Journal of the Quake, April 24, 1906, BL.

273 **"as curious mail as was . . ."**: Account of William F. Burke, assistant postmaster, *Arg.*, December 25, 1926.

273 **"S.F. Apr 20th Dear Mother . . ."**: Letter from Karl E. Kneiss to Rosa Kneiss, April 20, 1906, BL.

273 **"beautiful, well-groomed"** . . . : ConlonJr.

274 **"We had fourteen people living . . ."**: Dunne.

274 **"filled to its capacity"** . . . : Account of Edwin A. Freeman, December 4, 1919, RSS.

274 **"covered with glass & debris"** . . . : Letter from John Walter to his parents, April 26, 1906, published in Walter, *To His Parents, April 18, 1906.*

274 **"very much blistered and blackened . . ."**: Stetson1.

274 **"No one went to bed"** . . . : Miller.

275 **"flames mounting in huge billows"** . . . : Eugenia C. Murrell Poston, Personal Experiences from Apr. 18 to June 10, 1906: signed and amended typescript, BL.

275 **"large quantities of water"** . . . : Pond, p. 992.

275 **"The hardest fight we had . . ."**: Freeman.

276 **"With these four lines"** . . . : Account of Cpt. Daniel R. Sewell, Engine 9, *Arg.,* August 20, 1927.

276 **"several others which I fail . . ."**: Freeman.

276 **"When hope was almost gone . . ."**: Eugenia C. Murrell Poston, Personal Experiences from Apr. 18 to June 10, 1906: signed and amended typescript, BL.

17.

277 **"When the sea of flames . . ."**: Kendrick.

277 **"the almost total absence of life"** . . . : Letter from William Hancock to his sister Mary, May 31, 1906, CHS.

277 **"The smell of human flesh . . ."**: Letter from Hugh to Natie, April 21, 1906, Nine Miscellaneous Letters from Unidentified Eyewitnesses to the San Francisco Earthquake and Fire, 1906, CHS.

277 **"Walking down Market Street and . . ."**: Letter from William Hancock to his sister Mary, May 31, 1906, CHS.

278 **"most picturesque ruins"** . . . : Letter from Tom to Jessie, April 26, 1906, Nine Miscellaneous Letters from Unidentified Eyewitnesses to the San Francisco Earthquake and Fire, 1906, CHS.

278 **"We located the bureau and . . ."**: Letter from L. M. Simpson to George, May 14, 1906, Phillips-Jones.

278 **"The bugle-calls in the morning . . ."**: Burke.

278 **"[T]he entire waterfront from Fort . . ."**: Pond, p. 993.

278 **"Dead-tired when we reached"** . . . : Einstein.

279 **"The soldiers were parked about . . ."**: Laurence Klauber, Typed Annotations on Transcript of his 1906 letter, 1958, CHS.

279 **"People have been shot right . . ."**: DBrown.

279 **"they take a shot at . . ."**: Letter from Frederick H. Collins to his family in Placerville, April 24, 1906, VMSF.

279 **"All the men that pass . . ."**: Letter from Catherine to Elise, April 22, 1906, Nine Miscellaneous Letters from Unidentified Eyewitnesses to the San Francisco Earthquake and Fire, 1906, CHS.

279 **"but every man caught in . . ."**: Letter from Ernest H. Adams to Messrs. Reed and Barton, April 23, 1906, VMSF.

279 **"cleaning debris, building conveniences"** . . . : Letter from Tom Davis to his mother in England, 1906, CHS.

280 **"this abuse of authority shall . . ."**: *Presidial Weekly Clarion,* April 27, 1906.

280 **"I had an idea that it . . ."**: Livingston.

280 **Approximately 100,000 had been fed** . . . : Reports for April 19, 20, and 21 list "Number of persons (estimated) as 100,000, 150,000, and 200,000 respectively." *ReliefSurvey,* Appendix II, Methods of Distribution, Table 6—Daily Issues of Rations from April 19 to May 12, 1906, p. 11.

280 **"There was no starvation in . . ."**: Unsigned manuscript letter addressed to Uncle Wales (Wales L. Knox), BL.

280 **"Water is scarce, but food . . ."**: Letter from Bert Tuttle to Mary Butler, April 24, 1906, CHS.

280 **"putting the bread into . . ."**: Anonymous man, account of the earthquake and fire, April 25, 1906, SFPL.

280 **"It is a great sight to see . . ."**: Letter from Clarence Gault to his parents, April 23, 1906, SFPL (original in San Joaquin Pioneer and Historical Society).

280 **At least thirty-five thousand loaves had** . . . : "On Friday, April 20 . . . The bakeries that day furnished 35,000 loaves of bread." *ReliefSurvey,* Appendix II, Methods of Distribution, Section 2, Distribution of Food, p. 6.

281 **"The neighbors helped build a . . ."**: Unsigned manuscript letter addressed to Uncle Wales (Wales L. Knox), BL.

281 **"[W]e all have our stoves . . ."**: Letter from Catherine to Elise, April 22, 1906, Nine Miscellaneous Letters from Unidentified Eyewitnesses to the San Francisco Earthquake and Fire, 1906, CHS.

281 **"built an elaborate range from . . ."**: ConlonJr.

281 **"gone beyond repair"** . . . : Statement by Hermann Schussler, chief engineer, Spring Valley Water Company, April 24, 1906, VMSF.

282 **"use any water except for . . ."**: "Mayor Points to Grave Danger of Disease," *SFC,* April 21, 1906, p. 1.

282 **"reputation for scrupulous honesty . . ."**: Walsh and O'Keefe, *Legacy of a Native Son,* p. 108.

282 **"vastly inflated price"** . . . : *Ibid.,* p. 114.

283 **"[m]any thousands homeless"** . . . : Morrow.

283 **"the immediate and pressing necessity . . ."**: *Ibid.*

283 **"In the night it poured"** . . . : Burke.

283 **"We never closed our eyes . . ."**: Letter from Frederick H. Collins to his family in Placerville, April 24, 1906, VMSF.

284 **"Although I had seen plenty . . ."**: Carl Emil Peterson, Selection from "The Champion Globe-Trotter, Twice Round the World Without Money," 1928, Fifth Chapter, BL.

284 **Sunday morning the clergy of** . . . : "Ministers Will Hold Services," *SFE,* April 22, 1906, p. 2.

284 **"sanitary arrangements of the city"** . . . : Special Orders No. 27, April 20, 1906, Torney, p. 210.

284 **Six-year-old Emily Curran** . . . : Emily Curran, six, died April 22, 1906. *DeathIndex,* p. 2421.

284 **"inhalation burns"** . . . : Gladys Hansen Death Index, SFPL, *SFC,* April 24, 1906, p. 3; *SFCh,* April 24, 1906, p. 7.

284 **Jens Sorenson** . . . : Jens Sorenson, eighty-six, was a tailor found unconscious on April 18, admitted to Army General Hospital at the Presidio on April 19, died April 20, and was buried in San Francisco National Cemetery. Coroner's Book C, front fly leaf, Gladys Hansen Death Index, SFPL.

285 **Holber Mansen** . . . : Died at Army General Hospital on April 22, 1906, after being admitted for fracture of legs/bruises. Coroner's Book C fly leaf, Gladys Hansen Death Index, SFPL; *DeathIndex.*

285 **fire chief Dennis Sullivan** . . . : Dennis T. Sullivan (b. November 2, 1852) died April 22, 1906, at Army General Hospital. *SFC,* April 23, 1906, p. 3; Gladys Hansen Death Index, SFPL; *DeathIndex.* His funeral was held at the house he owned with his wife, Margaret, on 49th Avenue on April 24, 1906, and his remains were temporarily interred in Calvary Cemetery. *SFCh,* April 26, 1906, p. 6. His body was removed for burial to Holy Cross Catholic Cemetery in Colma, CA, on April 14, 1907. *SFC,* April 15, 1907, p. 7.

286 **"had been working day and . . ."**: *Arg.,* March 12, 1927.

286 **"Red Cross!"** . . . : *Arg.,* May 28, 1927; Account of William Harvey, *Arg.,* March 12, 1927.

286 **"The shots came rapidly"** . . . : "Witnesses Tell of the Shooting at Red Cross Automobile by Defendants," *SFCh,* September 25, 1906, p. 2.

286 **"You've got one of us"** . . . : *Ibid. See also* "Jury Secured To Try Slayers Of Heber C. Tilden," *The Recorder,* September 22, 1906, p. 1; "Tilden Shooting is Described," *SFC,* September 22, 1906, p. 16; and "R.G. Seamen Goes on Stand in Tilden Case," *SFE,* September 25, 1906, p. 5.

287 **"Clerk, foremen and general employees . . ."**: Ad for the John Bollman Co., *SFC,* April 23, 1906, p. 4.

288 **"uninjured"** . . . : Ad for the Paraffine Paint Co., *SFC,* April 23, 1906, p. 6.

288 **"report at the store"** . . . : Ad for Pacific Hardware and Steel Company, *SFC,* April 23, 1906, p. 4.

288 **"My route is burned up"** . . . : Angove.

288 **"knew I would have to find . . ."**: Livingston.

288 **"relaxing the rigidity of military rule"** . . . : "Funston Relaxes the Rigor of Martial Law," *SFE,* April 23, 1906, p. 1.

288 **"all who are regularly employed . . ."**: "Pay For All Who Work For City," *SFCh,* April 24, 1906, p. 7.

288 **"dangerous walls left standing in . . ."**: Report of Cpt. Le Vert Coleman, US Army Artillery Corps, to the Adjutant at the Presidio, May 2, 1906, VMSF.

289 **"to open a safe artery . . ."**: "Dynamites Fire Ruins," *SFE,* April 24, 1906, p. 1.

289 **"They appeared as if the . . ."**: Leach.

289 **"fell and crushed every bone . . ."**: *OT,* EXTRA Edition, April 28, 1906, p. 1.

289 **"some of them seven stories high"** . . . : Report of Cpt. Le Vert Coleman, *supra.*

289 **"pile of bricks and a wobbly wall"** . . . : Leithead.

289 **"would soon have fallen of . . ."**: "Dynamites Fire Ruins," *SFE,* April 24, 1906, p. 1.

289 **"as large a force of men . . ."**: "Cars Begin to Run on the Streets," *SFC,* April 22, 1906, p. 4.

289 **"new Market Street"** . . . : According to the article, "Fillmore Street . . . is the new Market Street at present," *ibid.*

290 **"endeavor and accomplishment"** . . . : Greely, p. 91.

290 **"no misunderstanding as to the . . ."**: *Ibid.*, p. 97.

290 **"be strictly confined"** . . . : *Ibid.*, p. 98.

290 **"9 deaths by violence"** . . . : *Ibid.*, p. 92.

291 **"Presidio Soldier[s]"** . . . : *SFE*, April 23, 1906.

291 **"most important duty"** . . . : Greely, p. 101.

291 **"unwarranted by law"** . . . : *Ibid.*, p. 102.

292 **sixty-four officers and five hundred enlisted** . . . : *Ibid.*

292 **"We have not yet gotten . . ."**: Sinsheimer.

292 **"OWNERS OF SAFES ACT TOO HASTILY"** . . . : *SFC*, April 29, 1906.

292 **"the contents burst into flames"** . . . : "Fire Destroys Assessor's Books," *SFE*, May 3, 1906, p. 1.

292 **"all danger from combustion is passed"** . . . : "Hotel Guests Ask Police to Get Their Money," *SFE*, May 3, 1906, p. 2.

293 **"There will be abundant money . . ."**: "United States Mint to Advance Millions to the Banks of Cities About the Bay," *SFC*, April 22, 1906, p. 2.

293 **"Every bank in San Francisco . . ."**: Leach.

293 **"Banker's Row"** . . . : *Biography of a Bank*, p. 27.

293 **"He knew every one of . . ."**: *Ibid.*, p. 28.

293 **"consisted of a plank counter . . ."**: *Ibid.*, p. 27. *See also A. P. Giannini: The People's Banker*, p. 45.

293 **"in *floridissime condizioni*"** . . . : "Banca d'Italia," *LI*, May 5, 1906, p. 2.

294 **"We are quite fully insured"** . . . : Letter from John Walter to his parents, April 26, 1906, published in Walter, *To His Parents, April 18, 1906*.

294 **137 different insurance companies** . . . : Robert A. James, "Six Bits or Bust: Insurance Litigation Over the 1906 Earthquake and Fire" (June 1, 2011), *Western Legal History*, vol. 24, no. 2 (Summer/Fall 2011): p. 131.

294 **"The Company sent for him . . ."**: Letter from Carrie Mangels, July 9, 1906, CHS.

294 **"the great fire"** . . . : In the article "Great Buildings Are To Rise From Ashes," it was reported that the San Francisco Real Estate Board met and "agreed that the calamity should be spoken of as 'the great fire,' and not as 'the great earthquake.'" *SFCh*, p. 1.

294 **"Dollar-for-Dollar"** . . . : "Dollar-for-Dollar List Now Numbers Thirty-Five Concerns," *SFE*, June 17, 1906, p. 1.

294 **"I represented The Emporium in . . ."**: Mark Lewis Gerstle, excerpt from Mark Lewis Gerstle Memories, 1946, BL, p. 46.

295 **$235 million was paid** . . . : Robert James, "Six Bits or Bust," p. 32.

295 **"We just received your letter . . ."**: Letter from Marie Mueller to Aunt Josie, April 25, 1906, Seawall Family Collection.

295 **"read the papers with tears . . ."**: Letter from Minnie Mueller to her sister Josie, April 24, 1906, Seawall Family Collection.

295 **"by the thousands"** . . . : Letter from Minnie Mueller to her sister Josie, April 25, 1906, Seawall Family Collection.

295 **"Not hearing from any of . . ."**: Letter from Minnie Mueller to her sister Josie, April 24, 1906, Seawall Family Collection.

295 **"to come stay with us"** . . . : Letter from Minnie Mueller to her sister Josie, April 25, 1906, Seawall Family Collection.

295 **"Leo Jacobs please let mamma . . ."**: *SFC*, April 24, 1906, p. 5.

295 **"Wanted—To know whereabouts of . . ."**: *Ibid.*

295 **"hip bones and other charred bones"** . . . : "Finds Bodies Among Ruins," *SFC*, May 19, 1906, p. 1.

296 **Sixty-year-old Sarah Boyle** . . . : Sixty-year-old Sarah Boyle, who kept a lodging house in San Francisco, went to Oakland with refugees and committed suicide by drowning; she died April 20, 1906. *OH*, April 21, 1906; Gladys Hansen Death Index, SFPL; and *DeathIndex*, p. 1103.

296 **Thirty-four-year-old Ethel Gross** . . . : Ethel Gross, thirty-four, died at 6:00 a.m. April 23, 1906, after committing suicide by jumping from the fourth floor of the hospital at Octavia St. and Golden Gate Ave. *SFCh*, April 24, 1906; *DeathIndex*; and Gladys Hansen Death Index, SFPL.

296 **"[c]razed by the experience through . . ."**: *SFCh*, April 24, 1906, p. 7.

296 **fifty-six-year-old Albert Smith** . . . : Albert Smith, fifty-six, died in Los Angeles on April 23, 1906. Gladys Hansen Death Index, SFPL, and *DeathIndex*.

296 **"despondent over the deaths of . . ."**: He committed suicide in his hotel room. He reportedly "came to Los Angeles two weeks ago looking for work" and died after getting the news of the deaths of his wife and son in San Francisco. *Oakland Enquirer*, April 27, 1906.

18.

297 **"drawn to the car as though . . ."**: "Cheers Greet the Return of the Trolley," *SFCh*, p. 1.

297 **"I rode it to the end . . ."**: Livingston.

297 **"practically ready to operate"** . . . : "Cheers Greet the Return of the Trolley," *supra*.

298 **"is wholly temporary"** . . . : *SFE*, April 26, 1906.

298 **"invaded"** . . . : "Trolley Cars in Operation—Market Street is Invaded for the First Time," *SFC*, p. 8.

298 **along with the sole surviving** . . . : This was Cal Cable Dummy no. 24, stored in the company's other car house on California Street past Central (present-day Presidio) Avenue. Its storage there allowed cars used in the morning to run from the outer end of the line without having to "dead-head" (run without passengers) from Hyde Street to begin service. Author interview with Emiliano Echeverria, June 24, 2022.

298 **began limited service on August 17** . . . : "Cable Runs on California Street," *SFE*, August 18, 1906, p. 2. The machinery was given its first full-speed test on August 5. "California Cable to Start Soon," *SFC*, August 6, 1906, p. 12. And it was reported that six of the twenty cars had arrived by August 13 and the first car was to be test-run the next day, August 14. "Old Cars for Old Hill Line," *SFCh*, August 13, 1906, p. 7.

299 **$9,673,057.94** . . . : *ReliefSurvey*, Table 1. Cash Receipts of the Finance Committee of Relief and Red Cross Funds, and its Successor, the Corporation, to June 1, 1909, p. 3.

299 **"able-bodied men, for whom . . ."**: *ReliefSurvey*, p. 47.

299 **"For Chinese"** . . . : No. 3. Presidio, Ft. Winfield Scott (For Chinese), List of Official Camps, *ReliefSurvey*, p. 404.

299 **"would be collected and placed . . ."**: "Location of a Chinese Camp is Opposed," *SFC*, April 29, 1906, p. 1.

299 **"All of the Chinese at present . . ."**: "Plan for New Chinatown," *SFCh*, April 25, 1906, p. 5.

300 **"as remote as possible from . . ."**: "Chinese Camp is Picturesque," *SFC*, May 13, 1906, p. 16.

300 **"gave us each a cup of . . ."**: Lily Sung on Her 1906 Earthquake Experience, interviewed by Connie Young Yu, *Earthquake: The Chinatown Story*, CHSA.

300 **"The big fire has obliterated . . ."**: "Plan for New Chinatown," *SFCh*, April 25, 1906, p. 5.

300 **"at once"** . . . : "The Plan to Remove Celestials to San Mateo County Is Opposed," *SFCh*, April 27, 1906, p. 9.

301 **"Westerners have suggested moving the . . ."**: Anna Naruta, *Chung Sai Yat Po* Translations by Danny Loong, "Relocation," *Earthquake: The Chinatown Story*, CHSA.

301 **"as soon as they could get an assurance . . ."**: "To Resist Moving of Chinatown," *SFC*, May 17, 1906, p. 1.

301 **"important business center"** . . . : "Oriental City is Planned," *SFC*, May 24, 1906, p. 14.

302 **"the Chinese style of architecture"** . . . : Philip P. Choy, *San Francisco Chinatown: A Guide to Its History & Architecture* (San Francisco: City Lights Books, 2012), p. 44.

302 **"The appearance and condition of . . ."**: W. E. Alexander, Account of the 1906 San Francisco Earthquake and Fire, CHS.

302 **"Thank goodness we have the . . ."**: Letter from Carrie A. Duncan to Mrs. Noitchey, May 23, 1906, CHS.

302 **"I have not slept in bed . . ."**: Letter from Halvor H. Berg, May 10, 1906, SFPL.

302 **"The majority of these people . . ."**: Letter from Carrie Mangels, July 9, 1906, CHS.

303 **"successful in trade, business, or profession"** . . . : *ReliefSurvey*, p. 172.

303 **2,032 people applied and 1,226** . . . : *Ibid.*, p. 173.

303 **"huckster or peddler"** . . . : *Ibid.*, Table 56, p. 184.

303 **"We started the office going . . ."**: Letter from John Walter to his parents, April 26, 1906, published in Walter, *To His Parents, April 18, 1906*.

303 **"Two weeks after the earthquake . . ."**: Account of Alex Paladini, *Arg.*, August 7, 1926.

303 **"a fully equipped studio waiting . . ."**: Genthe, p. 97.

304 **"Small houses are springing up . . ."**: Letter from Dr. Wilber M. Swett, May 27, 1906, BL.

304 **"that the new San Francisco . . ."**: Livingston.

304 **"turned carpenter again"** . . . : Letter from Percy H. Gregory to his mother in Australia, May 29, 1906, CHS.

304 **"THE CALL GETS FIRST PERMIT . . ."**: *SFC*, April 23, 1906, p. 1.

305 **"every cook and attendant connected . . ."**: "Owners of Palace Hotel WILL ERECT Temporary Hostelry," *SFC*, June 7, 1906, p. 12.

305 **"walls and steel structure were . . ."**: "Fairmont To Be Finished," *SFCh*, April 29, 1906, p. 18.

305 **"Let the whole idea be . . ."**: "Eastern Lecturers Will Be Set Straight in the Matter," Stockton Chamber of Commerce Circular, 1906, VMSF.

305 **"New San Francisco Emergency Edition"** . . . : E. H. Harriman, "San Francisco," *Sunset* magazine, vol. XVII, no. 1 (May 1906).

305 **"hyperbolic nonsense"** . . . : Simon Winchester, *A Crack in the Edge of the World*, p. 330.

305 **"for the purpose of studying . . ."**: *Structures*, p. 14.

306 **"mortar of poor quality"** . . . : *Ibid.*, p. 39.

306 **"Flimsy and loosely built structures . . ."**: *Ibid.*, p. 14.

306 **"on soft, marshy, or made ground"** . . . : *Ibid.*, p. 157.

306 **"In the earth's vibrations it . . ."**: "Pile Foundation is Considered Best," *SFE*, May 3, 1906, p. 3.

307 **"Bonus Plan"** . . . : *ReliefSurvey*, p. 239.

307 **$423,288.17 helped 885 residents** . . . : *Ibid.*

307 **"destitute"** . . . : Form for Special Relief, *ReliefSurvey*, p. 437.

307 **nineteen two-story, wood-frame "tenement houses"** . . . : Table 63, *ReliefSurvey*, p. 219.

308 **"Camp Cottages"** . . . : *ReliefSurvey*, p. 221.

308 **A total of 5,610 "refugee cottages"** . . . : Table 63, *supra.*

308 **"My father was able to . . ."**: Siegel.

308 **"payments of $50 down and $10 . . ."**: *SFE*, August 11, 1907, p. 31.

309 **"About October 1st our April-October . . ."**: ConlonJr.

309 **"prompt, determined action"** . . . : Editorial, *SFE*, May 31, 1906, p. 16.

309 **"the crowd of angry citizens"** . . . : "Crowd Tries to Get at Ruef and the Curly Boss is Scared," *SFCh*, October 27, 1906, p. 1.

310 **"although martial law did not . . ."**: "Jury Frees Vance and Simmons," *SFC*, September 29, 1906, p. 1.

310 **"I doubt if there were ten . . ."**: "Dismisses Case Against Boynton," *The Recorder*, October 10, 1906, p. 1.

310 **"the third of those brought . . ."**: "Makes Martial Law His Defense," *The Recorder*, November 22, 1906, p. 1.

310 **"I only did my duty"** . . . : "Denicke Shot at Disarmed Man," *SFC*, November 24, 1906, p. 6.

310 **"the rule of the bullet"** . . . : "City Governed by Law of Bullet," *SFC*, November 28, 1906, p. 4.

311 **Judge Cook dismissed the only** . . . : "Useless to Try Bechtel Case," *SFC*, December 5, 1906, p. 1.

311 **"the last of the series . . ."**: *Ibid.*

311 **"The only thing saved from . . ."**: "Mechanics' Library Has Temporary Offices," *SFCh*, May 26, 1906, p. 8.

311 **143,000 of** . . . : The May 19, 1906, report of the Library Restoration Committee found "that out of 166,344 volumes in the public library and its branches on April 17 there were only 23,000 accounted for on May 1." *SFC*, May 23, 1906, p. 5.

311 **"The greatest loss to the city . . ."**: Eastwood.

312 **"twelve-story Class A Building"** . . . : "Imposing Corner is Assured," *SFC*, November 3, 1906, p. 4.

312 **"Concrete Construction"** . . . : *The San Francisco Crocker-Langley Directory for the Year Ending October 1907* (San Francisco: H.S. Crocker Company, 1907), p. 1802.

312 **"Contractors—Building"** . . . : *Ibid.*, p. 1808.

312 **"Engineers—Construction"** . . . : *Ibid.*, p. 1836.

312 **"Engineers—Structural"** . . . : *Ibid.*, p. 1838.

312 **3,430,000 feet of lumber . . .**: Water Front Notes, *SFC*, December 14, 1906, p. 11.

312 **"You can stand up and look . . ."**: Account of Michael Maher, December 1, 1906, SFPL.

313 **"the rushing crowd instantly stopped" . . .**: "Ferry Clock Turns Over New Hands This Year," *SFE*, January 1, 1907, p. 1.

314 **"elaborately decorated" . . .**: "Society at Dinner in Tait's," *SFE*, January 1, 1907, p. 2.

314 **"chopped-up, multi-colored paper" . . .**: "Joyous Spirit of Carnival Bids the New Year Welcome," *SFE*, January 1, 1907, p. 1.

314 **"It was all like this—broken . . ."**: Austin.

Afterword

317 **"no man, no matter how . . ."**: "Schmitz Sentenced to Serve 5 Years," *The Recorder*, July 9, 1907, p. 1.

317 **The municipal and judicial spectacle . . .**: Information on the public corruption "graft" trials was obtained primarily from *Boss Ruef's San Francisco* and issues of *SFC*, *SFCh*, *SFE*, and *The Recorder* published between October 1906 and May 1912.

318 **set aside by the Court . . .**: *People v. Schmitz*, 7 Cal. App. 330, 94 P. 407 (Cal. Ct. App. 1908).

318 **"wholesale debauchery of the government . . ."**: "Schmitz Released from Indictments," *SFC*, May 26, 1912, p. 60.

318 **"ideas, investments, real estate" . . .**: *Crocker-Langley San Francisco Directory for the Year Ending June 1916*, p. 1639.

318 **"redeem his good name" . . .**: "Big Vote Seen for Primary," *SFE*, September 27, 1915, p. 4.

318 **"bring back the good old times" . . .**: "Schmitz Declares He Is Sure of Majority in Primary Vote," *SFE*, September 27, 1915, p. 4.

318 **He was decisively rejected . . .**: "Gamblers in New Contest of Schmitz," *SFE*, October 15, 1915, p. 11.

318 **"K.O." . . .**: "Joyful Jottings," *SFE*, November 6, 1919, p. 14.

319 **"wholly and undeniably unconstitutional" . . .**: "Praise the Army," *Topeka Daily Herald* (Topeka, KS), April 27, 1906, p. 2.

319 **"cowardly" . . .**: Letter from Gen. Funston, Presidio of San Francisco, Cal., July 2, 1906, *Arg.*, July 7, 1906.

319 **"for fighting the great San Francisco . . ."**: "Veteran of Three Wars Was Earthquake Battler," *The Kansas City Times*, December 25, 1959, p. 21.

320 **"her accuracy, good judgment" . . .**: Dora Thompson, National Park Service, https://www.nps.gov/people/doraethompson.htm.

320 **"Histories of the Army's role . . ."**: Carl Nolte, "We can't gather at Lotta's Fountain, but we can start a new ritual: Remembering the forgotten of 1906," *SFCh*, April 10, 2020.

320 **"[o]vercome by grief" . . .**: "Hero of '06 Quake Dies After Clearing Name in Navy Records," *OT*, February 19, 1941, p. 12.

320 **with his sister in Kentucky . . .**: World War I Draft Registration Card for Frederick Newton Freeman, September 12, 1918, US, World War I Draft Registration Cards, 1917–1918, www.ancestry.com.

321 **driving while intoxicated . . .**: "Driver Arrested," *The Times* (San Mateo, CA), July 29, 1929, p. 3.

321 **President Roosevelt granted Freeman a . . . :** "Hero of War and Fire—Vindication Comes—To Soledad Resident," *The Californian* (Salinas, CA), February 19, 1941, p. 1.

321 **"Navy Man Who Saved Piers . . .":** "Navy Man Who Saved Piers in 1906 Succumbs," *SFE,* February 19, 1941, p. 36.

321 **"Hero of '06 Quake" . . . :** "Hero of '06 Quake Dies After Clearing Name in Navy Records," *supra.* "Death Takes F.N. Freeman," *The Californian* (Salinas, CA), February 18, 1941, p. 2.

321 **It was only nine months later . . . :** John Pond's death was reported in "Naval Rites for Commander Pond," *OT,* November 27, 1941, p. 2.

321 **Two months after the fire . . . :** "Has Honorable Career as Firefighter," *SFE,* June 16, 1906, p. 3.

321 **"dedicated to the principle . . .":** Steve Van Dyke, superintendent, Bureau of Engineering and Water Supply, San Francisco Fire Department Water Supply System, San Francisco Fire Department, VMSF.

321 **"fire hero, chief of fire . . .":** "Old Comrades of Department at Fire Chief's Bier," *SFE,* October 18, 1925, p. 106.

322 **Assistant Chief John Conlon . . . :** "Asst. Fire Chief Dies of Injury," *SFCh,* March 3, 1919, p. 2.

322 **"Keep California White" . . . :** Robert W. Cherny, "City Commercial, City Beautiful, City Practical: The San Francisco Visions of William C. Ralston, James D. Phelan, and Michael M. O'Shaughnessy," *California History,* vol. 73, no. 4 (1994): pp. 296–307, https://doi.org/10.2307 /25177450.

322 **"save our country from the . . .":** "Phelan Rips C. Of C. Stand On Land Law," *SFE,* April 30, 1921, p. 8.

322 **"great leader of California" . . . :** "Ex-Senator James D. Phelan Dies," *SFE,* August 8, 1930, p. 1.

322 **"name linked with city growth" . . . :** *Ibid.,* p. 2.

323 **"weakened her and she never . . .":** "Lucy B. Fisher, Noted Nurse, Dies," *SFC,* November 26, 1910, p. 1.

323 **"nothing of intrinsic value" . . . :** Will Proof and Certificate of Estate of Lucy B. Fisher, Book D of Wills, no. 154, p. 391, May 3, 1911; California, US, Wills & Probate Records, 1850–1953, database online; www.ancestry.com.

323 **"We were not disheartened" . . . :** Mahoney.

323 **"pioneer physician" . . . :** "Mass Is Said for Woman Physician," *OT,* December 9, 1931, p. 16. The memorial service held by the Native Daughters of the Golden West was reported in "Last Rites Today For Dr. Mahoney," *SFE,* December 10, 1931, p. 17.

324 **Ng Poon Chew . . . :** Information about Dr. Ng Poon Chew was gained primarily from the Ng Poon Chew papers, ca. 1901–1964, BL; articles "Wa Mi San Po: Los Angeles' Chinese Newspaper and Its Busy Editor," *LAT,* July 23, 1899, p. 4; and "Chinese Talks on Exclusion: Ng Poon Chew Lectures Before the Academy of Sciences," *SFC,* September 2, 1905; *see also* "Chinese Editor to Be Buried as Occidental," *OT,* March 15, 1931, p. 1; "Prominent Chinese Doctor Succumbs," *La Grande Observer* (La Grande, OR), March 14, 1931; and "Ng Poon Chew Famed Chinese Editor Passes," *Medford Mail Tribune* (Medford, OR), March 14, 1931.

324 **Lily Soo-Hoo's . . . :** "A Pioneer Chinese Family" by Mrs. Wm. Z. L. Sung, collected in "The Life, Influence and the Role of the Chinese in the United States, 1776–1960," Proceedings/Papers of the National Conference at the University of San Francisco, July 10, 11, 12, 1975, CHSA.

324 **"there was not as much . . .":** *Ibid.,* p. 327.

324 **"too frightened"** . . . : Interview of Lily Sung, by Connie Young Yu at Lily's Palo Alto home, March 27, 1980; taped recording transcribed by Yu, January 26, 2006, *The Unshakable—Rebirth of Chinatown in 1906,* p. 16.

324 **"We could feel the fire . . ."**: *Ibid.,* pp. 16–17.

324 **"And when I smell hot coffee now"** . . . : *Ibid.,* p. 17.

324 **Lee Yoke Suey** . . . : "Chinatown, 1906: The End and the Beginning," by Connie Young Yu, *The Unshakable—Rebirth of Chinatown in 1906,* pp. 14–15.

325 **"victim of technicalities . . ."**: "Law Parts S. F. Chinese, Tots," *SFE,* March 10, 1925, p. 4.

325 **"fine old scrub-oak"** . . . : Genthe, p. 97.

326 **"[s]ince breathing San Francisco air . . ."**: "Noted Photographer Visits S.F.—Arnold Genthe Back in 'Home Town,'" *SFCh,* September 29, 1937, p. 1.

326 **Charmian and Jack London** . . . : Charmian London, *The Book of Jack London,* Volumes I and II (New York: The Century Co., 1921); Iris Jamahl Dunkle, *Charmian Kittredge London: Trailblazer, Author, Adventurer* (Norman, OK: University of Oklahoma Press, 2020).

326 **"a woman ahead of her time . . ."**: Dunkle, *Charmian Kittredge London,* p. 303.

326 **"embarrassed"** . . . : George C. Marshall, *Memoirs of My Services in the World War 1917–1918* (Boston: Houghton Mifflin, 1976), p. 95. *See also* Matthew Davenport, *First Over There* (New York: Thomas Dunne Books, 2015).

327 **"lawyer, war correspondent, football coach . . ."**: "Funeral Held for Writer J. B. Hopper," *SFE,* August 31, 1956, p. 8.

327 **"quarterback of the famous . . ."**: "Rites for Carmel Writer James B. Hopper Are Held," *Modesto Bee* (Modesto, CA), August 30, 1956, p. 19.

327 **"California's authentically great men"** . . . : "James Hopper," *OT,* August 31, 1956, p. 60.

327 **"to the use and benefit . . ."**: "Lotta's Fountain—Its Final Presentation to the City of San Francisco," *SFCh,* September 10, 1875, p. 3.

327 **"Lotta's Fountain!"** . . . : "Church Federation Wants to Know Where Visitors in 1915 Can Get a Drink of Water," *SFCh,* April 18, 1913.

327 **Luisa Tetrazzini** . . . : "Tetrazzini Thrilled S. F. Crowd of 250,000," *SFE,* April 29, 1940, p. 1.

327 **on April 18, 1956** . . . : "Civic Rites to Mark Anniversary Today of City's Destruction," *SFE,* April 18, 1956, p. 2.

327 **"placed on the fountain in . . ."**: *Ibid.*

327 **first in 1926 for the twentieth** . . . : *The Recorder,* March 11, 1926, p. 9; "South of Market Folk Celebrate at Grand Ball," *SFE,* April 18, 1906, p. 3; "Nation Lauds City 25 years after Big Fire," *SFE,* April 18, 1931, p. 7.

328 **"Californians long ago learned to . . ."**: "California Sits on Top of Quake 50 Years After Frisco Disaster," *The Knoxville Journal* (Knoxville, TN), April 15, 1956, p. 52.

328 **"California's Next Earthquake"** . . . : "CD Chiefs Talk On 'Next Quake,'" *Record Searchlight* (Redding, CA), April 17, 1956, p. 5; and "Meet to Set Quake Strategy," *The Times* (San Mateo, CA), April 17, 1956, p. 5.

328 **"California may go 10 . . ."**: "Great Disaster of 1906 Could Repeat Tomorrow," *Rocky Mount Telegram* (Rocky Mount, NC), April 15, 1956, p. 9.

328 **"for the first time since . . ."**: "Dramatic Stories of the Quake From 'Eyewitnesses' in S. F.," *SFE,* March 23, 1957, p. 2.

329 **108 years of ferry service . . . :** "Old-Timers Taken on Last Ferry Ride," *SFE,* July 31, 1958, p. 11. Note this was the Southern Pacific's final ferry service. Ferries resumed service years later but never in the same volume or frequency as prior to August 1, 1958.

329 **"hideous monstrosity" . . . :** The editorial read in part, "We oppose, and have consistently opposed, the hideous monstrosity which the State Highway Commission built along the Embarcadero in front of the Ferry Building, obscuring the tower." Editorial Staff, "The Boobery Goes On and On," *SFCh,* August 28, 1959, p. 32.

329 **"the handsomest office building . . .":** Michael R. Corbett, *Splendid Survivors: San Francisco's Downtown Architectural Heritage* (San Francisco: California Living Books, 1979), p. 85.

329 **"modernized" . . . :** "Claus Spreckels Building Will Be Modernized," *SFCh,* May 17, 1937, p. 5.

329 **"Economic forces prove stronger . . .":** *Splendid Survivors, supra.*

329 **"This, San Francisco's first fireproof . . .":** "Plaque Unveiled at Historic San Francisco Building," *SFE,* September 8, 1955, p. 21.

330 **But four years later, both . . . :** Oliver Perry Stidger: 12/31/1873–9/2/1959. Buried in Cypress Lawn Memorial Park, Colma, CA; "Landmark is Doomed," *SFE,* March 8, 1959, p. 14.

330 **"construction of a towering pyramid . . .":** "Transamerica 'Pyramid' Receives Go-Ahead by City," *SFE,* August 26, 1969, p. 3.

330 **"a practice drill" . . . :** "East Bay to Rehearse for Earthquake," *SFCh,* August 7, 1989, p. A9.

330 **"There was a loud noise . . .":** Recollection of Sgt. Diane Langdon, An Oral History of the Presidio of San Francisco During the Loma Prieta Earthquake, by Eve Iverson, VMSF.

330 **"I tell you what, we're having . . .":** Al Michaels, "1989 World Series Game 3—Battle of the Bay," *ABC Sports,* October 17, 1989, television broadcast.

330 **"looked down on the ground . . .":** Recollection of Sgt. Diane Langdon, *supra.*

330 **The earth's crust had ruptured . . . :** David J. Wald, Donald V. Helmberger, and Thomas H. Heaton, "Rupture Model of the 1989 Loma Prieta Earthquake from the Inversion of Strong-Motion and Broadband Teleseismic Data," *Bulletin of the Seismological Society of America,* vol. 81, no. 5 (October 1991): pp. 1540–1572.

331 **"History does not repeat itself . . .":** James Eayrs, *Diplomacy and Its Discontents* (Toronto: University of Toronto Press, 1971), p. 121. Note: this was one of several citations from the early 1970s exploring the origin of the quote and its attribution to Mark Twain (who passed in 1910 but was never attributed any variation of the quote in print until 1970). *See also* "History Does Not Repeat Itself, But It Rhymes," quoteinvestigator.com/2014/01/12/history-rhymes/.

331 **City Water Department workers . . . :** Art Jensen, acting general manager of Public Utilities Commission for the City and County of San Francisco, Report to the Board of Supervisors Concerning the Water Supply, November 21, 1989, VMSF; and Water Supply System Review, VMSF.

331 **"ask for the maximum bail and . . .":** "DEVASTATING REPORTS FROM BIG QUAKE AREA," *SFCh,* October 19, 1989, p. A1.

331 **forty-two over in Oakland . . . :** Bernard J. Feldman, "The Nimitz Freeway Collapse," *The Physics Teacher,* vol. 42 (October 2004): p. 400.

331 **nearly a mile-long stretch . . . :** The length of the collapsed portion was 1.4 kilometers (0.87 mile), *ibid.*

331 **one-tenth the size and one-thirtieth . . . :** "How Much Bigger . . . ?" calculator, USGS Earthquake Hazards Program, earthquake.usgs.gov/education/calculator.php.

332 **"dwindling band of survivors"** . . . : "San Francisco Journal; And Yet Again, the Earth Trembles for a Tiny Band of 1906 Survivors," *NYT,* April 19, 1990.

332 **"When his horse and buggy . . ."**: "Quake Survivors Look Back to 1906," *SFE,* April 18, 1906, p. 2.

332 **In 1994, the Fairmont Hotel** . . . : "Hotel Fete for Woman, 99, Fulfills Dream Deferred by 1906 Quake," *LAT,* November 27, 1994.

332 **In 1997, the Fairmont extended** . . . : Manny Fernandez, "At 102, She's Celebrating What Might Have Been," *SFGate,* November 28, 1997.

332 **"set aside the death toll of 478"** . . . : Resolution No. 53–05, File No. 041149, "Death Toll of 1906 Earthquake Victims," https://sfbos.org/resolutions-2005. *See also* Suzanne Herel, "A century later, quake's toll to rise," *SFCh,* January 27, 2005, p. B4.

333 **"what seemed like thousands of letters"** . . . : Tom Graham, "Gladys Hansen—90 Years Later, Quake Victims Get Names," *SFCh,* April 14, 1996, p. 3/Z1.

333 **"the names of 1,500 persons . . ."**: "SF Earthquake Fatal to 1,500," *Tyler Morning Telegraph* (Tyler, TX), April 18, 1985.

333 **"1906 List of Dead & Survivors"** . . . : "Integrated List All Deaths 7–22–10 992 Names, 75 Unknowns," VMSF, accessed February 24, 2023.

333 **The index cards completed with** . . . : Information from these cards cited herein as Gladys Hansen Death Index, SFPL.

333 **"Integrated List All Deaths"** . . . : *Supra.*

333 **"When the Big One Strikes Again"** . . . : Charles A. Kircher, Hope A. Seligson, Jawhar Bouabid, and Guy C. Morrow, "When the *Big One* Strikes Again—Estimated Losses Due to a Repeat of the 1906 San Francisco Earthquake," Study commissioned by the 100th Anniversary Conference, California Office of Emergency Services, and the Earthquake Engineering Research Institute, 2006.

334 **"seismically vulnerable"** . . . : *Ibid.,* p. 31.

334 **"The Bay Area is probably . . ."**: Terence Chea, "The big one," *The Standard-Times* (New Bedford, MA), April 18, 2006.

334 **at least eight of 7.0 or greater** . . . : California Earthquake Authority, https://www .earthquakeauthority.com/California-Earthquake-Risks/California-Earthquake-History -Timeline.

334 **"creeping section"** . . . : "Tectonic Setting," US Geological Survey, Earthquake Hazards Program, https://earthquake.usgs.gov/learn/parkfield/geology.php.

334 **"a large quake there is inevitable"** . . . : Kurtis Alexander, "'San Francisco earthquakes' went viral because of a report detailing the worst case scenario. Here's what it says," *SFCh,* March 4, 2022.

334 **"life safety and socioeconomic impact"** . . . : "Editorial: Lessons from the 1989 Loma Prieta earthquake," *SFCh,* September 20, 2019.

335 **And on October 17, 2019** . . . : Robert Sanders, "California rolls out first statewide earthquake early warning system," *Berkeley News,* October 17, 2019, https://news.berkeley.edu/2019/10 /17/California-rolls-out-first-statewide-earthquake-early-warning-system/. *See also* "Earthquake Warning California—Don't Let Earthquakes Catch You Off Guard," https://earthquake.ca.gov.

335 **Oregon and Washington were added** . . . : "Entire West Coast Now Has Access to ShakeAlert®," News Alert from Communications and Publishing, US Geological Survey, May 4, 2021, https://usgs.gov/news/entire-us-west-coast-now-has-access-shakealert-earthquake-early -warning.

335 **"grant people enough time to . . ."**: Jenessa Duncombe, "California Launches Nation's First Earthquake Early Warning System," *Eos*, October 24, 2019, https://eos.org/articles/california-launches-nations-first-earthquake-early-warning-system.

336 **" 'The house may not have . . .' "**: "A Midsummer Story—Concluded," *SFCh*, August 3, 1949, p. 16.

336 **"the high-ceilinged front room . . ."**: "Feusier Rites Monday—Services to Be Conducted in Octagonal House," *SFE*, July 7, 1951, p. 1.

336 **"due to a mile long fire . . ."**: 451 Jackson Street was built by A. P. Hotaling in 1866 and is San Francisco Landmark No. 12.

337 **"If, as they say, God spanked . . ."**: After a Los Angeles medium "attributed the earthquake to the wrath of God," Charles Field wrote this poem after learning "that 12,000 barrels of whiskey belonging to Dick Hotaling were saved." "Providence Questioned," *Evening Sentinel* (Santa Cruz, CA), May 26, 1906, p. 2.

Selected Secondary Sources

Accardi, Catherine A., *San Francisco's North Beach and Telegraph Hill* (Charleston, SC: Arcadia Publishing, 2010)

Adkins, Jan Batiste, *African Americans of San Francisco* (Charleston, SC: Arcadia Publishing, 2012)

Aitken, Frank W. and Hilton, Edward, *A History of the Earthquake and Fire in San Francisco: An Account of the Disaster of April 18, 1906* (San Francisco: The Edward Hilton Co., 1906)

Alioto, John, *Before the Gold: A History of San Francisco Before the Gold Rush, 1769–1847* (San Francisco: Norfolk Press, 2020)

Asbury, Herbert, *The Barbary Coast: An Informal History of the San Francisco Underworld* (New York: Alfred A. Knopf, 1933)

Banks, Charles Eugene and Read, Opie, *The History of the San Francisco Disaster and Mount Vesuvius Horror* (Chicago: C.E. Thomas, 1906)

Barker, Malcolm E., *Three Fearful Days: San Francisco Memoirs of the 1906 Earthquake & Fire* (San Francisco: Londonborn Publications, 1998)

Barrymore, John, *Confessions of an Actor* (Indianapolis: The Bobbs-Merrill Company, 1926)

Bean, Walter, *Boss Ruef's San Francisco—The Story of the Union Labor Party, Big Business, and the Graft Prosecution* (Berkeley: University of California Press, 1952)

Becker, Robert S. and Tillis, Jane, *Look Tin Eli: The Mendocino Visionary Who Helped Shape the Chinese-American Experience* (Mendocino, CA: Kelley House Museum, 2021)

Bennett, Milly, *On Her Own: Journalistic Adventures from San Francisco to the Chinese Revolution, 1917–1927* (Armonk, New York: M.E. Sharpe, 1993)

Benton, Lisa M., *The Presidio: From Army Post to National Park* (Chicago: Northeastern University Press, 1998)

Bolt, Bruce A., *Earthquakes, Fifth Edition* (New York: W.H. Freeman & Company, 2003)

Brands, H. W., *The Age of Gold: The California Gold Rush and the New American Dream* (New York: Anchor Books, 2003)

Brechin, Gray, *Imperial San Francisco: Urban Power, Earthly Ruin* (Berkeley: University of California Press, 2006)

Breuer, Karin, ed.; Binder, Victoria; Ganz, James A.; Görgen, Carolin; Terry, Colleen; and Misrach, Richard, *Among the Ruins: Arnold Genthe's Photographs of the 1906 San Francisco Earthquake and Firestorm* (Fine Arts Museums of San Francisco: Cameron + Company, 2021)

Careaga, Rand, *The United States Customhouse in San Francisco, An Illustrated History* (Washington, DC: General Services Administration, 2011)

Choy, Philip P., *San Francisco Chinatown: A Guide to Its History & Architecture* (San Francisco: City Lights Books, 2012)

Cohen, Katherine Powell, *San Francisco's Nob Hill* (Charleston, SC: Arcadia Publishing, 2010)

Corbett, Michael R., *Splendid Survivors: San Francisco's Downtown Architectural Heritage* (San Francisco: California Living Books, 1979)

Davies, Andrea Rees, *Saving San Francisco: Relief and Recovery after the 1906 Disaster* (Philadelphia: Temple University Press, 2011)

Dillon, Richard (author) and Monaco, J. B. (illustrator), *North Beach: The Italian Heart of San Francisco* (Novato, CA: Presidio Press, 1985)

Dunkle, Iris Jamahl, *Charmian Kittredge London: Trailblazer, Author, Adventurer* (Norman, OK: University of Oklahoma Press, 2020)

Dyl, Joanna Leslie, *Seismic City—An Environmental History of San Francisco's 1906 Earthquake* (Seattle: University of Washington Press, 2017)

Echeverria, Emiliano; Dolgushkin, Michael; and Rice, Walter, *San Francisco's Transportation Octopus: The Market Street Railway of 1893* (ebook: Michael Dolgushkin, 2013)

Echeverria, Emiliano and Rice, Walter, *San Francisco's Powell Street Cable Cars* (Charleston, SC: Arcadia Publishing, 2005)

Fracchia, Charles A., *Fire and Gold: The San Francisco Story* (Encinitas, CA: Heritage Media Corp., 1998)

———, *When the Water Came Up to Montgomery Street* (Virginia: The Donning Company sponsored by San Francisco Museum and Historical Society, 2009)

Fradkin, Philip L., *The Great Earthquake and Firestorms of 1906* (Berkeley: University of California Press, 2005)

Gann, Richard G. and Friedman, Raymond, *Principles of Fire Behavior and Combustion* (Burlington, MA: Jones & Bartlett Learning, 2015)

Garvey, John, *San Francisco Fire Department* (Charleston, SC: Arcadia Publishing, 2003)

Hansen, Gladys and Condon, Emmet, *Denial of Disaster—The Untold Story and Photographs of the San Francisco Earthquake and Fire of 1906* (San Francisco: Cameron + Company, 1989)

Hansen, Gladys; Hansen, Richard; and Blaisell, Dr. William, *Earthquake, Fire, and Epidemic—Personal Accounts of the 1906 Disaster* (San Francisco: Untreed Reads Publishing, 2013)

Hittell, John S., *A History of the City of San Francisco and Incidentally of the State of California* (San Francisco: A. L. Bancroft & Co., 1878)

Hitz, Anne Evers, *Emporium Department Store* (San Francisco: Arcadia Publishing, 2014)

———, *San Francisco's Ferry Building* (San Francisco: Arcadia Publishing, 2017)

Hooper, Bernadette C., *San Francisco's Mission District* (Charleston, SC: Arcadia Publishing, 2006)

James, Marquis and James, Bessie R., *Biography of a Bank—The Story of Bank of America, NT & SA* (New York: Harper & Row, 1954)

Keeler, Charles, *San Francisco and Thereabout* (San Francisco: The Stanley-Taylor Co., 1902)

Klett, Mark with Lundgren, Michael, *After the Ruins 1906 and 2006: Rephotographing the San Francisco Earthquake and Fire* (Berkeley: University of California Press, 2006)

Koenig, Bill, *Everything Took Time—The Actions of the San Francisco Fire Department During the 1906 Great Earthquake and Fire* (Evansville, IN: M.T. Publishing Company, 2020)

Lapp, Rudolph M., *Blacks in Gold Rush California* (New Haven and London: Yale University Press, 1977)

Lee, Erika, *At America's Gates: Chinese Immigration During the Exclusion Era, 1882–1943* (Chapel Hill: University of North Carolina Press, 2003)

Lipsky, Dr. William, *San Francisco's Marina District* (Charleston, SC: Arcadia Publishing, 2004)

Lotchin, Roger W., ed., *Narratives of the San Francisco Earthquake and Fire of 1906* (Chicago: The Lakeside Press, R.R. Donnelley & Sons Co., 2011)

Margolin, Malcolm, *The Ohlone Way: Indian Life in the San Francisco–Monterey Bay Area* (Berkeley: Heyday Books, 1978)

Morris, Charles, *The San Francisco Calamity by Earthquake and Fire* (Washington, DC: W.E. Scull, 1906)

Nee, Brett de Bary and Nee, Victor G., *Longtime Californ': A Documentary Study of an American Chinatown* (Stanford, CA: Stanford University Press, 1972)

Newhall, Ruth Waldo, *The Folger Way—Coffee Pioneering Since 1850* (San Francisco: J.A. Folger & Company, 1970)

O'Brien, Tricia, *San Francisco's Pacific Heights and Presidio Heights* (Charleston, SC: Arcadia Publishing, 2008)

Pfaelzer, Jean, *Driven Out: The Forgotten War Against Chinese Americans* (Berkeley: University of California Press, 2007)

Pincetl, Stephanie S., *Transforming California: A Political History of Land Use and Development* (Baltimore: The Johns Hopkins University Press, 1999)

Rice, Walter and Echeverria, Emiliano with Dolgushkin, Michael, *San Francisco's California Street Cable Cars* (Charleston, SC: Arcadia Publishing, 2008)

Richards, Rand, *Historic San Francisco* (San Francisco: Heritage House Publishers, 2011)

Schussler, Hermann, *The Past, Present and Future Water Supply of San Francisco* (San Francisco: C. A. Murdoch & Co., 1908)

Smith, Dennis, *San Francisco Is Burning: The Untold Story of the 1906 Earthquake and Fires* (New York: Viking, 2005)

Smith, James R., *San Francisco's Lost Landmarks* (Fresno, CA: Linden Publishing, 2005)

Starr, Kevin, *Americans and the California Dream, 1850–1915* (New York: Oxford University Press, 1973)

Tchen, John Kuo Wei (selections and text) and Genthe, Arnold (photographs), *Genthe's Photographs of San Francisco's Old Chinatown* (New York: Dover Publications, 1984)

Thomas, Gordon and Witts, Max Morgan, *The San Francisco Earthquake* (New York: Stein and Day, 1971)

Thompson, Erwin N., *Defender of the Gate: Presidio of San Francisco, CA 1900–1904* (Denver, CO: National Park Service, 1997)

Tobriner, Stephen, *Bracing For Disaster: Earthquake-Resistant Architecture and Engineering in San Francisco, 1838–1933* (Heyday Books, 2006)

Tyler, Sydney, *San Francisco's Great Disaster: A Full Account of the Recent Terrible Destruction of Life and Property by Earthquake, Fire and Volcano in California and at Vesuvius* (Harrisburg, PA: The Minter Company, 1906)

Valente, Francesca, *A. P. Giannini—The People's Banker* (Temple City, CA: Barbera Foundation, 2017)

Walsh, James P. and O'Keefe, Timothy J., *Legacy of a Native Son: James Duval Phelan & Villa Montalvo* (Forbes Mill Press, 1993)

Winchester, Simon, *A Crack in the Edge of the World: America and the Great California Earthquake of 1906* (New York: Harper Perennial, 2006)

Wollenberg, Charles, *Golden Gate Metropolis: Perspectives on Bay Area History* (Berkeley: Institute of Governmental Studies, University of California, 1985)

Yeats, Robert S.; Sieh, Kerry; and Allen, Clarence R., *The Geology of Earthquakes* (New York: Oxford University Press, 1997)

Yung, Judy and the Chinese Historical Society of America, *San Francisco's Chinatown* (Charleston, SC: Arcadia Publishing, 2006)

Index